Notes
from the
Last Testament

D0556890

Notes
from the
Last Testament
THE STRUGGLE FOR HAITI

MICHAEL
DEIBERT

SEVEN STORIES PRESS
New York   Toronto   London   Melbourne

Copyright © 2005 by Michael Deibert

A Seven Stories Press First Edition

All rights reserved. No part of this book may be reproduced, stored in a retrieval system, or transmitted in any form, by any means, including mechanical, electric, photocopying, recording or otherwise, without the prior written permission of the publisher.

Seven Stories Press
140 Watts Street
New York, NY 10013
http://www.sevenstories.com

In Canada:
Publishers Group Canada, 250A Carlton Street, Toronto, ON M5A 2L1

In the UK:
Turnaround Publisher Services Ltd., Unit 3, Olympia Trading Estate, Coburg Road, Wood Green, London N22 6TZ

In Australia:
Palgrave Macmillan, 627 Chapel Street, South Yarra VIC 3141

Library of Congress Cataloging-in-Publication Data

Deibert, Michael.
  Notes from the last testament : the struggle for Haiti / Michael Deibert.— A Seven Stories Press 1st ed.
    p. cm.
  Includes bibliographical references and index.
  ISBN-13: 978-1-58322-697-1 (pbk. : alk. paper)
  ISBN-10: 1-58322-697-4 (pbk. : alk. paper)
  1. Haiti—History—1986- 2. Aristide, Jean-Bertrand. 3. Deibert, Michael. I. Title.

F1928.2.D43 2005
972.94'06—dc22

                                    2005018780

College professors may order examination copies of Seven Stories Press titles for a free six-month trial period. To order, visit www.sevenstories.com/textbook or fax on school letterhead to (212) 226-1411.

Cover design by Julie Burke
Book design by Jon Gilbert

Printed in Canada

9 8 7 6 5 4 3 2 1

This book is dedicated to the memory of two journalists who I never met, but who gave their lives so that the story of what was happening to the people of Haiti should be known, Jean Dominique and Ricardo Ortega, and to the memory of one I did know, Jacques Roche; to the memory of Winston Jean-Bart, also known as Tupac; to James "Billy" Petit-Frere, wherever he may be. And to the memory of my grandmother, Leah Maude Breon.

Contents

Acknowledgments

THERE HAVE BEEN MANY PEOPLE whose presence in my life served as an inestimable asset to getting this book written.

Chantal Regnault, who patiently shared her accumulated years of experience with this turbulent, beautiful place. Nina Clara Schnall, who first lead me into a world of Haiti behind that of the headlines, a world of many, many people who didn't often get the opportunity to talk with journalists, but whose courage formed the heart of my experience there. Herby Metellus, maker of necklaces and provider of friendship in the lakou of figi beton, and Madame Claudette, who worried for her son as any mother would when he would go out with me.

Doctor Frantz Large, and Tacha and Ronschy and Menno, provided a boisterous family to keep me company during my long time away from home, and Frantz, especially, provided the intellectual companionship and sparring that kept me sane during long months of seeming madness.

Etzer Pierre, painter, musician and thoughtful gwo chef of ENARTS, provided measured context and fine company at *vodou* ceremonies, carnivals and demonstrations for many years.

James Petit-Frere, Junior Millard, Winston Jean-Bart and the people of Cite Soleil never asked to be born in the worst place in the world, and had much higher and more noble ideas than the political actors who cynically used them. This book is a tribute to their stolen youth and idealism as much as it is to anything.

Gerry Hadden of National Public Radio proved an invaluable traveling companion and friend, and I will always smile at the memory of our journeys to nightclubs in Gonaives, marches in Port-au-Prince and soul-searching late night talks on the roof of the Hotel Montana. David Gonzalez of the *New York Times* realized when it was time to break with expectations and admit to ugly truths. Alex Smailes was a fearless partner and great photographer who sensitively documented the experience of a people in the throws of great upheaval and, like me, wondered why more of the world didn't seem to care. I will join you for Trini Carnival one of these days, mate. Marika Lynch from the *Miami Herald* provided a sensitive sounding board for many of the issues discussed in this book. Amy Bracken of the Associated Press worked hard and still found time for languorous lunches at Trois Decks in the hills of Fermathe. Jim Rupert, Tina Susman and Kayne Rogers at *Newsday* and Anna Szeterenfeld at the *Economist* Intelligence Unit proved themselves to be thoughtful, dedicated editors.

Ben Fountain, the Texas author whose travels took him to Haiti over the years, provided encouragement when I sorely needed it, kept at me to keep going and dispatched wise advice within sight of the storied Oloffson pool. Guy Antoine imbued me with the love he feels for his homeland and the generosity he feels towards its people. Patrick Moynihan and his family and the staff of the Louverture Cleary School opened their doors to me and the revivifying gift of belief in the future. Cassio Leite Vieira and his family provided me with a lovely apartment in Rio de Janeiro, where much of this book was composed. George Mürer at Seven Stories Press kept pushing to bring this book out until he finally met with success. Raoul Peck lent his voice of support to a young author he had never met, and I owe him a great debt of gratitude for that.

My friends in New York stood by me through poverty and difficulty while I chased this story and this book through the years: Sebastian Quezada, Douglas Young, Philip Schnell, Kevin McCaffrey, Antonia D'Amato and Nomi Prins. Further afield, Sutton Stokes, Meli Glenn, Monica Campbell, Justin Cappiello and Eirin Mobekk.

Laura Parker shared the upheaval of the last days of the Aristide regime with me in a time I don't think either of us will ever forget.

Ettore di Benedetto and Javier Henrnandez of the international missions to Haiti all contributed to the success of the project in their own way. Anne Fuller contributed a series of essential interviews from Saint Marc and helped immeasurably with often difficult Kreyol translations.

The Trimble family gave me a place to stay and hot food to eat during some of Haiti's most chaotic days.

Madame Brunette Tondreau was a dignified, trustworthy and irreplaceable part of my household.

Richard Morse and the staff at the Hotel Oloffson provided me with a retreat that often vibrated with the joy of Haiti when that joy was in short supply.

Jorgen Leth entertained me with sparkling dinner parties at his fantastic house in Jacmel and shared cigars and political conversation deep into the tropical night.

The bloodied but unbowed Haitian press corps taught me what real grace under pressure was all about: Rotchild Francois, Wendell Theodore, Naomie Calixte and Goudou Jean Numa from Radio Metropole, Roosevelt Benjamin from Radio Signal FM, Pierre Richard from Reuters Television, Thony Belizaire from Agence France Presse, Daniel Morel and Jane Regan from Wozo Productions, Gotson Pierre from AlterPresse and Michele Montas and the entire staff of Radio Haiti-Inter. Jan Voordouw, Jean-Claude Louis and Nicole Simèon at the Institute Panos were always there with a free computer to write on and ready smiles of welcome even after the roughest of days on the streets.

Pierre Esperance and the staff of the National Coalition for Haitian Rights in Port-au-Prince were flickers of hope in a darkness that sometimes seemed to threaten to envelop us all.

My grandparents, James and Leah Breon and Joseph and Elizabeth Deibert, brought to me the accumulated wisdom of their years. My father, Caleb Deibert, perhaps put the first seed of travel in me with the knowledge of his early days in Argentina.

My brothers, Benjamin Deibert and Christopher Deibert, have never failed to make me very proud, and my mother, Jann Deibert, taught me more than a little something about the value of perseverance.

—Michael Deibert
New York City, June 2005

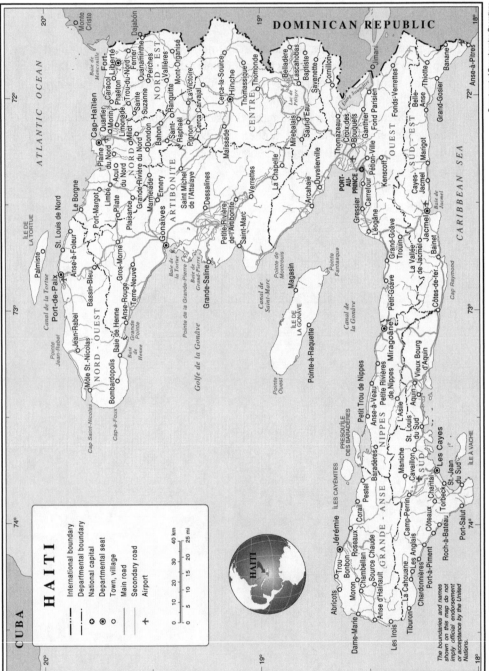

HAITI

International boundary
Departmental boundary
National capital
Departmental seat
Town, village
Main road
Secondary road
Airport

0   10   20   30   40 km
0   5   10   15   20   25 mi

The boundaries and names shown on this map do not imply official endorsement or acceptance by the United Nations.

CUBA

DOMINICAN REPUBLIC

ATLANTIC OCEAN

CARIBBEAN SEA

Map No. 3855 Rev. 3   UNITED NATIONS
June 2004

Department of Peacekeeping Operations
Cartographic Section

HAITI

We had fed the heart on fantasies,
The heart's grown brutal from the fare;
More substance in our enmities
Than in our love; O honey-bees,
Come build in the empty house of the stare.

—William Butler Yeats, "The Stare's Nest by My Window"

| | |

Introduction

WITH *NOTES FROM THE LAST TESTAMENT*, Michael Deibert has entered the long tradition of chroniclers of the history and politics of Haiti. Seductive and mysterious Haiti that, from Graham Greene to Anna Seghers, and Bernard Diederich to Amy Wilentz, has never ceased to fascinate either the occasional visitor or the one who will never let go. A country that will bruise you with its excesses, and still hold you hostage through the vitality, the endurance, the fantasies, the beliefs and the contradictions of its people. From its "discovery" on, Haiti was swept up in a political, social and economic whirlwind, and has been punished by its history. Many have tried to capture its mysteries only to create others along the way, have tried to explain its vibrations, only to fall prey to easy exoticism, have tried to rationalize its tragedies only to over-simplify them.

Of course, there is no miracle formula for understanding Haiti. A country that cannot restrain itself from baring its overpowering heart and soul, irrevocably intoxicating the credulous newcomer. But it is also a country that reveals its real pains, its real fears, and its dreams, only to the patient observer who lingers, comes back over long years with humility, patience, and modesty.

Aside from time and patience, what is needed, at the very least, to understand Haiti, is credulity, madness (a touch of it) and, above all, the ability and the willingness to descend barefoot alongside its poorest inhabitants, those most impoverished (from a material standpoint—never make the mistake of believing that they are spiritually impoverished). In Haiti, at every street corner, at every narrow path that winds through the *mornes* (mountains), you'll learn about things that make your heart beat faster, your blood boil, your imagination flare up. This is the price to pay for the truth. You have to pursue it, hunt it down, or simply wait for it, for long hours, weeks, months, with restraint and exhilaration, wisdom and madness. And maybe, just maybe, if you can see through the superficial baroque and the misleading exoticism, you might capture a piece of its puzzle.

Michael Deibert has dared to turn such a gaze onto my country. He was keen to plunge into this long unending voyage that leaves deep marks under your skin. He doesn't pretend to write as an insider, or to speak in the name of Haitians, but he comes close. He manages to show in the most intimate details how a democratic movement went wrong and how a heritage of valuable victories and painful sacrifice was slandered by a charismatic leader and his cronies, and how they fooled the rest of the world all along. The traditional reading of the history of Haiti, with its panoply of colorful, picaresque characters, indisputably linked to the apparent incoherence of its nature, systematically obscures the broader vision without offering to the accidental observer the least chance to put this suite of events into any rational context.

In these pages, Michael Deibert knows enough to avoid the subtle traps of the fascinating attraction to the romantical-tragical, and to provide us nonetheless with solid analysis. His book provides a formidable concentrate of our political memory of the past twenty years—a precious treasure for a country that has learned to forget in order to survive the daily challenges, and that, as if to avoid leaving any trace of its wounds and shame, never hesitates to burn all in its path. He recounts acutely the role and evolution of a number of Aristide's accomplices in their violent quest for power. The whole hierarchy of the Aristidean apparatus of repression is displayed in front of us in their tortuous biography up to their final self-destruction.

One cannot help but wonder why representatives of the American Congress, such as Maxine Waters and Barbara Lee, among others, are the first to demand with such amazing fervor the return of the "legitimate" predator and to repeat perpetually, in a stubborn anti-Bush posture, the absurd thesis of his kidnapping by the U.S. government.

What additional scandal will it take for the pro-Aristide lobby in the United States to recognize that they have been duping themselves (at least the most honest among them) and to simply renounce their dividends? With the black and white American political nomenclature it has never been a question of solidarity. Or to be fair, never exclusively. The services rendered here and there by "our black friends" or by our "Republican allies" or our "Democrat friends" have come to translate into gifts, payments, jobs, and lucrative arrangements. These manners are obviously long accepted practice in politics.

The ethical lines have long been blurred under the dirt of dubious "bipartisan" telecommunications business dealings between former and current U.S. policy makers and deposed Haitian president Jean-Bertrand Aristide at the expense of the hemisphere's poorest country; financial dealings with Fusion Telecommunications Inc., Digitech, Uniplex Telecom Technologies, Mont Salem Communications Group, Globo, and Terra Communications Group/Webcom, among others, never garnered the attention they deserved. Deals from which the likes of Congressman Joseph Kennedy III, Joseph R. Wright Jr. (the former Director of the Federal Office of Management and Budget under President Reagan), John Sununu (the former chief of staff under the first Bush administration), and Thomas F. McLarty III (the former White House chief of staff under President Clinton) seem to have profited.

Between 1993 and 1994, unprecedented mobilization in several major American cities demonstrated how popular the Haitian cause had become. Hundreds of thousands of Haitians were able to block all of downtown Manhattan and managed, without any prior publicity, to do better than the Pope, drawing more than 100,000 people in Central Park. Realizing the mobilization capacity of the Haitians and its influence on their own electorate, politicians jumped on this electorally lucrative "bandwagon." It suddenly became a "must" for the Democratic political class and the Congressional Black Caucus.

Aristide was excellent in using this enthusiasm for his own political agenda. Not even hiding his primitive racism from his closest collaborators, he favored the support of the white establishment since he doubted that the black politicians had any real access to the White House, with most Haitians viewed as nothing more than a convenient polemical toy for American domestic politics. During the last U.S. presidential elections, Aristide's failed presidency was used by the Republicans to refute Clinton's foreign policy achievements, while his exile was exploited by the Democrats to denounce George W. Bush's strong-arm tactics.

Remember the Eddie Murphy sketch in *Saturday Night Live*? Disguising himself as a Caucasian, just to experience for once, how "white people" behave when they are among themselves? As soon as the last black person gets off the bus, a spontaneous party breaks out on the bus, with champagne and hors-d'oeuvres. I feel the same when American politicians are talking about Haiti. Just change "white" to "American." Except they don't even wait for us to get off the bus. We are there but just don't exist. The partying starts right there in our face.

Today, after almost eighteen months of transition government and fifteen months with the presence of the United Nations Stabilization Mission in Haiti (MINUSTAH), which was supposed to guide the country toward free elections, acceptable to and accepted by all, the social situation and security conditions have degraded considerably. The Haitian capital is traumatized with incessant violence that affects every social sector. Threats, kidnappings, rape, assassinations and armed robberies all punctuate the daily life of a city thrown into a state of siege. It is the result of an offensive calculated and coordinated from Aristide's self-exile in South Africa to make the country ungovernable.

To describe our future in Haiti, President Aristide liked to use the metaphor of a cigar lit at both ends. As the favorite slogan of his partisans was, "If Aristide leaves, we'll chop heads and burn houses," one can only deduce that he is the one who lit the cigar. The sad truth for the millions of Haitians who had placed their destiny in the hands of Father Aristide in 1990 and again in 1994 is that he left a legacy of lies, intolerance, corruption, nepotism and conspiracy to eliminate his rivals and detractors. We should have known.

It became a habit among the tyrant's "friends," in particular among his

American friends in the pseudo-left sector, to downplay these trends, or to hold his entourage responsible. Is this to say that there are crimes condemnable in a western country but acceptable in Haiti? Are journalists' assassinations, threats, the dismissal of judges who are honest or not "flexible" enough, the forced exile of bothersome adversaries—are these "acceptable"? Do we only deserve a dime store version of democracy? A patronizing conceit that "low-end" democracy is good enough for "poor" Haitians? Justice and democracy as elastic concepts for the sake of "realpolitik"?

We have been hearing loud protestations about Aristide being "kidnapped" from some members of the Black Caucus, supported in their outrage by the ambiguous positions of South African President Thabo Mbeki and by the Caribbean Community (CARICOM). The added forces of this respectable triumvirate don't make their partisan stand more credible. Each one of these entities has their own particular agenda for which "poor" Haiti is only an easy excuse.

The Black Caucus's position is grounded in part on legitimate suspicion of U.S. strong arm tactics against a weak government, and on a stubborn belief that anything "black" must be defendable. But sadly enough, for some of the loudest voices, their position also stems from their sound and solid socio-economical advantages.

President Mbeki's position can be explained by his rather equally stubborn "black consciousness" attitude arising out of his known admiration of the Haitian revolution (which took place in 1789 for Christ's sake!), which transforms any black identity discourse à la Aristide, into a legitimate revolutionary stance. And Mbeki apparently does need this sort of discourse at home.

The CARICOM position, the most absurd of them all, giving our common Caribbean interest, is based on the geopolitical delusion that approving a forced removal of Aristide would be setting a dangerous precedent in the region. Despite many historical instances that show the absurdity of this position, where "Big Brother" just came and went without asking for permission (Grenada and Panama for starters).

It is interesting to note that, despite all the evidence to the contrary, much of it in this book, Aristide backers in the U.S. are still repeating that he was kidnapped, while cleverly avoiding mention that both the Clinton and the second Bush administration have been Aristide's strongest backers and the architects of many political settlements between him and the opposition, settlements that he never respected, of course. Still they kept supporting him though each crisis, until this last one, when a vast popular opposition to his rule finally took to the streets he has been monopolizing through years of terror. And sadly enough, even part of the progressive left in the U.S. is still holding fast to their fantasy of a "Western imperialist conspiracy." An intellectual cliché that only tired and lazy fighters in the west can afford. An easy way out of a deeper analysis of an admittedly complex political situation. The charismatic friend, "the leader of the masses" has taken a wrong turn. Let's have the courage and honesty to assess it. Too many people have paid with their lives just for admitting that.

When Haitian civil society decided to pick up the fight against Aristide through massive and peaceful protests in late 2003 and early 2004, bringing together democrats of all classes and political stripes—students' and women's organizations, businessmen and union organizers, intellectuals and simple citizens—one of the main purposes was to get rid of an authoritarian rule and of a kleptocratic business dealer. The people of Haiti have had to suffer this kind of intervention repeatedly over its two hundred years of independence. But we shouldn't see it as history constantly repeating itself. In the bigger picture, it is about the long and perilous road toward democracy or whatever the form or the term will be in the future. Despite unfavorable odds and unreliablefriends, Haiti has managed to survive (badly I admit). Friends, who too often mistook paternalism for advice, charity for support and collaboration, pity for solidarity.

But Haitians do not need pity or charity. Neither do we need patronizing advice or paternalistic lessons in democracy and justice. In this courageous and tireless country, there is a wide range of valid and critical opinions that are neither submissive to any local or foreign powers, nor aligned with the wealthy, the former military, the Lavalas extremists or the infrastructure of corruption.

One aspect of the erratic scrutiny given to the "poorest country of the hemisphere" (as most observers are prone to repeat) is its paternalistic and dismissive bent. The perennially arrogant pontification about "helping those poor Haitians," or, alternatively, about "being fed-up with these [same!] Haitians," or even—usually while throwing up both hands—about "the un-governability of this cursed country" is not really helpful to those in Haiti and abroad who have been fighting for decades for a better life, often paying a high price for doing so.

We Haitians, as a whole, do share the responsibility for the current mess. But we are not alone in this responsibility. The international community is an important actor as well. After many years of disappointing involvement and halfhearted support, as well as patent political miscalculation, they bear their own share of the debacle. Today there is a unique opportunity for this international community to be more discerning and consistent in its approach to our problems.

Most Haitians know what is wrong in Haiti, and with time, and solidarity from our real friends, especially those who are discerning, we can and will put Haiti on the right track.

And Michael Deibert's book is a good way to start.

Raoul Peck
Jacmel, Haiti
August 2005

| | |

Ti Goave

IT WAS SUCH A BEAUTIFUL DAY—characteristic of Haiti, with sea-smooth blue skies and wisps of clouds floating thoughtlessly through—that we almost forgot that we were going to a funeral.

It was beyond Carrefour Road, with its abandoned casinos and dancehalls. It was beyond its still functioning waterside brothels, clinging to the edge of the bay like a last temptation to the peasants coming into the capital to find work. Beyond this purgatory of caramel-skinned Dominican prostitutes and crowded lanes winding themselves back into the hills, Petit Goave was only thirty miles from Port-au-Prince, but it was decades away in look and feel. Known colloquially as *Ti Gwav* in Kreyol (though I had always preferred the archaic mixture "*Ti Goave*"), the city was a rambling, frontier place, full of dusty streets, swinging front doors, broad porches and verandas and a semi-defunct port that occasionally roused itself from torpor to accept a contraband load of clothes from Miami, rice or cocaine. The most distinctive feature of the town, aside from its massive, white and blue cathedral and signature tricolored candy, *douce marcosse*, was how hard old habits died. Almost twenty years after their fall, hotels there still had framed photographs of Haiti's disgraced playboy dictator Jean-Claude Duvalier and his disreputable light-skinned wife, Michele Bennet, hanging in their lobbies and guestrooms. Ti Goave had once been one of the largest bastions in the country for the Duvaliers' murderous secret police, the Tontons Macoutes, created by Jean-Claude's father, Francois, and in these convulsive days of the reign of Haiti's only truly dominant political personality to follow him, the diminutive and galvanizing orator and former priest President Jean-Bertrand Aristide, it soon became abundantly aware that precious little had changed.

We had crowded into the sweltering Radio Metropole van to traverse that road to Ti Goave. Early that morning, about half a dozen Haitian journalists and I had rendezvoused in Port-au-Prince's Champs de Mars plaza, which Aristide's predecessor in power, René Préval, had succeeded in transforming from a rubbishy wasteland to an elegant, piazza-style meeting place, replete with electric lamps, a band shell, overflowing greenery and splashing waterfalls. The orange sun was just beginning to crest over the mountains that held the capital in a maternal embrace as it faced the bay, and its glow and warmth was reflected in the puddles where the street boys were washing their faces. Beyond the ghastly, permanent traffic jam at the outer edges of Haiti's capital, the sense of oppressive physical crush lifted in an almost corporeal sensation. Passing the overgrown, shuttered sea resorts with names like Brisas del Caribe and La Siren and the stone-workers' outpost village of Leogane, soon we were in the company of only rainbow colored tap-taps speeding by, filled beyond capacity with passengers and pumping sinuous compas music in compensation, and silently padding women walking down the roadside, baskets on their heads filled with bananas, mangos and flowers.

Journalist, sometime schoolteacher and occasional employee of Ti Goave's notoriously porous port, Brignol Lindor had been murdered a week before, on December 3, 2001. A heady and explosive mix of politics, violence, drugs and corruption had been brewing around the country for some time, as elements affiliated with populist Aristide squared off on the political stage and in the streets with members of a noisy opposition, armed and dangerous former members of the disbanded Haitian military and various international and politico-criminal actors. Ti Goave, a city divided, had been where that brew had most poisonously concentrated. Lindor, a slight, dapper man with a fondness for antigovernment pronouncements and an easy smile, initially became caught up in the combination when he had conducted an exposé of Ti Goave's Lavalassian deputy mayor, Dume Bony, and his appropriation of thousands of dollars of government funds earmarked to improve the port where they both worked. Shortly thereafter, Lindor stepped out to work one morning beautiful as this one and paid for it with his life.

He had been driving back from teaching a law class, they said, a few towns over. Bony had declared the previous weekend that Aristide's policy of "zero tolerance" against Haiti's urban gangs and rural thieves should be applied to Lindor as well, who had spoken on his radio show to spokesman of the Democratic Convergence opposition coalition, one of whose most right-wing members, Hubert de Ronceray, hailed from Ti Goave and maintained a sizable power base there. A group of landless peasants calling themselves Domi Nan Bwa (Sleeping in the Woods), declaring affiliation with the government but in fact, many said, operating as little more than a gang, decided to put Bony's words into action after one of their number was brutally beaten in an altercation with Convergence partisans earlier that day.

Domi Nan Bwa—some had the mob numbering at nearly fifty that day—began to roam the roads leading to Ti Goave, machetes in hand, looking for someone, anyone they could take their anger out on. The reptilian brain at the back of all mobs took hold and when Radio Echo 2000 reporter, Love Augustin, drove into their midst, they saw their chance had arrived.

"They wanted to kill me," Augustin said to a local journalist later, recounting how the gang dragged him from his vehicle and started to beat him. "But when Brignol's car arrived in the area, one of them yelled, 'Leave him alone, there's Brignol.' I ran to hide."

Lindor, sensing the mortal implications of the mob's anger, tried to dash to a nearby home, but was seized by the mob, who set to work on him with machetes, stones and their fists. Soon, the news director of Radio Echo 2000 was reduced to the rent and violated corpse whose image decorated the signs held by demonstrators as we pulled into Ti Goave. Almost as soon as they had arrived, Domi Nan Bwa had disappeared back into the mountains and fields around the city, and it was left to Lindor's family to bury his body.

Goudou Jean Numa, our driver that day and an aspiring reporter, and Wendell Theodore, Metropole's affable, round-faced senior correspondent, were in the van's two front seats as we drove past the facade of Lindor's former radio station. Black banners reading *Adieu, Brignol* had been strung across the street, and the front awning of the building was hung with garlands of flowers and wreaths. Weeping women dressed in black and glistening with sweat and tears tugged on them as the radio station broadcast funeral elegies from speakers set out towards the street. A young bearded man in a dark suit wiped his shaved head with a handkerchief and held up a sign reading *Brignol, mon frere* as we passed.

Loss.

But there was more. At the funeral home a few streets away, hundreds more were gathered, most in dark mourning dress, some in blue jeans and peasant hats, some in the blue and khaki uniforms of Haiti's security force, the Police Nationale d'Haiti (PNH). The gathered assemblage continued to act out the surging tide of grief's manifestations. Men pounded on the hood of the long black hearse that sat dust-covered under the tropical sun at the door of the funeral home. On the building's roof, several more waved a placard containing a picture of Lindor's grisly, macheted head and unveiled a banner that ran, in part, *"Nou mande kominote entenasyonal retire Aristide/Li se yon Ousama Benn Laden nan peyi dayiti."* ["We demand the international community remove Aristide/In Haiti he is our Osama Bin Laden."]

Inside the stifling funeral home, atop a simple black coffin, a picture of Lindor as he had existed in life, slight, smiling and black, with the trimmed mustache of the Haitian male middle class. A stout woman leaned her head on another's shoulder and appeared to be overcome, whether from emotion or the heat was unclear.

It was too much, and I stepped back outside.

Naomie Calixte, Metropole's reporter, was walking through the screaming throng with the hipsway of a dancer, interviewing the men in straw hats as they screamed spittle into her face.

Micha Gaillard, a university professor who had run for mayor of Port-au-Prince and had been known as one of Convergence's more thoughtful members, was standing across the street with Claude Roumain, himself a former candidate. The near-white Gaillard, seemingly beefed-up and unrecognizable since I had seen him the previous summer, was dressed entirely in black and glowering at the crowd from behind designer sunglasses as Roumain surveyed the chaos with his sad eyes and thick, sensual lips.

"This is incredible," Gaillard said, seemingly to no one in particular. A truck full of riot police, the Corps d'intervention et de Maintien de l'ordre, though always called the CIMO, was trying to negotiate the narrow street that ran from the market past the funeral house to the road out of town, and the crowd was screaming and spitting at them, with the CIMO sweating and looking cornered in their bullet-proof vests and heavy helmets.

More wailing came from the funeral home, and several of Lindor's coworker's at the station appeared at the door, bearing his coffin toward the hearse. They lifted the coffin up and, being careful not to dislodge the halo of wreaths arranged around the vehicles roof, slid it in and slammed the door.

The procession began to wind its way slowly to the cathedral, sitting in the sandy coastal plain, a series of three crosses reaching its apex in the middle arch, some sixty feet off the ground.

"*Nou pa pe,*" the group sang. "We are not afraid."

I saw Guyler Delva walking near the front of the crowd. Delva, dapper and slightly portly, was the secretary-general of the Association of Haitian Journalists, or AJH. Scorned by many more conservative Haitian journalists for years for what they viewed as his excessive closeness with (and superior access to) the National Palace during René Préval's presidency, Delva had recently taken a more vocal role in criticizing what he viewed as government excesses. He had arrived in Ti Goave days after the murder and, traipsing into the bush, tracked down the members of Domi Nan Bwa, who freely admitted their role in the murder, but explained that they had only been following the deputy mayor's orders, and avenging the murder of their friend. Lindor, in their view, had gotten what he had asked for.

"And they're still sitting out there," Delva said, smiling a somewhat unnerved smile, pointing down the road running into the hills, past the market where the merchant women's stalls sat abandoned today.

The throng and the hearse had arrived at the Cathedral Saint Pierre, rising up out of the town like a moored ship just hanging on at sea. The angry crowd seemed to be growing exponentially as the minutes passed, and as Lindor's coffin was brought into the cathedral, a woman threw herself on it and fainted, having to be carried out and revived on the steps. The sight seemed to inflame the onlookers only more.

"Lindor was killed by Aristide! By a *vakabon*! I won't be eating my soup with him this year!" a muscular man yelled, somehow laughing, and making a reference to the traditional New Year's soup *joumou*, intimating that Aristide would not finish out the year.

In the midst of the chaos, a line of uniformed school children lay pink-and-white wreathes on the church steps as others jeered the masked and hooded riot police that stood guard.

After an oratory by a local priest and some mournful liturgical music, it was time to see Brignol Lindor off to his final resting place, the city graveyard on the south of town. Ti Goave's narrow streets were so full of people by now that several men had to half-walk, half-ride on the hearse's hood to push stragglers out of the way as they descended slowly to where the freshly dug grave waited. More convoys of CIMO were making their tenuous way through the masses as well, seeking to head off the crowd and set up positions in and around the graveyard first, just in case anything got out of hand. The crowd rocked their armor-plated personnel carrier back and forth briefly, but the black-clad and hooded men kept their cool.

Down at the graveyard, there was a lot of waiting going on outside of the cemetery walls as journalists gathered and waited for everyone who was going to make their way inside. Roosevelt Benjamin, the young news director for radio Signal FM, was leaning against his station's van, smoking a cigarette and talking to a correspondent inside the cemetery on a walkie-talkie.

As we stood by, watching the people file in, all of a sudden the air was filled with a sound like that of cars backfiring, and immediately we all knew what it was. We had seen teams of CIMO enter the cemetery earlier and the rumor had begun to circulate that they were barring the family from entering and forbidding them from burying Lindor. Some of the younger kids hanging around, most quite poor and many drunk on tafia and Prestige beer, almost immediately began turning their bottles into makeshift projectiles that broke on the helmets of the CIMO as they landed on their heads. At nearly the same time, a hysterical crackle of automatic weapons fire went up from within the cemetery, and the crowds that had been entering turned and began charging toward us, screaming in fear. Trailing plumes of smoke like primitive tracer missiles, tear-gas canisters (called *gaz lacrymogene*) began issuing over our heads, soon emitting their choking contents into the streets. Naomie continued to stand and watch the crowd with her microphone out as Wendell's eyes darted excitedly back and forth and I moved behind one of the van doors to escape the oncoming crowd and wicked gusts of tear gas. Gunfire exploded again and we could see the tops of the high stucco wall we were parked against kick up dust from the cemetery side as they ricocheted. The people living near the cemetery, who had been quietly watching the whole scene from the doors of their wooden shacks, had now disappeared behind the hanging blankets that functioned as doorways and pulled their children inside.

"*Aba Aristide!*" shouted one young man, looking at me as he took off his t-shirt and wrapped it around his face, bandit-fashion, to fend off the choking fumes. "You hear me?" he asked in English.

As the clatter of bullets and stench of gas grew, we opted to pull out and re-group. As the journalists squeezed limes under their noses to ease the sting, we took off to try and find a way out of the city. From time to time, on the deserted streets, a crowd of young men would run by, bottles and gas cans in hand. For a moment, finding ourselves back on Ti Goave's broad main street, we saw a con-voy of CIMO make a hair-pin turn around the corner and head down toward the cemetery, their AK 47s pointed in the air.

Retreating, we turned the corner and were face to face with a CIMO in full riot gear, menacingly pointing his machine gun at the car. The metal frame of the van suddenly seemed like a cartoonishly weak defense against such a weapon, but he saw the *Presse* banner plastered across the front windshield and waved us through. We set off without a moment to consider where exactly we were heading, when another figure began darting toward us.

A man was running toward us, holding an unconscious child in his arms, tears streaming down his face.

"Please, my child!" he wailed. "Don't let her die!"

The van came to a terrifying halt as the man and his daughter were dragged inside, and the CIMO at the intersection turned his attention back to us. She had evidently been overwhelmed by the tear gas. Not pausing to think, Goudou sped off in the direction of the local hospital. As the man held the child in his lap, journalists frantically slapped her face and tried to rouse her with limes under her nose.

Arriving at the decrepit local hospital, where a dilapidated gate opened onto several sick wards with broken windows and peeling white paint, it was obvi-ous that they had not been spared. Spent tear-gas canisters lay fuming in the street and from within the compound itself patients looked out, peering fearfully from behind windows. As the father got out of the van with his daughter, a white-coated intern came jogging along, a handkerchief held in front of his mouth and nose. As the child was whisked to a back room, patients in hospital gowns looked on. The child began to cry in the hot room, reaching out for her father, who wept some more and thanked the doctor profusely. We stood in the hospital's court-yard where shouting and gunfire could still be heard, but only sporadically. A PNH jeep drove casually by. They were mopping up. Power politics at its most naked seemed finished for the moment.

It would be a long drive back to Port-au-Prince, through the heat and swirl of Carrefour, now that the sun was beginning its slow languid descent from the sky. Before we hit the road again, we decided to stop at a row of *ti machanns*, as the market women in Haiti are called, who had set up shop across the street from the local police station on the eastern edge of town.

Three CIMO sat in a semicircle; one leaning back in his chair, his assault rifle balanced casually in his left hand. They were chatting among themselves and quietly regarding the reporters as they descended from their vans. A woman with a roadside stand was selling roasted corn, delicious and slathered with fatty butter, and another woman was selling *fritay*, the characteristic fried Haitian patty that serves as the backbone of many diets in the country. The journalists and the police eventually began to talk to one another—the journalists teasing the police about the day's chaos, and the police, not overly amused but friendly, shaking their heads and smiling. The tension dissipated quickly enough as to be somewhat disorienting, until I realized that a kind of dance was being done, and how often and in how many ways it would be performed. It seemed to speak of something hopeful for the country, if people could be involved in situations so dangerous and intense as the journalists and the police that had been teargassing them only minutes earlier, could, almost at once, put that trauma behind them and converse, joke, share the same humor.

I thought of how, at the edges of the protests, beyond the crowds and the mobs and the CIMO and the reporters, staring silently as we passed by the tiny lanes and the levees and the alley entrances, the poorest of the poor, the market women, their naked babies, their husbands in frayed jean-shirts or t-shirts, watching, almost cataloging everything as it went on.

What happens outside the fray can often tell you more than the fray itself. And that silence will call you in, every time.

One thought of the agonies endured by the slaves, chained in the airless dark of a ship's hull and then pushed out into the bright light of a terrifying new world. Of the massacres across the island as those slaves rose up and cast off their colonial masters, the killings then and after, as they fought for a decade to beat back repeated attempts at invasion by the European powers, as Jean-Jacques Dessalines brutally birthed a new nation. One thought of the civil war between Alexandre Petion and the surpassingly romantic figure of Henri Christophe, who built a palace and a fortress in the north of the country to rival any wonder of the ancient world, and then committed suicide in it rather than be captured. Of the Duvalierist massacres, and the slaughter that commenced when the army and paramilitaries had ousted Aristide almost as soon as he had begun his first term a decade ago. And now, yet more bodies. They were the currency of politics in Haiti.

In Haiti they have a saying, *deye mon gen mon*. Beyond the mountains there are more mountains—a beautiful expression, not only of hope and struggle, but of lineage, of history, of the ebbing of tides, the passing of clouds and breaths of thick wind covering the mountain ranges. They also have another saying. *Bay kou, bliye. Pote mak, sonje.* The one who gives the blow, forgets. The one who suffers the hurt, remembers.

| | |

|
Saint-Domingue

IT HAD ALL STARTED with such joy.

When I first landed in Port-au-Prince, a city I would visit continually over the years before finally settling in to live there, it was near the first day of November. A day, as any Haitian will tell you, not like any other because it is the first day of *Gede*, the two-day celebration of the dead. The cemeteries fill with *vodouisants*, adherents of Haiti's poignant spiritual blend of its African and European heritage, paying tribute to Baron Samedi, the guardian of the cemetery and a randy raconteur whose erotic commentary passes through the lips of those he possesses like the holy grail of Haitian bawdiness made writ. With the fall of the hated Duvalier family dictatorship a decade before, Haitians had seen off the scion of a family who had written a history of greedy thuggery and murderous bloodletting to rival that of any of the dime-store despots that bedeviled Latin American throughout the twentieth century. There had followed four long years of struggle as what would become known as "the popular movement" attempted to uproot the entrenched apparatus of impunity and gunmen military rule, and to bring something like representative democracy to a people who had never known any such thing.

The city was like nothing I had ever seen: an immediate chaos of people, cars, dust, noise, withering light and pungent scents. The airport road, devastated and potholed by years of tropical rains and neglect, staggered from the suburb of Tabarre into the city as if at whim. Traffic consisted of distinctive, beautiful collective buses referred to by the Haitians as tap-taps, squeezing as many as two dozen people at a time into the back seats of pickup trucks fitted with benches on the cab. Their hulks bore the images of popular Haitian singers, Brazilian football players, *vodou lwa*, and, occassionally, a smiling white Jesus. They had names like "I Love You" and "Express Pour Tout." Beneath them sped communal taxis, signified by a distinctive red ribbon dangling from the rearview mirror, in various states of disrepair and taking in great gulps of black smoke belched out by passing trucks hauling gravel, charcoal and garbage. The smell was overpowering, a heady mixture of bursting tropical flowers, choking exhaust, rotting citrus fruit peels and raw sewage canals that snaked through the city—open, black and fetid. Peeling signs still hung recalling the election of René Préval, president two years, now. *"Votez Préval!"* they implored.

My driver and I rolled over vaulting low urban hills, as befit the most mountainous nation in the Caribbean, yet every inch of their surfaces seemed built upon, with men gazing out from *borlette* lottery banks and bars, barefoot and straining cart haulers rushing beside the open window of our taxi bearing their back-breaking loads, schoolgirls with ribbons in their hair and abandoned shirtless little boys at every turn. The traffic was an ebb, a slow moving intravenous drip of people in and out of various parts in the city, from the once-elegant mountainside suburb of Petionville, now declining in status as the poor built slum dwellings clinging to the hillside, to the Carrefour neighborhood along the sea on the city's southern edge. The sun burned in a carnal yellow, informing even the dust blowing down the crowded lanes with a certain beauty and flair.

It was as intoxicating a place as I have ever been.

Haiti was a democracy now. That was what was said when René Préval, the mournful-faced agronomist and one-time bakery owner whose name decorated the campaign signs that had greeted me, had been overwhelmingly elected to replace former priest and president Jean-Bertrand Aristide. His inauguration in a peaceful transfer of power was a monumental thing in itself, given Haiti's history of mandate by bullet. Aristide himself has spent three years of his term in agonized exile, ousted in a military coup, and had only been returned by a U.S.-led multinational military force of some 25,000 troops, remnants of whom still rolled through the capital's narrow streets in their wide military vehicles, their blue UN helmets poking up from the green armored cars; I saw a convoy of them, Pakistanis, roll past what I would later realize was the main thoroughfare of Avenue Jean Paul II.

Haiti's history had never lacked for drama, though.

CHRISTOPHER COLUMBUS first set eyes on Haiti on December 5, 1492. Sailing around the northwestern claw of the island, he remarked that the bay his ships (the *Santa Maria*, the *Nina*, and the *Pinta*) weighed anchor in recalled the Bay of Cadiz in Spain. His men first set foot near what would later become the town of Mole St. Nicholas; continuing to skirt the northern shore, they named a large coastal island Tortuga, or Turtle, for that's what its sloping outline reminded him of. Columbus and his men went ashore several more times, where they were greeted by a peaceful and docile native people called the Arawak. The Arawak called their island Haiti ("mountainous land") and Quisqueya ("vast country"), but Columbus renamed it Isla Espanola ("Spanish Island"), which eventually became Hispaniola. Before Columbus had returned to Spain at the end of the year, he lost the *Santa Maria*, run aground on a reef near present day Cap Haitien. He set sail for Europe leaving some fifty men ashore to begin the foundations for a settlement. By the time Columbus came back, they had disappeared into the vastness of the island and were never seen again.

Diseases, enslavement and wanton killing by the Europeans who returned reduced the number of the native Arawak people, earlier estimated at three million by Bishop Bartolome de las Casas, to under fifty thousand by 1510. By 1540, the Arawaks were all but extinct, and within the next decade the population disappeared from the face of the island entirely. The Europeans introduced the crop of sugarcane to the island and, with the disappearance of the Arawaks, the colonizers needed a work force for the back-breaking labor of the cane fields. For this, they turned to Africa and the slave trade. By the mid 1500s there were over thirty thousand African slaves on the island—a sizeable number, but only the merest foreshadowing of what was to come.

The island's first group of Spanish invaders were more interested in conquest and plunder than farming, and so sugar production was gradually abandoned. While the eastern side of the island was firmly under Spanish control, the western side became something of a hemispheric redoubt for pirates and ne'er-do-wells from other parts of the Caribbean. The buccaneers first settled on Tortuga (now renamed Isle de la Tortue) off the island's north coast and gradually crept southward. A distinct French flavor took over this side of the island, as French sailors and fortune seekers took advantage of lax Spanish attention to insinuate themselves at various points along the coast.

When the Treaty of Ryswick officially granted the Western third of Hispaniola to the French in 1697, that swath of land was renamed "Saint-Domingue" and returned in earnest to the process of sugar cultivation to supply the product for a ravenous European appetite. By the end of the 1700s, Saint-Domingue supplied three-fourths of the world's sugar and its economy was generating more income than that of all thirteen original North American colonies combined. It quickly became France's wealthiest colony, but was also a tinderbox waiting to erupt. A population of forty thousand whites lorded over thirty thousand mulattos and free blacks and five-hundred thousand slaves. The everpresent threat of revolt and the colonists' reaction to it helped establish Saint-Domingue's infamy as the scene of some of the most sickening excesses of the institution of slavery. Visitors to the colony reported that the whites, vastly outnumbered by the slaves and convinced that any slackening of their fear could spell the colony's doom, routinely crucified disobedient slaves, burned them alive both at the stake and in large cauldrons, flayed them with whips until dead and drowned them in weighted sacks in the colony's bays.

UNDER SUCH A SCENARIO, it was not long before rebellion was brewing among the island's slave population, many of whom had been snatched from the West African kingdom of Dahomey, in what is present day Benin. The slaves had managed to craft a new language—Kreyol—out of the French tongue of their overseers, their native African dialects and a polyglot adaptation of Spanish and English words; and, to a greater degree than anywhere else in the New World, they managed to retain their native religious beliefs, often practiced under a guise of Catholicism in what would become known as *vodou*. At nighttime meetings throughout the summer of 1791, slaves came together from throughout the Plaine du Cap region near the northern city of Cap Francais to plot their liberation. In the midst of a dramatic tropical storm on the night of August 14, at a meeting led by a towering black overseer imported from Jamaica named Boukman, the slaves conducted a long, complex *vodou* ceremony pledging to fight for freedom, and a week later rose up against the whites, attacking plantations at Acul, Limbe, and elsewhere throughout the Plaine du Cap. Boukman was seized early in the uprising and beheaded at the Place d'Armes in Cap Francais, but soon thereafter the Plaine du Nord also erupted. Plantations were sacked and hundreds of whites killed in a manner as barbarous as that by which they had treated the slaves, and soon those very same slaves were laying siege to Cap Francais, the elegant city that had become the jewel of the colony. The prolonged battle for the city produced terrible carnage, with the British historian Bryan Edwards, who was in the city for part of its siege, estimating that some ten thousand slaves must have died in battle. The city fell on April 22, 1793, and its townspeople fled to the docks to board ships and escape, with over ten thousand setting sail for North America. Many of the Cap's slaves escaped and joined the rebellion.

THE MOST EXTRAORDINARY PERSONALITY of the rebellion was Toussaint Louverture, a former slave and coachmen who had taught himself to read and write and became the rebel's great military strategist. Famed for riding many miles in a single day and then appearing, like a ghost, unexpectedly, from place to place, Toussaint was referred to as the *centaure de la Savanne* because of his outstanding horsemanship. In 1796, in the midst of a brief British occupation of the western side of the island, Toussaint declared himself governor-for-life of Saint-Domingue, which he said would remain a colonial state—with slavery abolished—within the French realm of influence. As it struggled for its freedom, though, the new nation was riven with division. A split between the mulattos and the blacks was not long in coming, and by 1799, mulatto officers such as Alexandre Petion and Jean-Pierre Boyer rallied to the side of dissident general Andre Rigaud in the south, who sought to wrest the leadership from Toussaint and install mulatto supremacy.

On Toussaint's side, a brilliant English-speaking ex-slave named Henri Christophe, who had originally hailed from Grenada and fought alongside American revolutionary forces at the Battle of Savannah, commanded the forces at the Cap, while Jean-Jacques Dessalines, a brave and brutal general, took command of the south. The mulattos were finally defeated at the southern town of

Jacmel, and Toussaint traveled to the port of Les Cayes to proclaim Dessalines as governor of the region.

Not surprisingly, given such unrest, the economy of the colony was in tatters. Under the advisement of Christophe, from 1800-01, Toussaint established the fermage system, whereby the state took over abandoned plantations, gave them to army officers to administer and contracted laborers into a kind of indentured servitude to work the land. When Toussaint seized Santo Domingo from the Spanish in 1801 and abolished slavery there as well, it appeared that the moment of liberty for the island had finally arrived. However, the rise of Napoleon Bonaparte in France, so long distracted by its own revolutionary upheaval, spelled trouble for the new nation, and in 1802, Napoleon sent a force of some forty thousand troops, under the command of his brother-in-law General Charles Leclerq, to Cap Francais to bring the rebellion to heel. What followed was more scorched earth fighting throughout the island, as Christophe and Petion, both going over to Leclerq's side, eventually forced Toussaint and his lieutenant Dessalines to surrender. Toussaint was then kidnapped to France, where he died in a remote French jail in the Jura Mountains, but soon thereafter rebellion—under Dessalines's cry of *koupe tèt, boule kay* ("cut off their heads and burn down their houses")—flared again, this time with the local generals unified under a goal of a complete independence from France when it became evident that the French intended to restore slavery. Leclerq, beset by tropical diseases, died, and was replaced by Jean-Baptiste Rochambeau, who brought in dogs from Cuba to hunt the rebels. It was of little use, though, as guerilla tactics and yellow fever shattered the French military, claiming the lives of some twenty thousand French soldiers, and local forces under Dessalines's command finally won a decisive battle at Vertieres, near Cap Francais, in November 1803. On January 1, 1804, in the northern coastal town of Gonaives, Dessalines declared republic of Haiti, reverting to the Arawak name that had so long been abandoned. Upon hearing the declaration of independence read aloud, Boisrond-Tonnerre, Dessalines's secretary (Dessalines himself was illiterate) was overcome with emotion and shouted that, "This doesn't say what we really feel! For our declaration of independence, we need the skin of a white man for parchment, his skull for an inkwell, his blood for ink and a bayonet for a pen!"

"Long live independence!" Dessalines declared to thousands assembled at the Place d'Armes in Gonaives. "Swear now, with clasped hands, to live free and independent and to accept death in preference to the yoke!"

Dessalines declared himself *gouverneur general a vie*, as had Toussaint, and, proving that the sentiments voiced by Boisrond-Tonnerre were no idle remark, a wholesale slaughter of the remaining French and whites commenced soon thereafter. By the early months of 1804, the island was seized in the frenzy of a pogrom. French citizens and other whites, including many women and children, were sought out and butchered throughout the island. In the southern city of Jeremie alone, some four hundred were killed in a single day. Dessalines rode throughout the country, personally supervising the killing in Jeremie, Port-au-Prince, Archaie, Saint Marc back to Gonaives and then on to Cap Francais, now renamed Cap Haitien (often referred to colloquially as Au Cap). For every American or British subject that was spared, there were a hundred instances such as that which took place at Les Cayes, where the town's caucasian women were loaded aboard ships with their children taken out to the harbor, weighed down with rocks and tossed overboard alive into the sea. Petion and Christophe did what they could to save lives here and there, but Dessalines was implacable in his desire to rid the new land of any trace of French influence.

He largely succeeded, but in doing so he destroyed a huge reservoir of foreign expertise in agriculture, commerce and government that the country desperately needed if it were to succeed, and left in its place a military dictatorship enforced by often ignorant and rapacious generals. Haiti was free, but it was also in ruins, scorned and held in hostility by fearful slave-owning countries such as the United States, where refugees had arrived steadily, bringing with them stories of an inferno of violence. Haiti had become, in the view of many in the slave-holding United States, an upside down world of chaos where black ruled white, and killed them with impunity.

Dessalines set up a lavish court at the village of Marchand in the Artibonite Valley, and, in emulation of his foe Napoleon, he proclaimed himself Emperor Jacques I at a ceremony in Cap Haitien in October 1804. Christophe and Petion were both rewarded for their service by being entrusted with administering the north and south of the country, respectively, and the fermage system was redoubled with enforced servitude on the plantations. In February 1805, Dessalines led another ill-advised invasion of Santo Domingo, which left large-scale massacres and smoldering ruins of towns in its wake, but he was forced to make a humiliating retreat from his siege of Ciudad Santo Domingo upon catching sight of landing French warships. The army, which had been poorly provided for, was the source of murmurs of rebellion that rumbled throughout the country upon its return. On October 16 1806, while traveling through Pont-Rouge to put down a uprising near what today is the La Saline slum in Port-au-Prince, Dessalines was ambushed and killed by rebellious soldiers. He was shot down and his body then defiled by a mob who stripped him off his lavish uniform and cut off his fingers to steal his rings. Legend said that a madwoman gathered his remains to hide them from his enemies.

At the death of Dessalines, the tensions that had been present in Haiti since independence, between north and south, black and mulatto, finally resulted in the cleaving of the country into two. Henri Christophe, in many ways Toussaint's spiritual descendent, controlled the north, where he essentially reinstated slavery, using forced work brigades as the backbone of a state-managed agrarian economy. Taking a page from Dessalines, he declared himself King

Henry I and set up an elaborate court system modeled on Europe's absolute monarchies, building a stunning palace modeled on Versailles—Sans Souci—outside of Cap Haitien and a fort, Le Citadelle, to guard it. He also created a monetary system with a currency called the *gourde*, after one of northern Haiti's most plentiful objects, which is still in use in Haiti today. In the south, Alexandre Petion, from his capital at what was then the small harbor city of Port-au-Prince, scorned the idea of large plantations and instead doled out parcels of land to peasants in lieu of payment to soldiers in his army, to do with as they saw fit. As a result, productivity proved far less in Petion's south than in Christophe's north, but Petion proved a popular leader, and one of pronounced republican ideals. At one of the darkest hours of the struggle for South America, Petion opened the town of Jacmel to the Latin American revolutionary Simon Bolivar and his men, providing them with material and logistical support for their campaign to liberate the southern hemisphere. Upon Petion's death in 1818, he was succeeded by Jean-Pierre Boyer, a veteran both of the struggle for independence and of the mulatto secessionist battles that followed in its wake. Boyer launched a concerted effort to reunite the country under his rule—an effort that culminated with Christophe's suicide in his palace in 1820 as Boyer's forces approached his door. The new leader then marched on Cap Haitien and reunified the country under a reign that lasted twenty-five years.

Boyer championed the Petion policy of parceling out small plots of land in the north, as well, and productivity soon plummeted there, mirroring its decline in the south. Realizing Dessalines's thwarted dream, he invaded Santo Domingo in 1822 and succeeded in uniting the entire island under his rule. Menaced by a French fleet in 1825 that threatened to bombard Port-au-Prince unless he agreed to pay an indemnity for the "intemperance" of Haiti having seized its freedom and outlawing slavery, Boyer was forced to accept a debt of 150 million francs in exchange for France accepting the nation's independence. Eventually overthrown and exiled in 1843, Boyer's dream of a united island crumbled when the Dominican Republic declared its independence from Haiti a year later. Haiti thus settled into its life as a sovereign nation for the next seventy years, threatened at every turn by various French, American, German and British schemes and weakened internally by a series of endless wars among its competing political factions. Two more disastrous attempts to retake the Dominican Republic did little to win the good will of its neighbors, and thus history was played out on an insular, limited canvas until the early part of the twentieth century.

FOLLOWING A MASSIVE EXPLOSION that destroyed the National Palace and, along with it, the life of president Cincinnatus Leconte in August 1912, the reins of Haiti's government passed through the hands of a series of would-be presidents for three years until, in March 1915, a black general from the north named

Vilbrun Guillaume Sam finally wrested control from his opponents. As with virtually every other leader in Haitian history, Sam, a veteran of various campaigns throughout the country whose pleasant demeanor masked a brutal and ruthless nature, had an armed rebellion to contend with—this one spearheaded by an imperious, red-headed mulatto doctor (also from the north) named Rosalvo Bobo. Apprised of a Bobo-inspired plot to overthrow him in March 1915, Sam rounded up over two hundred hostages from the elite families of Port-au-Prince and locked them in jail, the implication of their fate should Bobo attack the capital thus obvious. While the capital remained relatively peaceful, peasant brigands loyal to Bobo, known as *cacos*, succeeded in overrunning several northern towns.

Despite the cost in men and treasure of World War I, which had begun a year earlier, when a riotous *caco* band invaded Cap Haitien in June—decapitating several prominent citizens and threatening to storm the local consulates, which were loaded with political refugees—a contingent of U.S. Marines disembarked from the *USS Washington* and declared that the city would henceforth be neutral ground during the conflict. For some time the United States had its eye on the Haitian port of Mole St. Nicholas, but, a few years earlier, U.S. Secretary of State William Jennings Bryant, upon receiving a briefing about the particulars of the Haitian situation, was able to muster no more insight than to comment in awed tones, "Dear me, think of it! Niggers speaking French!" With the political situation continuing to deteriorate throughout early July, Wilson was already seriously considering invading Haiti.

The American hand was set in motion beginning on the evening of July 26, when a band of Bobo loyalists attacked the new National Palace (built to replace the one destroyed in the explosion only three years earlier). President Sam fled to the French legation next door, and, in the capital's prison, as word of the attack spread, Sam's chief of police, General Charles-Oscar Etienne, executed over one hundred and fifty of the bourgeois prisoners Sam had taken the previous March as insurance against just such an attack. After discovering the massacre and burying their dead, on July 28, a mob consisting of members of the dead men's families dragged Sam from the French Legation, killed him and paraded his dismembered body through the streets of the capital. The same day, following a furious exchange of diplomatic cables between the U.S. mission in Haiti and Washington, the Marines landed in Bizoton, in the south of the capital, officially commencing a U.S. occupation that would last for twenty years. During that time, the Americans took over in their totality Haiti's finances and customs, built good roads throughout the interior through the labor of forced work brigades known as *corvees*, formed and trained a new Haitian military (the Forces Armees d'Haiti or FADH) and fought off a *caco* rebellion against their presence in the country. They also inflicted deep damage on Haiti's pride as an independent and free nation that would be very long in healing and, in their own way, set the stage for much of the country's political life in the second half of the century.

IT MAY BE SAID THAT much of modern Haitian political history begins with a largely forgotten figure, somehow swept aside by the personalities that came before and after him: Dumarsais Estimé.

Born in Verettes in the Artibonite Valley to a black Haitian farming family in 1900, Estimé had been educated in the port town of Saint Marc and then in the capital, observing in his role as a schoolteacher the social upheaval and wound in the Haitian psyche caused by the American occupation. Nevertheless, he first entered politics under American-mandated elections in 1930, where he won a seat as deputy from his home region in Haiti's lower house of parliament. Eventually, he would become that body's president, and was named Minister of Education under the presidency of Stenio Vincent, a fierce mulatto opponent of the American presence in the nation. With the Americans gone by 1941, Vincent was replaced in the presidency by another mulatto, this one a former ambassador to the United States and senator named Elie Lescot, who had altogether cozier relations with Washington. Lescot supported American efforts in its campaigns against the Axis powers in World War II and ruled his homeland with an iron fist, earning the nickname "Sieur (Sire) Lescot." Things went smoothly enough for a time, but a disastrous agricultural program—at first suggested and then abandoned by an itinerant American agronomist—was followed by a brutal suppression of a series of student-led strikes in its wake.

Soon, for the first time since its brief pause during an enforced mulatto hegemony under the U.S. occupation, Haiti was undergoing another one of its scrambles for control between the self-interested mulatto elite and their surrogates in the political realm and the populist black demagogues who said they sought to rouse their countrymen out of their feudal squalor. During his tenure in office, Lescot, a powerfully built man with a bulldozer personality to match, had committed some grave political sins in the eyes of many Haitians. These included bloating the government bureaucracy with like-minded light-skinned cronies and relatives, supporting an ill-advised campaign to stamp out the practice of *vodou* spearheaded by the local Catholic Church, and, perhaps the death knell, being revealed to have been on the payroll for many years of the Dominican Republic's dictator Rafael Trujillo, who had murdered twenty thousand Haitians, most of them desperately poor immigrant workers, in a single xenophobic spasm across the border in 1937. By 1946, the country was ready for a change, and Dumarsais Estimé, who seemed to represent all that Lescot had not been, seemed about the man to deliver it when Lescot fled into exile and was replaced by an interim military junta.

Estimé's only serious competition in the public realm came from another schoolteacher, a 26-year-old with a massive following among the capital's downtrodden masses, named Daniel Fignole. A rousing orator, Fignole had formed a political movement after Lescot's fall, Le Mouvement des Ouvries et Paysans (The Worker-Peasants Movement, or MOP) and could summon throngs of the poor into the streets to cause mayhem, referring to them as his *rouleau compresseur* or steamroller, with bitter rhetoric against the mulatto establishment that Lescot's rule had come to symbolize. Lacking a substantial base with the country folk beyond the capital, though, he appointed a young, preternaturally grave Haitian doctor with an interest in Haiti's folk culture as the party's secretary-general. That doctor's name was Francois Duvalier.

But Estimé also articulated that anger, from a peasant's perspective, whose rage at the political and economic elite in the capital was doubly felt because of their distance from it, and despite his slogan *un noir au pouvoir* ("a black man in power"), he was regarded by many as less threatening than the youthful Fignole. When Haiti's senators and deputies, elected in public elections the previous May, gathered to select Haiti's new president at the Palais Legislatif on August 16, 1946, they opted against the Fignole party candidate (Fignole was too young to run for the presidency himself) and chose Estimé on the second ballot. The *rouleau compresseur* rioted in the streets when it turned out their man had lost, but the army closed ranks around Estimé, and he assumed the ill-famed presidency a day later. Cannily doling out cabinet appointments, he tapped Fignole as his Minister of Education and MOP official Francois Duvalier as his Director of Public Health. Inheriting a robust market for Haiti's agricultural exports, Estimé was able to make good on some of his populism by raising the minimum wage and creating a series of public-works projects for the chronically unemployed Haitian labor force. When Fignole quit Estimé's cabinet two months later, Duvalier, the soft-spoken doctor, stayed on, impressed by Estimé's populism. In return for his loyalty, he later served as Estimé's Minister of Public Health and Labor.

But populism has a short shelf life when confronting problems as massive as those that plague Haiti's rulers. Estimé created the first glimmers of a black political—as opposed to economic—elite in Haiti, which sent the mulatto elite—who had always been hostile to him—again scanning the army for friends. Leftist student and union movements, some with ties to Fignole, some with ties to Haiti's nascent communist elements, pressed him for greater reform and progress on all sides. Faced with what he feared was an attempt to weaken his base among the unions by communists in the Federation des Travailleurs Haitians (Federation of Haitian Workers) and alarmed by what he saw as Washington's undue notice of the phenomenon, Estimé outlawed the Haitian Communist Party (PCH) in 1948 and booted its declared members out of government office. Attempting to institute constitutional revisions to allow him to succeed himself in the summer of 1949, Estimé provoked a violent student and labor strike. The next year, as the senate gathered and refused to amend the constitution to allow Estimé to stand again, they were attacked by a pro-Estimé mob that sacked the Senate chambers. On May 10, 1950, the general staff of the Haitian army demanded, and got, the president's resignation.

Estimé spent his remaining three years living in bitter exile in New York, dying of uremic poisoning in 1953. His body was returned to Haiti and given a state funeral by his successor, the military dictator Paul Magloire. By the time I had arrived in Haiti, though, Estimé's second tomb, to where he had been reinterred from his original resting place by his disciple Francois Duvalier in 1968, sat on a grassy bluff facing the Bay of Port-au-Prince within sight of Haiti's Parliament, and had fallen into shocking disrepair. Its walls and foundations were broken, grafittied and chipped away, its grass trampled, and homeless legions sprawling passed out or lounging all around its circumference. The waters in the bay had grown yet more fetid since Estimé's death, and the whole scene made a melancholy comment on the state of Haiti's supposed ongoing state of revolution.

But his heirs were not to be so quickly vanquished.

IT WAS SAID THAT his mother, who had died when he was only fourteen, had been mad, and that, indeed, madness ran in his family. There was nothing outwardly assuming about Dr. Francois Duvalier—who had served as both Estimé's Public Health and Labor Ministers before the coup—except perhaps a history that Haitians and outsiders could regard as a model of good works.

He had gained a name for himself through his work with a terrible affliction, through gazing into the wretchedness and malice that nature can sometimes throw at man. Yaws was a disease caused by a spirochete that maimed and twisted limbs and facial features, leaving its victims in agony, and for many years it seemed Duvalier's mission in life to eradicate it. Under the direction of the American Dr. James Dwinelle of the Inter-American Affairs Commission, Duvalier was entrusted with supervising an anti-yaws campaign in 1943 in Gressier, south of the capital. The campaign succeeded in wiping out the disease and introduced Duvalier as a benevolent figure to thousands of poor Haitian peasants who viewed him as having freed them from what was an endemic scourge. In preparation for a nationwide campaign against the disease, the Americans even sent Duvalier to the University of Michigan for training in public health medicine. Following his return to Haiti, Duvalier saw even more patients in newly mobile medical clinics in the south and central regions of the country, and his nickname, "Papa Doc," was born. When Estimé fled, Duvalier, angry about the way his mentor had been treated, refused to take a post in Colonel Paul Magloire's new government, returning instead to his health work with the Americans.

Born the son of a schoolteacher in the capital, Duvalier had graduated from medical school in 1934, the same year the marines left Haiti, and that same year began contributing bitter, angry articles to the nationalist *Action Nationale* newspaper under the pen name Abderrahman, in tribute to the emir who founded the medical school in Cordoba, Spain. In the late 1930s, the young doctor also had become part of a circle of Haitian intellectuals who referred to themselves as Les Griots, an African term for storytelling bards. The group founded an eponymous journal. which ran from 1938 until 1940, and Duvalier contributed socio-ethnologic musings to it from time to time. The writings of educator and ethnologist Jean Price-Mars, born in Grand Riviere du Nord in 1876, were of immense import to the intellectual foundations of Duvalier's little group. Price-Mars had been a high-school professor of Duvalier's and in 1928 he published *Ainsi parla l'Oncle* (*Thus Spoke Uncle*), a landmark book in the Negritude movement in the French Caribbean, which sought to look back to African traditions for cultural legitimacy rather than to those of the region's colonial powers, an argument that found receptive ears among Haitians enduring a humiliating U.S. occupation. Eventually, Duvalier would adapt the rhetoric of Negritude to his own ends, and create Noirisme, a political philosophy that sought, so he said, to empower Haiti's black majority at the expense of the mulatto minority who had so long manipulated the country.

COLONEL PAUL MAGLOIRE, Estimé's 42-year-old successor, was a different type altogether. A black military man close to the mulatto elite, Magloire was an extrovert whose enthusiasms ran to horses, drinking and dancing. His love of a good time was legendary enough that a popular song referring to him contained the memorable refrain *toujou m sou / se whiskey m bwe / toujour m sou / nan sein mama-m, se whiskey m bwe* ("Every day I'm drunk / It's whiskey that I drink / Every day I'm drunk / Even at my mother's breast, it was whiskey that I drank"). Nevertheless, as Magloire's rule commenced, things seemed to bode well for Haiti. A strong, unified army and police force kept a lid on the nation's often roiling political unrest, tourism to the western part of the island reached new heights, coffee prices picked up on the world market and Magloire christened the brand new Sylvio Cator soccer stadium in Haiti's capital. Magloire also granted land and buildings in the Artibonite Valley to an American couple, Gwen and Larry Mellon, who were just commencing their work on what would become the Albert Schweitzer Hospital, and his government commenced construction on the Peligre Dam, a hydroelectric project designed to provide power to the capital and help irrigate the Artibonite, but work on which saw several thousand villagers kicked off their land in the Plateau Central to make room for the endeavor. For the 150th anniversary of Haiti's independence, Magloire built a new modern cathedral in Gonaives and staged a massive reenactment of the battle of Vertieres outside of Cap Haitien, with the diplomatic corps and thousands of Haitian in attendance.

By the beginning of 1954, though, Magloire was sniffing rebellion among the capital's political class, and he ordered scores of his opponents arrested. For much of the next two years, Duvalier, who was one of the more prominent among them, went underground, hiding at the homes of friends in the capital and spending much of his time reading—Niccolo Machiavelli's treatise on the grim nature of power, *The Prince*, being a particular favorite. In January 1955, Magloire visited Washington, met with U.S. President Dwight Eisenhower and addressed Congress, but corruption in his government—every project cost twice as much as it should have and legislative elections, such as they were, continued to be riddled with fraud and vote-buying—began to spark more restlessness at home. By mid-1956, student demonstrations aimed at provoking general strikes against his government were met with violence by the army and police. Duvalier and other Estimé loyalists were frequently named as the possible causes for the unrest, and a state of siege was declared on May 21, 1956. Presidential elections were scheduled for January 1957, despite Magloire's stated desire to remain in office. Duvalier, Daniel Fignole and mulatto businessman Louis Dejoie all declared their intention to run, and a crude attempt by Magloire to hang clinging on to the reins of power was met with a general strike. Finally, on December 13, 1956, in time-honored Haitian tradition, Magloire slipped into exile with his family.

THE ELECTION SEASON OF 1957 thus began. Duvalier, who bitterly distrusted the army after their betrayal of Estimé, was a singularly grave, quiet presence on the Haitian political scene in terms of demeanor. What a first might have been ascribed to professional reticence, in time became something of a dark, compelling anti-charisma, that of a cat waiting patiently to pounce or the silence of a wise man. While everyone else would bluster, Dejoie wooing the mulattoes and Fignole whipping up the Port-au-Prince masses, Duvalier, quietly and with great focus, simply worked. He traveled the length of the country giving speeches casting himself as the logical heir to the thwarted legacy of Estimé; he met with the Army and flattered them with talk of their role as national liberators; he gathered a coterie of like-minded supporters around him, such as a women's activist from the central town of Mirebalais named Rosalie Bosquet (later Madame Max Aldolphe) and the Saint Marc schoolteacher Clement Barbot, whose loyalty to him was absolutely assured and of whose ruthlessness there was never any question. He also courted the peasantry and the *houngans*, the spiritual leaders of the *voudouisants* throughout the country that held such sway over them. Duvalier knew what he wanted, which was the National Palace, and while the others postured, he did everything to connect the dots to make the picture in his mind a reality.

Following Magloire's flight, a middle-aged judge from Cap Haitien, Joseph Nemours Pierre-Louis, lasted approximately fifty-five days as head of state, during which time he presided over bitter and often bloody political fighting among Magloire's would-be successors. He was replaced by another lawyer, Franck Sylvain, who himself lasted only fifty-two days. A revolving series of military leaders and street demonstrations followed in rapid succession until the men jockeying for the presidency—Duvalier, Fignole, Dejoie and former government minister Clement Jumelle—worked out a power-sharing agreement whereby Fignole would serve as president. The four men represented, in their own confused way, the splintered, fractious nature of Haitian society at the time, with Fignole as the champion of *le lumpen*, the urban proletariat of Port-au-Prince, and Dejoie catering to the whims of the imperious mulattoes. Jumelle, who had served under both Estimé and Magloire, was never regarded as a serious contender. That left Duvalier to pick up the slack, which consisted of the Haitian peasantry, his natural constituency given his work as a country doctor and amateur ethnologist, and, not coincidentally, roughly three-fourths of the voting population. Duvalier and Jumelle soon pulled out of the government in the hope of destabilizing the country and provoking a military coup. The coup did not occur, but Fignole panicked and cut another power-sharing deal with Duvalier, who in turn agreed to back Fignole for provisional president. Fignole lasted nineteen days before being ousted by General Antonio Kebreau. Although he was quickly put on a plane to a lonely exile in Jamaica and, eventually, New York (following in both Estimé and Magloire's footsteps), Fignole's constituency in the slums refused to believe that he would desert them. Believing that he was being held in Fort Dimanche to the north of the capital, a crowd several thousand strong marched from the slums to liberate their hero, only to be cut down by the guns of the Haitian army. Hundreds were said to have died, and bodies choked the streets leading from the prison back to the slums of Bel Air. International observers were outraged, demanding that the election move forward, and Kebreau, believing that he could easily manipulate the certain winner, Duvalier, agreed.

Small in stature, relatively reserved and halting in speech, Duvalier often played up the image of the simple country doctor for all it was worth. Through a series of brutal betrayals and cold, calculated planning, Duvalier had managed, in a few months, to allow his opponents to publicly whittle one another down while vying for infinitesimal constituencies, undo a power-sharing provisional government and rid himself of his only serious rival, driven out of the country by the Army he despised at the point of the gun. He won the election, held finally on September 22, 1957, a sham affair by all accounts.

THE NEXT THIRTEEN YEARS mark an outstanding and awful chapter in the history of tin-pot despotism and pointless bloodletting. Ever mindful of the military, Duvalier saw fit to create a paramilitary counterbalance, the Volontaires de la Sécurité Nationale (VSN), which became popularly known as the Tontons Macoutes after a Kreyol expression (the name translates as "uncle napsack") for a boogeyman who would stuff disobedient children into a thick burlap sack (*macoute*) like the ones the Haitian peasants carried. Madame Max Adolphe became the warden of the capital's Fort Dimanche prison, where hundreds, probably thousands of Duvalier's enemies were tortured and killed, and Clement Barbot became head of the Tontons Macoutes before turning against Duvalier and launching a brief but bloody rebellion against the dictator (which ended with Barbot's killing by government forces in 1963). Duvalier also reinvigorated the *chef de section* system, where government loyalists were put in charge of watching over rural municipalities as a combination of sheriff, enforcer and tax collector, thereby keeping closer watch on the peasants. The Catholic Church was humbled as Duvalier expelled scores of priests and eventually won the right to appoint his own bishops. The United States was squeezed as Duvalier played off their fear of communism for more financial support and the mulatto business class, now groaning under the living embodiment of Noirisme, was brought to their knees under exorbitant, arbitrary taxes and Duvalier's empowerment of his angry, violent followers, who carried with them the bitterness of decades of exploitation at the hands of Haiti's upper class.

Though he was likely never in any serious threat of being ousted, Duvalier had to survive a series of invasion attempts by exiles, who would periodically return to try to topple his rule. Among these, which included one accompanied by two Miami sheriffs that came within shooting distance of Haiti's National Palace, perhaps the most tragic was when a group of mulattoes from the southern city of Jeremie and a lone black comrade landed on Haiti's Grand Anse in August 1964. Calling themselves Jeune Haiti (Young Haiti), the invaders never stood a chance. Duvalier used the opportunity to exert his full homicidal wrath against the mulatto population of Jeremie, massacring the town's branches of the country's eminent Sansaricq and Guilbaud families, men, women and children and dumping their bodies in a mass grave out by the city's single-strip airport.

When I visited Jeremie shortly after arriving in Haiti in the fall of 1997, I saw a town that had sunk back slowly into tropical torpor. Ships still landed at its decaying port, and planes landed infrequently at the runway where Duvalierist forces had all but wiped out the Sansaricq family. A dreadlocked madman in a dress spouted Bible quotations in the Place de Trois Dumas where Grand Anse peasants haggled over the price of pots and pans and broad-brimmed straw hats. Four years earlier, in February 1993, a steamer called the *Neptune*—which carried merchants and others back and forth between Jeremie and the capital—had capsized, killing some two thousand. At night, at the decrepit Hotel La Cabane on a hill above town, I looked down over a black expanse nearly devoid of illumination and watched as schoolchildren came to study under the hotel's meager lights, produced by a sputtering generator. Finding out I was American, a small boy sought me out to practice his English. "I think you are a nice man," he said, as a million stars revealed themselves above us on a canopy of night sky.

Papa Doc, brutal as he was, could not live forever, and when he died in 1971, he was succeeded by his obese 19-year-old son, Jean-Claude ("Baby Doc"), who the Haitians referred to as "Baskethead" because of his great girth. Generally assessed as "not a very impressive figure" by those who met him, Jean-Claude nevertheless managed a relatively secure first decade in power, helped in no small part by his mother Simone and his sister Marie-Denise and the loyal Tontons Macoutes. The government was still brutal and ugly—Duvalierist official Lucker Cambronne made a fortune in the 1970s by using his company Hemocaribian to sell mass quantities of Haiti's antibody-rich blood as well as cadavers to North American medical firms such as Dow Chemical and Armour Pharmaceutical—but in general the violence was on a slightly less spectacular scale. Haitians, however, like most people, didn't like living under the whim of a dictator, and the first cracks in the dynastic facade began to appear when Jean-Claude decided to marry Michele Bennet, a mulatto divorcee of questionable reputation, on May 27, 1980. A product further from Papa Doc's Noiriste values could have been hard to imagine, but nevertheless, the Bennet clan, especially Michele's father Ernst, soon began to enjoy the fruits of government corruption.

Bad policy also was beginning to catch up with the regime. In 1980-83, the U.S-Canadian funded Program for the Eradication of Porcine Swine Fever and Development of Pig-Raising (PEPADEP) succeeded in destroying the 1.2 million Kreyol pigs (*kochon kreyol*) in the country that formed one of the backbones of its peasant economy when tests showed nearly a quarter of the island's pigs were infected with African Swine Fever. PEPADEP officials paid for the pigs before they slaughtered them, or, in many cases, promised to pay for them or replace them and never did. Most of the replacement pigs that were delivered soon expired, unable to adjust to the rough world the Kreyol swine had grown so accustomed to, and an already wretched economy suffered another blow. When Jean-Claude, in an effort to quell rumblings of discontent, named Roger Lafontant, a doctor and hated Macoute leader, as Minister of the Interior in September 1983, it was a fateful miscalculation. Lafontant's brutal tactics served to only further inflame an already restive populace, and Duvalier had to fire him in November 1983, allegedly because of Lafontant's involvement in the murder of an elderly Belgian priest that July, and his creation of an ill-advised "vote" declaring Jean-Claude "president for life," which only polarized matters more. Three schoolchildren were killed in protests in the northern city of Gonaives on November 28, 1985, and by January 1986, antigovernment demonstrations were sweeping the country. It appeared the regime's days were numbered.

|||

2
Rocks in the Sun

IN JANUARY 1985, just as opposition to the dictatorship was beginning to burst out into public view, a young priest returned to Haiti after having spent three years studying in Montreal. Father Jean-Bertrand Aristide had already traveled farther in his young life (he was only thirty-two at the time) than many Haitians of similar upbringing could have ever imagined.

Born to a family of land-owning peasants in a village near the southern town of Port Salut on July 15, 1953, Aristide had moved to the capital with his mother and sister Marie-Anne shortly after the death of his father, under mysterious circumstances, when he was still very young. Shuttling between various households with his mother and sister in the capital, he began his schooling with the Salesian brothers of the Catholic Church at age five, where, he later recalled, students were beaten when they "forgot themselves" and spoke to the brothers in Kreyol rather than in French. He continued his studies with them until he was fourteen, and over that time he said one of his most vivid memories was seeing squatters, who had been burned out of the capital's La Saline slum by a Macoute who wanted to take possession of their land, arrive at the Salesians' door, with what meager belongings they could salvage strapped to their backs. Finishing primary school in 1966, Aristide decided to join the priesthood, to the joy of his mother, and entered the Salesian seminary the northern city of Cap Haitien that same year. He would eventually finish seminary at the age of twenty-one, in 1974, and then leave Haiti to take his *noviate*—a period during which clerical aspirants take their first vows—in the Dominican Republic, where he learned Spanish. Returning to Haiti a year later, he entered the State University of Haiti to study psychology and philosophy and received a degree in psychology in 1979. Briefly working as a broadcaster for the station Radio Cacique in Port-au-Prince, Aristide then left to study in Israel from 1979 until June 1982; there he immersed himself in the study of Hebrew and also eschatology, or prophecies relating to the end of the world. Upon his return to Haiti, he was ordained into the priesthood by Bishop Willy Romelus of Jeremie on July 3, 1982, at age twenty-five, and appointed to the parish of St. Joseph in the capital. Aristide was also inducted into the Salesian order of the Catholic Church, a group set to live by the example of Saint Jean Bosco, a nineteenth century Italian priest who gained renown for his work with the homeless youth in Turin. After preaching in the capital for a time, he was again sent abroad—the result of pressure, some said, from the Duvalier government, who disliked the young priest's political bent in his sermons. Sent to Canada and somewhat at loose ends, Aristide began doctoral work in psychology at the University of Montreal. However, times were changing in Haiti, and when he returned this time, he was sent to minister at the Église Saint Jean Bosco, a parish abutting the squalid La Saline shantytown near Port-au-Prince's waterfront. For some time, Aristide had been a priest in search of a pulpit. Now he had one.

AS THE TIDE OF UNREST GREW and grew, with demonstrations against his rule in all major cities and his army increasingly turning against him, Jean-Claude Duvalier and his wife fled into exile on Feb 7, 1986, finally ending the 29-year Duvalier dictatorship, though not Haiti's troubles. FADH Lieutenant General Henri Namphy emerged at the head of the civilian-military Conseil Nationale de Government (CNG) to oversee a two-year democratic transition period. For the next year, revenge was taken on Macoutes throughout the country, and the military and their former paramilitary rivals did a complex dance around one another to see how they could find some sort of mutually beneficial relationship. Houses and property belonging to Duvalierists were sacked and destroyed in what the Haitians referred to as *dechoukaj*, a peasant term referring to the pulling up of a tree, roots and all, from the ground. The tens of thousands of residents of the capital's festering Cité Simone slum (so named after Francois Duvalier's wife) renamed their home Cité Soleil, in honor of Catholic Radio Soleil, which had done much to spread word of the rebellion. A march that Aristide helped organize on the Duvalier death prison at Fort Dimanche on April 26, 1986, and reported on for Radio Soleil, was cut short when the young commandant of the fort, Isidor Pignon, had his men open fire on the demonstrators, killing several when a high-tension wire severed by bullets fell on them. Shunning the traditional programs set up by the poor for Salesians, Aristide also formed Lafanmi Selavi ("The Family is Life") in July 1986; the organization, based out of building in the middle-class neighborhood of Turgeau, was something of a rooming house-cum-support center for street boys, of the type that surrounded Aristide at the parish in Saint Jean Bosco.

Despite all this, on March 29, 1987, over a year after the Duvalier dynasty had crumbled, Haitian voters approved a liberal constitution in a referendum that seemed to bode as an important first step toward representative government. The document called for presidential elections to be held the following November, created a post of Prime Minister to curtail the powers of the presidency, and commenced a ban on "architects" of the Duvalier dictatorship from participating in elections for ten years.

When Aristide's Salesian superiors attempted to transfer him from Saint Jean Bosco to the Macoute redoubt of Croix-des-Missions outside of Port-au-Prince at the end of July, some of the priest's young supporters began a hunger strike, lying on mats in the capital's National Cathedral and refusing to move until the order was rescinded. Eventually, the Church blinked, and Aristide stayed at Saint Jean Bosco.

Things were still very unsettled, though. While delivering a sermon on August 23 in the central town of Pont Sonde, Aristide was fired upon by a pistol-wielding gunman in the crowd of onlookers. None of the bullets found their mark. Later that night, attempting to drive back through a driving rain to Port-au-Prince, Aristide's car—which also included as passengers that night other progressive priests such as Jean-Marie Vincent, William Smarth and Antoine Adrien—was attacked at a roadblock in Freycineau just outside of Saint Marc. The priests were beaten and pummeled by a mob of young men looking for Aristide, who was hiding under a blanket in the back of the car. Only a blind acceleration through a small opening in the barricade by the driver—done amidst the downpour and with a smashed windshield—saved them.

On November 29, following a violent run-up that saw attacks on candidates' offices and the office of the electoral council itself, voters went to the polls to choose their new president. At the École Nationale Argentine Bellegarde off the capital's Ruelle Vaillant, a group of voters waiting to cast their ballots were set upon and massacred in a well-planned attack by a group of machete and gun-wielding assailants. Among the dead was Dominican cameraman Carlos Grullon, shot even as he declared that he was a journalist. Three radio stations, Radio Haiti-Inter, Radio Soleil and Radio Cacique, were all attacked, and later in the day, for good measure, the army opened fire on a crowd gathered on Rue Nazon. In all, at least thirty-four died that day. The United States immediately suspended $70 million in aid to Haiti and Henri Namphy immediately dissolved Haiti's electoral council. On Jan 17, 1988, in widely boycotted, army-organized elections, Haitian academic Leslie Manigat was elected president, but lasted only until June 20, when Namphy ousted the rotund professor after he tried to replace him as army chief.

Aristide, who never for a moment stopped attacking the government, even after the Ruelle Vaillant massacre, finally received his reply on September 11 of that year. Youthful gang leaders from the city's slums, in the pay—many said—of the brutal Port-au-Prince mayor and macoute Franck Romain, did the deed. Men with names like Gwo Schiller, Ti Chinois ("the Little Chinaman") and Kolachat shot, stabbed and hacked their way through Aristide's church as he said Mass, gunning down a man as he held his Bible, slashing and stabbing a pregnant woman in the stomach. According to a May 1990 Organization of American States (OAS) report, at least twelve died. The attackers then burned the church when they were finished but, perhaps thinking the shock of the slaughter had neutralized him, did not kill Aristide, nor the peasant leader Chavannes Jean-Baptiste, nor an agronomist named René Préval, all of whom were present.

The attack on Aristide's congregation marked the culmination of an era of large-scale public violence against the democratic sector following Duvalier's fall and, although some large scale killings would follow, they would largely be conducted in the hinterlands, in Haiti's remote mountains and rural departments and out of public view. A lesson that those ravenous for power in Haiti never seemed to learn is that of when to stop, when one step further will bring the whole house of cards tumbling down. For Namphy, the siege of Saint Jean Bosco was that step, the tipping point. Though the attack was viewed by some as a power-grab by Franck Romain, designed to put himself in front of Namphy in the country's struggle for post-Duvalier political power, when Namphy and the killers appeared on television a day later, gloating about the event at a slum called Lakou Breya, the wheels were already turning for the general's downfall. On September 17, Namphy was overthrown by the military, including a vocal group of progressive, noncommissioned officers who called themselves the "Ti Soldats" (little soldiers). General Prosper Avril, who had overseen financial matters for the Duvalier family, took over the reins of power, promising civilian rule. With Namphy packed off to the Dominican Concorde Hotel in the Dominican Republic, many of the young men who had actually committed the murders at Saint Jean Bosco were hunted down, stabbed or hacked by many hands and then roasted in the street by having tires placed around their necks and then set aflame—a practice referred to as "necklacing," and also widely known as *pere lebrun*, after the name of a Port-au-Prince tire company.

Barely having time to pause and count the dead, in early October, Aristide received a communiqué from his superiors in Rome dated August 23, informing him that he would soon be transferred out of Haiti. The deadline for his departure was given as October 17. As with his planned transfer to Croix des Missions the previous year, crowds of young men blocked the airport and said they would refuse to let him leave.

Addressing the country on November 22, 1988, Aristide told the radio audience, still traumatized by the attack on his church, using the imagery of a cleansing flood (*lavalas* in Kreyol) to stir the population's sense of their own power:

> *Yon sel, nou feb*
> *Ansanm, nou fo!*
> *Ansanm, nou Lavalas!*
>
> *[Alone, we are weak*
> *Together we are strong!*
> *Together we are Lavalas!]*

Let the flood descend, he cried out.

He went on to call on Avril to disarm the macoutes, arrest Franck Romain and end the country's state of insecurity. In other words, the priest had issued an ultimatum to the general.

"The matter is in your hands," Aristide concluded. "The people will write their own fate. The blessing of God is upon them. Thus, grace will descend until the flood brings down all Duvalierists, all macoutes, all criminals, forever and ever. Amen."

On December 8, Aristide received word that he had been expelled from the Salesian order. The message delivered to him read that, "His attitude has had a negative effect on his confreres. . . . His selfishness demonstrates a lack of sincerity and of a religious and priestly consciousness. . . . (He has committed) incitement to hatred and violence, and a glorifying of class struggle (and) the profanation of the liturgy." Aristide now had no church in Haiti that would hear his sermons.

IN HIS BOOK *Tout Homme, est un Homme*, coauthored with French journalist Christophe Wargny, Aristide wrote acidly and correctly later that, "I did not invent class struggle any more than Karl Marx did. I would even prefer never to have seen it. Perhaps that is possible, if one never leaves the squares of the Vatican or the heights of Petionville. But who can avoid encountering class struggle in the heart of Port-au-Prince. It is not a subject of controversy, but a fact, a given."

Now without a church, Aristide was also without the religious order that had been his home for the past six years. He retired to work at Lafanmi Selavi, licking his wounds.

INTO THIS VOID LEFT BY ARISTIDE being caught on the back foot by his expulsion, in January 1989, a new organization, the September 17th Popular Organization (OP-17) was formed by former soldiers who supported democratic reform both in the military and within the Haitian political spectrum in general. The group chose as its leader Marino Etienne, a former sergeant in the Presidential Guard who had served on active duty until 1982. Many of the Ti Soldats instrumental in the overthrow of Henri Namphy belonged to OP-17, and it was their hope that they could pressure Avril into adopting a more democratic path.

Avril stumbled along in an attempt to restart the spigot of foreign aid, but, on April 2 of that year, as if to underscore how shaky his regime really was, members of the military's counterinsurgency Leopards battalion (including a politically ambitious dissident colonel named Himmler Rebu) arrested Avril after he attempted to purge officers involved in drug trafficking. Avril was later freed by his Presidential Guard and, though the army's Dessalines Barracks later joined the rebellion, Avril survived the coup attempt. Thirty-five died in the violence.

Watching this incestuous power struggle and concluding that Avril had little intention of holding democratic elections any time soon, thirty-three political and civic organizations came together to form the Rassemblement National after a general strike held on September 27. Including elements as diverse as the Parti Agricole et Industriel National (PAIN) and Haiti's Communist party, the group sought to pressure Avril to step down and open up Haiti's political process. On October 31, Rassemblement National leaders Evans Paul—a well-known journalist and playwright who had been exiled under Baby Doc—and OP-17's Marino Etienne, along with Centrale Autonome des Travailleurs Haitians (CATH) union leader Jean-Auguste Mesyeux held a press conference calling for a monthlong spate of protests against Avril and demanding democratic reforms, to culminate with a massive demonstration of November 29, the second anniversary of the Ruelle Vaillant massacre.

THE FOLLOWING DAY, November 1, responding to overtures by several soldiers, Paul, Etienne and Mesyeux drove to the home of a soldier in Avril's Presidential Guard in the capital's sprawling southern Carrefour district in Mesyeux's jeep, ostensibly to hear information about soldiers who had been killed and imprisoned by the regime. As they arrived at the house around 6 p.m., dusk was beginning to settle in the bay that formed the neighborhood's western edge, and the trio arrived at the house to find a group of men in civilian clothes playing dominoes in the yard. Descending from their jeep and entering the house, they were almost immediately set upon by a group of men that Paul later labeled as numbering around forty. What followed next would speak volumes about Avril's sense of democracy.[1]

Etienne, former soldier that he was, immediately recognized three officers in Avril's personal security detail as those leading the assault. Knocked to the floor, kicked and stomped, beaten with rifle butts and then pistol-whipped, Etienne, Paul and Mesyeux had their hands bound behind them and were thrown facedown on the floor of a pickup. As the truck took off, soldiers climbed in, standing and stomping on Paul and the others, and continuing to beat them throughout the drive.

Driven to the yellow army headquarters near the National Palace, the prisoners could barely stand once they reached the building's courtyard, and as a result were beaten further there, in full view of milling officers. Another group of soldiers arrived driving Mesyeux's jeep, commandeered once the attack in Carrefour began. The soldiers demanded that the three remove weapons planted on the drive in the jeep, but Paul and the others refused, not wanting to put their fingerprints on the guns. Their refusal provoked even more savage torture, which lasted an hour, and then the three were dragged to a waiting room at the Anti-Gang division of the police headquarters where they were thrown, semiconscious, to the floor.

Interrogated separately, soldiers continued to torture Etienne and Mesyeux as they harangued them to give out information of the activities and whereabouts of various democratic activists. Paul was not beaten, but said that his captors were in regular communication with Avril, whose voice he knew well, via telephone. Etienne also reported witnessing FADH Lieutenant Colonel Ernest Prudhomme converse with Avril during the torture. Then the three captives, exhausted and covered in blood, were thrown into cells to ponder their fates.

The next day, November 2, the three were dragged back into the same office where they had been interrogated and tortured, only this time, Television Nationale d'Haiti (TNH) television cameras and microphones had been set up inside. Though their captors had made some attempt to wash the blood off their faces, the captives' bruised, swollen heads and twisted limbs, visible as police investigator Leopold Clerjeune read a government statement accusing them of complicity in a plot to assassinate Avril and military officials, made the nation groan. Etienne, barely conscious, had to be supported by Paul. A stack of weapons and ammunition lay next to the prisoners during the proceedings.

Transferred to the National Penitentiary, after two weeks Paul, Etienne and Mesyeux went on a hunger strike for nearly a month to protest their imprisonment. Initially refused medical treatment, they were finally relocated to a military hospital, where they were afraid to eat or accept medication for fear of being poisoned. Transferred back to the National Penitentiary on December 1, the three were finally released in a general amnesty on February 7, 1990. Examined at last by private physicians, the three were found to have suffered appalling injuries, including six broken ribs suffered by Paul and permanent loss of hearing in the right ear for Etienne. For over a year, Paul could not walk without the assistance of a wheelchair or a cane.

The brutality meted out to the *"Prisonniers de la Toussaint"* ("Prisoners of All Saint's Day") as the trio became known, removed any doubts in the minds of Haiti's democratic sector as to whether or not Avril was someone who could be negotiated with or should be uprooted, by force, if necessary.

AVRIL, FACED WITH GROWING UNREST, declared a state of siege in Haiti on January 20, 1990. That same day, the leftist politician Serge Gilles, head of the Parti National Progressiste Révolutionnaire (PANPRA) political party, was arrested at his home on Rue Chavannes in Petionville by five armed men in civilian clothes at around 2 p.m.[2] Thrown to the floor, beaten and handcuffed, Gilles was dragged away as the men ransacked his house and as his daughter, little more than a toddler, wandered around bleeding after cutting herself on broken glass from a table the men had smashed. Accused of having "annoyed" the government, and ordered to reveal the locations of other party members, Gilles refused, and was thrown into a jeep—belonging to the Direction Generale des Impots (tax office), where Komite Nasyonal Kongre Mouvman Demokratik

(KONAKOM) politician Gerald Emile "Aby" Brun and half a dozen other men already lay beaten—and driven to the National Palace. At the Palace, the beatings continued, and the men were then driven to the Anti-Gang Service of the Port-au-Prince police department and jailed. During his detention, Gilles was taken out of his cell and directed to a telephone where, on the other line, to his surprise, was Prosper Avril, who apologized, saying the executors of the raid had "gone too far." Gilles was later released. The next evening, Brun was thrown in his still blood-soaked clothes onto a plane bound for Miami, deported against his will for nearly a month and only to return to Haiti after Avril's fall.

EVENTS SUCH AS THESE finally forced Avril's ouster by hostile elements in the army on March 11, and, in time honored tradition, he was bundled aboard a plane to the United States. Power passed into the hands of Army Chief of Staff Brigadier General Herard Abraham who, to the surprise of many, turned the reins of government over to Supreme Court Justice Ertha Pascal Trouillot, as dictated by Haiti's oft-violated 1987 constitution. Trouillot was sworn in as interim president on March 13. The departure of Avril did not mean the end of military violence, however, and in the hamlet of Piatre near Saint Marc on March 12, soldiers from the Saint Marc garrison acting on the behest of local landowners burned dozens of houses and killed at least eleven peasants who had been agitating for agrarian reform in the region.

DEMOCRATS WERE NOT THE ONLY ONES who saw the potential of a new day in Avril's demise. Roger Lafontant, Jean-Claude Duvalier's former Interior Minister and a notorious macoute leader, saw an opportunity for political rehabilitation with the departure of his bitter enemy Prosper Avril, and returned from exile in Canada on July 7. With presidential elections set for December 16, Lafontant announced on October 16 that, despite the ban on Duvalierists running for office, he would be the presidential candidate for his own party, the Union for National Reconstruction (URN).

Following Lafontant's announcement, at the urging of a broad-based progressive political coalition named le Front National pour le Changement et la Democratie (FNCD) Aristide announced his candidacy for president on October 18. The FNCD, made up of political parties such as Evans Paul's Konvansyon Inite Demokratik (KID) and Victor Benoit's Komite Nasyonal Kongre Mouvman Demokratik (KONAKOM), as well as long-term democratic activists such as former priest Jean-Claude Bajeux, had intended to run Benoit as their candidate, but passed him over when the charismatic Aristide became available, much to Benoit's chagrin. Many in the movement would later say that they hoped they could ride Aristide's popularity to secure offices for other leading FNCD candidates and then, over the next several years, enact substantial democratic reforms in the country. Evans Paul, the political activist who had been tortured by Avril and himself a rousing orator, became the defrocked priest's campaign manager, throwing his own hat into the ring for the mayorship of Port-au-Prince. Robert Manuel, a progressive young mulatto FADH officer, helped by compiling a dossier bringing young, progressive officers such as himself to Aristide's side and served as the chief of Aristide's security during the campaign. Dany Toussaint, another young former officer in the FADH who had lived in the United States, served as Aristide's chief bodyguard. Opposing Artiside on the ballot was Marc Bazin, a former Finance Minister under Baby Doc, and a World Bank official thought to be the favorite of the United States, veteran leftist politician René Théodore, who was a former head of Haiti's Communist party exiled under Papa Doc, and a host of lesser candidates given scant chance of winning. The eventual disqualification of Roger Lafontant from running on the basis of the fact that he had not submitted his birth certificate to election officials seemed to only strengthen Aristide's hand.

Aristide's main financial backer as he campaigned was a left-wing millionaire of Palestinian extraction named Antoine Izmery and, as much as Aristide was an expression of a certain experience of his milieu, Izmery was also an expression of his.

"I remember the first time I saw him," the painter Jhomson Vidho Lorville said, recalling his initial sighting of Izmery, when Lorville at the time was a young man growing up in the city's southern *quartier populaire* Carrefour. "I had heard a lot about him, that he was some kind of pro-Aristide bourgeoisie, really militant. He was distributing food to poor people downtown in Port-au-Prince outside of his business. He saw me, some kid from Carrefour, staring at him, and he gave me a big smile, and a thumbs-up."

Izmery was a striking figure, with a Levantine nose and a head of hair that he would eventually grow into a flowing beard. He was known as an anomaly among the Haiti's Arab business class, who were mostly Syrian and Lebanese, and tended to be conservative (or reactionary, depending on one's politics) in the extreme. Izmery's passion for radical leftist political activism and pro-democracy credentials were said to be matched only by his other two chief pursuits: women and gambling.

"The toys of rich men," a friend who had known him once told me.

An American woman who had lived in Haiti for years and would reminisce at length about Izmery's prowess in preparing Middle Eastern dishes in the kitchen had a different theory.

"Antoine was Palestinian, you see," she said one evening over dinner with her family in the cool hills of Fermathe, above Port-au-Prince. "I think he had a lot of anger towards the United States government. I don't think he could ever forgive what had been done to his country."

That anger, palpable and in many ways righteous, was something that he shared with Aristide.

DESPITE A SERIES of pre-election attacks, including a bomb that exploded at an Aristide rally in Petionville on December 5, killing eight and injuring nearly fifty more, the elections went off relatively smoothly and, *nou se lavalas*, Aristide was elected Haiti's president with 67 percent of the vote on December 16, 1990. Evans Paul was elected mayor of Port-au-Prince. Thousands of Aristide's supporters paraded joyfully through the capital's streets brandishing palm fronds, singing and celebrating.

The euphoria proved to be short lived, as, on the night of January 6, Roger Lafontant kidnapped Ertha Pascale Trouillot, entered the National Palace and addressed the nation on television, proclaiming himself Haiti's president. But he had overplayed his hand. The Haitian army stormed the Palace the next day and arrested Lafontant and his cohorts, including a former Haitian army officer named Louis Jodel Chamblain. Pro-Aristide mobs wreaked terrible vengeance on those associated with coup, cornering and killing Chamblain's pregnant wife at their home in the capital's Delmas neighborhood and burning down the capital's ancient cathedral in an act of vengeance against the Duvalierist archbishop Wolff Lingonde.

The putsch had failed, and with Lafontant and his conspirators locked away in jail, Aristide assumed the presidency before thousands of cheering supporters on February 7, 1991. In a gesture of thanks for his securing of the elections and remaining loyal amidst Lafontant's assault, he appointed Lieutenant General Raoul Cédras chief of staff of the army and, at the same time, thanked six of Haiti's eight generals for their service to the country and retired them. In his inauguration speech, Aristide quoted from the Book of Isaiah:

> The spirit of the Lord God is upon me; because the Lord hath anointed me to preach good tidings unto the meek; he hath sent me to bind up the brokenhearted, to proclaim liberty to the captives, and the opening of the prison to them that are bound; to proclaim the acceptable *year of the Lord, and the day of vengeance of our God; to comfort all that mourn.* . . .

With his inimitable turn of Kreyol phrase, Aristide also advised that now *"woche nan dlo ap konnen doule woche nan soley."* ("The rocks in the water will know the suffering of the rocks in the sun.") The Aristide era of Haitian politics had begun.

PLEDGING THAT THE three defining themes of his government (he called them his three *woch dife* or firestones) would be justice, transparency and participation, and that his goal was to lift Haitians from misery to "poverty with dignity," on February 9, in a move that surprised many, Aristide chose René Préval, the agronomist who had been among the survivors of the raid on the Saint Jean Bosco church three years earlier and an unknown to most, as his

Prime Minister. Many hoped that Aristide would chose from the FNCD coalition that got him elected, and noted that, according to the Haitian constitution, the Prime Minister was supposed to be drawn from the majority party in parliament. Aristide did not submit Préval's nomination to the body for approval, a move that some thought did not bode terribly well for relations between the two branches of government.

Aristide's first few months in office, which are alternately described as chaotic class warfare by his detractors and inspired revolutionary reform by his supporters, were, in truth, something of a mixed bag. On the positive side, the new president began a literacy program for Haiti's poor, tried to reign in the country's unwieldy bureaucracy and attempted to raise the appallingly low minimum wage. He called on the estimated two million Haitians living in exile—a group he termed "the Tenth Department" in reference to Haiti's nine governmental divisions of territory, to return to Haiti and help rebuild the country. However, there were also some disturbing eruptions of pique. In April, the government arrested Ertha Pascale Trouillot and charged her with having taken part in the January coup rather than being a victim of it, though she was later released. At Roger Lafontant's trial on July 29 (trials in Haiti rarely last more than a day), crowds outside the courtroom carried pictures of Aristide and tires, threatening to necklace the lawyers if Lafontant got less than a life sentence. Lafontant was tried, sentenced to life in prison and hauled away to the National Penitentiary. In August, when parliament threatened to declare a no-confidence measure against Préval, whose name Aristide still had not sent before them for ratification, several thousand Aristide supporters surrounded the building and threatened similar action to the parliamentarians locked inside, then setting the offices of both Evans Paul's KID party and the CATH union ablaze. Essentially, it was the same heaving to-and-fro of competing political forces as had long existed in the country, but with one crucial difference: many people had voted for one of the sides in the contest, and so they felt they had a real stake in who might triumph.

By mid-September, things had grown more tense, with Aristide's more radical followers growing weary at what they saw as the slow pace of reform, elements of the army feeling increasingly threatened by the power Aristide could command through his ability to mobilize the Haitian poor, and the Haitian elite livid at what they saw as the assault on their long privilege to treat the country as their private farm. Following an address to the United Nations in New York on September 23, 1991, Aristide returned to Haiti and on the flight home was informed of an unfolding plot to overthrow him, being financed by some of Haiti's wealthiest families. Frightened by the specificity of the coup rumors, Aristide held a huge preemptive rally in downtown Port-au-Prince on September 27. His back to the wall, knowing that moves were afoot to topple him and perhaps kill him, and that lists of his supporters who were also to be killed were being drawn up, Aristide delivered an incendiary speech that would long echo in the ears of those who heard it:

> Brothers and sisters who are born into the bourgeoisie in Haiti and who don't want to see the bourgeoisie fighting the people, and you the people who would not like to fight the bourgeoisie, but who know that the bourgeoisie must play according to the rules of the democratic game, today it's in the name of this people, I come to tell you: YOU who have money yet who would not like to go live outside this country of Haiti, you who would like to live in the country, when you die, you won't take that money with you.
>
> Put people to work. You must invest your money any old way, so that more people can find work, for: if you don't do it, I am sorry for you! It's not my fault, you understand? That money in your possession, it is not really yours. You earned it in thievery, you carried it through bad choices you made, under an evil regime, an evil system, and in all other unsavory ways . . . give you a chance, because you won't get two, nor three chances. It's only one chance that you'll get. Otherwise, things won't be good for you! If I speak to you in that way, it's because I've given you seven months to conform, and the seven months are up to the day.
>
> Whenever you feel the heat of unemployment, whenever the heat of the pavement begins to make you feel awful, whenever you feel revolt inside you, turn your eyes to the direction of those with the means. Ask them why not? What are you waiting for? Why this long wait? Are you waiting for the seas to dry up? And if you catch a thief, if you catch a false, Lavalassian, if you catch one who shouldn't be there, don't hesitate to give him what he deserves.

Aristide spat out the words with the staccato refrain of a rifle report, as a crowd of thousands, delirious and in the grip of his oratory, hung on every word:

> Your tool in hand, your instrument in hand, your constitution in hand! Don't hesitate to give him what he deserves. Your equipment in hand, your spade in hand, your pencil in hand, your constitution in hand, don't hesitate to give him what he deserves. The Macoute isn't in this game. Don't hesitate to give him what he deserves. Three days and three nights watching in front of the National Penitentiary, if one escapes, don't hesitate to give him what he deserves.
>
> Everywhere, in the four corners, we are watching, we are praying, we are watching, we are praying, when you catch one, don't hesitate to give him what he deserves.

What a beautiful tool! What a beautiful instrument! What a beautiful piece of equipment! It's beautiful, yes it's beautiful, it has a good smell, wherever you go you want to inhale it. Since the law of the country says Macoute isn't in the game, whatever happens to him he deserves, he came looking for trouble.

Again, under this flag of pride, under this flag of dignity, under this same flag of solidarity, hand in hand, one encouraging the other, one holding the other's hand so that from this day forward, each one will pick up this message of respect that I share with you, this message of justice that I share with you, so that the word ceases to be the word and becomes action. With other actions in the economic field, I throw the ball to you, you dribble it, you shoot, shoot from before the penalty box, shoot on the goal adroitly, because if the people don't find this ball to hold it in the net, well, as I told you, it's not my fault, it's you who will find what you deserve, according to what the Mother Law of the country declares.

Alone, we are weak. Together we are strong! Together together, we are Lavalas! Do you feel proud! Do you feel proud!

The crowd roared its deafening approval while, behind Aristide on the stage, General Raoul Cédras, who had been seated with members of the military listening to every word, dropped his head into his hands.

THE NEXT EVENING, the trouble began. As he left a political meeting in the southern city of Les Cayes, the Protestant pastor Sylvio Claude, a longtime democratic activist and Aristide rival, was attacked and burned to death by a mob of young men. Soldiers declaring themselves committed to coup d'etat rose up at the military base in the capital's suburb of Freres and at the downtown police commissariat. At some point, Roger Lafontant was killed, gunned down in his cell in the National Penitentiary.

After the abortive Lafontant coup the previous December, this time the military were taking no chances, and fired on anything that moved in the capital's streets. Aristide's home in suburban Tabarre was under siege when French ambassador Jean-Raphael Dufour arrived at the residence to take the president to the National Palace. In a convoy moving towards the Palace, lead by Aristide's security chief, former Haitian army major Dany Toussaint, one soldier was killed, and the cars were fired on several times. Upon his arrival at the Palace, Aristide was arrested and taken to army general headquarters across the street, where he faced Raoul Cédras and soldiers debating whether or not they should execute him. Eventually the decision was made that Aristide should go into exile, and within hours he flew to Caracas aboard a plane sent by Venezuelan president Carlos Andres Perez.

In addition to the 45-year-old Cédras, who, though he became the public face of the junta, was considered to be the weakest, politically speaking, the new regime was comprised of two other main personalities. Lieutenant Colonel Michel Francois, misnamed "Sweet Micky" by Haitians, who are always fond of sobriquets, was the chief of police for Haiti's capital and by all accounts as paranoid, corrupt and ruthless a killer as Haiti had produced. Brigadier General Philippe Biamby had formerly plotted to overthrow Prosper Avril's government, but fled to the U.S. when the coup failed and spent several months cooling his heels in a U.S. jail, which had left him with an intransigent anti-Americanism and determination not to cede to U.S. pressure.

The junta installed Supreme Court Justice Joseph Nerette as provisional president on October 8, and Jean-Jacques Honorat—a former Duvalier Minister of Tourism and director of a leading human rights organization, the Centre Haitien des Droits et Libertes Humaines—who had grown rather crusty and conservative in his old age, as Prime Minister. The military rulers then also promptly picked a series of legal advisors, including a young, U.S.-educated female lawyer named Mireille Durocher Bertin and the attorney Calixte Delatour, as legal council.

FOLLOWING THE COUP, the OAS convened an emergency meeting and issued a statement calling for Aristide's return. The regime showed something of its view of international political opinion at Haiti's international airport on October 7, when Port-au-Prince mayor Evans Paul, arriving to meet with the visiting OAS delegation, was instead manhandled and arrested by Haitian soldiers and savagely beaten afterwards. He was imprisoned and only released hours later, with several broken ribs and a broken leg, after intervention by members of the international diplomatic corps. The OAS voted to impose an oil and trade embargo on October 25 and U.S. President George Bush ordered U.S. compliance on November 5, a move that hit the poor terribly but was described as "leaky" when it came to actually putting pressure on the putschists, who had received financial support from several of Haiti's elite families—people who were adept at skirting such moves. Meanwhile in October, for good measure, the army and its supporters in the Plateau Central region had trashed the headquarters of Haiti's largest peasant movement, the Mouvman Peyizan Papay (MPP) headed by Chavannes Jean-Baptiste outside of the central city of Hinche. In the initial days after the coup, many supporters of the ousted president were killed, and as the crisis wore on, some would be found in the lanes of poor neighborhoods with their faces hacked away, and many women associated with the democratic movement were raped as a weapon of terror by dissident soldiers and police.

After relatively fruitless negotiations were held between the junta and Aristide's representatives in Colombia, a massive wave of boat people, seven thousand in the first two months of the coup, began to be intercepted by the U.S. Coast Guard, and the Americans set up an internment camp for Haitian refugees caught at sea at the U.S. military base in Guantánamo Bay, Cuba. As 1992 loomed, Aristide and the junta began negotiating around the office of Prime Minister, which some saw as at least a first step towards leveraging the situation back toward representative government. On January 8, 1992, Aristide agreed to have leftist politician René Théodore put forward as Haiti's new Prime Minister, but before the month was over, Théodore had been beaten by the military and one of his bodyguards had been murdered. The nomination was dead in the water. A few months into 1992, Honorat stepped down and Marc Bazin, whose policies and platform were explicitly rejected by the Haitian voters in the 1990 election, was sworn in as prime minister on June 19. He would serve until June 8, 1993, when he would resign, the negotiations still deadlocked and the democratic sector in Haiti still hunted and fighting for its life.

THE SAME MONTH AS Bazin's appointment, the embargo originally implemented by the OAS against the de facto regime was echoed by the United Nations Security Council, who put in place a worldwide oil and weapons embargo for good measure.

United Nations-sponsored negotiations, heavily backed by new U.S. President Bill Clinton, took place on New York's Governor's Island in the summer of 1993, with Aristide and Cédras negotiating in separate buildings and refusing to meet face to face. The meetings resulted in both men signing on July 3 an agreement calling for restoration of democracy and Aristide's return to Haiti on October 30. In addition, the document stipulated that Aristide would name yet another new Prime Minister, sanctions would be immediately lifted against the country, reforms would commence in the army (including their formal separation from the police) and amnesty would be granted to the authors of the coup. With the embargo about to cease, Aristide chose Robert Malval, a businessman and owner of Imprimiere Natal, one of Haiti's oldest printing companies, as Prime Minister. Malval conditionally accepted the post on August 25, but gave himself a December 15 expiration date by which he said he would step down. A few days later, sanctions were lifted.

The omens for success were not auspicious, however. A September 8 attempt to reinstall Evans Paul to the mayorship of Port-au-Prince was violently disrupted when the ceremony at the capital's City Hall was disrupted by gunfire and men with knives. At least three people died in the melee. On September 11, the fifth anniversary of the attack on Aristide's congregation at Saint Jean Bosco, Antoine Izmery arranged for a Mass to be held at the capital's Sacre Coeur Church off Avenue Jean Paul II to remember the event, doubtless also remembering his own brother, George, murdered, some said, by military gunmen who mistook him for his more radical brother the previous year. As the Mass was underway, several armed men in civilian clothes entered the church, at one point asking the imposing, bearded Haitian news photographer Daniel Morel if he was Izmery. Eventually, they located the real Izmery, and, as they grew more aggressive, parishioners began flooding in a panic out of the church. Izmery was taken to the front of the church and out into the small square before it, surrounded by the armed men and executed, shot in the head a point-blank range. Several army contingents that had been observing the church throughout the morning did nothing to intervene.

DURING THE SAME TUMULTUOUS MONTH, a new group, the Front revolutionnaire pour l'avancement et le progress haitiens (Revolutionary Front for Haitian Advancement and Progress, or FRAPH, like the Kreyol word "to hit"), thought by many to be little more than a front for the army's death squads, announced its presence. Founded by Emmanuel "Toto" Constant, the forty-year-old disreputable playboy son of a general who had once served as Francois Duvalier's chief of staff, and Louis Jodel Chamblain, the former Haitian army officer and macoute leader whose pregnant wife had been killed by a pro-Aristide mob after he took part in Roger Lafontant's unsuccessful December 1990 coup attempt (he had subsequently been freed from jail after Aristide had been deposed), FRAPH portrayed itself to foreign reporters as a political movement, but its guns spoke louder than its words, and in place of "macoute," armed civilians now attached to the police and army were now referred to as "attaches." On October 11, as the USS Harlan County attempted to dock in Port-au-Prince, the first salvo in an envisioned UN-mandated landing force, it was met by a boisterous demonstration by about one hundred armed FRAPH members at Port-au-Prince's dock. Conferring amongst themselves, Washington and the U.S. Embassy in Port-au-Prince opted, unbelievably, to turn the ship around.

Given this turn of events, on October 13, the UN Security Council voted to immediately reimpose sanctions. As if in response, the day after the UN vote, Guy Malary, Aristide's Howard University-educated new Minister of Justice and one of Haiti's foremost lawyers, was mowed down in a hail of gunfire along with his driver and bodyguard as they traveled through the capital's Turgeau district. Malary had been the original lawyer associated with bringing the cases of Evans Paul and others against former dictator Prosper Avril and, in his new role of Minister of Justice, would have been in charge of, among other things, reforming Haiti's army and formally separating it from the police. On October 19, a UN embargo on army, military and police supplies and oil shipments to Haiti took hold, and the U.S. government froze the assets and revoked the visas of the Haitian leaders. The October 30 deadline for Aristide's return passed with little reason for optimism.

FRAPH CHOSE THE END OF THE YEAR to flex its homicidal muscle. On December 27, in revenge for the killing of local strongman Issa Paul, FRAPH members launched a raid on the capital's pro-Aristide stronghold of Cité Soleil, torching large swaths of the shantytown and killing pro-democracy activists. Amnesty International estimated seventy men, women and children died in the onslaught, including some thirty children. That same month, soldiers and attachés raided the Raboteau slum in the northern city of Gonaives, searching for Amiot Metayer, a former law student who had been at the front lines of Aristide's most radical supporters in the city, and who was known as "Cubain" or "the Cuban" for his revolutionary fervor. Unable to find Metayer, they arrested one of his younger brothers and several other men, took them to the headquarters of the Anti-Gang unit of the Goanives police and tortured them for many months before releasing them.

Several months later, on the night of April 22, 1994, a day after soldiers in Gonaives again failed to capture Metayer, they returned along with FRAPH members and rival street politician Jean-Pierre Baptiste, better known as Jean Tatoune, to the Raboteau slum that Metayer called home. Having burned Metayer's house and beaten his family members the previous evening, this night the gunmen began firing wildly, chasing residents into the putty-hued water that lapped in a polluted foam at the bidonville's beaches. Soldiers and attachés chased them, shooting at their backs and legs, while other gunmen fired on the shore and people attempting to swim away from boats stationed in the city's bay. Up to twenty people were said to have perished in the assault.

MAY 11 WAS MARKED with the junta appointing octogenarian Supreme Court Justice Emile Jonaissant as Haiti's new provisional president, and a week later Jonaissant named a cabinet sans Prime Minister and promised to organize new elections so a new president could take office on February 7, 1995. On June 21, most international flights in and out of Haiti were suspended, and a month later the United States, flailing at the ceaseless tide of boat people and interning thousands of refugees at its Guantánamo Bay naval base, announced that it would seek UN approval for an invasion of Haiti. Ten days later the UN Security Council approved the measure 12-0 with two abstentions. The following day, Jonaissant declared a state of siege in Haiti. On August 1, Reynold Georges, a slippery lawyer and former senator who had been a strident supporter of the military, found himself a target of its gunmen. He was struck down, though not fatally, in Delmas by a car full of soldiers and police who loosed a fusillade of automatic weapons fire at him, and some saw it as payback for recent statements Georges had made to foreign journalists criticizing the regime.

At the August 1994 culmination in Paris of a series of meetings with international banking institutions and American and European diplomatic and financial representatives to discuss the terms of his return, Aristide was presented with an extensive list of measures designed to restructure Haiti's moribund economy. The selling off of state-owned monopolies, elimination of thousands of government workers, the lowering of trade tariffs and a promise to keep Haiti's criminally low minimum wage (about a dollar a day) at a depressed level were all components of the Structural Adjustment Program (SAP), which would popularly become known as the "Paris Plan." The agreements amounted to a betrayal of the aspirations of the poor majority that had elected Aristide and then suffered through three years of terror during his exile, and stood in contrast to everything the former priest and then president had endorsed during his political life. But it was late in the day, and the clock was ticking past his presidency. Aristide signed the agreements.

A DEVASTATING LOSS STRUCK Haiti's progressive church on August 29 when, in the latest high-profile political murder, Father Jean-Marie Vincent—a priest who had acted as an advocate for peasants in Haiti's poverty-stricken northwest and had been in the car during the attempt to kill Aristide at the roadblock in Freycineau in 1987—was gunned down in front of the Holy Ghost Fathers' residence in Port-au-Prince. Vincent's attempts at radical land-reform near the town of Jean Rabel had spiraled into trench warfare between peasants and wealthy landowners, climaxing in a July 1987 massacre of hundreds of peasants affiliated with Vincent's movements by thugs in the employ of the local elite. On September 15, referring to Vincent's killing, U.S. President Bill Clinton addressed the U.S. public and outlined the reasons for the planned invasion.

In a last-ditch effort to avoid a shooting invasion, former U.S. President Jimmy Carter, former chairman of the Joint Chiefs of Staff (and future Secretary of State) Colin Powell and former U.S. Senator Sam Nunn were dispatched to Port-au-Prince on September 17 to attempt to convince Cédras and company that the United States meant business. On September 18, after marathon negotiations with Jonaissant and the coup leaders, the triumvirate gained an agreement for a nonopposed entry of a U.S.-led multinational force, for the junta to relinquish power by October 15 and for Aristide to return. The invasion was called off even as some Fort Bragg, NC, troops were already on airplanes speeding toward Haiti.

The first American troops landed at Port-au-Prince's airport early on Monday morning, September 19. They were greeted by thousands of Haitians straining against the airport's fences, cheering, celebrating their arrival.

The force would eventually grow to some twenty-five thousand United Nations troops and, after an unpleasant introduction where American troops operating under restrictive rules of engagement were basically forced to sit and watch as the Haitian army and FRAPH continued to terrorize the population, it became clear very quickly what a paper tiger the army and paramilitary forces had been, capable of victimizing a largely unarmed civilian population but utterly lacking the backbone or desire to stand up to international troops. After American troops raided FRAPH headquarters on October 4 and seized some one-hundred fifty thousand documents from there and FADH headquarters and sent them back to the United States, the act of doing so and the papers themselves would become a political football tossed back and forth between the Haitian and American governments for years afterwards.

In one of a series of surreal scenes that took place after the troops arrived, Toto Constant, surrounded by U.S. soldiers, said in front of the U.S. Embassy that, "The only solution for Haiti is the return of Aristide. . . . I'm asking every-body to put down the guns." As he was jeered by hundreds of Haitians, Con-stant also pledged that FRAPH would work as a "constructive opposition" after Aristide returned. Constant's jeep was attacked and its windows smashed as he drove away. Months later, he resurfaced in the United States, having entered on a valid tourist visa. It was later revealed that Constant had been on the CIA's payroll as an "informant" since at least 1992. Coupled with the *Harlan County* incident the previous year, many observers wondered if elements of the Repub-lican Party in the United States, nearly as hostile to President Bill Clinton as it was to Aristide himself, had deliberately undermined U.S. government policy in Haiti.

ARISTIDE FLEW BACK to Haiti from his three-year exile on a U.S. government plane on October 15 with U.S. Secretary of State Warren Christopher at his side. Landing at Port-au-Prince's international airport, he boarded a U.S. military helicopter, which whisked him to the National Palace. Addressing the throng that had awaited his arrival in front of the Palace, Aristide released a single white dove.

"Never again should one more drop of blood flow," he said. "No to violence! No to vengeance! Yes to reconciliation!"

The leaders of the coup against him were scattering to the four winds. Michel Francois, the Port-au-Prince police chief who many had thought spearheaded the revolt, had fled to the Dominican Republic, crossing over at the border town of Malpasse after being forced to spend the night sleeping in his car. As Cédras also fled (to Panama) Aristide named Major General Jean-Claude Duperval as the new head of the military. Doling out appointments to neutralize his oppo-nents, Aristide also named Carl Dorelien, a close ally to Cédras, as military attaché in Spain and sent Ernest Prudhomme, one of the chief torturers of the "Prisonniers de la Toussaint," to Argentina. Jackson Joanis, Michel Francois's right hand man and the former director of the capital's feared Anti-Gang unit, was transferred to army's downtown headquarters. Smarck Michel, Aristide's former Minister of Planning, was tapped for the new Prime Minister's post. On October 15, though, to the surprise of some, Aristide promoted an FADH officer with an unsavory reputation, Colonel Mondesir Beaubrun, from colonel to general and named him Chief of Staff for the army. Dany Toussaint, the former FADH officer who had driven with Aristide from Tabarre to the National Palace the night of the coup, was elevated to the rank of major in the FADH, and then appointed head of Haiti's interim police force. The day after Christmas, 1994, as soldiers wildly demonstrated at Haitian military headquarters in Port-au-Prince demanding pay, a panicked Mondesir Beaubrun barricaded himself in his office and opened fire through his closed door into his hallway, killing two of his own bodyguards. Few were surprised, then, when Beaubrun was among forty-three FADH officers dismissed by Aristide as the new year began.

THE YEAR COMMENCED in difficulty, with a February 19 riot erupting at the National Penitentiary, with prisoners upset at the continued misery of their living conditions setting the prison chapel aflame. Fifteen escaped before the building was cordoned off by troops from the multinational force. The same week, Aristide surprised many observers with the announcement that Brigadier General Mondesir Beaubrun, the former army chief of staff who had been among the forty-three officers dismissed only days earlier, would serve as his new Minister of Interior. American officials opposed the appointment.

On February 20, barely four months after Aristide's return, Haiti's newly-formed provisional electoral council called for new elections to be held in June, with all eighty-seven seats in the Chamber of Deputies and two-thirds of the Seats in the Senate to be up for grabs, as well as some two thousand local posts. The same month, by decree, Aristide inserted a provision in Haiti's electoral law whereby political parties had to pay less in registration fees the more candidates they fielded, which many smaller and fledgling parties denounced as an attempt to drive them out of existence by demanding fees far beyond their ability to pay.

SO FAR, THE SIGNS did not bode exceedingly well, and things were about to get much murkier.

On March 19, working on information supplied by a Haitian interpreter—Claude Douge—American troops in the capital detained two brothers, Eddy and Patrick Moise, who each had criminal records both in Haiti and the United States. The brothers were arrested while traveling in a gray Isuzu Trooper registered to the Ministry of the Interior and were carrying on their persons the phone number of Minister of the Interior Mondesir Beaubrun, as well as that of General Joseph Cherubin.

The Moise brothers had a long record of thuggish and opportunistic political allegiance, having alleged connections to the extreme left-wing Militant United Front and having served briefly on Aristide's security staff during his 1991 term. They had also led a 1992 takeover of the Canadian embassy in Haiti, calling for

Aristide's return to the country, but their arrest and subsequent release (at a time when people were being executed for far less) made some believe that the pair were in fact working in collusion with the military government.

Acting on information garnered in their investigation of the Moise Brothers, on March 22, U.S. officials in Port-au-Prince informed Aristide and new Minister of Justice Jean-Joseph Exume of a possible plot against Mireille Durocher Bertin, the young lawyer who had served as legal advisor to the coup government of Cédras and company. Aristide promised action. On March 23, Durocher Bertin was apprised of the plot against her and offered protection by Haitian government, which she declined, not seeming, said those who knew her, to trust it. The next day, Aristide sent a letter to American officials in Port-au-Prince informing them of Durocher Bertin's refusal. United States Ambassador William Lacy Swing, perhaps sensing something awful on the horizon, met with Aristide several days later, and again pressured him to investigate Beaubrun.

On March 28, while driving her white Subaru through the capital with a client, Eugene Baillerjeau, at her side, Durocher Bertin was caught in traffic when gunmen jumped out of a red Mitsubishi jeep, shot out her car's tires and raked its windshield with gunfire. Durocher Bertin, 35, died along with her client. Dany Toussaint, head of the interim police force, was announced to be in charge of the government's investigation. An FBI team was dispatched to Haiti to investigate the killing. They soon left, complaining of stonewalling by the Aristide government, who did not seem to want the crime actually investigated—a fact many American officials took worried note of.

It had been a disturbing performance by the recently returned government, and following President Clinton's visit on April 1, the Pentagon sent a classified cable to the U.S. Embassy in Haiti, listing twenty-seven Aristide opponents who they warned may have been targeted for assassination. That same month, Aristide finished what he had been wheedling at since his return, and demobilized the Haitian army. As the army was still enshrined in Article IX of the Haitian constitution, the move was illegal without a constitutional amendment, but, given the body's excesses over the years, few Haitians save the soldiers themselves were sad to see them go.

FURTHER DAMAGING any appearance of "transparency," from April to December of 1995, the Aristide government put some $3,763,422 from Haiti's public treasury into programs that became known as *Les Petits Projets de la Presidence*. Distributed to public works projects headed by such people as Chavannes Jean-Baptiste in the Plateau Central and Father Joachim Samedi in Jeremie, the programs also contained $207,156 for projects near Aristide's residence in Tabarre, and some $191,779 for "urban development" in the Aristide stronghold slum of Raboteau in Gonaives. Rumors of corruption swirled around the project, and little of the work that the money had been allotted for was ever finished.

In an echo of Haiti's recent past, in May 1995, the FRAPH leader Toto Constant, who had fled to the United States on a tourist visa after Aristide's return, was seized by INS officials on a Queens, New York street and imprisoned in Wicomico County Detention Center in Maryland. Evidently, Constant had been trying to rally the FRAPH remaining in Haiti from his New York exile, and the Aristide government had launched a diplomatic offensive to get the Americans to pick him up. Threatened with deportation, Constant would later begin talking to the press and threatening to divulge all he knew about his links with Colonel Pat Collins, a U.S. military attaché who had served at the U.S. Embassy in Port-au-Prince, and who, Constant said, had approached him to work for the CIA. Constant also fingered John Kambourian, another embassy official, as having had close contact with the paramilitary organization. The CIA had even, Constant claimed, encouraged the FRAPH protest during the *Harlan County* incident, intentionally scuttling the plan for Aristide's returns and undermining official U.S. policy, before severing ties with the group in the Spring of 1994. After he started talking, Constant was eventually quietly released back to New York, told to stay within the confines of Queens and report regularly to the INS. Still under a formal order of deportation, his return to Haiti was delayed indefinitely under official order of the U.S. State Department.

AFTER HIS RETURN, Aristide's relationship with his former campaign manager, Port-au-Prince mayor Evans Paul, had grown increasingly frosty, and so few were surprised when in advance of the June elections, Aristide and his political coterie shed Paul's FNCD and instead created a new political movement, the Platfòm Politik Lavalas (PPL), and a new party, the Òganizasyon Politik Lavalas (OPL), with left-wing intellectual and author Gérard Pierre-Charles, a longtime Duvalier opponent who had spent two decades living in Mexico with his wife, the historian Suzy Castor. The fissure marked the first significant public fraying in the social-democratic coalition that had brought Aristide to power in 1990; Paul—imperious, intelligent and on friendly terms with the Americans who had watched him endure three years of terror as Aristide sat in luxurious exile in the Georgetown district of Washington, DC—found himself increasingly frozen out from the Haitian political scene.

Aristide himself, not appearing to have the stomach to campaign for the draconian reforms he agreed to insure his return, after lowering most of Haiti's trade tariffs to under 10 percent, instead sent out new Prime Minister Smarck Michel to face the glare of cameras, explaining that, yes, the agreements meant that the state electric company Electricité d'Haiti (EDH), telephone company (TELECO), water industry (CAMEP), port administration (Administration Portuaire de Port-au-Prince), and state flour mill and cement plant were all to be privatized and hundreds of government workers fired.

Not all, though, were convinced by the president's attempts to distance himself from the reforms, and despite the creation of the Institut National de la Reforme Agraire (INARA) in June 1995, Haiti's peasants were chief among the skeptics. Speaking on Radio Haiti-Inter in September, Olry St. Louis—one of the leading spokesman for the Tet Kole (Heads Together) peasant movement begun by the murdered priest Jean-Marie Vincent—excoriated Aristide for accepting the reform package, saying, "Aristide always has a double-face, a double-game, at every juncture. He looks at the moment to see how to act so he can use it to his advantage and make political capital from it, and I think that is what is happening today. The first person who signed the thing at the beginning was Aristide. He could have refused, because the people were behind him."

IN THE RUNUP to the June elections, TNH director Constant Dominique raised a few eyebrows when he refused to air four debates between the political parties, despite having previously agreed to do so. The last debate, held in the capital on June 13, was instead edited for use in a program entitled "Elections 95" with Constant providing partisan, pro-government commentary throughout the show. Officials from the Washington-based National Democratic Institute (NDI) who protested the attempt at state propaganda were greeted hostilely by TNH programming director Jean Pierre Erl (Constant refused to meet with them), who told them free and fair media access was not his concern.[3]

On June 25, 1995, though, Haiti held its first elections since Aristide had returned from exile the previous September. Up for grabs were eighteen of the twenty-seven seats in the Haitian senate, all eighty-three representatives in the Chamber of Deputies, members of 133 local councils and 561 communal office boards. The Aristide-endorsed Organizasyon Politik Lavalas (OPL), his former coalition FNCD and Victor Benoit's KONAKOM were the main participants.

With three hundred OAS electoral observers deployed throughout Haiti's nine departments, the voting on June 25, despite problems with the distribution of electoral materials and voting stations in some areas opening up late, was generally viewed as a success, free of widespread intimidation and violence.[4] The U.S. Presidential Delegation sent by U.S. President Bill Clinton declared that while the elections represented "a step in the building of democracy in Haiti . . . the process was affected by irregularities and administrative flaws that need to be address for the second round and the future."[5] Ever the naysayers, the NDI's partisan counterpart, the International Republican Institute (IRI), the international arm of the U.S. Republican Party, in a press release the following day (June 26), took the Haitian authorities to task for failing to create "an open, transparent and viable process," going on to question balloting secrecy and security and assailing arbitrary disqualification of candidates.[6] Nevertheless, seven of the new deputies received an absolute majority of the votes, and discrepancies were assigned more to chaos and disorganization rather than partisanship. Evans Paul, in an event that would forever embitter him to Aristide, lost the mayorship of Port-au-Prince to leftist folksinger Manno Charlemagne, who had been endorsed both by Aristide and the Lavalas movement. Charlemagne was sworn in on August 4, 1995 with U.S. Ambassador William Lacy Swing— who had made no secret of his preference that Evans Paul keep that particular job—in attendance.

With all major political parties except Lavalas announcing that they would boycott the second round of elections, though, U.S. Undersecretary of State Strobe Talbot visited Haiti in late August to present a seven-point plan to Aristide and the opposition, designed to assuage their fears. On August 23, 1995, the CEP announced that the second round of balloting would take place on September 17. The elections held on that day featured 102 candidates representing fifteen political parties. After much posturing and back and forth on the part of both sides, the FNCD finally announced on September 3rd that thirteen of its members would participate in the coming ballot. The Electoral Observation Mission of the OAS said that voting for the second round of legislative elections held on September 17, 1995 "took place in a situation of calm and in an excellent climate of security. . . . [With] no widespread organized fraud and with respect to the training of staff, the management of the operations and the organization of voting day showed great improvement over the June 25 elections."[7] Vote turnout was estimated at around 20 percent. On September 28, the runoff election results were announced, and as expected, the Lavalas platform swept seventeen out of twenty-seven seats in the Senate and sixty-seven out of eighty-three seats in the Chamber of Deputies. Haiti had shown the world, though the world might quibble with the choices they made, that they could indeed hold a free, fair election, and the Haitian people hoped, at long last, to have a responsive government to help ease their misery.

BUT PERHAPS, ELSEWHERE, there were other plans. On October 4, in an echo of the Durocher Bertin killing seven months earlier, former Haitian General Max Mayard was gunned down by unknown persons as he tried to escape his car as it was sprayed with bullets on a busy downtown street. The gunmen fled the scene, and there were no arrests.

On October 13, Prime Minister Smarck Michel, whom Aristide had wisely let become the public face of the privatization measures he himself had agreed to in Paris in August 1994, resigned and was replaced by Foreign Minister Claudette Werleigh, a change that seemed unlikely to placate the United States, impatient with Aristide's foot-dragging over reforms. The next month, Washington suspended $4.5 million in pending economic aid to Haiti, citing the government's slow pace on adopting the agreed-to restructuring measures.

More momentously, perhaps, on November 7, a car carrying two deputies elected in the summer elections, Gabriel Fortuné and Jean-Hubert Feuillé , was fired upon in downtown Port-au-Prince. Fortuné was wounded, but Feuillé, a cousin of Aristide as well as a former member of the president's security detail, was killed. Reaction to the killings was volatile throughout the country and mobs in Les Cayes, which Feuillé represented in parliament, burned and sacked houses associated with Aristide opponents. This was relatively mild, however, to what came at Feuillé's state funeral on November 11, held at the National Cathedral in Port-au-Prince. With a corps of government officials, diplomats and young Aristide militants filling the cathedral, the president surveyed the scene from an elaborate, gold-hued chair as radical priests called for revenge against the enemies of the people in the most meagerly disguised terms. Rising from his seat, Aristide then erupted:

> The large guns of the international community are here to accompany the Haitian police to disarm all the criminals, all the terrorists, all the extremists. . . . If not, I'm going to tell them it's over. . . . I'm saying now, whoever tries to block the legal operation of disarmament if they're Haitian, we'll arrest them, if they're not Haitian, we'll send them back to their parents.

From the back of the cathedral, a mob of young men thundered their concurrence. Aristide continued, "We don't have two or three heads of state, we have only one. This is the first time I have spoken in these terms since my return."

U.S. Ambassador William Lacy Swing and UN Special Representative Lakhdar Brahimi, both in attendance, gazed icily up at Aristide from where they sat in front of the podium, but kept their cool and their seats. The nation, however, did not, and convulsed. In the capital, the Delmas and Carrefour Roads were blocked by burning tires and cars as roadblocks set up by pro-Aristide "vigilance brigades" went up around the city. Cars, including UN vehicles, were stopped and searched by armed civilian, riots erupted in ever-restive Gonaives and at least twenty-two people had to be evacuated from Les Cayes under UN military protection. At least nine died in the violence.

All of this made many wonder exactly what kind of government Aristide was looking to set up now that the Americans had returned him to power, so a palpable sense of relief went through the international community when, finally, on November 30th, Aristide told a group of foreign journalists that, despite having made sounds that he would like to "make up" for the three years he had lost in his term while in exile, he would leave office after the presidential elections in December as scheduled, but didn't rule out running for president again in 2000, when Haiti would shortly be celebrating its bicentennial of independence from

French rule. René Préval, Aristide's first Prime Minister, it turned out, would be the presidential candidate for the OPL despite not belonging to the party himself. The Haitians immediately dubbed Préval Aristide's *marassa* (twin).

HAITI'S PRESIDENTIAL ELECTIONS to determine Aristide's successor were held on December 17, 1995. Despite boycotts by Serge Gilles's PANPRA, Marc Bazin's Mouvement pour l'Instauration de la Démocratie en Haïti (MIDH) party and Leslie Manigat's Rassemblement des Démocrates Nationaux Progressistes (RNDP), the elections went off fairly smoothly, with the OAS Electoral Observion Mission declaring itself "satisfied" with the results of the election announced by the CEP on December 23, and lauding the fact that "voting occurred in a calm and orderly fashion, without serious incidents of intimidation or violence."[8] The U.S. Presidential Delegation declared the elections "a clear improvement over previous elections," especially referring to the muddled June 1995 legislative and municipal contests, and even the IRI noted that "Haiti's election authorities demonstrated a more responsive attitude to the basic requirements of a democratic electoral process . . . underscoring the positive impact of continued cooperation between Haiti and the international community."[9] When all was said and done and election results were announced on December 23, the mournful-eyed René Préval, a native of the northern hamlet of Marmelade, was chosen by the Haitian people as the man best hoped to guide them through what promised to be another tumultuous five years.

All that was left was the inauguration—in Haiti, no small thing.

THERE WAS STILL TIME for a few surprises.

On January 16, an angry demonstration by people demanding wages in front of a business owned by the wealthy Mevs family in Cité Soleil turned into a shooting match when members of the interim police force arrived and clashed with the crowd. Seven people were wounded by gunfire and a young local woman, Martha Jean-Charles, was killed. The demonstrators then attacked a police car and UN vehicles that were present. Attempting to calm the situation, Aristide himself visited Cité Soleil on January 19 during a meeting between police and residents, saying the he wished the people and the police force "to be one." At the meeting, which was broadcast on television and radio and which also included members of a criminal gang that had dubbed itself "the Red Army," a female PNH officer, Marie Christine Jeune, who had worked extensively in the district, vocally criticized the president's attempt to create a working relationship between the police and a group that she viewed as little more than a collection of thieves and murderers, bent on terrorizing their own community.

Later the same month, Haitians learned that Aristide, the former priest, was to marry Haitian-American lawyer Mildred Trouillot, who he had met while in exile in the United States, at his rebuilt mansion at Tabarre. Crowds of Aristide supporters filled the streets chanting *se pa bon*, that their "Titid" was getting married and that it would mean that he would forget about them. Trouillot had worked as a speechwriter and a liaison between the Aristide government-in-exile and U.S. officials. The ceremony held at Tabarre included on its guest list such notables as U.S. General John Sheehan, head of U.S. Southern Command, and U.S. National Security Advisor Anthony Lake.

On February 6, 1996, in one of his last acts in office, Aristide re-established Haiti's diplomatic relations with Cuba for the first time in three decades.

YEARS LATER, we were driving through the darkened streets, as gingerbread houses and political slogans scrawled on crumbling walls presented themselves to our headlights like a dreamtime vision of New Orleans a hundred years ago, or a hundred years from now. My friend, a light-skinned ophthalmologist and intellectual who had lived in New York for years and was the black sheep of one of the wealthiest families in Haiti, was driving. We had been drinking all night and, perhaps inevitably, the talk turned to America and its tumultuous relationship with the island.

"You know why I hated it when the Americans came?" he asked rhetorically, as our car descended the Canapé Vert road and Port-au-Prince lay spread out and glowing like a cinder beneath us. "Because they should have given us a real occupation."

"What do you mean?" This was coming from a man who had been written off by many for being too cozy with the Aristide government, and whose black wife had been jailed for putting up Aristide posters during the Cédras regime.

"They should have given us a real occupation. What they gave Japan and Germany after World War II. They should have destroyed this idea, this hateful, destructive idea. They should have completely changed the system of government, rebuilt the infrastructure, ripped out and replaced the educational system. They should have destroyed this destructive myth once and for all."

He paused for a moment to negotiate a sharp turn before the TELECO building, and soon we were passing the burned-out remnants of the offices of two political parties.

"Then we would have had a chance."

IN A SOMBER CEREMONY on February 7, 1996, René Préval was inaugurated as Haiti's president. Aristide placed the blue and red presidential sash on Préval's shoulders and, as the ceremony drew to a close, the priest-turned-president entered a white helicopter that ascended into the sky above the National Palace for the short flight to Tabarre. Above the heads of a throng of thousands of loyalists, the helicopter swooped once, twice, three times over the crowd, with Aristide stretching out his hand as if in benediction of those assembled. Then the helicopter turned and began its quick journey north. Within moments, it was gone.

CHAPTER NOTES

1. Evans Paul, declaration, Exhibit 1, executed in Haiti on April 23, 1994. Marino Etienne, declaration, Exhibit 3, executed in Paris, France on May 10, 1994. Gerald Emile "Aby" Brun, declaration, Exhibit 4, executed in Haiti on April 23, 1994.
2. Declaration of Serge Gilles, Exhibit 5, executed in Haiti on 10th May 1994.
3. Tanya L. Domi, field director in Haiti for the National Democratic Institute for International Affairs, Letter to Prime Minister Smarck Michel and CEP President Anselme Remy.
4. Elections Day Observations: Electoral Observation Mission Organization of American States (EOM/OAS), June 22, 1995.
5. U.S Presidential Delegation to Observe the Haiti Elections, departure statement, June 26, 1995.
6. International Republican Institute, Irregularities Mar Electoral Process, press release, June 26, 1995. U.S. Representative Porter Goss Details Challenges to Sunday's Electoral Process, press release, International Republican Institute, June 24, 1995.
7. Report on the 2nd Round of Legislative & Municipal Elections held on September 17, 1995, Electoral Observation Mission Organization of American States (EOM/OAS), September 1995.
8. Early OAS/EOM Assessments Affirm Calm, Orderly Elections, press statement, December 17, 1995.
9. Dr. Georges Faurial, Assessment of the Electoral Process In Haiti, statement on behalf of the International Republican Institute, December 18, 1995. Update on Haitian Pre-Election Activities From IRI's Port-au-Prince Office, December 13, 1995.

3
Marassa in the Kingdom

THE COUNTRY RENÉ PRÉVAL took over was one that had been decimated by decades of senseless political violence and economically ravaged by the three-year embargo. Lacking the kind of sweeping popular appeal that Aristide could work up so effortlessly, Préval instead decided to concentrate on the more mundane task of making concrete the meager gains Haiti had succeeded in gaining since the invasion. Naming Rosny Smarth, 56 years old and, like Préval, trained as an agronomist, as his prime minister on February 16, 1996, Préval more or less pleased the OPL, who had initially hoped for their leader, Gérard Pierre-Charles, to occupy the post. Chavannes Jean-Baptiste, head of the MPP peasant group and now also director of the 200,000 strong Mouvman Peyizan Nasyonal Kongre Papay (MPNKP) organization, was acting as Préval's transition chief, and he was also offered the job, but declined, preferring to continue working with the peasants in the Plateau Central, but still remaining a member of Préval's private cabinet of advisors. Smarth, for his part, had lived in exile in Chile during much of the Duvalier years, and had held government posts there under the administration of Socialist President Salvador Allende. Following Allende's ouster, Smarth, who was also, not coincidentally, the brother of Father William Smarth, one of the survivors of the 1987 roadside ambush against Aristide, had spent a decade living in Mexico. In short, he seemed like exactly the sort of modernizing bureaucrat a country like Haiti—which seemed to have exhausted its supply of messiah politics and revolutionary slogans—needed; taking office on March 6 after parliamentary approval, Smarth seemed prepared to set out and proselytize of behalf of the IMF-mandated reforms that Aristide had agreed to—but not implemented—in Paris before he was returned to power.

Many hard decisions lay ahead for Préval and the newly-elected Parliament. The Structural Adjustment Program (SAP) was seen as key to the Haitian government accessing some $135 million in international loans and grants, but was a bitter pill for many to swallow, boding as it did not only for the selling off of TELECO, EDH and CAMEP, but also a large reduction in trade tariffs and massive layoffs among state workers. That is, among the few who even had the promise of a regular income in the impoverished country. International lending bodies, hoping for brisk approvement of the moves by Haitian government officials, instead began to look somewhat alarmedly towards a future that seemed to promise raucous parliamentary debate on the subject.

The new parliament itself was a curious mixture of social democrats, Aristide loyalists and the odd right-wing holdover, but in its early days, it seemed to manifest something of a healthy, independent spirit. After parliament had opened on January 8, but before Préval had been sworn-in, one of its first acts was to refuse to ratify army dentist Lt. Col. Jean-Marie Fourel Celestin, Aristide's nominee to head the newly formed Haitian National Police and a former head of security at the National Palace. Despite no replacement having yet been found, Dany Toussaint, who had headed the interim police force and then the judicial police force since Aristide's return, resigned. By March 1996, Pierre Denizé was appointed by Préval and approved by parliament to be the director general position of the newly formed Police Nationale d'Haiti (PNH). That Denizé was also a friend of Haiti's new Secretary of State for Public Security Robert "Bob" Manuel, an affable mulatto ex-military man who had been an early conduit between Aristide and progressive elements in the military, seemed to bode well for cooperation within Haiti's new law-enforcement establishment. Smarth also named Jacques Edouard Alexis, founder and rector of the capital's well-regarded private Quisqueya University, as minister of education.

Among the first obstacles, literally, to confront the government, were the mountains of garbage piling up around the capital. Following Carnival celebrations in the early spring, the festering heaps only grew worse, with the Port-au-Prince mayor's office, the Ministry of the Environment and the local garbage trucking company all blaming one another for the mess. A February 27 protest at the Lycee Alexandre Petion (Francois Duvalier's alma mater) by students who were almost unable to enter the school because of a himalayan pile at its entrance, was broken up when police arrived and ill-advisedly fired in the air, panicking everyone in the neighborhood. A March 1 agreement between the government and with four private trucking companies alleviated the problem somewhat, but the capital still remained so dirty that one senator charged it had become "unlivable."

Plucking himself from the capital's morass in early March, Préval, son of Haiti's peasant heartland, in anticipation of what he said would be a major move toward land reform, became the first-ever Haitian president to visit the hamlet of Maribaroux near the Dominican border, where he was greeted by crowds of peasants lined up along the Diasa River, cheering his motorcade and waving their machetes and hoes in the air.

SEVERAL EPISODES in the capital, however, made one curious for what lay on the horizon, and exactly how quiet Aristide's retirement would be. Though the conventional wisdom was that Préval was little more than a front by which

Aristide would continue to exercise control of the executive branch of government, in reality a more complicated dynamic was developing, with Préval demonstrating more independence—and enduring far more assaults on his authority—than most ever gave him credit for.

On March 26, at the Hotel Christopher in the capital, a scuffle broke out between an entourage belonging to Port-au-Prince mayor Manno Charlemagne and one belonging to Annette Auguste (known as "So Anne," the "so" being short for *soeur* or sister), a sometime folksinger who had returned from years working in Brooklyn when Aristide landed back in Haiti in 1994 and had since ingratiated herself with the former priest. Barreling into a conference that Charlemagne, an erratic but nevertheless independent-minded individual, had organized on privatization, spouting "anti neoliberal" slogans, Auguste's contingent fired shots into the air before departing the building's premises.

At a weekend conference beginning on March 29 that was allegedly timed to celebrate International Youth Day and held at the newly founded Aristide Foundation for Democracy—ostensibly a body providing low-cost loans and assistance to the Haitian people and located next door to Aristide's palatial new residence in the capital's Tabarre suburb—groups of young Aristide supporters savaged the Préval government and its "neoliberal" privatization plan in speech after speech. Though Aristide had signed off on the reforms as a condition for his returning to power in 1994, the attendees of the conference stated that the plan was "working against the national interest" and was "diabolic," terming them an "economic coup d'etat." Some were not surprised to see Aristide use his surrogates to strike out at Préval, but many were surprised that it happened so quickly.

Also that month, the body of Marie Christine Jeune, the courageous young female PNH officer who had publicly criticized Aristide's attempts to link the police force with armed gangs the previous January, was found, raped and mutilated, after she had been missing for several days. No one has ever been convicted of her murder.

By June, the antipathy between the former president and the new parliament, at least, had become more evident. In a twelve-page letter released that month, Senator Jean-Robert Sabalat called into question a transfer to Aristide's Lafanmi Selavi orphanage of some $3.3 million from a US$20 million Taiwanese grant to Haiti. Noting eleven other withdrawals, including "Alpha pour le developpement" for $2 million and "Alpha," for $1 million that took place while Aristide was president, Sabalat concluded that only $7 million had ever in fact been put to public use, while the rest had disappeared. Sabalat called for a Senate inquiry, but none was ever held.

Aristide, returning from a two-week trip abroad that June, sat down for a two-hour interview with TNH, where, in his elliptical way, he seemed to be advising the new parliamentarians to oppose the structural adjustment plan that he had signed off on as a quid pro quo for his return. He also lashed out at those who charged him with improperly diverting state funds to his private charities while he was president, labeling them "vagabonds," a strong insult.

IN LATE JUNE, Préval's Minister of Health, Dr. Rodolphe Mallebranche, revealed that, since April, at least sixty-four children had been poisoned by two fever-reducing syrups made by the Pharval laboratories, directed by Rodolphe Boulos of the elite family of the same name. The Valodon and Afebrile medicine the children were taking apparently contained a toxic component, diethylene glycol, which caused kidney failure. The Boulos family, for its part, denied having ever used the chemical in the manufacture of the medicine and said that the product the children had ingested was in fact a pirated version of their brand, which it had asked the government to remove from the marketplace without success. Pharval had been founded by Francois Duvalier's former Minister of Health Dr. Carlo Boulos. Another Boulos brother, Dr. Reginald Boulos, was presently serving as the director of the Centres pour le Developpement et de la Santé (CDS), a hefty recipient of USAID health funding, with a major outpost in Cité Soleil. Despite the family's denials, a sense of popular anger festered against them after the incident, with Jean Dominique, the director of Radio Haiti-Inter who served as an informal advisor to his old friend Préval, being particularly scathing in his criticism.

In September, the third round of parliamentary voting went off with relatively little fanfare. After a cursory and biased trial that same month, with almost no evidence presented for the defense, Michel Francois and Louis Jodel Champlain—either of whom could had more than enough blood on their hands to warrant conviction in a just court—were convicted in absentia of the murder of Antoine Izmery along with fifteen co-defendants and sentenced to life at hard labor.

ON NOVEMBER 2, echoing his training as an agronomist and with the support of Jean Dominique, Préval launched an agrarian reform program set to begin in Haiti's Artibonite Valley under the direction of the Institut National de la Reforme Agraire (INARA). The body, which had been provided for in Haiti's 1987 constitution and created though not staffed by Aristide the previous year, was set to replace the ineffective, corruption-ridden Organisme pour le Développement de la Vallée de l'Artibonite (ODVA), which would never the less continue to sputter along for years to come. Préval saw title to land as something that would motivate peasants to work their property responsibly, helping to stem Haiti's near-total deforestation, and he believed that by empowering the country's peasant majority, it would also help shift the political balance of power that had long been centered around the politicians and their acolytes based in the capital. Land conflicts in Haiti's hinterlands often flared into violence, and ownership was seen as one way to reduce them. Préval and Dominique both sought to make Haiti's rice production more competitive, beset as it was by a flood of cheap imported American rice that had begun to arrive in the 1980s, and the Artibonite was seen as an appropriate pilot for such a move.

There was great historical resonance for Préval's desire to shift some of the Haitian government's attention from the capital to the countryside, as no Haitian could ever forget the toll the country's inability to support its rural inhabitants had exacted.

IT WAS 1937, and the United States was struggling in the midst of the Great Depression as sugar prices collapsed around the globe, and more Haitians than ever fled their homeland to seek employment in the cane fields of Cuba and the neighboring Dominican Republic. Having a hard enough time employing his own populace, the Cuban dictator Fulgencio Batista expelled most of the Haitians working in Cuban fields that year, many of whom had worked in the country for decades, and venally seized the assets they held in Cuban banks, sending them back to their homeland nearly penniless. More and more Haitians began streaming into the Dominican Republic, then under the iron-fisted rule of its own dictator, Rafael Trujillo. Trujillo, with the country groaning under the weight of the sugar crisis, was ill-disposed, politically or temperamentally, to deal with the immigrants and thus precipitated one of the most shameful chapters in the history of the island. For three days beginning on October 2, 1937, Dominican soldiers and police massacred an estimated 15-20,000 Haitians throughout the country, killing many with clubs and machetes. Often, the Dominicans even went through the process of rounding up Haitians and processing them for deportation, so as to able to disclaim all responsibility for the murders as the dead had already "left" Dominican soil. Though the killings occurred throughout the country, they were committed at a particularly furious pace along the aptly named Massacre River, which runs between the Haitian border town of Ouanaminthe and its sister village on the Dominican side, Dajabon, and for days afterwards, bodies could be seen flowing towards the island's north coast in its waters.

Exactly what prompted Trujillo, the vain, barbarous Dominican tyrant, to unleash such a crime has never been made entirely clear. Rumors abounded that it was a vengeful payback for the murder of several Dominican agents in Haiti by the nationalist president Stenio Vincent, or that Trujillo sought scapegoats for his country's own financial troubles. That he was driven by racial mania brought on by his own desire for "whiteness" in his country and the inescapable fact that some of his own relatives had been Haitian could have also played a hand, yet none go very far in explaining such a slaughter. The reaction of the Vincent government to the killings was pathetically weak for a nation that had once bred such warriors as Dessalines. In protracted negotiations over the course of several months, Trujillo finally agreed to pay Haiti an indemnity of $750,000, or about $30 per life of every Haitian murdered.

Haiti's greatest author, Jacques Stephen Alexis, was moved enough by the mas-sacre and what he saw as the role of venal Haitian politicians in creating the con-ditions that made it possible that he made it the denouement of his most famous book, *Compere General Soleil*, which was translated masterfully into English as *General Sun, My Brother* by the American professor Carrol F. Coates.

Alexis, born to a distinguished black political family in Gonaives in 1922, was the son of Stephen Alexis, who would eventually serve as Haiti's ambassador to France and Lyida Nunez, herself descended from Dominican heritage. A direct descendant of Haiti's revolutionary hero Jean-Jacques Dessalines, as a young man Alexis was deeply impressed by a meeting with the Haitian novel-ist, Jacques Roumain, who had founded the Parti Communiste Haitien in 1934. Though he was in Haiti and had taken a leading role in the student strikes that helped to oust Elie Lescot in 1946, for the most part, Alexis's education had been European, and he had even been briefly married to a French woman, who he eventually left, marrying a Haitian and returning to his native land. After Fran-cois Duvalier's election in October 1957, Alexis helped form the Part d'Entente Populaire (Party of Popular Accord) in 1958, and served as Haiti's representa-tive to the Thirteenth Congress of the Union of Soviet Writers in Moscow the following year, also traveling to the Conference of Communist Worker's Parties in Beijing in November 1960, where he met Mao. Returning to the Caribbean by way of Cuba, he and four other men set sail from that island on the writer's thirty-ninth birthday, April 22 1961. Their destination was Mole Saint Nicolas, wherefrom Alexis and his band hoped to spark a revolution that would topple Duvalier. Seized by Haitian soldiers almost immediately, the prisoners were eventually stoned to death by a group of peasants and street children under the urging of the local army and Tontons Macoutes. It is perhaps sadly apt that one of Haiti's greatest intellectual minds, who had done much to raise the country's profile in the French-speaking world, should be consumed by a product of its political culture, which had done so little to uplift its fellow citizens. Neverthe-less, Alexis produced several impressive works in his short life, large portions of which read like they could have been scratched out by firelight in the poor neighborhoods of the capital and elsewhere even today.

Compere General Soleil concerns the story of one Hilarion Hilarius, just after the end of the U.S. occupation in the time of President Vincent, who Alexis memorably describes as "an aging Casanova preserved in alcohol; lusterless eyes behind spectacles; full, sensuous lips."

Hilarion, a desperately poor worker and former *restavek* (a child from a poor family who goes to work in rich households as a kind of indentured servant) is arrested at the beginning of the book for theft and tortured while in jail. During his incarceration, he meets a mulatto Communist named Roumel, who inspires the first stirrings of political consciousness within him. Finally released from prison, Hilarion finds himself in the city's southern slum of Carrefour, even then known as one of the city's pleasure centers, and Alexis sensitively describes the lives of the urban poor there. Given the rudimentary awakening of a social conscience, Hilarion becomes more restless and questioning after being released from jail, even though he lacks much formal education. He falls in love with a young woman, Claire-Heureuse (also, not coincidentally, the name of Dessalines's wife), whose godmother had moved to the capital from Gonaives years ago to escape the warring between Haitian political factions there. The couple move in together for a time in a downtown neighborhood near the Saint-Anne Church; Hilarion finds a job as a laborer, Claire-Heureuse becomes pregnant and, for a time, they are happy. Writing about the couple's neighborhood with words that would have still been apt half a century later, Alexis penned the following:

> In this neighborhood, everybody lived on the street. The people were simple, plain and generous. But when you touched what was theirs, they fell into a rage. Misery had made them intractable on that. They lived on the borderline between instinct and intelligence. They were the products of a society that brutalizes people to a level of semi-animal existence, oriented towards their immediate and constant concern: food. Everything was transformed or deformed by an empty stomach; love, pride, willpower and tenderness. Lit up by the naked sunlight, their only entertainment was the theater, music hall and cinema of the bustling, noisy street . . . . What other joy could they take in life except to laugh excessively at anything—the quarrels, the street and the fleeting intoxication of a few popular holidays.

The couple struggles to make ends meet, Claire-Heureuse selling little candies that she makes, Hilarion continuing to work. He eventually loses his job, and though he finds another one at a mahogany-polishing shop, the reader is extremely conscious of the knife's edge on which rests the difference between mere survival and disaster for Haiti's poor majority. When their house burns down in a fire and Hilarion's workshop closes, the couple decide to join Hilarion's relative Jospahant, who had fled across the border to the Dominican Republic to cut cane after killing an army lieutenant who was trying to rape his girlfriend and also dispatching a corrupt sergeant who happens upon the scene. Discovering work cutting cane and setting up their household in a Haitian community near the cane fields outside of San Pedro de Macoris in the country's east, they exist in fleeting happiness, welcoming the birth of a baby, even as Hilarion's political awakening continues as he meets local Communist activists, both Haitian and Dominican, among the sugar cane workers. But the Trujillo pogrom is soon upon them, and as the Dominican army rounds up Haitian workers and massacres them in the fields, the couple and their child flee towards the border with the help of a sympathetic Dominican *campesnino* herder. En route, the baby, named Desire, dies when attacked by wild dogs, and crossing the Massacre River, Hilarion is fatally wounded by shots fired by Dominican soldiers and dies in Claire-Heureuse's arms, having just reached Haitian soil.

"The closer they came to the promised land," Alexis writes at the end of the novel, "the more they felt the net tightening around them."

HAITI'S OWN POLITICAL education continued when, on December 16, the sixth anniversary of his first election as president, Aristide visited Radio Haiti-Inter and sat across the table from Jean Dominique, a man who had a reputation as a champion of Haiti's democratic movement (having been twice forced into exile) and one of the few in Haiti's elite who consistently spoke truth to power. Dominique's afternoon show, *Face à l'opinion*, was perhaps the most widely listened to interview show on Haitian radio, with listeners always interested to see how the journalist would question and debate his often haughty and evasive guests. Commencing to question Aristide about the *Petits Projets de la Presidence* programs that had seen so much money disappear and caused so much controversy, Dominique granted that, though the stated intention of the projects had been to *"soulaje lamize pep la"* ("reduce the misery of the people"), the project had in fact been riddled with corruption and nepotism, and he asked Arstide if he was not disturbed that "Lavalas elements" were being perceived as responsible for that. Instead of directly addressing the charges though or taking responsibility for excesses that have might occurred under his administration, Aristide spoke of the all the people working in public administration and that it was impossible for him to be expected to know what all of them were doing at any given time, lacing his responses with platitudes about his government's "maturity" and "cool head" in the face of such charges. Though Dominique kept badgering Aristide for specifics and some sense of accountability for the shortfall, Aristide continued on, in the dreamy, unperturbed voice he often affected in interviews, urging critics to understand the "context" and "reality" of the abuses. By the time the interview ended amidst uncomfortable pleasantries exchanged by the two men, many listeners were left wondering exactly how bothered Aristide was by the corruption that had begun to wrap its fingers around the throat of the state since his return. The eloquent and brave words from the priest from Saint Jean Bosco seemed to have been swallowed in the mouth of the former president in the Armani suit who sat at Radio Haiti that day.

AS PRÉVAL'S FIRST YEAR of office drew to a close, the American military force—which numbered some twenty-five thousand troops at its height—had been scaled back in Haiti and had become the United Nations Support Mission in Haiti (UNSMIH), about 1,300 peacekeeping troops scattered around the country and three hundred civilian police to assist Haiti's fledgling police force, now including a new special crowd control unit, the Corps d'intervention et de Maintien de l'ordre (CIMO), in maintaining security and stability in the country. The Clinton administration had more wide-ranging plans to transform Haiti, but after the Republican Party secured a majority in the U.S. Congress in 1994, North Carolina Republican Senator Jesse Helms, who chaired the Senate Foreign Relations Committee and his counterpart in the House of Representatives, Republican Ben Gilman of New York—backwards and uneducated men when it came to understanding Haiti and long-term haters of the Haitian popular democratic movement—succeeded in passing numerous bills restricting the activities of U.S. troops there and ending or curtailing many initiatives designed to refurbish the country's physical and administrative infrastructure.

One wondered how many among the departing soldiers had studied the history on the first, far longer occupation of Haiti by the United States, and what lessons it might have held for Haiti's future. As the Americans left Haiti again for the second time in sixty years, it was useful to look back on their stay, from 1915 until 1934, as a yardstick for what force of arms could and could not bring to the republic.

THE CORRESPONDENCE BETWEEN U.S. President Woodrow Wilson and Secretary of State William Jennings Bryant at the outset of the occupation reveals not so much a carefully thought-out plan to exploit the supposedly ripe fruits of Haiti's economy, save for an interest in the port of Mole Saint Nicholas, but rather a musing for emergency contingency plans, such as existed throughout the region, for a rapid deployment of U.S. forces should the political situation spiral out of control, mixed with characteristic American hubris. Wilson bemoaned the country as a place where "revolutionary conditions constantly . . . exist."

Quickly after Guillaume Sam's murder in July 1915, the U.S. military entered in force both Port-au-Prince and Cap Haitien, where they quickly disabused the insurgent physician Rosalvo Bobo of any idea he might have of seizing power. The force seized Haitian government funds and put them into an account under the control of U.S. Navy Rear Admiral William B. Caperton; and Capterton's chief of staff, Captain Edward L. Beach, told an assembly of Haiti's senators and deputies that the United States was offering its support, providing the parliament elected as president a candidate who would put an end to the endless factional fighting. In any event, the United States would continue to control the customs and the Haitian budget. Momentarily grateful for their delivery from the abyss, but humiliated at the presence of foreign troops on their sovereign soil, the parliamentarians acceded. They had little choice.

The man the parliament elected was Senate President Philippe Sudre Dartiguenave, a mulatto lawyer from Anse-a-Veau in the country's south. Bobo, convinced his enemies were going to kill him, fled into exile in Jamaica.

Dartiguenave, the first mulatto to occupy the office of president in some forty years, was in a precarious position, as he had no army supporting him save for that which now occupied Haiti. As such, the United States made it known that he would be forced to accept a treaty affirming the U.S. right to choose a customs director and customs employees, form a new security force (which would eventually become the reborn Haitian army) and develop the country's natural resources; this treaty also gave the United States all discretion when it came to deciding Haitian affairs of state, with Washington threatening out-and-out military government if he refused. The Port-au-Prince political class and most ordinary Haitians reacted with anger and disbelief to the treaty proposal. A fact many of Haiti's American and European chroniclers have often misunderstood, in their effort to facilely divide Haiti along mere color lines, is the level of nationalism felt by Haitians, no matter of what political stripe, at the machinations that have so frequently been worked against their country by the great foreign powers. Nearly across the board, the great shame of an occupying foreign army for the first time since 1804 was doubled by the humiliating conditions of the treaty, which put the nation of Toussaint and Dessalines in utter fealty to their mighty northern neighbor.

In response to the uproar, Caperton established martial law on September 3. In a foreshadowing of the treatment of suspected terrorist detainees at the Guantánamo Bay Naval Base in Cuba a century later, U.S. military courts would try Haitians suspected of political offenses and the press was forbidden from publishing "false or incendiary propaganda against the Government of the United States or the Government of Haiti," a rather broad and changeable definition. The pressure brought by the occupiers was overwhelming. With the Americans controlling Haiti militarily and financially, the treaty was adopted on November 29, 1915.

But the Americans' diplomatic muscle meant very little beyond the capital and the Cap, as *caco* bands, those gang-pressed soldiers recruited throughout Haitian history to do the bidding of one would-be leader or another, had been running amuck since Sam's government had fallen, looting and pillaging through the Artibonite and Plateau Central. As U.S. troops fanned out into the countryside, they encountered particular resistance from the *cacos* in the north, where several marines were killed and where resistance to the new occupation took the form of local groups launching harassing raids against the invaders from bases located in old French forts scattered throughout the countryside. In suppressing these armed groups, the marines were obligated to fight several pitched battles—including one at Fort Riviere that killed over fifty Haitian fighters—a measure of just how intense resistance to the occupation was.

Dartiguenave, with American connivance, dissolved the senate on April 5, 1916, and the occupiers set about drafting Haiti's new constitution. In the meantime Admiral Caperton—who, despite his firm hand had always been something of a conciliator—had been transferred out of Haiti in May 1916 and replaced as the occupation's face by Colonel Littleton Waller, a banal and harsh man whose philosophy of mission was perhaps best summed up in a letter he dispatched shortly after taking up his appointment.

"I know the niggers and how to handle them," Waller wrote to another officer in June 1916.

After a few more personnel changes, finally, at end of 1917, Colonel John H. Russell, native of the state of Georgia and a much more measured and less abrasive personality, became chief of the U.S. occupation of Haiti. The new constitution was written, with hefty contributions from then-Secretary of the Navy Franklin Delano Roosevelt, and it was approved in a questionable plebiscite on June 11, 1918. Giving the Haitian president the right to decide if and when parliamentary elections would be held, it essentially transformed Dartiguenave into a dictator.

The main voice of civil opposition to the entire process was the Union Patriotique, formed in August 1915 and consisting largely of Port-au-Prince-based intellectuals such as Stenio Vincent and the author Jean-Price Mars. Basically a collection of naysaying, opportunistic politicians united only by what they saw as a common political opening—hatred of the occupation—the group was a motley collection that would be familiar to any student of modern Haitian politics, as would soon become clear.

A more serious well of public distaste for the occupation arose from the resurrection of the Code Rural, created by Boyer and making provisions by which peasants were drafted into public service and paid in food and *tafia*. When the Americans arrived, Haiti had approximately three miles of passable roads outside of its major towns and the occupation government felt that, by resurrecting the corvee system of work gangs first implemented in the Code Rural, Haiti's infrastructure could be rapidly improved. Doling out the responsibility for rounding up the corvees to local communal magistrates and administrative chiefs, the Americans oversaw a system whereby male peasants who could not pay a tax to the local authorities were forced to work; this effectively meant all peasants, as no one had any money to buy their way out of the labor. With peasants roped together like slaves, the corvees constructed 470 miles of road in three years, including the linking north-south highway between Port-au-Prince and Cap Haitien. The corvee was retired after, among other scandals, a report by Marine Lt. Col. R.S. Hooker and Major Thomas C. Turner in 1919 attested to the brutality with which the corvee had been implemented in the Plateau Central town of Hinche and its environs. The practice helped stir a two-year rebellion through the Plateau and Artibonite Valley, lead by former soldier Charlemagne Peralte and his deputy Benoit Batraville, both of them loyal to the exiled Bobo, before both men were killed by U.S. forces.

When Dartiguenave's term expired in May 1922, Louis Borno, Haiti's foreign minister, an educated, striking mulatto with a pince-nez and close-cropped mustache, was elected to replace him by the *Conseil d'etat*, the consultative body the United States had set up. Over the next seven years Borno, a lawyer by training and a conversant in both English and Spanish, oversaw what perhaps were the most positive fruits of Haiti's humiliating occupation. By the end of the 1920s, U.S. Navy civil engineers had constructed over one thousand miles of roads, over two hundred bridges, airfields at all departmental capitals and had revived the nation's moribund telephone system.

Despite an oft-repeated charge that the United States deliberately sent white Southerners to Haiti, as they would know how to "handle" the blacks, no authoritative contemporary evidence of this charge exists—not in U.S. Marine papers, not in the vehemently anti-U.S. publications of the Union Patriotique, nor via the congressional inquiries into the Haitian occupation that were held. In fact, academic research showed that the percentage of Southern officers in Haiti during most of the occupation was lower than that in the Marines as a whole at the time. But the social racism that the Marines practiced (who after all came from a country—the United States—where the most naked segregation and white supremacist ideologies still ruled as facts of the day), left the imperious, educated mulattos so used to lording over the peasants in no doubt that they were viewed as one with the most impoverished Haitians, and it came as a brutal shock to Haiti's privileged class. Student strikes at the end of 1929 spurred by Borno's desire to extend his two-terms in office and American reductions in the stipend given to Haitian students to attend school swelled into anti-occupation demonstrations in all the major cities. On December 5, as a crowd of about 1,500 marched on the southern city of Les Cayes, where they were faced down by a detachment of American troops. According to one's political ideation, accounts of what happened next vary, but most accounts hold that after a tense stand-off with well-armed Marines, a brawl between a protestor and a marine broke out and panicky troops opened fire on the crowd, killing a dozen and wounding twenty-three. The incident marked the finale of the United States' first attempt at nation building in Haiti. *Desoccupation* commenced shortly thereafter and, by 1934, the Marines were gone and Haiti was left in the hands of president (and former Union Patriotique leader) Stenio Vincent, the leader Jacques Stephen Alexis so loathed, but who was lionized by the left in the United States at the time as a fierce nationalist and apostle of freedom. Vincent soon revealed himself to be a dictator in very much the old Haitian mold. The rapidity of the reversion to type after the U.S. departure would have been useful as a template for further foreign intervention in the country, for Haiti's problems and resentments ran deep, and were not solved even by what was essentially a twenty-year military government by the wealthiest country in the world. The fact remained that however well- or ill-intentioned the American administration had been, Haiti's conflicts—mulatto versus noir, city dweller versus peasant, educated versus excluded—remained as pronounced as ever, as René Préval surely realized as he saw the second American occupation force in less than a century fly away from its shores.

ON JANUARY 9, 1997, in a move many had foreseen, Aristide, the object of the U.S. policy-makers' most recent attentions, broke from the OPL that he had attached himself to after abandoning Evans Paul two years earlier—and at the same time further distanced himself further from Préval—by announcing that he was forming a new political party, Fanmi Lavalas or the Lavalas Family. Though the reference was meant to mix the all-inclusive image of a family all seated around a table together (with Aristide, naturally, as the father), with the raging, unstoppable torrent evoked by lavalas, some joked that "family" in the *cosa nostra* sense might prove to be more apt.

Caught somewhat by surprise at his appropriation of at least part of their name, Gérard Pierre-Charles and the OPL would eventually rename their party as the Organisation du Peuple en Lutte (Organization of Struggling People) at a party congress, but still retaining the initials, in an effort to distinguish it from the former president. It was also announced that the new OPL would include among its members Rosny Smarth, the sitting prime minister.

Seven days after Aristide announced the formation of his political party, a general strike on January 16, which many believed to have been organized by the former president, shut down many street-level businesses and saw flaming barricades go up around the capital. Black-clad CIMO patrolled the city, clearing the roadblocks throughout the day. The strike was allegedly in response to the PNH's somewhat thuggish quashing of an anti-privatization demonstration in front of the National Palace on January 9, but was seen widely as yet another attempt by the Aristide camp to undercut the Préval government, with those manning the barricades calling for Smarth's resignation and an end to the IMF-backed austerity measures. The offices of the MPP peasant movement in Mirebalais were fired upon. Attempting to dedicate a water tower in the capital on February 6, Préval was heckled and insulted by a pro-Aristide mob.

The strike was significant as it illuminated a new phenomenon. Shortly after the formation of the Aristide Foundation for Democracy and, later, the Fanmi Lavalas party, certain organizations, claiming political independence from Tabarre but quite clearly taking their orders from Haiti's former president, began to spring up as armed quasi-political pressure groups. They called themselves *organisations populaire*, "popular organizations" or OP's, after the name given to the neighborhood democratic solidarity groups that had sprung up in the wake of Jean-Claude Duvalier's departure in 1986. But, in truth, there was very little spontaneous, grassroots or democratic about some of them. They were client organizations who paid frequent visits to Aristide at Tabarre and whose members, never numbering more than in the low thousands at most, stood in marked contrast to the highly moral and dedicated community groups that continued to support Préval and Aristide in the capital and elsewhere. The true nature of the closeness of their relationship with Aristide—and of Aristide's relationship with the far more numerous armed gangs in the slums of the capital and elsewhere—would only become clear later, but throughout Préval's tenure the groups were used effectively as a club to pressure the president, although few realized it at the time. Among the most visible to appear were the Ti Kominote Legliz (Little Church Community or TKL) of Saint Jean Bosco, which took its name from Aristide's former parish near the La Saline slum and was headed by a divinity student drop-out named Paul Raymond, and the Jeunesse Pouvoir Populaire (Youth Popular Power or JPP) party, which had as its spokesman a young man named René Civil, who hailed from the southern city of Jacmel and whose family owned a dry-cleaning business in the poor downtown neighborhood of Bel Air in the capital. Civil had originally been active in the progressive Protestant movement during the years leading up to and including Aristide's exile (during part of which time he hid in the home of American anthropologist Ira Lowenthal), but eventually he became concerned with more earthly pursuits, and the organization, known by its initial, JPP, had at first been called *"Jan l pase, l pase"* ("The way that it happens is the way that it happens") after a popular compas song, in reference to their often anarchic street demonstrations. Two criminal brothers from the La Saline slum, Ronald and Franco Camille—who also had close links with the former president, each at one time serving among Aristide's bodyguards—helped control that slum and the adjacent port for Aristide. As former officials in the Haitian military and other personalities who would have at first seemed anathema to the desires expressed by the first elections of Aristide in 1990 began to swell the ranks of Fanmi Lavalas and a struggle for supremacy began within the young institution of the PNH, these young, self-declared radicals would prove Aristide's first recourse in the political struggles that lay ahead.

ON JANUARY 22, one of those military men, Dany Toussaint, Aristide's former security chief, former head of Haiti's interim police force and a prominent member of the newly-formed Fanmi Lavalas party, was detained at Miami International Airport after arriving on a flight from Port-au-Prince. Toussaint had been a captain in the Haitian army, and he had been schooled by the United States in methods of war and surveillance when he resigned from the armed forced in 1986, refusing, he said, to take part in plans by elements of the armed forces to kill leaders in the democratic sector.

"In 1986, when the (Namphy government) wanted to stay in power, they wanted to eliminate all the strong leaders, like Evans Paul, Victor Benoit, Gérard Gourgue, Aristide himself," Toussaint told me as we sat in his office in Petionville early one Saturday. The walls were decorated with certificates attesting to his mastery in surveillance photography and martial arts, as well as a picture of his military class from Lackland Air Force Base in Texas. "They were strong political leaders, human rights leaders, and they wanted to eliminate them. When I came back from Fort Benning, Georgia in 1985, just a few months after Duvalier left, I had training in intelligence, and we had a file on every leader, but I thought it was so we would know who they all were. But after that, they decided to eliminate them, and I said that wasn't right, and I took exile. Aristide has known me since then."

Toussaint went into self-imposed exile after his resignation, shuttling back and forth between Miami and New York during the late 1980s, and then returned to Haiti to become an important part of Aristide's security detail after he was elected president in 1990, defending him on the harrowing trip from Tabarre to the National Palace on the night of the coup in 1991. After Aristide fled in 1991, Toussaint went into exile in Florida a short time later. Upon Aristide's return to Haiti in 1994, he promoted Toussaint to the rank of major, and then to serve as the head of the Haitian Interim Public Security Force. Toussaint resigned from the position in 1996, at which point he opened up a police supply store, Dany King, in Petionville.

When Toussaint disembarked from the plane at around 5 p.m. that January in 1997, though, he was pulled aside from the immigration line and held for three hours. Shortly after 8 p.m., officials from the Immigration and Naturalization Service (INS) began an interrogation of Toussaint that lasted until 2:25 in the morning. During the session, many of the questions posed to him were not involving his immigration status but rather concerned the 1995 assassinations of Mireille Durocher Bertin and Max Mayard in Haiti. After being questioned, Toussaint was transferred to Krome Avenue Detention Center and held by the INS for two days before being released and deported. While in custody, the INS began proceedings against him that eventually resulted in the revocation of the resident visa he had held since the mid-1980s. Representing Toussaint, unsuccessfully, in the proceedings, was a Miami attorney named Ira Kurzban, of the firm Kurzban, Kurzban, Weinger & Tetzeli. Kurzban had previously gained notoriety for representing Haitian clients in immigration proceedings, and had been retained as counsel for the Government of Haiti by Aristide upon his reinstatement to the country in 1994. A member of the board of the Aristide Foundation for Democracy, Kurzban, like Toussaint, would become a name very familiar to those with an interest in Haiti in the coming years.

IF *LE LUMPEN* (as the urban poor were frequently called) in the capital were lashing out over the austerity measures, Haiti's peasants, at least, Préval's natural constituency, had a few rays of hope to point to. On February 10, before thousands of cheering farmers and with Jean Dominique in attendance, René Préval went to Pont Sonde in the fertile Artibonite Valley to bequeath hundreds of plots of land to poor peasants in the area, averaging out to about one acre of rice paddies each for some 1,600 households. Progress, however small, was being made in the provinces, but you wouldn't have known it from watching how things were playing out in Port-au-Prince.

"It was part of Aristide's way of insuring his power," said one prominent Haitian who had been close to both men, of the strikes and demonstrations that continued to target Smarth throughout February and March. The other issue, perhaps even more damning from Aristide's point of view, was the fact that, through his work on reforms among the peasantry with Dominique outside of the capital, Préval also began to gain something of a following of his own.

"That really infuriated Aristide, because Préval was supposed to do things for him, for his [Aristide's] own popularity," said Michele Montas, a journalist and the wife of Jean Dominique, of that time: "He never wanted Préval to be a recognizable name in any way."

Ever his friend's loyal counselor, Dominique had taken Préval aside on more than one occasion when he saw him being unduly pressured by Aristide and told him simply, "You give too much."

ON MARCH 26, Smarth barely survived a parliamentary no-confidence vote, with parliament's seventy-six members members voting 37-29 in Smarth's favor with ten abstentions after fifteen hours of debate. Préval, in a strange move, chose to stay neutral during the voting, and some drama was supplied when the minister of planning collapsed during his ferocious grilling by the parliamentarians. Caught between Aristide, who seemed bent on undermining him at every turn, and the OPL, who were determined to block and scuttle any government initiative no matter how small, it was with trepidation that Préval approached the upcoming April 6 legislative elections, when the Aristide and OPL factions would at last have a chance to face off against one another in the polls. In the contest mandated by Haiti's electoral commission, the Conseil Électoral Provisoire (CEP), nine Senate seats, two in the Chamber of Deputies, and delegates for hundreds of Assemblées de Section Communale (ASECs) and town delegations would be up for grabs. At a peasant congress that same March, MPP leader Chavannes Jean-Baptiste openly accused Aristide of having had a hand in orchestrating the street violence that had roiled the country, and denounced the fact that formerly abusive members of Haiti's military and FRAPH partisans were suddenly transforming themselves into Fanmi Lavalas activists, with Aristide's tacit blessing. The erratic mayor of the capital, Manno Charlemagne, made similar charges and accused Aristide of organizing armed partisan groups in the capital's Cité Soleil slum.

AFTER A LENGTHY DELAY, on April 6, legislative elections were finally held, and they were almost at once rife with allegations of fraud and illegality. Préval himself went dutifully to the polls before the cameras, but only about 4 percent of Haiti's four million registered voters followed him. Tales swirled among peasants in the Artibonite Valley regarding how former FADH captain Medard Joseph, the former military commander for the region and the senatorial candidates for Fanmi Lavalas in the region, had sent armed men to intimidate and bully peasants at polling places throughout the agricultural zone. Similar stories also surfaced in the south, where former Colonel Jean-Marie Fourel Celestin, the Jacmel native who parliament had refused to confirm as PNH chief in 1996, was said to have applied similar pressure throughout his region. Villagers in Haiti's Plateau Central told of bands of armed Fanmi Lavalas partisans descending onto polling stations. When it was over, Celestin and another Lavalas senatorial candidate, Joseph Yvon Feuille, were declared to have obtained the majorities needed avoid runoff elections. The second round of voting to determine the fate of the other seven Senate seats however, was delayed indefinitely.

Chavannes Jean-Baptiste, who had aligned himself with the OPL but had up to this point been relatively restrained in his criticism of Préval, turned decisively against the government, and especially against Aristide, after watching the way the elections were conducted in his native Plateau Central region. Around this time, he had visited Aristide at his home in Tabarre and demanded that the former president denounce the acts that were being committed by people claiming to be his supporters, but Aristide had refused. Chavannes began characterizing Aristide as a dictator-in-waiting, laying the groundwork for his own return in 2000 and masterminding the whole campaign from Tabarre.

Following the victories of the Aristide-aligned candidates in the legislative elections, Prime Minister Smarth's austerity budget seemed doomed. Smarth, who was known to be extremely piqued, said that he thought the coming runoff elections shouldn't be taking place at all, given the first round's corruption at the ballot box. When it became ever more obvious that the CEP was indeed going to sign off on the elections, no matter what the prime minister thought and under great pressure from Pierre-Charles and the OPL, Smarth went on national television on June 9 to announce his resignation, saying that he refused to be party to electoral fraud.

"In our country, power is a sickness," he said simply. As if to underline his point, July 6 balloting for local political offices in Haiti was characterized by a thirty-eight-member OAS Electoral Observation Mission as "indifferent"; the members noted continuing irregularities, such as in the polling place in the capital's Delmas district, where the number of votes cast was seen to have tripled over a two-hour period without the arrival of any additional voters at the station.

TO REPLACE SMARTH, Préval tapped Eriq Pierre, a former World Bank employee who seemed well-suited to the technocratic job of implementing the structural readjustment plan. However, the April elections had embittered the

OPL, and Préval was already facing open revolt from the Aristide bloc in the congress. The nomination was scuttled in July 1997.

Haiti faced a tragic fall, during which a ferry sank about 160 feet off the coast of the village of Montrouis, killing more than one hundred and fifty people, and, three months later, forty people died when a sailboat loaded with passengers sank between the island of La Gonave and the Haitian mainland. Despite the diligent work of Secretary of State for Public Security Bob Manuel and PNH chief Pierre Denizé, a report by the human rights organization the National Coalition for Haitian Rights concluded that, between January and October 1997, the PNH had killed some forty-seven people, with about half of those killings appearing to have been serious human rights violations.[1] In the same report, Denizé labeled efforts to politicize the police as the major threat to the professionalization of the force. One bright spot, at least from the point of view of those supporting the Préval government's dual agrarian and privatization policy, came in October 1997, with the government succeeding in selling off a 70 percent controlling interest in the state-owned Minoterie d'Haiti flour mill to a private consortium composed of the Continental Grain Company, the Seaboard Corporation and Unifinance, a front company for a group of Haiti-based investors. The mill would later reopen in December 1998 as Les Moulins d'Haiti.

On November 3, Préval submitted the name of Haitian theater actor and director Hervé Denis as his new pick for Prime Minister. Though Denis had previously served as Minister of Information and Culture in the Cédras-era administration of Prime Minister Robert Malval, and boasted an economics doctorate from the Sorbonne, he seemed an odder choice for Préval than the methodical Smarth and Pierre had been. Less hopefully, Préval also announced that six of the nine CEP members charged with formulating and overseeing new elections had tendered their resignations, and he pleaded for time while a newly-formed presidential commission studied the April 1997 elections and submitted a report before a CEP—with six new members—would determine how to proceed with a new ballot. During his announcement of Denis's selection, Préval also bitterly attacked former Prime Minister Smarth and the five cabinet ministers who had quit in the previous two weeks as having abandoned their country in a time of need by not staying at their posts until their successors had taken up office, attempting again, he said, to make the case that it was institutions, not individuals, that made a country's democratic foundation solid. "These institutions are the people's guarantee of the right to life in this country, and of a stable political climate which encourages sustainable economic development to the benefit of everyone," Préval said.

Displaying the lack of vision that would become its trademark, Gérard Pierre-Charles and the OPL insisted that the remaining three members of the CEP resign and an entirely new electoral council be formed, while Evans Paul chided

Denis for declining to take up his newly-elected post as head of Haiti State University after he had been selected for the prime minister's post. At the end of the month, the UN mandate for its peace-keeping forces in Haiti ended and 1,170 soldiers prepared to leave.

The peace and stability that many hoped the UN mission would bring to Haiti was far from assured, however. In a December 23 vote in the Chamber of Deputies, with seventy-two deputies attending, Hervé Denis received 49 percent of the vote for approval, falling just short of the 51 percent needed for approval. Kelly Bastien, the chamber's president, announced that Denis's nomination had been defeated but, a short time later, stated that the chamber might yet again take up the subject when they met on January 7. The nomination was dead in the water, though, and by early 1998 it became apparent that Préval would have to seek yet another candidate to fill the government's top post.

AS 1998 DAWNED and the spread of various armed political actors in the capital continued unabated, Secretary of State for Public Security Bob Manuel gave the mayors in the Port-au-Prince metropolitan zone an ultimatum to give up weapons in their possession, citing Article 268 of the Haitian constitution and a May 23, 1989 statute relating to the control of firearms. Under the law, the PNH were to be the only body with the right to distribute and circulate weapons in the country, saying that uniformed police officers would take over security duties at the mayor's offices.

In the capital, Manno Charlemagne flatly refused to heed the decree, saying he had bought the weapons that armed his young bodyguards with his own money, and in a ranting interview given to the Agence Haïtienne de Presse, he said that gangs from Cité Soleil were planning to kill him, as well as OPL senators Irvel Chery and Paul Denis. He accused Manuel of being a CIA agent and said that, if police were looking for illegal weapons, that they should search Aristide's home in Tabarre.[2] As fevered as the declarations might have seemed at the time, Charlemagne had not survived as long as he had without keen survival instincts, and his comments about Haiti's former president and his gang allies in the slums would prove to be far more apt than many suspected at the time.

Charlemagne's unraveling had been sad to watch. A man once so pitch-perfect in his musical dissent against tyranny seemed to have lost his way once he himself assumed power. A friend of his from the early days in Carrefour, where Manno had grown up among the urban proletariat, was paralyzed with fear one day when a two-car convoy, its windows blackened, stopped beside him as he trudged through the Port-au-Prince streets under a hot Haitian sun. To his surprise, one of the window in the first car rolled down and inside he saw Charlemagne, motioning him over. The two old friends talked briefly, and the man was invited to come visit the mayor at his office in City Hall the next day. The man wanted to catch up with his friend, and so arrived promptly at the office the next day. When he entered Charlemagne's chambers, he saw the mayor sitting as his desk, wild-eyed, surrounded by half a dozen armed men. He looked up at his visitor.

"Want do you want?"

"I came to visit you," the man said, unsure of what to do.

"You want a gun? You're Lavalas, right? You want a gun?"

"No," the man said, flabbergasted. "I don't want a gun, I just wanted to come visit with you."

"Well, then get out if you won't take a gun, if you're not a militant. Go!"

The man left, saddened and confused by his encounter. Power had stolen over his old friend like a fever, he thought.

WITH DISPUTE OF THE PREVIOUS spring's election still simmering, on April 5, en route to a meeting of Caribbean foreign ministers in the Caribbean, U.S. Secretary of State Madeleine Albright touched down briefly in Haiti, meeting with Préval, Aristide and opposition leaders. Albright was said to have urged the approval of pending World Bank and Inter-American Development Bank loans by Haiti's parliament, loans tied to the privatization that Aristide and his allies had been so vehemently against. As might have been expected, nothing substantive came of the meetings and a sour Albright told reporters, "Frankly, we have been disappointed that Haitian political leaders have taken so long to resolve their differences. . . . The Haitian people deserve a democratic form of government, and they deserve the ability to have the fruits that the international community is trying to give them." She then took off, leaving for a place where the need for her presence and involvement was far less dire, but where her love of ceremony and pomp was more carefully catered to. A more substantive state visit occurred two months later. Leonel Fernandez, the New York City-raised president of the Dominican Republic, marked the first official state visit by a leader of that country in Haiti in nearly seventy years, and the first since the shameful massacres of 1937. He spoke with a receptive Préval about improving relations between the two countries and cooperating on such issues as the welfare of the thousands of Haitian laborers still toiling in the Dominican cane fields.

In July, making a third run at replacing a prime minister who had resigned over a year earlier, Préval announced the Minister of Education Jacques Edouard Alexis would be his new choice for the post. The OPL, to the surprise of many, announced that they would support Alexis, while the Aristide-aligned "anti-neo-liberal" bloc in parliament said they would support a candidate for prime minister only if a moratorium was called on economic reforms and the structural adjustment plan. Alexis, though not his cabinet, which had yet to be presented, was approved by parliament the same month.

As seemed to be Préval's lot, though, as one political crisis appeared to be nearing resolution, others brewed. On July 24, the final remaining members of the

CEP tendered their resignations to Préval, who accepted them. Thus the electoral body in charge of resolving the electoral dispute became inoperative, and the property and material of the CEP was placed under the jurisdiction of the Ministry of Interior.

On the heels of that blow, and perhaps in response to what appeared to be Alexis's easy ascendance into the government, on July 29 hundreds of demonstrators shouting *"Viv Aristide"* burned tires at intersections throughout the capital and shouted slogans against the government's economic program.

After the briefest of pauses, the days of killing had returned. On August 3 assassins struck down Father Jean Pierre-Louis, known as "Pere Ti Jean" to the peasants in Haiti's Plateau Central, on whose behalf he had advocated for many years. The fifty-year-old priest was a diminutive mulatto from a family of some means—his former sister-in-law, Michele Pierre-Louis, was the executive director of the respected Fondation Connaissance et Liberte (FOKAL)—yet he had chosen to work among Haiti's rural poor and had helped found the Sèvis Ekimenik pou Devlopman ak Edikasyon Popilè (Ecumenical Service for Popular Development or SEDEP). Pierre-Louis had just left the Unibank branch on nearby Rue Capois and was approaching the center's headquarters on Avenue du Chilie, near the Place de Jeremie that abutted the capital's storied Hotel Oloffson, when the gunmen neared his black Toyota pickup. Before he could make a move, Pierre-Louis was shot in the mouth and chest, the killers fleeing without taking any belongings. Taken to the capital's Canape Vert hospital, the priest was pronounced dead.

FOLLOWING THE KILLING, on August 7 Aristide's Fanmi Lavalas party's newly-appointed spokesperson Yvon Neptune, a bearded architect who had lived and worked for over a decade in Long Island, released a statement on the party's behalf attacking the Préval government, charging it was "indifferent" to the Pierre-Louis murder, accusing it of oppressing Lavalas partisans, and saying that he held "in contempt the demands of December 18, 1990," i.e., the date of Aristide's first election. At the priest's funeral at Mount Carmel Church on August 11, a group of Aristide supporters disrupted the service several times, hurling invectives at government officials seated in the front row.

On August 3, a PNH spokesman announced that three policemen had been arrested for involvement in drug trafficking and that customs agents at the capital's international airport had recently confiscated 21 kilos of cocaine hidden in a shipment of kitchen utensils coming from Panama. Later that same month, Pierre Fortin Jean Denis, director of the judicial police, resigned, charging that Police Inspector General Joseph Luc Eucher was stonewalling his investigation of the disappearance of 450 kilos of cocaine. The next month, Hurricane Georges slammed into Haiti and killed over one hundred and seventy people.

The parliament, which had not managed to pass budgets for the 1997/98 or the 1998/99 fiscal years, managed to rouse itself at the end of the year for one final act of defiance. With the mandate of eighty-three deputies and eighteen senators elected in the June and September 1995 elections due to expire in January 1999 and with no agreement on new elections in sight, on November 25 the parliament effectively voted itself term extensions, saying that the elections should be postponed until October 1999, in contravention of Haitian electoral law. The stage was set for a showdown in the coming year, and the storm clouds gathered.

CHAPTER NOTES

1. National Coalition for Haitian Rights, "Can Haiti's Police Reforms Be Sustained?" January 1997.
2. "Port-au-Prince Mayor Ready to Battle Haitian National Police," AHP, February 6, 1998.

| | |

4

The Crocodile of Delmas

IN A COUNTRY WHERE so few people are able to read, the role of radio news in Haiti has proved a powerful and dangerous one over the years since its advent. Since the late 1940s, Haiti's myriad governments have used state-controlled media as a bully-pulpit to present themselves as defenders of sovereignty, inheritors of the tradition of Louverture and Dessalines, and the only bulwark against the multitude of seen and unseen forces always charged, sometimes correctly, with wishing to destabilize Haiti. It goes without saying that vilifying their enemies has been part of this strategy, as well. Several radio stations, especially the Catholic Radio Soleil, played a pivotal role in broadcasting news and commentary about the rebellions around the country that eventually forced Jean-Claude Duvalier to flee Haiti in 1986; and by 1999, five years after Aristide was returned from exile and Haiti's political process had supposedly returned to its democratic path, the country had hundreds of radio stations giving voice to a multitude of opinions. Radio Nationale, the state-owned radio company, was predictably supportive of René Préval's political and economic program, while Radio Timoun, despite its name and stated aim to serve as a voice for the youth from the Lafanmi Selavi orphanage, served as the mouthpiece for the behind-the-curtain machinations of Aristide and his Foundation for Democracy in Tabarre. Radio Vision 2000 and Radio Metropole appealed to the middle and upper classes, but especially in the latter's case, made at least some attempt to present balanced coverage of the country's political crisis, while Radio Ginen appealed more to the *lumpen* proletariat of the capital with its mix of street-level reporting and *racine* music. In the provinces, dozens of stations had sprung up, giving voice to every group from Baptist missionaries to activist peasants.

None of these stations, however, for better or for worse, had come to match the moral authority wielded by one station in the capital whose story seemed to be the story of Haiti itself—one of resilience, terror, defeat, return and, ultimately, hope. That station was Radio Haiti-Inter, and the man who made it a voice that millions in the country listened to as the genuine arbiter of the health of Haiti's political climate was named Jean Léopold Dominique.

It has been written that by the late 1990s, Jean Dominique's angular, elegant mulatto features had matured into lived-in edges that gave him the appearance of an aging French movie star. Along with his second wife, Michele Montas, Dominique had, as Préval's term in office neared its final two years, lived a life that seemed as if it should have been penned by one of Haiti's great novelists, and he wasn't done fighting yet.

Born into a wealthy, politically conscious mulatto family in Port-au-Prince in 1930, just as the twenty-year-long U.S. occupation of Haiti was drawing to a close, Dominique told the American film director Jonathan Demme that one of his first memories was of his father, a wealthy importer, bristling with nationalist pride at the presence of foreign troops on his country's soil.

"I was 4 years old when the Marines left Haiti, the U.S. Marines left Haiti, I was a kid," Dominique said. "And every time a Marine battalion passed in front of the house my father took my hand and said 'Don't look at them, don't look at them.' And every May 18, Flag Day, defiantly, he put the Haitian flag in front of the house. I said, 'Father, what does that mean for you?' He said 'That means that you are Haitian. That means that my great-grandfather fought at Vertieres. Never forget that. You are Haitian. You are from this land. You are not French, you are not British, you are not American. You are Haitian!'"

Dominique's father often took the young boy with him on business trips throughout the Haitian countryside, where he witnessed the plight of the Haitian peasantry in stark relief.

In 1955, Dominique left Haiti to study at the Institut National Agronomique in Paris. The experience of studying there was of twofold importance for the young man, igniting as it did through his study of agronomy a lifelong passion for and understanding of the issues that confronted the poor peasant majority in his homeland, and also exposing him for the first time to the cinema, of which he became a devoted acolyte and promoter. Upon returning to Haiti, he began putting his agronomy studies to use, working among the peasants in the Artibonite Valley; but he had been home only a brief time when tragedy struck in July 1959, when Jean's older brother, Philippe, an exiled lieutenant in the Haitian army, took part in a failed invasion against Francois Duvalier along with two other Haitian exiles, Alix Pasquet and Henry Perpignand and a Miami sheriff. Landing on the Cote des Arcadins, the small band eventually made their way into eyesight of the National Palace, taking hostages and ordering Duvalier to step down. When a nostalgic love for Haitian cigarettes got the better of one of them, a boy sent out to fetch the invader's brand of choice was seized and revealed the group's small size, and Duvalier's forces raided the building they were in and Philippe Dominique was summarily executed along with the rest of the men. Shortly after his brother's death, Dominique, whose work among the peasantry was well known to the regime, was also arrested and imprisoned in squalid conditions for six months in the Gonaives jail.

Prison did nothing to tame Dominique's rebellious spirit, though, and upon his release, he threw himself back into his boosterism for the cinema—no small act in impoverished, authoritarian Haiti. He made a droll documentary on Haiti's mulatto-obsessed beauty pageants titled *Mais, Je Suis Belle* (*But, I Am Beautiful*) in 1961, and also founded a cinema club that was promptly banned by Papa Doc after it dared show Alain Resnais's renowned Holocaust documentary *Night and Fog*, whose depiction of the nature and bureaucracy of institutional evil did not sit right with the nation's despot.

Eventually, in what could be seen as a combination of his interests, Dominique drifted toward radio as a means to encompass both his intellectual curiosity and his social conscience. Shunning the Francophone tendencies of Haitian radio stations that never addressed local listeners in their native tongue, Dominique introduced Haiti's first daily Kreyol-language program in the late 1960s, and purchased the station Radio Haiti and changed its name to Radio Haiti-Inter (for Internationale) in 1971. Though the capital's Radio Metropole, which had been founded a few years before by Herbert Widmaer, had many fine journalists in its employ, it was largely, and with some justification, regarded by many as the voice of the upper class in Haiti. Dominique was out for something, a point of view, that was decidedly different.

AS MUCH OF AN EVENT as entering radio broadcasting was for Dominique, one of similarly earth-tremoring proportions, at least for him, occurred when a striking young journalist named Michele Montas returned to Haiti in 1971 after attending the Graduate School for Journalism at Columbia University in New York. Having attended school in the United States for her undergraduate degrees as well at the University of Maine, Michele began work for Haiti's main newspaper, *Le Nouvelliste*, a less than vibrant operation at the time, for two years upon her return. "Radio seemed to me the most dynamic media in Haiti," she said, and so, after meeting Dominique by chance, she began working for Radio Haiti in 1973. At the beginning, Montas, the one with the foreign journalism degree, was training reporters at Radio Haiti and having her own show broadcast in the evening. Eventually, she and Jean married.

"Radio Haiti was practically alone," Montas told me one day, as we sat in the cafeteria of the United Nations in New York City, where she was working at the time, as tugs pulled past the building out on the East River. "Of course, there was Radio Metropole, which was very much the voice of the bourgeoisie, but Radio Haiti was more along the lines of what I thought was important. Radio Haiti started very early with Kreyol programs and I always felt that the great asset that radio had was to be able to speak to the majority and to let people speak in their own names."

When American ambassador and longtime Duvalier apologist Clinton Knox was seized by leftist radicals in 1973, Dominique's running coverage of the crisis proved a pivotal moment for the station. Knox, an African American whose overly credulous adherence to the Duvalier dynasty's claims of revolutionary black empowerment had lead to him being referred to as an "honorary Macoute" by some Duvalierists, was as roundly reviled a figure by the Haitian masses as has ever served in the country.

The radicals seized Knox on January 23, 1973, holding him hostage inside the ambassador's residence in Petionville, and presented Jean-Claude Duvalier with a list of demands, including a $70,000 ransom, safe passage out of Haiti and the release of dozens of political prisoners. Though the Americans refused to negotiate for Knox's freedom, the Haitian authorities proved more pliable, perhaps fearing an even greater humiliation than the one already suffered should the ambassador come to harm. Aided in negotiations by the French ambassador, Bernard Dorin, and the Canadian Charge d'Affaires, Duvalier eventually agreed to release twelve prisoners, among them Haitian Communist party member Antonio Joseph—a capitulation on which Radio Haiti provided running commentary throughout. As Knox was escorted out of the embassy by the French ambassador and the kidnappers themselves the next day—en route to the airport where a plane was waiting to fly the latter and the freed prisoners into exile—he was visibly intoxicated and clutching a bottle of rum in one hand, a surreal scene that Dominique, broadcasting live along with then-correspondent Marcus Garcia, could not resist including in his coverage. One of the first times that any depiction of the dictatorship's fragility and fallibility had ever made in to the airwaves in Haiti, the coverage resulted in Dominique's being summoned to the National Palace, where he was questioned by the Duvalier's torturer-in-chief Luc Desyr. Desyr sat across a long wooden table from Dominique, a Bible on one side of it (Desyr was a Baptist), a machine gun on the other, as two soldiers stood behind him.

The story of Radio Haiti, though, was also the story of Richard Brisson. Brisson, a "dreamer," as Michele Montas referred to him, was the handsome scion of a well-off mulatto family in the capital, with a penchant for avant garde theater and classical music. When Jean-Claude Duvalier announced rigged legislative elections in 1973, Brisson promptly presented himself as an opposition candidate for a city seat. Predictably losing his quixotic quest for office in the authoritarian state, for his trouble, Brisson also lost his job at a car dealership in the Haitian capital. Sensing something kindred in Brisson's hybrid personality, Dominique hired him to work at Radio Haiti immediately afterwards as the station's program director. A dynamic, charismatic figure, Brisson started a classical music program on Radio Haiti, broadcast in Kreyol—something absolutely unique at the time—where he would explain the joys and nuances of Mozart to his fellow countrymen in their native language.

"We kept getting bolder and bolder, we were covering things that were considered unthinkable at the time," Montas said to me of the era when the 1970s, along with the human rights-centered foreign policy of the government of U.S. President Jimmy Carter, were drawing to a close. "First we started covering social issues, peasant issues, and then we started talking about the boat people, and that was a taboo subject. Boat people and drugs were the two taboo subjects, because it meant you were denouncing the government directly. . . . And the station was getting more and more popular."

During a demonstration of secondary-school students regarding a controversy surrounding the nation's baccalaureate exams in 1979, a time when demonstrations were not something you found easily in Haiti's streets, some thirty young students, being pursued by the police though downtown Port-au-Prince, sought refuge in Radio Haiti's studios on Rue du Quai, near the capital's City Hall. Armed police promptly surrounded the station for some five hours, waiting to arrest the teenaged refugees, and Dominique had to negotiate personally with the Port-au-Prince chief of police for the safe exit of each of the students, driving them in relays, five at a time, back to their homes in his own car.

As the station became more outspoken in its criticism of the regime, Duvalier tried a number of different means to silence its voice. At the government's behest, a specious lawsuit was brought against Dominique by Radio Haiti's previous owner. When that failed, the Duvalierist lawyer Constantine Mayard Paul issued directives freezing the Dominiques' accounts, and Jean-Claude Duvalier himself personally called many of Radio Haiti's major advertisers, telling them to stop selling their advertising spots to the station. The station's advertising income from these businesses stopped overnight, though several of the advertisers honored their contracts by continuing to pay Radio Haiti but with the understanding that none of their ads would be aired. Listeners of the station also rallied, with a Catholic nun bringing in donations that she had collected from the peasant community she served to enable the station to keep running. At one point, Richard Brisson even rented his car out for use as a taxi in order to drum up revenue to keep the Radio Haiti signal up and running.

"None of that worked," said Montas. "So they had to find a way to destroy us. Before Reagan's election, they couldn't do it openly. It was supposed to be the era of freedom of the press and human rights and all this, but they tested us."

Over this time, Radio Haiti had served as an incubator for journalists who would fan out through the airwaves to create their own stations. Correspondents Marvel Dandin and Lilianne Pierre-Paul founded Radio Kiskeya, while Marcus Garcia went on to found both Radio Melodie FM and the newspaper *Haiti en Marche*. One of Radio Haiti's most popular correspondents was Konpe Filo, the nom de broadcast of journalist Anthony Pascal. Pascal, along with Evans Paul, who used the name Konpe Plim or K-Plim ("the cock's feather") during his radio days, was one of the country's most well-known media personalities. When Pascal was arrested while doing a story about the red light districts in

Port-au-Prince, including the infamous brothel-rich seaside strip in Carrefour just before the 1980 U.S. presidential elections, he was supposedly taken in by the Haitian equivalent of the vice squad, but his detention was in fact a thinly veiled political move, and Dominique saw it as such. When Pascal still had not arrived at Radio Haiti-Inter by 3 p.m., Dominique broadcast live on their air that, "They have arrested Konpe Filo and we will not continue our programs until he is freed."

"There was such an uproar in the streets, the city froze," Michele Montas recalled. Pascal was released only hours later, but the station was running on borrowed time.

Evans Paul himself, at the time also the leader of the Cabiga theater troupe, twice sought refuge at Radio Haiti around this time, as did Protestant Pastor Sylvio Claude.

"Radio Haiti had become some sort of an embassy, you know, where they didn't dare to strike us because of that so-called human rights season," said Montas.

The night of Ronald Reagan's election proved pivotal. Every election eve in the United States, Radio Haiti would have a program called *La Nuit Américaine*, "The American Night," which would provide running reports on the returns from the United States elections as they came in, in implicit criticism of Haiti's cult-of-personality state. In a nod to his cinemaphile days, the title of the evening was chosen by Dominique in reference to a François Truffaut film of the same name.

The day of Reagan's election, November 2, Montas and Dominique were at Radio Haiti-Inter, providing coverage of the U.S. ballot and discussing the returns with a U.S. Embassy official. When it became apparent that the former California governor had defeated Jimmy Carter to win the U.S. presidency, crowds of Macoutes appeared on Rue du Quay in front of the station, shooting in the air and bellowing, "The cowboys are in power! Human rights are over!"

"Jean was a survivor though," Michele Montas says of this time, as they were waiting for the hammer to fall. "And we at Radio Haiti were all together in this."

THREE WEEKS LATER, at 3 p.m. on November 28, 1980, panic seized the Haitian capital. With word spreading that political activists and journalists were being rounded up and arrested by the Duvalier government, Michele Montas took to the airwaves of Radio Haiti to announce that Jean Dominique, Richard Brisson and Anthony Pascal had all disappeared. Human rights activists, including Centre des Droits et Libertes Humaines director Jean-Jacques Honorat, who would later briefly serve as prime minister under the Cédras junta in the 1990s, began arriving at the station to show their solidarity. At 5 p.m. the Haitian military police raided the station, smashing and racking the equipment with bullets and arresting everyone present. Taken to the Casernes Dessalines barracks near the National Palace, Montas and her staff found that other journalists—from Radio Cacique, Radio Metropole and the print review *Le Petit Samedi*

Soir—had also been picked up. Richard Brisson had already been seized by the military and was repeatedly tortured over the next several days until he had completely lost his hearing in one ear. In addition to his crime of being an independent journalist, Brisson had produced a stage piece called "Potpourri" that year, which included among its theatrical sketches a song chiding Michele Bennet, Jean-Claude's wife. Despots, it would seem, have little sense of humor about themselves.

Traveling in the countryside, Dominique returned to Port-au-Prince to hear that his station had been sacked, and his friends urged him to go into hiding. Three days after the arrest of the Radio Haiti staff, Dominique offered publicly to surrender himself in exchange for the freedom of Michele and the rest of the staff. Rebuffed by the government, Dominique then entered the Venezuelan Embassy. On December 5, with the Duvalier regime under intense pressure from the Carter administration, five journalists, including Montas and Brisson, were taken from jail, put on a plane without being told where they were going, and sent to the United States.

There followed nearly six agonizing, frustrating years in exile in New York City, with Michele busy working and Jean meeting frequently with the Haitian activist community leaders such as Father Antoine Adrien in Brooklyn, attempting to interest the world in what was going on in their homeland.

FOR RICHARD BRISSON, though, his patience in waiting for Haiti to be free of its tyrant had worn out.

"Richard was sick of exile, he couldn't take it, he was really unhappy," said Montas in Manhattan years later. "He was in New York first and the he went to Miami and it was in Miami that he connected with Bernard Sansaricq. Richard was a very generous, very affectionate guy, but to him, somehow, he felt they had to make them pay for what they had done to us."

Sansaricq, who hailed from the Les Cayes branch of the family Francois Duvalier had massacred in Jeremie in 1964, had long been mulling over the idea of invading Haiti as had been done to topple Papa Doc so many times before. Finding a like-minded soul in Brisson, he had soon rallied some thirty-nine men whose hatred for the dictator overpowered any fear of death they might have. Departing from Miami to Turks and Caicos in January 1981, Sansaricq dropped eight of the men, including Brisson, by boat on the island of Ile de la Tortue, six miles off the coast of the northern Haitian port city of Port-de-Paix. Afterwards, either Sansaricq or his men had second thoughts, because Brisson and his men were abandoned on the island. Following several chaotic run-ins with the Haitian military, the rebels were captured on January 21. Taken from the island to Port-de-Paix, and then likely to Port-au-Prince, the surviving invaders were killed. Their bodies, including Brisson's, were never recovered.

In a strange footnote to the whole disaster, a former news editor at Radio Haiti over the years had rather radically switched his allegiances, and at the time of the invasion was serving as a public information officer with the Duvalier regime. Sent to the scene of the uproar to explain the government's position, the man found himself face-to-face with Brisson, now a prisoner of the government he himself served, on Ile de la Tortue. He attempted to engage the journalist in conversation, remembering that they were once coworkers. Brisson spat in his face.

When Jean and Michele returned to Haiti aboard an American Airlines flight less than three weeks after Duvalier had fled in 1986, Dominique was mobbed by some fifty thousand well-wishers at the Port-au-Prince airport, where they hugged, embraced and kissed him. Footage of Dominique that day shows him looking utterly overwhelmed by the crush, the throng, the outpouring of love from his homeland. Lifted up on the brawny shoulders of several working-class Haitian men, Dominique is handed a microphone attached to a portable speaker.

"I am the last person in the world who would have believed this," he says to the cheering crowd. "I expected to land and find everybody dead. But instead I find a people full of life!" Then, to the cheers of the people assembled, he raises his hands and flashes a sign. "V" for victory.

THE RADIO HAITI-INTER STATION at Rue du Quay had been so thoroughly destroyed that a decision was made to open at a new location, on the upper reaches of the capital's Delmas Road just before it headed into Petionville. Working day and night to get things up and running at the new location, it nevertheless took almost a year before everything was set to go. The night before the aborted 1987 elections, Radio Haiti's newsroom was again full of journalists, preparing to cover them the next day.

"There was a *viejo* who had some experience with how things usually went who said that we should have some kind of defense," Montas recalled. "So they accumulated rocks on top of Radio Haiti's roof."

Election day saw attacks on two electoral bureaus, the homes of councilors on the electoral council, and the massacre at Ruelle Vaillant. People called Radio Haiti and told them, "They're coming." Some of the staff went onto the roof of the building to survey the city and, in the words of one staffer, "We saw Port-au-Prince burning." Soon afterwards, three or four men were dropped off by car and stood in front of the station and began shooting in. The reporters began throwing rocks at them, and the men, almost unbelievably, started running. "It was quite a pleasure," Montas says now with a smile. But then cars began arriving in front of the station, with men in military uniform on board who hurled at least two grenades into the station's compound. "At that point, there was nothing we could do," Montas says. The staff went back inside the station, where they did interviews with some American stations, including CBS. At around five o'clock the next morning, they received a call that the military and their new macoute allies were planning to launch an organized, military attack on the station that day. Jean declared, "Everyone evacuate the station," and the staff took off home through the streets under a hail of gunfire.

But Montas and Dominique stayed in Haiti, even after Jean-Bertrand Aristide was forced from the country on September 30, 1991. The couple interviewed him from exile on Radio Haiti in October of that year and did not leave for their own exile, again in New York, until the end of December. This time, rather than slamming the door on them on their way out, the Haitian military attempted to stop them from leaving, with Haitian immigration officials boarding the charter flight they were on and insisting that their immigration papers were illegal. When the couple was dragged off the plane, the other passengers informed the pilot that the plane wouldn't leave the ground unless Dominique and Montas were on it. Finally, a call from then-Prime Minister Jean-Jacques Honorat—the man who had sought to show solidarity by visiting Radio Haiti the day Montas had been arrested some eleven years earlier—pressured the military at the airport to let the couple leave, and off they went to the United States.

JEAN AND MICHELE RETURNED again to Haiti in 1994 and once more had to rebuild their station, which this time took about seven months. Radio Haiti's FM antennae in the mountain retreat of Boutilliers had been wrecked and then, after Aristide's return, with the American soldiers already in the country, armed men destroyed the station's AM antennae in Cité Soleil. Gigi Dominique, Jean's daughter from a previous marriage, was made executive director, the position once held by Richard Brisson. Dominique's voice again emanated from radios around the country as he hosted two daily programs, the news-oriented "Inter-Actualites" (cohosted with Michele) at 7 a.m. and "Face a l'Opinion" in the afternoon, during which he interviewed important politicians and newsmakers of the day. Uniquely among Haiti's major Port-au-Prince-based stations, Dominique often used his microphone on the latter show to give voice to peasant activists and advocates from Haiti's countryside, allowing them to bring a dose of balance to urban listeners of the media's coverage of what was still largely an agricultural society.

Dominique, who had been a supporter of Aristide's candidacy for president and a close personal friend of René Préval's for thirty years, noticed some disturbing changes about the former man after his return in 1994. He told those close to him that Aristide seemed determined to stay in power and to have accommodations with the military, as well as the bourgeois elements who had funded the coup. How else to explain the appointment of someone like Mondesir Beaubrun to a ministerial position? Or the prominent role that figures like Fourel Celestin and Medard Joseph had gained within the Fanmi Lavalas party? Dominique was also savvy enough a political observer to realize how deep the rift between Préval and Aristide was growing, some two years after Aristide had founded his Lavalas partly in response to Préval's perceived independence. The interview Dominique had done with Aristide in December 1996, the *"petits projects de la presidence"* interview, as it had become known, still rang in the ears of many.

PRÉVAL, WHO HAD OFTEN complained that he found the president's chair a "lonely" place, would be in sore need of Dominique's sage political advice in his upcoming political struggles. Having finally lost patience with the recalcitrant parliament, he announced at the beginning of 1999 that he would be sticking to the principal that the legislators' terms would end on January 11, at which point he dismissed the entire Chamber of Deputies and all but nine of Haiti's senators, declaring quite simply that, although the elections for their replacements in December 1999 had not yet been held, their terms were over. Correct in fact though questionable in intention he may have been, the action created a predictable reaction. The OPL parliament cried "coup d'etat" and filed suit against the government in the Court de Cassation, which would eventually decide that it lacked the jurisdiction to rule on the matter. The next day, gunmen opened fire on Préval's sister, Marie-Claude Calvin, as her car sped through Port-au-Prince, wounding her and killing her driver. Préval finally withdrew the parliament's funding and canceled diplomatic passports for its members on January 29, promising that an electoral council would soon be formed and elections would soon be held.

In an address to the nation on February 2, Préval mourned the loss of yet another life and thanked the country for their condolences.

"I'm talking with people in good faith. I want to tell them that I'm doing everything in good faith," Préval said, calling for the creation of an electoral council and national and international observers for the new elections. "I give them my guarantee that my duty and my conviction is to respect the constitution. That is the guarantee to continue building democracy. . . . We will not take too much longer."

At the beginning of March it was announced that Jacques Edouard Alexis, the former Minister of Education approved as prime minister by parliament in July 1998, would now be filling that role and be forming a cabinet, as there was no longer a legislature to approve it. Several opposition political parties, including Evans Paul's KID party and Serge Gilles's PANPRA, announced that they were banding together to form a coalition, Espace de Concertation (Common Ground).

BUT THE LOSS OF LIFE continued. On March 1, Yvon Toussaint, a high profile member of the OPL and one of the nine remaining senators, was ambushed at his home in the capital, dying in a barrage of gunfire. The next month, three former OPL deputies would seek refuge in the residence of the Chilean ambassador and flee into exile after attacks on their homes. On March 8, Pierre Esperance, the executive director of the National Coalition for Haitian Rights (NCHR), which had originally been formed as a refugee advocacy group in New York and expanded with an autonomous office in Port-au-Prince to become the nation's premier human rights organization, was fired upon by gunmen speeding past him in a car, but, unlike with Yvon Toussaint, the assassins' aim was not as sure as it could have been. Wounded in the knee and shoulder, Esperance survived. That same month, Préval announced that an agreement had been reached on the formation of the new CEP, with an elderly, eminent Haitian lawyer, Leon Manus, at its head, and that elections would take place on November 28.

Quickly, however, as the massive administrative tasks facing the CEP became evident, especially regarding the registration of candidates and voters, Préval announced that the elections would be delayed until March 19, 2000. Secretary of State for Public Security Bob Manuel had acted as Préval's chief advocate in negotiations with the OPL to secure their agreement to elections, but that did not seem to curb the climate of violence, not all of it political, swirling around Port-au-Prince. Guy Philippe, the diminutive police chief of the capital's Delmas district and a former soldier, had trained in Ecuador along with several other prominent policeman during the Cédras years, and was said by residents to have initiated a take-no-prisoners war against street gangs and common criminals—now referred to by Haitians as *zenglendos* in a refrence to breaking glass—in Delmas as well as in Cité Soleil, which fell under his commissariat's jurisdiction. Philippe's deceptively cheerful smile and easy manner belied what was an often violent personality, according to officers who served with him, and during his tenure in Delmas, bodies of several prominent gang leaders, shot execution-style with their hands bound, appeared by the roadside over a period lasting several months

On April 9, half a dozen thieves, led by Hyppolite "Chuck Norris" Elize—also known as "Ti Elize," the rumored trigger man in the Pere Ti Jean Pierre-Louis killing the previous year—robbed and murdered a CIMO officer in Martissant. Despite an exchange of fire in which Elize was wounded, all of the thieves escaped. His freedom was short-lived, though, and ten days later, Elize was tracked down and killed by police at his sister's house near the College Canado in Turgeau. Pure gangster to the end, Elize let loose rounds from a .38 in his hand until he died.

Sensing political opportunity amidst the crime wave, Aristide sent out Paul Raymond of the Tabarre-affiliated Ti Kominote Legliz (TKL) of Saint Jean Bosco OP to denounce Préval and the PNH at an April 13 press conference, where he labeled the Haitian president and Secretary of State for Public Security Bob Manuel as traitors to the popular movement.

The calls for Manuel's head by the Aristide-aligned OPs grew even louder when, on May 28, police raided the Carrefour Feuilles neighborhood in central Port-au-Prince and shot eleven men dead—most shot in the head while in police custody. Though three of the men were suspected criminals turned over to the police by local vigilantes, a local justice of the peace called in to certify their deaths witnessed in horror as the police executed the eight others, all of whom were unarmed. In the aftermath of the Carrefour Feuilles massacre, Port-au-Prince police commissioner Jean Coles Rameau, the commander of the operation and a former military man with a reputation for brutality, fled to the Dominican Republic, but was there arrested and then returned to Haiti. Around the same time, fourteen bodies were found in Tintanyen—a favorite dumping ground of bodies for the military—and were presumed to be the remnants of Guy Philippe's Cité Soleil purge, or perhaps of Ti Elize's gang, victims of the ungentle justice of the brethren of the murdered CIMO.

SIGNIFICANTLY, THE CLIMATE of violence and insecurity was not only affecting the poor, who had so often borne its brunt in Haiti.

On May 28, the morning of the massacre in Carrefour Feuilles, a rally against the country's "insecurity," spearheaded to by Haiti's Chamber of Commerce and its president, Oliver Nadal, had been scheduled to take place on the capital's Champ de Mars square. The rally, a reaction to the recent high-profile assassinations and assassination attempts as well as a spate of carjackings and kidnappings in the capital, had been heavily promoted on Haiti's bourgeois radio stations in the preceding week, especially on Léopold Bérlanger's Radio Vision 2000. Nadal, the rally's driving force, was an extremely polarizing figure with many facets of Haitian society. The land on which peasants had been massacred by soldiers in Piatre in 1990 had been owned by his family at one time; Nadal was eventually indicted for helping to organize the murders, and many continued to believe that he was in some way responsible. Nadal's name had also been on a list of supporters of the 1991 coup whose assets were to frozen by the U.S. government before Aristide was restored to power three years later. Unsurprisingly, the Foundation 30 September, an Aristide client OP ostensibly representing victims of the September 30 coup and led by an opportunistic psychologist named Lovinsky Pierre-Antoine, denounced the planned rally, questioning "how can they call for peace when they never called for justice" during the coup d'etat. Aristide's Fanmi Lavalas party issued a statement calling for "peace of mind, peace in the belly" and demanded justice for the victims of the 1991 coup. Nadal and Haitian Chamber of Commerce Vice President Jean Robert Wawa even paid a visit to the pro-Aristide stronghold of Bel Air on the night before the rally, surrounded by PNH officers, in which they attempted to rally skeptical locals to their cause. As several hundred demonstrators began to gather on the Champs de Mars shortly after noon on May 28, though, they were met by a howling crowd of several thousand young, mostly male Aristide supporters rallied from the capital's Cité Soleil and La Saline and from Bel Air itself. Under full view of the police, who were outnumbered by the roaring crowd, the mob, many carrying photos of Aristide, hurled rocks and bottles filled with urine at the demonstrators, driving most of them off the plaza and sending many scrambling for their cars, whose windows were shattering under the assault.

It was not greatly noted at the time, but it was a foretaste of things to come, and it was an illustrative vision of the Haiti that Aristide envisioned building if and when he returned to power in the coming elections. For his part, Olivier Nadal appeared to have sated his appetite for Haitian politics. A little over a year later, he left Haiti for exile in the United States, where he has remained ever since.

AMIDST ALL OF THIS, perhaps remarkably given the level of unrest, there was some progress being made. Fulfilling another one of the goals of the privatization plan Aristide had signed in Paris in 1994, Préval finally succeeded in auctioning off the state-owned Ciment d'Haiti on May 7, 1999. Three companies—the Swiss-owned UmarHolderbank, the Colombian-owned Colclinker and the Haitian-owned National Cement Company—bought 65 percent of the concern. In June, the Préval government requested the deployment of an OAS Mission to Haiti to observe the upcoming elections, and the OAS, to the surprise of some, accepted the invitation.

RUMBLINGS WERE NEVER far off. On June 24, in the wee hours of the morning, a group of young gunmen, alumni of Aristide's Lafanmi Selavi youth home, stormed Selavi's headquarters in the Turgeau neighborhood in the capital. Declaring that Aristide was stealing international donations earmarked to help the orphanage's youth and that they had been promised jobs for their political work by the former president that had never materialized, the next morning the occupiers began tossing stones and bottles at passing vehicles. More protestors supporting the gunmen arrived, and the scene provoked a police response, with PNH firing tear gas into the building. At that point Dany Toussaint, the former Haitian army man who had been deported from the United States in 1997 and since become one of the most public faces of Fanmi Lavalas, showed up on the scene to negotiate a solution. Speaking on the radio later, Toussaint charged that the protestors had been paid to create problems for Aristide.

In late July, the United States announced that it would be withholding more than $10 million in aid for Haiti's upcoming elections, because, when Haiti's new electoral law overriding the results of the contested 1997 elections appeared in the official government publication *Le Moniteur*, it lacked the signatures of Préval and the CEP, therefore not making it legally binding. An embarrassing screwup on the government's part, the dispute was eventually smoothed over.

AS HAITI'S TORRID SUMMER drew to a close, the arrival of fall was heralded with a pair of attacks. On September 5, a grenade exploded in front of the headquarters of Haiti's Chamber of Commerce—the organization that had sponsored the previous May's march—damaging it slightly. More seriously, en route to the Port-au-Prince airport with his family on September 6, OPL politician Sauveur Pierre-Etienne's car was fired upon by unknown gunmen. Etienne's family escaped injury, and he returned fire with his own weapon, wounding, he believed, his attacker.

Faced by further logistical hurdles, on September 8, the CEP announced that it was again postponing the elections, this time until December 19 with a second round on January 10, from their original scheduled date in November. The same month, the U.S. Agency for International Development (USAID) disbursed $3.5 million to Haiti in order to cover the cost of new photo voter identity cards. A little over a month later, though, on October 6, the CEP would announce yet another rescheduling, declaring that Haiti would finally hold local and legislative elections in two rounds on March 19 and April 30 of the coming year, with the entire eighty-three-seat Chamber of Deputies, nineteen seats in the twenty-seven-seat Senate, 133 municipal councils and hundreds of local offices up for grabs. The CEP also announced that a second round of voting would be held for parliamentary candidates should any one candidate fail to win more than 50 percent of the overall vote.

Despite the haggling over its timing, Jean Dominique felt the upcoming elections would be critical and, with René Préval's help, he encouraged the organization of a new peasant movement in the Artibonite, where much of Préval's agrarian reform program had been concentrated, under the leadership of a dignified local peasant leader named Charles Suffrard. The organization, which adopted as its name Komite Zafè Elektoral Peyizan pou Eleksyon Pwop (Electoral Affairs Committee for Clean Elections or KOZEPEP) marked an important step in bringing in Haiti's oft-shunted-aside peasant majority to the electoral table and organizing so their voice could be weighed against that of the country's urban population—the only population that most Haitian politicians ever paid attention to.

SEPTEMBER HAD ALWAYS been an auspicious month for Haiti's former president, marking as it did the date of not only his ouster from power in 1991 but also the attach on his church in 1988. On September 11, eleven years after the attack at Saint Jean Bosco, several hundred Aristide supporters, lead by TKL spokesman Paul Raymond, held a rally in the ruins of the church, plastering photos of the victims of the attack on the walls. Aristide, dressed entirely in black, made a brief appearance. Grimfaced and silent, he waved to the crowd and drove away in a small convoy of SUV's. As if energized by the patron's public show of support, on September 14 and 15, some one hundred demonstrators, lead by Raymond and René Civil, burned tires in front of the TELECO building and hurled rocks at passing cars and police, injuring two officers before the PNH grew weary of the dance on the second day and lobbed tear gas canisters and opened fire, wounding one of the protestors. The protest was again aimed at Préval—who was rumored to be about to replace Julio Cadet, the director of the notoriously corrupt agency—and seemed like yet another example of Tabarre flexing its disruptive muscle against the government. Préval held his ground, though, and on September 20, Cadet was replaced by Jean-François Chamblain, fresh from his tour managing the recently privatized Minoterie d'Haiti sugar mill. Things also heated up in the coastal outpost of Jeremie, where, on September 27, after a month of demonstrations, a pro-Aristide group called the Kowodinasyon Resistans Grandans (KOREGA) attacked the local electoral office, furious, they said, that it and local electoral mechanisms were in control of Espace de Concertation members. When police arrived to stop the assault, beating demonstrators with their batons and firing into the air, a brawl ensued through the city, resulting in the death of one protestor, killed when she ran into traffic to escape the melee.

THROUGHOUT SEPTEMBER, the murky links between elements of the PNH and the drug trade began to bubble to the surface. First, the police chief for the capital's sprawling Carrefour slum was arrested for suspicion of involvement in drug trafficking, then six PNH officers were arrested and charged with stealing pounds of cocaine discovered aboard a boat in Cap Haitien. Then, with Bob Manuel pushing strenuously, four top police commissioners, including those from Petionville and Croix-de-Bouquets, were questioned for possible involvement in drug activity after a Colombian national was stopped at Port-au-Prince airport with six kilos of cocaine in his possession. The questioning of the four led to a meeting between the police command and René Préval and the police hierarchy and the PNH headquarters near the end of September.

By the fall of 1999, Manuel himself, though, the former military man who had been part of the democratic movement since the days of Saint Jean Bosco and who was viewed as the best assurance that upcoming elections would be free and fair, had discovered how finite and complex power can be. He had been apprised early on by foreign military experts who had been brought from abroad to professionalize the Haitian army and police about the malicious ambitions of Dany Toussaint, and the PNH had discovered in their own investigations of Haiti's banking industry the existence of financial links between Toussaint and two other former army officers, Jacques Aurelus and Pierre Cherubin, with Colombian drug cartels. As Manuel began to aggressively implement counter-narcotics measures in the country, he often found that elements of the PNH would be actively undermining him and police chief Pierre Denizé, and that squads of officers would often break up one narcotics ring not in order to stamp out drugs, but in order to strengthen another illegal syndicate. After he balked at a face-to-face meeting with Aristide, at which the latter asked him to make sure the upcoming elections "went well" for the Fanmi Lavalas party, ominous graffiti reading *"Bob Manuel vle touye Titid"* ("Bob Manuel wants to kill Aristide") began appearing around the capital. Manuel, who had won praise for helping Pierre Denizé construct a semiprofessional, independent law-enforcement body out of a politicized and murderous army and who held the view that "the most revolutionary thing you could do in Haiti is strengthen an institution," had seen those gains run up against a wall when he attempted to move against allies of Haiti's former president. Finally, as the pressure grew ever greater from Aristide-aligned client organizations for his resignation, after a meeting with Préval, Manuel resigned. It was widely assumed that former Colonel Jean Lamy, a friend of Manuel's who had helped him substantially in his spring negotiations with the opposition parties to secure a date for the upcoming elections, would succeed him.

The resignation of Manuel represented a significant escalation in the tension between the National Palace and Tabarre. Manuel had very much been Préval's man, and the professionalization of the police force was one of his crowning achievements. Now that all seemed to be threatened.

And yet there was also a third current flowing in this struggle.

"It was obvious that Dany Toussaint was positioning himself to be the next president of Haiti in 2000 and in the meantime positioning himself to be head of the police," said one prominent voice in the democratic movement, active in Haiti for many decades. "For this he had to get rid of Bob Manuel. Never forget, Bob Manuel had been of the first Saint Jean Bosco team, so he wanted in one clean sweep to get rid of Bob Manuel and discredit René Préval."

But the plan was not yet in its final act. As he descended toward Port-au-Prince from his home in the cool reaches of Laboule in the mountains above the capital, the man rumored to be Manuel's possible replacement, former FADH Colonel Jean Lamy, was killed by gunmen on Avenue Pan-Americaine in his car on October 8, the day after Manuel had resigned.

ALMOST IMMEDIATELY after the killing, Dany Toussaint took to the airwaves to accuse Manuel of Lamy's murder.

Manuel was shattered by the death of his friend, and when his phone rang late that night, with the clock inching towards three o'clock in the morning, the streets of the capital sat dark and silent under another blackout.

"You need to come to the Palace." The voice belonged to René Préval.

"Why?" Manuel asked. "It's so late."

"Because Dany [Toussaint] and [Pierre] Cherubin are here and they are saying that they're going to kill you if you don't come and explain yourself."

Manuel drove down toward the Champs de Mars through the capital's empty streets, entering through the back gate. As groups of PNH and tough young men, all armed, milled menacingly about the palace grounds, Manuel was shown into Préval's office, where Dany Toussaint, Pierre Cherubin and several other former military officers involved in the new police force stood surrounding Préval at his desk.

"We know you killed Jean Lamy," Toussaint said. "And you're going to have to pay for that."

"What? What are you talking about?" Astonished, he looked at Préval sitting at his desk. "I did not kill Colonel Lamy."

The exchanges went back and forth like this for some time, with the military men accusing Manuel of involvement in Lamy's death and Manuel denying it. Throughout it all, Préval sat nearly motionless at his desk, looking like a prisoner in his own palace. Finally, Cherubin came to the point of the meeting:

"Okay, perhaps you were not, perhaps we know you weren't responsible for Lamy's death, but still, we have to come to some type of understanding. . . ."

Manuel immediately realized what Cherubin meant. This had all been planned. They wanted leverage on him so he could pressure any new PNH director to stop the body's anti-narcotics activity in Haiti.

As he left, Manuel looked into the sky, which would soon be turning the yellow-crimson of the Caribbean morning. He would have to get his affairs in order. He went back to his home, packed all that he could carry and left Haiti with his family on a plane that same day. He hasn't looked back since.

Speaking years later in a restaurant in a tony section of Guatemala City, where he was overseeing security for that country's UN mission, Manuel, freshly returned from six months with a similar posting in Afghanistan, mused on the circumstances of his departure.

"I still don't know if I've overcome the disappointment," Manuel a light-completed mulatto with a solid, military man's frame told me, as a cool breeze blew over the open veranda we were sitting on.

Manuel, who had been a friend of René Préval's for twenty years before his exile, said that he hadn't spoken to the Haitian president for two years after he left the country, but that even so, and in contrast to the claims of many observers who felt that Préval had been little more than Aristide's bag man, at a certain point the two men's goals had begun to diverge.

"There were two different projects after a certain point, Aristide's and Préval's," Manuel said, looking across the leafy business park where we sat in as if recalling another life, another time. "René Préval was not uncomfortable with institutions, he wasn't threatened by them, or by knowledge, or by working collectively. But Aristide can't work with someone who has a base independent of being bought by the state, he wouldn't listen to anybody. And René Préval is not a killer."

Days later, at around 10 p.m. on the night of October 14, the Directeur de la Police Judiciaire, Mario Andresol, whose department was in charge of investigating the Lamy killing, was driving to his home in Delmas when gunmen sped past in a car and opened fire on his vehicle, hitting it at least five times. Andresol, miraculously, escaped unharmed.

THE FLIGHT OF MANUEL—and the propaganda campaign that had preceded it—enraged Jean Dominique. The destruction of the name of a person he viewed as a decent man, and the demagoguery and playing of the color card that went along with it, all struck him at his core as intolerable. As Radio Haiti-Inter and other reporters covered Jean Lamy's funeral at the National Cathedral on October 17—with René Préval, Aristide and his wife Mildred, Dany Toussaint and Pierre Denizé all in attendance—a mob of young men entered the cathedral and began to shouting and screaming that they were going to take Lamy's body away to bury it. Attempting to attack Pierre Denizé and seize Lamy's casket, the band even managed to briefly knock over "Minouche" (Madame Aristide). Surrounded by a chanting, shoving throng, Denizé was forced to flee in Aristide's car. As PNH officials took Lamy's body and began to move toward the cemetery with it, Toussaint, who had been observing the scene with a rather pronounced calm, was hoisted on the shoulders of the young men, who began shouting "Viv Dany." "It was an insane scene," said one observer.

The day after Lamy's funeral—October 18—a mob of young men from René Civil's Jeunesse Pouvoir Populaire organization arrived at Radio Haiti, shaking and banging on the station's front gate, saying that they wanted to come in and speak on the radio. They also began spray-painting slogans and aggressively harassing passers-by. Dominique himself stepped out to speak with the young men after they said they wanted to "negotiate."

"Well, what do you want to negotiate?" Dominique asked.

"We want to talk to you," one man said. Some of the graffiti they had sprayed denounced both Bob Manuel and Dominique himself as *ti wouj*, or "little red ones"—a racist slur against the color of the mulattos' skin.

"You won't talk to me until all that graffiti is erased," Dominique replied.

The young men then erased the graffiti they had so recently put up, and five of them entered the courtyard of the station and spoke with Dominique. They explained that they wanted to go on the air and explain why Bob Manuel had killed Jean Lamy, as well as the involvement of Pierre Denizé. Dominique said no.

"Jean knew who had sent them," said Michele Montas. "So Jean made his editorial the next day directly addressing Dany Toussaint. But in fact he was addressing Aristide, saying, 'This is what you are facing; if you don't act the right way, they will have you!'"

Brilliant and startling, Jean's voice ebbed and flowed on the October 19 editorial, but was anchored in a tone of implacable determination. It was a performance that was classic Dominique.

"Can a screaming mob pretend to take Radio Haiti hostage to force it to broadcast their defamatory accusations against honest public functionaries? And their racist, anti-mulatto comments?" Dominique began. "This is the question we asked ourselves yesterday morning when about forty fanatics blocked for four hours the Delmas Road in front of our building. Screams, vociferation, rocks thrown at the front of our building, our iron fence violently shaken. Confronted with our resistance to their terrorism, they took me on personally, with the obvious macoute slogans against the 'ti wouj,' against the 'mulattos,' and so forth and so on."

Giving the license plate numbers of one of the two trucks that had brought the young men "from Petionville," Dominque continued:

Drivers and demonstrators questioned freely admitted to having received a few dollars from the major to demonstrate in front of Radio Haiti. From the major? Dany Toussaint to be sure.

But why Radio Haiti for God's sake? During the campaign unleashed by Dany Toussaint against Robert Manuel, Pierre Denizé and the leadership of the police, the following slogan was circulating in Tabarre, "Bob Manuel, Pierre Denizé and Jean Dominique are *ti wouj.*" I have thus been for some time the target of Dany Toussaint's clique within La Fanmi. Our enemies never miss an opportunity to destabilize us. . . . With the dismissal of Manuel, a padlock that was blocking Dany Toussaint's ambitions was knocked out of the way—rather carelessly, it must be acknowledged. Then Dany Toussaint turned against Denizé . . . at the cathedral and today against me. What was circulating at Tabarre as a rumor is being implemented.

Recounting the chaos in front of the station the previous day, Dominique then addressed Toussaint directly, saying:

The person who paid you to try and terrorize me made three mistakes. The first was on Saturday at the cathedral when he and his followers tried to take advantage of Jean Lamy's funeral service to organize an accusatory and slanderous demonstration. . . . To be sure they desecrated under the eyes of Father Aristide a place that should be sacred for all: namely the cathedral of Port-au-Prince, a sacred place for believers and non-believers alike.

After outlining the pathetically small numbers of demonstrators, Dominique faulted Toussaint for poor military strategy for displaying such weakness of support in public. Then, with a single turn of phrase, he dismissed all of the intricacies of the power struggles being played out at Tabarre as so much useless noise:

His second mistake . . . [was to have the demonstrators] carry him in triumph on their shoulders under Jean-Bertrand Aristide's enigmatic gaze. . . . Titid has a sharp eye, he knows how to decode ambitions and his sibylline smile says a lot about the future, but that is their business! It is not mine! I have not fought for thirty years to waste my time deciphering the quarrels among the satraps of Fanmi Lavalas!

And then, finally taking Toussaint to task for daring to attack him at Radio Haiti:

The mistake of Dany Toussaint was to think that a bit of terror on the part of a few street gangsters of the JPP would give him access to our microphone. . . . Here we don't give the floor to anyone! We don't give the floor to slander. We know that true justice is not created by screaming fanatics, more or less well paid. . . .

The murder of Jean Lamy, the attack on Mario Andresol, the recent assassination of a dozen police officers, the murder of Yvon Toussaint, the murder attempt against Marie-Claude Calvin Préval all aroused from us on Radio Haiti the anger of the citizenry and the indignation of Lavalas, prompting us to fight again for justice, transparency and popular participation.

I will close with this last consideration: If they keep trying to use these mobs in front of Radio Haiti-Inter to shut down the Delmas Road, he will break his teeth! The microphone of Radio Haiti will stay closed to him! But I know that he has weapons! I know that he has the money to pay and arm his followers. Here, I have no other weapon than my journalist's pen! And my microphone and my unquenchable faith as a militant for true change! And let me be perfectly clear, I will not turn over to any free-rider in the world a monopoly over Lavalas, no matter who it is!

If Dany Toussaint tries anything else against me or the radio and if I am still alive, I will close the place down after I have denounced these maneuvers one more time and I will go in exile once more with my wife and children.

In 1991 the friends of Dany Toussaint [an allusion to the military that toppled Aristide] tried desperately to take over Radio Haiti, I resisted them alone! With my faith, intelligence and professional experience. At the time I understood that behind the politicians preparing the coup d'état, behind certain friendships—because there were dissidents among them who frequented the salons of the great ladies of Lavalas!—there was a stubborn will on the part of one, and I had understood on

September 30, 1991 and later on, Jean-Bertrand Aristide and René Pré-val told me, "You were right!" They wanted to take over Radio Haiti to prepare a coup d'ètat. That's what happened!

Today I ask the same question: Is this the same maneuver? The parish priest of Dessalines was saying on Sunday in the presence of the head of state that new coup plotters were trying to destabilize the government. In 1991 I told Jean-Bertrand Aristide and Renè Prèval, "Don't trust Cédras." Titid replied, "Cédras and I, we are married." Sad marriage! With AIDS. Titid is stubborn. Although he is stubborn he must understand that it is not his person alone nor his sense of power that hangs in the balance in this affair.

Over Radio Haiti, there is a silence to awaken the dead, the five thousand dead of the coup d'ètat; this is the truth that must emerge from this insignificant exercise in intimidation today. This is the truth that it is right to speak of this morning, the truth of a free man.

Earlier I cited another free man, Laclos. I close with Shakespeare: "The truth will always make the face of the devil blush!"

Thank you!

As 1999 drew to a close, so did the U.S. military mission in Haiti, the sparse remnants of the invasion that had returned Aristide to power in 1994. After Aristide was returned, the soldiers had built and repaired 134 miles of roads and bridges, dug sixty-four new wells around the capital and elsewhere, refurbished forty-eight schools and provided 117,000 Haitians with medical care with their medical unit. Soon the U.S. camp out near the airport would be abandoned, its watchtower unguarded and the sandbags settling into the ground. Given how high the hopes had been with the return Aristide those short years ago, some said it was as if the Americans had never been there at all.

People with memories of the bad old days could be forgiven their déja vu as the year drew to a close. A November 6 political rally by Aristide opponents in Petit Goave was disrupted by young men trucked in from Port-au-Prince who pelted the crowd with rocks and bottles filled with urine and feces while shouting *"Viv Aristide."* In the capital on November 28—the fifth anniversary of the massacre at Rue Valliant—a rally by Espace de Concertation calling for legitimate, nonviolent elections degenerated into a brawl when a gang of young men shouting pro-Aristide slogans attacked the crowd. This time, however, police intervened and arrested several of them. The violent pro-Aristide demonstrators had started to be referred to by a new name—*chimere*—which referred both to a mythical, fire-breathing demon and the French word for a wild or upsetting dream.

The new millennium dawned with the news that Léopold Bérlanger, owner of the Aristide-hostile Radio Vision 2000, had been elected head of the CNO (Conseil National d'Observateurs), a body mandated by Haiti's electoral law that incorporated the Catholic Church, the Plateforme des Organisations Haïtiennes Droits Humains (POHDH) and KOZEPEP, and was charged with watching the tallying of the votes in Haiti's upcoming elections. In preparation for the vote, the OAS Electoral Observation Mission requested by Préval was deployed to Haiti on February 23. With Dany Toussaint now running as a senatorial candidate under the umbrella of Aristide's Fanmi Lavalas, on February 9—speaking from New York to the radio station Radio Liberté, run by a beret-wearing notorious Duvalierest named Serge Beaulieu—two of Toussaint's lawyers, Jean-Claude Nord and Gérard Georges, made veiled threats against Jean Dominique, accusing him of launching a campaign against Toussaint to deprive him of his place in the Senate, and intimating darkly that "the heart of Roger Lafontant will be buried at Radio Haiti."

On March 3, citing continued organizational difficulties that had left an estimated one million voters still unregistered, Préval, in consultation with the CEP, yet again postponed the elections that were due to take place on March 19, with elections set for April 9. The voter registration period was extended until March 19 to allow more voters to register, but things were still difficult. The opposition parties howled that Préval was trying to delay the elections until November 2000, when Aristide would surely be running for president again. When elections material arrived at the BEDs (Departmental Electoral Offices) at the beginning of March 2000, the body was unable to distribute them to the Communal Electoral Offices (BECs) or Local Offices (BIs) in a timely manner because they lacked vehicles to transport the materials. BI workers, paid in an erratic fashion by the cash-strapped CEP, in some areas took to opening registration centers whenever they felt like it, resulting in long lines and frustration on the part of those trying to register. At one point, several disgruntled BI workers attempted to set fire to the Port-au-Prince BEC, but only succeeded in causing minimal damage. Eventually, though, and despite the replacement of two BEC officials at the BEC there under charges of registration fraud, a May 2000 OAS report on the registration process concluded that "despite these difficulties in registering, the BI's managed to eventually register almost everyone who sought a voter card."

In a prophetic poll by the U.S. State Department Office of Research conducted in nine Haitian cities (comprising 1,502 interviews between February and March of 2000), the observers found that many Haitians looked toward the upcoming elections, with 80 percent of respondents thinking it "very" important that Haiti be a democracy, with particularly committed voting blocs to be found among women, supporters of Aristide's Fanmi Lavalas party and university-educated respondents. Respondents also rated character, honesty and a positive program as being the most important attributes for potential candidates.

Troublingly, though, some three-fourths of respondents said that Haiti was heading in the wrong direction, and that conditions, especially crime, had worsened since the past year. Slightly under half of respondents said they still had confidence in the PNH. And whereas Lavalas supporters seemed to be, on the whole, more optimistic that things would improve after the scheduled elections, only 30 percent expressed confidence in the Préval government. Fanmi Lavalas still had the widest public support of the political parties, with 62 percent in Jeremie, 59 percent in Cayes but—strikingly—only 18 percent in Hinche. The OPL was viewed unfavorably by 53 percent of respondents nationwide. The interviewing, though, significantly, had excluded the capital's vast Cité Soleil shantytown, home to over 200,000 of the capital's residents and, as would be seen in coming years, a force to be reckoned with in terms of political power.

Protests continued to flare periodically throughout March, and, on March 27, the venerable Agence France-Presse photographer Thony Belizaire was stopped and his film confiscated by armed *chimere* after he had photographed them extorting money from motorists at a roadblock near Saint Jean Bosco. In the tense city of Petit Goave at the end of the month, Legitime Athis, the local campaign coordinator for the Mouvement Partiotique pour le Sauvetage National party of former Duvalier minister Hubert Deronceray, was murdered by a mob along with his wife. Though the OAS mission denounced the killing and called on the government to "open a serious investigation into this crime, to find the culprits and to condemn them," no arrests were made.

AS THE RHETORIC surrounding the CEP and the date for new elections became ever more contentious, Dominique used his March 27 commentary as an opportunity to lash out at fellow news director Léopold Bérlanger, the owner of rival station Radio Vision 2000 and now president of the CNO body charged with observing the elections. Dominique accused Bérlanger, who had a long history of hostility to Lavalas in general and Aristide in particular, of attempting to manipulate the results of a 1990 senatorial election in the West department, and he also claimed Bérlanger was too partisan a figure to be trusted with overseeing the accuracy of the upcoming ballot. Particularly troubling to Dominique was the discretion of the CNO-appointed observers to put together, if they wished, and report of the balloting "as they observed it." As Dominique saw it, this overstepped the observers' charge of action.

"The electoral law is clear. . . . The written process of the balloting is drawn and signed by members of the electoral bureau and in some cases by the representatives of the party, group or political groups who are officially recognized. . . . The written report is prepared in at least six formally signed originals. If the representative of a party or group . . . refuses to sign this report, they will state the reason invoked or alleged for their refusal to sign and these protests have no immediate value, and are only for future reference. The refusal to sign a report by the representative of the electoral bureau has no effect on the validity of the electoral operations. . . . The word observer never appears in Article 158. Never!"

In other words, Dominique was saying, the anti-Préval and antiprogressive forces were already setting the means in motion by which they could cry foul if that party won a plurality of the votes, and the CNO would be their megaphone to do so.

But many others were not so convinced. "I don't think the Bérlanger people were there to deliberately sabotage the elections at all," said one veteran of international observer missions to Haiti who was involved in monitoring the 2000 elections. Another, recalling a meeting between Dominique and OAS officials in the last week of March, recalled how the journalist seemed fevered with the idea that "the elections would be very bloody and that many would not be registered because of macoutes, neo-macoutes and people working against the people's project. He said that the Haitian people were not going let themselves be cheated out of their right to vote."

AS JEAN DOMINIQUE arrived for work at Radio Haiti a little after 6 a.m. on the morning of April 3, there was little to suggest that this day would be different than any other. Jean-Claude Louissaint, Radio Haiti's gatekeeper, opened the station's heavy metal gates and Dominique drove inside to the station's parking lot. Though Michele Montas had been accompanying her husband to the station in recent days because of a back problem, today she had opted to drive herself, and had not yet arrived. Dominique paid little mind to the red Nissan Pathfinder parked near the station's entrance or two other cars—a white Cherokee jeep and a small truck—also parked nearby. As Dominique parked, exited his car and began to walk toward Radio Haiti's entrance, a man who had been loitering near the front of the station slipped through the open gate past Jean-Claude Louissaint, pulled an automatic pistol and shot Dominique seven times—hollow-point bullets ripping into the journalist as he crumbled and fell to the ground. Then the gunman turned and shot Louissaint, killing him as well. The killer then ran back to the Pathfinder, and all three cars sped off. Arriving at the station minutes later, Michele Montas approached the gates of Radio Haiti-Inter in her own car and discovered, to her horror, that the deed had been accomplished and the killers had fled.

A correspondent from Radio Metropole who was driving up Delmas saw the commotion in front of Haiti-Inter's gates and called news director, Rotchild Francois, to inform him. Within minutes a huge crowd of journalists, friends and neighbors had gathered in front of the station's gates. As the news of Dominique's murder spread throughout the capital, both Préval and Prime Minister Alexis rushed to the hospital where Dominique had been brought. Aristide arrived at the hospital some time later. Despite the doctors' best efforts, there was little they could do. Both Louissaint—a member of the poor whose cause the journalist has championed for so long—and the journalist himself were dead. On the airwaves, the voice of Radio Haiti was silent and still.

5

Putting Our Heads Together

DOMINIQUE LAY IN HIS CASKET on April 8 in a state funeral with full honors that followed a three-day period of mourning ordered by President Préval. An estimated twenty thousand mourners filled the capital's Sylvio Cator Stadium where Dominique's body lay in state, its skin pallid again the warm Caribbean sunshine. On a dais sat Préval and his wife, Jean-Bertrand Aristide, Aristide's wife Mildred Trouillot and Michele Montas. Several times during the three-hour service, Préval lost his composure and sobbed inconsolably into his hands. He pinned on Dominique's lapel Haiti's National Medal of Honor and Merit, Haiti's highest honor, which he had awarded posthumously to his old friend. Aristide sat, silent, watchful, unreadable. At one point during the service, in a bizarre gesture as mourners filed past Dominique's casket, a young man tried to drop a playing-card-sized picture of Aristide in with Dominique in the open coffin. Observers, incensed, removed it. As the ceremony ended, a crowd of young men began shouting "*Viv Aristide*" and declaring that Evans Paul had been responsible for Dominique's killing. Charging out of the stadium, they said they were going to kill Paul, but could not find him. Instead, they burned down the headquarters of Paul's KID political party, and a group of chimere then marched to Radio Vision 2000, pelting the station with rocks and bottles and calling for the heads of journalists there. A stone-throwing mob also surrounded the house of Micha Gaillard, a professor of Haitian-French descent turned KONAKOM candidate for mayor in the capital. Born in Bulgaria while his father, the great Haitian historian Roger Gaillard, was teaching there, Gaillard had been on a committee to help work out the details of Aristide's return during the Cédras years. Though he was not home at the time, his wife and young sons were, and as rocks rained down on the house, they fled over a back wall to seek shelter at a neighbor's. A week later, over one hundred Haitian journalists marched through the Champs de Mars demanding justice for Dominique and Louissant. Dominique's ashes would eventually be scattered in the Artibonite River. On April 12, Préval announced that elections would finally be held on May 21.

Attacks on the political opposition continued throughout the month. Late on the evening of April 12 Merilus Deus, a MOCHRENA candidate for the rural assembly in Savanette, was shot and then hacked to death by a mob of attackers who then slashed his daughter for good measure. On April 18 axe and machete-wielding assailants hacked Ducertain Armand to death in his Thomazeau home just north of the capital. The seventy-year-old was an advisor to Marie-Denise Claude, the daughter of murdered pastor Sylvio Claude, who was a senatorial candidate for the Haitian Christian Democratic Party and whose sister, Marie-France, was running under the party's banner for the mayorship of Port-au-Prince. Meeting with political parties following the killing, CEP President Leon Manus warned that, "If in the coming days popular organizations continue to promote violence . . . the elections intended to change the economic and social situation of the nation, will not take place." On May 6, Ary Bordes, a prominent physician and author, was shot and killed by gunmen as he sat in a Port-au-Prince traffic jam. Préval again promised, however, that the elections would indeed go ahead as scheduled. In a May 5 press release, the OAS concluded that "despite certain difficulties observed during the registration process, the majority of the Haitian electorate who wished to register were able to obtain a voting card and will therefore be able to exercise their right to vote on 21 May."[1] From Tabarre, on May 18—Haiti's flag day—Aristide released what many viewed as a rather disingenuous call for peace, writing, "To you, dear candidates in the opposition, we send you our wishes for peace."

MAY 21—A SUNDAY—DAWNED with people already forming long lines at polling stations around the country, and 22,500 local and two hundred international observers mobilized to monitor the vote. Despite a controversial decision late Saturday night to postpone elections in the southwestern Grand Anse department due to what officials there termed huge logistical difficulties, fear and rumors that the day would be plagued by violence proved largely unfounded, save for a fatal shooting at a polling place in Croix-des-Bouquets, north of the capital and, again, in the Plateau Central, where a group of armed men stole ballot boxes from three polling places in Hinche. The opposition, which had largely stopped campaigning weeks earlier in the face of the attacks launched against it, boycotted completely the vote on the massive Ile de la Gonave, charging that the polling stations there were staffed solely by Lavalas partisans. Despite the late openings of many polling stations and often chaotic scenes that erupted when they did open, the vote was carried off by an estimated 60 percent of Haiti's eligible voters, some two million people. Haitian and American officials lauded the high turnout, but the latter, as well as the OAS Observer Mission, continued to voice caution about the circumstances of the ballot.

By Monday, though, things began to look a bit strange. Some observers noted ballot tallying centers that were littered with ballots, some being trod underfoot, some still in boxes, and thousands of discarded ballots were found littering a downtown Port-au-Prince street. A report—confirmed by electoral observers—revealed that in the KOZEPEP stronghold of Verettes in the Artibonite Valley the previous day, a group of armed men seized and burned electoral materials in seven polling stations, stopping the vote.[2] An attack Monday afternoon by Lavalas partisans on the headquarters of a minor political party in the capital resulted in the death of mayoral candidate Jean-Michel Olophene, after his skull was cracked open by a hurled rock.

ON MAY 22, the opposition parties came together to form a new coalition that they soon named the Convergence Democratique (Democratic Convergence or CD). The group consisted of the old Espace de Concertation grouping (basically Evans Paul's KID and Serge Gilles's PANPRA parties) with the addition of Gérard Pierre-Charles's OPL, the KONAKOM bloc of Victor Benoit and Micha Gaillard, Leslie Manigat's centrist RNDP and the more right-wing of Hubert de Roceray's Mobilisation pour le Développement National (MDN) and Reynold Georges's Alliance pour l'Avancement et la Libération d'Haiti (ALLAH). At a press conference on May 27, this newly formed coalition called for a boycott of the runoff elections.

Shortly after the elections and the opposition's announcement, police sweeps throughout the country picked up scores of political activists. Former OPL senator Paul Denis and was arrested along with four others arrested in the South Department on May 23 and charged with illegal weapons possession, which Denis denied, only to be released four days later. On May 25 it was the turn of former president of the Chamber of Deputies and OPL member Vasco Thernelan, as well as a senate candidate from that party, Mellius Hyppolite, both arrested in Gonaives. The same week, over a dozen Espace de Concertation activists were arrested in Petit Goave. On May 23, with the results of the election still not announced, Lavalas spokesmen Yvon Neptune and René Civil were already on the radio declaring a landslide for their party.

Despite all this, in a late May press release, the OAS Observation Mission, while criticizing the violence that had led up to the vote and the chaotic scenes that were witnessed at some polling places on election day, "initial reports gathered from over 200 international observers deployed throughout the country during Sunday's polling indicate that the credibility of the elections is so far acceptable."[3]

DURING THE MAY ELECTIONS, I arrived back in Haiti after an extended absence. I took an apartment in Pacot, a genteel, declining middle-class neighborhood of winding, leafy streets and half-empty great houses that clung to the foot of the mountains that rose up from the capital and headed up toward the more affluent suburb of Petionville and, eventually, the mountain town of Kenscoff. In my apartment complex, the middle-class kids and toddlers would go out to play soccer on the dead-end street we lived on with poor children who would trudge up the hill from downtown to do odd jobs and beg for money. One of the poor boys learned my name, "Michel," and insisted on shaking my hand every time we passed. After the first time, he never even asked for money. He just wanted someone to talk to.

"The world is moving forward, faster all the time," said an acquaintance of mine, a libertine mulatto who had formed something of a *blan* bidonville out of the apartments in his complex. "And we're being left behind. Internet, fax, everything. And we're still trying to master elections." He sighed. "It makes me sad."

The disillusionment was palpable. A friend of mine, an aspiring artist who had grown up in the working-class urban donnybrook of Carrefour, had, over the months of political crisis, gradually changed the theme of his paintings from vodou-inspired material to a caste that perhaps more accurately reflected the country's mood: a group of homeless people sprawled and starving in front of the National Palace, which glowed infernally from fires burning within it; a peasant family carrying their dying mother beneath the lights of a glittering society party; and a street tough's face, bandannaed and wearing mirrored sunglasses that reflected twin scenes of burning tires and police on the march while a crowd of street people cowered behind them. "Figi Beton," he called that one. "Downtown Face."

I walked around the town, as I always did when I returned to Haiti, to get the pulse of the place back into my bloodstream, to feel the warm Caribbean sun on my face again, to listen to the conversation of the *ti machanns* as they sat under their umbrellas selling their wares, to inhale the combination of life and decay that informs the air of Port-au-Prince. Walking through Carrefour Feuilles, I met an English teacher, thin and in a frayed suit, a man who had lived near my own home in Brooklyn for some fourteen years before returning to Haiti on the wave of jubilation and hope that accompanied Aristide's return. He walked with me for many blocks, peppering me with questions about what New York was like these days and asking me that I tell people what "they [Lavalas] did in this election."

I continued on, a long way, to the downtown campus of the Université Quisqueyea, where I found Mirlande Manigat, wife of Haiti's former president Leslie Manigat, sitting in her office. Manigat, a professor at the university's constitutional law faculty, looked destined to lose her senate race as the candidate for Manigat's RDNP party to Fanmi Lavalas spokesman Yvon Neptune.

"These are difficult times in Haiti," she said. "The many political parties in here reflect the polarization of Haitian society, and one party wins over 90 percent of the vote? Impossible. We are heading for a gloomy time in Haiti."

Manigat, a pleasant, highly educated woman, was part of what was regarded by the majority of poor Haitians—that is, a vast majority of the country—as an opportunistic political class with no real interest in helping them out of their misery; nevertheless, her disappointment seemed genuine.

"My political party doesn't believe in violence or dictatorial force, so we now have no recourse," she said, adding, despite her husband's cooperation with brutal Namphy government thirteen years earlier. She looked down at her desk, and then wistfully out the window of her university office. "I didn't expect this for my country, now."

Later, when I crossed the Champs de Mars, the park in front of the National Palace that for years had been a rubbishy wasteland, I found it had been transformed into an elegant piazza-style meeting place, complete with lamps, a band shell, overflowing greenery and splashing waterfalls. When I would return at night, I found Haitians of all ages studying, debating politics or simply relaxing among its soothing perimeters. The improvement was a noticeable one.

I met Yvon Neptune, the Lavalas party spokesman, at his family home located just off the Champs de Mars. Neptune—who had spent decades living and working as an architect in Long Island and spoke perfect English—greeted me in a suit, despite the hot weather. His neatly-trimmed, graying goatee added to the slight sense of hauteur with which I thought he spoke. We sat around a table inside the house where the room was cool and quiet, away from the noise of the street. Cabinets were arranged around the room, lined with books in several languages. A bird chattered away from somewhere in the garden out back.

"You must be very pleased with the outcome of the election," I said.

"The Haitian people are pleased with the results of the elections; the majority of voters are pleased because the elections have been an opportunity for them to state their position on the situation in Haiti," Neptune replied firmly.

Over the course of an hour, Neptune spoke of the policy of agrarian reform begun under Préval, and also about encouraging the private sector, local and foreign, to invest in Haiti. He alluded to the pending approval of agreements with the IMF and World Bank by the new parliament, and of the necessity of modernizing the administrative infrastructure of Haiti. When I asked him about Lavalas's commitment to democracy, and about the violence preceding the election, Neptune commented that "we continually stated our position on violence in Haiti: denouncing the violence, condemning the violence. We encourage everybody, everybody," he continued, "not to let themselves be intimidated and to come out and vote. And that's exactly what they did."

When I questioned him about the attacks on the opposition headquarters, specifically the arson of Espace de Concertation's offices after Jean Dominique's funeral, Neptune shifted blame back to Evans Paul, and those he characterized as his party "cronies." The fire, he implied, was probably set by Espace themselves. "That particular organization failed to pay the rent on that building for almost five years."

"It is difficult to accept the value of the opposition, the weight of the opposition," he went on, "because it is practically nonexistent except for a few politicians who would use the airwaves to make accusations. They often commit violent acts or delegate people to commit violent acts, and they go as far as posturing as Fanmi Lavalas partisans. It is very easy for them to do that."

Now that Fanmi Lavalas seemed on its way to achieving dominance in all branches of government, what were their plans for the next few years in Haiti? I asked, as the interview drew to a close.

"With a strong government and parliament, and a strong political program," he said, "we'll spend less time bickering over power, so the majority who represent the people will have enough time to concentrate on their jobs. I think that's what needs to happen. And it is about to happen."

NEPTUNE'S WORDS SEEMED prophetic when, on May 29, CEP spokesman Jean-Gardy Lorcy announced partial results from the May 21 ballot, stating that Fanmi Lavalas had won fourteen of twenty-seven seats in Haiti's senate and sixteen of the eighty-three seats in the Chamber of Deputies. More partial results, this time for the populous West Department in which Port-au-Prince was included, were announced on May 31, and they showed even further gains for Lavalas, including senate victories for Neptune and Dany Toussaint, who scored more votes than any other candidate in the electoral contest. The FL bloc thus rose to outright wins for sixteen out of twenty-nine senate seats, and twenty-three out of eighty-three seats in the lower house, and Toussaint and Neptune joined such figures as the notorious former Army Colonels Fourel Celestin and Medard Joseph in heading to parliament under the FL banner.

When the initial results of the election began to filter out, something curious was quickly apparent. Haitian election officials would eventually report that all nineteen of the contested Senate races had been decided in the first round, with Lavalas victories straight through, thus precluding any need for runoff contests. With high-profile non-Lavalas candidates such as Mirlande Manigat in the running, it seemed highly unlikely that every single Lavalas senatorial candidate would have received the over 50 percent of the vote needed to avoid a second round. The senatorial results also stood in marked contrast to the results arrived at for the eighty-three deputy seats being contested, only a third of which were resolved in the first round.

A pair of OAS observers visiting the Haitian electoral offices quickly ascertained the reasons for the stunning sweep. Comparing the percentage of the vote awarded the victorious Senate candidates with the actual number of votes cast, the OAS observers realized that a large number of votes were simply not being counted. Rather than count all the votes cast for the candidates in total in any one race, the Haitian electoral council had instead only counted the votes of the top four contenders, thus ignoring the votes cast for all other candidates and awarding the Lavalas candidates with a false 50 percent plus of the vote—

that is, artificially inflating their percentages to push them over the threshold of victory.

"They could have gotten a respectable 70 or 80 percent of parliament and that might have pleased the U.S. Senate, but they wanted it all and they went for it," said one member of the OAS observers' team, who had been working in Haiti for six years at the time of the elections.

The OAS, in the person of its chief of mission Orlando Marville, was not inclined to roll over, however, and the same day as the West Department results were announced, Marville sent a letter to CEP president Leon Manus. Calling Manus's attention to the fact that "a review of the results announced by the CEP and in particular the percentages stated for the leading Senate candidates shows a serious error affecting the number of parliamentary races won in the first round," Marville reminded the body that Haiti's electoral law "clearly establishes in Articles 53 and 64 that to be elected to parliament in the first round you have to get an absolute majority of the total valid votes."[4] He went on:

> The numbers distributed by the electoral-operations office indicate that it did not follow the procedures established in these articles but that it decided to add up only the votes of a small number of candidates who obtained the most votes. As a result, the operations office got the wrong percentages. Our own analysis indicates that the political party Fanmi Lavalas is leading in all departments but that in many of them there will have to be a runoff election. . . . As you will understand, Mr. President, this is a serious error which if not corrected can place in doubt the validity of the whole electoral process. . . . Confident that the CEP will quickly correct this situation in strict conformity with the provisions of the electoral law I present my compliments.

I found Richard Morse—the eccentric owner of the capital's storied Hotel Oloffson and the driving force between the vodou-rock band Ram—in a gloomy mood when I stopped by the hotel one afternoon. I walked up the hotel's long driveway, where the imposing white building—one of the finest examples of gingerbread architecture in the Caribbean—disappeared into a hillside clinging deep-green with vines and trees. A swimming pool, lit at night so that one could see the tropical bats drinking out of it in great relief—was set to one side. The hotel's terrace was a long clapboard affair with white wicker chairs and tables and views toward downtown and the bay, but it was empty today.

"They're trying to set up a system where there's no opposition and they're willing to use any means necessary to do that," Morse said as we went to sit down in the lobby, referring to the violence that had roiled the electoral season. "Freedom of speech is winding down. The precedent has been set again that if you want to be involved in politics in this country, you've got to get your gun together. Nothing's changed, the name's have changed but not the modus operandi."

Morse, who was the son of the eminent Haitian singer Emerante de Pradines and an American university professor, had lived in Haiti since 1985, when he took out a lease on the Oloffsonn after graduating from Princeton and tiring of playing in punk rock bands on New York's Lower East Side. He had seen fifteen years worth of political machinations in Haiti, and during Aristide's exile in the United States, his band, which played songs viewed as supportive of the deposed president, had been menaced and his hotel frequently subject to threatening visits from the military. After Aristide's return, he had watched as the president gradually revealed an ever more ruthless side, and he had famously evicted Port-au-Prince Mayor Manno Charlemagne from a room at the Oloffson, where the latter had camped out for months with gun-toting heavies, refusing ever to pay a bill. Shortly after that, Ram's Carnival float was sabotaged during Port-au-Prince's celebrations, causing an accident in which several died.

"I came down here in 1985 to research voodoo rhythms," said Morse, a tall man with his hair braided into a pony tail, smoking a cigarette as we sat in the lobby of the hotel, while fans circled slowly through the torpor overhead. "I took over the hotel in 1987, formed a band in 1990 and stopped counting governments in 1996. And now the OAS is saying, 'There were some discrepancies, but everything's okay.' Well everything's not okay. They're killing people. They're killing people and people are going into hiding. And that's not okay."

He believed that Lavalas had essentially terrorized the opposition into hiding until two weeks before the elections and then, with the statement from Aristide calling for peaceful elections, the violence miraculously ceased and the opposition was told to field their candidates in what was to be a competitive election.

"Yeah, right, everything's fine, now go vote," said Morse cynically.

As I left him that day to walk back to my apartment, Morse said simply, "You can get killed here for saying the shit I just said."

Around this same time, Nina Clara Schnall, an American anthropology student living in Haiti, introduced me to a young Haitian who would become a good friend. I say "young," but in fact he was a few years older than I was at the time, just getting ready to exit his late twenties. We walked into a warren of alleys off Rue Oswald Durand—named for one of Haiti's most beloved poets—near the national stadium and sat in a common courtyard (*lakou* in Kreyol), talking and drinking with a young man with short dreadlocks and a fluid command of street-level American English. His name was Herby Metellus, and as we spoke, he showed me beautiful necklaces, made out of seashells and beads and leather, which he had fashioned to sell on the streets of Port-au-Prince. He kept dozens of pigeons in a complex tin cage system that stretched above the *lakou*, and a sleeping dog was tied gently to a post near an outhouse. Over the scene, Herby had scrawled a message in English on a white chalk on a board, a paraphrase of Proverbs 12:10. "A good man takes care of his animals, but wicked men are cruel to theirs," it read. As we spoke, a little girl with braids and ribbons in her hair danced and sang along to disco music playing from a ghetto blaster, and she braided and rebraided my companion's hair.

Taking a taxi out to the Aristide Foundation for Democracy in the naive hope that the man himself might let me interview him, I found myself cooling my heels in the waiting room for some time before walking back out to the dust-blasted midday street. About to hail a cab or a camionette, I was instead offered a lift by an evangelical minister who spoke a lilting, musical English he had learned in Brooklyn as he drove me the whole way back to the Champs de Mars and then refused to take payment for his troubles.

"*Nap toujou renmen w Titid*" was scrawled on a wall as we drove: "We will always Love you Aristide."

ON JUNE 11, the vote was finally held in the Grand Anse department, and saw long lines of those wishing to participate but no serious violence. Nevertheless, with cryptic utterances from the Préval government, Fanmi Lavalas representatives, and the CEP, a serious dispute appeared to have broken out regarding the certifying of the final election results. On June 15, speaking from New York, United Nations Secretary General Kofi Annan said that the body stood firmly behind the OAS observers and that he was "troubled by continuing irregularities in the way the votes for Senate candidates were being calculated." The next day, Lavalas partisans set up barricades of burning tires across Port-au-Prince and attacked passing cars with rocks and bottles, threatening more violence if the CEP didn't publish the final electoral results by 2 P.M.

AT FIRST, CEP PRESIDENT Leon Manus was resistant to the OAS concerns, and even sent off a contentious letter to OAS head Orlando Marville for interfering.

"My impression was that when Manus was presented with what had gone wrong by the OAS he had this onslaught of Haitian pride, thinking people were trying to push him around, humiliate him, show him that the Haitians had gotten it wrong," said one member of the OAS team who had observed the elections, by way of explaining Manus's initial recalcitrance in the face of criticism.

But eventually, the lawyerly side of Manus's personality came to the fore, and he asked for a recount of the electoral results, at which point it was concluded that only five, not sixteen, of the senatorial candidates for Fanmi Lavalas had secured a sufficient number of votes to avoid a runoff election. After Manus announced these findings, in an echo of the summons received by Robert Manuel the previous year, he was summoned to the National Palace by René Préval. Entering Préval's office, he found the president looking stressed and somewhat emotional. Préval explained to Manus the importance of certifying the election results, and Manus refused, saying that the method that was first used to tabulate the votes simply wasn't correct. Préval continued to plead with him. Manus said, in good conscience, he could not certify the votes. Then Préval's phone rang. Préval spoke briefly and deferentially to the caller, before handing the phone to Manus.

"Listen, this has gone on long enough, you better certify the electoral results soon." Manus immediately recognized Aristide's voice on the other end of the line. "Bad things could happen if this continues, the situation could get out of control. . . ."

And so it was that, in the middle of the protests that paralyzed the capital on June 16, Manus entered the U.S. Embassy on Boulevard Harry Truman, later that day to cross the border into the Dominican Republic, eventually arriving in the United States. When he arrived in exile, he released a letter that sent reverberations throughout Haiti's political elite. He wrote:

> May 21 was a day that gave great reason for satisfaction both to the CEP and the country. Contrary to forecasts, [the elections] were calm and in spite of certain delays and logistical problems . . . the most intractable national as well as foreign critics had to recognize that the day and the vote of May 21 were a success. Glory and Honor to the Haitian people!
>
> However, as of the following day, protests, both by those who shouted for victory and those who charged fraud, built and placed the CEP in the crossfire. From both sides, the pressure was increasingly intense. As often in this kind of situation, the truth lay somewhere in the middle. But inflamed passions were placing the CEP on one camp of the other, whereas its responsibility was to respect to the letter the provisions of electoral law concerning all operations, including the tabulation of votes, the management of disputes and the proclamation of a final result.
>
> The publication of certain partial results was exploited by all and sundry to throw discredit upon the CEP. Even the OAS electoral mission considered it necessary to issue a warning which was interpreted in various ways. . . . [But] the final results for the candidates for senator of the republic saw only five senators elected in the first round. The majority of those which placed first in the partial calculations would have to go on to a second round. That was the final calculation of the votes and tabulation of results according to the provisions of the electoral law.
>
> As soon as I made my decision available to the Executive, the pressure increased to convert the partial results into final results. This would be with absolute contempt or all considerations of justice and

respect to the electoral law. . . . The highest levels of government sent me unambiguous messages of the consequences of any refusal on my part to refuse to certify the final results. Moreover, groups of individuals claiming allegiance to an influential political party began to carry out their threats to immerse the capital and provincial towns in fire and blood.

Addressing an ultimatum to me to immediately proclaim results that I regarded as illegitimate and incorrect, I felt incapable of such an act of treason against my country at this watershed in its history. I understood that conflict between my legal and constitutional position and the intransigence of the government and the orchestrated fury of so-called "popular" organizations became inevitable. Such a situation left me no choice but to temporarily leave the country to avoid the worst and to lower the tension.

I continue to believe in a democracy that puts an end to dictatorship and brings to man freedom, justice, the spirit of unity and dialogue, greater comfort and development. I know that vindictive men . . . do not accept that on the ground of Haiti men of integrity are able to live with dignity. They do everything in their power to sully the honor of an honest people. Citizens of my country, I continue to believe in the redemption of our fatherland, because despite everything, the vicissitudes of his existence, no people can live indefinitely in ignorance, division, insecurity, misery and injustice.

After Manus's flight, the electoral results that Manus refused to sign off on were announced as official. In a press release on July 7, the OAS Electoral Observation Mission concluded that "the final results for the Senate elections as proclaimed by the Provisional Electoral Council (CEP) are incorrect, and the mission cannot consider them accurate or fair. . . . The Mission believes that the methodology used by the Provisional Electoral Council to calculate percentages for the Senate races violates both the constitution of Haiti and its Electoral Law. Both state clearly that in order to be elected in the first round, a candidate for the Senate must obtain an absolute majority of all valid votes."[5]

The mission announced that it was refusing to observe any second round of elections. The second round took place on July 9, with voters called upon to cast their ballots for forty-four seats of the eighty-three-member Chamber of Deputies. After the debacle of May, most refrained.

CONCURRENTLY WITH the election upheaval, the investigation into the murder of Jean Dominique was leading to some interesting places. Michele Montas had defiantly reopened Radio Haiti-Inter three weeks after her husband's murder, addressing "Bonjour, Jean" to the listeners and, in a strong and determined voice, told them that in fact Jean had never been killed, and that he had been rendered invisible to his assassins by a magic spell that protected him. "Jean Léopold Dominique, free man, citizen of this torn land, is alive. Good morning, Jean."

Shortly after the killings, the suspected triggerman in the shootings, a young thug named Jamely Millien, known as Ti Lou, was arrested along with his brother, Jean Daniel Jeudi, known as Gime, who was thought to be the second gunmen who covered Ti Lou during the shooting. Both brothers were members of the capital's notorious Route Neuf gang, a theft and murder-for-hire racket based out of Cité Soleil that took its name from the potholed road that ran through the district. They were known to associate with Ronald Camille, a gang leader and former member of Aristide's security detail, who along with his brother Franco controlled various criminal enterprises in the capital's La Saline slum, including extorting protection money from the impoverished merchants in the district's congested market. Camille's reputation as a killer in his home neighborhood was so fierce that he had earned the nickname Ronald Cadavre (Cadaver), and his name had frequently come up as having been the potential triggerman in the 1999 murder of OPL senator Yvon Toussaint, though he was never formally charged. A young man named Philippe Markington, an employee of the capital's port (where both Ronald Camille and René Civil worked), as well as a member of the Aristide Foundation for Democracy who sometimes worked as an informant for the U.S. Embassy, presented himself to those investigating Dominique's murder a few days after the crime, claiming to have witnessed everything. But his descriptions were so detailed, including descriptions of the two getaway cars and the license number of the white Cherokee, that police soon concluded that he had in fact taken part in the killing. A policeman named Ralph Léger was arrested in possession of the white Cherokee present at the crime scene soon thereafter.

While looking into the origin of the getaway cars, police arrested a small-time hood named Jean-Wilner Lalanne, a thirty-two-year-old former FADH soldier and an employee of a crime syndicate that fenced stolen cars around the capital; he was later released, however. On June 15, police rearrested him, as suspicion had grown that he was somehow the link between the intellectual authors of Dominique's murder and the actual killers. During the arrest, Lalanne was shot and wounded in the buttocks and thigh, and left to lie in the general hospital bed for thirteen days without treatment. Lalanne told several visitors that he feared he would be killed.

Then the investigation took an odd turn. On June 28, Lalanne was transferred from his fetid hospital bed to Saint-Francois de Sales hospital where he was operated on by, curiously, an orthopedic surgeon, Dr. Alix Charles, who was assisted by two anesthetists, Marie Yves-Rose Chrisostome and Gina Georges. Lalanne's lawyer, Ephésien Joassaint, had recommended Dr. Charles to the prisoner. Joassaint himself had been recommended to Lalanne by none other than Jean-Claude Nord, the lawyer for Dany Toussaint who had threatened Jean Dominique's life on the February radio broadcast from New York. Dr. Charles himself knew both Toussaint and his right-hand man, Richard "Cha Cha" Salomon. During the procedure, Lalanne died—killed, Charles said, by a pulmonary embolism. Lalanne's death certificate stated that he had died of a heart attack.

The reaction of those monitoring the case was immediate and swift, and they demanded that an autopsy be performed on such an important link in the investigation who had so conveniently died. When officials sought Lalanne's body in the hospital morgue to perform an autopsy, it was discovered that the body had disappeared.

The investigating judge in the case, Jean Sénat Fleury, had been provided with substantial resources and security by the Préval government, but he began receiving serious death threats telephoned to him almost daily as soon as he took up the case after the murder. When he finally succeeded in summoning Dany Toussaint to the Palais de Justice for questioning in the case on July 26, Toussaint arrived with a group of chimere in tow, who protested wildly outside of the building, further rattling Sénat Fleury. As the summer wore on, it became obvious that Sénat Fleury had become spooked enough to tread very carefully.

THOUGH THE EXPLOSIVE behavior of some groups linked to Fanmi Lavalas at the time of the May elections led many foreign observers to assume that all Haitian popular movements were inherently violent, community organizations have always played a more important role in Haitian civic and political life than they have in many nearby countries. In a country where there is so little, and where the government often cannot be looked upon to provide any help whatsoever, the power of collective bargaining among the powerless to make their voices louder and to make those in a position to listen to their concerns and perhaps change something has always been a key facet of Haitian life. While it sometimes manifests itself in spectacular ways—bouts of tire-burning at major intersections, for instance—more often than not it is the quiet, steady organizing of neighbors in urban communities such as Port-au-Prince's Delmas and Carrefour districts, and rural outposts such as L'Estere in the Artibonite and in the Plateau Central, where people try to collectively come up with solutions to the myriad of potentially catastrophic problems that face Haitians on a daily basis and, somehow, to productively deal with the extremely difficult and stark existence life has handed them. Part of what many foreign journalists found so hard to understand was that the rampaging chimeres who had become more and more visible during the Préval administration were, in the words of the painter Etzer Pierre, "a political tool," not a political force, whereas the other groups—peasant collectives, Christian community groups, labor and student organizations—were political forces, whose support couldn't easily be bought but whose ability to squeeze whatever assistance they could out of the government had far more practical effects for those living in their communities in the long run.

WE WERE SITTING in an open-air, borrowed pavilion in a dusty, crowded section of upper Delmas, just before the thoroughfare begins its climb into the chaos of the Petionville market and then breaks off into the multitude of narrow streets that criss-cross Petionville's finer restaurants and shaded gardens. The community organization, the Organisation de la Providence Unie pour le Développement Socio-Economique de Pétionville or SOPUDEP, had called the meeting to discuss postelection strategy, yet seemed both surprised and pleased to have a journalist in their midst. Foreign journalists, or at least the ones who cover Haiti, don't often like to spend time in popular neighborhoods. The Lavalas and Convergence spokesman were all available in their refined offices not so far away from the creature comforts of the salubrious Hotel Montana, with its steady supply of electricity and its Wednesday night sushi served on the terrace overlooking the bay and Haiti's skeletal Titanyen mountain range. Even lower-class neighborhoods that don't fall into the extreme depths of despair-inducing poverty that Cité Soleil and La Saline sink toward are still chaotic, noisy affairs, full of lanes with jackhammered edges on concrete able to knock out the surest alignment in an SUV and are populated by the vast majority of Haitians who don't speak English, don't have easy answers to explain the multitude of problems in their day to day lives and don't, it must be said, have experience with any group of international reporters who have ever attempted to fit their opinions into a dialogue about where Haiti should go. I sat and looked out on over a hundred pairs of eyes regarding me curiously, though not with hostility. There were men and women, young and old, and this represented the true power of the OPs and the crux of Aristide's support, far away from the violent histrionics of those who had come one day to rattle Radio Haiti-Inter's gate so close by. SOPUDEP's secretary general, an impassioned young man in his late twenties named Dol Joseph Bozer, stated the everyone present would give journalists, who contain so much power to shape perceptions of Haiti, "interviews in all frankness and with all our soul, even though it puts our lives at risk." As if to punctuate his words, the sounds of evangelical hymns from a nearby church drifted across the cement lot. It was decided that, in order to facilitate an easier conversation, we would go to a local home to chat with a few SOPUDEP representatives. As I walked there, someone on the road said they wanted to talk to me.

"I've got something that I want to tell the international press," the muscular man, named Jean, said in the middle of the road, the night darkening and children running through the dusty lanes calling to one another. "Why are all these countries giving so much attention to these little political groups that don't have any support? We had them already. They were in Parliament. They didn't do their work. We threw them out and we don't need them back. I don't want a job from Aristide. I want all Haitians to have the freedom to put their heads together to solve their problems."

We entered the house where we were to meet. The home was being rented by an odd sort, a heavy-drinking American filmmaker who had spent years in Central America during the 1980s and had now washed up on the shores of Haiti, aligning himself with the Lavalas movement and working at TNH, the state television company. The apartment abutted another one owned by, of all people, the right-wing lawyer Reynold Georges. The foreigner and Georges feuded violently over everything imaginable, as Georges plotted the demise of the Aristide government and the American filmmaker opened his home to the government's partisans every night.

In the sparsely furnished room, we sat in a semicircle on folding chairs. A young woman handed me a handwritten list detailing the names and positions in the organization of those present: secretary general, representative for women's issues, representative for cultural issues, and so on. She said that the only reason to be anonymous would be if they were doing something that should be hidden.

"From 1957 to 1986 this country was being destroyed, and it was being destroyed by the Macoute system, where they would steal and kill," explained Dol Joseph Bozer. "But it is still that Macoute system that is in place today, and they are the ones that are really still in power. They are the ones who have the money and the arms and all the intellectuals behind them."

"The problems of this country are the same problems we've suffered since 1804; we've never really taken our freedom," said another man, Yves Marie Lamé. "The treason against Dessalines is the same treason that's going on today. You go to work from six in the morning until six at night and at the end of the month you still can't find enough to eat. That's the situation of exclusion the Lavalas movement wants to change."

But what about the violence that had been committed across the country in the Lavalas movement's name since its founding in 1997?

"Lies always dominate over the truth in Haiti, and what they're saying about Aristide now couldn't be less true," said Bozer. "He's the one who took us out of the chains that we were in; he's the one who helped us to see when we couldn't see."

"In 1991 Aristide was like a political baby, and he was mistaken about a number of people who were false prophets," said Yves Marie Lamé. "Aristide has always emphasized the importance of OPs, because it's those organizations that bring people together to struggle for a different country, to make a difference for their children. It's not the politicians in power who are going to do anything for the country, it's the people. That is the political base of the new Aristide.

"Aristide is going to have a government of competence. He will give people jobs who have been trained to do them, and if they don't do them, they will be fired," Lamé continued. "Aristide is mature now. He's not going to make the same mistakes twice. He's had time to understand the situation. It's like the difference between cold water and hot water; once you've touched the hot water, you won't go back."

It was hard not be impressed with their sincerity and how articulate they were—these decent, honest people who were working so hard and putting so much faith in the hope that their communities and their country, despite the weight of history, could change and get better. But every instinct within me worried if they were about to be betrayed yet again.

"They say that Lavalas is a bunch of chimeres, that they're not educated," declared Yves Marie Lamé, with air of someone finally being able to get something off his chest that he'd wanted to say for a very long time. "But we're educated. I'm an engineer; this man's an engineer, so is he. You can take anybody on the street who doesn't have anything and pay them to say they're Lavalassian, but it doesn't mean that they represent us. A true Lavalassian is what you do, not what you say. A true Lavalassian is one who is a patriot and trying to do something for their country."

"We don't have money; we almost have nothing," concluded Dol Joseph, leaning close to me on his chair and looking me directly in the eye. "But we just put the money we do have together and the capacity we have to work and think together to make things better in our community. It's the action, what we're doing, that's important, not what we're saying. We are clean and proper people."

The fact of the matter was that, despite the increasing and in some cases overwhelming evidence of Aristide's corrupt and criminal behavior, he still represented the only slender ray of hope that many in Haiti's poor majority saw in their daily epic and heart-rending struggles to lift themselves out of *la misere*. Throughout the election season of 2000, there were thousands of groups like SOPUDEP throughout Haiti, quietly organizing for Aristide's reelection away from the street theater and bravado of TKL and JPP; they represented the true base of Aristide's support, and they would not be convinced that Aristide was not their champion. This is something that Aristide's political opponents, both domestically in Haiti and abroad, failed to reckon with, as it was the heavy anchor that held the ship of his Fanmi Lavalas political machine, increasingly awash in guns, drugs and murderous treachery, anchored to the popular base that had supported his first election in 1990. And no amount of campaign rhetoric against him and no amount of withheld foreign aid would make them believe otherwise. They had made an emotional bond with Aristide—during the Saint Jean Bosco years, during the first election, during the coup d'état and the difficult years of his return— and it would not be severed except by his own hand.

ON AUGUST 17, an OAS mission led by OAS Secretary General (and former Colombian president) Cesar Gaviria arrived in Haiti. After two days spent talking to Lavalas, Convergence and civil society representatives, the delegation left, with Gaviria telling reporters, "We're concerned that maybe the presidential elections may have the same problems that we had with the May election, and in general we're worried about the way the whole democratic process is going." An OAS human rights mission that visited the country the same week concluded that the climate of political intimidation had increased markedly in the country since the beginning of the spring electoral season.

After a summer that saw the Convergence repeatedly demanding new elections and Lavalas refusing to back down, Haiti's new parliament, made up of the senators accorded victory under the flawed vote count, was convened on August 28. Lavalas controlled eighteen of nineteen contested seats in the Senate, and seventy-two out of eighty-two seats in the Chamber of Deputies. Yvon Neptune, the Lavalas party spokesman, was appointed Senate president. As had begun after disputed parliamentary elections in 1997, a suspension of international aid to the country would continue, shutting Haiti off from some $522 million in Inter-American Development Bank loans and grants, some $145.9 million of which was destined for improvements in basic human services such as HIV/AIDS prevention, potable water and road rehabilitation.

I spoke to Micha Gaillard, the defeated KONAKOM mayoral candidate for Port-au-Prince whose home had been attacked by Lavalas partisans on the day of Jean Dominique's funeral.

His house was airy, but somewhat faded in its charm, and located on a small street off the capital's busy Avenue John Brown—not at all where the Haitian elite live. His French wife made us coffee as his two young sons practiced football in the yard. His father, the historian Roger Gaillard, who had done so much to chronicle Haiti's history of dictatorship and occupation, had passed away recently. Gaillard seemed adamant in his conviction that the opposition would not back down.

"After May, the political class and the civil class decided that the conditions did not exist for national elections, and we will never, ever accept the results of these two elections," he said. "The struggle is not the struggle against Aristide and Lavalas. It is a struggle against the two-century tradition of electoral coup d'états."

ON AUGUST 22, in a small step forward against Haiti's usual impunity, proceedings began in the trials of Port-au-Prince police chief Jean Coles Rameau and five others accused in the massacre that occurred in Carrefour Feuilles on May 28, 1999 and resulted in eleven deaths. Several dozen protestors outside of the courthouse chanted for justice and held up photos, not of the accused men and their victims, curiously, but of former Haitian army officers, an act whose significance would not be clear until some time later. Two officers were eventually acquitted, but four others, including Commissioner Rameau, received the minimum sentences of three years each. Nothing to sing about, but more than they would have gotten a decade earlier. But Haiti's search for justice was far from over.

ON THE AFTERNOON OF SEPTEMBER 6, nine men dressed in PNH uniforms and one more in civilian clothes entered the Port-au-Prince offices of the Fondasyon Kole Zepól, ("Shoulder-to-Shoulder Foundation") in an alley off Avenue Jean Paul II in downtown Port-au-Prince. The organization, always referred to by its abbreviation, Fonkoze, was essentially the sole bank in Haiti that would offer its services to the poor, usually impoverished *ti machanns* and peasants, who comprised the majority of its eleven thousand account holders. Only days earlier, the bank had announced that it was initiating "Ayiti Direk Direk," a money transfer service by which people could send any amount of money to Haiti from the United States for a flat fee of $10, far below the 10 percent assessed by most other agencies and Haitian banks, and a boon for struggling Haitians with relatives in the United States. This day, as the men entered, they identified themselves as police officers and said they were there to check on the firearms registration of Fonkoze's security guards, but, once inside, they drew their weapons on the staff and proceeded to empty the bank's safe of its contents. As they left the bank, they asked by name for Amos Jeannot, Fonkoze's trusted money courier, who was responsible for transporting deposits and withdrawals from the bank's accounts around the city, and shoved him roughly into the Honda jeep they were riding in and sped off. For three tense weeks, the staff waited and worried about Jeannot's fate, with only an anonymous call phoned in ordering them to cease operations if they ever wanted to see Jeannot alive again. Their wait ended when Jeannot's body was found in the morgue of Port-au-Prince's General Hospital three weeks later, bearing the signs of horrific torture. He left a wife and three-year-old son.

Naturally, rumors swirled about who could have been responsible for the killing, from Fonkoze's competitors among Haiti's banking sector to members of Haiti's former military. All agreed, given the coordination and confidence with which the assailants operated on the day of the robbery, that it was a sophisticated operation, and that whoever its intellectual authors were, they had obviously had some money behind them.

Fonkoze had been created in 1994 in the midst of the junta that ousted Aristide by the soon-to-be-slain liberation theologian priest Jean-Marie Vincent and another Holy Ghost priest, Father Joseph Philippe. It was recognized as a foundation by the Haitian government in October 1995 and opened its first savings accounts soon thereafter. A gem of Haiti's talent for collective endeavor, anyone could open a Fonkoze savings account, but to become a member of the bank and get access to credit, one had to be part of an organization—which usually meant a group of five or more *ti machanns* pooling their money, as each person vouched for the other and if one couldn't pay their share one month, the others agreed to cover them. After passing through a couple of cycles of on-time payment, the group would pass onto another level of membership where they could get business loans and more targeted technical assistance. It was the first national microcredit institution in Haiti, and soon had offices in all nine departments.

I spoke with Fonkoze's executive director, an American woman named Anne Hastings, a few months after the murder, in her office on the top floor of the Fonkoze bureau situated incongruously at the back of an alley off of Avenue Jean Paul II in downtown Port-au-Prince. The organization was preparing to move to more spacious and secure quarters just across the street, and workmen and movers came in and out, hauling tools and boxes of supplies.

Hastings had been feeling "burned out" after having worked as a management consultant for fifteen years in the Washington, DC area, and she was thinking of joining the Peace Corps when she first came to Haiti in 1996.

"I met Father Philippe and I realized after twenty minutes talking to this guy that he had more vision than all of my clients put together and absolutely no resources to achieve that vision," she said, smiling, remembering that first trip. So Hastings had moved down to Haiti to help Philippe oversee the operation. With Hastings's business skills at work, Fonkoze brought in microcredit experts from around the world, and they created a Fonkoze USA entity in order to get pro-bono legal services and put out a prospectus. The organization was being financed mostly through private individuals and foundations in the United States that would loan Fonkoze money and agree to be paid back with a very small amount of interest. By the time Hastings and I spoke, Fonkoze's microcredit line had over eleven thousand active borrowers; its new literacy and business skills course had some eight thousand graduates, and the bank had branches as far afield as Port-de-Paix in the north, Jeremie in the west and the massive, little-visited island of La Gonave in the Bay of Port-au-Prince.

More impressively, the bank had developed a literacy and business skills program, *Jwe korlit la* (Game to Reinforce the Struggle), which Father Philippe had based on the methods of Paulo Freire, the Brazilian liberation theology priest and author of the classic treatise *Pedagogy of the Oppressed*. The game set forth letters, words, numbers and calculation problems all in kreyol, dealing with such themes as agriculture and democratic movements, and put out books explaining to *ti machanns* how to calculate assets (such as benches to sit on while selling, knives and burlap sacks) and expenses (transportation, food for animals and the like) that would help them devise business plans and increase their take-home money.

"It was one thing to have a democratic government, but people looked around and saw that the economy was controlled by the same people, the people who controlled the banks. So it was at that point they decided they would need a bank that the poor could call their own."

The murder of Jeannot had obviously shaken Hastings terribly; he had been her right-hand man. But her determination to carry on, along with that of the Fonkoze staff, was heartening.

Jeannot's death was to remain shrouded in mystery. After what the Fonkoze staff characterized as a "very professional" investigation by the PNH that appeared to successfully identify seven of the ten assailants, and the issuing of several arrest warrants, no one was ever charged. When the presidency changed hands the next year, the ongoing investigation into the murder was stopped. Most of the men who robbed the bank that day were later said to have been killed on the streets of Port-au-Prince. The crime remains unsolved.

IN REMARKS TO THE OAS Permanent Council in Washington, DC on September 5, Ambassador Luis Lauredo, the permanent representative of the United States to the OAS, stated that, "We have reached a crossroads. The elation experienced on May 21, when millions of Haitians demonstrated their trust in the ballot box and democratic elections, has turned sour as a result of the unwillingness of the Haitian authorities to address the serious irregularities and deficiencies arising in the elections' aftermath.

"Haiti's leaders have chosen to proceed unilaterally down the wrong path," Lauredo continued. "The decision to install a Parliament based on a flawed methodology for determining Senate winners and to prepare for the November 26 presidential elections with a compromised Provisional Election Council, indicates an unwillingness to cooperate with the international community regarding the most serious challenges facing democracy in Haiti. . . . Absent new concrete steps to end the impasse, the United States will not be able to conduct 'business as usual' with Haiti. Instead, we will pursue a policy that distinguishes between helping the people of Haiti and assisting the Government of Haiti. . . . Therefore, in the absence of meaningful change, the United States will not support the presidential and legislative elections of November 26, financially or through observation missions."

In other words, no money and no observers to smooth Aristide's return to power.

WHILE ARISTIDE'S PORT-AU-PRINCE-BASED opposition, fearing the huge number of chimere in the capital, were content to launch their protests over the airwaves, Aristide's opponents among the peasantry, long used to living in state of siege from the successive governments and their surrogates in the military and possessing a proud tradition of independent political thought, had no such reservations. On September 18, Chavannes Jean-Baptiste, the MPP peasant union leader who had broken with Préval after the disputed 1997 elections, lead an estimated eight thousand MPP and other peasant leaders on a march from the group's homebase in the village of Papay to the nearby Plateau Central town of Hinche to protest what Jean-Baptiste charged was the "return of the *chef de section* system" and the deteriorating security and political situation in the country. At several points, shots were heard on the periphery of the march, but the activists held their ground, at times lying on their stomachs in the dirt, and they succeeded, in their number, in traversing the small country road into the departmental capital. Despite Chavannes's often acerbic comments about the relative worth of the Democratic Convergence, one of their number, OPL's Paul Denis, participated in the march.

The situation in the Plateau Central had deteriorated rapidly after the May election with the installation of Dongo Joseph—a Lavalas member and former petty criminal from the Artibonite Valley town of Saint Michel de l'Attalaye—as the mayor of Hinche, the region's main economic and transport hub. Widely viewed among locals as an outsider, Joseph set about attempting to break the peasant movement, interrupting meetings with armed men, harassing MPP members on their way to and from functions, and spreading malicious gossip about Jean-Baptiste and his two brothers. The night before, the MPP office in Hinche had been set aflame by unknown arsonists, though it caused only minor damage.

"We do not now and we will never recognize the authority of those people elected May 21," Jean-Baptiste said as he addressed the throng as they gathered in Hinche's main square. "And we will never participate in fake elections."

THE RACE FOR HAITI'S PRESIDENCY was announced to be underway by new CEP president Ernst Mirville (replacing the exiled Leon Manus) on September 20. With all of the major opposition parties boycotting the vote, though, and the only individuals truly capable of challenging Aristide at the ballot box (Jean Dominique, Chavannes Jean-Baptiste, Préval himself) out of the running, it didn't look like it was going to be much of a horse race. Eschewing the impartiality called for in a CEP by Article 194 in Haiti's 1987 constitution, Mirville dismissed the Convergence as a "puppet opposition." Facing a handful of unknown businessmen and religious leaders, Aristide's reelection seemed assured.

Word spread quickly around the capital that Aristide was likely to register his candidacy for the presidency at the CEP headquarters on Delmas on October 2. From early in the morning, government TELECO trucks and Service Plus busses had been ferrying Aristide supporters to the site, until several hundred jammed the street in front of it. Among them was Ronald Camille, the gang leader and habitué of Tabarre, whose name had been mentioned as a possible link between the killers of Jean Dominique and what, if any, connection might exist between them and Aristide. On the morning of October 2, Camille was strutting in front of the CEP headquarters, visibly drunk and brandishing a gun. At one point, when his men engaged in a shoving match with others in the crowd that seemed likely to degenerate into something more serious, Delmas Police

Chief Jacky Nau, who was on the scene, moved in and told Camille to surrender his weapon. At this point, Camille's gunmen, some of whom were also intoxicated, began shoving and pushing Nau. At one point, a tire was thrown around the police chief's shoulders in a clear intimation of the grisly, incendiary *pere lebrun*. When a shaken Nau was finally extricated from the crowd by his bodyguards, Camille partisans used rocks to shatter the windows of their car as they drove away.

Aristide didn't register his candidacy on the Delmas Road that day, but when he did, on October 9, he was greeted by a crowd of several thousand chanting supporters; for posterity, he brought his wife Mildred and Yvon Neptune along with him.

At this point, the fact that Aristide—in collusion with the Aristide Foundation for Democracy and front groups like TKL and JPP—was arming and patronizing violent gangs was apparent to all but the most deluded of his foreign supporters, and made many who had struggled so hard for the Lavalas movement over the years wonder exactly where it was heading.

"Personally, I realized in 2000, maybe three or four months after Jean's assassination that Aristide was consciously constituting armed gangs," said Michele Montas. "And I remember saying so in the microphone and warning him that it would lead to a destruction of the state."

ON OCTOBER 14, gunmen on motorcycles fired on the car carrying Lavalas Senator Lans Clones, but missed him and his bodyguards. A day later, René Civil went on the radio claiming that a JPP meeting had also been fired upon. Several days later, TNH ran a curious editorial that darkly intimated that a group of Haitian policeman and former soldiers "who had studied abroad" were planning a coup d'etat after an October 8 meeting "with a foreign embassy official." The editorial particularly noted "a police chief transferred to the provinces" was maintaining both an expensive hotel room and a private residence.

Despite the lack of named participants, it wasn't hard for Haitians to figure out who the government was referring to. The "Ecuadorians," as a group of police officers who had received training in Ecuador during the Cédras years were called, included former Delmas Police Chief Guy Philippe, now transferred and serving as police chief in Cap Haitien and living at the Mont Joli hotel, the city's fanciest. Also rumored to be in collusion were Philippe's replacement at the Delmas commissariat, Jean-Jacques "Jacky" Nau (whom Ronald Camille had attempted to "necklace" days earlier) and Police Chief Gilbert Dragon of Croix de Bouquets. It was said that Prime Minister Alexis had been apprised of the impending coup by a visit from Don Steinberg, an aid to U.S. National Security Advisor Anthony Lake, who was temporarily stationed in Port-au-Prince.

Summoned before PNH Director Pierre Denizé to explain themselves, the police chiefs gave contradictory, prevaricating responses as to their activities before fleeing across the border to the Dominican town of Dajabon on the night of October 17. Arrested by the Dominican military, the six were taken to the capital Santo Domingo. They were later released, and granted asylum in the Dominican Republic.

AMIDST ALL THIS PLOTTING, Jean Sénat Fleury, the investigating judge in the Jean Dominique murder investigation, resigned, apparently having had his fill of daily telephoned death threats. He was replaced by a thirty-six-year-old, Paris-educated barrister named Claudy Gassant, who had gained a reputation for honesty and tenacity among those who knew him. In one of his first moves in his new position, he summoned both Radio Vision 2000 owner Léopold Berlanger, whom Dominique had lambasted in his last editorial, and Dany Toussaint, now a Lavalas senator, to appear before him for questioning in the investigation. Berlanger appeared, but Toussaint refused. Determined to draw Toussaint out, Gassant set about petitioning the Senate to, if not lift that parliamentary immunity that all Haitian senators enjoyed, then to at least direct him to appear before the judge investigating the nation's most notorious murder. Gassant saw much work to be done, which he imagined would take him into the new year.

EVEN AS THE Jean Dominique investigation was being stonewalled, on November 9, Haiti reached a major milestone in its legal history that, if properly nurtured, could have proved the building block for an aggressive and effective judiciary; but instead it registered as a spark in the darkness of what would continue to be a politicized, corrupt and incompetent judicial night. After a six-week trial by jury in Gonaives, a verdict was rendered on those accused of being responsible for the April 1994 attack on the city's Raboteau slum. Following the testimony of more than thirty witnesses, including a visibly intoxicated Amiot Metayer (the Aristide militant whose presence in the slum had served for the impetus for the raid) sixteen defendants, including ex-FADH and FRAPH members, were convicted. Captain Castera Cenafils, the FADH commander in Gonaives at time of assault, and Jean Tatoune, the street activist who had played a key role in the protests in Gonaives in 1986 that lead to the ousting of Jean-Claude Duvalier and who later became a member of FRAPH, were both sentenced to life in prison, along with ten others. Four others received lesser sentences and six were acquitted. Thirty-seven others, including Raoul Cédras, Toto Constant, Michel Francois, Philippe Biamby and Louis Jodel Chamblain, were tried in absentia and sentenced to life in prison.

The trial was conducted with extensive logistic and legal support from the Bureau des Avocats Internationaux (BAI), a body consisting of mostly American attorneys led by the gifted lawyer Brian Concannon and funded through the

Miami office of Haitian government counsel Ira Kurzban. Additionally, the Préval government had established a special office to help with the logistics of the complicated case, and also with organizing assistance, both medical and economic, to those going through the long process of preparing for the trial. The Ministry of Justice also formed a special police squad that was charged with locating and arresting many of the suspects in the case. Broadcast live on national television, Haitians could watch the testimony of, among others, CARICOM Ambassador Colin Granderson, the American forensic anthropologist Dr. Karen Burns and two Argentine military officers who outlined military legal responsibility and chain of command issues regarding the attack.

The trial was especially instructive in how it demonstrated, when the government was committed to doing so, even highly politicized, dangerous legal proceedings—supported from a sitting administration and backed up with the help of concerned parties both in Haiti and abroad—could be effective in bringing those guilty of high crimes to justice. The Raboteau Trial, as it became known, provided an impressive new yardstick by which to measure the willingness of the powers that be in Haiti to end the country's long tradition of impunity and lack of transparency. As much as he would have bequeathed a new president in Haiti anything, René Préval, along with his Justice Minister Camille LeBlanc, would be leaving them a muscular example that showed how those who spoke with guns could be made to answer for their crimes. For relatives and friends of Jean Dominique, it was seen as a heartening development.

"For the first time," Brian Concannon wrote in a commentary on the verdict, "human rights victims, judges and prosecutors throughout the country believe that the justice system can provide justice to the victims. For this reason, the Raboteau massacre case will not be the end of the fight against impunity, but the beginning."

WHILE JUSTICE WAS being served in Gonaives, across the Artibonite plain in the mountains of the Plateau Central it was being undone. On October 26 in the remote Plateau hamlet of Maissade, Lavalas Mayor Wilo Joseph responded to two arrest warrants for theft being issued against two local FL partisans by setting up flaming barricades in front of the Tribunal de Paix and seizing administrative materials and motorcycles provided to the judiciary there. The men had been transferred to the jail in Hinche earlier, though, but the justice of the peace in Maissade, Ossagnol Servil, felt threatened enough to go into hiding. Two months later, Servil would be fired by the Ministry of Justice.

Elsewhere on the Plateau Central, the MPP had organized a meeting of some of its most important members to take place in Hinche on November 2. After the shooting that occurred during its September 18 march, the organization thought it wise to write to the PNH to officially request protection for the event. The November 2 meeting took place at the Recif Night Club, an airy dancehall near the town's market. Earlier in the day, a scuffle had erupted with some Lavalas activists putting up pro-Aristide political posters around the venue—a move the MPP members strenuously objected to. When the meeting finally got underway at around three in the afternoon, Chavannes, his younger brother—a sweet-natured agronomist named Dieugrand—and several hundred peasant activists from surrounding villages were present. The meeting continued for about two hours, with the assembled discussing political strategy and other concerns, before finishing up shortly after 5 P.M. As the attendees began to leave the nightclub, stones began raining down on the top of the building, striking some of those present who had already made their way into the street. After a sustained barrage of stones that lasted several minutes, a terrifying cacophony of gunfire from Uzis and T65s began to crackle from assailants who had surrounded the nightclub, causing four PNH officers who had arrived to protect the meeting to dive back inside the Recif with the participants, being heavily outgunned and having only sidearms at their disposal.

Many witnesses said that employees of Hinche mayor Dongo Joseph, as well as the mayor himself and Maissade mayor Wilo Joseph (no relation), did the shooting. One MPP member, stunned as he was struck by stones hurled at him, was shot in the side. Another activist was shot in the neck. A mechanic working nearby the scene was shot in the ankle and a merchant pushing a cart was shot in the back. Chavannes's brother Dieugrand was shot in the chest as he tried to take cover inside the building where the meeting had taken place.

Chavannes himself was flanked by bodyguards and rushed from the scene. His two-car convoy was struck by bullets multiple times as it fled. An MPP truck that had been used to transport people to the meeting was consumed by flames, as were half a dozen motorcycles used by the organization. As the meeting participants scattered in panic, the gunmen attacked the house of the local coordinator for the Espace de Concertation, driving the man's wife and small children from the building as the attackers looted, ransacked and burned it.

It was an appalling display, made even more so by the apparent duplicity of what came afterwards. Following the carnage in Hinche, Prime Minister Alexis went on the radio to state that only the police, not mayors, performed law-enforcement functions in Haiti and that the efforts of local elected officials to create their own armed forces would be considered illegal. The news had evidently not reached the town of St. Louis du Sud on November 4, where a meeting between the playwright Hervé Denis—Préval's rejected PM nominee who had served as Aristide's Minister of Culture before the 1991 coup—and local Espace de Concertation members was broken up by the local Lavalas mayor and a group of armed men firing their weapons into the air.

SHORTLY AFTER THE ATTACK, I traveled to Hinche to see Chavannes, who had sequestered himself, sleeping at a different house in the area most nights.

Leaving the capital before daybreak in a car with, among other passengers, another of Chavannes's brothers, Bazelais, in the passenger seat, and an MPP driver, we climbed over the steep precipice of Mon Kabrit, looking down the bony spine of the mountain and the swirling dust in the parched fields beneath. Once we reached the top, however, the landscape became less stark. As we entered the Plateau Central on Route Nationale 3, we passed startling mountain vistas and lakes, beautiful doe-eyed children walking to school in pink and blue uniforms and t-shirt clad toddlers carrying buckets of water on their heads. Fording a river, the road rose into a grove of lemon trees as the tap-tap "Justice" passed by. Upon entering Hinche, despite the recent troubles the difference in pace and mood from the capital was striking. People moved slowly and smiled easily. Bazelais, ever the dutiful son, insisted that we stop at once and visit his mother, Iliénise Israel. A stout, white-haired old peasant woman of great dignity, she lived in a nondescript two-room house off one of Hinche's main roads. Bazelais kissed her, greeted her and proudly pointed out that at seventy-seven she was teaching herself how to read and write with the aid of a blackboard and some secondhand textbooks. The woman looked a bit shy at all the attention, and looked away to the board, chalk, and books sitting in the corner, ready for the day's lesson. Bazelais's own home was built around a simple courtyard, and in the coming days when I would sleep there, I would wake up to the dueling sounds of evangelical music and the strains of Mexican ranchera music mysteriously wafting over the hills.

It was much later that night by the time Chavannes Jean-Baptiste was located, at the end of a rocky dirt road, in the guarded MPP compound where he stayed most nights when he could, in contrast to the lavish homes of many politicians, set amid papaya fields lit by a high country moon. When I arrived, he had just stepped out of the shower and seemed healthy and vigorous, greeting me with a hearty, very Latin-American laugh, seemingly possessed of a great energy despite the late hour. We spoke at length on a small, gazebo-shaped meeting area toward the back of the complex, illuminated by a single light-bulb, with owls hooting and crickets humming an incessant rhythmic song.

"I was born into a peasant family," he began, in a forceful, gravelly voice. "My father couldn't read or write but he made sure that his children went to school. He didn't want his children to suffer from this problem. My mother couldn't read or write either, but she's teaching herself now, at seventy-seven years. In 1973, we formed two groups to advocate for change on behalf of the peasants, one in Papay and one in Bassin Zim. In one year we had three new groups. Then we had nine new groups form the year after that.

"We realized that we had rights before we died on this earth that the landlords and the *chefs de section* [the rural enforcers of the Duvalier government] did not respect. The *campesinos* [Chavannes used the Spanish word] were taxed on everything they grew and received nothing in return. No services, no schools, no food, no clothes. Nothing. The only thing we had were numbers; there were more of us than there were of them. When we realized this, more and more peasants wanted to join our groups. Little by little, we began creating cooperatives and lending credit, building on that base, until today we have a national organization, with 15,000 groups and over 200,000 members."

By the time Jean-Claude Duvalier fled in 1986, most of the country knew about the MPP's work in the Plateau Central. In 1987, the MPP held its first national congress in Papay and invited Aristide, who was then the parish priest at Saint Jean Bosco, to attend.

"On the day of the 11th of September massacre at Saint Jean Bosco, I was with him," Chavannes continued, an edge, lingering somewhere between anger and sadness, creeping into his voice for the first time. "I saw the killing. We barely escaped, and hid together, side by side, that night. When he was having his problems with the Catholic Church, the MPP was defending him. We had marches and protests supporting him. And when he assented to become a candidate for president in 1990, I was with him. I served on a presidential commission and would consult with the state about rural agriculture, advising and struggling with Aristide for our common goals."

During the years of Aristide's exile, the MPP suffered terribly: property was seized and members of the movement were jailed, beaten and murdered. Building on the MPP, Chavannes had helped form the Mouvman Peyizan Nasyonal Kongre Papay (MPNKP) in 1990, a nationwide group that sought to unify the peasantry throughout the country. But after Aristide returned in 1994, as so many had said about president, Baptiste said the two men found it difficult to resume their former friendship.

"There was tension between us," admitted Chavannes. "He wanted to extend his presidential term for three more years. There were a lot of *gran manje* [a Kreyol expression for high-living political types that translates literally as "big eater"] in the Palace and in the parliament. This began to be a factor between us. We began to have two separate projects.

"In 1995, the Lavalas movement had to decide on a candidate, and many people thought that I would be that person. But I decided that no, I wasn't going to be that candidate, and I decided to support Préval. I was thinking that with Préval, things would get better. But, around '96-'97, it was hard for me to reconcile with myself what I saw the new Fanmi Lavalas becoming. There were all kinds of people—drug traffickers, many ex-military people. We couldn't have dealings with those kinds of people. I was certain that we had two different projects now."

And then, it seemed, the struggle began in earnest.

"In March of 1997, in a park in Hinche, I denounced Aristide as a criminal. Since then, we've tried to dismantle and kill this heroic image that has been created of Aristide, so he is doing everything possible to eliminate us. At this point, we have two projects that are colliding."

From there, things seemed to deteriorate even further, with the disputed May elections marking a new low in relations between the two, and a deepening of Chavannes's personal sense of outrage:

"We denounced the theft of the May elections. There were armed groups that were sent from the National Palace in Port-au-Prince to the Plateau Central because Aristide wasn't about to win anything here. And instead he won everything—he stole everything. So these illegitimate officials, these Lavalas mayors, started to steal from the people, and began imposing new taxes. For example, they raised the tax on selling pigs, which was five Haitian dollars [a little under a dollar at the time] and is now twenty-five dollars. The *chef de section* system returned to the countryside. The Lavalas judges have decided that the MPP doesn't have a right to organize and hold meetings. These are the practices of a dictatorship that, for us, ended a long time ago. This isn't just in the Plateau Central but all over the country.

"We went to Hinche with over eight thousand people. The chimere Lavalas were all over the place, screaming at us, throwing things at us, but we were able to get to the park and deliver our message. This was historic because of the number of people who came out to support us. The opposition wasted $25,000 trying to organize and we did it on the pure strength of the MPP. It was a complete rejection of Lavalas and their elections. We were saying that there was no election and there is no authority."

Chavannes then proceeded to give a chilling account of the events of November 2.

"We decided to hold a meeting to address this lack of democracy, this illegitimate authority. Over one thousand people attended, even though we had received threats not to hold it. We have been given a right by the constitution to assemble and to protest and we were not willing to accept anyone terminating that right. At the meeting, with the backing of the local mayors, there was an attack on the people with stones and firearms. They burned our cars. They even burned down the house of the guy who let us use the space. It was something that was unthinkable, but it happened. . . . Now he [Aristide] wants to enforce his image through fear, so people shut their mouths and have the silence of the cemetery. So he can go on with all the stealing and all the trafficking he wants.

"After the massacre of November 2, where my brother almost died, Aristide lost even more support in the community. And so now everyone in the country knows what happened on that night. It's an example of what Aristide plans for the country as a whole."

How, I asked, could the movement that brought Aristide to power in 1991 have fragmented so brutally in a mere nine years?

"The movement of 1991 included many types of organizations: peasants, women's groups, students. Their main goal was opposing the Duvalierists and we believed that Aristide represented this goal. The coup tried to eliminate the movement that allowed Aristide to come to power. But what happened is that it wasn't Cédras but Aristide who almost eliminated the popular movements. Aristide has terrorized or bought out their leaders to form the chimere Lavalas. Aristide always used to talk, now Aristide keeps his mouth shut and they do his talking for him."

I asked him what he saw as the role of the MPP in the future of Haiti.

"Our fundamental objective is the construction of a green Haiti, a Haiti where there's food and life for everybody. We know it's a long process, which takes a lot of patience, a lot of struggle and fighting. But we're growing amidst this crisis. Every action they take against us only makes us stronger. We will send a message that we will proceed peacefully and lawfully, because we're fighting for democracy, not just for us, but for everybody."

By now it was very late. Beyond the glow of the bulb hanging above him, the night was black. In the darkness, the fertile fields and hills of Papay rolled historically on, impassive to the drama of men.

"For me, Aristide is nothing but a political cadaver who will pass like garbage through the history of Haiti. He has only one chance, and that is to come out and say that there was no election in 2000, and agree to start the process over again. He should say, 'I will win, but I'll win a fair election.' I know that he's too sick with power to say that. I would tell him to enter the Palace provisionally and organize clean and fair elections. But if not, he will bury himself face down in the history of the country and humanity."

DESPITE THE ATTEMPTED murder of one of Haiti's most long-standing and respected democratic activists, the Haitian government's chief legal counsel in the United States, the Miami-based attorney Ira Kurzban, dismissed the years of work by democratic activists like Chavannes Jean-Baptiste and the wave of attacks against opposition figures by writing in a November 16 *Miami Herald* editorial that, "On November 26 Haitians will vote in a free and fair democratic election for their next president. . . . The large turnout will be due to one person: former President Jean-Bertrand Aristide." For his trouble that year, Department of Justice filings attested, Kurzban was paid $631,332 by the cash-strapped Haitian government.[6]

THE RUNUP TO THE presidential vote was violent in the capital, as well. On November 22, seven bombs exploded around Port-au-Prince, killing a teenage boy and injuring fourteen people in advance of the weekend's vote. Later that same week, a similar mysterious explosion in Carrefour killed a seven-year-old girl walking to school and injured two others. That month, Fanmi Lavalas had put out a glossy booklet entitled *Investir Dans L'Humain*, which consisted of extracts from Aristide's book of the same name and presented its economic and social programs for the next five years. Within its pages, in a form that would be familiar to any glad-handing politician of a country in less stark circumstances, were soothing words about improving the economy, reforming the judiciary and implementing a national education plan, though lacking many specifics on how these goals would be accomplished or even financed, after the promise to create 500,000 new jobs and build 11,520 new homes for the poor.7

When November 26, the day of the big vote, arrived, turnout was very light, characterized by Prime Minister Alexis as "timid" in response to fears of further bombings. For an event so long both prayed for and feared by so many, the actual vote was fairly anticlimactic. Holding his first press conference since he left office over four years earlier, Aristide on November 28 declined to fully declare victory as the margin of his victory against his six virtually unknown opponents was not yet known, but he told reporters that, "There will be a place for everyone in my government." The opposition, as was by now routine, rebuffed Aristide's comments, again calling the elections fraudulent and saying that he had no mandate to govern the country. On November 28, the CEP declared Aristide winner of the presidential elections with nearly 92 percent of the vote and announced that Lavalas had also won all nine Senate seats up for grabs, thus giving the party all but one seat in the legislature's upper house. It was announced that Aristide would take the oath of office on February 7, ten years to the day he first entered the National Palace and fifteen years to the day that the Duvalier dictatorship had crumbled, propelling him onto the national stage.

ON DECEMBER 10, International Human Rights Day, I watched from the audience as Michele Montas returned to her alma mater, Columbia's Graduate School of Journalism in New York, to see her late husband memorialized by the New York branch of the National Coalition for Haitian Rights. During an emotional evening, speakers eulogized the slain journalist, and the film director Jonathan Demme screened scenes from a documentary he was making about Dominique and Montas that would eventually become his film, *The Agronomist*.

"I was asked by a student earlier today, 'Where do you establish the boundary between objective reporting and activism?'" Montas told the crowd. "I said that you don't establish it, it comes to you."

Back in the country where that calling came so forcefully to Montas, the Democratic Convergence upped the pressure on the incoming Aristide government by declaring on December 14 that they had begun forming a "provisional government" that would assume offices parallel to those of any new Aristide presidency on February 7—the day of Aristide's scheduled inauguration. In an effort to forestall an escalation of the crisis, an American diplomatic mission persuaded Aristide to send a December letter to outgoing U.S. President Clinton offering to rectify the May election results, include opposition figures in his government, and appoint a new electoral council. The Convergence rejected the overture, calling for completely new elections.

THE CONTINUED SIMMERING of the electoral crisis as Haiti entered 2001 was mirrored by the increasing pressure being put on Claudy Gassant as he attempted to investigate the Dominique murder. As Judge Jean Sénat Fleury had before him, Gassant evidenced great interest in conducting a thorough questioning of Dany Toussaint, given his acrimonious relationship with Dominique. After Toussaint had assumed his senatorial post in August, however, he was protected by the cloak of immunity provided to all senators. As such, Gassant was obliged to send a formal request to hear Toussaint to the Senate body as a whole, which rejected it in February, with Senate President Yvon Neptune dismissing Gassant as "a small judge that cannot summon someone from such a great body" and threatening to launch an investigation into Gassant's "exact motives."

As the issue was being decided, I watched as Dany Toussaint made his way through the Senate chambers. What I will always remember about him that day is that, despite his strapping physique, he moved with a singular, languid slowness. The expensive silk of his Italian suit, the glittering rings on his fingers and the mirrorlike shine of his black shoes all seemed to flow at a pace divorced from the commotion around him. He always seemed unhurried, in charge. He was Dany King. When he fixed you with his liquid dark eyes and spoke in his deep baritone voice, you could picture the figure he would have cut before his JPP devotees in the slums. More than a politician, more than a military man or the rumored killer that he was, there was a sapient, palpable charisma there, as if he were a rock star.

Following the Senate's refusal, though, the constant anonymous phone calls threatening Gassant's life increased, and the only thing that kept him confident enough to continue working were the two armed guards that the Préval government had provided him with. Further complicating Gassant's job, the PNH assistant traffic chief Evans Sainturné, a former bodyguard of Aristide's, was demanding that Gassant return an armored vehicle that had been given to the investigation by Préval. A member of Ronald Camille's gang who went by the street name Gasoline, who authorities were interested in questioning, was gunned down in a daytime hit on a Port-au-Prince street before he could be brought in. On January 30, driving through Port-au-Prince, Gassant's car was cut off by a vehicle full of armed men belonging to Millien Rommage, a Lavalas deputy who led an armed Aristide faction in the capital's seedy Carrefour suburb. As the men brandished weapons at Gassant from the windows of their vehicle, Rommage shouted that they could kill Gassant anytime they wanted. That month, in one of his last acts as president, an emotional Préval addressed Haiti's parliament and charged them with continued vigilance and collaboration with the Dominique investigation. "Jean Dominique was a Lavalas independent," Préval said. "And he was shot for his independence, not because he was Lavalas."

The new senate applauded politely.

CHAPTER NOTES

1. Organization of American States Electoral Observation Mission in Haiti, press release, May 5, 2000. Organization of American States, Report on the Registration Process, May 2000.
2. Organization of American States Electoral Observation Mission in Haiti Press Release, May 24, 2000.
3. Organization of American States Electoral Observation Mission in Haiti Press Release, May 24, 2000.
4. Orlando Marville, letter to Leon Manus, May 31, 2000.
5. Organization of American States, Organization of American States press release, July 7, 2000.
6. United States Department of Justice, Foreign Agents Registration Act (FARA) filings for Kurzban, Kurzban, Weinger & Tetzeli, P.A., 2000.
7. Organisation Fanmi Lavalas, "Investir Dans L'Humain," November 2000.

|||

6

La pe nan tet, lape nan vant

IN THE RUNUP TO Aristide's inauguration, huge billboards bearing the future president's smiling, waving visage appeared all around Port-au-Prince, the phrase *la pe nan tet, lape nan vant* (peace in the head, peace in the belly) written beneath the beatific image. A gasoline-filled container was thrown into the yard of Radio Kiskeya—which Lavalas groups had taken to task for referring to the May ballot as a "contested election"—but failed to ignite. A meeting between Aristide and the opposition at the Papal Nuncio's residence in the mountains overlooking Port-au-Prince produced little, and a new American ambassador, Brian Dean Curran, fluent in both French and Kreyol and fresh from his posting in Mozambique, arrived to further stir the pot. In Washington, after the United States resolved its own disputed election, the Republican governor of Texas, George W. Bush, was sworn in as president and named as his Secretary of State Colin Powell, whose diplomacy had been so instrumental in facilitating Aristide's return half a decade before.

On February 6, a day before Aristide was set to take office, talks between the government and the Convergence Democratique collapsed, and the latter announced that they were naming the elderly lawyer and educator Gérard Gourgue, whose possible election as Haiti's first post-Duvalier president had been scuttled by the election day massacre in 1986, as Haiti's "provisional president" for its "alternative government." The group also said that an as-yet-unnamed Convergence prime minister would rule by decree and that general elections would be held sometime in 2003, and Evans Paul called for the populace to "rise up" and peacefully demonstrate against Aristide's inauguration. Additionally and even more provocatively, Paul stated that forming the parallel government would be equivalent to "loading a cannon" in their struggle to oust Aristide. Reaction to the announcement was mostly confined to sarcastic chuckling at its self-important, politically tone-deaf and profoundly undemocratic tone, but Aristide and his supporters were not amused, as they would make clear in coming weeks.

The day of judgment arrived on February 7. At a ceremony before Parliament, the forty-seven-year-old Aristide took the oath of office, the former priest holding his hand on a Bible before Préval slid the red-and-blue presidential sash around his predecessor and now-successor's shoulders, looking almost physically relieved to be rid of the thing, many observers thought. Aristide supporters gathered in the United Nations park in front of the Palais Legislatif and in the roads leading to the building, though the object of their curiosity was now among the elected Lavalas officials inside, behind thick walls, and unable to be seen by them. Absent among the assembled thousands, though, were members of KOZEPEP, the peasant organization from the Artibonite Valley founded by Jean Dominique and Préval. Despite a request from Tabarre that KOZEPEP members gather in state-provided buses to attend the function, their leader, Charles Suffrard, told government officials that the group was not keen to participate in that type of political theater. France and the European Union declined to send representatives to the ceremony, while the United States was represented by Ambassador Curran. Children were excused from school for the day, and some lampposts, where wire from Haiti's near-moribund telephone system was strung, were painted in patriotic red and blue.

ARISTIDE ANNOUNCED THAT Jean-Marie Cherestal, a fifty-six-year-old economist and boyhood friend of the president's from Port Salut, would serve as prime minister on February 9. Approved by the Lavalas senate, Cherestal and his cabinet were sworn in on March 2. Though some appointments, such as that of veteran diplomat and former Communist Antonio Joseph as foreign minister, seemed to fit nicely with Aristide's public pronouncements, some others were quite jarring. Stanley Theard, who served as Minister of Commerce under Jean-Claude Duvalier and who had been indicted in 1986 for embezzling $4.5 million from the Haitian treasury, returned to that position under the new administration while Marc Bazin, prime minister from 1992-93 under the military regime that ousted Aristide, was appointed Minister of Planning and External Cooperation. Jocelerme Privert, fired from Haiti's tax office by Préval for corruption, returned as the Secretary of State for Finance. As with the Lavalas parliament installed the previous August, each minister was supplied with, at minimum, two new bullet-proof SUVs (known as *tet boefs*, or cow's heads, in Kreyol, in reference to the logo of Toyota, which produced many of the cars), and the cars, with blackout windows and distinctive *Officielle* license plates, could be seen speeding through Port-au-Prince, past street children washing their faces in puddles of rainwater. Jean-Nesly Lucien, a head of palace security under Préval, was named the new director general of the PNH and was replaced at his former job by Oriel Jean, a former member of Aristide's private security detail. Mario Andresol, the director of the judicial police responsible for investigation of high-profile crimes such as the Jean Dominique and Jean Lamy killings, was informed that his service would no longer be needed in that capacity and, awaiting reassignment, he was replaced by Harvel Jean-Baptiste, a Lavalas party member.

Beyond the levers of power within the government and police, there were also significant changes in the Aristide who had returned to office from the man who had been elected in 1990. Replacing the slain Antoine Izmery as Aristide's chief contact among the elite was Gladys Lauture. A wealthy former confident of Jean-Claude Duvalier's wife, Michele Bennet, Lauture had helped set up contacts between Aristide and wealthy Haitian families in her social sphere. A murky figure whose links with Aristide stretched back to his Saint Jean Bosco days, Lauture had a history of floating opportunistically between Haiti's power brokers, be they Lavalas or military. Another difference most immediately apparent about Aristide this time around were the hulking white American bodyguards that surrounded him. Aristide had first begun paying the San Francisco, California-based Steele Foundation to supply him with security guards in 1998, but their presence had been largely kept out of he public eye while Aristide was working from Tabarre. Now, though, the former Navy SEAL and Delta Force men to whom Aristide entrusted his personal security were everywhere in evidence. Ironically, the man who liked to portray himself as the personification of Haitian nationalism would not entrust his own safety to the Haitians themselves, but rather preferred those succored at the military breast of a government he often excoriated in his speeches. Initially consisting of about a dozen men, the guards eventually cost Aristide nearly $6 million a year—a price that would soon be picked up by the Haitian government.[1,2] As the president traveled between the National Palace and his home in Tabarre, residents of the capital became accustomed to seeing his caravan of vehicles sweep past, guarded by Steele and Unité de Securité Palais Nationale (USPN) personnel, machine guns at the ready as a helicopter carrying yet more armed men hovered overhead.

THE DAY CHERESTAL'S nomination was announced, Paul Raymond and René Civil, surrounded by their supporters, called a press conference at the ruins of Aristide's church at Saint Jean Bosco. Reading from a list of names purportedly concocted by the opposition for inclusion in any potential "parallel" government, in addition to the usual opposition political figures, Raymond named Radio Kiskeya programming director Lilianne Pierre-Paul and Le Nouvelliste newspaper owner Max Chauvet, among seventy others, giving them three days to publicly reject participation in the plan or else, Raymond told reporters, quoting Boisrond-Tonnerre, Jean-Jacques Dessalines's fiery secretary, "after that, we'll eliminate them personally. Their blood will serve as the ink, their skulls as the inkwells and their skin as the parchment for writing Haiti's second declaration of independence."

Raymond and Civil, who in the coming years would be the faces of the government pronouncements that Aristide couldn't say himself, were a study in contrasts. Raymond, a brawny, former divinity student with crooked teeth whose face was pockmarked with acne scars, was the shouting, saliva-spitting firebrand of the two, mixing near-fanatical religious fervor with extremist populist politics, which the February declaration perfectly encapsulated. René Civil, on the other hand, was a different matter entirely. Tall and slight, with his most distinctive feature being his abnormally large ears, Civil traveled around the capital in a Palace-provided SUV after Aristide assumed office with a coterie of assistants and National Palace security personnel. Appearing at rallies and demonstrations, Civil would hold a walkie-talkie in one hand as he rallied hordes of chanting JPP supporters around him. Unlike Raymond, Civil was soft-spoken, rarely raising his voice in anger or emotion, but he was thought of by those close to the popular organizations as the more dangerous of the two, given his stated political ambitions and previous close links with Dany Toussaint, who had reportedly used Civil and the JPP to organize the get-out-the-vote effort for his Senate campaign. After Aristide returned to office, both were rewarded with government jobs: Civil at the capital's port and Raymond at TELECO on Avenue Martin Luther King, where he was provided with a spacious office overlooking the OPL and KONAKOM headquarters across the street. For his part, Ronald Camille was also granted a new job, as chief of security for the port.

FAIRLY QUICKLY, IT BECAME apparent that, despite their electoral "victories" and the slow-burn fizzling of the Convergence's pathetic provisional president ploy, all was not well within the Lavalas house, and the Dominique murder revealed itself as the tread that ran through the divisions. At the beginning of February, Michele Montas shut down Radio Haiti-Inter for two days to protest what she charged were the "deliberate and arbitrary attempts by the Senate to obstruct the judicial investigation into the contract killing" of her husband. In Haiti's Senate chambers on February 21, Lavalas Senator Prince Pierre Sonson, a physician hailing from the southern city of Jacmel, supported by Senators Lans Clones and Gérard Gilles, lashed out at Dany Toussaint for the latter's refusal to appear before Claudy Gassant.

"Let's be honest with ourselves," Prince said. "It's a simple question, but it's being posed in a complicated way. We must not try to hide the truth, because that would open our veins to the venom of impunity. Senator Dany Toussaint should present himself before investigating judge Claudy Gassant."

Though Toussaint himself was not present in the Senate chamber at the time, René Civil was, as was Paul Raymond. Both men cornered an aide to Prince and, according to the senator, threatened his life, a move that he then returned to the Senate floor to denounce. At one point, several senators stormed out of the chamber. Following the flare up, Yvon Neptune announced that the Senate would be closed to the public and reporters from now on when in session. So much for transparency.

Much to Gassant's shock, Toussaint showed up at his office unannounced the next morning, offering all his assistance in the investigation. Gassant asked Toussaint if he could return the next day, when he would be prepared to question him, and Toussaint agreed. The next day, Toussaint never returned, and instead went to Tabarre, where he met with Aristide and other top Lavalas officials in a closed-door session. Again, transparency appeared not to win the day.

Gassant had slightly more luck with Radio Vision 2000 owner Léopold Berlanger, who again sat for questions. Visiting Radio Haiti-Inter on March 3, Aristide assured Michele Montas and the station's listeners that he would do his utmost to see that justice was done in the case.

SAYING THAT LAVALAS and the Convergence "needed one another," Aristide announced the unilateral formation of a new nine-member CEP on March 2 to oversee runoffs for ten of the disputed Senate seats. Somewhat less than reassuringly, the CEP included both former Duvalier Minister of Health Volvick Remy Joseph as well as Duvalier's former Chief of Protocol Yves Massillon, but no members of the political opposition. Unsurprisingly, the Convergence again announced their refusal to have anything to do with elections, which begged the question of the point of the whole exercise. Perhaps deciding to try a different tack, on March 17 flaming barricades were erected throughout the capital by chimere who were quoted as calling for the arrest of not only Gourgue, but also Evans Paul and Gérard Pierre-Charles. Gunfire erupted at one roadblock at Delmas, wounding two. Three days later, on March 20, armed pro-Lavalas gangs attacked Gourgue's private residence and for two hours terrorized two hundred students at his Gérard Gourgue School in the leafy Pacot neighborhood, hurling bottles and rocks at the structure and shouting that they were going to come inside. The OPL and KONAKOM headquarters across the street from TELECO were also stoned and fired upon. In neither case did police intervene. Far from denouncing the attacks, Minister of the Interior Henri-Claude Ménard instead released a statement intimating that Gourgue's arrest could come at any time.

Throughout the month of March, political events around the country continued to be volatile. On March 6, several hundred former soldiers marched through Port-au-Prince, chanting, "Long live the army." In Gonaives on March 22, Amiot Metayer, whose rough-and-tumble band of followers had by now matured into a street gang full of tough longshoreman known as the Armée Canibale (Cannibal Army), led several thousand demonstrators in a protest in Gonaives, calling for Gérard Gourgue's arrest, and a later confrontation there that same day at a local opposition-party headquarters resulted in two people being wounded by gunfire. On March 26, several hundred opposition demonstrators marching past the town hall in Petit Goave were fired upon by the security guards of local mayor Emmanuel Antoine, a Lavalas party member.

Five people were wounded, and opposition members erected flaming barricades around the city and forced the town hall to close later that day.

IT WAS LATE ONE AFTERNOON, and the painters Etzer Pierre and Jhomson Vidho Lorville and my friend Nina Clara Schnall and I were sitting together as the day ebbed away, drinking Barbancourt rum and a corrosive red alcoholic concoction called Sweet Dick bought from street vendors. A bearded artist and former activist from the democratic struggle, with a serious manner and deep, authoritative voice, Etzer invited us to sit out on the street front of his crowded, dilapidated apartment-cum-studio just off Grand Rue in the capital. As we sat and talked and Etzer tucked his neat dreadlocks under a leather cap, I realized that he appeared to be sharing his living quarters with several people, including an older man who made about a million trips to the icebox set on the steps for more drinks, and a quiet, serious woman with a small son, Ti Johnny, whose smile and laugh could have electrified several city blocks if human goodwill could be transformed into current. When we had first entered Etzer's apartment, one of his paintings, a deep green bull's head festooned with attached stones and an earring, gazed down from its easel. The sound of many radios and traffic and human voices trickled in through the porous wooden walls. All around, life. Despite his disengagement from the arena of political activism, Etzer, a teacher at the l'Ecole Nationale des Arts—ENARTS—state art school who hadn't been paid in months, remained immensely interesting as a source of information on the maturation of the Haitian political left as well as a sober analytic voice of the country's current turmoil.

"This conflict between Fanmi Lavalas and the opposition isn't a real conflict," Etzer said, showing exasperation with the political posturing on both sides. "It's comparable to two intellectuals sitting down and not being able to get along because one is coming on to the other's girlfriend."

He laughed, but soon turned serious.

"During the 1980s there were student organizations working with popular organizations working with labor organizations, etc,." Etzer said, contrasting those present at the time with the new political actors like Civil and Raymond. "Now there's a new generation of political activists who have come onto the scene since the return of Aristide without the level of political maturity that a lot of the older ones had developed over the years. A lot of the people who are acting now are acting neither with the same vision for global change nor the political autonomy that they were acting with in the 1980s. I mean, three-fourths of the people who are now making speeches on behalf of Lavalas had nothing to do with the political struggle that I was involved with. And that's one of the big problems that I have with Lavalas as it's functioning now. Why can't they control the people who speak in their name?"

In part, Etzer believed some of the political problems Haiti was facing were problems that were common to any populist movement, bred with a certain

poverty, desperation and sectarianism, and having to come to terms with actually holding the reins of power and being forced to confront some of their more
radical populist promises.

"One of the biggest problems we're facing right now is that of corruption in
the state." Etzer spoke as we sat on a set of low steps, smoking cigarettes. Night
was falling, but the streets were still full of people. An orange aureole glow
from streetside cooking fires caressed people in silhouette as they walked by:
men and women, the outline of the small head of a child. "You have an emer-
gent *ti bourgeoisie* political class who decided to enter into the government to make
it responsive to the population. But these people have come face to face with a
contradiction. They become their own class, a political class, and then they
begin to want to defend their interests and the interests of their class, such as
their jobs and the privileges that those jobs provide.

"I think that both sides in this conflict are involved in the chimere problem.
There's a huge population of people who will do anything for money. They're
not a political force, they're a political tool. They're always looking for jobs, and
any time there's going to be a political action, intermediaries are going to organize them to go do that action. But I don't believe that anybody gave René Civil
a mandate to speak. There's no profound political project going on there; it just
is what it is, which is a lot of posturing. Anybody can get on the radio and say
the price of food has to come down, the price of gas has to come down. But the
difference will be in what capacity that person has to analyze the situation and
understand why the prices are high."

To Etzer, Aristide was little more than a symptom of the wider forces of
Haitian society.

"I never believed that Aristide was 100 percent a leftist. He was the servant
of the masses of Haitian people. He was following a revolutionary impulse of
the people. I imagine, if I were in Aristide's place, the struggle would be
between the needs of the poor in this country and the impositions and the
restrictions of the international community. The space that existed for radical
critique and radical action doesn't exist anymore. A lot of people such as myself,
who were educated to believe in radical change, and who were educated to have
an analysis of the situation that was more profound than just liberation theology, have no place in the current political situation, not just in Haiti but all over
the world. Political struggle is a science."

I asked him if he still believed in the dream of building a new society.

"Well, there's something that makes me very sad. Because the Haitian people
missed two occasions that we will never be able to make up for again. First there
was the 16th of December [the date of Aristide's first election]. That wasn't an
election; it was a popular insurrection. What the population wanted was work,
justice and food. The second occasion was the coup d'etat. Aristide preached nonviolence because the international community put pressure on him to preach

nonviolence. But the majority of young people were ready to burst the situation wide open. They were waiting for Aristide to give them the word, but it never came. And that's how the coup d'état passed. But the activists were ready.

"But I don't have any regrets at all about all the struggles we've gone through over the years." Etzer sighed as he lit another in the night's litany of cigarettes. "Now, at the very least, I can sit on my steps and talk to a journalist."

THE BEGINNING OF APRIL brought—as it had the previous year—a flurry of developments. As the first anniversary of the murder of Jean Dominique arrived on April 3, a march of several hundred people, organized by Guy Delva and held under the banner of the Association of Haitian Journalists (AJH) snaked through the Champs de Mars to the Ministry of Justice, the gates of which were plastered with flyers bearing Dominique's smiling face, and then continued on all the way to Radio Haiti-Inter on the Delmas Road. Meeting with journalists' representatives the day before the anniversary, Aristide had pledged to uphold the principals of a free press in Haiti, but it was painfully obvious to everyone that government commitment to seeing the investigation through was no longer there. The same month, the effort to eliminate the peasant organizations in the Artibonite Valley that had been most closely associated with Jean Dominique and René Préval appeared to reach a new level of intensity. Speaking before Claudy Gassant as he continued to investigate the killing, KOZEPEP leader Charles Suffrard said that Lavalas Senator Médard Joseph, who represented the Artibonite in parliament and had been harshly and publicly critical of Préval for permitting the inquiry into the Dominique murder as it could implicate high officials in the government, had sent gunmen to repeatedly threaten Suffrard personally, along with other KOZEPEP members, with death should they continue pressing for the investigation. Even as Suffarard spoke, the security that had enabled Claudy Gassant to continue his very dangerous work was gradually being peeled away, as were his resources such as vehicles and supplies—a sharp contrast with the Préval government's commitment to the case. Michele Montas commented that the difference "was like night and day."

For those who still had faith in the Aristide government, the real tragedy was that, for many people, the government's interference with the successful prosecution of the Dominique case was undermining and tainting any of Aristide's other efforts at progress. Government partisans were forced into the uncomfortable suspicion that Aristide's was a ruling clique that wore one face to its foreign supporters and another face at home. The same day as the anniversary of Dominique's assassination, a policeman from the Fire Department named Beauvoir Davilmarand and his girlfriend were killed under mysterious circumstances in the capital. The following day, a Colombian-born U.S. citizen, Alejo Morales, who had worked at the Haytian Tractor company for years, was found shot to death in his car on the outskirts of the capital.

Another American citizen, the businessman Marc Ashton, who owned the Toyota concession in Port-au-Prince, was kidnapped the following day. The Ashton kidnapping stood out, as it was known that the Aristide government had expressed interest in purchasing Villa Rosa, Ashton's palatial multistructure home along the Canapé Vert road between Port-au-Prince and Petionville, for some time. Ashton, an American by birth who had spent his entire life in Haiti, was not interested in selling. He succeeded in escaping from his captors and quickly returned to the United States. Shortly after Ashton's flight to Florida, he evidently reconsidered the government's price as right, and the Aristide government, which had pleaded poverty at every turn in order to get international aid restored, purchased Ashton's home for US $1.734 million. It was stated that the buildings on the estate would serve as Jean-Marie Cherestal's home. Later, perhaps realizing appearances, it was designated as the official residence of the prime minister of the republic.

As the standoff between the government and Convergence dragged on, a new group, dubbing itself the Initiative de la Societé Civile, appeared on the political landscape. Drawn from elite business and religious organizations and consisting of figures such as businessman Rosny Desroches—who had briefly been education minister in one of the revolving-door juntas that held power between the fall of the Duvalier dynasty and the election of Aristide in 1990—and Protestant Federation of Haiti leader Edouard Paultre, the group offered to "mediate" between the warring political factions. Many, though, thought the Initiative's sympathy for the opposition was quite plain.

In late April, five months after the attempted murder of peasant leader Chavannes Jean-Baptiste, Aristide's new Minister of Justice, the well-known lawyer Garry Lissade, displaying a lapse into independence not to be repeated, ordered the arrest of Hinche mayor Dongo Joseph. It was not to be, though, and Minister of the Interior Henri-Claude Ménard promptly dispatched a delegation consisting of, among others, Petionville's Lavalas mayor Sully Guerrier, to Hinche to "investigate" the arrest, and Joseph was freed after their arrival.

ON MAY 3, International Press Freedom Day, speaking into the microphone of Radio Haiti-Inter that her husband had so long used, Michele Montas marked the station's return to the air one year before after the killing of her husband and Jean-Claude Louissant by addressing, once again, her remarks to the late journalist:

> Good morning, Jean. . . . For many months, just as they did with you each morning, people whom I do not know and who do not know me have been calling me daily to comment on current events and express their confusion and disarray with the same words, as if they were a *leitmotiv*: "This is why they killed Jean. Had he been alive, this would not be happening. . . ." The dangers that you had stressed would result

from a short-term strategy aiming at the blind conquest of power while systematically pushing aside the agenda of real change have led to what you had predicted—yes, at the time, they had called you a Cassandra. Today, a political party theoretically controlling the totality of power, from the ASECS to the presidency, sees its hold over the state apparatus challenged by opposition political parties with a meager capacity to mobilize and organize and which are betting more on the support of the international community than on their own political strength. Yet, a more fundamental challenge is emerging from the diverse fissures that threaten to cause the implosion of the party in power. . . .

Were you assassinated, Jean, so that you would not point to these ambitions for power that cannot even wait for this first false crisis involving Fanmi Lavalas and Convergence to be "negotiated"? Were you assassinated, Jean, because you saw too far and too clearly? There is word of the creation of a parallel party, which would keep in suspense militarily—oh pardon me!—simply keep in suspense, the government. There is word of last-chance negotiations, not between Fanmi Lavalas and the Convergence, but among the factions of Fanmi Lavalas. Today, the party in power, incapable as it is of getting rid of its own filth early enough, is in the process of imploding, perhaps endangering the very life of the head of state. . . .

You often spoke to me of your concerns regarding the general rise of a certain "macoute" mindset, of orchestrated violence, which sooner or later would crush, as during the time of the coup d'état, the timid progress achieved towards participation. With fierceness, you stressed, beyond the headlines of most media, the attempts by a peasant association to administer an irrigation system here, or the internationally-financed projects aimed at managing the water supply in popular neighborhoods of Port-au-Prince there, or the sewing of school uniforms contracted by the Ministry of Education to tailors' associations. You had once asked the question, "Who is afraid of participation?" Had you imagined that elected officials would meddle in the meetings of associations, that mayors with guns in hand would prohibit "unauthorized" meetings?

We know that they assassinated you, Jean, because you had the credibility to say NO to politicians of all stripes, greedy for power and money; NO to violence; NO to corruption; NO to exclusion; NO to impunity. What should give you hope today, my marathon runner, is the fact that one after another, organizations of this civil society, from the cities and the countryside, are brandishing you as their flag bearer, are themselves saying NO; that beyond petty political interests, more and more voices are clamoring, in the name of a country bled white and in the process of balkanization and collapse, for a nation more just, more decent, and more serene.

Good day, Jean, on this 3rd of April, International Day for Freedom of the Press.

Addressing a crowd of supporters on Flag Day at Arcahaie on May 18, Aristide declaimed that there had been "Too much suffering. Too much delay. Too much aid blocked. . . . Too many innocent people are afflicted by the crisis. Under the same flag of our father Dessalines, the government and the opposition cannot be enemies. Opposing, yes. Adverse, maybe. Enemies, no." A different message was communicated in the southern city of Les Cayes; on May 21, former deputy Gabriel Fortuné, who had been wounded in the attack that killed Aristide's cousin Jean-Hubert Feuillé in 1995, was arrested after a shootout erupted when Lavalas partisans stormed a Convergence meeting in the town. Police told local journalists that Fortuné was being held for his own protection, but as he sat in prison, Lavalas mobs plundered a food warehouse belonging to him, as well as a co-op affiliated with Chavannes Jean-Baptiste's MPP. After stewing in prison for two weeks, Fortuné was finally released without charge on June 4.

Prosper Avril had worked long and hard on his newest treatise on what he viewed as Haiti's ills, titling it *Le Livre Noir de l'Insecurité* (*The Black Book of Insecurity*). Little as it was known, Avril in fact had been steadily churning out his own version of Haiti's history in book form ever since he was deposed from office in 1990, alternately absolving himself from any wrong-doing in the assaults of the three democracy activists in 1990 (*An Appeal to History: The Truth About A Singular Lawsuit*) and bitterly attacking the disbanding of the Haitian army (*From Glory to Disgrace*). This book, though, struck more to the heart of the Haiti that Aristide had helped shaped since his return in 1994, consisting as it did of a litany of those killed in the preceding five years, including Mireille Durocher Bertin, Ti Jean Pierre-Louis and Jean Dominique, and resting the culpability for most of the killings squarely at Aristide's door. Avril, who, returned from his first exile, had fled Haiti with U.S. help in 1995 after the murder of Jean Hubert Feuille, had returned again in the late 1990s and had recently been stepping into the public eye, founding a political party, CREDO (Latin for "I believe") and appearing at a meeting of Convergence leaders and business men on April 19: bold moves for a man who was sued in a Miami court for his 1989 torture of such Convergence notables as Evans Paul and Serge Gilles and ordered to pay his victims some $41 million in compensation. As Avril sat at a Petionville restaurant on May 26, signing copies of his new book's laundry list of those killed—many with military connections—since Aristide returned in 1994, it was known that his reemergence had angered the government, which was anxious to portray itself as the rational element in the seemingly intractable negotiations with the Convergence. As

Avril sat at a table, six masked men dressed in black—Haitian SWAT—stormed the building, handcuffed the former dictator, and hauled him off to jail. A week later, government prosecutor Josué Pierre-Louis said in a statement that Avril had been arrested for ordering the torture of Evans Paul, Marino Etienne, Serge Gilles and others during his tenure in office a decade earlier. The fact that Paul and Gilles, betraying a disturbing political opportunism, had recently publicly forgiven Avril appeared to bear little weight.

The day after Avril's arrest, the Convergence seized on the move, with Gérard Gourgue telling reporters that the opposition would never negotiate with the government as long as Avril remained in jail. Gourgue's declaration seemed to insure that the work of a joint OAS-CARICOM delegation lead by Secretary-General César Gaviria that landed in the country on May 28 would be doubly hard. After meeting with both the government and the opposition, the delegation left empty-handed, with Gaviria saying time wasn't right for an agreement, that the political environment was too acrimonious. Sensing an opportunity to appear magnanimous, on June 4 Aristide, in a letter delivered to an OAS meeting in Costa Rica, announced that seven of the senators in the disputed elections would resign to clear the way for a new vote, that a new electoral council would be set up in thirty days and new elections held within ninety days. With a sad predictability, the Convergence rejected Aristide's overture to rerun the races, instead demanding new elections for all seven-thousand-plus elected offices decided in the May and July ballots. OAS head César Gaviria announced that he was appointing Mexican diplomat Sergio Romero Cuevas as the body's special representative in Haiti. Taking a break from political wrangles while receiving eight delegations of newly certified literacy tutors at the National Palace on May 29, Aristide announced that a major *alfabetizasyon* (literacy) program would soon be launched in the country.

At the end of May, the Dominique case again exploded onto the airwaves. On May 30, Dany Toussaint spoke to several radio stations in Port-au-Prince, denouncing what he claimed was a conspiracy to frame him and charging that René Préval, Bob Manuel, Claudy Gassant and others were colluding to destroy him, and that Gassant had been put on the case with the express purpose of carrying out the plot. He also charged Préval and Manuel with involvement in drug trafficking, and questioned the jailed informant Philippe Markington's connections with the U.S. Embassy. Even as he spoke, Claudy Gassant finally delivered a preliminary report on the Dominique killing to the public prosecutor's office, whereupon public prosecutor Josué Pierre-Louis asked Gassant to provide more information. As Gassant began to review his presentation, Toussaint announced that Justice of the Peace Jean-Gabriel Ambroise was now carrying out a "parallel" investigation of the crime and had interrogated both Philippe Markington and Jamely "Tilou" Milien as they sat in prison where, Toussaint said, they had admitted to having been bribed by Gassant with $50,000 and the promise of U.S. visas if they implicated him. Josué Pierre-Louis, the public prosecutor to whom Gassant had submitted his findings, told reporters he saw nothing at all wrong with Toussaint's actions, but he was overruled by an embarrassed Garry Lissade, who announced the Minister of Justice was exploring possible sanctions against Ambroise. On June 12, a heretofore-unknown organization calling itself the Komite Solidarite ak Dany Toussaint (KOSOLDAT), featuring La Saline gang leader Franco Camille as its spokesman, released a statement proclaiming the senator's innocence and announcing their willingness to fight any moves to arrest him.

All of this proved too much for Gassant, who had long ago sent his family into exile in the United States and, following his public a war of words with Justice Minister Lissade over the peeling away of his security detail, Gassant announced he was resigning because he was being blocked from being able to carry out his investigation. He left Haiti on a plane for the United States. The same day, June 14, Toussaint supporters erected flaming barricades in Petionville and along the Delmas Road, charging the investigation was going in the wrong direction.

"We ask the Haitian government and the Haitian judiciary to proceed immediately with the arrest of Judge Claudy Gassant so that he can explain before the law why he resigned," René Civil told Radio Signal FM. "If Judge Claudy Gassant is not part of a plot, if [he] is not a wrongdoer in the investigation of the Dominique murder, then he cannot resign. Because we have learned from reliable sources that he has been provided with all the material, weapons, vehicles and sophisticated equipment to carry out the investigation."

On June 20, KOSOLDAT activists again blocked roads, this time Route Nationale 2 leading into the western town of Grand-Goave. The demonstration was broken up by local police but not before the protestors had spray-painted the towns wall's with "Down with the plot against Dany Toussaint! Up with Toussaint, president for 2006! Do not touch him!" Heightening the tension, Radio Haiti-Inter correspondent Fritzon Aureus was forced off the road by a red Tracker SUV on the Delmas Road on June 21. After armed men who identified themselves as police and identified the car as belonging to Radio Haiti corralled the journalist into an Esso gas station, they smashed the driver's side window before letting him go.

Justice Minister Lissade, under immense public pressure, announced that he would "not accept" Gassant's resignation and pledged that he would satisfy Gassant's demands. Hesitant but determined, Gassant returned to Haiti on June 25. Justice of the Peace Ambroise was suspended for six months for his "parallel" investigation.

IN LATE JUNE, a ghastly gang-inspired massacre took place in the Fort Mercredi, on the capital's southern fringes. The locals at Fort Mercredi had grown tired of being extorted by members of a chimere gang lead by Felix "Don Fefe" Bien-Aimé, an Aristide loyalist who served as director of the Port-au-Prince cemetery and lived in the adjoining Grande Ravine area. Finally snapping, Fort Mercredi residents killed two Bien-Aimé gang members. Not long in taking his revenge, Bien-Aimé stormed the slum with his men that same night, looting houses, setting them ablaze and firing upon anyone they came across. Several injured persons were burned alive and at least two were decapitated. When it was all over, thirteen people had perished and over one hundred homes had been destroyed. The next week, Bien-Aimé met with Aristide at the National Palace along with what was left of the local Fort Mercredi gang. Under Aristide's gaze, the gangs signed a joint statement declaring their conflict over. No one was ever arrested for the killings.

VISITING PNH HEADQUARTERS on June 20, Aristide had a firm message to deliver the new recruits. Referring to *zenglendos*—the Kreyol term for common criminals that had become an all-purpose catch phrase for referring to people that those in a position of power in Haiti wanted to eliminate—Aristide issued a dynamite charge for how the police were to conduct themselves in the country.

"If a *zenglendo* stops a car out on the street, takes the car keys, forces the driver to get out and drives away with the vehicle, then that person is guilty," Aristide told Haiti's police force. "You do not need to take him to court to answer to the judge, because the car does not belong to him. If a criminal carries out physical violence against somebody out in the street with intent to kill that person, you do not need to wait for that criminal to appear before the judge, you can prevent that murderer from taking action. When it has to do with criminals it is zero tolerance. Period and full stop."

When Pierre Esperance and the National Coalition for Haitian Rights (the Haiti branch of the organization long since having outdistanced its all-but-defunct New York counterpart) denounced the speech as irresponsible and as opening the door for all sorts of mob justice, both René Civil of the JPP and TKL's Paul Raymond called publicly for Aristide to show "zero tolerance" toward NCHR and similar human rights organizations. A June 30 editorial in the *Haiti en Marche* newspaper warned Aristide and the opposition that, "Radicalism is the only winner. The two sides are likely to lose feathers, and not minor ones, in this fight. . . . One does not engage in [this] kind of trench warfare—ferocious, lengthy and in which all blows are allowed—and expect to come out of it smelling like a rose."[3] Before the month ended, in a move that had as much of an element of farce as the first group's declaration, a Fanmi Lavalas organization declaring itself the "Majority Civil Society" (MSCM) announced its existence at the capital's Plaza Hotel, declaring itself an alternative to the Rosny Desroches-led elite Civil Society Initiative. "Who gave Desroches a mandate to speak on behalf of the Haitian people?" a spokesman for the organization told Haitian radio. "In order to defend the rights of this civil society majority, which we represent here, we are creating today the MSCM and we solemnly declare it."

ON JULY 3 ongoing talks at the Montana Hotel aimed at choosing a new CEP collapsed, with Lavalas and Convergence failing to reach an agreement and blaming each other for the talks' failure despite the attempted smoothing of the rough patches by a joint OAS and CARICOM delegation.

Before flying to the Bahamas for a meeting of CARICOM the next day, Aristide told reporters that, "We will continue the dialogue." At the conference itself, things were awkward, as both the Dominican Republic's Hipolito Mejia and Bahamian PM Rupert Ingraham noted the one million and sixty thousand Haitians that had migrated to their countries, respectively, when discussing any future Haitian plans to join the body as a full-member and thus be subjected to eased migration rules. Aristide pledged to increase the standard of living in Haiti so that fewer of his countrymen felt the need to emigrate. Earlier on the same trip, Aristide addressed thousands of cheering Haitians at the Church of God Prophecy Auditorium, telling them, "When you are suffering, I am suffering with you." Some observers noted that, as had become a pattern, Aristide was the last to arrive (a day after the conference had started) and the first to leave. The CARICOM leaders ended their meeting by urging international aid donors to make technical and financial assistance to Haiti available again "without delay."

Visiting the harbor city of Port-de-Paix on July 9, Aristide spoke to a crowd estimated at over twenty thousand people outside of the city's cathedral. With Madame Aristide by his side, the president promised the curious peasants and fisherman that he would build an international airport and that he had cleared the Ministry of Agriculture to spend $22 million to help increase agricultural production in the district. He also announced that ten public transport buses and four tractors would be given to local authorities. Across town, Dany Toussaint, due to appear before Claudy Gassant in the capital, failed to materialize as the judge waited for him in his chambers.

But there may have been a slender ray of hope. On July 16, amidst negotiations between Aristide's Lavalas party and the Convergence being held at the Montana Hotel, the parties seemed to intimate that they were near a breakthrough of sorts. Speaking to Radio Metropole, the Convergence's Paul Denis said, "We certainly made some progress. We may reach a compromise on the basis of a political agreement as soon as possible."

That same day, Aristide arrived in Havana, where he praised Cuban President Fidel Castro for the hundreds of doctors it had provided to Haiti. Aristide, who was visiting at Castro's invitation, also expressed optimism that the negotiating parties in Port-au-Prince would reach some type of agreement.

BUT THOSE WHO irritated the government were still at risk. On the evening of July 22, armed men in civilian clothes, identifying themselves as members of the Unité de Securité de la Garde du Palais National d'Haiti (USG-PNH), raided the home of thirty-nine-year-old Dr. Blondel Auguste, the director the Association for the Promotion of Integral Family Healthcare (APROSIFA) and former director of the Hospital Sainte Catherine Labouré in Cité Soleil. Dragged from his residence by some of the men directly responsible for Aristide's personal security, August was first driven to the National Palace and then to the Port-au-Prince police station, and at which point he was charged with possessing illegal firearms and plotting against the State, though none had been found in his possession nor on his person. He was released five days later. No satisfactory explanation for the arrest was ever provided, either by the government or by Auguste, but the latter darkly hinted that he was being "targeted" by Minister of Health Dr. Henri-Claude Voltaire for unspecified reasons.

A LITTLE-NOTICED declaration was carried over the airwaves of Radio Metropole on July 27. Speaking from exile in the United States, a former Lavalas militant leader named Yvon Bonhomme, who had lead the Oganizasyon pou Sove Ayiti (Organization to Save Haiti, or OSA) for several years called the station to explain why he would never return to Haiti as long as Aristide remained in power; and in the course of his declaration, he made some stunning allegations.

"If the Lavalas government thinks they can arrest me and attack me today, the only thing they can charge me with is the fact that I contributed to the lying and brainwashing of the *pep la*, as did a lot of other people, in order to drag them into the situation that they are in now," Bonhomme told startled Metropole staff in a statement.

> I want to let the Lavalas government know that I still stand firm and remain a consistent political militant who believes in the establishment of a state of law in the country. I believe in the law of my country and in the application of Articles 19 and 22 of the constitution [guaranteeing the right to life, health and respect of human rights, as well as the right of citizens housing, education, food and social security], which are in the interests of the masses. I want to remind [the Aristide government] that I am not Jean Dominique; I am not Father Jean Pierre-Louis; I am not Mireille Durocher Bertin, and so on. I want to let them know once again that they will not shed my blood and that they have shed enough blood in the country. It will probably be Dany Toussaint's turn soon, but they will not find me and I shall not change my position. I shall never stop defending the masses.

I believe that one day the people will wake up and realize that they are mistaken. I recognize that a lot of members of grassroots organizations who fought, as I did, and who are family men, as I am, don't have the opportunity that I had to flee the country, and that they continue to suffer. I also know that there are a lot of them who are opportunists and who will be used to say things against me. . . . Haitian people, open your eyes! You lost the 16 December elections and you have lost them forever. Ideology does not stand anymore. It's a matter of people who are making money. And that is one of the things that caused me to be persecuted, because I refused to speak in their favor on the radio, hold demonstrations or do other things. Therefore, that is why I am in a difficult situation today.

I have chosen to go into exile over a government for which I shed my blood. I have chosen to go into exile over a regime for which I did things I should not have done. But today, I am facing an awful situation. I declare that I shall not return to Haiti as long as Aristide remains in the country. I give up.

From his lonely exile, Bonhomme had thrown down a gauntlet to Aristide's supporters among the popular organizations. It would be over a year before one of them picked it up.

IN THE EARLY MORNING hours of July 28, some half a dozen armed men attacked the Petionville police station on Place St. Pierre. With PNH officers fleeing at the first sounds of gunfire, the men occupied the station for nearly an hour. Prisoners, coerced or not history may never know, said the men forced them to shout "Long live the army!" before leaving with carloads full of weapons, ammunition and documents. On the heels of the raid, a larger contingent of men in military fatigues attacked the police academy situated along Route de Freres, which also served as the base for PNH's SWAT unit. In the assault, Eddy Cantave, the administrator of the academy, was killed, along with a young cadet and an officer on guard duty. Occupying the academy for several hours, the assailants, now joined by those who had attacked the Petionville station, fled into the early morning light, utterly evading a PNH dragnet that had been set up to capture them when word of the assaults spread, as well as the attention of hundreds of chimere who had set up barricades of burning tires throughout the capital. Over the same period, Plateau Central police stations in Belladere, Mierbalais and Hinche were also attacked and their weapons seized, resulting in the deaths of two policeman. Wilner Jean Louis, a former FADH soldier, was killed in Hinche under what a joint report by National Coalition for Haitian Rights and the Plateforme des Organisations Haïtiennes de Droits Humains later characterized as suspicious circumstances.[4] The legal offices of the MPP in

Hinche were gutted by fire. Hermione Leonard, the cherubic female police director of the West Department and one of Aristide's many liasons to the chimere gangs in the streets, that morning declared on national radio that, "Now zero tolerance will begin across the entire country." As Aristide and Prime Minister Cherestal visited some of the fourteen wounded policeman in their hospitals the next day, the opposition, frightened by the size and the intensity of the mobs that had taken to the streets, denounced the attacks as "theater."

LIKE ROBERT MANUEL before him, Mario Andresol had felt like he was fighting a losing battle when it came to tackling criminal elements who appeared to have ties to Haiti's president. The former head of the judicial police put in charge of the investigation of the Jean Lamy murder in October 1999, Andresol had already survived one assassination attempt when Aristide had informed him, following his inauguration as president in February 2001, that his services would no longer be needed in that role. Told to report to the general directorate of the PNH for reassignment, Andresol was in professional limbo at the time of the police station attacks. But when he received a summons to appear before the Ministry of Justice on July 31 to discuss what had transpired, he went willingly, ready to play a role in any investigation. After speaking to the investigating committee, which was headed by Secretary of State for Public Security Gérard Dubreuil, Andresol left, but was tailed by two carloads of heavily-armed men in black ski masks. Careening into the parking lot of a busy gas station, Andresol was ordered to get face down on the ground by the men or else he would be shot. At this point, Andresol realized the men were policeman and it dawned on him that his quick turn into the filling station might have very well averted an assassination. The men communicated on walkie-talkie, asking a third party what they should do, as Andresol, his wife and his driver all lay face down on the pavement. Finally a decision was made to arrest them all. The other two captives were released the next day, but Andresol was kept in custody. An August 7 court order deemed Andresol's arrest "illegal and arbitrary" and demanded that he be released immediately, but he was held in a fetid 10-by-15-foot cell with seven other men until August 25. Finally freed and told to wait at home while a judge decided on whether to pursue coup-plotting and murder charges, Andresol eventually went into exile in Florida.

At the funeral on August 8 for those killed on the attack at the Freres police academy, Aristide gave what appeared to be an emotional appeal for former soldiers not to support any attempts to oust him from power.

"Former military, you are the sons of the Haitian nation. Haiti needs you. Don't allow yourself to be manipulated by those who thirst for power," he said.

The full significance of the event lay elsewhere, though.

The attack on the police academy and the arrest of Mario Andresol signaled a new drive by Aristide and the Lavalas party to firmly turn the PNH into yet another arm of the imperial presidency. In place of trained, skilled men such as Bob Manuel, Pierre Denize and Andresol himself were put the likes of new PNH director Jean-Nesly Lucien, Rudy Therassan, who had been fired from the PNH for abandonment of his post but was reintegrated by Aristide and promoted to head the Brigade de Recherche et Intervention (BRI) unit of the force, and Hermione Leonard, the police director for the West Department whose links with armed gangs in the capital's Cité Soleil slum were long-standing. Policemen such as Normil Roboam, who had been dismissed from the PNH for possible involvement in summary executions in October 1996, Carol Lochard, dismissed for human rights abuses the same month, and Patrick Guillaume all were returned to active duty. The common denominator? They were all individuals known to be loyal partisans of Aristide and Fanmi Lavalas party militants, and their fortunes, therefore, were closely linked to that of the current government.

WITH ANDRESOL, who had served as the chief police investigator on the case, now in exile, on August 10 Minister of Justice Garry Lissade forwarded to Haiti's Senate Claudy Gassant's petition to lift Dany Toussaint's parliamentary immunity in the Dominique slaying, as well as, for good measure, a decision by a judge in chambers questioning Gassant's impartiality. The Senate agreed to form a committee to study the question. In a August 20 letter, the National Coalition for Haitian Rights pleaded with the Senate to "take [it's] historic responsibility" by lifting Dany Toussaint's parliamentary immunity, concluding "The nation is watching you." After their menacing of Prince Pierre Sonson in the Parliament the previous February, Gassant also summoned René Civil and Paul Raymond to give evidence in the case. On August 28, the second-in-command for René Civil's JPP organization, Jocelyn Lundi, was arrested while waiting to enter Gassant's chambers, a 9 millimeter handgun stuck in his belt. Lundi, from prison, would later say that he had come bearing a "message" from Civil and TKL spokesman Paul Raymond that the two would submit to questioning in Gassant's investigation into the Dominique murder, but the handgun begged the question what "message" exactly Lundi intended to deliver. Exasperated, Gassant had an arrest warrant issued for Raymond and Civil.

On August 22, police stormed the headquarters of Evans Paul's KID party and arrested six party activists, after allegedly finding weapons and ammunition stashed in a false ceiling. A judge dismissed the charges and those arrested were released four days later. Somewhat amazingly, as if he had nothing else to do, the case of the KID militant arrested in the PNH sweep the previous month landed in the lap of Claudy Gassant as investigating magistrate and, proving that the politician's contempt for the beleaguered judge wasn't confined to the Lavalas camp, Evans Paul refused to submit to Gassant's questions on September 3, instead calling Radio Metropole to say that there had been a plot to assassinate him on the courthouse steps.

IN SEPTEMBER, Amnesty International released a report titled "Steps Forward, Steps Back: Human Rights 10 Years After the Coup," which warned that, "Efforts to repress freedom of expression, political pressure on the police and the judiciary, and the failure by both police and justice officials to fulfill their duties to protect the right of Haitian citizens have reversed some gains of recent years." Noting with concern the Dominique murder seventeen months earlier, subsequent attempts to undermine the investigation of the killings and the growing evidence of police collusion with armed pro-government pressure groups, the report warned that, "This is a crucial case for Haiti's future: impunity cannot be permitted if the country is to be truly committed to freedom of expression and to justice."5 On the thirteenth anniversary of the raid on Aristide's church at Saint Jean Bosco, September 11, 2001, NCHR issued a press release questioning why "the persecuted of Saint Jean Bosco have today been transformed into the persecutors maintaining with impunity a dangerous climate of violence (verbal and physical) in the country." In particular to be deplored, the communiqué said, were the "assassins as the result of fortuitous acts, disguised by the seal of the 'Zero Tolerance' phenomenon."6 The previous day, during a melee in front of Haiti's parliament, Ronald Camille killed another Aristide partisan, Fritzner Jean alias Bobo, by shooting him down, and then fled the scene.

FOLLOWING THE SEPTEMBER 11 terrorist attacks on New York and Washington by the al-Qaeda organization of Islamic militant Osama bin Laden, while the rest of the world alternately sat in shock and rallied to the side of a besieged America, throughout the Haitian capital, in distinctive red Lavalas spray paint colors, walls were daubed with slogans such as, "Thank you Osama bin Laden For This Blow" and "The Whole World Thanks Bin Laden." On September 29, marking the tenth anniversary of the coup that had ousted him in 1991, Aristide traveled to Gonaives, where he walked, surrounded by his Steele Foundation bodyguards, from the Decahos bidonville at the city's entrance to the Place de Armees. Thousands of residents, many roused and organized by Amiot Metayers's gang, walked with him. With the world still reeling and the United States still grieving for its dead, Aristide used his speech to recall the attack on the Saint Jean Bosco parish and the murder of Antoine Izmery (both of which occurred on September 11), as well as the coup itself. Then he denounced the suspension of aid to his government as "economic terrorism" and claimed that a conspiracy, not voting irregularities, had caused the crisis that had led aid to be suspended in the first place: "[They] fabricated a false crisis, which holds us as a people, as a nation, by the throat."

INTERESTINGLY, AS ARISTIDE was goading the United States over the terrorist attacks, members of Haiti's small Muslim community—numbering in the low thousands and counting Lavalas deputy Nawoon Marcellus among their number—opted to take a different path.

Tucked away on a corner of the Haitian capital's dusty, congested Delmas Road, the modest white building bore a curious sign, painstakingly stenciled in green Western and Arabic script.

"*Mosquee Al-Fatiha*," it read. "*Communauté Musulmane d'Haiti.*"

An attendant was splashing water on the ground when I arrived, and he greeted me as I approached the gate. "As-salaam aleikum [peace be upon you]," he said, breaking into a smile.

"Welcome to the mosque."

Sitting and speaking to Abdul Al-Ali, the Delmas mosque's white-bearded, commanding imam, or spiritual leader, and the congregants, was an enlightening experience.

"I returned to Haiti in 1985 just to preach Islam. I converted while I was in Canada and we bought the space for the mosque in 1993. The Pakistani and Bangladeshi soldiers came to our mosque to pray and enjoy our faith and they encouraged us with this belief."

There was murmured approval from the men, about half a dozen, some in distinctive Muslim kufi headwear and finely groomed beards.

"Haitians would like to have the truth and Islam will bring it to them. If we follow Allah, peace be upon him, I think things can change," said Al-Ali.

At another mosque I visited, in Carrefour-Feuilles, a neighborhood that snakes up the mountains surrounding Port-au-Prince, a plangent, timeless sound echoed. Among the market women haggling over prices while portable radios blared compas, the muezzin's call to prayer goes forth from the new Islamic *masjeed*, or prayer center.

Allahu Akbar, Allahu Akbar Allahu Akbar, Allahu Akbar, La ilaha ila Allah— "God is great, God is great, there is no god but God."

"If you see someone who is in need, the ones who need help, whether it's education, money or what have you, we Haitians as a whole tend to be very generous in helping with one another," said Racine Ganga, the imam of the Carrefour-Feuilles center, who attended college and was introduced to Islam in New York. "Those who don't have anything tend to help out. It is in some way inborn to us as Haitians, as well as Muslims, to help out. So that principle of responsibility, of helping those less fortunate, resonated very well.

"Allah says that if a man kills another man it is as if he has killed all humanity," said Racine Ganga. "The people who did what they did in New York, they are not even human. Islamic people should use the weapon of their love, because violence, as we've seen here in Haiti, will not take us anywhere."

IN MORE EARTHLY MATTERS, when Radio Haiti-Inter reporter Jean Robert Delciné visited Cité Soleil on October 13 to investigate reports that police had summarily executed three gang members there, he spied police inspector César Yrvens drag a wounded man into the street, apparently to shoot him. Seen by the police, Delcine was seized by PNH officers and beaten in the presence of Delmas police chief Camille Marcellus before being released. Paul Raymond and René Civil casually held a press conference in the capital on September 28, despite the arrest warrant hanging over their heads. As Haiti entered October, something of an elliptical and secretive power struggle between Cherestal and Interior Minister Henri-Claude Ménard appeared to have broken into the open, with graffiti lauding Ménard and damning Cherestal appearing throughout the capital.

On October 15, yet another OAS mission to Haiti, this one led by Assistant Secretary-General Luigi Einaudi, failed to get the government and the Convergence to come to anything like an agreement. Interestingly, though, this time Einaudi pointed the finger at the Aristide government for the talk's failure, telling Radio Metropole that, "We have found very significant cooperation on the part of the members of the Democratic Convergence during these series of discussions, and I do not want to deny the fact that there have been difficult moments with certain representatives of the Fanmi Lavalas."

On the last night of October, a group of armed men broke into the headquarters of the health agency APROSIFA, whose director, Dr. Auguste Blondel, had been seized and jailed by Aristide's Palace security forces the previous July. Finding the teenage daughter of the building's security guard present, the men gang-raped her before leaving with materials and equipment valued at nearly US $3,000. No one was ever arrested for the crime.

The Haitians have a saying. *La recherche continue.* The investigation continues.

PIERRE ESPERANCE, the longtime human rights activist who served as the director of the National Coalition for Haitian Rights, sent an open letter at the end of September to Jean Marie Cherestal in the latter's capacity as president of the Superior Council of the Haitian National Police (CSPN). In it, Esperance bemoaned "the dangerous downward spiral of this institution, an institution given the task of guaranteeing order, peace and societal stability."[7]

"The situation is disturbing," Esperance continued. "Intolerance, ideological conflicts and political seizures of land, illegal police operations that are deplored by civil society, security forces that appear to have obtained a carte blanche allowing them to kill or let others kill with impunity. In this climate of reprehensible and unacceptable insecurity, human rights violations have reached an inconceivable level."

Mentioning the events of July 28, the arrest of Auguste Blondel and the KID activists, and the government's refusal to arrest René Civil, Paul Raymond and Ronald Camille, Esperance questioned if "it is the return to favoritism as such during the time of the Army. What has changed?"

CHAPTER NOTES

1. "Haitian president expands guards," *The Baltimore Sun*, February 10, 2002.
2. Banque de la Republique d'Haiti (BRH) internal report, May 2005.
3. "The Crisis Leaves Both Adversaries Equally Weakened" editorial, *Haiti en Marche*, June 30, 2001.
4. Platform of Haitian Human Rights Organizations, National Coalition for Haitian Rights and Committee of Lawyers for Respect and Individual Liberty, Report on the Situation of Human Rights in Haiti Following the Events of July 28, 2001, August 2001.
5. Amnesty International, "Steps Forward, Steps Back: Human Rights 10 Years After the Coup," September 27, 2001.
6. National Coalition for Haitian Rights, September 1988–September 2001: Thirteen Years After, NCHR Remembers, September 10, 2001.
7. National Coalition for Haitian Rights (Haiti), "Open letter to the Superior Council of the Haitian National Police (CSPN)," October 18, 2001.

$$| \quad | \quad |$$

7

Small Hours in the Night

IT WAS NOVEMBER 2001, and Aristide had been in office for nearly a year. During that time, Haitians had watched with increasing concern as the police academy in Freres and the police station in Petionville were attacked, as members of Aristide's new government began to exhibit conspicuous signs of great wealth incompatible with their incomes as ministers, senators and deputies, and as the administration appeared to begin to disappear behind its phalanxes of security guards and heavily armed police and the tinted-windows of the gleaming new SUVs in which they sped through town. I returned to Haiti once more, this time to report on the country for Reuters, and descended into Port-au-Prince on an airplane from which we could see the warm light of the Caribbean falling in layers over the country's bald, deforested mountains and the shacks of Cité Soleil. In advance of Christmas, Haiti's always picturesque National Palace was strung with white lights and lit up like a Christmas tree, sending a festive glow across the humble homes that surrounded it. Taking a new flat in Pacot, I found it inhabited by the brilliant green lizards that Haitians call *zandoli*. Too poor on my reporter's salary to afford a car, often at night I would trudge up the hill in the darkness to visit a friend of mine, a brilliant and eccentric mulatto ophthalmologist who lived in a tumble-down apartment with his black Haitian wife and their two sons, and was always riveting intellectual company. Conversant in half a dozen languages and deeply read in art, literature and philosophy, the mulatto doctor had interned at a hospital in New York, and could have stayed there in private practice. "But I loved Haiti, you see," he would confess, and so he came back to struggle to support his family. Sometimes we would climb the stairs to the apartment of an itinerant Dutchman who lived in the compound—he was in Haiti running a media-training NGO—and talk long into the night, watching the staggered specks of light beneath us in electricity-starved Port-au-Prince. Again, I walked down Avenue Jean Paul II, across the Champs de Mars and onto busy, congested Avenue Monsignor Guilloux, where tap-taps cruised in a fury of roaring engines and exhaust and *ti machanns* sat selling cigarettes, wafers and deep-fried patties from boiling black metal pots. I entered the gates of ENARTS, the state university art school, and there I saw Etzer

Pierre, for the first time in many months, in a classroom with one of his music students. The young man played piano as Etzer drew out the elegant, jaunty melody of "Englishman in New York," of all things, on his violin. When he saw me, a smile spread across that wise face of his, framed by tumbling dreadlocks underneath his leather cap, and he nodded my way.

By now, as I looked around, it had become obvious that Aristide fully intended to ignore Article 7 of Haiti's constitution, the article that stated unequivocally that, "The cult of personality is categorically forbidden. Effigies and names of living personages may not appear on the currency, stamps, seals, public buildings, streets or works of art." Billboards bearing Aristide's image covered the capital, and on my television TNH showed ceaseless homages to the president, the most frequent of which depicted a dove flying down a long stretch of road from the words "1991" to the words "2001" and toward a rising sun. The sun, as it ascended, turned out to be the top of Aristide's balding head, his smiling visage lighting the world.

As Aristide was lauding himself on television, U.S. officials, having compiled an impressive dossier of his alleged drug-trafficking activities while serving as police chief in Cap Haitien, revoked Santo Domingo resident and Aristide foe Guy Philippe's U.S. travel visa, despite the fact that he was married to a U.S. citizen, an NGO worker he had met while training with the Haitian military in Ecuador.

At the beginning of November in La Saline, a gang war between the Camille brothers and the gang of their rival Roland Francois for control of the La Saline market left six dead and climaxed when residents' homes were firebombed and riddled with bullets by attackers in a nightlong siege. During the height of the fighting, locals said they saw Ronald Camille being shuttled through the slum's narrow lanes in a police vehicle. Police and firemen responding to the scene were shot at. Angry residents called for the brothers to be driven from the neighborhood and subsequently torched Franco Camille's house but, three days later, some two hundred protestors marched on the National Palace, shouting their support of the criminal duo. When Aristide visited the slum a few days later, at the invitation of the Camilles themselves and Annette "So Anne" Auguste, a sometime folksinger who had lived in the United States for many years and had immersed herself in the most rancid criminal-political underbelly of Aristide's entourage since returning to Haiti, he doled out money to the victims of the weekend's violence but offered no apologies.

Back in the United States, a November 8 Congressional Black Caucus letter to U.S. President George W. Bush demanded a meeting on Haiti and stated that the United States should "remove its blockage on aid to Haiti," specifically citing the Inter-American Development Bank (IDB) loans. The letter was the brainchild of Ron Dellums, a former U.S. representative from California and former member of the Caucus, who continued to exert great influence, especially with Congresswoman Barbara Lee, who began her political career by working as an intern in Dellums's office and became his chief of staff before winning Dellums's congressional seat in Congress. Over the next year, as Department of Justice records would attest, Dellums's lobbying firm would collect over $200,000 from the Aristide government.[1] Not solely among the Caucus, Aristide was able to continue to rally various interest groups to his side. Ira Kurzban, the Haitian government's chief counsel in the United States, was particularly effective, writing articles and giving interviews and speeches as he collected $870,449 from the Aristide government during 2001.[2] The Catholic peace movement Pax Christi also continued to voice its support for Aristide, partially as a result of their chief liaison in Haiti, Ron Voss. Voss, an accused fugitive pedophile American priest from Indiana who had settled in Haiti after fleeing the United States and, many said, likely child molestation charges, for his loyalty was rewarded by being allowed to live in one of Antoine Izmery's old homes, which he dubbed "the visitation house," and where he frequently held court surrounded by groups of young street boys. It was a sad state of affairs for a leader who had been able to rally such pervasive support during his 1991–1993 exile.

PANEL RENELUS, a small-time criminal with a nasty history of theft and rape and links to both the Camille brothers and Port-au-Prince's Assistant Mayor Harold Sévère, had been arrested by police in Leogane, just west of the capital beyond Carrefour, and linked with a recent crime spree in the area. When Claudy Gassant heard that Renelus, an individual he had wanted to question for some time, had been detained, he immediately set out for Leogane from the capital to take possession of him. Gassant had been on something of a winning streak lately, having succeeded in having René Civil and Paul Raymond before him on November 28 after the two had met with Aristide at Tabarre, and thus rescinding the arrest warrants ordered for them. As he arrived at the Leogane jail, though, a conflagration with many agitated people, most of them young men, was flaring in front of its doors. The crowd was demanding that the police turn Renelus over to them, so they could administer "zero tolerance." As Gassant watched, the Haitian police shoved the terrified Renelus out the prison's front door, toward the mob.

Cameron Brohman, a Canadian working to save a tropical forest on the former estate of American choreographer Katherine Dunham in Carrefour, happened to be passing through Leogane at the time, en route to Jacmel, and witnessed the killing.

"They dropped a rock on his head," Brohman told me later on the veranda of the Hotel Oloffson. "It sounded like they were breaking glass."

A shaken Gassant headed back to Port-au-Prince, again one interview short.

ON NOVEMBER 15, a general strike called by the Convergence in Cap Haitien saw schools and businesses shut down, though most banks remained open. In a reversal, a group of pro-Lavalas demonstrators who attempted to gather were sent home under a hail of rocks by Convergence partisans. On November 20, René Civil called a press conference at which he announced the beginning of a nationwide movement to force Cherestal's resignation, saying that the prime minister had "bought luxurious houses for personal purposes and luxury vehicles," an ironic thing for an Aristide supporter to call attention to, no doubt, but in no way unusual, as Smarck Michel and later René Préval had previously fallen victim as the targets of anger Aristide successfully diverted from his own failings as a leader. Two days later, protesters calling for the resignation of Jean-Marie Cherestal attacked the cars of Lavalas Senators Lans Clones and Gerald Gilles as they passed through Saint Marc north of the capital, forcing the the men to seek refuge in the town's city hall. The building was then surrounded by protestor's chanting "Long live Aristide!" until police arrived to rescue the senators some two hours later.

HE WAS SPEAKING to a group of peasants when I first saw him face to face. It was in one of the reception rooms at the National Palace, and as the subsistence farmers and market women shifted uncomfortably on the hall's straight-backed chairs, Aristide spoke to them from a podium on the dais that was nearly big as he was, a small man on a big stage.

"The peasants are hungry, but together we will move forward together. There is a marriage between literacy and agrarian reform," Aristide told the gathering, his large head, seemingly too big for his body, bobbing expressively behind a large microphone.

The peasants ranged from young women in modest, spotlessly clean dresses to elderly men sporting the traditional wide-brimmed straw hats of the Haitian countryside. Some dozed in their seats as Aristide spoke, no doubt exhausted by the long tap-tap rides from the provinces to the capital.

"We must make room at the table for the peasants," Aristide said as he stood underneath one of the Palace's ornate golden chandeliers. "The peasants may not know how to write, but they know commerce. They are very smart. They have experience, they're intelligent, and we need their input."

"They set up a literacy center in our town and never came back," a young woman from a village on Haiti's northern coast near Cap Haitien complained. "We called on our people to help organize the election but they're discouraged, they're angry and we can't call on them again!"

"The literacy program can't work if you're hungry," concurred one young man.

Aristide gazed upon them, even, unflappable.

"We don't have a chance without you!" exclaimed a rail-thin, white-haired old man from the lush Grand Anse peninsula.

IN HAD BEEN a week of great tension in the coastal city of Petit Goave. A rally of Convergence partisans from nearby districts held in the town on November 24 had resulted in a call for a general strike there on November 29, with the stated aim of increasing the pressure on Lavalas officials there. On November 28, several Convergence activists—Déus Jean-Francois, Panoski Roger and Frantz Sagaill—spoke on the evening "Dialogue" radio program of journalist Brignol Lindor, carried on the local Radio Echo 2000 station, speaking out strongly against the Aristide government and local officials. The day after the strike—which itself transpired with little violence or effect—the triumvirate of mayors in charge of administering the town, along with the local directors of TELECO, the port and the leader of the Domi nan Bwa (Sleeping in the Woods) OP, Raymond Jean Fleury, held a press conference at City Hall. During the course of the press conference, Deputy Mayor Dume Bony called for the application of "zero tolerance" to be directed at Brignol Lindor and several other individuals from the municipality associated with the opposition, including the guests on Lindor's radio show. Observers said that Bony was "particularly vehement" in his declarations. Three days later, on the morning of December 3, an attempted Convergence demonstration in the city was violently broken up by PNH officials and, as the crowd dispersed, they came upon and seized Joseph Céus Duverger, a security guard at the local port and a member of Domi Nan Bwa, beating him and slashing with a machete. It was at this point that Domi Nan Bwa—bent on revenge—found Brignol Lindor on his way to Miragoane. As is recounted in the chapter that begins this book, they spared him no mercy, and after stabbing, hacking and lynching him, all that was left was for Lindor's family to come and pick up his mauled corpse.

Reached by local journalists later, the Domi Nan Bwa group boasted of their crime with Joseph Céus Duverger, the original victim that morning, stating flatly, "Lindor is a criminal, he was asking for it. He wasn't killed by one, two or five people. If ten, fifteen or twenty people kill someone, nobody should be arrested. He's dead and gone. Brignol isn't king, he's a cheat, a customs official who steals public money and who's trying to fuck up this country. That's is why zero tolerance was meted out to him."

Following Lindor's murder, Aristide's Minister of Information Guy Paul commented that, "They did not attack Lindor because he was a journalist. They killed him because he was a member of the Convergence and things like that. Whether it has to do with a journalist or a member of the Convergence, we deplore it because that should not take place. It has nothing to do with freedom of the press."

THROUGHOUT LOCAL COVERAGE of the unrest in Petit Goave, local Haitian media always referred to it as *la ville de Faustin Soulouque*. Curiously, Petit Goave's most famous native son was also the Haitian ruler first closely associated with loosely-grouped, politicized armed bands. Faustin Soulouque was born in Petit Goave, the son of slaves who had been born in Africa, in 1788. He became a soldier in his youth, serving in the presidential guards of both Alexandre Petion and Jean-Pierre Boyer, and in his drive to better himself he learned, as contemporary records show, an impeccable French rare among men of his background on the island. Perhaps inevitably, given his proximity to the nexus of power, Soulouque was elected president of Haiti as a compromise candidate between several political factions in a Senate ballot cast on March 1, 1847 but he showed himself to be anything but a place-holder. Somewhat distrustful of the institution of the army as a whole, although not without his supporters among the officers with whom he had served, Soulouque, shortly after taking office, began to build up a network of black, lower-class partisans called *zinglins*, a precursor of the word, *zenglendo*, that would be used to describe criminals some one hundred and fifty years later. Feeling threatened by the mulatto political class in the capital shortly after assuming power, Soulouque had his Palace guard gun down dozens of leading mulatto politicians after having them gather on the Palace grounds. When the mulatto-heavy south of Haiti revolted upon hearing the news, Soulouque personally led his forces on a sweep through the region to put down the revolt, stating famously that, "My sword will never return to it's sheath while a man survives among the traitors who have plotted the betrayal of the country." Returning to Port-au-Prince from the campaign, *zinglin* bands greeted Soulouque at the entrance to the city waving palm fronds.

Like the Haitian leaders before and after him, Soulouque was beset by problems beyond his borders, as well. Haiti had stopped paying its onerous "debt" to France in 1843, and France, England, and the United States (where slavery still flourished) were all vying for some level of dominance in Santo Domingo, just across the border. Believing that revenue from Santo Domingo's ports would both enable him to repay the French debt as well as forestall further European and American expansion onto the island, Soulouque invaded in 1849, only to be beaten back in a humiliating retreat by the Dominican General Pedro Santana. In 1852, Soulouque, hearkening back to Christophe, crowned himself Emperor Faustin I, and doled out to his generals and other supporters a peerage that included dukes, barons, marquises and others. An enthusiastic *vodouisant*, Soulouque kept among his Palace staff several bocors and mambos, and vodou was openly practiced in the capital during his reign, marking perhaps the first time in Haiti's history when a governing ruler gave the much-maligned religion semi-official status.

The spirits however were not enough to ward off a series of Dominican navy reprisal raids along Haiti's south coast. The great powers feared that Soulouque might have grander ambitions, including both the islands of St. Thomas and Guadeloupe where, during civil unrest, mobs of black residents had chanted, "Viv Soulouque!" in 1851. A British and French dual navy squadron blockaded

Port-au-Prince that same year, withdrawing only after assurances that Soulouque had no further international plans. Within Haiti though, things were not well. *Zinglins* robbed travelers at roadblocks throughout the country and, due to economic management, the gourde lost four times its value. Unable to restrain himself, again, in 1855, Soulouque lunged toward Santo Domingo—an excursion that ended disastrously for the Haitians in Dominican triumph.

Four years later, he was ousted in a Palace rebellion, and exiled along with his family to Jamaica. When he arrived in Kingston, some of the local Haitians who had been exiled by his regime threw a party celebrating his downfall in a hotel near Soulouque's residence. From where he sat, the old man could hear their waltzes and laughter.

AROUND THE TIME of Lindor's murder, I went to visit Yvon Neptune again, whose offices had now moved from the modest home in downtown Port-au-Prince that I saw to those of the president of the Senate in Haiti's Palais Legaslatif. Neptune greeted me, dressed dapperly in a dark suit with a Haitian flag pin in the lapel, and as we spoke he sat behind a large desk, the air-conditioning system humming frigidly along. I asked about the killing.

"Ti Goave has always been perceived as a place that has been under the control of the Duvalierists. As a matter of fact you have Hubert de Ronceray from Ti Goave, he still lives there. He was a member of the Duvalier government, a minister, and he still lives there," Neptune said, folding his hands and peering at me through his glasses. I thought that statement conveniently overlooked the many Duvalierists in Aristide's own government, but I let him continue.

"Given now the creation of the Convergence, that has complicated the situation, because now you have different politicians claiming to have a following, but trying to focus on Ti Goave. From time to time, you have different conflicts that end in violence, but that the violence has been provoked, and more often than not, it is the people of the Convergence provoking the violence, using language, using threats, that provokes a certain reaction. Lindor was a journalist, but he was also an employee of the customs office at Ti Goave. So both he and Joseph Duverger were state employees, but the difference is that maybe Duverger may be a sympathizer of Fanmi Lavalas, while Lindor, his neighbor told me that he is an OPL member, so that means a member of the Convergence, while he's a journalist. Journalism shouldn't be used as a cover to do political work."

Changing the subject, I asked him how the government's announced plan for agrarian reform and modernizing the country's infrastructure was proceeding amidst the political and economic impasse.

"To tell you the truth, as far as I know, the situation being what it has been since President Aristide took office, although there might have been efforts made, it's been very difficult, so many of the things that the government has projected to do have been put on hold. We're trying to use whatever funding we can use to keep whatever we can keep alive, alive. As far the agrarian reform, I don't think that there's been any real activity."

He said the government was trying to put together an electoral council with the opposition, and that the stumbling block had been a rerunning of the local elections, which the Aristide government would not agree there was ever a problem with. I asked him if he felt that the behavior of some local mayors, such as Dongo Joseph in Hinche, was reflective of the party's attitude as a whole.

"If there are some who are unacceptable because of their behavior, if they don't respect the law, the government will use its power to dismiss them. That case you mentioned is a case that is under consideration. There is an investigation underway to determine if he is a liability, not for Fanmi Lavalas but for the population of Hinche."

I asked also, now that he was Senate president, given his statements after Jean Dominique's murder that the killing sent a threatening message to people who wanted elections and wanted justice in Haiti, what would be done about lifting Dany Toussaint's parliamentary immunity? Basically, I asked him why the Senate was stonewalling the investigation.

"We've been acting on it, but we've been acting on it as legislators. We make laws, so we are the first to show that we can use the law and the constitution in a serene fashion to make decisions that have relation to the justice system. . . ." Neptune then launched into a long, legalistic defense of the Senate's delays, and the necessity for studying and restudying the documents submitted by Claudy Gassant.

"As a matter of fact," he concluded. "We are at the point where the report is being written. Despite what some sectors are saying, we are doing our best." He said he expected a decision to be announced before the Christmas holidays.

I shook his hand as I left, and stepped out into bright, blinding sunshine— the Place Nations Unies, with its myriad flags fluttering and its empty fountains, stretched before me.

ONE GOVERNMENT PROGRAM that I did find impressive was what seemed to me to be a massive and spirited AIDS-education campaign. On World AIDS Day 2001 (December 1), I watched an AIDS-awareness event held at a clinic in Petionville that was attended by U.S. Ambassador Brian Dean Curran and Haiti's Minister of Health Henri-Claude "Claudy" Voltaire. Surrounded by posters of smiling couples holding packets of condoms, students, educators and officials spoke honestly about the disease, and amid raucous cheers, a young man barely out of his teens told the assembled crowd: "This may be difficult for some of us to talk about. We may be embarrassed, we may want to laugh. But we need to talk about it." Around the capital, brightly painted banners bearing public health slogans, posters promoting condoms, frank public discourse and a growing number of clinics were all part of the campaign Voltaire had spearheaded for a country still on the front lines of the AIDS war. About thirty thousand new cases of AIDS had been diagnosed in the country the previous year and, though the spread of the disease had stabilized somewhat, about 4.5 percent of the population—some 360,000 people—were infected, the highest rate in the Caribbean.

One of the program's main boosters was Aristide's own wife, Mildred, the Bronx-raised lawyer who now sat next to the president in his golden chair at public functions. When I spoke to her that month at the Hotel Plaza in the capital, she complained bitterly about the delay by the IDB in disbursing a $22 million loan to reinforce Haiti's national Health Care System, though the body had dispensed a pitifully small $1 million grant.

"We need the loans so we can have clinics throughout the country to provide free testing and assistance to people in their own communities, so they don't have to travel all the way to the capital to get testing or to get treatment," Madame Aristide said.

A few days later I visited Henri-Claude Voltaire—a thoughtful, bearded young minister who gazed out at the world from a pair of gold spectacles and hailed from a peasant family near Miragoane—at the Ministry of Health just across the street from the National Palace. Voltaire had often been the subject of swirling controversy with regards to corruption and the arrest of APROFISA's Dr. Auguste Blondel who had publicly accused him of wrongdoing. For my part however, I always found him to be among the most dedicated, thoughtful, and humble members of the Lavalas government, with an ascetic sense of mission that Aristide could have done well to study.

He spoke in a soft but firm voice of the detailed plan the Ministry had put together on how to combat AIDS in Haiti, beginning in October 2002 and continuing through October 2006, which was minutely detailed in booklets and outlines unlike most government policies, and the temporary plan they had set up before the program was to begin. The program included such steps as putting HIV treatment centers in each general hospital in the departmental capitals as well as two more in Port-au-Prince, which already had two locations where people could be tested.

"We had to go into every department and ask them what their problems are," said Voltaire, who felt that without decentralization and participation, nothing would work if centered in Port-au-Prince. "Once we finished all that work, we had a meeting to put all the data together in November with national and international health experts who shared their views and we tried to make a synthesis of the information. It's a plan that was created by experts, not government ministers, although they are certainly involved."

"We're starting a national campaign of consciousness raising," Voltaire continued. "And we're very conscious of the feminization of the AIDS phenomenon, that more women are getting it, and that young people are getting it. Mobilization and consciousness-raising of the population is the basis for the battle. If the ground is not prepared, you can throw all the money you want at it, nothing will happen."

Haiti's Ministry of Health estimated HIV infection rates in Haiti as highest in the poor, rural Northwest and Northeast departments, with 13.9 percent and 6.25 percent of the population infected, respectively. That number is substantially higher than the national average of 4.5 percent and the government said it is acutely aware of the need for community-based health programs.

"We are very conscious that it is a sickness tied with poverty, and the first tendency of a lot of people is to hide the symptoms of the disease. But we want to help liberate these people so they can come forward and speak. We have to arrive at a consciousness-raising so people can support each other. But just since the first of December, my hope has been raised that people will react more positively. In Jacmel, for example, and Petionville, where we are offering testing, people are coming in voluntarily to be tested."

Noting a small grant to Haiti by the IDB the previous month, Voltaire said that of the portion to reinforce the public health system and hospitals, 50 percent would be eaten up by administrative expenses, and that the full $22 million would be needed for the program to work.

"This money to combat AIDS is still dependent on the rerunning of the May 2000 elections, as if AIDS were a political issue," Voltaire said. "Well, it's not, and that's not logical. There's no justification, no effective reason whatsoever why they haven't freed up this money."

As we spoke, as if to underline his point, the lights went out in the office where we sat, leaving us in the dark.

In my email correspondence with the American doctor Paul Farmer, a Harvard-educated physician and author who had for two decades been devoting himself to building a public health infrastructure in the Plateau Central, he echoed Voltaire.

"In my view, people who argue that the Aristide government is anything less than committed have little historical memory for the past two decades," Farmer wrote from his hospital in the hamlet of Cange, where a recently launched initiative included a tuberculosis facility, a women's center and a clean-water program. The hospital had launched Haiti's first community-based HIV program in 1999, enrolling over fifty patients with advanced AIDS into a regime of therapy and support services.

Farmer said Aristide's was the only Haitian government that had worked HIV into its platforms and public speeches and provided assistance for training, serologic kits and medications for AIDS patients.

"The Haitian government is completely broke and still does these things," he wrote.

With a trace of anger, Farmer noted that at one point, the foreign donors had pulled together a $175-million aid package for HIV programs in the Caribbean—none of it destined for Haiti, the country with the region's worst HIV burden.

"If the architects [of the suspension of aid] are trying to strangle Haiti, they're doing a pretty good job," Farmer wrote. "And they're sure making our work difficult."

IN EARLY DECEMBER, Minister of Foreign Affairs Antonio Joseph and Minister of Finance Gustave Faubert traveled to Washington at the invitation of the Congressional Black Caucus, where they met with Caucus members to apprise them of the government's take on the situation in Haiti. The pair also met with U.S. State Department and Treasury officials to plead their case for the release of the IDB loans, but with no success. Further heightening the feeling of insecurity back in Haiti, on December 7, men wearing police uniforms stormed the home of Jean Astrelle Dimanche, owner of the city's ubiquitous Chez Toto lottery banks, and kidnapped his two small children, Kipler and Anderson. Negotiating down from an initial $1 million ransom demand, the children were eventually returned, unharmed, for substantially less. Dimanche himself had been kidnapped only the previous April, and was released only after his family paid an undisclosed—though presumably large—sum. On December 8, Aristide visited the Cité Soleil slum and called for peace and development in the zone.

THE NEXT WEEK, on December 11, Petit Goave exploded into violence with Brignol Lindor's funeral. After a day of calm, the city was again rocked by antigovernment protests on December 13, as anti-Aristide demonstrators erected barricades and burned tires along Route Nationale 2 leading into the city and in front of City Hall. Attending the funeral, which forms the first chapter of this book, at one point I leaned down into Petit Goave's dusty main street and picked up a piece of paper blowing up against a sun-blasted porch. *"Gade Yon Machinn Fenwa,"* it read; "Look at the infernal machine."

> *Nan peyi dayiti fos fenwa preski kouvri nou*
> *Nan PotoPrens machinn fenwa pase kraze jounalis Jean Dominique*
> *Nan Ti Gwav machinn fenwa kontinye desann li kraze jounalis Brignol*
> *Nan tout mond lan se yon mobilizasyon pou demokrasi blayi tou pa tou . . .*

At the bottom of the page were written the words *"sete yon elev lise nan klas 8e 1."* It had been an elementary-school writing assignment. Protests flared in Petit Goave again on December 13, with anti-government demonstrators setting up burning barricades and one protestor receiving a bullet in the head. There was little hope for those who sought to flee the country for the country to the north as, in December, the U.S. Justice Department initiated a policy toward Haitian refugees that could be termed little more than brutal and stupid. Under the direction of Attorney General John Ashcroft, administration policy toward Haitian asylum-seekers arriving by boat became one of automatic detention until those detained were either deported or gained legal status. This included entire families and unaccompanied children. "The Bush administration will be remembered for its mistreatment of the Haitian boat people," the *Miami Herald* wrote in a scathing editorial on the topic.

Speaking on TNH regarding the disturbances in Petit Goave, Dany Toussaint said that the country was on the verge of a coup that could come "at any time," and that the population should remain vigilant. On December 16, celebrating his first election as Haiti's president over a decade earlier, Aristide visited the working-class Saint Martin neighborhood, to inaugurate what he dubbed "a park of peace," a concrete public space that included a playground.

IN THE EARLY MORNING hours of December 17, around two in the morning to be precise, two brothers from the capital's Cité Soleil slum, Winston Jean-Bart and James Petit-Frere, better known as Tupac and Billy, were awakened by phone calls from the PNH director for the West Department, of which Port-au-Prince was a part, Hermione Leonard. Leonard, a cherubic, deceptively cheerful woman, was a close confidante of Aristide—who was said to have fathered a child with her—and for some time had acted as one of his closest conduits to the street gangs in the capital's slums. Married and with children, she was nonetheless known to have a wandering eye for the flashy but impoverished young gang leaders, occasionally passing evenings with one of them, a young tough named Rodson Lemaire, although better known as Kolobri.

For his part, Tupac—handsome and, like his younger brother, an alumnus of Aristide's Lafanmi Selavi institute for street children, and multilingual after having studied English in free courses after the U.S. troops had arrived in 1994—had declined Leonard's affections, which was why he was surprised at the phone call. He was even more surprised at the tone of excitement in the police commander's voice.

"There has been a coup! You must come to the National Palace!" she told him.

Tupac and James, indeed the whole contingent of gang leaders and political militants from Cité Soleil, seized their weapons from their hiding places (loaded with ammunition that had been given to them by Leonard and the PNH only weeks earlier), rounded up cars and took off toward the Palace. Tupac and his men were the first to arrive. The Palace and the Champs de Mars were oddly silent, with no sign of activity beyond the normal somnolent pace of the capital in its wee hours. Tupac sensed something amiss and opted, with the two cars he and his men had, to head back to the slum. On the way back, Tupac was separated from one of the cars carrying his men, and the car lacking the gang leader was stopped by a heavily-armed contingent of PNH troopers, who drew their guns on the young men, took their weapons and beat several badly before throwing them in jail.

James, slightly slower to rally his troops than his big brother, was also heading at breakneck speed toward the Palace when the cars his men were traveling in were hailed by, of all people, Hermione Leonard. She demanded to know what kind of weapons the men had, and when they showed her the pistols and shotguns they were carrying, she told them to go back to the slum and get the "big guns," the Uzis and M14s the boys had stored away for times of real trouble. This they did, and by the time they were crossing down toward the capital's Champs de Mars park, a strange scenario was already playing itself out.

Around the time Tupac's men were arrested, and James was sent back to Cité Soleil to fetch larger weapons, somewhere between ten and twenty heavily armed men dressed in camouflage began strafing the northern and western side of the National Palace with gunfire from three pickup trucks.[3] As one group of men scaled the northern fence, the on-duty guards fled their posts and another group entered through the Palace's western gate. In both cases, guards and Palace security retreated without offering substantial resistance. As they entered the Palace's main building, the men swept the grounds and street with a .50-caliber machine gun mounted on one of the pickups, and also let loose volleys from Uzis and Galils. A man named Claude Dieuveu, passing by the western gate of the Palace at this time, was struck by a bullet. Curiously, the assailants were able to occupy the main building of the Palace for nearly three and a half hours without being challenged by either the Unité de Sécurité Présidentielle (USP) or the Unité de Securite de la Garde du Palais National d'Haiti (USGPNH). In that time, they damaged a USP office, the office of Aristide's Steele Foundation bodyguards, the office of the First Lady, the Diplomatic Lounge and the offices of Aristide and his private secretary. PNH members would later state that the assailants had broadcast statements over PNH radio transmitters stating that Guy Philippe, the Cap Haitien PNH commandant who had fled into exile in 2000, was in command of the National Palace, and that a new president would soon be named. At around 5:30 a.m., though, the men inside the Palace began to make a break to leave, at which point Shavre Milot, a former USGPN employee who was said to be with the invaders, was killed in circumstances that were unclear. Palace security would later say he was killed in a gun battle, but the nature of his wounds, doctors said, suggested execution. In the course of the wild firing, two more policeman, PNH officers, were killed.

The three pickups fled west, firing at points along the way and injuring and killing people at Rue Pavée, in Tabarre and at Croix des Bouquets. Following the cars was a contingent of PNH SWAT officers as well as Aristide's personal helicopter, piloted by his chief of security, Frantz Gabriel. A first vehicle was abandoned at Ganthier, said Gabriel, and then a second at Thomazeau. At Mon Kabrit, where the city's suburban western plain rises up toward the Plateau Central and the Dominican Republic, it was said that the men abandoned their last vehicle, the one containing the .50-caliber machine gun, and that their pursuers then lost the trail. Gabriel, who had made a refueling run back to the capital, said he saw the men enter and emerge from a cave near the top of Mon Kabrit, having changed into civilian clothes from their fatigues, and then scatter in different directions. PNH officers would later say they had found an arms cache there.

I WAS WALKING DOWN Avenue Jean Paul II alone, just as the sun was beginning to bring the shapes in Port-au-Prince's lightless streets into greater relief. It must have been around 6 a.m. A phone call had appraised me of the attack and, lacking a car, I set out from my apartment in Pacot on foot. As I descended the empty street, I saw clutches of frightened people gathered in front of their homes, or in front of the snaking alleys that led back to their *lakous*, gazing fearfully down the street in the direction of the Champs de Mars, their transistors held up to their heads.

"*Yo te atake Palais?*" I asked one man, barrel-chested, a bushy mustache resting atop his lip. (They attacked the Palace?)

"*Wi, nou te tande sa.*" (Yes, that's what we heard.)

"*Ki moun?*" (Who?)

"*Nou pa konnen.*" (Nobody knows.)

I continued walking downhill until I got to the intersection of Avenues Charles Sumner and Lamartiniere, just before the Champs de Mars, where a group of individuals were gathered in front of a shuttered gas station, gazing warily downhill. I was about to inquire as to the state of the streets further downtown when a pickup careened around the corner on two wheels in the direction on the Palace. From the back and sides of the truck hung about a dozen men, young and dressed in bandannas and Rasta tams, waving a myriad of shotguns, machetes and automatic rifles. They gazed at me with anger and shouted something I couldn't make out before they sped past and down toward the Palace.

Then, as I stood there, a car stopped and I saw the shadow of someone walking toward me. It was Guy Delva, from the AJH. We greeted one another.

"So, have you been down there yet?" I asked him, motioning to the Champs de Mars.

"No, not yet," he said.

"So let's go."

What awaited us was a scene of utter chaos. We drove down through a square that was thronged with thousands of armed young men, some brandishing shotguns and pistols, other charging toward the Palace brandishing machetes and nail-studded clubs. As we parked near the back of the Palace and got out, a CIMO said that the shooting had begun around 5 a.m., but declined to say whether or not Aristide was there.

"There are some things we can't comment on," he said, fingering his M5.

As I threaded my way through the huge crowd—many armed and hostile, and screaming "*git mama w blan*" ("Fuck your mother, white man") in my face—I saw a police vehicle parked at an odd angle just in front of the building. I peered in, and inside saw two policeman laying dead, still in their tan PNH khakis, dark halos of blood radiating around their shirts.

"We are going to find all the ex-military in Port-au-Prince and put them to the gun!" shouted one young man, as he banged a machete on the ground. "We are going to send all the Dominican people back to Santo Domingo! We are going to go house to house in Carrefour and send them out!"

At the front gates of the Palace, several men drove a bulldozer that stopped just short of knocking the fence-links down.

"Turn them over to us! We know what to do with them!" screamed a young man holding onto the Palace gate. They said they had launched an ultimatum to those they believed were still inside, saying that if they didn't come out by noon, they would go after ex-military and Convergence members in the city. At about the same time as I gathered their plan, and for the first time heard the rumor that Guy Philippe was said to be behind the assault, another group of about a dozen shrieking chimere, armed with machetes, some with pistols tucked into their belts, surrounded me. Screaming so loudly I could see their spittle landing on my shirt, they asked if I was Dominican.

"No, I'm American," I told them, not knowing if that would be any help but figuring it best not to start constructing a web of lies in such a situation.

"The Americans come to Haiti just to fuck up things! What your country is doing in other countries we see, but we won't let you kill Aristide!" shouted one man, missing a few of his teeth, as he waved his machete. "We know that the American Ambassador paid these people to do these things! *Git mama w blan!*"

"We will burn the whole country rather than let coup d'etat pass," said another, pointing his finger at me.

A slight, dreadlocked man parted the group and approached me, speaking in a lower, more composed voice than the rest.

"We only want Aristide," he said. "We want Aristide forever. But if someone wants to kill him, we will kill them first! Tell the international community that for me!"

"2004 will be freedom for all black people in the world," he continued. "The Palestinians who are black, the Afghanis are black, but the Americans call them terrorists. Osama bin Laden will win the war with America in the end, because America tries to fuck up everywhere."

As he spoke, several journalists descended from the Radio Metropole van for a few moments but were surrounded by chanting chimere and hopped back

in the car, which took off under a shower of paving stones and other projectiles. Sensing that my presence was somewhat less than welcome, and having
been at the Champs de Mars now for more than an hour, I began to cautiously
retrace my steps over the park toward the streets that led back to Pacot, careful
to move confidently and not run so as not to set off the scent of panic. As I did
so, a few hundred yards from the Palace gates, I watched two more truckloads
full of chimere, holding automatic rifles above their heads, drive several circles
around the Palace in two SUVs. A small boy, barefoot, shirtless and no more then
seven, lugged a stick that was almost as big as he was into the midst of the mob.
When he saw me, he smiled.

"What are you doing?" I asked him.

"I'm protesting, too," was his response.

About halfway to the Hotel Plaza, I came across a group of people regarding
something halfway nestled onto a curb. I peered over their shoulders and was
sickened to see a burned corpse, barely recognizable as human and singed the
color of gray charcoal, crumpled on the street. Someone had thrown orange
peels on top of the body. It helped things burn faster, someone later told me.

Walking over to the gate of the Palace Hotel where many diaspora Haitians
were staying as they visited their families in advance of the Christmas holiday,
I saw several frightened women looking down the steps at the chaos on the
street. Down Rue Capois, a crowd of several hundred young men came charging past, brandishing automatic pistols and rifles, shotguns, machetes and
knives, singing the old song "Grenadier, to arms!" that had been sung at the time
of the U.S. occupation. I followed them for a time and, as police watched and
one police vehicle followed slowly behind them, a crowd of several hundred
more charged up Avenue Lamartinierre in the direction of the OPL and KON-
AKOM offices.

I did not know it at the time, but the mobs would by the end of the day reduce
both buildings, situated directly across from the TELECO state telephone company, nearly to ashes, also burning down the neighboring home of the man
who had rented them to the politicians for good measure. The bulldozer that I
had seen at the National Palace earlier slowly made its way up to Turgeau, where
it was put to use battering in the gates of the OPL compound to open it to the
sack. After the destruction of the OPL and KONAKOM offices was complete,
the mob moved on to the headquarters of Evans Paul's KID party, destroying it
with fire for the third time in ten years. Private residences were not excepted,
and four carloads of armed, masked men arrived at KONAKOM leader Victor
Benoit's house and set it on fire, room by room. The Petionville home of OPL
leader Gérard Pierre-Charles and his wife Suzy Castor was also attacked, with
some fifteen men, arriving in trucks owned by the government-owned National
Center for Equipment (CNE) and, in one case, a police vehicle, first throwing
stones and then shooting at the house. Pierre-Charles was at a conference in

Miami, and Castor and her servants fled in terror. In her absence, and in full view of the police as well as Lavalas Senator Prince Pierre Sonson and Petionville Mayor Sully Guerrier, the mob burned the couple's home and in their ignorant blind, bought rage, Pierre-Charles would later write, they incinerated "a whole collection of classics about Marxism, my books about Cuba, about 500, that had helped me write 'Genèse de la Révolution Cubain,' whose manuscript in French disappeared into the flames as well as some of my books, leaving me without a single copy." The irreplaceable library of Latin American and Carribean political thought, including many original manuscripts dealing with Haiti's early history at Castor's CRESFED center, a frequent source of study for grassroots groups and impoverished students, was looted and burned to the ground.

Attempting to walk home, at the crossroads of Rue Waag and Avenue Henri Christophe I came across a mountain of burning tires in the otherwise deserted street, but managed to thread my way through back alleys until I arrived more or less intact at my home. When I again passed the headquarters for Reynold Georges's Alliance pour l'Avancement et la Libération d'Haiti (ALAH) party on Avenue Jean Paul II a short time later, all three of the buildings in the compound were in flames, and the inferno was being watched by a crowd of curious onlookers.

There will probably never be an accurate estimation of how many people died in the violence. In addition to the three bodies I saw in front of the Palace, there was another dead civilian I did not see and the dead gunmen inside. Nor was the rest of the country spared. In Gonaives, members of the pro-Aristide Cannibal Army street gang led by Amiot Metayer, whose Raboteau slum had been the scene of such terror during the FRAPH years, attacked the home of Pastor Luc Mesadieu, who was the head of the Mouvement Chrétien Pour une Nouvelle Haiti (MOCHRENA) party, and who was viewed as an increasingly important force in the spread of evangelical Protestantism throughout the once solidly Catholic country. When Mesadieu's assistant, Ramy Daran, tried to intervene, he was seized by the mob. Refusing to reveal the location where Mesadieu was hiding, on Metayer's orders Daran was doused with gasoline (distributed from the gas station owned by the city's Lavalas mayor) and burned alive. The gang also torched twenty other houses in the city before they were through. In the Plateau Central, a group of chimeres carrying jugs of gasoline piled into two taptaps provided by the Lavalas mayor of Hinche, Dongo Joseph, and went to burn down the nearby headquarters of MPP, the peasant organization headed by Chavannes Jean-Baptiste, Aristide's bitter political enemy who had been the subject of an assassination attempt the pervious fall. Arriving at the MPP compound, though, the chimere beat a hasty retreat away when dozens of machete-wielding peasants descended into the road to defend it. In Petit Goave, the scene was even more chaotic, with Convergence supporters flooding the streets and burning property belonging to Lavalas members when news of the attack became public, and Lavalas in turn attacking and burning homes of Convergence partisans when word reached the town that the attack had failed.

Rather than make any attempt to reign in the chaos, Lavalas officials instead fueled it.

"The people have identified their enemy. This coup was an act of terrorism and terrorism will not be tolerated in Haiti," Senate President Yvon Neptune said on national radio.

"It is time to be patriots; the nation is in danger," said Aristide, in a speech broadcast to the nation from the National Palace hours after the attack. "I thank the population and the police for defending democracy."

Later in the day, Palace security officials led reporters on a tour of the rooms in the presidential Palace that had been damaged, with bullet holes pockmarking the white walls and Shavre Milot's body, dressed in a camouflage uniform and with U.S. dollars having been clumsily stuffed visibly into his pockets after the fact, lying dead facedown on the floor. Guy Philippe, for his part, speaking to the Miami-based Radio Carnival from his exile in Santo Domingo, denied that he had been the organizer of the assault, later asking reporters, "How am I going to mobilize troops? By remote control?" He then promptly fled Santo Domingo for Ecuador.

AS CHAOTIC AS December 17 was, many felt that it was only a glimpse of what Aristide was capable of should he ever feel truly threatened. Many in Haiti recalled the lessons of the *semaine sanglante* (bloody week) of 1883.

In August 1878, Lysius Salomon, a towering black lawyer who had been born in Les Cayes in 1815 and served as Faustin Soulouque's Minister of Finance for eleven years, was brought to power in a chaotic election over the Liberal party and was in turn backed by a supportive coup. Salomon, who had traveled widely in Europe and even taken a French wife, entered office promising Haiti's down-trodden that he was going to modernize the country, reform the army, give aid to peasant farmers, and put the treasury in order. Before ascending to the presidency, he had watched several members of his immediate family, including two brothers, die in political violence, and he had no affection whosoever for the mulatto elite in the capital.

After he took office, Salomon made strides in restructuring Haiti's education system, staffing and funding often forgotten schools, and traversed the country giving public speeches urging his fellow Haitians to modernize and leave behind the litany of fratricidal struggles that had bedeviled it since its independence. Tellingly though, he also imported French and Belgium machine guns to arm his expanded 16,000-man military. In order to recapitilize the Haitian national bank with loans from French financial institutions, Salomon also had to begin repaying the onerous 1825 "debt" to France, which, though he managed to do so in under two years, nearly bankrupted the country.

But Salomon's Liberal and mulatto enemies, especially in Cap Haitien, who resented perceived domination by a southerner, ceaselessly schemed against him, and, in the spring of 1880, Salomon responded by arresting scores of them. A smallpox outbreak in December 1881 had soon claimed thousands of lives, and an abortive coup led by dissident soldiers beginning in Saint Marc that same December prompted Salomon to arrest hundreds more political enemies and have twenty-eight of them shot after summary trials. In April 1882 the president, having endured months of plotting against him, addressed a throng of supporters of Champs de Mars in a speech recounted in *Written in Blood: The Story of the Haitian People, 1492–1995* by Robert Debs Heinl and Nancy Gordon Heinl, that would find echoes in one given on the square a century later:

> I'll betide the Cap if a single shot is fired. That shot would be the signal for massacre, incediarism, and, I will add, for I want to be truthful, pillage. . . . Soldiers! Isn't it right you should be paid before civilian employees? The money has been sent here to pay you; if you haven't been paid, it is because the funds have been diverted to other pockets. . . . Wrongdoers have said I wish to have myself proclaimed emperor. If in 1848 it was an error to found an empire, today it would be insanity. . . . Blood that flows from explosion of powder is a heady drink. Those who commence to drink it are devoured by thirst. Let us be careful not to arouse the anger of the people. My friends, I pray, I entreat you, I adjure you, support me in my work of pacification. Be my disciples, preach to all: Peace, Union and, Concord.

Gloomily confiding to his aides a month later, Salomon is reported to have said, "I have been pushed to extreme measures."

A year later, on March 27, 1883, a group numbering some hundred of Salomon's exiled Liberal enemies landed and seized Miragoane. Small rebellions by Liberal forces flared in the north and south of the country, and they finally overcame government forces in Jeremie and Jacmel, effectively splitting off the southern claw of the country for siege warfare that went on throughout the summer. Arson fires gutted poor sections of Port-au-Prince, and with the September 22 murder of one of his generals by rebel forces, Salomon finally revealed what extreme measures he had referred to.

Shortly after the general's murder, military loyal to the president and paramilitary volunteers under Salomon's orders commenced to burning homes belonging to the president's enemies and gutting the capital's business district, where they looted stores and murdered merchants where they found them. Individuals and families associated with the Liberals and the mulattos were subject to gruesome deaths throughout the city, which hung over a pall of black smoke, and the madness continued for three days until foreign diplomats threatened an invasion unless Salomon put an end to it. When he did, the capital's economy had been destroyed utterly and the unrest had claimed over a thousand lives. A president who had held great promise as a modernizer and a hope for his people had instead given vent to the darkest impulses in the hearts of his supporters, re-cleaved the chasm of color and class, and, despite the eventual victory over the rebels in the south, mortally wounded his own presidency. His enemies never paused in their efforts to oust him, and, six years later, they succeeded. Salomon joined a long list of Haiti's leaders to know the bitter fruit of exile.

ON DECEMBER 19, accompanied by Evans Paul, U.S. Ambassador Brian Dean Curran toured the charred-out remnants of the OPL and KONAKOM offices. The buildings, singed-black, were utterly gutted, and as we stepped through them, we stepped over half-burned Convergence flyers depicting Aristide as a ravenous cat with the words "Zero tolerance for stolen elections."

"It's clear that the coup was a pretext to justify the systematic repression of the opposition," Evans Paul said to me as I walked beside them. Paul, a distinctive-looking black Haitian man with pursed lips that made him appear as if he was always about to launch an acerbic barb or two, had never forgiven Aristide for what he regarded as the character assassination committed against him after the latter returned from exile in 1994. Paul had endured multiple beatings and arrests after Aristide fled, but Aristide had sent the OPs out to accuse him of complicity in the coup after his return, and supported the folksinger Manno Charlemagne in the latter's successful bid to unseat Paul from the Port-au-Prince mayor's office. For him, the struggle against Aristide was personal as well as political. "Jean-Bertrand Aristide and Lavalas don't only want to destroy political parties, they want to assassinate history as well, as you can see by their actions at the homes of Gérard Pierre-Charles, Victor Benoit and at CRESFED," he said. "This was no coup d'etat; it was a coup de théatre."

I had watched earlier with some amusement, as some OPL activists relit some of the charred embers of the building to give it an added smoky flavor for the ambassador's arrival, deferring always to the Haitian bent for dramatic flair. Seeing the incinerated building though, and hearing stories from the political activists and neighbors about the armed gangs that had attacked the structure two days earlier, Dean Curran looked anything but amused.

"I've come here today to see with my own eyes what the officers of the American embassy have seen for the last two days," Curran said, addressing the reporters in Kreyol. "Here at Convergence headquarters, the result of a crowd, out of control, on Monday. It didn't happen only here, it happened at several other party headquarters and it happened at the homes of several party leaders. This is completely unacceptable. The United States strongly condemns this action just as we have condemned the attack on the presidential Palace. We are particularly concerned about the attacks on political party headquarters, on individual's homes and the intimidation of the press, because the police were unable or unwilling to intervene."

The Aristide government would eventually end up paying (from the state treasury as opposed to from the budget of the Fanmi Lavalas party, whose partisans had caused the damage) four million gourdes to Evans Paul, ten million gourdes to Reynold Georges and twelve million gourdes to Victor Benoit in compensation for the destruction.

That same day, Ecuador's deputy foreign minister confirmed that Guy Philippe had been detained there after arriving from Panama on an investor's visa, which was then revoked. Rather than holding him, though, the Ecuadorian government deported Philippe back to Panama, from where he slipped back into Santo Domingo.

ON DECEMBER 20, five days after the attack, PNH spokesman Jean-Dady Simeon told a news conference that Guy Philippe was responsible for the assault. Simeon also blamed Guy Francois, a former army colonel who served as Minister of the Interior in the 1991–1994 military regime, for complicity, and he said that Francois had been arrested at the international airport the previous day attempting to board a flight for Venezuela. Simeon said testimony from Pierre Richardson, an alleged co-conspirator police said had been arrested that Monday at the Dominican border with a wad of cash and an M16 rifle, had provided the information. The same day, a group of chimere, led by René Civil, marched past the restaurant where I was eating in Petionville with a police escort, screaming "Down with the Convergence."

THAT CHRISTMAS, spent by the events of the previous weeks, I whiled away the holiday in Jacmel, the lovely colonial town situated on Haiti's southern coast and blessed with 24-hour electricity courtesy of a project by Hydro-Quebec. I went by tap-tap, alone, and while there renewed a friendship with a French photographer, a woman who had lived in Haiti off and on since 1979, and who had deeply inhaled the particular bug that keeps some foreigners returning to Haiti again and again. An invaluable source of perspective, we soon became fast friends. I also met and was befriended by a European diplomat who had moved to Haiti a decade earlier when he had grown weary of life on the continent. He was also a respected filmmaker and journalist, and another attraction for him, he said, was that being so far away in Haiti allowed him to do his work in peace. The night I arrived, though, crowds of hundreds of Haitians danced in the streets to music on Christmas Eve, while others ascended the steps of their churches for nighttime services and the sounds of Catholic and Baptist Kreyol hymns resonated through the town's narrow streets.

I slept in the otherwise empty Hotel Florita on Rue St. Anne, two streets away from the polluted beach, a rambling four-story white-washed building that for many years had been the home of the American author Selden Rodman and his family. The most recent owners had only recently moved out and turned it into a hotel, and rooms were still piled with boxes of their belongings and books, as if they might be returning to claim them at any time.

Rodman was as interesting and eccentric a character as Haiti ever drew to her bosom. A writer and citric born in New York City in 1909, he had written a play, "The Revolutionists," about Toussaint Louverture, and along with De Witt Peters, a California artist who came to Haiti to teach English during World War II, he had opened the Centre D'Art, Haiti's first professional art school, in 1944. On one of my first visits to Haiti, I wandered around the steaming, fume-choked lanes just north of the National Palace and had stumbled upon the Episcopal Cathedral Saint Trinite, possibly one of the most extraordinary churches on earth. Unassuming from the outside, once inside the silent, dim chamber I saw the walls illuminated by stunning indigenous murals depicting scenes from the Bible: a black John the Baptist painted in bright primary colors, a near-nude Adam and Eve with an apple and a snake in between them, all created by such eminent Haitian painters as Wilson Bigaud and Philome Obin, many thick with vodou references. I would later discover that Rodman supervised the painting of the cathedral for the open-minded Reverend C. Alfred Voegeli in 1949.

A fan of Rodman's book on Haitian art, *Where Art Is Joy*, I had visited him at his home in Oakland, New Jersey in 2000. Elderly but still vigorous, he shared rum punch with me after he came into his ranch-style home from a game of tennis. The house, which he shared with his wife Carole, was adorned from floor to ceiling with Haitian canvases, exquisite examples of work by painters such as Stevenson Magloire, who had been killed mysteriously during Aristide's return in 1994, and Magloire's mother, Louisiane Saint-Fleurant, one of the members of the highly regarded Sans Soleil school in Haiti. Speaking to him over drinks, I wondered how much of his soul the old man had left back in Haiti.

This town—which had given Simon Bolivar shelter during some of the darkest days of his struggle for South America—worked a similar effect on me, with a white-sheeted four-poster bed and opened double doors on the terrace allowing a sea-breeze to blow through the hotel. Still mourning for those who had been killed in my city, New York, the previous September, I sat at the Yaquimo, an open-air bar directly on Jacmel's rubbish-strewn beach, as pigs roamed freely up and down and the hull of a ship lay rotting in the bay. Underneath the high tropical moon, a group of children splashed their feet in the blue-green waves of the sea.

BACK IN THE CAPITAL, once Guy Philippe returned to Santo Domingo, the Aristide government attempted, unsuccessfully, to have him extradited.

"The government believes he is in the Dominican Republic and we are actively seeking his extradition," Jean-Dady Simeon told reporters on the day after Christmas.

The police also announced that two more people had been arrested for complicity in the attack, including one Anthony Saati. Saati, a Haitian-American businessman with a food distribution company in Miami, later ended up being rushed to the hospital from his jail cell when someone switched the water he had been drinking with cleaning fluid.

Visiting Saati at the Canapé Vert hospital a few days later, I was surprised to bump into Evans Paul walking down the hallway from the direction of his room. I asked him what he was doing there and Paul just smiled.

"I'm just visiting an old friend," Paul said, betraying nothing.

Once I passed the PNH guard posted outside of Saati's room, I found the man himself, a burly, bearded 47-year-old mulatto, sitting on his bed in a hospital gown, playing solitaire and evidently bored out of his mind, grateful to receive visitors.

"I had absolutely nothing to do with this coup attempt," he said. "I'm here because of people taking advantage of the trust the government put in them."

Saati then told a fevered tale of a business dispute involving Eddy Deeb, a former partner of his and close associate of Lavalas senator Fourel Celestin. Arriving at Deeb's place of business a few days after the coup, Saati said he was beaten and arrested by Haitian police in Celestin's employ. Since his poisoning he had been trapped in the small hospital room, as Judge Bernard Sainvil delayed his court appearance repeatedly because of Saati's supposed ill health.

"Do I look like I'm too sick to stand trial?" he asked me. Amidst embarrassed official silence, Saati was finally released without comment three weeks later.

On December 27, the government announced that Minister of Justice Garry Lissade had appointed Judge Bernard Sainvil to investigate the attack on the palace ten days earlier and the ensuing mob violence.

After the attack, Aristide had upped his contract with the Steele Foundation by some forty men, increasing the total number of American security personnel on his staff to nearly fifty and increasing the financial burden on the Haitian government from $6 million to $9 million a year for the president's personal security. An additional weapons package for the guards topped nearly $1 million. A good place to spy on Aristide's million-dollar men was always Le Petit Saint-Pierre, a restaurant just off Petionville's Place Saint Pierre. There you could see the burly white men as they drank and caroused, often with very young black Haitian prostitutes on their laps, enjoying the balmy Haitian winter nights and thanking their lucky stars that they had landed such a well-paying job in such an agreeable tropical locale.

EARLY ON IN THE NEW YEAR, I sat chatting with Bob Moliere, a barrel-chested, gap-toothed Lavalas militant, on the grass behind TNH, the state television company, just off the Delmas Road. Moliere was frequently a face among the pro-Aristide mobs that paralyzed the streets from time to time, and when he had begun spouting pro-Aristide lines at a restaurant nearby, the owner had responded by shouting, "Get out of here, I don't want you talking that kind of shit in here!" and promptly kicked us out. Moliere had been born in La Saline, but his home was burned down in 1969 on the orders of Tonton Macoute leader Madame Max Adolphe and then his family had moved to Cité Soleil. After a falling out with some gang leaders in Cité Soleil, he now shifted from neighborhood to neighborhood.

"Aristide is the one to replace Dessalines," Moliere told me. "Because Dessalines's dream after slavery was to give people liberty, and to let them know what was the right thing to do, because we know he has a dream to help the people to know a better day, to have a better life. And that's why they killed him in 1806. But right now we have Aristide who has the same dream that Dessalines had; it's the same dream that Aristide had. To help the country, to help the people, to help the majority."

In the countryside, strange things were happening. In the northern hamlet of Saint Raphael on January 6, Lavalas Deputy Jocelyn Saint-Louis machine-gunned the town's Lavalas mayor, Sernand Sévère, to death in the climax of a long-simmering feud between the two for political supremacy in the region. At a January baptism held for the son of Reverend Phéde Civil, René Civil's brother, in the idyllic Vallée de Jacmel, the gunmen who accompanied René Civil from Port-au-Prince posed with the impressive variety of weapons they brought along, pictures that eventually found their way onto the Internet. At a January 7 meeting with representatives of Haiti's local media institutions, Aristide attempted to soothe them, saying, "The government must do its best to protect the press and political parties." The same day, the Inter-American Press Association issued an appeal for greater press freedom in the country, saying that "the lack of respect and tolerance in Haiti has forced dozens of journalists into exile and to remain in hiding, since they feel that by staying in their country, they live in constant fear for their lives." Several journalists urged Aristide to reappoint Claudy Gassant, whose mandate as investigating judge in the Jean Dominique killing—which it was Aristide's personal responsibility to renew—had expired two days earlier, but Aristide refused to commit himself.

"When Radio Haiti is a victim, our brother journalists are victims, too," said one reporter. "We ask that you please lift the immunity of Dany Toussaint."

Aristide, polite in a gray suit and red tie, listened and even appeared to take notes at times. As he did so, doves fluttered outside the curtains drawn against the sun, casting fantastic shadows on the drapes behind him.

"I would appreciate it if the Haitians could find a political solution themselves, without having to call on the OAS, the UN and the OAS," said a journalist from Tele Haiti.

That same month the OAS Permanent Council adopted Resolution 806 on Haiti, calling on the Aristide government to resolve the political impasse with the Convergence, take steps to stem growing violence and the deterioration in human rights and authorized establishment of OAS Special Mission in Haiti to support the resolution's implementation. An OAS Special Mission, under the aegis of Canadian diplomat David Lee, was set to begin operations in March.

I HAD MET HIM before, briefly, on the porch of one of the capital's hotels where the international press often hang out on the rare occasions they're in town—a tall, skinny kid with close-cropped hair and a tattoo on one bicep that said, "Don't Trust No One." He carried himself with a polite authority, switching back and forth between English and Kreyol, yet he could not hide the gnawing sadness he felt that his brother Winston, the gang leader better known around the city as Tupac, had been picked up and thrown in the National Penitentiary after the events of December 17. With his group of gunmen arrested by the police the morning of the Palace attack, Tupac had been livid, and called Hermione Leonard, asking her to explain to the police that they were working for the government and that the police could look and see that all the bullets in the guns were police-issued. The youths were eventually released, but the police kept their weapons, which had irked Tupac, who had paid for them himself. When he had pressed Leonard on the subject, she refused, saying that, given the events of the last weeks, the Aristide government needed all the firepower it could get. The calls had gone back and forth, culminating in a conversation between Tupac and officials from the National Palace, during which the officials promised to reimburse the guns. Instead, though, Tupac was thrown in jail on kidnapping charges that he was never formally convicted of, where he remained for two years.

His name was James, though he went by the nome de guerre Billy and, like his half-brother, he hailed from Cité Soleil, the shantytown that now held some 200,000 souls and slumps from the northern edge of Port-au-Prince toward the marshlands that bleed into the polluted Bay of Port-au-Prince. He was a child of Aristide. His mother, a community activist, had been killed in Cité Soleil shortly after the coup against Aristide in 1991, and his father during the FRAPH raid on the bidonville in December 1993. Afterwards, for a time, he had become a habitué of Aristide's Lafanmi Selavi organization and a favorite guide for English-speaking journalists who wanted to visit his home district. Following Tupac's incarceration, he had also become the boss of his older brother's group of armed militants.

Here we stood in the first month of 2002, in the warren of alleys and lanes that made up Soleil 19, his home base in the area; James looked at the world through dark aviator sunglasses, giving him a menace that vanished once he removed them and the smiling 21-year-old beneath was revealed.

"They burned these houses down in December 2000," he said, gesturing at the charred tin and cement shells that people once called home. Pointing across a stream bank choked with refuse, he said, "They burned those down a few months ago."

James's faction, the gang from Soleil 19, and other gangs from the Boston and Belakou neighborhoods of the district, had recently engaged in a spate of fighting with rival groups from the Brooklyn and Tracks zones. The latter gang, which took its name from the railroad tracks that ran by the abandoned Haitian American Sugar Company headquarters near their base, had a fierce reputation for violence and drug abuse, with residents telling tales about the orange glow of their crack pipes illuminating the alleyways.

"My mother was killed by FRAPH and so was my father," James said as we walked through his neighborhood. "So my brother and I were on our own when we were very young. I got involved in politics first when I was fifteen, trying to understand my life and my situation. We want to try and help our people now and President Aristide has been the only president who has tried to do something for poor people like us."

James told me—and other gang leaders from the neighborhood later concurred—that they were proud of their actions on the morning of December 17. They told me how Hermione Leonard had called them in the early morning hours, telling them that the Palace was under attack.

"The police called us, early in the morning, and I took my gun and my people and was gone, to defend my Palace and defend my president."

The poverty of Haiti reached staggering proportions in Cité Soleil, and before my eyes thousands were literally clinging to the city up to the very edge of the rank water. In claustrophobic lanes swarming with flies, a small child played with a kite fashioned out of a plastic bag, while schoolgirls in pink uniforms walked delicately, hand-in-hand.

"We are tired of all this killing," James said. "We want to concentrate on community projects, help our country, teaching people how to read, how to speak English. Me, I would like to be a policeman, or a doctor."

I walked around with James, the length of the long road that stretched from his neighborhood, which abutted the sea, up to the Boston zone, which almost touched a pot-holed artery of Route Nationale 1, which ran from Port-au-Prince all the way to Cap Haitien. As we talked, I listened to how James had followed packs of journalists around when the American troops had landed in 1994. A photographer from the *Washington Post* had even given him some camera equipment at the time, which the young boy, at that time all of thirteen years old, had worn around his neck with obvious pride. He talked of how he had seen journalists come and go from Cité Soleil, but how nothing ever seemed to change for him and his brother, how the poverty remained. Yet he still hoped Aristide could change things. Working together with the police, as they had on December 17, and despite the fact that they themselves were no angels, James and his friends felt they had a larger vision, and that they could protect the bodies and the interests of the poor.

As we reached Boston, James introduced me to two more young men standing at the entrance to the neighborhood. One, a fierce looking natty dread, was Rosemond Titus, who was running the Boston baz while it's nominal chef, named Robinson Thomas but known to all as Labanye (Banner), was locked up, under what charges he declined to specify. The other, a smiling, easy-going boy with a whisp of mustache, was named Junior Millard and also hailed from the zone.

I told James that I hoped I would see him again. He told me the gangs were having a meeting, trying in the interest of their community to come together, and that they would be having a press conference to that affect soon. Would I like to come? Absolutely, I said. We shook hands on it, and then I hailed a red ribbon cab to take me back uptown.

Several days later, at a news conference held at the CATH union hall in downtown Port-au-Prince, James and the boys read their declaration.

"Honor and respect to President Titid," James read, his voice shouting above the din of those assembled and the rumbling coming from Rue des Miracles outside. "Cité Soleil bows down to you to thank you for the beautiful Christmas we spent in Cité Soleil, without forgetting to give a special tip of the hat to the police, especially the D.D.O. [the Directeur Department d'Ouest, Hermione Leonard].

"President Titid," the statement continued. "The *alfabetizasyon* program cannot happen with war going on. *Alfa-ekonomik* cannot happen with war. No development can blossom if there is no peace in Cité Soleil. In that sense, President Titid, the only thing that can establish peace is to open another police substation in Cité Soleil.

"In Tracks and Boston, ever since Cité Soleil was called Cité Simone, it was always these two areas which were fighting for control of Cité Soleil. This is exactly why, President Titid, we would like you to open a substation, so no time will be lost for the *lambi* of peace to blow in Cité Soleil, and 2004 will be a success."

Seated with him were a virtual who's who of Cité Soleil gang leaders, young men with names like Amaral, Doudou, as well as Rosemond and Junior. Probably the biggest gang leader in all of Cité Soleil, though, the baby-faced Labanye who commanded the loyalties of the gang in the Boston section of the slum, was still cooling his heels in jail.

"I was raped three times," said Dadent, a small, fine-featured woman who sat next to me on a battered, stiff-backed wooden chair, her hair braided in a mass of cornrows. "I have to move from house to house every night because those guys always come back."

"Look at what happened to that journalist," said Lise Lande, a careworn woman in a pressed blue dress and a straw hat; she was referring to the Canadian reporter Mathieu Prudhomme, a 27-year-old who was shot and wounded while interviewing people in Cité Soleil for the Haitian Press Network in January. "They shot him because they want to make people afraid to come and talk to us, so they can do whatever they want."

"We would give up the guns if we could," said one gang member, a strapping young man with sensitive, Chinese eyes. "Who would want to live like this if they didn't have to?"

"President Aristide wanted two representatives from each of Cité Soleil's thirty-four different groups to find a solution, but those five gangs want to run the whole thing themselves," said Junior.

"We hope the president hears us and helps us."

WRAPPING UP A weeklong investigation in Haiti into the Brignol Lindor murder and the status of the Dominique investigation, Robert Ménard, secretary-general of the Paris-based press freedom group Reporters Sans Frontières, called a press conference at the Hotel Plaza on the Champs de Mars for the morning of January 11. With Guy Delva at his side, Ménard, arrogant and passionate, delivered a scathing indictment of the Aristide government before the local press, and I sat in the audience, watching him assail the regime for its obstruction of the investigations into the journalists' murders and saying that an official policy of press repression existed in Haiti.

"President Aristide is personally responsible for this situation," Ménard said. "And he is personally responsible for the impunity that has been manifest in the Haitian government."

Ménard then called on countries that respected freedom of the press to revoke the travel visas and freeze the assets of Aristide, his wife Mildred, Yvon Neptune, Minister of Justice Garry Lissade, Interior Minister Henri Claude Ménard and Dany Toussaint, as well as those of nineteen other individuals.

As Ménard spoke, from our location in a conference room on the second floor of the Plaza we could hear a growing commotion down on the street. At first we thought it might be a traffic altercation, but then we could hear the distinct sound of chanting, though the words were indecipherable. Excusing myself, I stepped out onto the Plaza's terrace and looked down on the street to see Paul Raymond, in a ludicrous day-glo green shirt, shouting into a bullhorn before a group of about three-dozen protestors. Several us walked down to the Plaza's entrance to see what all the commotion was about and were treated to the crowd chanting *"Aba imperialis!"* Raymond himself launched into a shrieking tirade that his supporters greeted with more chanting.

"We are a free nation!" Raymond said. "Today they are trying to assassinate our liberty! Robert Ménard is not working for journalists; he just working for his own country, and he is a colonizer!"

"Robert Ménard *se vakabon!*" the mob responded.

Despite a police presence in front of the hotel, Raymond and his supporters charged into the Plaza, saying they would drive Ménard out of the country, but Ménard and Delva had fled out a back door. The Aristide partisans came back out into the street empty-handed.

FOLLOWING THE EXPIRATION of his term as investigating judge in the Jean Dominique case, Claudy Gassant, whose security had always been in jeopardy, was left without any official protection at all. After fifteen months spent investigating Haiti's most notorious murder, Gassant arrived in Miami on January 8, and entered exile. A final encounter with police in front of the National Palace had been too much for him. On December 21, just after the Palace attack, while caught in traffic near the National Palace, Claudy Gassant's car was front-ended by another vehicle, shattering its headlight. Four police officers suddenly appeared on the scene to jeer him, one of them pointing an automatic rifle directly at Gassant's head before withdrawing. Rather presumptuously, speaking to the *Miami Herald* after Gassant's flight, Brian Concannon—the Aristide government attorney who had prosecuted the Raboteau case and whose commitment to human rights evidently did not extend to those who would challenge the government that paid him—said that Gassant "had more (resources) than any other judge in any other case in Haiti's history," and went on to blame Gassant for provoking confrontations with police.4 In the future, the government-funded Bureau des Avocats Internationaux that Concannon worked for, while claiming an interest in prosecuting human-rights violations in Haiti, would studiously avoid pursuing any that could have lead back to the Aristide government, including the Dominique case.

Shortly after Gassant's flight, I went to visit Michele Montas at Radio Haiti. I asked her about Yvon Neptune's statement a month earlier that the Senate was looking into lifting Dany Toussaint's parliamentary immunity.

"They've had the whole thing in front of them since August, so it's been a while," she said, idly toying with bullets and spent shell casing that had been fired at the station over the years, which she kept in a bowl on her desk. "They haven't acted on it so far. . . . We can't believe words on this any more, we've waited long enough. They are not asking the senate to hold a tribunal or to be a court in anyway; all they are asking the Senate is to lift parliamentary immunity, so if Mr. Toussaint is innocent or guilty, a court can decide."

The investigation was at a standstill, said Montas, who was an often disarmingly witty woman, but someone within whom I could sense a well of deep sadness. The Préval government had established a special fund for the investigation—as they had done for the Raboteau and Carrefour Feuilles trials before—but Aristide had personally cut that funding once he returned to office in 2001.

"Judge Gassant has done a very professional job," Montas told me. "And he has at times been quite rebellious when he had to face the Minister of Justice, who has said he is on the side of this investigation, but has shown absolutely no commitment to it.

"Judge Gassant has had a tremendous amount of courage to go this far."

Evidently, with Gassant now safely out of the country, Aristide disagreed. On January 23, the government announced that a panel of three new judges—Josué Agnant, Bernard Sainvil and Sinclair Joachim—had been named to investigate the case. At the end of the month, as the Senate debated lifting Toussaint's parliamentary immunity inside, Toussaint partisans demonstrated wildly outside, shouting vows of violent reprisals against those who voted in favor of rescinding the privilege. In typical fashion, Senate President Yvon Neptune showed little chagrin when citing an internal report to the Senate that advised against lifting the immunity and he faulted Claudy Gassant's handling of the case. Neptune announced the Senate would give the case further study; he sent Gassant's file on Toussaint back to the judiciary for "clarification," and a nation winced.

I WAS AT THE CROWDED, dilapidated Electricité d'Haiti (EDH) office on January 14 in downtown trying to negotiate yet another ludicrously exorbitant electric bill, the cost of which increased every month in inverse proportion to the amount of power we received. Looking up, I saw Cherestal on the office's television set, sweating, looking trapped and addressing the grim-faced Lavalas parliament to defend his government. He looked like a man whose days were numbered and, having been squeezed dry of the last bit of usefulness that Aristide could get out of him, was about to be jettisoned. On January 17 Cherestal tendered his resignation to Aristide and on Jan 21 the resignation became official, leaving Haiti without a head of government. The day before, Aristide had visited the Dominican Republic, with his by-now standard large coterie of ministers and "aides" in tow, and discussed the possibility for Dominican factories to begin operating on Haitian land with the country's rotund president, Hipólito Mejia.

Dominicans were apparently far more welcome on Haitian soil than the French. From the northern town of Saint Marc on January 18, Figaro Desir, a spokesman for the Bale Wouze (Clean Sweep) street gang that had been formed by the local Lavalas Deputy Amanus Mayette, told Radio Signal FM that Association of Haitian Journalists president Guy Delva would be killed if he ventured to Saint Marc.

"We have not used a middleman to deliver the message. We have sent a clear message, and everybody knows what Bale Wouze can do," Desir said. "If Guyler Delva ever dares to come to Saint Marc, he will deserve whatever happens to him. . . . He came with that little hoodlum Robert Ménard to sully Haitian soil on the eve of 2004. We do not accept that. [Our forefathers] said, 'Cut off their heads and burn their houses.' As for us, we will burn all the people and their properties."

THE YOUNG MAN arrived at the house in Delmas with two bodyguards. One man, unsmiling with close-cropped hair, was sharply dressed in a suit-coat and wore wrap-around sunglasses while the other, dressed in the gray-black uniform of a CIMO officer and carrying an Uzi, told me he worked at the National Palace. The object of their attention smiled and shook my hand as we met, and we retired to the inside of the house to speak. René Civil's only request, as he sat across from me, was that we shut the open front door directly behind me. He could be shot at otherwise, he explained.

Civil had been born in Jacmel some twenty-nine years earlier, and throughout his youth been involved in the popular movement, first growing up in the progressive Protestant church in the country, watching the movement against the Duvalier government and the military governments while a secondary-school student, and acting as a campaign worker for the FNCD during Aristide's first run for office in 1990. Though he, like Aristide, said he saw his political activism growing out of his faith, he said he now questioned the priorities of the Catholic and Protestant churches in Haiti.

"If you see the pastor's house, it's big, his car is fine, yes, the pastor's house is very beautiful, but the fidel's house is very small," Civil began, in a soft measured voice that nevertheless betrayed an intense timber. "They share God's word but the daily bread they keep for themselves."

At this he laughed—a trace cynically, I thought.

"When Jesus went to the temple and saw people selling things and making money, he said that he didn't build the temple to make money, he built the temple for people to share what they have," he continued. "Jesus knew that we must share what we have, but the religious missions in Haiti have forgotten their mission. They see people with no house, no work, no peace of mind, and all they preach to them is resignation, the hope of the next world."

"The majority of people don't have roads, don't have schools; we are struggling together for this change. This is a struggle for democracy, but a particular type of democracy—a democracy that is responsive to the power of the people. It's not just a political movement that we have in Haiti; it's a movement to truly change social, economic, political realties in Haiti."

Civil said that JPP and Tabarre-aligned groups like it had really come into their own upon Aristide's return from exile in 1994.

"After the coup d'etat—when you have a lot of diverse organizations in Cité Soleil, in Carrefour Feullies, in Martissant—we decided we needed to form a unified organization to change things. Our decision was redoubled when we saw the Rosny Smarth government began to push a radical neoliberal agenda on the country. In 1996, we had the Préval government, and we had the parliament blocking the country. They weren't working for democracy, nor for peace, nor for justice."

What role did he see the international community playing in Haiti's ills?

"The international community is committing violence against Haiti by blocking aid, they are blocking the country," he said, jabbing the air with a long finger to emphasize his point. "For ambitious politicians here in the opposition, this aids their plans. They don't have a program. The government has a program to refurbish roads, hospitals and schools and to create work, but the foreign donors give all the money to nongovernmental organizations in Haiti, to foreign people working here, and the problems of the people are not getting any better.

"The press, as well, has a responsibility to aid in the development of the country, but the journalists never talk to the popular organizations," he went on. "For example, look what happened in Ti Goave in December: the Convergence attacked people there, slashed them with machetes, burned their houses, and we heard nothing about it. And the international press takes their cue from the local press; they don't talk to peasant organizations or popular organizations. So the journalists in their own way begin working as well to destabilize the country."

I asked him if he thought the problems of Haiti could be solved peacefully and without violence.

"The situation today is very delicate, because today we have an economic blockade in effect. People are hungry and they have no work; they are existing in misery," he said. "It's not peace when you always have stones in your pathway; it's not peace to have nothing at all, nothing to eat, no proper housing. For all the people to be dying. These are terrible things. Every day these conditions exist for people. It's only because of the good nature of the Haitian people that nothing has happened yet.

"We are willing to sit together, to talk together and to work extraordinarily to avoid a violent resolution to this conflict, but there is much frustration, much hunger and black misery. The people want this country to change and they won't accept this misery forever."

We shook hands at the end. It was a difficult interview. Civil's points were righteous and well-taken, but he was the servant of a government whose commitment to the Haitian poor as opposed to its own party cadres and, especially, its maximum leader, had so far been demonstrated to be minimal, at best.

Civil got into the SUV with his two gunmen and drove away, and, as I did so often in Haiti, I wondered what this man could have been in a different context, a different country, how his oratorical gifts and seemingly genuine outrage at the impoverished stupor he saw his countrymen wallowing in could have been put to better use by a leader with even a trace of greatness in him—in other words, a leader far different than the one Aristide had thus far shown himself to be.

IN LATE JANUARY, the Aristide's government was shaken by its most serious scandal up to this point when a riot erupted in Cité Soleil. Residents of the slum had poured out of their homes when they discovered that rice being imported free of customs duties by the Pou Nou Tout (For Us All) food cooperative, affiliated with the Aristide Foundation for Democracy and Fanmi Lavalas, was being loaded into trucks and official vehicles. It seemed that, despite the government's statements that the rice was being given to senators to distribute among the hungry in their home districts, the Lavalas chiefs had been in fact regularly taking the rice and then reselling it at a profit. Angry Cité Soleil residents, whose lives clung on the knife's edge of starvation, surrounded dozens of cars loaded down with the cheap *diri*, as rice is called in Kreyol. CIMO arrived, tear-gassing the crowd and firing into the air, but couldn't prevent them from ransacking the warehouse where the rice was kept. Oddly, the government sent out Jonas Petit, the spokesman for the Lavalas party, rather than anyone from the cooperative itself to try to calm matters. The uproar eventually died down, but it was in any event a deeply cynical and short-sighted ploy, as by flooding the market with cheap rice, Aristide was only increasing the pressure on the already desperately poor Haitian farmers whose rice sold at a higher rate given their struggles with eroded soil, very basic farming techniques and transport on tap-taps over collapsing roads.

NEAR CITÉ SOLIEL, in the hollowed-around ruins of the Duvalierist torture chamber once called Fort Dimanche, there lies a desperately poor enclave built in and around the ruins of the prison that its residents have named Village Demokrasi. It is here where, famously among foreign journalists who visit Haiti, people are so poor that they subsist on cakes made out of clay and seasoned with inexpensive cubes of chicken or beef bouillon. Shortly after Cherestal resigned, I led a BBC journalist down to the district.

"We need work here; we need schools for the children," said a man named Jackson who had his name tattooed on his left arm, as we stood next to a row of dozens of clay cakes drying in the sun, with pools of fetid green-black water lapping at our feet from where puddles collected after the previous night's storm. "We have no hospitals when we are sick. No one comes to see us from the government. No other countries help us. We are in pain here."

The ruins of the fort had been flooded with water and, in my effort to avoid falling into a puddle, I accidentally planted my size twelve boot in a row of clay cakes. I closed my eyes for a split second, expected to be, at the very least, virulently excoriated for my faux pas, but when I turned around to face the women patting away to make the cakes with their hands, they just smiled and laughed at me. "Look at the crazy *blan*, walking in our supper."

"*Tout moun gen gran gou,*" said a little boy in a t-shirt and black shorts, causing the rest of his diminutive posse to explode into hilarity. "Everyone is hungry here." Climbing down from his perch where his family lived around the edges of a mostly crumbled floor, Jean-Baptiste, a handsome young man in a bright yellow football jersey, chased after me as I was leaving.

"Village Demokrasi is not a good place," he said, taking my tape recorder to his lips as he spoke. "Water passes through our home, we have such a bad life. Someone should participate with us, to help the children's lives here."

I've rarely felt the guilt of man's indifference to the suffering of his fellow man weigh on me more heavily than I did that day. I still do.

DURING THE FIRST WEEK of February, the Aristide government decided to celebrate its newly restated commitment to press freedom by clapping Genet Morin, a reporter for Radio Magik Stereo FM, in jail along with several members of Evans Paul's KID party, accusing the journalist of being part of an urban kidnapping ring.

Upon his release without charges being filed a week later, Morin seemed perplexed and angry.

"They never even told me why they wanted me or what I was being charged with," Morin said. "I think this was just an attempt to humiliate me. I told them that as a citizen I have no problem answering their questions, but this situation was unacceptable."

Though Morin claimed no political affiliation, that was certainly not the case with the eight KID activists arrested in the same sweep, including Jean Mandave, a former deputy in Haiti's parliament. Ever ready to milk a government misstep for all it was worth, Evans Paul immediately took to the radio charging that the arrests were "another example of actions to thwart negotiations and intimidate the opposition and the press."

At a news conference held on February 4, Aristide told reporters gathered at the Palace that he sought a negotiated settlement to the 2000 election dispute and pressed the Convergence to agree on a timetable for new elections.

"I don't have enemies in the opposition, I have opponents, and they are my brothers," Aristide said, his voice quiet and syrupy. He reiterated his offer to hold new elections for the seven contested Senate seats in November, as well as for the Chamber of Deputies. Surveying the ruins of his burned home, Gérard Pierre-Charles said substantive discussion about new elections would be a prerequisite for any meeting.

On February 6, Lavalas Senators Prince Pierre Sonson, Gerard Gilles and Lans Clones announced publicly that they had asked for increased security details as a result of death threats they had been receiving, which they blamed on partisans of Dany Toussaint. Having pressed for parliament to lift Toussaint's parliamentary immunity to allow him to be questioned and possibly charged in the Jean Dominique killing, Toussaint had recently taken to charging that the senators were in fact CIA agents who were planning to kill him.

On February 7, the first anniversary of Aristide's reinnauguration, fifteen people died when a high-tension electricity wire collapsed on the Carrefour Feuilles market in the capital as vendors were busy cleaning up their wares for the day. For two days, angry residents took to the streets of the district to protest, blaming the national power company, EDH, for negligence and for failing to respond to the previous complaints of residents about the instability of the cables, as well as demanding that EDH make restitution for the accident and help pay for the funerals of the dead. Police spokesman Jean-Dady Simeon arrived at the scene and told reporters, "I appeal for calm in the face of this terrible tragedy."

The same day, following a meeting with Caribbean leaders in the Bahamas, U.S. Secretary of State Colin Powell sounded unenthusiastic about resuming aid to Haiti, saying, "We do not believe enough has been done yet to move the political process forward to assure ourselves that additional aid will be used in the most effective way at this time." The Caribbean leaders disagreed, with Guyana's foreign minister Rudy Insanally being particularly insistent on the resumption of aid, and praising the Aristide government's efforts toward compromise.

Later that day, speaking at the Darbonne sugar factory in Leogane, Aristide blamed the opposition and the elite for the country's ills.

"I come to tell you that you are going to get more help this year, if the people who are persecuting you have more understanding," Aristide said, speaking to a crowd swelled by the Cité Soleil militants the government had rallied and bused in for the occasion. "If they had not blocked the money that was supposed to come to the country in the past year, we would have accomplished wonderful projects. If they had not plotted with the others [the international community] to block the money, a lot of roads would have been built. A lot of hospitals would have been built. A lot of schools and universities would have already been built. We would have completed a lot of projects.

"We say thank you to the Caribbean countries, to CARICOM, for the solidarity they have shown when they asked for the lifting of the economic sanctions against the country. Let us say a big thank you to CARICOM."

Three days later, on February 10th, just down the road in Petit Goave where tensions had never really abated following the murder of Brignol Lindor and the riot at his funeral, a policeman was killed in an early morning attack by unknown gunmen at that town's commissariat. No arrests were made.

IT WAS A CLEAR, sunny winter afternoon on Sunday, February 17, as Lavalas Deputy Marc-Andre Durogène was driving through traffic in the capital with his wife and small daughter. The politician, a young representative for Gonaives in Haiti's lower house of parliament, had recently been gaining a name for himself speaking out about what he charged were corrupt and illicit practices going on in the port of Gonaives, a stance that was known to be widely unpopular with both Lavalas Senator Medard Joseph, who also represented the region, as well as gang leader Amiot "Cubain" Metayer, whose brother, Butteur, worked as assistant director there. Two young men on motorcycles approached Durogène as he sat stuck in traffic and had a brief discussion with him, before opening fire on him in full view of his family. Durogène was struck twice in the head and died instantly. Television cameras arriving on the scene videotaped Durogène's hysterical wife wailing over his blood-spattered body and his daughter watching, seemingly frozen, nearby.

Two of Durogène's bodyguards, who witnesses said did nothing to protect their boss, were taken into police custody. "This killing is the consequence of the political and security degradation on the country," said Micha Gaillard when I spoke to him on the phone that day. Dr. Jean-Claude Desgranges, the director of Aristide's personal cabinet, released a statement to the press saying that Aristide "One more time . . . condemns without reservation all acts of violence," and sent his sympathies to Durogène's family and hoped the culprits would be identified and arrested. For days after, protestors in Gonaives set up flaming barricades made out of tires and overturned vendor carts at the entrance to Gonaives, demanding justice for the slain deputy. Durogène's bodyguards were quietly released from jail several weeks later. The case has never been solved.

On February 22, Patrick Merisier, a monitor for the National Coalition for Haitian Rights in the South Department, was shot and wounded by unknown assailants on motorcycles while visiting Port-au-Prince. The shooting came after death threats in the form of anonymous leaflets were left at Merisier's home and community radio station, pressuring him to cease broadcasting and monitoring human rights. Berthony Philippe, another monitor from the central town of Ennery, went into hiding after receiving similar threats.

"We are working to establish law and justice in Haiti, but for weeks now, there has been a campaign against our organization both at the street and the official level," an exasperated Pierre Esperance told me in NCHR's shady offices on Rue Riviere in the capital, around the corner from the TELECO building. Esperance, a serious black Haitian man in his early 40s, said that the trouble began when NCHR published a report highly critical of the human rights situation in Haiti timed to coincide with the one-year anniversary of Aristide's inauguration as president. The report alleged the Lavalas supporters involved in gang violence in the La Saline slum had escaped prosecution because of their links to the ruling party. Days later, the state-funded *L'Union* newspaper published a Lavalas press release accusing the NCHR staff of defamation and threatening to have them arrested.

Through spokesman Luc Especa, Aristide issued a flat-out denial, as per usual.

"The president has made it clear that everyone in Haiti has the right to express themselves in the spirit of diversity," Especa said. "This is pure exaggeration on the part of the human rights organizations as they know the government supports their work and there is no systematic pressure against them."

Echoing NCHR's concerns, however, Amnesty International issued a statement voicing concern for the NCHR staff, saying it feared that they were "in grave danger," and the U.S. State Department's annual report of human rights said the Aristide government continued to commit serious abuses of human rights in 2001 and that "its generally poor human rights record worsened."

TAP-TAP IS BY FAR the best way to see Haiti, and its chaotic, colorful structure is perhaps the best parallel for how a country as dysfunctional as Haiti is in so many ways can somehow always be on the verge of falling apart and still manage to function. You arrive at the station, where buses congregate waiting for enough passengers to begin the journey. The place is usually a blur of mud, dust and flies. The *ti machann*s sit among the towering machines, selling fritays, batteries, razor blades and anything else that may bring money. Porters rush back and forth trying to direct passengers to the right destination (and get a cut of the driver's profits), occasionally pushing and fighting with one another and the street boys who surround the vehicles to beg. Compas and *racine* music blare from the tap-taps' sounds systems, and the hulks of the transports themselves are slapped with exuberant primary colors and festooned with images of saints, soccer players and vodou spirits. Passengers crowd into the rear cab while others strap their belongings down and sit on the roof. The driver marches back and forth, checking the volume level of the music. Finally, after a seemingly interminable wait—and that's what a great deal of life for the poor majority of Haiti consists of, waiting, for a job, a ride, a chance—the driver climbs into the front of the bus and, with a triumphant signal of the horn, the tap-tap is off. Somehow the whole noisy, rude, ready-to-collapse-at-any-moment proceeding has worked, and life continues.

I rode on the tap-tap today with James at my side. We were going back to Jacmel, for the town's famous *carnaval national*, which always took place a week before the real thing in Port-au-Prince and had become the repository for the traditionally colorful, costumed Haitian carnival that had been lost in the music-and-float focused, one-million-plus plus person party that took place on the Champs de Mars in Port-au-Prince every year. The year's carnival songs—witty, ebullient, arberic Haitian compas or driving- committed *racine*—played as we went along. This year, in honor of the rice scandal that had erupted at the port, Haiti's most famous musician—a lewd, rough-and-tumble compas singer named Sweet Micky—had dubbed his entry "Carnaval Diri" ("Rice Carnival") in honor of the upheaval and laced it with sarcastic references to government officials arriving in their big cars.

Micky himself—born Michel Martelly—was a curious Haitian hybrid. The grandson of Auguste de Pradine, a protest troubadour songwriter from the occupation era, Martelly had grown up in a middle-class family in the capital's Carrefour red-light district. Enrolled in the Haitian military academy, he dropped out after allegedly impregnating an officer's daughter. Over the years he had made some interesting friends, including former Port-au-Prince police chief Michel Francois, with whom he shared his nickname, and Dany Toussaint. Having lived in Miami off and on for the better part of a decade, Micky spoke a fluid, musical English and was given to such gestures as performing in the 1996 carnival in full drag and announcing that he would perform nude atop Haiti's National Palace if ever elected to the presidency. During a moonlit drive through the darkened streets of Port-au-Prince one January night, Micky turned to me and patted the 9 millimeter that sat on the seat between us.

"I trust the Haitian people, but. . . ." He guffawed.

Other times, though he was a coffee-colored mulatto with relatively "black" facial features, he would evidence a realization of how bad a situation his country was in.

"You know these people, they have so much money and they wouldn't even build one fucking fountain for the people to get water from," he said to me during the same drive, taking in the poverty around him.

Micky was slated to play in Jacmel that weekend, which promised to increase the always large turnout. Luckily, James and I had an invitation to stay at a beach house outside of town in a small fishing village called Ti Mouillage. We arrived in Jacmel town that Friday evening, and took a tap-tap from Jacmel town out along the coast road, with the warm Caribbean evening wind blowing over us. The rocky shore of the beach curved around to our right, splashing blue water up to the palm-lined shore. To our left, vegetation was broken by denuded mountains lurching toward the sky. At the beach house—more a thatched hut fitted with electricity—James walked down to the water and dipped his feet in. Most Haitians can't swim and have a healthy fear of the open sea, but James, looking at the light, the open space, feeling the calm, seemed happy enough. He even began hitting on the young daughter of the matron who would ordinarily take care of the place, with the girl not knowing what to make of the tattooed, beret-wearing, gold chain-draped city boy in her midst.

Late that night, at a small, smoky club on the town's outskirts where Sweet Micky was in the middle of a typically exuberant, sweaty set, I spied an white-bearded, middle-aged man, staggering drunk, his ocular gleam seemingly wall-eyed from cocaine. It wasn't until he climbed teetering to the stage and I saw the duo of bodyguards with him that I realized it was Fourel Celestin, the Lavalas senator from Jacmel. It was actually painful to watch, as Celestin danced by himself on stage behind the band, directed a phantom orchestra with his hands, put his arm around Micky and made an attempt to play his keyboards. Returning later that night to the beach, we slept outside on the porch, the sound of compas echoing through the night.

"I could live here, man, no problem," James said before he went to sleep.

Riding back into Jacmel in the light of the next day, we passed peasants leading their livestock into town for Saturday market, tying them together with old rope, as little girls and boys riding on donkeys behind the herd licked the beasts lightly with switches to increase their pace. The streets of town were full of revelers, walking under balconies of old houses that were overgrown with bougainvillea and vines, and dancing to the year's carnival songs. As we stood there laughing, James danced under the sun of Jacmel to the strains of the King Posse band—his head back, his eyes closed and a beatific smile on his lips, as for a moment all worries seemed to fade away.

Several days later, I saw James again, but this time his face was among those seated at a table with Aristide at the National Palace, as a "peace conference" for Cité Soleil was broadcast live on state-run television. Sitting with youths that his government was actively arming, Aristide told the cameras, "This is no good, it's no good. If there is solidarity in Cité Soleil, we will see *zenglendo*s live in fear, we will see *zenglendo*s be scared to do any harm in Cité Soleil. The population should not be afraid. Fear should not be in the citizens' hearts in Cité Soleil. Fear should be deep in the *zenglendo*s hearts and heads. *Zenglendo*s are cowards. *Zenglendo*s are cowards and only the weapons they hold in their hands can make them feel a little stronger, can make him feel he can do what he wants. We can't let them scare us like that. This is why I ask the police to respect the people, to respect the people's rights, to stand together with the people so they can find all the information. I ask you to stand united so there is zero tolerance in the Cité, so the light of justice can shine again, so the light of peace can shine again."

"TODAY IS MARCH 3," Michele Montas began in her morning editorial on Radio Haiti-Inter. "And twenty-three months ago a journalist committed to the struggle for change was assassinated. That shameful crime aroused indignation throughout the entire country. Such an example of growing impunity brings the attention of the world upon Haiti today."

Port-au-Prince then listened as she called out the president at his own game.

"On this same date last year, March 3, 2001, President Jean-Bertrand Aristide came to Radio Haiti to express his support publicly for the judicial inquiry and pledge that the executive branch of government would make available to justice the resources needed to investigate the April 3, 2000 assassinations at Radio Haiti. Today, twenty-three months later, facts are speaking louder than words: Fact: The Chief of State, who has the direct and exclusive authority to renew Judge Gassant's mandate, has still not done so although that judge diligently and systematically conducted the investigation for sixteen months with courage and competence. . . . Facts: All the resources, i.e., logistical, technical and financial made available in this judicial case by the preceding government have been cancelled. The special and relatively modest funds which had helped in the success of the trials of Raboteau and Carrefour Feuilles, as well as the funds allocated, among other resources, to the work of the first two investigating judges assigned to the murder cases of Jean Dominique and Jean-Claude Louissaint, allowing them to follow the leads of a difficult investigation in several areas of the countries, were cancelled. . . . Fact: The Senate of the Republic, composed exclusively of members of Fanmi Lavalas, returned the Jean Dominique file to the investigating judge, asking for a number of documents prior to any decision about lifting Senator Dany Toussaint's parliamentary immunity, as requested by Judge Gassant; according to jurists, the release of such documents would amount to a flagrant violation of the investigation's confidentiality. By doing so, the Senate conferred upon itself the authority of a court, in violation of the separation of powers. Fact: The Police, which theoretically answers to the Ministry of Justice, has taken no action on some arrest warrants. Witnesses who have refused to appear in court, alleged assassins or individuals who have openly committed illegal acts go about their businesses freely, in this case as in others. . . . Will you say to me: The investigation is making progress? Senator Toussaint, charged by Judge Gassant, bragged and claimed victory. It is not a common practice for an individual who has been charged to select the investigating judge by whom he will be interrogated. Will you tell me that the investigation is also making headway, since things are apparently moving?

"Because of those very facts, serious questions arise about the political will to render justice to Jean Léopold Dominique, after twenty-three months and many other assassinations. In the case of Judge Gassant, one could mention the need for the regime to be careful with a few rich and powerful party members that the investigating judge had not spared, or with members of the judicial branch resentful of that judge who spent several months in the spotlight. In the interest of the State: Appease, in the name of forced reconciliation, adversaries or possible political rivals within the same party facing accelerated implosion. There are still more serious questions arising: Would it be the case that the healthy wing of this party, who expressed itself for an independent and transparent judicial investigation, is being sacrificed in favor of those who constitute a mafia within the party? Putting the 'continuing investigation' on the back burner and forgetting the demands for justice formulated in the emblematic case of Jean Dominique, is that one of the prices that the regime must pay? Power at what price?

"Seriously, what has been Judge Gassant's professional mistake? Why is the chief of state keeping so silent? We have the right to know. You may remember, Mr. President, the three famous *woch dife*: Participation, Justice and Transparency. If it is confirmed, that decision not to renew the mandate of a competent investigating judge after he conducted an investigation for sixteen months may seem like an easy way out, in the short term; however, even if it is never explicitly announced, that decision will exert a powerful effect undermining the credibility of the chief of state. How can someone really expect that Judge Agnant, no matter how competent or dedicated, will manage to bring himself up to date in a matter of days, and work effectively on a difficult and eminently dangerous case, while obviously he will have no special police protection? Is it possible to believe that the purpose is just 'the investigation continues?'

"In the case of the majority party in the Senate of the Republic, as in the case of the Police, the inability to impose guidelines and to clean up, control and manage is dramatically eroding the authority of the already weakened State, by projecting the image of a lack of cohesiveness, planning, and, above all, the absence of political will. But is that just an image?

"Today, beyond words and promises, the facts indicate that the balls are biased and the regime is affected with a dangerous gangrene. Principles and moral guidelines are compromised every day by political opportunism. Those ideals shared by Jean, including a generous but rigorous socialism, respect for liberties within the framework of democracy, nationalist independence, based on a long history of resistance, those ideals that Jean used to call 'Lavalas' are trampled every day in this balkanized State where weapons make right, and where hunger for power and money takes precedence over the general welfare, causing havoc on a party which, paradoxically, controls all the institutional levers of the country. Our concerns run deep, since the cracks are widening and the building will eventually collapse over all of us. Today, it may be politically incorrect to demand truth and justice, twenty-three months after the murders of April 3, 2000. All we want is a decent country, and we will never accept a new assassination of Jean Dominique, even perpetrated insidiously."

ON MARCH 4 Aristide announced that Yvon Neptune, the 55-year-old former Long Island architect who had been the spokesman for Aristide's Fanmi Lavalas party and then become the president of Haiti's Senate, would become Cherestal's replacement as prime minister. Fourel Celestin, the staggering drunk I had seen in Jacmel a week before, would become the new Senate president.

"They all agreed Senator Neptune was a good choice, and his first act as prime minister will be to tackle corruption in government," Jonas Petit told reporters on the day of the announcement.

In the new administration, there were some new faces and some old ones. Jocelerme Privert, the Secretary of State for Finance who had been fired by Préval from Haiti's tax office for corruption in earlier years, took over as Minister of Interior from Henri-Claude Ménard. Lovinsky Pierre-Antoine, the spokesman for the Aristide-affiliated 30 September Foundation organization, was also rewarded in March for his work on Aristide's behalf by being appointed head of Haiti's Office National pour la Migration (ONM), a plumb government job. Marc Bazin became minister-without-portfolio in charge of the government's negotiations with the Convergence. Perhaps the most hopeful nominee was that of respected jurist Jean-Baptiste Brown, replacing Garry Lissade as Minister of Justice. Maintaining a pattern, a man with well-known links to the Tontons Macoutes, Dr. Haendel Carré, joined the National Palace staff as one of Aristide's spokesmen.

The newspaper *Le Matin* reported on March 5,that the U.S. government had cancelled the travel visas of several top officials in Haiti's government, including Médard Joseph; a report later confirmed by officials at the U.S. Embassy. Days later, a report by the State Department's Bureau of Democracy, Human Rights and Labor found that Haiti's "generally poor human rights record worsened" during 2001, and went on to cite arbitrary arrests after the July police station attacks, the government's failure to bring action against parties implicated in the Dominique case and the abuses by the mayors in Maissade and Hinche. The report characterized PNH candidates as having been "chosen based on political and personal favoritism" and that "allegations of corruption, incompetence and narcotics trafficking affect all levels" of the organization.

Finally acting on what had become overwhelming pressure, while at the same time, as he had done before and would do again, ridding himself of an ally who had outlived his usefulness, Aristide ordered the arrest of Ronald Camille, who was seized on March 23 while Camille and his gang were waiting to "welcome" Aristide back at the Port-au-Prince airport from a conference in Monterrey, Mexico. Unlike many who wallowed in Haitian jails without ever having been formally apprised of exactly why they were being held, Camille was charged with manslaughter in connection with the shooting death of Fritzner "Bobo" Jean outside Parliament on September 10 of the previous year. At the end of March another criminal, Jackson Joanis, a former army captain and head of the Anti-Gang unit of the police under the Cézdras regime, was deported from the United States to Haiti and promptly jailed in Port-au-Prince for his alleged role in the murder of Guy Malary, Aristide's justice minister during his first administration. In 1995, Joanis had already been convicted to life at hard labor in absentia for his alleged role in the 1993 murder of Antoine Izmery. Though he had entered the United States on a tourist visa in 1994 and sought political asylum after the coup regime had fallen, the murder conviction had made him ineligible for residency in the United States, and the U.S. government ordered him deported. He unsuccessfully had contested the deportation order, arguing that he faced torture if returned to Haiti.

I WAS DRIVING with my friend, a young American who had spent most of his life in Haiti, up the Kenscoff Road to the mountains. We climbed up the narrow paved vein of mountain lane, passing dreamy-eyed peasant girls walking by the roadside and children in pink school uniforms. A cool wind made the altitude more bearable than the often-baking downtown Port-au-Prince streets, but if you stopped at certain vantage points, you could still see all the way down the hillside to my neighborhood of Pacot, the Champs de Mars, the National Palace, Cité Soleil and the Titanyen Mountains leading into the Artibonite Valley beyond. Stopping off this day at the home of a wealthy mulatto businessman from the north of the country to see if his son, who was to accompany us, was home, we found the man dining with a Colombian visitor, guarded by two men clutching glocks, hanging on their every word. Failing to find anyone but the father at home, we drove on alone, as mist began seeping onto the road through the hillside blades of grass and the temperature dipped as the altitude climbed. Eventually, we stopped at a soccer game being played in the chilly climes of Obleon, on the grounds of what had been one of Jean-Claude Duvalier's mountain retreats. Country people on donkeys rode in to watch, buying *clarin* from a makeshift stand. A contingent of mountain Rastas sat on a rise, cheering the teams and smoking ice-cream-cone-sized spliffs of ganja. Clouds rolled in over the valleys with enough chill and moisture that dew would form on your hair.

Haiti was a hard place like that sometimes—hard when such beauty existed next to such misery, such pause and space and reflection next to such an overwhelming crush of people and such generosity of the humble, gentle, honest people that made up the population against the treachery and bulldozing blind personal ambition of those who ruled them with such brutality. It was enough to drive you mad, really. Or keep you coming back, again and again. Being an outsider, one would always have more and more to learn in Haiti; but she was a generous mother, in many ways, and had much to teach, if her visitors would listen.

CHAPTER NOTES

1. United States Department of Justice, Foreign Agents Registration Act (FARA) filings for Dellums, Brauer, Halterman & Associates, LLC, 2001- 2002.
2. United States Department of Justice, Foreign Agents Registration Act (FARA) filings for Kurzban, Kurzban, Weinger & Tetzeli, P.A., 2001.
3. Organization of American States, Report of the Commission of Inquiry Into the Events of December 17, 2001, in Haiti, July 1, 2002.
4. "Haiti judge in murder case flees country amid fears," *Miami Herald*, January 18, 2002.

8

Bizoton

CARREFOUR, THE SPRAWLING slum that takes up the entire southern swath of Haiti's capital city all the way from the Theatre Nationale and running nearly to the Leogane police station, had always, for many reasons, been one of the most chaotic and alarming parts of town. Having exploded in population over the last twenty-five years as peasants teetering on the edge of starvation crowded into the capital, decaying luxury homes and decrepit tin shacks begin at the polluted waters of the city's bay and climb high into the mountains running along its western edge. Once a semi-affluent retreat and home to various pleasure palaces during the relative stability of the Duvalier dictatorships, Carrefour is now home to tens of thousands of immigrants from the countryside who arrive in the city every year looking for work, bringing with them an intense commitment to the religion of their ancestors. The roads are often awash with overflow from the bay or Port-au-Prince's sewers, and a course, insalubrious nightlife still thrives, with rowdy late-night dancehalls continuing to do business and a string of brothels specializing in imported caramel-skinned Dominican prostitutes still boasting parking lots full of cars—the specter of AIDS still apparently not enough to ward off the lonely or the wanton from the sweet pleasures of the flesh.

Shortly after the gunmen had stormed the National Palace, on one of my visits to the neighborhood I found myself descending through the maze of muddy alleys and lanes of the district's Bizoton quarter. Goodwin Jacques, one of the local *houngans* (vodou priests), referred to by everyone as Ti Papi (Little Daddy), was having a busy day. Ti Papi was a big man, rumored to have done time in the Dominican Republic for drug dealing in his youth, whose once-muscular build was giving way to the softness of middle-age, and whose theatrical, somewhat effeminate manner belied his imposing physique. His wife, a woman from Martinique, also practiced vodou, and the pair traveled back and forth between that Francophone island and Haiti, performing ceremonies for expat Haitians and initiating locals into traditions that had somehow faded on neighboring islands as they had never done in Haiti. This week, Ti Papi had been presiding over the initiation of a dozen converts from Martinique into his temple, referred to in Kreyol as a peristyle. He greeted me and my friend, an

American anthropologist doing research on Christian revival cults in Haiti, with an embrace, and took us toward his house, where he promised *ti bwe* and *ti manje*—in other words, a drink and a snack—would be in order.

"This area was something of a virgin territory, years ago," he said, adjusting his seashell necklace as neighbors eyed us, smiling shyly and treating him with obvious deference. We were walking up the muddy slope of hill from where the peristyle was to his home, a non-decrepit poured-cement box whose interior tables were festooned with plastic flowers and family pictures. Ti Papi with his wife on their wedding day, Ti Papi with jherri curls from his youth. Ti Papi's lovely, near-white grandmother, the daughter of the liaison between and Englishman and a Haitian woman, he tells us. Behind us rolled the muddy waves of the bay.

"There weren't a lot of people here, but there were a lot of trees here, and a lot of water, these being strong attractions for the spirits: the sea, the river and the trees. I'm lucky, because I have clients from Martinique, Guadeloupe, French Guyana. When you do good work for someone, word gets around, and those who are interested come to me."

Ti Papi's wife whipped up a quick meal of spicy pork for us, and we quickly downed it along with strong Barbancourt rum. Ti Papi would occasionally shout out the door at his children who were playing in the street, correcting them for their rambunctiousness in self-consciously correct French. He had his daughter fetch me a Prestige to help wash down the rum, and when it was discovered that we lacked a bottle opener, the young girl bit down on the bottle tap with her teeth and twisted it off in that manner. We ate quickly, and then strolled to the temple.

At Ti Papi's temple (also known as *ofou* in Kreyol), initiates go through many purification rites, including ritual baths and forty-one days of sexual abstinence, before being sequestered in a windowless room, the *devo,* for seven days, emerging only to take part in rituals that will go on, day and night, for the entire week of their stay.

"My mother was from Martinique and my father from Israel," said a young, white-clad, coffee-complected man, sitting with other initiates as we entered. "My grandfather was a *gengen* (vodou priest), but after he passed on there was no one to carry on the tradition. Over the years, I had very strange dreams, dreams of a man with horns, of repeated visits to an *ofou* in the countryside. I went to the priest but the priest told me I was crazy. Eventually, I realized the problems were coming from the spirits that had been abandoned. They were trying to claim me, but because I had lost the knowledge, I didn't know how to properly respond."

In addition to being initiated, the man was set to be symbolically married to two manifestations of the vodou spirit of love, the *lwa* Ezulie. Necessary, Ti Papi said, because if he married only one, the competing sides of Ezulie would fight and potentially drive the young man mad.

"In Martinique, they have almost entirely lost their African traditions," interjected Ti Papi, waving a bejeweled finger in the air. "I would say that they have almost become too French. We all came from the same people, but Haiti, with its early independence was able to keep their traditions strong. In many of these countries now, when people have problems with their ancestors and problems specifically relating to spiritual matters, they turn to specialists from Haiti to help them."

With paper Haitian flags hanging from the temple ceiling, the booming rhythms of the kata drums beating out its fast, driving *petro* rhythm announced the arrival of the six initiates, barefoot and dressed all in white. They replicate a complex series of salutations learned from Ti Papi before the assembled congregation, as Ti Papi and his assistants strike the *poto-mitan* (center post) and the ground fiercely with machetes.

"With respect, honour and respect," he shouted.

The ceremonies had already been going on for a while and, despite the breaks, would last long through the night and well into the following day. Haitians in fact often call a vodou ceremony "a dance," and commonly a ring of worshippers, dressed in white referred to as *hounsi,* take a lead in the chants, prodded on by the *ongeikon,* or "queen singer." Ti Papi, already bathed in sweat in the sweltering room from dancing with and saluting the initiates, stepped behind the drums, taking a deep swig from a bottle of Barbancourt rum he had stationed there. He was pacing himself for a long night.

"When there's tires burning in the streets, when there's coup d'etat, when there's everything else, we are still doing our ceremonies, we are still beating our drums," he had said to us as we sat in his home, referencing the chaos and blood that had descended on the city in the wake of the coup attempt only weeks earlier. "Politicians come and go but vodou is always here. If it wasn't for vodou, we would already be occupied, either by the Americans or the Dominicans. Vodou? It's been our sovereignty, over the years."

IN HIS BOOK, *Voodoo: Search for the Spirit,* the Haitian sociologist Laennec Hurbon writes that the faith's origins can be described as "a cult dedicated to the spirits that rule the different realms of nature and human activities . . . first encountered in Africa among the Fon, the Yoruba and the Ewe in the Gulf of Benin, in an area that stretches from Ghana to Nigeria to Togo. More specifically, it was developed in Dahomey (today the Republic of Benin)." Many of Haiti's slaves were drawn from the Fon tribe of Dahomey and the Yoruba of Nigeria, and were sold into slavery by Dahomey's royal family, which lorded over several small fiefdoms on the West African coast. Thousands departed Africa, never to return, from the Gulf of Guinea, in the seventeenth and especially the first half of the eighteenth centuries. The pantheon of vodou *lwas* (spirits) is full of manifestations of Dahomian gods, such as that of Legba, who

opens the channel for other deities to reach humans and as such is invoked
first at ceremonies, Dambala Wedo, symbolized by a dual rainbow/snake image
and thought of as the link between the sky or thunder and the sea, and Agwe,
the god of fishing. The spirits serve beneath an overarching deity—called *bon
dye* in Kreyol—who is though to be too distant and aristocratic to be invoked and
entreated for help with the day-to-day problems and questions that the other *lwa*
can deal with. The *lwa*s themselves are said to belong to a number of nations
(*nanchon*) for which specific rituals must be performed, distinctive music must
be played and particular animals sacrificed. The shape of the *veve*—a symbolic
shape evoking a particular *lwa* traced out, most usually with corn maize, on the
floor of the *ofou*—is also determined in part by what nation a *lwa* belongs to.
Among the main families of nations, there are Dahomey, Rada, Kongo and
Petro. Dahomey rituals are performed in tribute to Dahomian spirits and are considered in some ways to be the most "pure" African form of the religion (Lakou
Souvenance, a famous place of worship outside the northern city of Gonaives,
is a Dahomey temple). The Rada rituals, closely related to those of Dahomey, are
the ones used when one is being initiated or pledged to a *lwa*, such as the initiates at Ti Papi's temple. Kongo rituals speak to *lwa* of Bantu lineage, while
Petro rituals evoke spirits mostly drawn from the island of Hispaniola (or Saint-
Dominique, as it was called in the time of slavery) itself. Coming into being in
a place of such trauma and violent upheaval, the Petro *lwa* are often thought of
as violent and angry, and the drumming that accompanies Petro ceremonies is
the most frenzied on the island. Kongo-Petro rituals appear to dominate vodou
rituals in urban environments such as Port-au-Prince. In all, there are twenty-
one nations in vodou—and each one supposedly represents a different tribe
that left Africa and came to Saint-Dominique, so in total are representative of
all the different tribes that make up Haiti. Of the more prominent *lwa* often
evoked in ceremonies, Ogou—part of the Rada rite—is a warrior associated
with the Catholic Saint Jacques whose color is red, his provenance is fire, and
he has a special relationship with the feminine *lwa* Ezulie, with complimen-
tary, romantic overtones. Ezulie herself personifies beauty, sensuality, and is
thought to live in the waters. Mater Dolorosa in Catholicism transforms a bit into
Ezulie Freda. The Gede family of spirits is headed by Baron Samedi, guardian
of the cemetery, also known as Baron Cimetiere or Baron La Croix. Black is
their color. Since colonial days, vodou *lwa* have often intermingled their traits
with those of Catholic saints, a practice that enabled the continued conducting
of worship under sheen of Catholicism at times when the faith was banned.

The role of vodou in Haiti's political life has been a serpentine one over the
years, slithering along and insinuating itself in the form of the "societies
secret"—as the name would imply, secretive mystical brotherhoods throughout
Haiti broadly similar to the Freemasons of which Bizango is perhaps the most
famous—that date back to slavery days, and also in the devotion and adherence

of certain politicians, who, be they vodouisant or not, have always realized the potential power wielded by the *houngans* and *mambos* over their flocks. The belief system played an important role in the ceremonies with which the slaves girded themselves to rebel against the French, who had banned its public practice on the plantations; and vodou priests, adept at concocting complex mixtures of natural materials into powders used in their faith's ceremonies, at times proved themselves skilled prisoners of their colonial overseers. After the revolution, Dessalines and Boyer both feared vodou enough to proscribe it—with Dessalines, who partially blamed vodou leaders for fomenting unrest that led to flights from the forced plantation system, killing several of note. Boyer's 1835 penal code demoted vodou to the level of "superstition," and the faith only truly flowered as an aspect of state-craft in postrevolutionary Haiti with the rise of Faustin Soulouque, the Petit Goave soldier who crowned himself emperor in 1852 and included in his court hierarchy various vodou priests and *mambos*.

Haiti's leaders since have had a love-hate relationship with the faith. Whereas Elie Lescot actively suppressed it with help of the Catholic Church, Francois Duvalier actively recruited local vodou leaders such as Zachary Delva from Gonaives into the Tontons Macoute, and later leaders like Arsitide courted people like the *mambo* Annette "So Anne" Auguste, the middle-aged Haitian woman who had lived in Brooklyn working as a maid for many years, but who was also a folksinger who returned to Haiti with Aristide in 1994 and had long-standing links with the violent Camille brothers. Auguste was said to be Aristide's chief liaison with the vodou community, and since Ronald Camille's arrest, she was said to have taken over the running of the La Saline market with his brother, Franco, where the two continued to profit from protection fees extorted from the poor merchants there. Aristide himself, despite his Catholic credentials, had long been said to be an active and observant devotee of the faith.

ON APRIL 3, as the second anniversary of Jean Dominique's murder approached, banners bearing Dominique's smiling face and reading "Les assassins sont dans la ville" ("The killers are in town") were strung across several key intersections throughout the capital by the Eko Vwo Jean Dominique, an organization headed by a former Aristide Secretary of State for Public Security Patrick Elie, that had pressed for a resolution to the investigation of the murder. With one banner strung across Avenue Pan-Americaine, the Lavalas officials had to look at it everyday when they returned to their mansions in the mountains after working at the ministries downtown. On April 3 itself, two years after his murder, most radio stations around Haiti held a minute of silence at noon to mark Jean Dominique's death and call for a resolution to the long investigation.

The staff of Radio Haiti had scheduled a press conference in the morning, and, as I went to the station on Delmas Road, my taxi driver, a white-haired man named Felix Louis, when he found out where I was going said that, "Jean

Do was a militant for us; when they killed him, they tried to kill the Haitian people. We lost one of our best friends, and the politicians have done nothing about it."

When I arrived at Radio Haiti and was let in through the gate, I saw Michele Montas, pasting up photos of Jean's return in 1986, when he was greeted by tens of thousands at the airport. Not ten feet away from where Jean and Jean-Claude Louissant were killed, signs hung that read *"Jean Dominique tonbe, batay la ap rapouswiv."* (Jean Dominique fell, but the struggle continues.) Pictures of the station's murdered caretaker, Jean-Claude Louissant—a somber vision of a Haitian manhood looking unsmiling into the camera—were also hung up. Then Montas went back inside, and three reporters from Radio Haiti sat at a table awash in microphones and tape recorders.

"President Aristide is chief of a political party that controls the executive, legislative and judicial branches of government and he has blocked this investigation at every turn," said Radio Haiti journalist Sony Esteus, as he went on to denounce the government's refusal to execute, among other arrest warrants, that which had existed for Dany Toussaint confidant and former army officer Richard "Cha Cha" Salomon since November 2000. "We demand the president renew the mandate and ensure the security of Judge Gassant."

I visited a careworn looking Michele Montas at her office after Esteus had finished speaking and found her in a not very hopeful mood.

"People, particularly poor people, feel that if Jean doesn't find justice, there's no hope for them," she told me. "This case carries an enormous amount of expectations for many people, not just mine, and something must be done."

In a surprise move that night, Aristide announced through National Palace spokesman Jacques Maurice that the long-suffering Gassant would have his mandate renewed, a Pyrrhic victory if there ever was one, as Gassant had already fled for his life to the United States.

Trying to reach Michele Montas that night at Radio Haiti-Inter, I instead reached Nadine, Jean's daughter, busily fielding calls at the station about the case from Haiti and abroad.

"We are pleased that the mandate of Gassant, who we have always had faith in, was renewed," she said, the sounds of a busy radio newsroom chattering away behind her. "But now the government must give him the means to do his job in security, free from interference and intimidation."

Given Aristide's active undermining of the investigation thus far, one could be forgiven the Dominiques' lack of faith on the last matter.

A HUGE PRO-LAVALAS rally was held at the capital's Theatre National on April 5, with thousands of members of pro-government OPs, both legitimate and criminal, filling the stands of the structure to listen to rousing speaker after speaker and listening as the RaRam rara band played driving indigenous groove and danced through the aisles. Dozens of *baz,* as the Lavalas grassroots organizations called themselves, from around the city were there—the Kodinasyon Baz Fanmi Lavalas Portail Leogane, the Baz Nazon, the *baz* from Lakou Watson in Martissant—as was the ubiquitous Bob Moliere.

"When it's voting time, they're after our support, but after that, they don't give a fuck about us," he said, by way of explaining why Lavalas could still draw such a large crowd while the opposition couldn't. He was wearing a paper hat made to resemble the Haitian flag. After a group singing of the national anthem, Ernst Vincent, a deputy from the Ouest Department addressed the crowd.

"We believe in one simple leader, Aristide!" he said. "We must work together and support our president."

As barefoot street kids in ragged clothing ran before the stage, the crowd roared its approval.

Georges Mikano, a former comedian who had become one of the government's chief public speakers and who was dark and slim in a short-sleeved shirt in the tropical heat, then took the microphone and the stage.

"Haiti is not for sale!" he cried, as if there were any buyers, before launching into a line of thought that sounded like it might have come straight from Aristide's pen in his less guarded moments. "The *blan* wanted to give Aristide a chief of police! The *blan* wanted to give Aristide a prime minister! But he said no! Everything the president does, the foreigners are watching, everything the Haitian people try to do, the foreigners keep them from being able to do it."

"If there is a coup d'etat, we stand up! If Aristide is going to die, he's going to die with the people!," he cried. *"Liberté! Liberté! Liberté!"*

"Liberté! Liberté! Liberté!" the crowd responded, loud enough so that they might have even been able to hear them in the National Palace.

Speaking in Cap Haitien on April 7, Aristide again appealed to his base as he looked ahead to 2004.

"We need a communion with the spirits of Louverture, Dessalines and Petion to illuminate the hope of Haiti as we celebrate our bicentennial. We need to repell a new deaths of Toussaint Louverture with our power before 2004. I am working for the people of the north!

"Are you preparing for 2004?"

"Yes!" the crowd at his feet responded.

"We must then work against this political and economic blockade. *Viv l'homme du Nord!"*

A few days later, Aristide invited members of the press corps for a characteristically cool and detached question-and-answer session. A master of keeping the press off-balance, Aristide had the journalists herded into a small, ornate antechamber on the opposite side of the Palace from the usual reception room. We were left there to cool our heels for about an hour. When we were finally received, we found Aristide sitting beneath a large portrait of Toussaint

Louverture in the National Palace. He responded to questions about impunity and corruption by saying that, "The legal and peaceful participation of the people is absolutely necessary for us to win this struggle. Journalists, with honest criticism, can accompany us in this work, by identifying, without false accusations, those involved in corruption. The chief of state wants all people's right to be respected."

Jacques Stephen Alexis had once written, "Cruelty is easy to learn, and it changes faces." So it had been with Aristide. As we stood there and watched him speak, I couldn't help but notice how the pop-eyed wonder and intellect so readily visible in early photos of the priest had now been replaced by sharp, darting glances that alternated with sullen, slit-eyed stares, the arrogant purse of the mouth, and the haughty slight incline at which the president tilted his forehead. They all stood in contrast to the soothing words he spoke, but in Haiti as in many places, what people say tells only part of the story.

Outside of the Palace, about a hundred people who had recently lost money in a banking scandal were hanging on the Palace gates, screaming in protest, and their screams at times threatened to overwhelm Aristide's near-whispered declarations. Very soon, the entire country would hear their voices.

THEY APPEARED WITHOUT warning on the green and fertile Maribaroux Plain, skirting the Dominican border on Haiti's northeastern fringe. Beginning in March, Haitian government bulldozers began tearing through the carefully tended small plots of land developed by the region's farmers under the gaze of heavily armed Unité dé partementale de maintien d'ordre (UDMO) riot police. The very land René Préval had visited in March 1996 and helped re-irrigate in order to help the small farmers improve their meager rice production was being pulverized and, helpless, weeping peasants watched as their corn and bean plants were torn asunder.

Soon the peasants found out the reason for the destruction. Without any public consultation or debate within the government, and before any law approving or regulating such activity was passed by the Haitian parliament, Aristide had directed Minister of Finance Gustave Faubert to sign on behalf of the Haitian government an agreement with the Dominican investment body Grupo M, which, it turned out, would be creating a free-trade zone on the land where the peasants' farms had stood, promising to supply 1,500 low-wage factory jobs during the project's first three years. Over the next several weeks, the Aristide government seized 15,000 hectares for production on some of the most fertile land in the region, evicting fifty-four farmers, only fourteen of whom were ever compensated in any way. An association of Haitian agronomists projected that the free- trade zone would annually cost a loss of $1 million to $2.4 million worth of agricultural production. In a press release, the Groupe d'Appui aux Rapatriés et Réfugiés (GARR) and the Plateforme Haïtienne de

Plaidoyer pour un Développement Alternatif (PAPDA) eventually cried out that, "No official act declaring these lands State property has been published, nor has any information explaining the clearance operation, backed up by armed force, been given. [We] deplore the attitude of the government in ignoring the demands, recommendations and concerns about the free zone on the border that have been voiced by citizens from a variety of social sectors."[1] Aristide and Dominican President Hipólito Mejia, surrounded by phalanxes of security personnel to protect them from the hostile gazes of hundreds of angry peasants, attended a groundbreaking on the site on April 8.

Why the Aristide government would choose one of the few fertile spots in the increasingly arid country to decimate farming with a free-trade zone was never entirely clear when other areas, such as those near the ports of Gonaives and Port de Paix, for instance, with just as close proximity to shipping routes and an arguably more impoverished population were available. Perhaps Aristide wanted to rid the country of any remnant of his successor's work among the peasantry, or perhaps he feared the region's independence, as he feared that of the Plateau Central. Perhaps the cut that Gustave Faubert arranged for Aristide to get from the enterprise was too attractive to resist. Whatever his motivations, the move became widely viewed as another example of Aristide using the country as his own private cash cow, and it made the region's peasants—so loyal to René Préval, who was now in retirement in nearby Marmalade—eternally hostile against the government in the capital. Despite a May 1 government-sponsored rally that attempted to lure attendees with promises of free food and alcohol as well as free agricultural tools, hundreds of farmers gathered in the nearby town of Ouanaminthe on that traditional worker's day, chanting "Down with the free-trade zone" and carrying signs accusing Aristide of selling out the peasants.

THE REGIME HAD a momentary fright in mid-April when, unexpectedly, an appeals court judged ruled that the Aristide government had presented insufficient evidence when arresting Prosper Avril the previous year on charges of plotting against state security, and ordered him released. Aristide saw this as only a momentary setback however, and soon government officials succeeded in pressing Saint Marc magistrate Henry Kesner Noel into signing an arrest warrant charging Avril with orchestrating the 1990 massacre of peasant farmers in the village of Piatre, in central Haiti, even though the massacre occurred after the dictator had been ousted from power. The resulting scene—Avril believing he was leaving the National Penitentiary to a triumphant welcome home on April 12 and then being scooped up by a SWAT team on the street outside of the prison as his son Gregor and his lawyer Reynold Georges looked on—reminded people to some degree that humiliation, rather than simple victory, was also part of Aristide's envisioned future for his enemies, be they culpable or not.

Following Avril's arrest, Justice Henry Kesner Noel, who had signed the warrant, fled Haiti for Florida, saying that Aristide officials had forced him to sign the warrant and he feared for his life should he remain in Haiti.

"I was brought to the office of Secretary of State for Public Security Gérard Dubreuil and the warrant had already been printed," Noel said once he had arrived in Florida. "They informed me that they strongly suggested I sign it, so I did and left. When representatives of this president tell you to sign something, you better sign it." Aristide's actions in this event were a blatant violation of Article 60 of Haiti's constitution, which delegated firmly the independence of the executive and judicial branches of government.

Speaking on Radio Metropole on April 17, four months to the day of the attack on the National Palace and the attendant orgy of violence, Paul Raymond and René Civil denounced the deployment of the impending OAS mission as part of a conspiracy to topple the Aristide government. Around the same time, graffiti reading "*Ipokrit debloke peyi a / Viv Titid*" (Hypocrites, unblock the country/Long live Aristide) began appearing on walls all over the capital, daubed in red Lavalas colors, in obvious reference to the suspension of international aid to Haiti.

"Where is the morality and credibility of the OAS when we know that George Bush and Colin Powell, those Nazi criminals, are leading it?" trilled Raymond, going on to cite a recent attempted coup attempt against Venezuela's leftist president Hugo Chavez as proof of U.S. malfeasance in the region before returning to the subject of the OAS. "If we allow them to come to our land we can say that we are condemned to return to slavery once again. We say never again! In the name of the blood that flowed in the veins of Dessalines and in our veins, they will not be able to penetrate our land, because we shall defend it with every means." Speaking a few days later, the new spokesman for Fanmi Lavalas, the polished and urbane Jonas Petit, said that those coming with the OAS on its mission were "friends" of Haiti, Aristide once again displaying the double game he played with regards to internal and external politics.

Raymond's doubts about the OAS mission were echoed on Radio Metropole from a different perspective several days later by Chavannes Jean-Baptiste.

"Despite the hope that people have in the OAS mission, we don't believe that it will resolve the country's problems; even if a political agreement were reached, we clearly say that nothing will make Fanmi Lavalas honor its commitments," Jean-Baptiste said. "The country's only chance is for people to organize and mobilize in order to overturn the catastrophic situation and finish off the Lavalas hurricane that is ravaging the country. Our organization is ready and we're on the move. Whenever a level of awareness develops in all sectors of the population, then we're ready to take the lead."

The ungentle spring rains came to the capital, and on April 26, torrential storms descended, killing four people and driving some two thousand from their homes. Cité Soleil was particularly badly hit, and when I spoke to James on the phone, he was bemoaning the water falling through the cracks in their roof onto his wife and little daughter.

THE PARIS-BASED press advocacy group Reporters Sans Frontiéres, whose director, Robert Menard, had been chased from the Hotel Plaza by Paul Raymond some months earlier, announced on May 2 that Aristide had been included in their annual worldwide list of press predators, joining such august company as Iraq's Saddam Hussein, Zimbabwe's Robert Mugabe and Russia's Vladimir Putin. Saying that "impunity has been at the root of the authorities' strategy of cowing the media," RSF then went on to note the Aristide government's active obstruction of the investigation into Jean Dominique's murder, and cited the murder of Brignol Lindor. "At best, Aristide is protecting the killers," the statement said. The Aristide government greeted the announcement in stony silence. That same day, gunmen attacked a provincial police station in the town of Belladere on the Dominican border, killing Jean Brochette, a local Fanmi Lavalas coordinator. Jean-Dady Simeon said there had been no arrests, but sources close to the police identified one of the attackers as Winson Salomon, a former chauffeur and bodyguard to exiled Port-au-Prince police chief Michel Francois. Perhaps spurred on by the RSF declaration, on May 3, around two hundred journalists rallied at the bandshell on Champs de Mars and marched to the Ministry of Justice to demand justice for Jean Dominique and Brignol Lindor. Many were wearing white t-shirts with blue lettering on them that read, "Jean Dominique and Brignol Lindor fell so that the press could live."

As the month wore on, a violent power struggle erupted within the Catholic church in Jeremie, on the country's Grand Anse peninsula. A young priest, Father Jude Berthomieux Frederic, who had become very popular in the diocese with his impassioned speeches against government corruption and thuggery as well as corruption in the local Catholic church, was said to have been banned from celebrating Mass or speaking in public by his superior, longtime Aristide supporter Bishop Willy Romelus. In response, demonstrators descended into Jeremie's streets, pelting the local Catholic radio station, Radio Tet Ansanm, with rocks and shattering the car windows of vehicles belonging to the priests. They were finally dispersed by CIMO shooting tear-gas through the town's ordinarily placid streets. The following day, Gérard Dubreuil arrived in town to meet with Romulus and Frederic himself returned on May 9. Trust between the rebellious young priest and Romelus, though, had been poisoned, and the split between Aristide loyalists and opponents in the church would only grow more pronounced over time.

Addressing the Annual Conference of the Council of the Americas in Washington, DC on May 6, U.S. Secretary of State Colin Powell, who had been instrumental in facilitating Aristide's return some eight years before, said that, "It is a source of personal disappointment to me that nearly eight years after my mission with President Carter and Senator Nunn to help restore Haiti's elected government, Haiti has made so little progress. It is still far from supporting a democratically competitive political environment, in which human and civil rights are respected and economic growth is made possible."

IN THE SOUTHERN HAMLET of Cayes Jacmel on May 7, an incident occurred that revealed just how fractured and factionalized Aristide's party had become. For some time, Cayes Jacmel residents, a small fishing village about ten minutes outside of Jacmel proper along the coast road, had grown weary of the behavior of the local mayor, a Lavalas cadre member named Ernest Fils, who pocketed any funds earmarked to improve the hamlet and, in the final unforgivable humiliation, had stolen all the money set aside for the village's Carnival celebrations that year. The residents ran Fils out of town in no short order and, hearing this, Fourel Celestin, Haiti's Senate president and senator from the Jacmel region, raced to the mayor's office, concerned that evidence of questionable business practices he was involved with the mayor might be brought to light. With his security contingent, Celestin locked the mayor's office and forbade anyone else to enter. Several hours later, Prince Pierre Sonson, the Lavalas senator and also a local and, apparently, also frantic that evidence of suspicious business dealings might come to light, arrived at Cayes Jacmel surrounded by his own bodyguards. Breaking into the mayor's office, Prince was busy rooting through various papers as his bodyguard, Robert Belmur, walked onto the beach road the cut through Cayes Jacmel from Jacmel proper on the way to Marigot, where some witnesses say he fired his pistol into the air to frighten curious locals away. Someone fired at Sonson's contingent, sending a bullet into Belmur's head and killing him.

Though at first Sonson attempted to link the shooting to his urgings for the Haitian Senate to lift Dany Toussaint's parliamentary immunity, the convoluted nature of the actual story was soon revealed. Several nights later, unidentified arsonists set ablaze the home of Sonson's mother, who fled to Port-au-Prince with her son after Belmur's murder.

Amidst all this, in New York City on May 10, as Aristide addressed a United Nations-sponsored conference on children, a few hundred protestors, lead by Annette "So Anne" Auguste, who had been flown to the United States along with about fifty other Aristide government officials on the Haitian government's tab for the occasion, chanted for the United States to unblock aid to Haiti and carried signs repeating Aristide's "economic terrorism" refrain. The reliably pro-government Agence Haitian de Presse (AHP) swelled the crowd in its report of the day to over fifteen thousand. The AHP, as it was known, was headed by Georges Venel Remarais, who had served as the information director for the Catholic station Radio Soleil from 1978 to 1989 and, like Aristide himself, would

barter every ounce of his hard-earned credibility over the next years by cranking up an increasingly shrill propaganda machine. AHP, along with the government-owned TNH television station, Radio Nationale, the Venel
Remarais-directed Radio Solidarité (which, documents from Haiti's central
bank would later reveal, recieved an unexplained stipend via TELECO of 40,000
gourdes monthly[2]), the reborn *L'Union* newspaper and Radio and Tele Timoun,
became the Aristide government's main bully pulpits in its battle against the
reporting coming from Haiti's independently-owned radio stations. At a press
conference after the U.N. address, Aristide said that he hoped Haiti would have
new elections before November.

HOLY WEEK WAS APPROACHING, and as the spring winds picked up,
brightly canvassed, exquisitely delicate kites began to appear for sale on the
streetcorners of Port-au-Prince. If you drove out to the Artibonite Valley, you could
see them, tied to the ends of tenuous strings, floating above the scrub brush and
rice fields, with dancing, twirling children holding the strings on the ground
beneath them. At that time of year, the winds blew across the flatlands, whipping up dust in the streets and alleys of Gonaives and boring away at the backs
of the *rara* bands marching day and night on Route Nationale 1 on their way to
Lakou Souvenance.

You leave Port-au-Prince to drive north on Route Nationale 1 and soon you
are on a mere ribbon of paved road, the brown and ash gray Titanyen Mountains
rising up prehistorically to your right and a flat flood plain of scrub growth sinking toward Cité Soleil and the Bay of Port-au-Prince to your left. Shortly out of
town, a modest sign adorns the roadside. "*Justice! Pour Jean Marie Vincent!,*" in
honor of the slain priest and peasant-activist that helped found the Fonkoze
credit bank. Shortly thereafter, about the time you pass a commercial firing
range, the Caribbean edges up so blue that it almost appears green under the
high sun. You drive through Cabaret, the former Duvalierville, which Francois
Duvalier had envisioned as Haiti's answer to Brasilia, but that simply ended
up with a massive, strangely-shaped cockfighting arena and graceless neo-futur-
ist architecture lording impassively over the thriving marketplace. Through
Archaie—where Dessalines created the Haitian flag by ribbing the white out of
the French tri-color and stitching the blue-and-red together, and where a massive celebration is held every May 18—you pass Jean-Claude Duvalier's old
beach house at Castries, now turned into a public wharf, and the beach resorts
of Kyona and Wahoo Bay where the bourgeois kids from Petionville come to play
and flirt. Shortly beyond the city of Saint Marc, the road disintegrates into a
surreal moonscape of powdered gravel and trees and homes turned white by the
swirling dust kicked up by passing tap-taps. Here the blue sky above Haiti seems
to stretch on forever about the chalky, choking abyss, as if someone had painted
it on the roof of the world.

Lakou Souvenance is one of the oldest vodou *lakous* in Haiti, and pure African Dahomey vodou has been practiced at the location from before the time of Haiti's independence. In recent years, three brothers from the Bien-Aimé family, whose father was the *lakou*'s highly regarded chief priest for decades, took over after his death. The elder Bien-Aimé had passed from this world at the age of eighty-six only a few years before, and he remembered ceremonies being practiced at the same location all his life, as had his father before him.

During this same season sixty years earlier, members of Haiti's Catholic clergy, including Goanives fierce Breton bishop Paul Robert, engaged in a thuggish and uncomprehending attack on vodou *lakous* throughout the country, trashing peristyles and breaking sacred drums and instrument. This offensive had been done with the blessing of Haiti's then-president, the mulatto Elie Lescot, Estimé's immediate predecessor in the National Palace, who, viewing Haiti's always complex political geometry, estimated that giving the Catholic hierarchy the freedom it wanted to destroy vodou would be a way of currying favor with them for other political considerations. Ironically in the present day, Lescot's great granddaughter, the filmmaker Anne Lescot, would later, along with filmmaker Laurence Magloire, sensitively and empathetically document the experience of a group of working-class Haitian gay men with vodou in their film *Des hommes et des dieux.*

"For us, he was worse than Estimé, Magloire, the Duvaliers, the CNG and Aristide, people could not even get together to play drums," Roger Bien-Aimé, one of the three brothers responsible for maintaining the *lakou* told me about Lescot one day at Souvenance in the midst of a noisy ceremony. Bien-Aimé, a bespectacled, patrician middle-aged man, lives part-time in Canada and is a man of the world, yet he takes seriously his commitment to the tradition at Souvenance.

In a pastoral letter from February 1941, at the height of the Church's "anti-superstition" campaign, Robert wrote that: "The results obtained revealed the depth of the disease, the breadth of the deviation and the amplitude of the encroachment, which we could only suspect. Compelled to renounce completely their superstition in order to take part in the Sacrament, eight percent of those who communicated preferred to give up communion instead. . . . They think they can serve God and Satan at the same time, even giving the better part of their devotion to the demon, since in making a choice, they chose the latter." Later in the letter, Robert urges the inhabitants of Gonaives to break ties with "ignoble superstition" and "dispense the sacrileges committed by thousands of false Catholics."

Not surprisingly, perhaps, Robert fell into disfavor with the vodou-infused government of Francois Duvalier, who eventually exiled him from the country and had local macoute leader (and vodou priest) Zachary Delva sacrifice a pig on the altar of the cathedral in Gonaives in a gesture to consolidate his own power some time later.

On the dirt road that turns away from ramshackle, frontier Gonaives to Souvenance, our path was blocked by a *rara* band. We had encountered others on our drive, but this one was bigger, with several hundred people jammed into the street dancing to the incantory sounds of the *vaksins*, drums and conch shells. Women in green scarves and flowing robes shook and gyrated in moves as loose as boiled lambi while an outrageous costumed array of characters—a soldier in full green army dress and sunglasses cracking a whip, skinny peasants boys dressed in black foam vests in attempted representation of the CIMO—chanted and joined in a spontaneous burst of applause. A young man in a Haitian flag-themed bandanna waved both the American flag and a drapo of Bob Marley. With the sun sinking into the flat Artibonite plain, I walked inside the *lakou* to see the modest collection of thatch and mud huts orbiting around the poured-concrete main temple, where the words *"Souvenance Mystique"* were painted on the entrance along with a five-pointed star. As the night wore on, the sky dancing with an immeasurable number of delicate stars, a Rasta sat under a tree near me and began playing Haitian folk songs on an acoustic guitar. Aged farmers in straw hats were walking around the improvised stands of food and drink sellers holding hands, and round-hipped high-school girls with their hair braided for the occasion swayed and shimmied with no partner save for themselves.

The next day, in one of the festival's biggest events, white-robed devotees, driven on by thundering drums inside Souvenance's concrete temple, hoisted a dozen goats above their heads, slashing their throats and allowing the blood to spatter their white garments. The sweet-sour smell of fresh blood filled the temple in the April heat and, later, a large steer was sacrificed, dispatched by machete slices, beneath the shade of a tree. In a sacred pool of water, devotees dove in and writhed ecstatically, communing deliriously with element. U.S. Ambassador Brian Dean Curran arrived, much to the surprise of the attendees, and chatted amiably in Kreyol with the vodouisants and watched the proceedings with great interest. The next day, the faithful would conduct a daylong prayer, chanting and dancing session at the base of a giant mapou tree on the outskirts of the *lakou*, beginning early in the morning as the sun crested the bare mountains ringing the city of Gonaives. Mapous, the huge, gnarled trees with the expansive branches found throughout Haiti, are thought to be favorite dwellings of the *lwa*, hence they are given great importance in the faith of vodou and despite the country's rampant deforestation, never, ever cut down by the faithful. The scene was a beautiful and moving testimony of the Haitians commitment to their heritage and history, lost in that long voyage in the hulls of slave ships hundreds of years ago. The ancient sound of the drums, full of life, affirming its existence in a country that at times seemed about to drown in death, echoed from the drummers' powerful arms, deep into the night.

"We are not modernizing vodou here; we want to preserve it as it is. It's a pure tradition, pure Dahomey," Roger Bien-Aimé told me. As we spoke, a young girl, in full thrall of possession by one the often light and airy Dahomey spirits came up, giggling and coquettishly batting her eyelashes, and ran her fingers through the white man's strange hair.

THE AVANT-GARDE filmmaker Maya Deren, born in the Ukraine but raised mostly in Syracuse, New York, arrived in Haiti in September 1947 under the auspices of a Guggenheim Fellowship for "creative work in the field of motion pictures." Deren had originally intended to film Haitian dance, but she would visit Haiti three more times over the next four years, spending a total of eighteen months in the country studying its vodou rituals and shooting footage. Her writings would eventually become the seminal anthropological text *Divine Horsemen: The Living Gods in Haiti*, and a compendium of her footage shared the same title. Deren was particularly fascinated with the phenomenon of possession, the method by which the *lwa* incarnate themselves in their human hosts. For this to be accomplished during the vodou ritual, the soul of a person must be driven out, which often brings on trembling and convulsions and then a helpless, fainting state as the person waits for the *lwa* to enter. When it does, the relationship between the *lwa* and the possessed has been likened to that of a horse and rider, hence the title of Deren's book. The possessed person is "mounted" and "ridden" by the *lwa*, a state that lasts a variable amount of time and intensity depending on the *lwa* at work—from the various manifestations of the Erzulie, including the sensual and particular Ezulie Freda and the often violent and "hot" possession that characterized Erzulie Ge-Rouge, to the warrior-hero archetypes that came forth in those possessed by Ogou. The departure of the *lwa* often produces a collapsing condition and the possessed remember nothing that transpired as they were being ridden.

Deren visited Haiti at the height of Estimé's reign, and at the beginning of Papa Doc's political career, and returned to the United States transformed by her experiences. Then, as in Haiti today, there is much to be gleaned about the Byzantine workings of Haiti's political system by studying the dynamics and hierarchical structure of vodou. As the *houngan* is seen as a paternalistic figure with great possibility for both good and ill in his community, so has Haiti's imperial presidency, with very few exceptions, been seen as the means by which a leader and his *ofou* of supporters can preside over, lead or exploit their "children" in the Haitian populace. Much as the *lwa* ingratiate themselves into the bodies of their hosts in a beautiful, in some ways democratic, experience where the most impoverished peasant can be the heroic Ogou, one can see echoes in the way in which Duvalier and, later, Aristide, reigned as the *bon dye*, looming over their underlings, first the macoutes and then the chimere, and, especially in Aristide's case, insinuating themselves into the legitimate dreams of democracy of their supporters with their own grand vision of setting up a personal realm, where they alone decided who would triumph and who would weep, who would live and who would die.

Beyond that, the concept of the zombie, a dead person brought back from the grave to serve its living master, has also had great political resonance in Haiti. No one has ever been able to determine precisely what is in the potion that *bokors* use to render their victims into zombie-like states, but one of the active ingredients is believed to be tetrodotoxin, a nerve agent produced by the puffer fish and found plentifully in the water off Haiti's coast. Tetrodotoxin or TTX helps produce paralysis, respiratory distress and produces a death-like state before the final coup de grace actually descends. Once subjected to such a state, legend says, only a taste of salt will bring the zombies back to consciousness of their fate.

In the middle of the U.S. occupation of Haiti at the beginning of the twentieth century, the American writer William Seabrook was living in Port-au-Prince, and he collected the story of a man who led a group of zombies out to cut cane in the fields and then collected their paychecks at the end of every week. He gathered many other such anecdotes from a gentleman-farmer acquaintance who divided his time between the capital and the massive, roadless Ile de la Gonave, visible in the Golfe de la Gonave as one drives north from the capital. Seabrook was initially arrogantly dismissive of the phenomenon, but he was sobered considerably when a learned Haitian acquaintance pointed out to him Article 249 of Haiti's Code Penel which states: "Also shall be qualified as attempted murder the employment of substances against any person which, without causing actual death, produce a more or less prolonged lethargic coma. If, after the administering of such substances, the person has been buried, the act shall be considered murder no matter what result follows."

In more recent times, the British writer Ian Thomson, traveling through the village of Passe Reine near Saint Marc shortly after the fall of the Avril government came upon a man at the Baptist mission there, Clarvius Narcisse, who was listed as having "died" at the nearby Albert Schweitzer Hospital in 1962; Narcisse said he had been exhumed by members of a secret society and then set to work in the fields for two years until being freed by tasting salt for the first time since his exhumation. He wandered the countryside for sixteen years before returning to his family. The French photographer I had befriended had met a man outside the southern city of Les Cayes whose parents claimed he had been kidnapped and turned into a zombie and, indeed, his mental state seemed to evoke one who had been through a terrible ordeal.

It would be hard for those coming up through slavery to imagine a fate worse than slavery that would continue even beyond the grave, and any observer of Haiti would be foolish to dismiss the seriousness with which vodou cosmology inhabits both everyday and political life in the country. One of the trademarks of the Tontons Macoutes for many years was their sunglasses that, while perhaps seeming like a sartorial flourish to the visitor, in fact were meant to evoke the blank-eyed stare of the zombie, with the macoutes intimating that they were hiding just such a gaze from public view, always adding to their image of fear.

BEYOND THE SHORES of Haiti, and its legacy of a people whose identity was born in the hulls of slave ships and forged with the fire of the 1791 revolt, far from offering anything more than feel-good regional solidarity with the Aristide government, members of CARICOM, where Haiti had been actively lobbying for membership, appeared to shudder at actually getting their hands dirty in any attempt to help the hemisphere's second independent republic. A May 24 column in the *Nassau Guardian* typified this attitude:

> Haiti is a country populated by millions of people that appear to have no knowledge of family planning or birth control, and they are coming here in droves with this same mentality. . . . Illegal immigrants and Haitians in particular are committing the ultimate act of terrorism on this country. They by illegal means enter our country, plunder our resources and establish a pipeline through which to smuggle more illegal immigrants into the country. But amazingly, they can use our medical facilities, have children and register them in school, obtain drivers license etc, under the noses of the Bahamian people and the government while violating our constitution.

Sadly, the rank bigotry to which the Haitians have been subjected from the Caribbean nations was often at least as virulent as that which has been heaped on them by their white neighbors.

I ARRIVED BY CAB and hopped out at the entrance way to Cité Soleil when I saw James standing by a huge tap-tap.

"Hey, Michael!" he said, hugging me. "You ready to go to Plage Préval?"

I saw all the gunmen I recognized from Soleil 17 and Soleil 19, and some from Boston, as well, piling aboard the tap-tap. The boys had pooled their money to rent one for the day, and they were bringing their wives and girlfriends and babies along on an excursion, thirty miles to the north of the misery of Cité Soleil, to the public beach that had been renamed Plage Préval in honor of the ex-president. The beach sat amongst the moneyed resorts of the Cote des Arcadins, where Jean-Claude Duvalier used to have his beach house. The Cité Soleil crowd never used the beaches at the resorts where the bourgeois went, though. They all charged an entrance fee and kept armed guards around to discourage uninvited visits from the downtown crowd. The crowds from Petionville and up above in Laboule and Thomassin had to be allowed to eat their lobster, drink their rum, and snort their cocaine in peace, after all. We all hopped aboard and set off amidst a cacophony of children shrieking in delight, girls on board giggling as they flirted with the young men, and compas and dancehall music blaring from boom boxes as the sweet smell of marijuana filled the tap-tap's cabin.

We cruised north for about an hour until we arrived, pulling left off Route Nationale 1 to the beach, which was already crowded. Cheering, singing and laughing, the throng poured off the bus and onto the sand, receiving many curious glances from the working-class families already there as their ghetto blasters still pumped out tunes. They had brought some beer and sandwiches and pork to grill up from the Cité, and those that didn't go swimming stripped off their shirts and began grilling the meat up. Some of the poorer kids began washing their hair with the beer from half-empty Colt 45 bottles they found. For a moment there was respite, among the blue-green waters, of all the wars fought and those left to come. James and Junior sang along to the King Posse songs, which had become anthems during the previous carnival season, and the boys—they really were boys—for the first time looked as young as they were in actual chronological terms, bobbing up and down underneath the waves, deprived of any street poise or attitude. James looked out on the scene, his shirt off but a black beret on his head, and smiled as he scooped up a paper plate of grilled pork into his mouth. The sun peeked out of the clouds now and then, and from next door, at the nice resorts, we could hear fancy sound systems playing the latest compas hits. After several hours of respite, though, it was time to return back to Cité Soleil, and the tap-tap barreled down the highways the way it had come, back toward the slum, nearly rear-ending a Texaco gas truck that passed us (its red lettering reading incongruously in English "Star of the Haitian World"). When we pulled into Cité Soleil through the Boston neighborhood, I thought I saw several people running, but James did not seem unduly alarmed, so I paid it no mind. However, as we descended into the street in Soleil 19, far down from the entrance near the water, several of James's grave-faced young underlings, who had stayed behind, approached him and quickly pow-wowed in a rapid-fire Kreyol that I couldn't understand. I was about to ask what was going on when I heard an exploding crackle of gunfire behind me and turned to see several women and children running down the road in our direction.

"*Sak pase?*" I asked James, not wanting to seem too alarmed.

"The police killed Rosemond," he said matter-of-factly. "And Doudou and Super, as well."

Rosemond had been one of the gang leaders I had met in Cité Soleil at the beginning of that year and, as it turned out, he had arrived with two of his lieutenants at a prearranged meeting with police in the slum while we were away at the beach set to discuss work the Boston gang was going to do for the Aristide government, but the police instead opened fire on the three.

"Boston's fighting the police in Cité Soleil now," James said.

After a few more bursts of gunfire, the road began to clear and I debated my options. A friend of James's, a young man in wrap-around sunglasses and a Miami Dolphins cap, arrived on a motorcycle. James suggested he take me out to the main road, where I could hail a taxi, but the man didn't want to travel through Cité Soleil with a white man alone in the middle of a gun battle. So the three of us—me, James and the friend—all piled onto his tiny motorcycle and were soon careening through the muddy back alleys of Cité Soleil, water and muck splashing up around our legs from the tires and gunfire resounding ever closer as we drew near the exit of the slum. James, who knew the warrens of the zone with his eyes closed, directed his friend on a back way, skirting Boston and exiting at the abandoned Haitian-American Sugar Factory building. Cars and tap-taps were circulating, so I thanked James and climbed aboard one, heading back toward the city center. My last glimpse as I entered my communal taxi was of James on the back of the motorcycle, descending back in to Cité Soleil and the political battles that never seemed to give him a moment's rest or reward.

IT WAS A MODEST request, really. In the northern region of Guacimal, workers had been agitating for some time to be provided with gloves to wear while harvesting the oranges, which would reduce their exposure to stinging insects and other workplace hazards as they harvested the oranges, whose extract was the key ingredient in the French liqueurs produced by Cointreau. As might be expected, those assembled also voiced their opposition to the nearby free-trade zone on the Maribaroux Plain. But evidently the requests angered some powerful people. On May 27, a meeting in Saint Raphael of union workers affiliated with the Guacimal orange plantation was attacked by an armed mob led by local Lavalas officials, including Saint Raphael Mayor Adonija Sévère, brother of Sernand Sévère, the mayor machine-gunned to death four months earlier. Much as Chavannes Jean-Baptiste's November 2000 meeting in Hinche had been assaulted, except in this case with fatal consequences, two elderly attendees, Francilien Exine and Ipharés Guerrier, were decapitated by machetes and over a dozen people were severely injured. Nine union members and two journalists who had been recording the scene were thrown into jail.

The next day, the prisoners were airlifted to Port-au-Prince in Aristide's private helicopter and imprisoned in the National Penitentiary, with the two women prisoners sent to the women's prison at Fort National. Sévère, who had close links with the wealthy landowner Jacques Novella, who operated the Guacimal plantation, denounced the protestors as "terrorists."

Many said that it was an attempt to break the back of the local workers' movement in advance of Aristide's stated desire to develop the region as a free-trade zone for Dominican and American factories. Aristide, whose power base had always been strongest among the urban poor and much less secure in the countryside, was said to find the independent movements typified by MPP and the Guacimal worker's movements as intolerable challenges to his authority to operate the country as he saw fit. TNH referred to those arrested as "terrorists-uprooters attempting to use force to take land."

At a June 4 press conference in the capital, the worker's union Batay Ouvriye, the Plateforme des Organisations Haïtiennes Droits Humains (POHDH) and the Plateforme Haïtienne de Plaidoyer pour un Développement Alternatif (PAPDA) all called for the release of the Guacimal prisoners, with PAPDA's Camille

Chalmers saying that, "The events of 27 May at Guacimal are part of the neoliberal war and the anti-peasant politics violently orchestrated by the current regime." An NHCR delegation was refused admittance to the National Penitentiary to ascertain the physical condition of those detained. The Brussels-based International Confederation of Free Trade Unions (ICFTU) also stepped into the fray, lashing out at the Aristide government in a report for "flagrant violations of workers' trade union rights, including violence against trade union activists." Two journalists among the prisoners were released on June 8, but the rest were held over, Aristide once again pitting his will against that of local and foreign human rights advocates.

In a letter sent to OAS Secretary General César Gaviria the day the Guacimal workers were attacked, exiled Judicial Police Chief Mario Andresol recounted his struggles against drug-trafficking and impunity in the PNH after Aristide's return and his subsequent arrest and imprisonment:

> The Police institution, the cornerstone in the building of a legitimate State, is held hostage today by politically influential external groups who intend, through their allies in the government holding key positions, to install a system of corruption. . . . I remain convinced that, on July 31, 2001, the plan to assassinate me had fallen through. My assassins and their accomplices had no choice but to have me arrested and to send me to prison in order to perpetrate their crime away from indiscrete eyes. Since coming home after my liberation, I live almost underground, not wanting to give my ever more powerful enemies an occasion to try again. . . . I follow with great interest the moves of Investigative Commission of the OAS, hoping that it will finally bring out the truth. I remain at its disposal and wish it success in its work.

THE COMMERCIALS WERE what stuck in your mind. Tonton Bicha, a young Haitian comedian whose trademark character was a lecherous old peasant man, popped onto TV screens across Haiti, and his distinctive cracked voice emanated from the scratchy transistors that Haitians often held their ears to get news and, more importantly, football scores as they went about their business.

"Douze pour cent par mois!" Bicha said, breaking into gales of laughter as he shilled for the Coeurs Unis (Hearts United) cooperative bank. The cooperative phenomenon, which had begun spreading throughout Haiti rapidly in the fall of 2001 and liked to link itself with Haiti's long-standing tradition of peasant cooperatives, was little more than a classic, many-headed pyramid scheme, really; but for Haitians desperate for economic relief and with a penchant for games of chance anyway (as was evidenced by the country's preponderance of *borlette* lottery banks), it represented a chance to lift themselves out of *la misere*.

By early 2002, there were over two hundred and fifty cooperatives operating around Haiti, many with close links to the Fanmi Lavalas party. Usually offering

12 to 15 percent per month interest compared to commercial banks' 2 to 7 percent annual interest. the co-ops never explained how they could afford to pay such high rates, but tens of thousands of desperate and poorly educated people nevertheless lined up to invest—some going as far as selling their homes to gather the money they thought could act as a down payment on their futures. One of the biggest co-ops was the Jacmel-based Coeurs Unis, run by David Chery, who was said to be a business associate of Dany Toussaint. During its heyday, which lasted for only a few months, Coeurs Unis bought bus fleets that ferried passengers around the capital at a low charge, and Chery also bought a 28-room beach hotel on the outskirts of Jacmel for over $3 million—four times the hotel's true value. Said to employ over forty people, the hotel most often sat empty. Rumors swirled that the co-ops were being used as a front for laundering drug money, and these rumors got back to the commercial banks in which the co-ops were depositing their cash. The fact that these new financial institutions had taken off shortly after the passage of a law obliging banks to notify authorities of deposits exceeding $10,000 in mid 2001 only strengthened rumors, as the regulation didn't apply to the co-ops themselves. In February one of Haiti's largest banks, Sogebank, insisted that some twenty cooperatives depositing there funds in Sogebank accounts reveal their books and accounting methods to bank auditors. When the co-ops refused, the bank returned over $9 million in deposits and closed the accounts. By the beginning of June, still holding depositor's accounts standing somewhere between the $200 million range, over a dozen co-ops shut their doors and disappeared with their depositor's money, and almost all the others would soon follow.

As the scandal mushroomed, Aristide, who lived in his palatial Tabarre home and had demonstrated increasingly conspicuous signs of wealth during his second term even as he praised the cooperative system, told reporters that there was "no crisis in the cooperative" movement and that and "the state won't abandon anybody who deposited money in a cooperative and was victimized," a curious statement for the head of state in a country with a $400 million external debt, but Aristide never explained where in fact the government would find the money to reimburse them. Depositors in one of the cooperatives, CADEC (Insurance, Savings and Loan Cooperative), went on Radio Signal FM in early June to charge that the Aristide government had taken much of the principal capital from the co-op to help finance its "Alpha Economic" literacy program and to pay government employees, including street gangs affiliated with the government. One irate investor, a passionate and articulate young man named Rosemond Jean, helped form and became the spokesman for the Coordination Nationale des Societaires Victimes (CONASOVIC), which would become a thorn in the side of the government pressing the cause of the co-op's now-ruined investors for months to come. The scandal, like disputes in Maribaroux and Guacimal, was telling and saddening in terms of how it illustrated the way Aristide and his government were perceived as having perverted Haiti's traditional support systems and took advantage of the desperation and lack of financial savvy of Haiti's poor majority for nothing more than cold profits. As I traveled throughout Haiti that summer, I found in town after town people who had voted for Aristide in 1990 and 2000 now saying that unless he brought the money investors had lost on his next trip to their region, they had no desire to see the president ever again.

Despite the growing public dissatisfaction with his government, Aristide and several opposition leaders finally met face to face for the first time in nearly two years on June 15, in a meeting arranged by OAS Assistant Secretary General Luigi Eniadi, who had arrived in Haiti on June 10 to push for a resolution to Haiti's two-year old electoral crisis. The meeting took place at the residence of Haiti's papal nuncio, Luigi Bonazzi—the same location where the sides had met two years before. Leaving the meeting, Luc Mesadieu, whose bodyguard had been burned alive by the Cannibal Army in Gonaives seven months earlier, said that, "Aristide assured us that he will act to satisfy the conditions needed to restart the negotiations." Conditions, as always, included reparations for the victims of political violence and the disarming of the chimere. Gérard Pierre-Charles and Hubert de Ronceray also attended the meeting.

THE CAPITAL WAS BROUGHT to a standstill on June 19 as PNH units backed by armored cars set up roadblocks in an operation Secretary of State for Public Security Gérard Dubreuil said was designed to seize illegal arms. Heavily-armed personnel from anti-riot units and police officers searched through cars and checked identification papers at main intersections, though there was no information on how many weapons had been seized. On June 24, in Belladere on Haiti's border with the Dominican Republic, gunmen shot to death five relatives of Lavalas party official Cleonor Souverain, including a three-year-old child. Souverain was not home at the time. Calling the killings "an odious and horrible crime," PNH spokesman Jean-Dady Simeon said that the government would use every means at its disposal to find the killers. Rumor had it that the murders were the work of demobilized Haitian soldiers operating from across the border in the Dominican Republic and led by one Remissainthe Ravix, the former commander of the military garrison at Saint Marc. On July 6, in a major diplomatic victory for the Aristide government, at a summit in Georgetown, Guyana, Haiti was admitted as the 15th member of CARICOM, at once becoming the trading bloc's most populous and poorest state.

THE COLLAPSE OF the cooperatives was the beginning. If the murder of Jean Dominique had marked the opening salvo of the disintegration of Lavalas, and the December 17 attack on the National Palace and the attendant violence marked a crescendo in Aristide's political miscalculation, it was the summer of 2002 that would finally, violently, rupture the Lavalas base, sever Aristide from those he had claimed to champion all along and turn some of his most natural allies—the poor, the students—irretrievably against him.

As before, it was the utter lack of perspective that he had brought to his party—the complete refusal to entertain the concept that, when a wave meets no resistance, it quickly dissipates in the water, but when it meets an unyielding stone, it breaks even larger and sprays into thousands of streams—that would be his undoing. There would be many streams that would collide against Aristide's government that summer, and when he met them with force and terror, they would spray bigger and bigger and bigger until not even he, his police, his gunmen or all his beautiful words could control them. The genie would not be put back into the bottle.

Things started off well enough when, on July 4, finally bowing to international and domestic pressure, Aristide had Amiot Metayer arrested, ostensibly on charges of arson stemming from an attack on the stronghold of rival gang leader Guy Poupoute in the Decahos neighborhood. Told he was being driven to the National Palace to meet with Aristide, the burly Metayer was enraged when he was instead taken into custody and flown by helicopter to the National Penitentiary in the capital. Angry at what they termed the "kidnapping" of their don, the Cannibal Army rioted in Gonaives for several days, disrupting the port and burning down the customs house until Aristide relented and had Metayer transferred back to the prison in Gonaives on July 12.

But events soon took a more ominous tone. On the steaming, starless night of July 15, Radio Caraibes reporter Israel Jacky Cantave was dragged from his car by gunmen on Delmas 19. Cantave, an investigative reporter known for his work in Cité Soleil and La Saline, was, along with his cousin, shoved at gunpoint into a waiting car that disappeared into the night. Caraibes staff members said anonymous death threats against Cantave had been phoned in to the radio station in previous days, but no ransom note had been sent. The next afternoon, gunmen stormed the house of Jean Claude Bajeux, founder of the Centre Ècuménique des Droits Humains and a former Minister of Culture, in the Péguyville section of the capital, beating his wife Sylvie and the family maid before fleeing with several valuables. Late that afternoon, the skies above Port-au-Prince darkened and broke with a deluge that sent water rushing down the Canapé Vert road and sweeping the *ti machanns* off of Jean Paul II. Explosions of thunder echoed around the mountains behind Port-au-Prince and brilliant bursts of lighting played tag with one another in the sky. That night, Jacky Cantave and his cousin were found, bound and beaten in a hole dug in the ground of an empty Delmas house, but the capital was rife with speculation as to who was behind what many had feared was a kidnapping and murder plot similar to that committed upon Amos Jeannot. Cantave himself declined to provide many details about the kidnapping and, several days later, quietly slipped into exile with his family.

July itself was stretching out for what seemed an eternity, rainless and tor-tuously hot. Walking down Avenue Jean Paul II near my apartment in Pacot, I would often hear a woman singing litanies for the afternoon service from inside the Sacre Coeur Church, her voice echoing ethereally out onto the busy road, where *ti machanns* sat selling cigarettes, tins of powdered milk, and crackers underneath straw hats to ward off the sun. With no press and few international organizations left in town, often that summer I would be the sole diner at Sun-day breakfast at the Hotel Oloffson.

On July 24, a group of seven self-described radical students at the twelve thou-sand-member State University of Haiti occupied the body's administrative offices and began a hunger strike, calling for more say in the running of the school and calling for the departure of the university's rector, the popular Pierre-Marie Paquiot, whose term had expired before scheduled faculty elections. As it turned out, one of the protestors, Guichard Prince, was the brother of Lavalas Senator Prince Pierre Sonson, and another, Marjorie Michel, was a well-known govern-ment activist. A day later, the Lavalas-dominated Senate passed a resolution sup-porting their actions and urging Minister of Education Myrtho Celestin Saurel to fire Paquiot. Ever happy to do her master's bidding, Saurel promptly dismissed Paquiot, naming Charles Tardieu as his replacement and announcing that stu-dent and faculty elections would be suspended. The move was met with outrage by most of the student body at the university, almost all of whom were from poor and lower-middle-class families and had viewed the school as one the few bas-tions of independence in a highly polarized society. In a moment of unusual elo-quence, Gérard Pierre-Charles referred to the government's move by saying, "We are witnessing the chimerization of the university system in Haiti."

It was a fateful and clueless move on the government's part, another exam-ple of its over-reaching desire to control every aspect of Haiti's civic life; over the coming months, this move and Aristide's reaction to the protests that it sparked, would have significant consequences.

In his book, *Tout homme, est un homme*, Aristide wrote of his own time studying at the State University that, "the vast majority of (students) came from the middle classes, the upper bourgeois preferring to send their children abroad to institutions that were better equipped and more prestigious. Many were there only at the cost of heavy sacrifices on their own part and that of their families. The regime kept a close eye on the university, which it viewed as a highly risky place for it, but there we breathed a little of the foretaste of democracy." How Aristide could have ignored the historical echoes of student protest in Haiti, which tended to begin small but have the effect, if suppressed, of starting a motor than can topple governments, speaks to his lack of vision. One of his greatest flaws as a leader was always his inability to think beyond the expediency of the moment and so, despite whatever ramifications it might have for the future for flaring higher, any movement against him must be stopped immediately even, or perhaps especially, if it came from Haiti's poor majority. One of Aristide's main psychological quirks was that, as he saw himself as the only possible legitimate representative of the victimized Haitian underclass, any criticism of him was by extension a criticism and attack on that whole group of victims which he saw himself as exemplifying, and he was willing to go to any lengths to snuff out any challenge to this self-perception.

The night of July 30, a violent lightning storm struck Port-au-Prince, lighting up the sky and knocking out power lines all over town. Venturing downtown to visit a friend who lived near the national stadium early the next morning, I found the roads choked with debris: empty bottles, rotting cardboard crates, even what appeared to be the rotting flank of a steer. In the taxi, a woman in a cheery yellow dress surveyed the scene and remarked *"Lavalas desann"* to the muted laughter of everyone in the car.

THE GOVERNMENT OFFICIAL had returned from abroad with some good news. Despite the continued suspension of financial aid to Haiti, he had succeeded, through careful application to international lending bodies, to secure a substantial sum of money, chiefly designed to improve the country's health system and infrastructure. He had returned to the country from his trip full of optimism and energy for how he would use the money to tackle the great problems confronting the nation. The political situation was still dismal, it was true, and the government was still rife with rumors and evidence of corruption, but nevertheless, no one could object to the plan the money would help implement, to improve the health and well-being of the country's most vulnerable citizens. To this end and to secure the funds, the official arranged that, when they were disbursed, they would be deposited in a special account guarded by USAID. When he returned home and heard that the prime minister had arrived to see him, he was sure that Yvon Neptune was paying a call to congratulate him on a job well done. The prime minister entered his office alone and they exhanged pleasantries for a few minutes before Neptune got to the point.

"The president and I, as I'm sure you are, as well, are very concerned that when this money for these programs is disbursed we can ensure that none of it will be used for purposes other than that which it was intended, to help the Haitian people."

"I couldn't agree more, Mr. Prime Minister," the official said.

"That is why the president thinks it important that only three individuals—and no more—be able to draw from the account holding these funds. The office of the president, the office of the prime minister, and your own office should be the only ones able to access this money."

The official explained that he had made all the arrangements to put the money in a guarded account that, with oversight from USAID, would be administered solely by the branch of government he worked for. The exchange grew testier and testier as the official pleaded that, while he certainly trusted the president and prime minister's good intentions, he felt that his original plan was still the best and safest to insure that the funds were actually put to the use for which they were intended.

"Are you disobeying a direct order from the president?" Neptune finally said curtly.

"If it's a direct order, then put it in writing," the official said, bristling and feeling cornered by the prime minister's approach.

With an icy gaze, Neptune got up and left the room without another word.

WE WERE TRAVELING over the rainless northern plain just outside of Au Cap. No water had fallen from the skies here in two months and the roads were a swirl of dust. We had driven outside the city's old colonial gates and past the Caribbean Disco and the marshy, waterfront slums that ringed the city. On the eastern side of Route Nationale 1 we saw them, tap-taps lined up, private cars and pilgrims on foot, all trying to pass through the small corridor the mayor of the town of Plaine du Nord had set up to make pilgrims fork over a few gourdes for the privilege of paying homage to Saint Jacques, the warrior spirit represented by Ogou in the vodou pantheon. They were arriving in Ogou's colors, red and blue, walking past the thatched-roof stands set up along the road by the *ti machanns* selling *fritay, clairin* and bananas. We drove past them down the long dirt road, finally descending in the midst of a smoking, belching traffic snarl and marketplace of the kind only Haiti can create on a moment's notice. The air was thick with the smell of frying fat and exhaust, and barefoot street kids were rallying passengers for the tap-taps departing and begging spare change from those arriving.

The vodou tradition runs long and deep across the northern plain, like an unwritten history of the country. Francois Makandal, a rebel slave leader said to be a Muslim from Guinea, led a mass poisoning of white colonists before being arrested in 1758. Condemned to death, he was set to be burned at the stake in Cap Haitien, but, according to legend, he leapt out of the fire—an incident that was the subject of a famous painting by the Haitian artist Wilson Anaceron. It was also near Cap Haitien on the night of August 14, 1791, that the slave vodou priest Boukman, who was brought to Haiti from Jamaica and who worked on the Lenormand de Mezy plantation, presided over a massive vodou ceremony in a clearing called Bois Cayman, where slaves were said to have made a pact to die while struggling to overthrow their masters rather than continue to live as slaves, and they killed a pig and drank its blood and commenced their rebellion on August 22. (Interestingly enough, Haiti's Muslim community has its own interpretation of these events. Boukman is said to have in fact been called "bookman" because he was always said to be reading an "upside-down book," which Muslims have taken to mean the Koran, outsiders being confused by its Arabic script. Bois Cayman, they also say, was in fact Bwa Kay Imam, "the woods of the house of the imam.") During the uprising, two hundred sugar plantations and 1,800 coffee plantations were destroyed and countless slaves and colonists lost their lives. Boukman himself was killed in an ambush shortly after the rebellion commenced, but what began at that summer night ceremony would eventually lead to the country's complete independence from France and the abolition of slavery.

In front of the yellow and white Cathedral as we arrived, a sign stood. "PAROISSE PLAIN DU NORD." Beneath it, and spilling out into the road, devotees held candles, sang beautifully and began to seize up when they felt the spirit move them. An old woman, rocking back and forth and holding her scarved head with her hands, seemed to undergo a transformation, and opened eyes that were dancing with the animation and vitality of a twenty-year-old girl, before striding spryly away.

Walking past the boiling cooking pots and vendors shaving blocks of ice and covering the slivers with sweet syrup, we passed down a tight corridor of bodies all traveling toward the mud pool, which initiates possessed by Ogou dove into. Votive candles flickered on every available surface and crowds of women and men in red and blue dresses and scarves formed whirling, dancing circles around the drummers who fiercely beat out Ogou's rhythms over a surface of muddy earth.

From the walled-in mud pool, a man ascended. Covered in mud from head to toe, he carried the severed head of a bull he had been swimming with, and didn't seem to notice as it rained down blood on his head. In the pool itself, delinquents from a local gang stood waist deep in mud in which they also urinated and assailed pilgrims for money before they could swim. Above them, on a mud rise, an armless man had somehow stripped off his shirt and was dancing to the wild tambourine beats of a woman in a blue dress, both of them bearing the rail-thin frames of very impoverished Haitian peasants.

"*Erzulie Dantor / Ti Jean Petro / Travay pou nou / Travay pou nou,*" they sang. ("Erzulie Dantor / Ti Jean Petro / Work for us / Work for us.")

A young man with hugely defined biceps descended into the mud pit, snorting, staggering and drinking rum from a dusty bottle. He began to pour the rum in the pool. A murmur went through the crowd and Evans Paul, a Plaine du Nord native, arrived to survey the scene with his bodyguard.

This was Plaine du Nord in the Summer of 2002. Angry, desperate and in many ways endemic of what was going on in the country as a whole.

A steer was brought into the entrance of the mud pit, covered in red and blue flags, and quickly dispatched with the slash of a machete. As a *gengen* began carving it up where it had fallen in the mud, a beautiful teenage girl with the whites of her eyes radiating out of her face descended into the pool and began covering herself in mud, a look of post-orgasmic bliss on her face. A heavyset older woman who had been lying in the pool seemingly comatose after a writhing possession earlier, slowly raised herself up, took the girl in her arms and began braiding her hair.

Attempting to exit the walled-in area around the pool, a toothless old peasant man who had been sent by the mayor to get money from the pilgrims accosted me.

"W bezwen gen lajan," he shouted, as we stood over the space where the bull had been slaughtered and adopted the most belligerent posture an aging, frail peasant could. ("You need to pay.")

"Men m se journalis," I told him, trying a smile, not wanting to open my wallet in front of the vulturous street kids in the mud pool. ("But I'm a journalist.")

"Journalis Dominicain? Aba Dominican!" ("A Dominican journalist? Down with the Dominicans!")

"No, mwen pa Dominicain!" ("But I'm not Dominican!")

"Ah! Cubain! M te konnen!" He threw an arm around me. ("Ah, you're Cuban! I knew it!")

"N'ap renme w," he said, suddenly staggering away. ("We love you.")

I wound my way through the crowd until, at last, I came out behind a row of squat buildings, where pilgrims sitting in front of cooking fires looked quizzically at the *blan* who had somehow stumbled into their midst.

As I sat down on a rock, under a tree, to wipe the sweat off my brow with a red Saint Jacques bandanna, I looked down. My boots were covered in blood.

"W renmen Saint Jacques," a thin man said, eating a sliver of mango and leaning on a barbed wire fence in front of me. ("You must really like Saint Jacques.")

Flying back to Port-au-Prince the next day, we boarded an ancient Caribintair twin-prop two hours late and sailed right into the midst of a ferocious storm over the Montagnes Noires. Lightning crackled about the tossing plane as we sailed over the bare mountains, and rain beat against the windows. To the east of the place, black, black, black. But toward Port-au-Prince, the fading rays of clear sunshine. Taking note of my worried demeanor, a Brazilian photographer I was sitting with patted me on the leg.

"Don't worry, man," he said with a smile. "Nobody dies on their birthday."

LISTENING TO THE RADIO as I returned to the capital, with an old song by Manno Charlemagne playing in the background, a voice issued a call to action.

"We call on all students, teachers, parents and professionals of all disciplines," it said, "to defend autonomy and resist this attempt by the government to seize power of our university."

Visiting the university's Faculty of Economics, I found dozens of students milling about inside, caught somewhere on the emotional scale between anger at the government, which they felt was forcing them to act, and fear at what the consequences could be should they do so.

"We have a problem when they are trying to make us afraid," said Pierre Jean Jacques, a student sitting amidst a large group in the facility's shady garden. "But we'll defend our university."

"This government wants to hold the university in its hands," said another young student from Haiti's Plateau Central region who declined to give his name, while looking uneasily down the street. "The government wants to control all institutions in our life: the police, the airport, the port, and now they want to control the university."

Many students, exhibiting a keen grasp of their own history that Haiti's leaders would have been wise to study, said that the controversy reminded them of stories they had heard about life under former dictator Francois Duvalier. In 1961, Duvalier seized de facto control of the university by banning unauthorized demonstrations and requiring students to pledge allegiance to his government and authoritarian ideology. One of his chief agents in the takeover had been a young medical student named Roger Lafontant, who would later become Jean-Claude Duvalier's Minister of Interior.

"They don't want autonomy because we will learn all forms of government here, and not just incompetence, or dictatorship, which is all we've had here in Haiti," said Pierre Jean Jacques as I was leaving. "This government wants the whole nation working for it."

On July 31, the respected feminist organizations Kay Fanm, Solidarite Famn Ayisyen (SOFA) and the Centre national et international de documentation et d'information des femmes en Haiti (ENFOFANM) sent out a press release denouncing what they characterized as the government's "coup" against the university students. The release went on:

> We cannot remain voiceless in front of such an outrageous aggression, for the University's autonomy is the result of a struggle waged by the progressive forces within the university community, joined by various sectors of Haitian society. . . . Haitian women's organizations have joined the mobilization called by the defenders of the University autonomy, because, as concerned citizens, we agree with the righteousness of their cause. . . . (We) call upon all Haitian women to join the solidarity front that is being built with all concerned citizens who are willing to stand up for their rights. . . . A people united will never be divided! Long live the autonomy of the University!3

THE FRENCH PHOTOGRAPHER and I were going down to Cité Soleil. James had shown up at the photographer's house in Pacot some hours earlier, and he and I sat chatting on the photographer's breezy front porch, as the photographer looked through her cameras to find the right lenses for the stark brightness of the treeless slum. The photographer wasn't terribly enthusiastic about taking her car, a small gray Subaru, over the atrociously potholed roads that led to the slum, so we hailed a taxi driver who, surprisingly, seemed happy enough to take us there. We descended from Pacot through the snarled, exhaust-laden traffic of downtown and then along Route Neuf which cleaved the district away from the rest of the city. Car-sized potholes of gray water made our driver take it slow even as he tried to avoid tap-taps grinding their way along with the ubiquitous compas music emanating from their sound systems. Fort Dimanche and the Haitian-American Sugar Company factory—abandoned symbols of terror and industry—rose up on our left as the capital's dark, mysterious mountains loomed over the whole scene.

We descended from the cab and paid our thankful driver when we reached the Boston zone, just at the entrance to Cité Soleil. We walked around a bit, James saying hello to everyone, the photographer taking pictures and chattering away in Kreyol and me just watching, taking it in. We passed a graffiti mural memorializing a fallen militant, dressed in a football uniform and holding a soccer ball. "*Brave Jude*," it read, "*decede le* 29 Dec 2000."

Eventually, we settled on leaning against the remaining concrete porch of a burned-out house, waiting to speak with some of the militants who were supposed to see us. As was my habit in Cité Soleil, I kept eyeing the rooftops, mindful of the fate of the Canadian journalist who had been wounded in the neighborhood months earlier. James always laughed at this.

"I'm not going to let anything happen to you, man," he said.

As we were sitting, a crowd gathered, curious about the *blan* in their midst, their number increased, as always, by innumerable delicate, shy small boys and girls in ragged clothing who would laugh if you spoke Kreyol to them and wrap their tiny fingers around yours if you would let them lead you somewhere.

As we sat there, James called out to a friend passing by, and Wilson Saville, a studious, bearded young man, came to sit and talk with us. Saville had founded a political group, the Organizasyon Revolisyone Chalo Jaklen, named after a pro-democracy activist murdered in the late 1980s and designed to press for improvements to the lives of the residents in Cité Soleil. When I asked him when the organization was formed, he told me "December 17th," the day of the attack on the Palace, without any trace of humor.

"We cannot forget what Aristide has been for us, and we will always be on his side when we see things being done," Saville said, choosing his words carefully. He was carrying a manila envelope containing the freshly printed stationery explaining the ideology of the new movement. "But we will not support this or any government when we see nothing being done, and right now we see him sitting with the *gran manje* and living like them. Now is not like the days of the coup d'état. We're armed and we're very determined to change this country and they know that, and they will have to deal with us."

As he spoke, James was fingering a 9 millimeter a friend had brought to show him. A little girl with ribbons in her hair peeked around the corner to see what he had in his hand and, instead of turning away, she continued to stare, transfixed. The French photographer snapped a shot of the scene.

"We were expecting a lot of things from this government that didn't happen," Saville continued. "It seems that we as the Lavalas movement have failed. Things are not changing. Aristide gives people jobs at APN, at the airport, and CAMEP, but they don't last. This government is moving very timidly with its literacy programs. We don't have any *alphabetizasyon* clinics here. We have one from the Catholic Church, but none from the government."

As Saville spoke, a group of young men came striding toward us. They called out to James and shook hands all around.

"A lot of these weapons you see are army weapons, the same kind of weapons that killed our fathers, and other relatives. But now the arms of Cité Soleil are the arms of the government, the arms of the nation; they are the arms that assure there are no more coup d'etats," Saville said finally. "We could have loved him for five years, we could have loved him for ten years, but someday, he is going to have to account for what he's doing, we are not going to let go and just not say anything."

I looked up from Saville and saw the boyish face of the gang leader Labanye gazing at me from behind James. I stood up and said hello.

"A lot of the guys here would like to talk," he said. "But we should go somewhere more private."

The French photographer, James, and I walked back through a maze of alleys in the slum until we came to a squat cement building at the end of a lane, surrounded by similar humble cottages on three sides and thus relatively secure. We all entered the tiny room, with the boys insisting the photographer and I sit on the bed while they—about a dozen of them—sat in a semicircle around us on the floor. I asked them what they thought of the political situation.

"Three days before the attack on the Palace they told us ,'You must protect the government, if you don't open your eyes you'll lose Aristide and his power,'" said a militant who called himself Dessalines, unexpectedly jumping ahead to a question I had intended to ask later. He had been wearing a tank-top and blue running shorts, but he had stripped off the shirt as we entered the apartment to reveal a broadly muscular chest. "There was no coup December 17, we realize that now. It was probably a drug thing. But the response was part of a strategy, just like it's a strategy when they kill someone like Lindor. We used to be Aristide's puppets, but now our eyes are open."

"When we were working for Aristide as militants, they didn't call us *zenglendos*, but now they call us *zenglendos*, and when we die, they are going to say that's why," said Labanye, his voice rising expressively. "You've got to understand that now, under Aristide, we are losing more people here in Cité Soleil than we lost under the coup d'etat. The difference with the macoutes is if you were a militant macoute, when the macoutes were in power, at least you had some protection. But we are the militant base of Aristide and now we have no protection, we can be shot anytime."

Labanye himself, already an established gang leader, had supported an independent political candidate in Cité Soleil for the May 2000 elections, and had been kept in jail for ten months until he accepted to work for the Lavalas government, which is why he was locked up during my first forays into Cité Soleil.

"He knows the activists—Lanbanye, Dessalines, Rosemond, Billy—and he knows that we are able to mobilize a lot of militants here," responded Dessalines. "Aristide has promised us a lot of things—school, work, that things would be better—and he's done absolutely nothing. And I can't go outside of Cité Soleil now, because if Aristide's cops find me, they'll kill me, because he knows he can't control me anymore."

The group then chimed in—saying that certain police commissioners had been entrusted with eliminating troublesome militants, and singled out Camille Marcellus, serving as the commissioner for Delmas at the time, and police at the downtown Cafeteria precinct as the worst offenders.

"These are the people who murder us," they said.

I asked if I could see the weapons they had and, after some discussion, the boys agreed.

Several runners were sent out and returned with about half a dozen large, heavy burlap rice sacks, full of automatic and semi-automatics, bolt-action rifles, glocks, a variety of pistols, about half a dozen hand grenades and several of the hybrid, homemade weapons the Haitians call *zanm kreyol*. The French photographer raised her camera to take a photo.

"Sorry, honey, no photographs," Labanye said curtly.

"We are not militants out of the blue," said Dessalines as I examined the guns. "We are militants because our mothers, our fathers, were already militants, because it's always been bad here and we always had the dream that things could change. We could form a new political movement, but naturally we can't do it on our own. It would have to be everybody, all nine departments, to try and do this change, and also the tenth department, because we are children of the tenth department, and they know that we are suffering here."

"Ironically, before 1994, the situation was better, because we had NGOs here," said Labanye. "We had the famous CDS center [the Centre pour le Développement et la Sante, run by Reginald Boulos, a major recipient of USAID health funding]. We had a hospital. When Aristide told us to drive Boulos out, we did it. And we organized the demonstrations and drove them out. And now we have nothing. Nothing has replaced them. If Boulos were to come back, everybody would support him."

I asked if the gangs' patrons in the PNH couldn't help them in some way.

"One of the biggest fears of Aristide is that another potential leader will come along, so he will eliminate anyone who is gaining momentum and has popular support—for instance Jean Dominique, for instance Dany Toussaint," said Labanye. The boys had previously told us that, shortly after the May 2000 elections, they had received orders from the National Palace that they should no longer cheer and rally for Toussaint. "I think Hermione [Leonard] is squeezed, right now. She's a true militant; she likes the people but she's also working for the regime, so if she gets too close to the people, they'll eliminate her."

"Yes, I can't walk the streets in peace because they can seize me, they can frame me, they can put a gun in my hand, say I was attacking them and kill me," said a young man named Maxon Moreau, although he said went by the name Kolonel. "We are ready to call the American ambassador and the international organizations to let them know about this situation because we want to create a new movement; we want to know also that we have support and protection because today we can be dead at any minute."

I asked them when they thought things might change in Cité Soleil.

"When we die," was the mordant response, said in unison and met with bitter laughter.

I left the meeting heavily dispirited, a feeling that was not lifted as I walked down the rubbish-strewn lanes with James to visit his wife and daughter.

"One day, man, I'd like to be able to give up this politics," says James, as we picked our way down a hill of shacks and were met by naked, laughing children. "If not, I'll die and I couldn't do anything for myself."

We met James's wife, a shy-eyed beauty, and James cradled his baby in his arms.

"You know, my mother died in '91 and FRAPH kidnapped my father in 1994 and killed him, too," he said, looking down at the child in his arms.

"And now I've sat with Aristide many times and I still have nothing, I still have this same room. I've done too much work for politics. Now, too many people hate me, and they hate what I say. But it's for this I try to help my little son, so we can arrive at a new place."

IT HAD STARTED early in the morning of Friday, August 2, a Haitian former U.S. Marine who owned a bar across the street from the jail in Gonaives told us later. The previous day, Cannibal Army members, still furious at their leader Amiot Metayer's detention in the prison there, had sacked and burned the city's customs house.

"I was walking down the street, and the first thing I heard was a couple of gunshots," he said, looking out toward the street and nervously chain-smoking cigarettes. "Coming toward the police station, all I heard was gunshots left and right, so I had to dart from house to house to get back here."

Arriving at the bar, what he saw alarmed him.

"There were two groups of guys shooting at the police station. At the same time they're doing this, they took a front-end loader from where some workers were building a house and, as the other group kept the front occupied, from the back of the jail you heard the 'boom boom' from the loader. And the police were shooting out at the street.

"The gang out front set a truck on fire in front of the police station. Next thing you know you hear them all screaming 'He's free! He's free!' and then they were gone."

He snapped his fingers to indicate the rapidity with which the crowd disappeared.

"Just like that."

After a month in jail, Amiot Metayer had been liberated. The Cannibal Army, after weeks of violent disturbances in Gonaives, had leveled the wall of the prison there with a bulldozer. One hundred and fifty-nine prisoners fled into the streets that day, among them Jean Pierre (a.k.a Jean Tatoune), who had been convicted in the November 2000 trial for his role in the 1994 killing of Metayer's supporters in Raboteau. Throughout the day and into the night, Cannibal Army members set government buildings on fire and shot their weapons off in the air in a confluence of celebratory and intimidatory impulses. Metayer and Tatoune walked through their respective neighborhoods, their arms draped around one another like long-lost brothers. The PNH contingent stationed in Gonaives gamely tried to respond with tear gas and their own guns, but after a police vehicle was burned and its occupants forced to flee for their lives, they essentially abandoned the city to wait for reinforcements.

On Saturday, recovering their equilibrium somewhat, riot police poured into Gonaives. Speaking to Radio Metropole from Raboteau, Metayer did the unthinkable for a street-level gang leader in Aristide's employ and, as Yvon Bonhomme had done on radio a year before, he broke the code of silence, admitted government collusion with the political violence that had been roiling the country, and denounced the Haitian president as a despot and a tyrant.

"I was kidnapped by Aristide and forced under threat of violence to appeal for calm," Metayer said. "Aristide has betrayed the people and I call on the people of Gonaives, of Cité Soleil, of Petit Goave, to fight. We will fight until the death!"

As he spoke, one could hear a helicopter circling overheard, and Metayer then cut the broadcast short to say the chopper was full of armed policeman.

GERRY HADDEN, a correspondent from National Public Radio in the United States who was based in Mexico City, and I headed up Route Nationale 1 to Gonaives only days after the disturbance. Leaving Port-au-Prince, we crossed a bridge bearing a red banner reading *"Jésus nous préparent"* ("Jesus, we are prepared") just after the turn off for Route Nationale 1 near Aristide's home at Tabarre. We cruised up toward the Titanyen Mountains in the morning sun, leveling out with the sand flats beyond Cité Soleil to our left, once a killing field, where a friend had told me FRAPH had left bones as far as the eye could see. With the hills rising up in the strong morning light, we thought of the old Kreyol expression: "The mountains are showing their bones."

The road seemed more desperate, somehow, this time, the villages more crowded and cacophonous, the resorts along the beach more fading and deliquescent. Past L'Estere, a thin shirtless man sat on the porch of his shack, head in his hands, as tap-taps roaring past blew white dust on him, and he seemingly didn't notice.

Arriving in Gonaives just as the late afternoon summer rains were beginning to fall, we saw the remnants of tires and burned-out tap-taps pushed off to the side of the road. The town was busy, and after we checked into the by-now familiar, waterless hotel, seemingly staffed only by sullen teenage girls, we ventured back downtown for a look at the maligned prison. The rain was falling heavily now, as two beautiful girls in red and green t-shirts stood talking, oblivious, as the rain drenched them in the street. We took shelter in a small bar, owned by the mayor's son, across the street from the prison and got pleasantly inebriated on ice-cold Prestige served for 15 gourdes a piece. As night fell, before our scheduled entry the next morning, we got bolder, and went cruising with a local friend past burned-out hulks of cars and curling ribbons of incinerated tires into the lightless heart of Raboteau.

We arrived at the Chandel nightclub, a series of gleaming new pickups and SUVs parked outside, all with rifle-toting men sitting on their hoods, watching. The club was located in the back of a cavernous, never-finished shopping complex, and we sat drinking with heavy, black-hat-wearing Raboteau gangsters, listening to compas and rap as they danced with their dolled-up molls in front of jarring, day-glo wall murals. A man we were with, older but still bearing the jittery eyes of a street fighter, took a look at the scene, sipped his Prestige and smiled.

"Raboteau's in the house," he said.

When we rendezvoused with our friend again the next day, we once more backtracked gingerly through the debris. The streets of Raboteau seemed curiously lethargic, although there were clutches of young men standing on either side of the sewage drain gutters that ringed the streets, watching us. The houses here were mostly made of wood and concrete, but seemed a rung or two above those in Cité Soleil, with the obvious, poisonous rot of waste and decay less overpowering here. Finally, our local friend motioned us to slow down, and our rental car came to rest in front of a nondescript squat gray building. In the yard of another building in front of us, we couldn't help but notice as we sat that an American flag had been incongruously hoisted up a pole and fluttered in the breeze coming off the Bay of Gonaives—as if that would be the ultimate insult to Aristide, to see that banner flying in this, one of the country's poorest urban enclaves.

Metayer, for understandable reasons, was laying low, fearing for his life at this time, and, as such, he wasn't terribly disposed to chatting away to two *blan* who had somehow climbed over his barricades to get his opinion on the current state of Haiti. It turned out that Gerry and I wouldn't be seeing Cubain that day, but were instead pawned off to Winter Etienne, Metayer's most feared deputy, and a squad of armed henchmen. Directed inside the half-finished cement block home with hammers, lengths of rope and hacksaws scattered around the floor, Etienne, in a moment of inspiration, told us that he was the "Spokesman for the People's Committee in Solidarity with the Liberation of Amiot Metayer," which no doubt he realized had a better ring to it than "Cannibal Army."

"We've struggled for a long time," he said, fixing Gerry and I in a rapt stare and speaking in fluid, precise Kreyol. "We have always been struggling against dictatorship here, for years. When Jean-Claude Duvalier fell, we were only young boys, but now we are still fighting."

I remarked that, as Jean Tatoune went to jail for the Raboteau massacre that occurred during that struggle but now was parading through the streets with Metayer, that must be a rather complicated situation.

"That's Haiti," Etienne said, with a laugh. "When you're in hot combat, you get really angry. But then, as time passes, people come together again for different reasons. That's the way it is in Haiti."

I asked Etienne why his group acted as they had.

"They say that Cubain was involved in burning down Pastor Luc's house, but Cubain was not there. He was here in Raboteau talking with me the way we're talking now," he said. "We heard this week that they were going to send Aristide's helicopter back here to take him back to Port-au-Prince to prison again, and that is why we had to attack the jail. Cubain must remain free. This is non-negotiable because he is innocent; Cubain is one of the people trying to save the people of this country. Like in the Bible, Joseph was accused by his brothers and thrown into jail though he was innocent, that is what happened to Cubain, and that's why he had to be liberated. The reason we are calling on Aristide to leave is that Aristide arrested an innocent man."

Etienne sat back and folded his arms across his broad chest, evidently pleased at his rhetorical flourish.

What, I asked him, did the people of Raboteau think now of the government they had worked so hard for?

"People in this government have gotten fat since Aristide came back to Haiti, but for a lot of other people, life has gotten worse, and there's a lot of frustration because of this. I have four diplomas and I haven't gotten any work."

"Remember, in 1986," he said, with the air of a man imparting a lesson of history. "The movement to oust Jean-Claude Duvalier started here. It was the people for Raboteau and Gonaives who had to start that movement, and it took awhile for the rest of the country to catch up to us, to get together, so it's probably going to take a while for the country to get together and organize themselves to struggle against Aristide. I don't think either Lavalas or Convergence are going to solve this country's problems. But everybody wants justice, social justice and political justice, and that's not what we have right now."

BY MONDAY, AUGUST 5, hundreds of antigovernment protestors fought police in Gonaives, while police responded with tear gas and live ammunition, and Amiot Metayer continued his call that Aristide must resign.

"Today we know that Aristide no longer works for the people," he told Haitian radio again. "Therefore he must go."

Echoing Metayer, Jean Tatoune told reporters that, "We call on the entire population of the country to demonstrate against Aristide."

Fearful of a government counterattack, Raboteau residents began streaming out of the neighborhood, as Cannibal Army members burned tires around the city and fired their weapons into the air as they protested.

Dismissing the protestors as "nothing more than a small group of criminals and delinquents," Prime Minister Yvon Neptune said that, "when the time was right," Metayer would be returned to jail.

Nevertheless, the next day, Aristide announced that he was appointing Jose Ulysse, an employee at various government ministries with long-standing links to the gangs in the capital and elsewhere, as the state's special representative to negotiate an end to the crisis in Gonaives and come to a "peaceful solution" regarding Metayer's jailbreak. Though there was no official response from Raboteau, Gonaives remained generally peaceful on the day of the announcement. The OAS, for its part, in the person of its own special representative to Haiti, Sergio Romero Cuevas, asked the Aristide government to "assume its responsibility in apprehending these fugitives" and offered "assistance to the government (to do so) in the event of any request."

On August 8, Gonaives was blanketed with anonymous leaflets calling for the deaths of Dany Toussaint and Medard Joseph, and Paul Raymond and René Civil announced that they would hold a mid-morning press conference at Saint Jean Bosco in the capitol. Driving through the San Martin slum on this almost-raining, eerily deserted morning, a new sign had been erected in the park Aristide had opened there. "When we resist together, we are Lavalas," it read.

The parking lot of Saint Jean Bosco was full of *tet boefs*, Rastas and street kids. Bob Moliere was working security at the door, and ran up to me, his barrel-frame embracing me and announcing that "a *blan* militant" had arrived. In the church itself, where its burned-out roof had been now open to sparse raindrops, Raymond and Civil were standing on the rise where Aristide's pulpit had once stood, and Civil looked up and shot me a wan smile when he saw me.

"The enemies of Haiti are trying to destabilize the country," Raymond began, reading from a typed statement and wearing stylish gold sunglasses and a tan shirt and pants. "They are trying to snatch the power of the people away. Today we are fighting to defend our independence!"

"We'll never give up! We'll never surrender!" the Rastas shouted, clapping as elderly *ti machanns* danced to the rhythm.

"The international community has created only one thing for Haiti," Raymond continued, his voice seeming to break with emotion as the throng and reporters leaned in to catch his words clearly. "This fabricated political crisis. We must mobilize, we must not panic. Haiti is sick, this is true, but we have many doctors to save her. We know the disease, it is Kaplim [a nickname for Evans Paul], Gérard Pierre-Charles, Paul Denis. But we will beat back this disease!"

After another outburst from the Rastas, René Civil unfolded his arms and stepped forward.

"When the opposition talks about mobilizing to force the removal of the government, they are speaking in the language of the coup d'etat, and someone better tell him that we won't sit back and let a coup d'etat pass," he said, then addressing Evans Paul directly by using his nickname, accentuating his Kreyol vowels for maximum dramatic effect. "Kaplim its going to hurt! Kaplim, where do you get your weapons? Kaplim, who bought you?"

Then, to even more riotous shouts of those assembled, who had also begun to chant, "We don't want any sweet talk!" after a popular compas song by the group Chandel, Civil brought his message home.

"They want to create division! They throw money around! They are distributing arms!" he cried. "We ask the militants of Raboteau, but especially Amiot Metayer, return to the house of your country. Return for the democratic justice of the people! The criminals who massacred the people in Gonaives were arrested and judged, and we plead the militants of Gonaives to remember that we are in a war to transform to the country, and to defend democracy."

Shouts and defiance, and then the crowd began to disperse with the same electric energy as it had performed. The crowd continued, as always, to regard the *blan* in their midst curiously. Dupuy Delince Desance, a soft-spoken geography teacher at a public-learning annex in the capital, greeted me with a handshake and a sunbeam smile and thanked me for coming.

"I supported the students when they formed this," he said. "I thought it was good for the youth to have some organization politically."

A shoeless boy stood next to me, regarding me curiously, and he laughed when I bounced the back of my palm on his head. Raymond and Civil got into their huge, government-funded rental cars, the Rastas poured out to hail a tap-tap on Grand Rue, and pretty soon it was just the street boy, peering into the ruins of Saint Jean Bosco and watching the rain collect on the parking lot's broken gravel.

Dramatically, on August 9, Metayer called for an end to the demonstrations against the Aristide government after, he said, the government agreed to "review" his case. Secretary of State for Communications Mario Dupuy said it was "up to the judicial system to decide" the question of whether or not Metayer should go back to jail, as if the government itself had ever let the role of the judiciary stand in the way of its locking anyone up before. But, gradually, in Gonaives things went back to normal. Aristide, it appeared, had successfully wooed Metayer back into the Lavalas fold with a promise not to arrest him. On a crumbling wall near my apartment in Pacot, some wit had scrawled the words "Bulldozer forever."

"ARISTIDE ARMED THESE PEOPLE and he can no longer control them," said Michele Montas when I stopped by Radio Haiti-Inter. She and the Radio Haiti-Inter staff were busy preparing a series of reports on the murder of Marc-Andre Durogène, the Lavalas deputy from Gonaives who was gunned down in the capital the previous February. Durogène had been a vocal critic of corruption and contraband in the customs office of Gonaives before his murder, sending a letter to then-Prime Minister Jean-Marie Cherestal to that effect shortly before his killing. Perhaps not coincidentally, one of Amiot Metayer's brothers held a prominent post at the customs house.

"We felt that this was a case that was very similar to what happened to Jean. Someone who was investigating and had denounced corruption, not as a journalist but as a parliamentarian. He was challenging forces within the Lavalas party and they apparently decided to get rid of him. The police weren't doing anything, the judiciary wasn't doing anything, so we thought it was our job as journalists to do something."

She seemed to have accepted Claudy Gassant's flight to the United States ("I can't blame the man"), but she seemed to worry about the new investigating judge, Bernard Sainvil.

"He has a different character from Judge Gassant," she said. "Very prudent, very cautious, he doesn't like the limelight. It's difficult to tell what he will do. How independent is he from the different political sectors? I don't know, I have no way of judging that. That remains a big question."

Unfortunately, one of the great champions for a resolution to the case, Charles Suffrard, the leader of the KOZEPEP peasant union that Dominique had helped found, had been forced to flee into exile in the United States some months earlier, after receiving a steady stream of death threats.

LATER THAT SAME MONTH, another jail off of Route Nationale 1 was stormed, although this time the crowd had distinctly different intentions. Early in the morning hours of Tuesday, August 27, an enraged mob burst into the prison in the provincial city of Archaie, where Dessalines had torn the French tricolor in two to create the Haitian flag so many years before. The mob dragged out a murder suspect reporters could later only identify as "Ti Blan." Ti Blan had been arrested the previous day for allegedly killing another man in an argument with a knife, but, not wanting to wait for the tortuously slow wheels of Haitian justice, the mob instead lynched him near the penitentiary, and then set his corpse ablaze for good measure. After waiting a respectable amount of time, PNH forces began firing live rounds above the heads of the crowd, finally driving them off and leaving what remained of Ti Blan smoldering by the roadside. "We have dispatched additional units to Archaie to make sure that calm prevails," Jean-Dady Simeon told reporters later, though no one took that very seriously.

IN BAHAMIAN WATERS on August 12, the Royal Bahamas Defense Force picked up 204 Haitians sailing in a 40-foot wooden sloop near Inagua, bringing the total picked up by Bahamian authorities up to 2,500 so far for the year. Around the same time, closer to home, Ornis Freddy Pe'a Mendez, the Dominican vice-consul to Haiti, was arrested in a Santo Domingo slum with 90 pounds of cocaine, a machine gun, and a slew of fake Dominican and Haitian passports. Police said the drugs had been smuggled into the DR from Haiti aboard a tour bus.

On August 14 a group of students protesting the government's decision to remove Pierre Marie Paquiot and calling themselves the Front de Resistance pour la defense de l'Université d'Etat D'Haiti (Front to Defend the Autonomy of the State University), attempted a peaceful sit-in in front of the Ministry of Education. As they did so and local media gathered to cover the protest, chimere began hurling stones and bottles at the frail, impoverished scholars from the windows of the Ministry and later from the street itself. The windows on several cars, including press vehicles, were also smashed by government supporters.

"The executive branch wants all the power, they want to control the university as they want to control the rest of the country, in all aspects," said one young man when I went to survey the aftermath of the melée. "The only solution is for the university to retain its autonomy."

BETWEEN THE STUDENT PROTESTS and the Metayer jailbreak, Aristide's government had this far undergone an unnerving summer. Not surprisingly, it reacted the only way it knew how. On August 19, the day after students and journalists were attacked at the Ministry of Education, the Cité Soleil boys and several gangs from Carrefour were directed by the National Palace to set up barricades along the northern and southern approaches to the city. With James and his crew creating a wall of burning tires on the Croix de Missions bridge on the way to Cap Haitien, as well as outside Leogane just before the police station there, the boys went on the radio to say that they were protesting a destabilization campaign by the Convergence as typified by the student protests. For human rights advocates, the only good news thus far of the month came on August 20, when seven of the nine people still imprisoned after having been arrested at Guacimal the previous May were finally released from jail in Port-au-Prince.

I WAS SITTING in my apartment in Pacot on the night of August 21, writing and watching the bright green lizards that Haitians call *zandoli* perch on the chairs next to my desk when my cell phone rang. It was some of the boys from Cité Soleil.

"Michael, you heard that the students are going to march tomorrow."

I told them that I had.

"The Palace called us, they told us that we shouldn't let them march, that people should not be able to walk through the streets singing 'Down with Aristide.'"

"So what are you going to do?"

"We are going to stop them, at the gates of the École Normale, tomorrow morning. You should come; it will be a good story for you."

Come I did, and the morning transpired exactly as the Cité Soleil boys said it would. As hundreds of students and faculty members gathered at the École Normale Superieure of the State University of Haiti just behind the National Palace, thousands of young, mostly male protestors blocked the building's entrance, and before long they began throwing the ubiquitous bottles, rocks, and pictures of Aristide over the École's walls, all the while shouting "Down with Convergence! Aristide or death!" Riot police standing by occasionally pushed the pro-government crowd back, but generally did not intervene. Several students were assaulted as they attempted to leave the building, including one who was beaten with a board before my eyes. Students attempting to exit through the back of the building were greeted by a group of chimere holding wooden planks with nails driven through them, and quickly retreated to the inside of the building. My friend Etzer, a professor at the university, stood with me for a time on the sidewalk and watched the scene unfold, his arms crossed on his chest, as he sadly shook his head from side to side.

"We are here defending the autonomy of the university," said one student, speaking to me as we stood inside the school's grounds and rocks thudded against the roof and sailed over the front gate. "This is a student demonstration, not a political one. We are independent."

It was true. Not a single member of the Convergence, most of whom had seemed good at talking shop but little else, was anywhere to be seen—not even Micha Gaillard, a science professor at the institution. The crowd was made up almost exclusively of young students from lower-class neighborhoods around the capital and the provinces, kids from places like Carrefour, Delmas and Hinche, who were almost to a person the first ones in their families to receive any kind of secondary education, which in many ways helped explain what they saw as their passionate stake in something as seemingly abstract as faculty appointments. They waved banners saying, "We are not afraid," and pictures of the Argentine-born revolutionary Che Guevara, and they demonstrated a street-level courage that the traditional opposition decidedly lacked. Not only were they willing to talk, but they were willing to put their bodies on the line and march and demonstrate, getting beaten and bloodied only to return again and again, unbowed and utterly convinced of the moral righteousness of their cause—something no amount of meeting with the IRI at the Hotel Montana or any cadre of well-paid foreign lobbyists could ever buy Aristide and his traditional opponents.

I left the scene gravely depressed, realizing for the first time the full depth of Aristide's involvement in the violence that seemed to be tearing his country apart, upset at the cynical use of my desperately poor friends from the slums, humbled by the courage I saw in the frail, young student protestors facing down such a ruthless and megalomaniacal enemy, and nearly despairing, with the world's attention elsewhere, that there was any way I could make the outside world care about what was going on in Haiti.

"The situation is getting worse and worse every day," said Pierre Esperance from NCHR when I spoke to him later that day, not sugarcoating anything for me. "This government doesn't want any element of society that doesn't agree with them to be able to speak."

On August 23, the government sent the Cité Soleil boys to again burn tires and block the bridge at Croix des Mission Route Nationale 1 in an anti-Convergence demo, for which they carried carefully-stenciled signs reading "Down with Convergence" and "Arrest Convergence."

That same week, Aristide walked across the Champs de Mars to pay a very public visit to the DGI (Direction General des Impots), Haiti's tax office, the very place Jocelerme Privert had been fired by Préval for corruption before becoming the minister of chimere under Aristide. Sitting next to Jean Desroches, the agency's seemingly petrified director, and surrounded by white Steele Foundation security personnel, Aristide delivered a homily before a crush of reporters about how "Everyone in the country needs to help us combat corruption. . . . With the difficulties we are experiencing in Haiti, we encourage all people to pay their taxes. All people, merchants large and small, must understand this responsibility."

As Aristide spoke, a roaring crowd could be heard outside the windows of the office. *"Viv Aristide! Aba macoute!"* they shouted. *"Aba convergence!"* As we descended to the garage that marked the entrance way of the building, Oriel Jean, Aristide's chief of Palace security, was standing in a gray suit and sunglasses, directing the protest of a few dozen young men.

ON AUGUST 29, the OAS released a grim assessment of the deteriorating human rights in Haiti, saying that armed gangs were acting with impunity while health conditions were worsening. The report by the organization's Inter-American Commission on Human Rights said that it was "deeply preoccupied by the weakness of human rights in Haiti, the lack of an independent judiciary . . . the climate of insecurity, the existence of armed groups that act with total impunity and threats to which some journalists have been subjected." The rights delegation also cited higher rates of illiteracy, maternal-infant mortality, and undernourishment, which, it said, "represent by themselves human rights violations."

As if to underline the report's accuracy, during the end of August and beginning of September, a bloody two-week gang war raged in Cité Soleil between the Boston *baz* of Labanye and his deputy Kolobri ("Hummingbird") and the Bois Neuf gunmen headed by young, permanently high Emmanuel "Dread" Wilmé, so named because of his long, irregular dreadlocks, and who, like James and Tupac, was an alumni of Aristide's Lafanmi Selavi youth home. Though at least twenty people died, including a Wilmé deputy named Valentin, and scores of homes were burned, fighting together, Labanye, Kolobri (real name Rodson Lemaire) and their cohort Maxon Moreau (the "Kolonel Gay" or "Ti Fre" I had met with Labanye some weeks earlier) succeeded in driving Wilmé out of Cité Soleil, and killed several of his gunmen as they tried to get back in. The victory marked something of a personal watershed for Labanye, as he was now the undisputed *chef* of *chefs* in Cité Soleil. As such, he felt it appropriate to hold a "Fete de Guerre," and so, the gunmen dancing with their guns and machetes through the slum's streets to the accompaniment of vodou drums and blaring *vaksins*.

In the midst of the battles, hundreds of angry protestors from Cité Soleil descended through the Champs de Mars plaza to the National Palace to demand that Aristide rein in the gunmen.

"People are attacking us, they are burning our houses down! We have no work, no food for our children! We're sleeping in the streets!" one man from Soleil 4 told me as I watched the throng try to gain access to see Aristide through a side gate to the Palace.

"They set our house on fire when I was asleep inside," said one barefoot boy—who could not have been more than six or seven years old—looking in wonder at the swirling demonstration around him.

"We can't sleep at night because we're always so afraid," another woman told me.

When the Palace tried to fob off the protestors by sending out some Palace lackey in Aristide's place, the crowd grew even more incensed, and began threatening passing vehicles with clubs and metal pipes. Fistfights began to break out between protestors and motorists. The residents of the Palace let it continue for a while, but eventually, probably realizing their was no political mileage to be milked out of it, someone sent the CIMO, who tear-gassed the crowd and beat and chased the protestors away from the Palace gates.

Shortly after the Cité Soleil protest at the Palace, I watched as several hundred Lavalas supporters, marching in a demonstration cosponsored by Petionville Mayor Sully Guerrier, met up with a group of anti-Aristide protestors in the hill suburb's streets, and the two sides nearly physically pulled me apart while demanding that the other not be allowed to speak. Eventually, though, the pro-Aristide march continued down Avenue Pan-Americaine, lead by well-spoken young men in pressed shirts and ties, blowing on conch shells and chanting; the march, which also included a substantial number of women, appeared to be an attempt by some of the legitimate grassroots movements that still supported Aristide to recapture the civic, nonviolent momentum of the original democratic movement from the government's gunmen. Members of the pro-Lavalas community group SOPUDEP, who I had interviewed around the time of Aristide's reelection two years earlier, were there in force. The SOP-UDEP activists had recently taken over a disused mansion off Avenue Pan Americaine, on the way up to Petionville, that had formerly been owned by a Ton-ton Macoute leader named Lionel Wooley who, according to a 1988 report by the Washington, DC think-tank called the Committee on Foreign Relations, became a powerful drug lord in Miami after fleeing Haiti following the fall of the Duvalier government. SOPUDEP was cleaning and refurbishing the house, including a hidden room underneath the swimming pool said to have been a torture chamber, in hopes of opening a school and soup kitchen there for needy children. I had written a story concerning the project and sent in in to the Reuters office I was affiliated with in Miami, but an editor there, who preferred that Haiti be painted in broad black-and-white strokes, opted not to run it—not the first time I would run into difficulty attempting to explore the subtleties of a poor, black country that news outlets often felt they had little reason to pay much attention to. This day, singing from printed song sheets even as a pickup blaring the song lyrics "We don't want no sweet talk" rolled by, the group marched all the way to Yvon Neptune's office just below the Hotel Montana. A little girl in braids ran from the roadside to grab her younger brother, who had broken free from their family as they stood watching the march and began to follow, excited at the spectacle. "Aristide for five years," the marchers chanted. Two trumpet players, who said they were from an organization calling itself the Kon-federasyon Komite Tet Ansanm pou Developman Dayiti, struck up their instruments, lending the march a bit of the air of a jaunty New Orleans-style funeral, as they descended toward Delmas 60.

But cracks in the regime's facade of popular legitimacy had grown throughout the summer. On Aug. 30, Rosemond Jean, who had begun speaking out in solidarity with the student protestors, led a roiling CONASOVIC demonstration of those who had lost their money in the co-operative scandal from the U.S. Embassy to the National Palace, with marches shouting that Aristide was a *zen-glendo* who had stolen their savings along the way. When depositors surrounded the Coeurs Unis office in Port-au-Prince several days later, they were beaten and chased away by security guards. Aristide had promised that all investors would have at least part of their money back by the time the school year started on September 2 and Henriot Pétiote, director of the government's National Council of Cooperatives had been promising much the same; but as the date approached, he soon reversed himself, pleading that there were too many claims to be handled briskly and that his office was overwhelmed.

ON SEPTEMBER 4, the Organization of American States passed Resolution 822, calling on "the normalization of economic cooperation" between Haiti and international financial institutions while seeking free and fair local and legislative elections in 2003. In a written statement, U.S. Ambassador to the OAS Roger Noriega called on the government, as did the OAS body as a whole, to disarm the militants in its employ and pay reparations to victims of political violence, stating that "grave social and economic problems continue to confront the Haitian people. . . . [This] resolution calls on the Government of Haiti to fully comply with past OAS resolutions and take further steps to ensure free and fair elections, end impunity and strengthen democracy." While government cheerleaders would take to the airwaves in Haiti to hail the resolution as an unblocking of the $500 million of withheld international aid, some were more circumspect. Speaking to one senior government official who spoke to me on the condition of anonymity, he said that, "It doesn't mean anything in terms of actual disbursement of funds. There are many conditions to be met, and huge financial and technical obstacles in the way."

At Port-au-Prince airport the next day, Aristide was scheduled to be returning from his trip to the United Nations World Summit on Sustainable Development in Johannesburg, South Africa. James and the Cité Soleil boys had called to tell me that they had been told by the Palace and the Minister of the Interior to put on a big show for Aristide's arrival, and when a visiting colleague from Miami and I made our way to the airport, the lanes heading into the entrance gate were choked with young men waving signs that said, "We are defending a change that the foreigner does not respect," and, "End The Economic Blockade." As we squeezed our way past the noisy throng at the diplomatic entrance, I saw Junior, who gave me a thumbs-up. A National Palace guard I had previously seen guarding René Civil was admitting reporters through the front door.

Inside, after passing through security, in the special arrival lounge set aside for V.I.P.'s, Haiti's Lavalas elite were mingling. Minister of Health Henri-Claude Voltaire was there, and greeted me warmly. Hermione Leonard watched the proceedings with a deceptively innocuous smile on her plump baby face and Jean-Dady Simeon, one of the boys, as always, laughed and joked with reporters and dignitaries, dapper in his police uniform.

"Reuters, how are you doing?" he said to me with an outstretched hand, and we exchanged brief pleasantries before being rudely interrupted.

"What do you foreign journalists think you're doing?" a man who interjected himself between Simeon and myself said, in a louder-than-necessary voice. "You white journalists from the *Miami Herald* and the *New York Post* (I would only begin contributing articles to the *Herald* two years later and never wrote for the *New York Post*), you don't respect Haiti."

The man seemed in near-staggering state, and I could smell the rum on his breath as he began to poke a finger at my chest.

Having no idea who the man was, I basically told him to fuck off.

"All you write are lies about the president. You are all liars," he said, then staggered off toward the tarmac where Aristide's plane was landing.

"What on earth was that all about?" I asked Simeon, who looked mortified. "Who was he?"

"That," Simeon said, putting his police cap back on as he walked to the tarmac, "that was the president's new spokesman, Dr. Haendel Carré." Carré, an alleged former Tonton Macoute from the northern town of Pignon who had studied medicine in Minnesota, had been named a member of Aristide's private cabinet and presidential spokesman since Yvon Neptune had become prime minister that March. Inside the press briefing room, Haitian reporters joked and laughed with one another as a scowling, hulking white Steele security officer examined the dais from which Aristide was to speak. In a measure of just how bad the president's relations with the Haitian press had gotten, Goudou Jean Numa, one of the journalists from Radio Metropole who had been there the day of Brignol Lindor's funeral and whose widowed mother always fretted about her son's involvement in journalism, refused to even stand up as Aristide entered, as did several other journalists.

"Dear citizens," Aristide began, speaking into two microphones, one blue and one red for the colors of the Haitian flag, as Yvon Neptune stood woodenly at his side. "The people of Africa expressed solidarity with our historic legacy." After recounting a meeting with Nelson Mandela, Aristide then quickly digressed to begin a lengthy sermon on Haiti's environmental problems, and how they must be addressed along with the country's political problems. Finally arriving at, "In 2004, we will celebrate two hundred years as a free people. 2004 is not a year for Lavalas or a year for Convergence; it's a year for everyone, and should be celebrated."

Then came the question-and-answer session. I asked Aristide about the killings that had occurred of gang members loyal to his government in Cité Soleil and, fixing me with a placid gaze, he offered that, "The people of Cité Soleil are the sons and daughters of the country. Their rights are violated when they cannot eat; their rights are violated when they cannot go to school. We must work with all sectors, the opposition and the elite, to improve their lives. We are committed to working with them and we will not rest until we do that.

"We have to protect the rights of every citizen," Aristide added, "but we must also protect those who are visiting Haiti and who live in Haiti."

Then Goudou from Radio Metropole stood up, and, pointing out a recent report by the Berlin-based anticorruption organization called Transparency International listing Haiti as one of the most corrupt countries in the world, said that Aristide's stated anticorruption efforts had thus far been an obvious miserable failure, and so what was his plan now to stem the country's decline?

Aristide's face looked almost expressionless, but he leaned slightly forward, rigidly toward the podium, as he stared at Goudou.

"The state of press freedom in Haiti is obviously very healthy if you would even pose a question like that." The crowd laughed, but Aristide wasn't smiling. "I find it very interesting at this moment when Haitians are working together, that certain sectors speak ill of Haiti and its people, and drag its name through the mud. This is unacceptable."

After some more pleasantries, the crowd eventually dispersed, with Aristide returning to Tabarre, and the journalists heading toward their cars and news vans in the parking lot. But Aristide's declaration hung in the air as it had gone out over the airwaves, pregnant with meaning.

As we drove away, David Chery, the head of the Coeurs Unis cooperative investment group that had been so closely linked to Aristide's Fanmi Lavalas party, was being arrested with his mother, brother, and maid at the Dominican border town of Dajabon, and flown back to the National Penitentiary in Port-au-Prince in Aristide's helicopter. He had been banned from leaving the country prior to answering a summons to appear before Haiti's state prosecutor.

IN THE CAPITAL'S Martissant slum on September 17, Felix Bien-Amié, the Lavalas-affiliated gang leader who had scored a patronage job as the director of Port-au-Prince's main cemetery and who was responsible for the June 2001 massacre in Fort Mecredi, was arrested by PNH officers led by Commissioner Ralph Renand Dominique near his power-base in the district after a traffic dispute. Though PNH spokesman Jean-Dady Simeon said, rather ominously, "He is not in police custody" when asked about Bien-Aim, the next day, the gang leader's abandoned car was found burned out at Titanyen, once one of the favored dump grounds for the victims of political murders by Haiti's previous dictatorships. Immediately thereafter, Martissant erupted into anti-police riots, with hundreds of protestors burning tires along the Carrefour Road, surrounding the local police commissariat, and hurling rocks and bottles at police who tried to stop them. Only repeated volleys of tear gas, followed with live ammunition, succeeded in driving the protestors back into the warren of waterside shacks that they inhabited; but, with echoes of Amiot Metayer's words in August still ringing in their ears, the uprising was nonetheless duly noted as one of the first times that Aristide's lumped urban base in the capital had moved violently against his police department. Critics wondered if Bien-Aimé's disappearance was a foreshadowing of how Aristide intended to implement OAS Resolution 822.

IN LATE SEPTEMBER, while traveling in a taxi across the Champs de Mars, I was party to a conversation between two men in the front seat of the cab and the woman sitting in the back with me, all of them working-class Haitians who were used to being crammed into the capital collective *camionettes*.

"What about the next election?" said the driver. "Who do you think will run?"

"Yvon Neptune, probably. Maybe René Préval?" said the man in the front seat.

"René Préval was a good president; he was a good man," said the woman, as they all clucked in agreement.

"I would vote for René Préval," said the driver.

"What about Yvon Neptune and Dany Toussaint?" said the driver.

"That's no choice at all," snorted the other man.

The government's intolerance of dissent was highlighted dramatically on the evening of September 18, when a concert by Boukman Eksperyans, Haiti's most popular band, on the Champs de Mars within easy earshot of the National Palace was broken up by armed riot police who stormed the stage, saying that orders had come from "high up." The band had formed in 1978 and helped popularize its "vodou rock" style as a vehicle for social commentary, continuing the Haitian tradition of music as both political statement and rallying cry. Their lead singer, songwriter and visual focal point was Theodore "Lolo" Beaubrun, Jr., the tall, dreadlocked son of a famous Haitian comedian, who had in his earlier life gained renown as the comic character "Barnaby" on Haitian television—a name by which many Haitians still referred to him. Boukman's 1990 entry for Haiti's carnival, *"Ke m pa sote"* ("My Heart Doesn't Leap"), obliquely targeted political malefactors and was considered pivotal in the struggle to oust the Avril dictatorship. Vocal advocates who were exiled for their support of returning Aristide to power after the 1991 military coup, Beaubrun and the group had been very circumspect about Aristide since his decision to accept the IMF structural adjustment plan in 1994, and Beaubrun's disgust had been further reinforced when he had begged Aristide to institute a real disarmament plan after the first flaring of Cité Soleil gang wars in 1995. Aristide had rebuffed him coldly, and nine members of a legitimate OP that Beaubrun had worked with there were killed in the following months.

This night, as the band commenced the concert by launching into their song "We Don't Want No War"—interpreted as a critique of political violence under Aristide and containing the line "Mr. President, it's you I'm talking to"—a feared PNH officer named Jackson Bernard but known to all as *Gwo Jack* (Big

Jack) climbed up on the stage and began haranguing the band.

"You have to leave the stage," Jack said.

"I'm not leaving the stage," Beaubrun responded. "Who gave you that order?"

"The highest people in the country."

"Higher? What do you mean? Someone who is taller than you? I'm going to finish the concert."

"You're finished now." And with that, Gwo Jack roughly yanked the amplifier cable out of the band's keyboard and armed CIMO stormed onto the stage. A livid Beaubrun began screaming into the still-live microphone, "What kind of *zenglendo* behavior is this? This is not justice what you are doing here! We need a revolution! No one can play politics like this!", as CIMO shot into the air to disperse the angry crowd.

"This was one of Aristide's first real tries at dictatorship," Beaubrun told me later. "Afterwards, people who were inside the National Palace said that Aristide was frightened, that he thought I was talking directly to him."

Beaubrun went on the radio and television the day after the concert denouncing the government for its actions, but, later that afternoon, he was surprised when Fourel Celestin, Haiti's Senate president and a friend of Beaubrun's from his youth, called and said that he had to see him, immediately. Beaubrun arrived at the Tiffany Restaurant, downtown near Haiti's parliament and as he sat there, chatting awkwardly with the politician, Celestin passed Beaubrun his cell phone, saying, "Someone one wants to talk to you." Beaubrun immediately recognized Aristide's high-pitched voice on the other end.

"Oh Lolo! This is impossible!" the president said. "We cannot accept that! My daughter Christine loves Barnaby! Did you see the badge of the guy who did it?"

"Wow, I said," Beaubrun recounted to me later, laughing at the absurdity of the incident. "What a *bluffeur*."

MARC BAZIN, the former World Bank official and former prime minister that Aristide had named minister without portfolio to end Haiti's two-year-old electoral crisis, had enough and announced his resignation on September 20, citing frustrations with government policy.

"When I took this job, I gave myself a deadline of seven months to show substantive progress in the negotiations, and, while we have had some small successes, the difficulties between the government and the opposition remain," Bazin told me when I reached him by phone.

He then lashed out at the Aristide administration's record on human rights, corruption, economic policy and privatization.

"We've seen a 16 percent rise in inflation, the gourde has lost 32 percent of value in a year and the government's economic policy, if you can call it that, has been absurd," he said. "We need to privatize state industries to make them competitive and change the system we have now, which is one of no transparency and no accountability. Corruption is a system and the entire system needs to be reformed."

Bazin had succeeded in getting Aristide and opposition leaders to sit down together only once, at the papal nuncio's Port-au-Prince residence in June.

BAZIN'S EXIT FROM the public eye was done more gracefully than that of Rosemond Jean. On September 23, a SWAT team raided Jean's home in a suburb of the capital. Claiming they had found a grenade in the house, the police handcuffed Jean, threw a plastic sack over his head and dragged him away, charging him with possession of illegal weapons. First taken to the Petionville police station, Jean was then brought to the National Palace, where he was punched and kicked by CIMO and Palace security officers. That the leader of the victims of the co-operative scandal would be treated in such a manner by a government that had claimed solidarity with that group was met with outrage and indignation by Haiti's poor, and the airwaves were alive with editorials and broadcasts denouncing the move.

In response, several days later, the capital's popular Radio Kiskeya, run by veteran journalists Marvel Dandin and Lilianne Pierre-Paul, was forced off the air on September 26 amid a flurry of threats and warnings. When I phoned Dandin that night, he told me that Kiskeya had been obliged to suspend broadcasting after receiving "very serious and grave" intimations that something violent was about to happen.

"We received information from a reliable source that the station was to be burned this evening, so we were obliged to cease operations and evacuate our employees," Dandin said.

Other reporters at the station said that the threats were communicated to Kiskeya employees by a person present at the meeting where the attack was being planned, apparently as a warning to independent journalists. They said the station was being targeted as a result of its coverage of the disappearance of gang leader Felix Bien-Aimé and the arrest of Rosemond Jean. Caraibes FM also went off the air in response to similar threats the same day.

At a gathering of Lavalas officials and supporters held at the former ranch of Jean-Claude Duvalier in the hills above Port-au-Prince on September 27, the day after the threats to Radio Kiskeya, Aristide seemed to signal that, coupled with the breaking up of the Boukman Eksperyans concert earlier in the month, the government's attacks on free expression would come in a more full-frontal nature than previously witnessed.

"When you use lies and scenarios to try to make people believe that the press is muzzled, and when certain sectors utter threats against the press to throw people into disarray, it is again an extension of the coup d'etat," Aristide said.

Following the speech, on September 29, Minister of Justice Jean-Baptiste

Brown became the second member of Aristide's government to step down in a month, citing obstacles to reforms he wanted to institute in the police and judiciary.

"I arrived in this position with a plan of action and I was not given the means to implement this plan," Brown told Radio Metropole, but declining to elaborate further. "I found myself unable to substantively address serious issues such as the professionalization of the Haitian police and fighting against impunity." On September 30 the anniversary of the 1991 coup against him, Aristide named Calixte Delatour, who had once served as legal advisor to Raoul Cedras and was rumored for many years to have taken part in the killing of Senator Max Hudicourt in political upheaval during the government of Dumarsais Estimé, as Haiti's new Minister of Justice.

As September drew to a close, the investigating magistrate in charge of the investigation into the murder of Brignol Lindor released a farcical investigative report that refused to name any of those who had called application of "zero tolerance" against Lindor proceeding his murder or praised the act after the fact.

SPEAKING TO Lilianne Pierre-Paul on Radio Kiskeya, now back on the air, on October 11, U.S. Ambassador Brian Dean Curran said bluntly, "There are police officers involved in drug trafficking. . . . We know these people, and the [Aristide] government knows their names. . . . We must restructure the police." Going on to say that U.S. officials estimated that 15 percent of all the cocaine feeding the ravenous drug appetite in the United States in the previous year had passed through Haiti. Curran noted that the amount of cocaine passing through Haiti under the Aristide government was "growing, not diminishing."

On October 12, Dread Wilmé's gunmen killed twelve people in Cité Soleil areas allied with Labanye in revenge for being driven out the previous month, but Labanye's men then again routed Wilmé in a series of running gun battles throughout the slum. In response to domestic and international pressure to do something about the exponentially increasing number of gunmen under National Palace command, around midday on October 17, Hermione Leonard, following a meeting with Aristide, called Labanye and his deputies to inform him that the PNH would be staging a search for weapons in Cité Soleil the next day. Driving to the slum with a contingent of officers, Leonard collected weapons from the gang members and stashed them at various points around the city. Returning to Cité Soleil that evening, she provided four gang leaders, including Labanye, with police uniforms and the ski masks of the type the CIMO would use to disguise their identities on their more brutal missions.

The next day, as the police staged their search for weapons throughout the district, Labanye, his deputy Kolobri and four others were right alongside them in police uniforms, their identities thus disguised by the masks and without even all the police involved knowing the notorious gunmen were standing right next to them. Leonard returned their sequestered weapons the following day.

Ironically, over the same time period, frequent roadblocks by machine-gun-carrying plainclothes PNH officers supported by uniformed policeman began popping up around the capital at regular intervals, though only on heavily-traveled roads leading to middle-class areas such as Pan Americaine, Canape Vert and upper Delmas. Traffic was frequently backed up for miles, leaving thousands of motorists sweating under the sun, their autos stalling as they ran out of gas.

"They know who has weapons, and it's not us," said one disgruntled taxi driver, whose car I was sitting in as we crawled slowly through the roadblocks toward downtown. "This is pure cinema."

BY MID-OCTOBER, rumors that Aristide's cash-strapped government was about to convert U.S. dollar-denominated accounts into local currency at an unfavorable rate led worried investors to withdraw $20 million in three days. Though denied by both Aristide and Minister of Finance Gustave Faubert, the rumor was unusually detailed, stating that all accounts held in U.S. dollar denominations in Haitian banks would be bought up by the government and then returned to depositors at a rate of 15 gourdes to the dollar, far lower than the real exchange rate, which had hovered around 30 gourdes to the dollar for months. Coming after the collapse of the co-ops, the bank run only served to further undermine public confidence in the government's economic policies.

The world beyond Port-au-Prince also continued to prove problematic for the government. Even if Amiot Metayer had been seduced back into Aristide's camp, Jean Tatoune most emphatically had not. On October 22, Tatoune led several hundred supporters on an anti-Aristide march throughout his Jubilé slum stronghold, telling Radio Metropole that he would "keep the pressure on (and) paralyze Gonaives until Aristide goes and we have new elections."

IN A WRENCHING SCENE broadcast live across television screens around the United States on October 29, more than two hundred illegal Haitian migrants—including many children—on an overloaded steamer that had been hemmed in by the U.S. Coast Guard, jumped overboard and rushed onto a major Miami causeway, scattering, attempting to elude police and Coast Guard personnel and begging motorists to give them rides away from the scene. The images brought attention to the plight of a people desperate to escape the unending violence created by Haiti's politics and poverty, and threw into stark relief the United State's blatantly discriminatory immigration policy vis-à-vis Haitian and Cuban refugees. Any Cuban who touched land in the United States was automatically entitled to apply for asylum, while Haitians had no such privilege and often ended up at the stark prison of the Krome Detention Center before being unceremoniously dumped back in Haiti at the Coast Guard station at Bizoton. The boat, it turned out, had originated in Choucou Beach, in the north of Haiti.

When I spoke to Micha Gaillard that day, he seemed genuinely upset by the scenes he had witnessed.

"The government wants to manipulate this terrible situation of our compatriots for political gain," he said. "It is a problem of governance of this country, regardless of the status of international aid. Our country needs to find a way to keep its children at home."

The next day, Mario Dupuy blamed the freeze on foreign aid to Haiti for the scenes in Miami.

"The economic sanctions are responsible for this situation because the population is desperate," he told Radio Metropole. "Perhaps this event will pressure the international community to lift them."

"AT ALL-HALLOWS," writes the anthropologist Alfred Metraux in his pioneering 1959 study *Voodoo in Haiti*, "the Guede spirits of the dead overrun the countryside and towns, clad in black and mauve, and people possessed by them may be met not only in the sanctuaries but also in the markets, public places and on the roads."

And so it was in the fall of 2002. A friend of mine, an attractive young woman from New York who was active in the human rights community, had decided to come down to visit for, of all things, Gede, Haiti's Day of the Dead, the time when the family of spirits headed by Baron Samedi, guardien of the cemetery (a.k.a Baron Cimetiere, Baron La Croix or simply Baron) hold sway. Historically, the spirits are believed to have flowed from a group of slaves conquered and shipped to Saint Domingue from Benin, but, in Haiti, black is their color and the tomb is their favored abode, so it was to the massive main cemetery in downtown Port-au-Prince we went to find them. The sign above the cemetery entrance, beneath which a river of raw sewage was running with its attendant olfactory assault, said everything one needed to know.

"*Souviens—Toi Que Tu Es Poussiere*," it read. "Remember you are dust."

We stepped inside—my friend, Herby Metellus the necklace maker, the painter Etzer Pierre and I—past flower vendors, and saw the blue, green and black tombs, many above ground stretching out nearly as far as the eye could see, creating a city of the dead that hobbled toward the mountains, easily visible today in the blinding sun beyond the cemetery walls. Several tombs in the cemetery had been vandalized, broken open and emptied of their contents by grave robbers. The empty tombs are one of the places where the city's myriad of homeless people often find themselves sleeping at night.

Soon after entering, at the intersection of two rows of graves, we came upon a man in a black hat and sunglasses, leading a crowd in singing, all of them drunk on Haiti's raw rum, *tafia*, in perfect encapsulation of Gede, who are known for their obscene banter.

"Everything is so expensive, we have only pussy!" they chanted.

"Today is a nasty day," said Herby, laughing and sucking on a cigarette.

Beyond them, another crowd had surrounded a man playing an acoustic guitar who repeated the same refrain over and over again: "We are singing for the dead, we are singing for the dead, we are singing for the dead."

My friend, tall and blonde, attracted considerable attention among the revelers.

"How do you want it, *blan*, with a condom or without a condom?" screamed one young man, shoeless but with a black winter ski cap on, to her or me I couldn't be entirely sure.

Another tomb that had been robbed sat in front of us, a freezer-sized hole in the ground where the body had been removed and large black painted letters over it reading *"a demolir."*

A drunken man swathed in purple and seeming to be in a trance approached my friend, and with a blank stare he took her hand and whispered *lazan*, a slurring of the Kreyol word *lajan* (money).

A crowd of little boys circled around my friend and then squealed in delight when she took their picture. We exited the cemetery out a side entrance that looked more like a hole broken in the wall—a wall on which there was painted, some yards away from us, a faded mural of Karl Marx.

Later that day, we drove from the downtown inferno to the cool mountains of Kenscoff, and found the crossroads of the town filled with smiling people celebrating the holiday, dancing to compas music and drinking *tafia*. Bourgeois families were riding donkeys led by peasants holding the bridles. As we walked down a quiet country lane away from the din, a trumpet and trombone player practiced a mournful version of "Oh Come, All Ye Faithful" from somewhere nearby. We set off for the beach house in Jacmel that afternoon, driving the back way into Carrefour down what is colloquially called "Fifth Avenue," avoiding huge puddles in the middle of the road, which the smaller tap-taps half-disappeared into, and piles of garbage putrefying amidst clouds of flies and packs of dogs in the afternoon sun. We passed the El Caudio nightclub, and a row of coffin makers working outside a funeral parlor with a makeshift chapel for memorial services. Past the Crystal Ciné, advertising a Jet Li martial arts film and something called "Black Cheerleader." The Meridien nightclub, the Lisha Beach Hotel, the Taxi Motel, La Mariniere Hotel. . . . Finally, after an hour in the city's stop-start traffic, we began to pull beyond the southern suburbs and onto winding Route Nationale 2, speeding along past the flat grassy field Haitians call terrain dotted with towering royal palms. Driving past the Leogane police station, where Panel Renelus had been killed by a mob, we watched a shoeless young boy in an oversized muscle shirt that covered him like a tent struggle by, carrying two buckets of water down the road. Over the high rolling mountains that cleave central Haiti off from the south coast we drove, in a drizzling rain.

Toward midnight, we found ourselves parking in the deserted middle of rolling fields inland from the southern coast. We got out of our car at the end of the road and stood at the beginning of a moonless, starless path. We could hear the sounds of the drumming in the distance, though, and began to feel our way along further into the countryside. I led the way, my friend following behind me, and I clasped her hand tightly as we walked along.

"Ghede[sic.] is the dark figure which attends the meeting of the quick and the dead," Maya Deren had written. "Repository of all the knowledges of the dead . . . wise beyond all others."

So it was when we found the temple. First greeted by two immense wooden crosses, painted red and hammered into the ground at the end of the path through the fields, we saw beyond them what appeared to be a red-painted shed in a clearing from where the drumming throbbed into the night. As we approached, a crowd of well-over a hundred people regarded us curiously, though without malice, and we realized that in fact only the poles supporting the roof of the open-air peristyle were red, and that the shining of the bare white light bulbs hanging down from the temple ceiling made the structure appear to glow and throb with a rouge-hued light. As we entered, the *ounsis* were dancing and singing in the middle of the temple to drummers lined up along one wall. I sought out the *houngan*, a whisp of a man with a thin black mustache and liquid, distant eyes, and introduced the two of us, asking his permission to observe the ceremony.

"*Oui, oui,*" he said, running his fingers over a black and purple silk scarf draped around his neck. He wore a black top hat on his head. "*Bienvenue lakay nou.*"

As we turned back to the crowd, those sitting in chairs watching the ceremony immediately and graciously offered their seats to the newcomers, and, as we accepted, they came back with two icy Prestiges. As we watched the ceremony, the level of the lights, powered by a whirring generator, seemed to ebb and flow along with the energy of the music.

We drove back to the thatched hut in Ti Mouillage and fell asleep to the churning sea. We awoke the next morning to discover that our neighbor, a somewhat odd woman at the best of times, had been possessed by a Gede spirit overnight and now was sitting on her front porch, her face painted white with ash, a white handkerchief wrapped around her head, and tissue stuffed in her nostrils in imitation of the dead. She wore sunglasses and muttered unutterable obscenities to a highly-amused group of young children. The French photographer's boyfriend, a high-spirited man from Les Cayes, ran to grab a boom box on which played blaring *racine* music so that the possessed woman would dance.

"*Danse!*" the crowd yelled, laughing, as the old woman sashayed about, dancing obscenely. "*Balanse gede!*"

We drove into Jacmel town, and found that Prince Pierre Sonson, the maverick Lavalas senator from the region who had recently been attempting to make amends with the Aristide government, was holding a rally on the beach there. We could not see them, but I could make out his amplified words—denouncing the suspension of international aid to Haiti and denouncing the foreign presence in the country—interspersed with cheers from whatever crowd was listening to him. We parked our car and approached the Hotel Florita.

As we walked through the hotel, on this day eerily empty, all the doors and windows were open and white curtains fluttered in through the doors on the breeze from the Bay of Jacmel. The bed where I had slept, and the room where the American ambassador had stayed during Carnival, were now empty. The moss and vines in the courtyard hung with exceptional melancholy, and my friend and I kept close to one another as we walked through the rooms and looked down from the balcony onto a deserted street.

After returning to Port-au-Prince, we found out that Selden Rodman, the famous patron of Haitian arts whose home the building had been for thirteen years—and whose house in Oakland, New Jersey I had visited years before—had died the very afternoon we were walking through the Florita. Perhaps the melancholy, sapient aura, the presence that my friend and I had felt so strongly that we commented on it during the ride back to Port-au-Prince, had been the ghost of Selden Rodman, after all, come back to Haiti to be among the *lwa* on this of all days.

Later, the mulatto doctor, who had known Selden Rodman during his days in Jacmel, felt compelled to write a commemoration of him and, by extension, to commit some of his thoughts to paper about the state of Haiti.

"What is at stake is the Dignity of a people, the Future of a race, the Fate of a Nation. . . . The fate of a nation of outlaws which, thanks to men as Toussaint Louverture, as Dessalines, as Petion, but also thanks to men of the Universe as Wilberforce, l'Abbé Gregoire, Abraham Lincoln . . . [proclaims] to the face of the World the beauty of its soul and the splendour of its mission. Yes, we believe in the Renaissance of Jacmel. We believe in the renaissance of the black race. And we do believe in the renaissance of Haiti. We believe that a country that did so much for the cause of Beauty cannot and will not die."

CHAPTER NOTES

1. Groupe díAppui aux Rapatriés et Réfugiés (GARR) and Plateforme HaVtienne de Plaidoyer pour un Développement Alternatif (PAPDA), "Peasant farmers' fields are destroyed to make way for the construction of a free trade zone on the Plain of Maribahoux," March 28, 2003.
2. Banque de la Republique d'Haiti (BRH) internal report, May 2005.
3. Kay Famn/SOFA/Enfofamn, press release, July 31, 2002.

9
Among the Masters of the Dew

THE PLATEAU CENTRAL has always felt in some ways like Haiti's most unknowable region. Cut off from the rest of the country by its atrociously bad roads and without the benefit of a coastline and ports to facilitate trade and contact with the outside world, the Plateau is forced to look inward or across the border to the Dominican Republic for sustenance. A surprisingly large number of people in the region speak at least some Spanish, with many having worked as laborers either in the Dominican cane fields, or in the large northern city of Santiago on the Dominican side of the border. The area's feeling of isolation is increased when low, dark storm clouds roll over from the east and dusk's sunlight, peeking through the cracks, gives the terrain an unearthly, half-lit appearance, as if the countryside has somehow revealed itself to be a twilight world of secrets inhabited only by the winds blowing, singing through the trees.

This is the area from which Charlemagne Peralte launched his guerilla attacks against the U.S. soldiers that occupied Haiti and the beginning of the twentieth century, an episode as instructive of any to one trying to understand the Haitian national character and the ability of the country's inhabitants to carry on against what would often seem hopeless odds.

Peralte had been the commandant of the Leogane garrison south of Port-au-Prince when the Marines landed in 1915, and he had returned to Hinche after being unceremoniously relieved of his post by the new occupiers. Peralte, though, had caught the attention of the country's new American administrators, both as a supporter of Rosalvo Bobo, the exiled Cap Haitien doctor who continued to plot from across the channel in Jamaica, and also as a potential source of trouble among Haiti's ragtag former military forces. Court-marshaled on what many believed to be baseless charges in January 1918, Peralte was sentenced to five years hard labor and put to sweeping the streets of Cap Haitien, an unnecessary humiliation that showed a bad misreading of his emotional and intellectual makeup. He escaped in September of that year and lead his first attack on Hinche on October 17, a disaster during which his forces lost over thirty men. Peralte attacked again, though, this time down the road at Maissade on November 10, and succeeded in chasing off the local Haitian gendarmerie. His rebellion quickly spread, and he sent off impassioned letters to American military commanders, accusing them of having reestablished slavery with the corvee system. While he directed operations in the Plateau and the North, a loosely affiliated deputy, Benoit Batraville, also a Bobo partisan, attacked police stations throughout the Artibonite Valley. Peralte continued his hit-and-run attacks against the Marines for over a year before an attempt to attack the capital in October 1919 ended in failure. Betrayed by one of his men, he was killed by a U.S. Marine who snuck up on him disguised in blackface on November 1, 1919.

After Peralte was killed, in a precursor of the foreign policy decisions of a later U.S. government, American officials, in an effort to convince the rebels that their leader had in fact died, took a photograph of Peralte's near-nude dead body propped outside of Marine headquarters in Hinche, looking for all the world like the body of a martyr and with more than a touch Christ-like in its wretched pose. Peralte's eyes were closed in death but his face was still aristocratic and composed. The photo was circulated throughout Haiti and made Peralte an icon of Haitian resistance to foreign domination ever thereafter, as well as becoming the subject for a renowned painting by the artist Philomé Obin.

Though Peralte was dead, Benoit Batraville persisted between Gonaives and Mirebalais for another six months, stubbornly refusing to surrender though an attempt by some three hundred of his band to storm Port-au-Prince resulted in the loss of sixty of his fighters. His wife, Madame Benoit, was said to have helped his men by riding into market towns and buying supplies for them, all the while gathering information. On May 19, 1920, though, Benoit was shot down near Lascahobas. The rebellion against the invaders was over, but the region's tradition of independence from the central authority of Port-au-Prince did not stop there. Many of Haiti's leaders continued to regard the region as a hotbed of potential sedition. In the 1950s, the military ruler Paul Magloire evicted thousands of farmers from their land in order to build the Peligre dam, which never brought any electricity to those it displaced, and earned him the enmity of its inhabitants. Francois Duvalier constructed a huge military base to guard the dam against a feared Dominican attack and also to keep a boot on the neck of the locals. Jean-Claude Duvalier, the military chiefs and Aristide all feared the peasant unions that had sprung up in the region since the early 1970s, and none more so than the Mouvman Peyizan Papay, the group Chavannes Jean-Baptiste helped found when he was still a Catholic lay worker in 1973. The MPP had been targeted for repression by every government since it was created to work on irrigation, crop diversification and to agitate for the rights of the peasants to the *classe politique* in the capital. The attempted murder of Chavannes by Lavalas officials in November 2000 was only the latest in a long list of efforts to break the back of the peasant organizations, but in the fall of 2002, the MPP showed no signs of letting up.

HERBY, THE YOUNG jewelry-maker who lived downtown and raised pigeons in his *lakou* near the stadium, was accompanying me, and we climbed aboard a clattering tap-tap together, leaving Port-au-Prince for Hinche on the anniversary of the assassination of Dessalines at Pont Rouge. The spot where Haiti's fearsome independence leader had met his final betrayal was now the station near the La Saline slum for *camionettes* heading toward the Plateau Central. A fiery orange sun was rising in the sky as we pulled away from the capital, and we passed three boys sitting in the shell of a half-constructed Texaco station in an otherwise empty landscape just before we began the ascent over Mon Kabrit to the plateau.

Hinche, only fifty miles away from the capital as the crow flies, in many ways feels like it might as well be a different country altogether. One climbs the steep, treacherous face on Mon Kabrit, where a look out the tap-tap window reveals only hundreds of feet of sheer rock heading downwards toward the expanse of parched plain below. Once the mountain incline is cleared, there is a slow, inching progress over deeply rutted roads, past poor peasant shacks made out of wood and mud on either side and valleys rolling on between the deforested mountains. As we drove along, jostled to and fro by our enthusiastic driver, in the middle of the road hundreds of green butterflies fluttered in the morning light. An elderly peasant led a burro by rope as two little boys rolled a bicycle wheel down a mountainside with a stick in an echo of games played in wealthier countries at the turn of the century.

Herby and I arrived in Hinche at the beginning of Saturday night, and the town was much as I remembered it—a few decaying churches, a large prison and its raucous Saturday market still running strong with peasants buying sows, donkeys and goats. As we arrived, the tap-tap was flagged down by PNH officers who took me out of the vehicle and questioned me by the roadside, wanting to know my business in town. Not wanting to tell them I was there to visit the MPP, I simply showed them my National Palace-issued press credentials and told them I was a journalist. This seemed to satisfy them and without emotion they waved us on. On several walls had been daubed the slogan, "Down with the stolen parliament / Viv MPP!" Herby and I retired to a waterless hotel without electricity—The Maguana—and as we sat down at the restaurant's table, we heard the shrieking of chickens next door as they were slaughtered for our dinner.

We set out early the next morning on foot to Papay, the village near Hinche where the MPP is based. The sun rose warm in the sky as we walked down the road, passing ravines running with thin trickles of water and wood and thatched peasant cottages. Soon, we passed a butcher who was guarding a flank of beef that he had set on a table for purchase by passersby; its stench carried in gusts of wind down the road. He stood over it, swatting it in an attempt to keep at bay a ravenous cloud of flies that had gathered. As I passed, I stopped to greet him, and from the house behind him a toddler, bare but for a t-shirt, ran out to regard the strange visitor. As I turned to leave the child screamed in Kreyol, "*Blan*, come back and talk to me!" When I picked her up and then put her down after some slight banter under the amused eyes of her father, she ran back to the house yelling, "I shook hands with him!" where his family was laughing under the shade of their front porch.

Though the Plateau Central is a traditional stronghold of the near-subsistence farming that forms the backbone of the lives of Haiti's poor, rural majority, one only needs to take a look at its rolling hills, green and brown but nearly devoid of trees, to realize the dire environmental problems confronting the country as it tries to feed its eight million people. In the last fity years, 90 percent of Haiti's tree cover has been destroyed for charcoal and to make room for farming, with the resulting erosion destroying two-thirds of the country's arable farmland. That this happened even as the population increased fourfold only exacerbated the desperate scramble for plots on which to farm, further depleting the land. As there is nothing to hold the topsoil when the Caribbean rains fall—often torrentially after prolonged spells with no precipitation at all—it rushes in torrents down Haiti's steep mountains, carving gullies and carrying crops and seeds along with it, sweeping vital minerals into the country's rivers to be deposited, uselessly, in the sea. The rate of hunger in Haiti is now ranked as the world's third highest, surpassed by only Somalia and Afghanistan.

For the last thirty years, the MPP, later along with its 200,000 member national umbrella organization, Mouvman Peyizan Nasyonal Kongre Papay (MPNKP), has worked on a myriad of projects to stem this decay, including attempting to grow a special grass better able to withstand Haiti's brutal rainless spells and thus better feed livestock, introducing new approaches to animal husbandry and reirrigation of fallow lands in the Plateau and elsewhere, promoting the use of solar energy derived from solar panels to power water pumps and other farming equipment and reintroducing to rural communities the *kochon kreyol*, the pig that was slaughtered en masse by an ill-advised North American attempt to halt African Swine Fever in the region some twenty-five years earlier. From the first stirrings of the nationwide peasant movement when groups of farmers began meeting in the enclaves of Papay and Bassin Zim here under the aegis of a sympathetic Belgian priest in the early 1970s, to the pivotal moment in 1975, when nearly fifty peasants marched on the local army barracks to demand the release of a farmer falsely accused of stealing a pig, both the movement's practical work and its political bent have made powerful enemies among the Port-au-Prince politicians and their enforcers on the ground in the countryside. The hated Lavalas mayor of Hinche, Dongo Joseph, had by now been removed after he had beaten a judge who displeased him, but he had been replaced by James Joseph (no relation), who himself was one of the gunmen who fired on the MPP rally in November 2000. In Maissade, yet another

Lavalas official named Joseph with a reputation for brutality, Wilo Joseph, continued on as mayor.

The sun was climbing higher now as we reached the small *lakou* off the Papay road that housed Radio Vwa Peyizan, the MPP-affiliated radio station in the area. I walked in through the compound's gate, into the courtyard that also housed the home of Chavannes's brother, Bazelais, now in the United States, and found a slim peasant sitting with a shotgun across his lap dozing in a chair, guarding the radio station. Burned bicycles and motorcycles that Lavalas partisans had torched were leaning against one wall. On another wall was painted a large mural of the MPP logo, which consisted of mapou tree, a rada drum, two hoes, a machete, a conch shell and the words "Mouvman Peyizan Papay." Stopping to chat for a moment, we were greeted by Delanour Exil, an elderly man who said he was a member of the original Bassin Zim peasant collective.

"The government is still pressuring us, but they're not going to keep us from doing our work," he said as Herby and I stood sipping Coca-Colas he had brought for us. His statement was not an idle one, as, in addition to the frontal attacks utilizing violence, the Lavalas government had also attempted to institute a police whereby a member of the local CASEC (the Lavalas-dominated local governmental councils) had to be present during any meetings of peasant groups around the country, or the meetings would be considered illegal and broken up. Exil proudly took us to the back of the complex and showed us a grain-storage facility overflowing with rice. "I don't know what they have in mind but they want to destroy and destabilize everything we have. It's the same pressure we had with the Macoutes, except now it's with the chimere *Lavalas*. But we're not going to stop, the chef de section system can't return."

It wasn't much further now, and soon after leaving Exil, we were walking up a steep incline to the MPP compound. One could see peasants tilling fields in the distance, and hear the occasional gunshot from somewhere in the valley. A young man, glistening with sweat, was walking up the hill with his hoe over his shoulder.

"It's very hard work," said the man, who told me his name was Mario Hubert, as he looked over the fields in his tattered shirt and shorts, taking a break from work. "But if we work hard, the corn and manioc isn't so bad. And when the land is so green after the rains we could plant almost anything. The animals like it. I build fences, but they always run away over the hills."

Chavannes was standing on the front porch of the compound, speaking with an assistant, and smiled when he saw us. He was much as I remembered him: intelligent eyes behind gold-framed glasses, with a hoarse, emotive voice that often breaks easily into a laugh. He was fifty-five years old this year.

"Do you remember me?" I asked, not sure if the intervening years might have banished me from his mind.

"Yes, of course!" he said, laughing that gravelly laugh of his. "Welcome to the house of MPP!"

This weekend, it transpired, the MPNKP were having a meeting. Not a proper, several-thousand strong party congress, which they did at least once a year, but rather an invitation for the leaders of the peasant organizations around the country to form some kind of coherent plan for addressing the nation's spiraling troubles, from the repression and thuggery the Aristide government was meting out to their members to concerns about irrigation methods that had been newly tried in the Plateau Central and may have proven effective enough to be tried elsewhere.

"I have to finish some work, would you like to eat lunch with them?" Chavannes asked.

"Absolutely," I said.

Soon I was sitting with some of the representatives, men from here in the Plateau, the Artibonite Valley and the Grande Anse peninsula in the country's southwest who had come to congress with Chavannes and together we shared a simple peasant meal of chicken, rice and plantains inside the organization's graceless dining hall in its compound. As we ate, I asked them if the situation had gotten better or worse for the peasants since Aristide returned to power, and my question was greeted with derisive laughter.

"We're in a position right now where we haven't been in a while," said a young man who hailed from the Plateau. "This government doesn't respect human rights at all. On November 2, they shot us, they burned our motorcycles and homes, on July 28, the chimere Lavalas in Hinche burned down our office there. They tried to come here on December 17, but we were here and we made sure they knew they would have a fight on their hands if they tried anything."

Unlike the often seemingly stage-rehearsed pronouncements of government front organizations like JPP and TKL, the peasants spoke in direct and conversational sentences, with a great deal of ease and no seeming fear of saying the wrong thing. I asked them how they felt about the free-trade zone being constructed in Ouanaminthe.

"Well, they produce a lot of corn and other things in that region, and they are taking the best land in there for that free-trade zone," said a weathered, middle-aged farmer from the Artibonite. "Aristide is looking to intimidate the peasant movement there by negotiating over their heads with a foreign government. They're only doing this for money, and they are longer standing with the poor people of this country."

After lunch, I went to sit with Chavannes next to neatly tilled rows of earth in which the MPP were trying to grow seedlings in a new irrigation method. Chavannes, who can be a bit overemphatic in his belief in his own leadership abilities, had nevertheless worked tirelessly on the ground to improve the lives of the peasants of the Plateau Central for three decades, living in a simple room on the MPP compound, sporting one battered SUV as opposed to the shiny new ones most government officials supplied themselves with, and he seemed genuinely liked by the people in the surrounding country.

"You know, I wanted to understand the situation of the peasants in Papay and elsewhere," Chavannes said, as a gentle afternoon rain began falling across the countryside. "At the time Haitian peasants were borrowing money and having to pay back to landlords at a rate up to a point of 300 percent interest per year. We started organizing when we realized the problems of the peasants weren't technical ones, but rather ones of exploitation and lack of education. . . . Now we want to promote cooperative work, agricultural techniques, conservation and unity among the peasants. Water conservation and food production, production and distribution of rice. . . . We have a lot of nurseries for trees and replanting the trees in this country is one of our missions. In MPP, we also have a democratic structure; we have elections every three years, and that is good for people to learn."

MPP had been among the first organizations in Haiti to attempt to branch out and sensitize the masses beyond the male urban poor, forming a youth organization in 1979 and a women's group in 1981. I asked Chavannes, with all its stated utopian and progressive goals, why the peasantry had fallen out so badly with the Lavalas movement.

"You know, we made the first public rally for Aristide here in 1990, and we put twenty thousand peasants in the streets?" said Chavannes, looking out over the fields where the men were beginning to return home from work. "He slept that night in my house."

"The problems between the peasants and Aristide began after his return in 1994, when he wanted his three years back that he had lost while in exile, and there was a division between the people who wanted to continue with our scheduled elections and those who wanted for Aristide to continue for three years more. We supported elections . . . and we pressed him on the question of agriculture and rural development. But he began to have a lot of *gran manje* in the National Palace, and money meant for the state passed through there and disappeared. From the time Aristide returned until the time Préval took over, millions of gourdes disappeared from the national treasury that supposedly went to fund projects through the National Palace, projects that were never undertaken."

"Before Préval was inaugurated, he vowed to fight against corruption. On February 6, the day before Préval took office, as his transition chief I gave him a list of people involved in corruption who should not be allowed to leave the country and he told me thank you, but did nothing. That's when I realized nothing would change with him, either. Finally, in 1997 the chimere attacked the MPP members in Mirebalais; they caused a lot of disorder. They came with cars and guns and attacked the office. I didn't want to denounce Aristide because we had been brothers, so I told him that he had to denounce what had happened in Mirebalais, before I left for a trip to Washington that January, to work on one of our microcredit programs, but he refused to do it. That's when we had the big demonstration against him in Hinche. In 2000, when the OPL wanted to run candidates here who were not honest, we decided we could not support them, either, so we stopped throwing our weight behind any one political party."

I asked him if anything had changed in the two years since we had spoken.

"Well, after two years of this government, all of a sudden we have a lot of Lavalas millionaires," he responded, laughing loud enough so that several men who had been standing nearby talking stopped to look at what was so funny.

But he rapidly got serious.

"Stolen elections, corruption, this will do nothing to help the people here, and we refuse to accept it. We have always fought against this and will continue to do so, and with our work today, it is obvious that Aristide considers the independent peasant movements a threat to be eliminated. And that is why Aristide needs these bandits to work for him in the Plateau Central and elsewhere. If Dongo Joseph is not here, he will just send another criminal. We have a catastrophic economic, political and social situation right now and we need unity between the peasants, urban workers and professional organizations, because the political class doesn't have the capacity to change the situation here."

"The Convergence are like *manje lwa*," Chavannes said, referring to the elaborate, banquette-like offerings that peasants leave for the *vodou* spirits. "Manioc, bananas, corn, beans, everything together, that is Convergence. We need free, honest and honorable elections, that would be the first step in helping the people participate in changing this country. The military regimes and all that oppressed the Haitian people had to go. Today Lavalas is creating a mentality of fear. People are afraid, but I am not afraid."

Before I left, Chavannes gave me a book, a history of the MPP written in Kreyol.

"To help with your Kreyol!" he said.

"We need a long time, there has been so much damage done to this country, so many trees cut down, and we've just begun to reverse it."

As we spoke dusk was beginning to fall and starling, near-horizontal light was throwing odd shadows around the valleys below us. From the distance, the rumble of thunder could be heard.

"Our project is a long-term project, but we think right now if all the sectors of the nation can come together, we can begin to change this country."

ONE THING THAT remained as true about Haiti at the end of the twentieth century as it had been at the beginning was that the country remained a majority peasant society, and, by extension, neither Aristide and his volatile, impoverished urban base nor the social-democratic *classe politique* of the opposition really in any way represented this, the largest sector of the country's population. That is why the peasant left was perceived as the greatest threat to Aristide's political power in Haiti, far more so than the Democratic Convergence. Besides strengthening its institutions, the single greatest thing any president could ever do for Haiti would be to devolve more political and governmental power back into the hands of its rural citizens who know much more intimately their own strengths and needs and frailties than the politicians in the capital ever could. That is what made the work of men like Chavannes Jean-Baptiste, Jean-Marie Vincent, Pere Ti Jean Pierre-Louis and Jean Dominique so important, because their consciencization and active involvement of the peasantry is paramount if anything is ever going to change in Haiti. The peasant farmers and their families who have seen the very ground erode beneath their feet know better than anybody what is at stake, and they are very hard to buy off with pretty words, promises, money or threats. They live life much as their ancestors did, and they've seen it all before. The capital's politicians come and go. Only the soil, the spirits and the suffering remain.

"WE'RE ALL GOING TO DIE."

Thus begins Jacques Roumain's *Gouverneurs de la Rosée (Masters of the Dew)*, completed in 1943, just a year before the author's untimely death at age thirty-seven. These opening lines, spoken by a desperate peasant woman as she clutches a handful of dry dust slipping through her fingers, could sadly enough have equally described the lot and desperation of Haiti's peasants in 2002 as it did sixty years earlier.

Like his disciple Jacques Stephen Alexis after him, Roumain was born to a well-known affluent family, in this case in Port-au-Prince in 1907. Educated chiefly in Belgium and Switzerland, he returned to Haiti in 1927 and became active in agitating for an end to the U.S. occupation, by then in its twelfth year. Roumain helped found *La Revue Indigène* magazine, attempting to articulate an authentically Haitian and nationalist voice in the face of the U.S. presence in the country. More significant was Roumain's role in founding the Ligue de la Jeunesse Patriote Haitienne, which took a leading part in the student strikes. For his trouble, he was jailed by the government of President Louis Borno in December 1928, and released eight months later. Roumain's early writings largely depicted his own elite class in withering relief, but by the time of his book *La Montagne Ensorcelée* in 1931, the influence of the writings of the Haitian ethnologist Jean-Price Mars—whose pivotal book *Ainsi parla l'Oncle (Thus Spoke Uncle)* was published the year of Roumain's first arrest and had proved so influential in the growth of the Negritude movement in the French Caribbean—was becoming more pronounced. Having displayed leftist sympathies for some time, Roumain formed the Parti Communiste Haitien in 1934. Jailed again, this time by President Stenio Vincent, Roumain spent three years in prison, released in 1936, at which point he went into exile, traveled in the

United States and Europe and made the acquaintance of the black American author Langston Hughes.

When he returned to Haiti in 1941, developing a sensitivity to the heart of Haitian existence, Roumain established the Bureau d'Ethnologie, which sought to institutionalize and legitimize the study of Haiti's peasants, and help preserve Haiti's folk lineage. The organization had come about partially after Roumain had befriended the French anthropologist Alfred Metraux, and, during President Elie Lescot's anti-*vodou* pogroms, the two had traveled the Haitian countryside, documenting *vodou* traditions in research that would eventually become Metraux's acclaimed book, *Voodoo in Haiti*—the first serious, scholarly study of the religion. Lorimer Denis, one of Francois Duvalier's closest friends and a member the soon-to-be-dictator's Les Griots intellectual circle, was assistant director at the Bureau for a time.

Appointed *chargé d'affaires* to Mexico in 1943 by President Lescot, who chose a more delicate way to deal with the troublesome author than prison, Roumain used the time abroad to complete *Gouverneurs de la Rosée*. Over the same period of time, Roumain completed a book of verse, *Bois d'Alene*, which contained a line referring to "les dammés de la terre," which would be later appropriated by the Algerian author Frantz Fanon as the title for his own book of anticolonial polemics, translated into English as "The Wretched of the Earth." Like so many of Haiti's brightest lights, Roumain's candle did not flicker for long, and he died at age thirty-seven in August 1944.

Masters of the Dew tells the story of Manuel, a young peasant who returns to his impoverished village of Fonds Rouge after having cut cane in Cuba for fifteen years. Though Roumain delicately and sensitively describes the peasants' lives and work, including a beautiful depiction of the *konbit*—a traditional communal work detail in rural Haiti—the pain of exile and dislocation, both in those who go and those who remain, is suffused throughout the book. Manuel nearly despairs looking around him at the state the country is in, but speaks aloud of calling "a General Assembly of the Masters of the Dew, a great big *konbit* of farmers, and we'll clear out poverty and start a new life."

Manuel's mother bemoans that God has forsaken them, to which Manuel replies:

> There's heavenly business and there's earthly business. They're two different things, not the same. The sky's the pastureland of angels. They're fortunate—they don't have to worry about eating and drinking. Of course, they have black angels to do all the heavy work. . . . But the earth is a battle day by day without truce, to clear the land, to plant, to weed and water it until the harvest comes.

Vowing to help his family and neighbors, who are feuding in a murderous land conflict over the estate of a dead *caco* soldier that he finds pointless, Manuel falls in love with a delicate country girl, Annaise, in the process. The portrait Roumain paints of the Haitian personality—from the sentimental, slightly jealous father Bienaimé to the obscene, boastful Simidor—is finely drawn. When Manuel finally finds the water with which he hopes to help his neighbors, he kisses the spot of earth where he finds it. But tragedy is not long in coming, as it seldom is in Haiti's novels, and the book's penetrating question lingered on in Haiti in the fall of 2002:

> Life had dried up at Fonds Rouge. One only had to listen to this silence to hear death. One yielded to this torpor and felt himself already buried. The regular and repeated blows of the mallets in the mortars had become stilled since there wasn't a grain of millet to husk. How far things were from the good old days of the *konbit*, from the virile joyous chants of the men folk, from the sparkling, swinging hoes in the sun, from those happy years when we used to dance the minuet under the arbors with the carefree voices of dark young girls bursting forth like a fountain in the night. . . . Can a man die like that, as a breath of air blows out a candle, as a pruning knife cuts a weed, as fruit falls from the tree and rots?

Away from the peasants and their generations-old connection with the land, back in the slums of Port-au-Prince, the brutal reign of Aristide's gunmen continued. On November 9, Labanye's deputy, Maxon Moreau a.k.a. Kolonel, who had been irritating his boss and the National Palace with his criminal entrepreneurship, was killed by Labanye himself and his partner, Kolobri, acting in collusion with the police in Cité Soleil. It appeared that Moreau's criminal activities had become bothersome to some of the powers in the National Palace, so Moreau was summoned to a meeting in the district that became an ambush, and witnesses said Moreau was shot some dozen times. For good measure, the gang leaders and their police back-up also killed one of Moreau's brothers and then found yet another brother, a schoolteacher with no involvement in politics or crime, and forced him to push his brothers' bodies through the slum in a wheelbarrow and then dig a grave for them. When he finished, he was executed at point-blank range and dumped into the pit along with them. "Kolonel" was all of twenty-four, and, together, the killings of the brothers left eight small children fatherless.

Cité Soleil had recently been officially designated as a city, and Aristide had marked the occasion by appointing Fritz Joseph, one of the most notorious FRAPH attachés there from the Cédras era, as its mayor, entrusting him with organizing and controlling the armed youth gangs that had become the president's chief means of clinging to power as he watched his popular base erode amidst the university upheaval and the co-operative scandal. Joseph had been an active FRAPH participant in the 1993 fire that had razed hundreds of homes and killed at least a dozen people.

Some time earlier, as I was entering the Ministry of Health near the National Palace, I saw a bunch of young guys I knew from the neighborhood hanging around outside the Ministry of Interior, which was right next door. They approached me to tell me that James was inside and wanted to speak with me. As I was running late for an interview, I told them I would call him and went toward the Ministry, but not before I saw a screaming woman in a wheelchair wheeled down the Interior's steps, a wet towel over her head. When I went down to visit James and his friends there later that month, I found them in a depressed mood.

"Aristide promises us one thing and gives us another," James said as we sat eating lunch with two of his boys at a humble restaurant off one of the slum's main roads, a .38 resting on the table next to the plates of spaghetti. "He gave me a job and jobs to the other bosses in Cité Soleil at the government, CAMEP, TELECO, but after a few days, they let us go."

"We don't understand where Aristide is taking this country," said one of the boys with us, young and usually retiring. They usually held back in deference to James, who after all was the boss and the one used to dealing with foreigners. "He said he's going to put *alfabetizasyon* in Cité Soleil, but he doesn't do it."

"Don't try to kill the youth of Cité Soleil, give them jobs," said the other.

We finished eating and James stuffed the .38 back inside the waistband of his baggy jeans.

"When Aristide would have problems, he would send Hermione to bring us to Petit Goave, to Leogane," said James, as the restaurant's owner eyed us uneasily. "He should do something for the people that have guns in their hands, make security work for them."

ON NOVEMBER 4, the Aristide government had missed an OAS-mandated deadline to create a new CEP, telling reporters as late as that evening that he expected a council to be in place the next day. It proved to be wishful thinking on his part, with opposition and civic groups still saying they would not name representatives to the body unless Aristide would establish a climate of security that would permit valid elections.

"The problem of insecurity is a reality and one needs only to recall the bloody events of December 17 to realize that," said Pastor Edouard Paultre on Radio Metropole. Paultre was spokesman for the Protestant Federation of Haiti, one of the group's expected to name representatives to the council.

ON WEDNESDAY AFTERNOON, November 13, I watched as hundreds of students from the State University protested around Haiti's parliament and then charged through the center of Port-au-Prince chanting, "*Dictateur, no! Autonomie, wi!*" Beating on *vodou* drums and chanting slogans against Charles Tardieu and Aristide, the group massed in front of the parliament.

Bob Moliere, the Lavalas chimere, happened to be passing by and stopped to watch the scene, folding his arms and staring before he entered the parliament.

"They have all their rights," he said, his broad arms folded over his *Pwodiksyon Nasyonal* t-shirt. "This is pure politics."

Under a steaming sun, I walked along with them as they marched down Rue des Miracles to the curious looks of *ti machann*s sweating under the hot afternoon sun and a scattering of applause from people walking through what had been Port-au-Prince's lively business district in years past.

"Duvalier had the Macoutes/Aristide has the chimere," they sang.

"We are here to protest against the growing threat of dictatorship in our country as represented by the actions of the Aristide government at the university," said one student to me, his white shirt daubed with antigovernment slogans.

Two days later, Friday, November 15, I heard that the students were holding another march, this time up to the university's rectory, far from the heat and swirl of downtown and near my own apartment, in the leafy climbs of Turgeau. Imagining that it would be little more than a repeat of the week's previous event, I was skeptical when Pierre Richard, a cameraman working with Reuters, called me to tell me that I better hit the streets.

"It's big, man," he said. "Really big."

I walked from my house to Avenue Jean Paul II, the long road that snakes down to the Champs de Mars from the middle-class districts. I was stunned to look downhill and see thousands of students and others, extending as far as the eye could see, a sea of black faces with only the faintest sprinkling of lighter shades here and there, surging past the Sacre Coeur Church in the direction of the rectory.

Some were wearing Che Guevara t-shirts in an echo of the previous summer's protest that had been broken up by the chimere, and one was wearing a home-made model with the words "*Hasta la victoria siempre!*" (Guevara's slogan) scrawled on it. The students charged in a jogging rush through the leafy streets of Turgeau and had me jogging to keep up with them, eyeing the curves in the road as I did so for anywhere a surprise attack from Aristide loyalists might come from.

Spying Hervé Saintilus, one of the group's leaders, as we caught sight of the rectory, I asked him why so many young people were on the streets.

"The university is for the students and the faculty, not the government's political games," Saintilus, an excitable, slight, bearded Haitian man said. Then we watched, riveted, as young students climbed the walls of the rectory, leaping over barbed wire and shards of broken bottles put there to discourage thieves and threw open the locked front gates of the vacant, undistinguished two-story building. Others then rushed inside, shouting "Down with Lavalas criminals!" and began plastering pictures of Guevara and Haitian flags over its walls.

"The government enacted the situation which brought about the action you see today," said a young agronomy student, Jean David, as he stepped into the street to talk with me. Standing next to me, a mulatto university professor was cheered by the black students as he arrived to observe the scene. A group of CIMO had also arrived, looking surly and spent, and leaned on their rifles in their gray uniforms under a shade tree. They watched, but did not intervene.

"Nou bouke!" the crowd thundered. ("We're fed up!") But their appetite was not yet sated.

After venting their frustration on the rectory, now awash in Haitian flags and covered in anti-Aristide graffiti, the students poured out onto Avenue John Brown, marching down toward the Palace. Paralyzing traffic as they did so, they were now joined by high-school students getting out of school. Chanting *"Lavalas/Zenglendo/Marassa"* and waving Haitian flags, some of the university protestors ringed themselves with a huge expanse of white rope, thus to keep them from breaking ranks in the event of an attack by the chimere.

"Autonomie oui! Dictateur non!" they sang, some wrapping Haitian and American flag bandannas around their heads. A handful of pro-Aristide protestors attempted to yell, "Aristide for five years" from the street corners, but the change in the crowd was palpable. Children cheered from the windows of the College René Descartes as the marchers passed, and as the crowd stormed past the Digital Graphic Services company, little children in ragged school-clothes standing on the roof held up two little puppies that they made dance in time to the music. Tap-tap drivers were blowing their horns and pumping their fists in support and an SUV with "Officiel" plates and tinted windows was surrounded and rocked back and forth by the crowd, as they yelled "You stole the rice, now you want to steal the university!" and "Aristide stole the money from the co-operatives." As the crowd surrounded the vehicle and came to a momentary halt, an enterprising ice-cream vendor pushed his cart out into the marchers' midst, happy at the prospect of so much business. Wringing wet with sweat, I stopped to catch my breath before the group continued on.

"Aristide is destroying practically every institution in Haiti, but the constitution says the university should be independent," said one young man sweating in a t-shirt. "We want the international community to know what's going on here." One protestor, wearing a Zanmi Lasante t-shirt, advertising doctor and Aristide-supporter Paul Farmer's health clinic, gave me a thumbs up as he walked by.

Then it was off again, down the hill, toward the Palace. *Ti machanns* on the roadside were dancing to the music by their big steaming pots, with some running into the mass of bodies to join in, and a group of giggling schoolgirls danced in time down the hill through the crowd.

Then, across the great expanse of the Champs de Mars, they made one last, adrenaline-fueled dash to the very seat of power. With motorists and vendors looking up in astonishment, the students brought their anger to the front door of Aristide's National Palace, climbing onto the gleaming white front gates and screaming, "Aristide, you're a murderer!" loud enough so that anyone inside would surely hear them. It was a small step perhaps, but after a summer of being victimized, it was a victory, and that was all the students needed to keep on going. Eventually the crowd dispersed, but a few die-hards still were hanging on the Palace gates when I left.

"Aristide, get out!" they called. "Aristide, your time is finished!"

IN THE NORTHERN CITY of Cap Haitien over the weekend of November 16-17, two local anti-Aristide forces, the Initiative Citoyenne (Citizens' Initiative) headed by Frandley Denis Julien and Robert Lalanne, director of Cap's Radio Maxima, announced they would sponsor a "Unity Weekend" of protest and dialogue, the climax of which would be an opposition march through the city to the independence monument of the Battle of Vertières commemorating Dessalines's victory over the French there two hundred years earlier. Private radio stations promoted the event heavily throughout the week before, and opposition politicians from the capital and Cap Haitien said they had invited former army officers, peasants and student groups who had met to plan strategy against the Aristide government. One of the opposition's newest voices was a former FADH colonel (and author of a slim volume of erotic poetry) named Himmler Rebu, who had been part of the bloody 1989 coup attempt against Prosper Avril and who had advocated for years on behalf of Haiti's disbanded military. Pouring further fuel on the fire, a curious piece in the November 16 edition of the Dominican newspaper *Listin Diario* reported that the United States would be donating twenty thousand M16 assault rifles to the Dominican army in an effort to help the country reinforce its border with Haiti, citing a recent visit to the country by Southern Command (SOUTHCOM) U.S. Army Major General Alfred Valenzuela to the Dominican border.

I awoke with the dawn on November 16 and swung down near the stadium to pick up Herby. We drove and drove and drove, past the beach road, through the devastated area between Saint Marc and Gonaives, into the fertile Artibonite, through Gonaives and then we were climbing. The hills after Gonaives are spectacular, high and mist-shrouded vistas that, despite their brevity, equaled those on the ride to Jacmel. Arriving in Au Cap in the late afternoon, we checked into the Roi Christophe hotel, an elegant, Spanish-style mansion dating from 1724, and began to stroll leisurely through Au Cap's colonial streets, the smell of salt air thick on the breeze. As darkness fell, the streetside bars in the Carrenage section facing the bay were filled with Haitian journalists, drinking, carousing and sniffing a big story, utterly different in mood than when I had visited Au Cap the previous July for Plaine du Nord and found the district deserted, the only sign of life being three boys playing marbles against the sea wall. Metropole reporter Goudou Jean Numa and AFP photographer Thony Belizaire sat drinking at a bar as I passed, and, at the top of a long driveway where the Hotel Mont Joli sat on a bluff overlooking the entire city, Micha Gaillard sat relaxing in a t-shirt and jeans, drinking a Prestige and discussing politics with KONAKOM activists and students.

On the morning of November 17, Herby and I walked from our hotel through Au Cap to the Église Sacre Coeur, where the rally was supposed to begin. A gaudy, faux-art deco pyramid abutting the city's cemetery, the church stood with its colors awash in the bright Sunday sun. Some people had begun gathering in the parking lot already, but most of the Capois were watching in clutches from in front of the Unibank building across the street and from the broad veranda of the Securi-Cap Agence de Securité Privé. I walked over to speak to a group of peasants that had gathered, and one old man grabbed my tape recorder and told me he was from the hamlet of Saint Raphael.

"We wish that Aristide will leave after the manifestation because he has given us nothing, no work, no food, only hunger," he said, pulling up his tattered shirt to reveal his emaciated rib cage.

"I was with Aristide for many years, so if I'm here, there is a problem," said another. "They say the Americans pay us to come here, but that's a lie. I didn't even have two gourdes to come here from Saint Raphael, so I had to borrow some money from my friend."

"We need to get together and change this situation so the descendants of Dessalines, the descendants of Toussaint Louverture can live in freedom, real freedom," said a young man who had been listening to our conversation, his forehead swathed in an American flag bandanna.

Shortly after 9 a.m., truckloads of heavily-armed CIMO rolled by in the direction of the city gates. A truckload also got out and began patrolling the courtyard of the church. The tension was thick, and no one could tell what would happen.

"Hey, *blan*," said an older man, tapping me on the shoulder. "You see that? We can't live anymore in this country; he has to go. There will be no elections with Aristide because he is a thief and he'll steal them. He was poor and now he's rich."

Suddenly from several blocks toward the town, a great roar went up and we turned to see a solid wall of demonstrators heading toward us. Evidently having expected trouble, the Initiative Citoyenne had begun the march from near the Mont Joli instead, and now they were heading straight for the city gates. I saw Micha Gaillard and Jean-Claude Bajeux among those in the front row, carrying a banner that read, *"Vertières: Rendevous avec l'histoire."*

"Aba, Aba, Aba Aristide / Aba, Aba, Aba Lavalas," the marchers—whose ranks included a lot of young people, probably students, and peasants this time—

sang monotonously as they walked, interspersed with lustier shouts of, "Aristide, eat shit!" and *"Git mama w, Aristide!"* Vans full of heavily-armed CIMO! were rolling down the street, observing the progress. Before long, I spied Himmler Rebu, a tall and hale middle-aged Haitian black man with a distinct military bearing wearing a black t-shirt with the words "Haiti" on it and a straw farmer's hat, along with Evans Paul, dressed in a dapper dark suit for the occasion, and René Théodore.

"I don't want those chimere to see me and think I'm one of those Convergence folks, man," said Herby, tying a bandanna around his face as he spied television cameras and news photographers.

As we began to walk toward the Cap Haitien's city gates toward the Vertières memorial, which consisted of statues of Dessalines's soldiers built on a small rise, people were smiling and chanting along, pumping their fists from the rooftops. Cries of *"Unité!"* and *"Nou gen gran gou!"* were interspersed with the demand *"Jugez Aristide!"*

"Aristide better have his bags packed to go," said a middle-aged man, speaking in English, when he saw that I was a journalist.

As we passed some of the areas at the city gates, people rushed out of the bidonvilles and hopped over the sewage-strewn canals to join the march, and street children joined in, singing happily.

"Do you hear what they're saying?" Herby asked me of a crowd of respectably-dressed poor people who had been shouting slogans at the CIMO.

"No." I had not been listening. "What?"

"They are saying that unless Aristide brings the money from the cooperatives the next time he comes to Au Cap, all they're going to have are some cakes for him!"

"Cakes?"

"Of shit!"

Herby was laughing uproariously under his bandanna.

When we finally reached the monument, thousands of people converged on it, climbing onto the rise and spilling down both sides of the street. A sizeable number wore green and white OPL headbands, but many more appeared in ragged street clothes. Looking around, I asked a scowling CIMO how many people he thought were there. He said eight thousand, give or take, but in retrospect I think it was likely closer to twice that. The demonstrations leaders—most notably Himmler Rebu, Evans Paul and René Théodore—raised the Haitian flag at the memorial and led the crowd in singing Haiti's national anthem "La Dessalinienne" ("For our nation / For our Ancestors / Let us march together / With no traitors in our ranks / The soil is our only master") to thunderous cheers and applause.

"Man, I think it is over for Aristide," said one man to his companion as they stood next to me and regarded the scene.

"Thank you to the population of the north who braved the menace of violence to come together today," said Rebu through a bullhorn, removing the straw hat he had worn throughout the march. "They are going to hear our message loud and clear! We thank the Haitian National Police for providing security for the people. The struggle begins today, and we need every facet of the population. It requires intelligence, determination, and a clear head."

Then it was Evans Paul's turn to speak. Recapturing the fire that many had noted when he was Aristide's campaign manager and running for mayor of the capital in 1990 but which I had never seen in action, Paul took the bullhorn, asking those assembled to make a pledge, and he then shouted out a message that had a rousing effect on those assembled.

"All those who want to build hope for their country, raise their hand; all those who want to get rid of Aristide, raise their hand, all those who want to respect human rights, raise their hand! We will fight against dictatorship, we will fight for liberty! Citizen alongside citizen, without division, with violence."

"*Viv Ayiti!,*" he shouted.

"*Viv Ayiti!*" the crowd roared back.

"*Aba Aristide!*"

"*Aba Aristide!*" they thundered.

The organizers then cautioned the massive crowd to disperse peacefully and they did so, though many set to work tearing down Aristide posters around the city on their way home.

Later that day, at a hastily-called press conference at the Mon Joli with the sun sinking into the bay behind them as a backdrop, the organizers seemed surprised by their own success.

"Today, November 17, 2002, is a great day for freedom in Haiti," said René Théodore. "A great day in the struggle for the Haitian people for democracy. We salute the courage of the people of the north."

At this, the assembled Haitian press corps applauded.

That night, a crowd of about a thousand Aristide supporters, young men to a one, led by official government cars, paraded through the streets of Au Cap by torchlight, shouting anti-opposition and antiforeign slogans. At one point surrounding the Roi Christophe, where we were staying, they completely blocked the entrance. I stood on the street with a Prestige in my hand and watched them.

"Aristide, the country is yours," they shouted.

"What are they supposed to be doing, marching on Frankenstein's castle?" asked one guest, a bemused American fireman who had come from Maryland to help train the city's fire department, as the braying, flame-brandishing mob continued on past the hotel.

The next morning, we were awakened by a preacher on the street, shouting out a sermon about the approaching end of the world. We began the long drive back to Port-au-Prince.

THE OPPOSITION had every intention of keeping the pressure on Aristide's government, which was said to have been extremely frightened by the size of the Au Cap demo. Three days later, on November 20, police in Petit Goave opened fire on a group of high-school and college students protesting an increase in final exam fees from 500 to 750 gourdes when they attempted to storm the town's police station in order to lower the Haitian flag, which they claimed should be flown at half-staff until Aristide resigned. Eight students, the oldest twenty-three and the youngest ten years old, were wounded. On November 21, with large-scale protests already being reported in Gonaives that day, I decided with Pierre Richard, a hardworking Haitian cameraman who at the time was my colleague at Reuters, to drive out to Petit Goave, where a huge demonstration was planned in solidarity with the eight wounded high-school students. As we drove out, we heard PNH director Jean-Nesly Lucien speaking on Radio Metropole.

"I don't understand what the protestors were thinking, attempting to storm the police station," Lucien said. "I appeal to the population for calm."

Fat chance of that, I thought, as Pierre and I pulled into a very tense Petit Goave, with CIMO patrolling the streets and a group of youths barreling forcefully down Avenue Liberté to join a group waiting in the grounds of the local high school. There were already several thousand people, mostly young students, in and around the school grounds, and about a dozen Haitian journalists watching the scene from the streets, where the CIMO regarded them with undisguised contempt. Goudou Jean Numa, Radio Metropole's fearless street correspondent, was there, as was Thony Belizaire, the venerable AFP photographer, whose hand I shook as I walked into the school.

The gate of the low-slung, whitewashed building was closed, and the solemn students guarding it let me in as masked riot police took up positions in the street outside. The courtyard was full of students, with no one over the age of about twenty-one seeming to be present inside, and they kept arriving in their blue uniforms throughout the morning. Some had dropped to their knees where they were daubing slogans on signs made out of poster-board and, often, discarded cardboard. "Aristide = AIDS, Blackout and Chimere" read one. Some sang a song, to get their courage up, recalling the murdered journalist Brignol Lindor.

"W te touye Brignol, nou pa gen jistis
W te vole lajan kooperatif
W pa gen konsyans
Nou gen blakawout e mize"

("You killed Brignol, we have no justice/
You stole the money from the cooperatives/
You have no conscience/
We have blackout and misery")

When I saw the march was about to begin, I stepped back out onto the street to begin observing it and was immediately approached by a man in his mid-thirties in PNH khakis, wearing sunglasses. His badge had been covered with tape.

"What are you doing here?" he asked.

"I'm a journalist."

"I need to see some identification," he said, which I thought odd as, save for visiting the Palace, I had rarely been asked to produce ID by anyone in Haiti. I showed him my press card, complete with photo, issued by the National Palace.

"This is unacceptable; this is fake," he said, by now backed up by a black-clad, helmeted CIMO with an assault rifle who had come up behind him. "You'll have to come with me."

"Listen, I've got a job to do; I can't come with you."

"You have to."

As we spoke, sensing the situation, Thony Belizaire had come up from behind the officer and began snapping away pictures of the two of us talking, the CIMO and everything else regarding the scene. Finally realizing he was there, the man in khakis turned to him, a look of irritation on his face.

"What do you think you're doing?"

"I'm taking pictures for Agence France Presse. This man is a journalist, too," Thony said. Goudou, coming from another angle, also asked what was happening.

"Fine," the officer finally said, shrugging his shoulders and walking away, the significance of his actions only becoming clear to me later. As the three of us were left in the road to ponder what had just happened, the CIMO began roughly frisking the students for weapons as they began to leave the school.

Finally, the march commenced, with several hundred students, boys and girls bringing up the front and singing "*Aristide allez/Nou pa vle Aristide.*" One little girl who looked to be about sixteen in a green-and-white checked dress carried a sign that read in Kreyol: "Aristide get out! You will never have the school in Ti Goave!"

The march moved past the green and white Hospital Notre Dame that had been tear-gassed during Brignol Lindor's funeral. Black-clad masked CIMO marched along with the students along the periphery, glaring at them, with their beefy, well-fed bodies looking like they could snap the wispy youths in half with one arm. People began coming out of their houses, and some people who were waiting at various street corners to join the march did so; the number began to swell exponentially. As I looked back from near the head of the march, I saw protestors, carrying signs and chanting, snaking as far I could see through Ti Goave's narrow streets, and I estimated the crowd must have been at least four or five thousand strong. An old, white-haired man with glasses smiled and waved to the crowd from the porch of his dilapidated house as they passed. "Fuck your mother!" one schoolboy screamed at a burly CIMO, then disappearing into the immense crowd when the policeman turned around to thrash him. As the clapping and chanting—all some variation of "Aristide get out!" at this point—intensified, an old peasant woman and a young blue-clad schoolgirl, laughing, danced together to the beat by the roadside. At the front of the march, the students had unfurled the blood-stained shirts of the students who had been wounded the previous day, holding them high as a banner.

"Now with the rest of the country, Ti Goave will mobilize and we will drive Aristide from power," said one boy, a bit older than the rest, who said he was a university student who was from the town.

At one point during the march, a second stream of demonstrators, easily as big as the one we were in, began marching to link up with our group in front of Ti Goave's cathedral. The police, amidst shouts that they were "drug dealers" and "kidnappers" were having none of this and stood between the two groups, weapons at the ready, as graffiti reading, "*Aba misere, Aristide se chef de gang*" hung on a whitewashed building above their heads. The two groups, separated in this manner for about twenty minutes, finally managed to link up when the police pulled back slightly and the assemblage began marching down Route Nationale 2 where it ran toward Ti Goave's downtown.

"They have money to pay the chimere but none for the cooperatives," yelled a teenage boy riding by on a bicycle.

As the marchers entered a section of the road surrounded on both sides by high walls and a few forlorn-looking lottery banks, the police, speaking on their radios, suddenly packed up all their equipment and gear, got into their cars, and left for a position several hundred yards down the road, where they dismounted with their weapons—a sight that made me very uneasy, standing exposed as I was with the now several-thousand strong march in the middle of the road.

As if on cue, the rocks began falling. Chimere that I later learned had been bused in by Aristide's National Palace the night before had been hiding in trees and behind some of the impassive walls, and, waiting strategically for the moment when the marchers were hemmed in on three sides, they began a furious fusillade of stones and glass bottles, many of which found their mark, shattering on the heads of teenagers and thumping peasants and sending some in the crowd scattering into the *borlettes* to hide, though most stood their ground. The police, looking on from their vantage point, did nothing. Some of the high-school kids, emboldened, even picked up their own stones and began hurling them back over the walls. But they were no match, and, the demonstrators and the press corps covering them thus left defenseless, things deteriorated quickly. More rocks and bottles began to descend, shattering on the road and thumping against the backs and shoulders of the students. Occasionally a wail would go up as a projectile found its mark on the head of a running student. I saw one, then two, fall, one boy in a blue uniform bleeding profusely from the head as he was carried away by his fellow students. Then the crackle of gunfire. We couldn't tell exactly where it was coming from, somewhere over the walls, but the marchers started running and scattering, and the small clutch of kids that I followed charged first along down Route Nationale 2 and then veered sharply left down a wide dirt lane, with bottles shattering at our heels and rocks breaking against the hoods of cars parked alongside. Students were tearing their uniforms off, afraid to be caught wearing their school colors and beaten or worse by the chimere. As I ran, a small metal gate opened and a middle-aged woman in a faded peasant dress motioned me quickly in. I entered her small *lakou* and heard the mob braying outside.

"Come in here," she said. "You will be safe."

We entered her cramped two-room house and I was confronted with a group of frightened students huddling together, and we all jumped when we began to hear the distinctive cascade of glass as it shattered on the roof. "*Viv Aristide!*" we heard from the road. None of the kids inside—there must have been about half a dozen—could have been over the age of eighteen, and all seemed quite fearful at having been driven inside, they said, by the chimere. As one teenage boy arrived and began to strip off his school uniform to ward off attack, he turned to me and said "You see what they do to us here?"

"Be careful, *blan*," said another. "The chimere don't like white people very much. We'll take you out when you want to leave."

Eventually, after being pinned down in the house by the mob for nearly an hour, I was able to make phone contact with Pierre, who drove back with Goudou to collect me. At that point, the streets had emptied only to be patrolled by menacing, masked CIMO, some of whom were likely gang leaders in disguise—the same police who had stood complicit and impassive as the children of their country were set upon like sacrificial lambs on the altar of Aristide's messianic, infallible self-image.

Driving back, ringed with sweat and spent, Pierre, Goudou and I looked out at the passing countryside. Looking out the window from the back seat, Goudou took a drag of a cigarette.

"It can't last much longer like this," he said.

THE SAME DAY as the attack on the students in Petit Goave, Radio Haiti-Inter reported that Minister of Education Myrtho Celestin had resigned, to join her husband who had recently been appointed Haiti's ambassador to France, though the government refused to give details about the circumstances of her departure. The students had scant time to savor this cosmetic change, though, as the capital awoke on Friday, November 22 to a rampage by the government's street gangs. Along Boulevard Harry Truman and along the streets near the National Stadium, gunmen firing from the backs of pickup trucks sent residents fleeing in terror while, attempting to drive down the

Delmas Road, one Haitian journalist found himself prevented from continuing by a wall of burning tires.

"Aristide was elected and he will never leave power," shouted one of the young men manning the barricade.

Darline Carré-Théodore, a Haitian obstetrician-gynecologist who was the sister of Aristide spokesman Dr. Haendel Carré and a naturalized U.S. citizen, was shot five times in her neck, shoulder, arm and chest when unknown gunmen firing from the street raked Petionville homes with gunfire seemingly at random, in the early morning hours. Discovered groaning in a pool of blood by her fifteen-year-old daughter, Carré-Théodore was flown to St. Mary's Medical Center in West Palm Beach, Florida, where she survived, though just barely. Two people were killed by gunfire in downtown Port-au-Prince. The city's businesses, banks and schools remained closed.

"We are in the streets to control the situation. Aristide must continue in power," said René Civil on Radio Metropole, taking credit for the disturbances.

When I called Lavalas spokesman Jonas Petit, he at first made a reference to the government not being able to control its supporters.

"They protest to make people respect the democratic decision of Haitians," he said finally. "Aristide was elected for five years and he will serve five years."

IF ANYONE HAD WONDERED by what methods Aristide intended to respond to the rising tide calling for his resignation, the events in Petit Goave and the capital served as a clear illustration.

The truth of the matter was that Aristide had set up several tiers of coordinating and occasionally competing gunmen to do violence in his name. At the bottom of the barrel were the chimere, who Aristide knew were trapped in their slums and utterly dependant on any largess the government might throw their way. They made an easy bludgeon to use to break up demonstrations, harass students and paralyze traffic around the capital; and, if necessary, they were easy to eliminate. In circumstances as desperate as Cité Soleil, there was always someone to step up and kill a chef to take his place.

On the next level were the leaders of various criminal enterprises and government patronage jobs around the capital and corrupt low-level police officers. People like René Civil, Paul Raymond, Ronald and Franco Camille, Annette "So Anne" Auguste and their like had benefited more from their close connections to the National Palace than the teenage gunmen in the slums. Many of these individuals handled tougher jobs, such as organizing high-profile political murders and kidnappings in collaboration with such corrupt and politicized police stations as the ones at the Delmas 33 commissariat in the capital (which Pierre Esperance and the National Coalition for Haitian Rights would soon label "a true bastion of armed gangs") and in Carrefour, where police actively recruited and armed chimere without any formal or official vetting process as required by Haitian law, these individuals represented the vital link between Aristide's National Palace and the destruction of the authority of the PNH, which many had done so much to build up over the years.

Finally, at the top tier, were the killers in uniform or fancy suits that Aristide surrounded himself with. Jocelerme Privert, Hermione Leonard, Delmas police director Camille Marcellus and, in the future, longtime Aristide ally Jean-Claude Jean-Baptiste were all people who had much blood on their hands and whose worst, most brutal tendencies were not only encouraged but rewarded by the Aristide government, as Aristide's elevation of the notoriously corrupt Privert to head the Interior Ministry evidenced. It was through this system, rather than through the poor masses he had spoken so eloquently to a decade before, where Aristide's power sprang from by the end of 2002. And it was through this system of complex loyalties, alliances, counter-alliances and betrayals that the thread would began to unravel his government in the months to come.

THE DAY AFTER the chimere rioted, November 23 the Association des Industries d'Haïti, the Chambre de Commerce et d'Industrie d'Haïti and the Centre pour la Libre Entreprise et la Démocratie, eighteen businesses and chambers of commerce from around Haiti in all, stepped into the fray. In a letter sent to local radio stations and *Le Nouvelliste*, the representatives of Haiti's private sector accused Aristide of having set up a "climate of terror" in Haiti, denounced the violence in Petit Goave, Port-au-Prince and Gonaives and went on to demand the arrest of Amiot Metayer, René Civil and Paul Raymond and the government's compliance with OAS resolutions 806 and 822.

"In unison we raise our voices in indignation" the group's statement read, at the criminal actions of "people acting under the protection of high authorities. . . . The private sector cannot accept orchestrated criminal actions planned and implemented with the money of taxpayers and the equipment of the state."

"We're having another meeting today to determine our strategy," said the mulatto doctor who helped draft the declaration, when I saw him driving past on the street in front of my house in Pacot. "My wife doesn't want me to go, but being a representative of the private sector from Jacmel entails responsibilities. I still believe that the problems of this country go further than personalities, but it's a very passionate moment right now and it's very difficult to voice those feelings."

At a press conference, responding to the private sector's statement denouncing the government's role in orchestrating that Friday's violence, Yvon Neptune sounded a threatening tone.

"The private sector is trying to provoke us and push us to the road of foreign intervention," Neptune said at a press conference. "The situation is very delicate and we fear civil war."

The following Sunday, as people around the capital stocked up on food amidst rumors than an equally chaotic pro-government explosion was planned for Monday, the Radio Etincelle station of Gonaives was partially burned down. The following day, Amiot Metayer's Cannibal Army attacked anti-Aristide marchers in the city, severely injuring five people, and the Association Nationale des Médias Haitiens said it was "highly worried by direct threats" to the journalists trying to cover demonstrations there and in Cap Haitien. In a statement, the OAS applauded the Aristide government's efforts to form an electoral council but deplored its handling of Metayer, who had now been allowed to roam Gonaives at will for almost four months since his August escape from prison, linking it to the previous Friday's tire-burning pro-government demonstrations in the capital.

"The authorities appeared to make no effort to keep roads open or to detain those committing illegal acts," the body said.

As if in response to the criticism, on November 26, unidentified gunmen fired on a marked OAS car in Gonaives, and, in a separate incident, three people were wounded by gunfire as antigovernment protestors were again attacked and beaten. In Petit Goave, a demonstrator was shot and marchers stormed a government building, seizing firearms there and parading through the city's streets with them, calling for Aristide's resignation.

ON NOVEMBER 27, I went to visit Evans Paul at his home on a quiet side street off Christ Roi, where he lived in a rambling, semimodern house built over a ravine and surrounded by coconut palms. It wasn't an easy street to find, and Paul had previously told me that a retired French army officer lived nearby, as did some other foreigners, all with their own security, which he said helped ameliorate his own security situation a bit. Let through the gate by an elderly *gardien*, I was shown to a nearly-empty downstairs room overlooking a drained swimming pool, where paintings on the wall depicted various Haitian folk scenes. Paul came down from his office to greet me, dapper in black slacks and a white shirt as always, and we went back to speak in his study. On his desk rested a black plaque on a little stand reading, "Evans Paul, Maire de Port-au-Prince," and on the wall were paintings of a charging brown horse with the letters "KID" stenciled on its rump and another of Toussaint Louverture. Despite his words, I knew there was more than a little of a personal vendetta in Paul's opposition to Aristide, and I had seen more than a hint of the demagogue in him.

"We must combat and prevent the establishment of an Aristide dictatorship in Haiti," he said to me, leaning across his desk and speaking in quiet, conversational tones far different from his forceful public speaking voice. "We'll continue with our peaceful national mobilization until we free the country from Lavalas control."

The opposition, Paul said, planned to hold continuous nationwide demonstrations until Aristide stepped down, and he jotted down a note on his personal stationary outlining for me a schedule of antigovernment protests to be held on November 28 in Gonaives, November 29 in Saint Marc and on December 3 in Petit Goave and Port-au-Prince. The Gonaives and Petit Goave rallies would commemorate, respectively, the shootings of three schoolchildren by the Haitian army during the dictatorship of the Duvalier family in 1985 and the mob murder of Brignol Lindor in December of the previous year.

"All the people who are demonstrating against Aristide now are the people who were demonstrating for Aristide in 1991," Paul said.

As we spoke in his office, thousands of university and high-school students marched against Aristide in Cap Haitien. In the capital, Secretary of State for Communications Mario Dupuy characterized the demonstrations as "provocations by the opposition."

ARISTIDE TOLD REPORTERS gathered at Haiti's National Palace on November 28 for his press conference with Taiwan's Ambassador to Haiti Michel Lu that he had no intention of resigning.

"I will not leave office, coup d'état is not a solution to Haiti's problems," he said. "Haiti is a democracy and the people have a right to express their opinion."

The same day—the anniversary of the shooting of three schoolchildren there in the last days of Jean-Claude Duvalier's regime in 1985 that helped bring the dictatorship down—thousands of anti-Aristide protestors in Gonaives marched past barricades of flaming tires and burning cars before being savaged by Cannibal Army members. In Jacmel, hundreds of students marched through the city demanding Aristide's ouster and the reinstatement of three local teachers fired for participating in antigovernment demonstrations. In the tense Plateau Central, Christophe Lozama, a Lavalassian justice of the peace from the border town of Belladere, was killed when a melee erupted between Lavalas and Convergence protestors in the hamlet of Poulie on November 28. The shooting erupted when Lozama and eleven other Lavalas partisans attempted to break up an opposition meeting in the town.

In the coming days, the government and its foreign supporters would turn Lozama's killing into a *cause du jour* as they attempted to deflect attention from government-sponsored attacks on demonstrators and the press and, in the time-honored tradition of authoritarian regimes facing popular revolt, Haiti's state-run media, such as TNH and Radio Nationale, portrayed the rampaging pro-government mobs as helpless victims, while the mauled and bloodied students were portrayed as politically co-opted agitators. It was a technique the Haitians, with some experience in how governments of this nature react when challenged, saw through immediately, but it was something that Aristide's supporters abroad would continue to cynically deny.

In one of the largest shows of support in many months, on November 25 Aristide had Paul Raymond, René Civil and So Anne Auguste organize a large-scale demonstration emanating from the capital's slums. Hopping out of a taxi near a mass of demonstrators in Bel Air, I saw Civil leading several hundred people down toward the National Palace, all of them waving palm fronds, Haitian flags and photos of Aristide. A *rara* band pumped up the crowd, with thumping drums and the plangent cry of the *vaksin* carried through Bel Air's curving streets. I was greeted with some hostile glares until Civil saw me, and I walked over and we shook hands, which drew some curious expressions from the assembled crowd.

"Aristide is the power of the Haitian people," he said. "You can see all the young people marching for him. He is here for five years, *mon chère.*"

And off they went. From Bel Air they marched to the Champs de Mars and passed the National Palace where they joined a far larger group of marchers, all of them young and, in a change from much of what I had seen from Lavalas recently, fairly evenly distributed among men and women. Standing watching the march next to the Albert Magones's statue, *"Le Marron Inconnu,"* I was showered with Aristide flyers and pro-Lavalas leaflets by the passing throng.

"Without Aristide the country will burn," they chanted. "Without Aristide, there is no country."

As the marchers approached the American consulate (always referred to as "the Embassy" by Haitians), groups of chimere hanging off pickup trucks drove back and forth shouting "Aristide or death" and "Viv Osama bin Laden." Wilson Sanvil, the head of the Oganizasyon Revolisyonè Chalo Jaklen from Cité Soleil, dressed in Lavalas red, tapped me on the shoulder to say hi. At one point a man in a suit—who I was later told was a Lavalas deputy—was hoisted on the shoulders of fellow marchers, shouted "Down with Convergence," drew a pistol from his belt and began firing into the air, sending people scattering onto the Champs de Mars (Haitians always wisely skittish at the sound of any gunfire). Later, the Patriyot Band, playing *rara* and blowing on conch shells, marched in front of the Embassy. Aristide's helicopter frequently swept up from the National Palace lawn and hovered above, filming the protests for use on state television later that night. By the end of the day, speakers and a stand were set up in front of the National Palace, and speaker after speaker addressed the crowd with anti-Convergence and antiforeign rhetoric. Rather stage-managed for what TNH would portray as a spontaneous "people's" demonstration, I thought.

As I stood with a clutch of taxi drivers listening to a hand-held radio outside of the Hotel Plaza on the far side of the park, I heard that the day again saw blood flow in Gonaives, where five people—including two high-school students—were wounded by gunfire amidst continued clashes by Aristide loyalists and opponents, and Amiot Metayer's Cannibal Army continued to mete out bloody street justice to its opponents.

"This is completely unacceptable," said Pierre-Robert Auguste, president of the Association of Artibonite Business Leaders. "The police and the government support these criminals, and now we must mobilize to change the situation."

I watched as the Lavalas demonstrators surged back and forth across the park.

"This country is already dead," said a man nearby, shirtless and washing cars from a dirty bucket, as he observed the scene.

THE NEW MONTH began in tumult. Over the first weekend in December, bloody gang fighting erupted in Gonaives between Amiot Metayer's Cannibal Army and Jean Tatoune's supporters from the city's Jubilé district, after two Tatoune supporters shot and killed Cannibal Army member Evans Auguste. In response, Metayer's forces torched some twenty homes in Jubilée and killed a resident. On December 2, *Le Nouvelliste* ran a dramatic photograph on its front page of the seven journalists who had been driven from Gonaives due to the threats from Metayer's gang the month before. The journalists, who included the local correspondents from Radio Metropole, Radio Kiskeya and Radio Signal FM, were picture huddled around the flame of a burning lamp, their faces grim and spectral in the flickering night. The article announced that, since they had been forced into hiding during the chaos of the chimere rampages on November 22, the journalists had arrived in Port-au-Prince, where they were holed-up in an unnamed local hotel. In the piece, the AJH Secretary General Guy Delva, who had engineered their trip from Gonaives to the capital, again called for the arrest of Amiot Metayer and Jean Tatoune, to no reaction from the government.[1] The same day, to cheers from their families, the last of the prisoners seized at Guacimal in May, the union members Urbain Garçon and Jéremie Dorvil were released without charge.

December 3, the first anniversary of the murder of the journalist Brignol Lindor ("*une anniversaire triste*" the announcer on Magik Stereo FM called it), began with a Mass at the Église Saint Pierre in his honor and the honor of all the other journalists who had died, been attacked or been forced into exile during the Aristide years. The church's gate had been plastered with Aristide flyers the night before, and earlier that morning, a couple of glassy-eyed chimere had strolled through the church with Aristide posters taped to their chests, walking through dropping Aristide flyers in every pew and all over the platform where the priest would be speaking. As the assembled journalists and opposition politicians arrived, they tore them down and trampled them under foot.

As mournful liturgical music filled the cathedral, Michele Montas, dressed all in black, sat in the first pew, along with Radio Metropole owner Richard Widmayer, Radio Kiskeya programme director Lilianne Pierre-Paul and U.S. Ambassador Brian Dean Curran. Quite surprisingly, Senate president Fourel Celestin was also in attendance. As if on cue, sunlight began to filter through the windows over the hundreds of mourners assembled as the congregation began to sing, "*Un jour a la fois / Doux Jesus c'est tout ceque je peux donner.*"

Throughout the service a throng of young men stood across Place Saint

Pierre glaring at the mourners, journalists and diplomats as they entered the cathedral. Every once in a while one of two particularly thuggish-looking guys in dark macoute glasses would wander in and glare around the church. Toward the end of the service one of them, just beginning to sprout dreadlocks, though he seemed to me in his late twenties, went back outside to give the signal, and, on cue, the lackeys across the street began to shout and bring out Aristide fly-ers and posters. Very quickly, Ambassador Curran was evidently given the word to leave, and he walked, calmly, down the steps of the church over the torn-down Aristide posters, escorted by his Haitian security guards. Hermione Leonard was sitting in an SUV with other police, quite visibly directing the action, gesturing to the chimere to tell them when to advance and when to retreat and so on, and from time to time chatting on a walkie-talkie.

I stood on the steps and watched as journalists who had been honoring Lin-dor began to come out and the chimere advanced to the cathedral steps, flinging Aristide pictures at them, shrieking *"git mama w, blan"* and about how they worked for *"colon blan"* (white colonialists). As Michele Montas descended the stairs, one stood screaming *"Aristide a vie"* about five feet away from her. She smiled a wan smile in her black mourning dress and continued on with her bodyguard, Maxime Seide, a big guy rippling with muscles who put himself between her and the leaflet tossers. A mulatto guy came out of the church, and tore down another Aristide poster that had been affixed to the church's gate. Patrick Elie, the of head the Eko Vwa Jean Dominique organization that had strung those damning banners around Port-au-Prince on the second anniver-sary of Dominique's death, shook his head and looked disgusted.

Then, descending to Place d'Italie with Daniel Aguilar, a colleague from Reuters who was being loaned out to Haiti from his base in Mexico, we pre-pared to cover the opposition's scheduled demonstration for the day. When we arrived at the square, also known as the Place des Nations Unies because of its small park fluttering with flags from around the world and located in front of Haiti's parliament and the American Embassy, things did not look good. The chimere, so they told me, had been instructed to gather there by the Palace and the Ministry of the Interior at around seven that morning. The opposition march was set to begin around ten o'clock, and as the few hundred people—with only a few famous faces such as opposition politicians Mirlande Manigat and Daniel Supplice among them—began to coalesce, a crowd of thousands of chimere (almost exclusively young and male, this time) began to charge across the plaza and around the corner from the American Embassy at them. The heavily armed CIMO present casually walked into the middle of the street, their machine guns present but not used.

"I'm a citizen of this country and Aristide is the only legitimate president of this country and we are here to show this opposition that he will remain in office," one young man told me in the pro-Aristide crowd.

Fairly quickly, the chimere began picking up the stones they had gathered over the heads of the CIMO at the marchers, with the CIMO moving backwards until the marchers were finally essentially backed up against a wall. Then the bottles came. Marchers who tried to escape were caught by chimere and beaten with whips, slapped, clubbed with metal bars and forced to scream "*Viv Aristide.*" As this was happening, CIMO were raiding various faculties at the State University of Haiti. At the Ecole Normale and the Faculté d'Ethnologie, where students had pulled down the Haitian flag and hoisted a black flag in memory of Brignol Lindor, CIMO and chimere broke in, led by Gwo Jack (the same policeman who had stopped the Boukman Eksperyans concert on Aristide's orders in September), where they joined in, together, in clubbing and beating students. Several required hospitalization, including two with head injuries at Canapé Vert, one of which nearly cost a young man his eye.

Back at the Place d'Italie, people were running for their lives. I saw a woman shedding blood from her arms and a man staggering along holding his head. I saw taxi drivers have their cars pelted with rocks and bottles for simply being in the area. Shots were fired. The police never lifted so much as a finger. Again, nothing but Aristide posters and flyers everywhere—the cult of personality, though expressly forbidden by the Haitian constitution, in full flower.

"Now is not the time to be afraid; now is the time to be brave!" shouted one mulatto woman as bottles shattered at her feet and rocks cracked car windows around her.

"Aristide or death!" shouted one young man, carrying a poster of the president, in response.

Among the mob that day was Annette "So Anne" Auguste, cementing her image as Aristide's contemporary version of Francois Duvalier's feared macoute leader Madame Max Adolphe, and Lovinsky Pierre-Antoine, the 30 September Foundation director upon whom Aristide had lavished a job heading the Office National pour la Migration (ONM) and who this day stood near a *rara* band, observing the scene. In the Place d'Italie, opposition supporters caught there were held down and beaten, with some set on benches and slapped and whipped with *rigwaz*—small cowskin whips—as television cameras rolled. Some chimere would later tell me that So Anne had "blessed" some of the whips in a *vodou* ritual before the demonstration had commenced. I looked at the boys, staggering, drunken, armed and all but certain to be abandoned when expedient, and thought of how Aristide must see them, in the final analysis, as the refuse of his rule. To be used and burned like the tires that formed their most ready form of protest: incinerated and with more on hand always at the ready to be thrown onto the fire.

I made my way back to where my rental car was parked—though not before I jumped to avoid a shower of bottles that seemed to come from nowhere, managing to drop and lose my wallet in the process. A trio of protestors—

middle-aged, well-dressed and with just a dollop enough of cream in their complexions not to be considered black in Haiti's color scheme—frantically flagged down my car as I drove away from the hail of bottles and rocks toward Haiti's parliament. Somewhat fearful of lingering in the area after witnessing the savaging of the students in Petit Goave the previous month, I nevertheless felt I could not in good conscience abandon these people to the mercy of the mob. So I pulled up a short stop.

"God, thank you, we've got to get out of here," a man said as he climbed into my front seat, along with two women. Before I knew it, others who had been hiding behind a low wall nearby leapt from their hiding places and began jogging, and in one case limping, toward my car. Before long, the compact rental was doing a good imitation of a Haitian taxi, with three people in the front and four in the back as we sped through the streets.

The radio was saying that the opposition, now calling itself the "Comité de Vertières," would be holding a press conference any moment at a home in Tuergeau, so I let my passengers out on Avenue Henri Christophe and sped up to the conference's location. I made my way through a crush of reporters and past two cars with shattered windshields to find Evans Paul, Himmler Rebu, René Théodore and Carline Simone, head of the Fanm Soley Leve (Women of the Rising Sun) feminist group, sitting and simmering with anger at a table full of microphones. Attempting to drive down Lalue to join the demonstration that morning, they had been attacked, they said, and forced to turn back. As radio reports filtered in from the provinces, we heard that antigovernment protestors in Cap Haitien and Gonaives were also attacked, and that a protestor in Petit Goave had been shot and wounded.

"Today we saw the Tontons Macoutes of Aristide, in Port-au-Prince, in Cap Haitien, in Gonaives," said Théodore. "We will continue to struggle until we uproot the Aristide dictatorship. We don't have money, and we don't have the money to kill and terrorize that Aristide does, but we are asking the population to observe a general strike tomorrow in protest."

"This is democracy," Mario Dupuy, one of Aristide's spokesman, told incredulous radio reporters later that day, as the demonstrators limped home to nurse their wounds. "People, including government supporters, may take part in any march they want to."

THAT NEXT DAY, as most businesses, schools and banks remained tightly shuttered in the capital, Cap Haitien and Jacmel, in the city of Les Cayes—a stone's throw away from his birthplace—Aristide spoke to one of his largest crowds in months, numbering perhaps twenty thousand. All the local Lavalas loyalists from this southern region, which had benefited from the largess of their local son in recent years, as well as party loyalists bused in by the government from the capital and other urban centers, applauded enthusiastically as

Aristide delivered a fiery Kreyol speech that reminded some listeners of his days as a preacher in Saint Jean Bosco.

"Should I pay them more?" Aristide asked rhetorically, referring to sizeable amounts of money the Haitian government had doled out to the victims of the violence of the previous December's Palace attack and aftermath.

"No!" roared back the crowd.

"It's not for ten years, it's for five years! It's not President Aristide they don't like, it's the Haitian people they don't like. They don't want to respect your rights. Do you want war or peace?"

"Peace!" the crowd thundered.

"Do you want war or peace?

"Peace!"

"Do you want war or peace? "

"Peace!"

"You are peasants; you are poor. You are the same color that I am. They don't like you. Your hair is kinky, same as mine. They don't like you," Aristide continued, the irony of his light-skinned wife behind him notwithstanding. "Your children are not the children of big shots. They don't like you."

Aristide vowed to stay on until the end of his mandate three years later.

"Not one day more, not one day less," he said and the crowd roared their approval.

As Aristide addressed the faithful, his nemesis and sometimes protector, the U.S. State Department, called on his government to restore a "climate of security" in the country.

"We are particularly troubled by the violence and intimidation perpetrated by government-backed 'popular organizations' and their allies in Port-au-Prince, Gonaives and Cap Haitien," said State Department spokesman Philip Reeker in Washington, referring to the previous day's donnybrook. "The United States deplores the deterioration of the political climate in Haiti that these events represent."

AS WAS EVIDENT by the events of November and December, Haitian society had become much more divided and complicated since the downfall of the Duvalier dynasty and, especially, since Aristide's return in 1994, than those who continued to use the facile noir against mulatre and right versus left definitions were willing to admit. Singularly among countries I have covered as a journalist, I think political ideology mattered less in Haiti than anywhere else in the Western Hemisphere, especially after the emergence of the nouveaux riche black political class that took off after Aristide's return in 1994. Politicians, most though not exclusively affiliated with the Fanmi Lavalas party, were able to enrich themselves through government contracts, corruption and drug trafficking, which they then laundered through legitimate and semilegitimate fronts such as the co-operatives and the myriad of Lavalas-owned businesses that sprung up around the capital and elsewhere to create a new strata of Haitian society that had heretofrefore barely existed. Whereas the fruits of government business as opportunity had historically fallen to Haiti's mulatto entrepreneurs, Aristide, like Francois Duvalier before him, managed, at a terrible cost, to bring the eternally oppressed and exploited black underclass a few steps forward in the sense that, as opposed to just being soldiers or street fighters, now they had money, access and influence to the real levers of power.

Conversely you could also have two left-wing parties—such as OPL and Fanmi Lavalas were, at least in rhetoric, in the late 1990s—fighting brutal, take-no-prisoners political battles in what would be, almost right up until the December 2001 Palace attack when goodwill evaporated entirely, a war amplified if not defined by clashing personalities, between Aristide and Gérard Pierre-Charles, between Aristide and Evans Paul, between Aristide and Chavannes Jean-Baptiste. The factor that brought it out of the realm of personal feuding was the overwhelming, pervasive corruption of the state that took place during Aristide's second term, the bulldozing of Haiti's nascent institutional structure to exclusively serve the executive branch, and the government's empowering of armed pressure groups and irregular militias to act as a bludgeon against threats—right or wrongly—that Aristide saw as everpresent. Eventually power—and its propagation—became an end unto itself for Aristide's government, and any populist ideological underpinnings were jettisoned in all but a rhetorical sense to permit the president and his small circle to grow ever richer at the expense of the Haitian masses.

It was an old and very cynical ploy. As Aristide denounced foreign designs on his country and demanded, as he would soon, that France pay restitution for Haiti's colonial debt with one hand, with the other hand he invited in Colombian drug traffickers and Grupo M, working his country for all its worth with about as much emotion as a battle-hardened pimp would set a withered prostitute out on whore's row. He would denounce the mulatto elite, even as he sat with his mulatto wife and made business deals with those among their number. He would blame the Americans, and yet was so distrustful of Haitians that he would entrust his security only to American bodyguards. That is what finally began to coalesce over the summer of 2002 and into 2003—a movement whereby you could have social democrats like the black Gérard Pierre-Charles and Evans Paul and the near-white Micha Gaillard sit down at a table with ex-military men like Himmler Rebu and peasant leaders like Chavannes Jean-Baptiste and even, eventually, industrialists like André "Andy" Apaid, Jr.—all spurred on by the courage of the student movement of the summer of 2002, actors who had nothing in common finding unity in their loathing of Aristide.

Other players on the scene at this time, albeit one with a far less significant an impact beyond hardening the "zero option" prevalent among Aristide's domestic opposition, was the ever-meddling International Republican Institute (IRI), an arm of the U.S. Republican party funded by the National Endowment for Democracy (NED), USAID and private donors that had been operating a political party-building program in Haiti since 1998. Until 1999, when he fled to the United States, the IRI's main point man on the ground in Port-au-Prince had been Stanley Lucas, a wealthy young Haitian whose family in the Northwest Department was said to have helped organize the Jean Rabel massacre that marked the bloody climax of Jean-Marie Vincent's attempts at land reform in the region. As early as 2000, the IRI had spent some $34,994 to ferry leaders of the Democratic Convergence to Washington to meet American elected officials and the body had set about trying to make Haiti's endlessly quarrelsome political class see the value of presenting a united front against Aristide, opposition to whom had long been something of an unofficial religion among Republicans in the U.S. capital.[2] Throughout 2003, USAID, contracting chiefly through IRI and its partisan counterpart, the National Democratic Institute (NDI), would continue to play a role, providing $875,000 in direct aid to Haiti's opposition parties by helping to "strengthen their constituencies, both inside and outside of Port-au-Prince; formalize party structures; and formulate issue driven platforms," according to one of their bulletins.[3] USAID also disbursed $625,000 that year to Haiti's independent media to help set up small community radio networks throughout rural Haiti.[4]

Another organization, the Washington, DC-based Haiti Democracy Project, was headed up by James Morrell, who had helped found the left-leaning Center for International Policy (CIP) in 1975 and was forced out of his role there in 2002 when he criticized Aristide's extensive lobbying payouts in progressive circles in the United States. Operating on a slim budget that saw $167,000 in donations—including one from the philanthropic San Antonio Area Foundation—over a three-year period, the Project also received financial support from Rodolphe Boulos, the CEO of Pharval Laboratories, the Haitian medical company that had been at the center of the poisoned fever-syrup controversy that erupted just after René Préval took office in 1996. Starting in the fall of 2002, the Haiti Democracy Project would regularly present Aristide's opponents at symposiums in Washington and do their best to interest an otherwise-occupied U.S. congress in their particular take on the Haitian situation.

Despite all the money poured into these activities and the IRI's occasional in-country powwows with the likes of KID and KONAKOM party members at the Hotel Villa Creole, by the fall of 2002 the Convergence had all but collapsed as a united front and all of the aid to its affiliated parties proved incapable of rallying any widespread public support to the opposition's cause or even a coherent game plan. In the summer of 2002, however, the collapse of the cooperatives and the brutal suppression of the student movement, combined with the increasing unchecked violence and criminality of the chimere, pushed large swaths of the urban lower-middle class, who had formed the base of Aristide's remaining support since his November 2000 election, into the camp of those hostile to his government, where the political opposition, independent peasant movements, middle-class intellectuals and of course Haiti's elite had been for some time. Aristide seemed unable to react to dissent in any other way than to violently suppress it, and the bravery of the student demonstrators, drawn from the lower to middle-class urban black poor that represented Aristide's most logical base, finally spurred the political opposition from an effete talking shop into some sort of collective action.

During all this time when I was covering the growing demonstrations against the Aristide government, not once did any of his mostly handsomely-compensated defenders observe any of the attacks meted out by Aristide's forces on the Haitian population and thus perhaps provoke what remained of their eviscerated consciences to assess what it was they were really being paid to defend. Ira Kurzban, Ron Dellums, Randall Robinson, University of Miami law professor Irwin Stotsky, the attorney Brian Concannon, U.S. representatives Maxine Waters and Barbara Lee and the rest of those who attempted to silence the voice of the people of Haiti by virtue of their media access and the Haitian government funds that were at their disposal have much to answer for to the Haitian people. But, as in many cases in Haiti, following the money told one a great deal more than following the rhetoric.

By law in the United States, all those formally representing foreign governments in the United States must declare their work and level of compensation with the U.S. Department of Justice under the Foreign Agents Registration Act (FARA). According to FARA figures available from the DOJ, between the beginning of 2000 and the end of 2002 Ira Kurzban's Miami law firm—responsible for funding Brian Concannon and the BAI in Haiti as well as the Haitian government's domestic representation in the United States—received nearly $2 million from the Aristide government of behalf of its lobbying efforts.[5]

During the same period the public relations firm of former Black Congressional Caucus member California Representative Ron Dellums—Dellums, Brauer, Halterman & Associates, LLC—was paid almost $600,000 by the Aristide government for its lobbying efforts.[6] The "agreement for professional services" between the government of Haiti and the Dellums firm signed on April 25, 2001 stated that the firm would "provide strategic advice to the Government of Haiti on how to achieve improved relations with the United States Government [including the United States Congress], multi-national financing agencies, United States business and business associations, the media and other entities." Among the firm's tasks were to be constant lobbying of Congress, production of bulletins delivered to U.S. politicians, activists and journalists and "placement of periodic stories, opinion pieces and editorials favorable to the Government of Haiti in U.S. Media sources." The agreement went on to state that the firm would be paid a monthly retainer of $33,000, with an invoice presented to Ira Kurzban at the first of each month and payment to be made within thirty days of receipt.

Hazel Ross-Robinson, wife of TransAfrica founder and vehement Aristide defender Randall Robinson, had served as Dellums's senior foreign policy adviser before going into the private sector. Her firm, Ross-Robinson & Associates, was paid $367,966 by the Haitian government starting in 1997.[7] Congresswoman Maxine Waters has long been listed as an "advisor" to Robinson's TransAfrica organization, and Barbara Lee, one of the Aristide's government's most strident supporters in the U.S. Congress, had been Dellums's chief of staff before taking his congressional seat upon his retirement. Waters, Robinson and Dellums were all official advisors to the tax-exempt Foundation for Democracy, the body that Aristide had set up to raise and administer funds for projects in Haiti but that in reality served as little more than a recruiting ground for the chimere gangs that were terrorizing the country.

Waters, for her part especially, may well have felt at home in the maze of conflicting interests and backroom deals that characterized the Aristide government, given her own questionable record on such matters. Her family in the United States had grown fabulously wealthy from deals her husband, Sidney Williams, a former U.S. ambassador to The Bahamas under the Clinton administration, had secured in his role as a consultant for the California company, Siebert, Brandford & Shank, for whom Williams procured bond-underwriting assignments from constituencies dependant on his wife's political support, such as the city of Inglewood. Waters's daughter, Karen, had also long accepted payments of more than $1.7 million over an eight-year period in exchange for placing her mother's endorsement of local candidates and ballot-measure sponsors on a political mailer in her local congressional district in California.[8]

"Plumez la poule, mais ne la fait pas crier," Jean-Jacques Dessalines had commented about such activity nearly two hundred years earlier. Pluck the chicken, but make sure it doesn't squawk.

GERALD KHAWLY, the 64-year-old scion of a prominent Jacmel family and brother of former Jacmel mayor Jacques Khawly, was mowed down by two men on a motorcycle as he stepped out of a gas station he owned near the Sylvio Cator Stadium on December 6. Khawly, whose mansion on the south coast had been built amid rumors of involvement in drug trafficking, was taken to Canapé Vert hospital along with his son-in-low, Pascha Vorbe, who had been shot in the neck. When I arrived at the hospital that night after hearing the news—having walked through the darkened Friday streets to get there—I found the hospital overflowing with pained-looking white Haitians and mulattoes.

A serious looking middle-aged mulatto man, slim and with a neatly groomed mustache, walked down from the operating room, shaking his head.

"Mr. Khawly was shot, yes?" I asked him.

"Mr. Khawly is dead," he replied.

Vorbe was later airlifted to Jackson Memorial Hospital in Miami and survived.

As I hailed a taxi, the driver asked me what was happening inside. I told him the story of the killing.

"Se Ayiti," he said, shaking his head. "Securité zero."

The night of Khawly's murder, arsonists set fire to the downtown Port-au-Prince headquarters of politician Hubert de Ronceray's Mobilisation pour le Developpement National (MDN) party, two days after the party had received threats that the attack would happen.

"We were threatened on Wednesday that this would occur, but the police would do nothing," de Ronceray told local reporters. "President Aristide is responsible for this as he supports this kind of action, and this is another step by the government making it clear that he must step down."

As murder and arson rocked downtown that night, gunfire also lit up the streets further uphill when, on the Kenscoff Road, unidentified gunmen opened fire on a car carrying Dany Toussaint. No one in Toussaint's entourage was injured, but the colorful senator and his companions returned fire, with Toussaint reportedly firing from his own gun on the assailants, who then fled. Toussaint told reporters that the PNH had withdrawn his security detail earlier in the day.

"This may have happened because I am speaking out on sensitive issues in parliament, regarding the police, regarding kidnapping," said Toussaint to Radio Metropole. "No one was injured on our side, thank god, though we may have shot some of the assassins."

Days later, speaking to the mourners at Gérard Khawly's funeral, the mulatto doctor, swathed in black, stood inside of the cathedral and called out from the pulpit.

"Assassins of Gerald Khawly," he said, "you can dance around his corpse if you want to, but the Southeast is watching you. You can at this moment enjoy the spoils of your crime, but the true people of our country have already catalogued you for what you are: villains and cowards. You can continue to do the only thing that you can do: to kill our men, to kill our wives, to kill our children, to kill our country, but the history we will read our children, our children's children, already assigned you your place: to its dustbin."

In apparent retaliation for the murder of Judge Christophe Lozama there the previous month, on December 7 a contingent of CIMO under the direction of Ministry of Interior employee Amos Metellus swarmed into the Plateau Central hamlet of Poulie, beating residents and ransacking and burning homes. Several days later, on December 10, a mysterious group of armed men killed a man as they seized the local police station, taking weapons, freeing prisoners and commandeering a police vehicle, which they later set ablaze.

That night, three men rumored to be police informants were killed in and around the town.

Speaking to the OAS Permanent Council on Haiti on December 9, OAS Assistant Secretary General Luigi Einaudi again noted the failure to form an electoral council and opined that, far from acting on Resolution 822, the Aristide government had in fact helped further destabilize the situation.

"Disarmament is only too obviously still a major problem," Einaudi said. "We need look no farther than Gonaives where a fugitive from justice whom the Commission of Inquiry had implicated in the violent incidents of December 17, 2001 is effectively in control of the streets. . . . Government supporters with limited democratic credentials have been allowed, some would say encouraged, to harass opposition supporters, retaliate against demonstrators and threaten the press. If we are engaged in a process that will lead to credible elections, then this situation, whose continuance has obvious implications for an electoral campaign, is unacceptable."

Einaudi then begged the government and opposition "to reflect hard on the implications of the course Haiti is lurching onto at the moment, and its potential for worsening the lot of each of them, further shattering their political hopes and ambitions—to say nothing of the well being of the long suffering Haitian people."

IN THE CAPITAL'S swampy, brothel-infested popular quarter of Carrefour in the predawn hours of December 8, three brothers—Andy Philippe, Angelo Philippe and Vladimir Sanon—were kidnapped from their mother's arms by hooded men in police uniforms who the young men's families recognized by their voices as being local PNH officers employed at the Carrefour commissariat. The three brothers had been among a group of protesters who had scuffled with police officers the previous week, protesting the robbery and attempted murder of a Carrefour man by a group of off-duty policeman, and one of the brothers had also been involved in a complicated romantic rivalry with a local policeman for the affections of a young woman in the neighborhood. There had been a rash of summary executions of at least a dozen young men in the district in previous months, along the zone's Route des Rails section near a disused railroad bridge. Residents said young men would be brought there, forced out of cars with their hands bound and then shot in the back of the head execution-style. Some hours after their abduction, the three Carrefour brothers were found dead, bullets in their heads, in the State University Hospital morgue.

Even as his police force and gangs were slaughtering his country's impoverished citizenry, Aristide, content to play Papa Nwel, would have none of this. On the steps of the National Palace on December 23, Aristide and his wife Mildred hosted a breakfast for street children at which they received a meal of hot soup and also gifts. On Christmas Eve, a U.S. Coast Guard patrol pulled forty Haitian migrants from the sea where their rickety sailboat was capsizing in the Florida Straits, bringing to 985 the number of Haitians intercepted at sea that year.

In a bloody denouement to the holiday season, as Michele Montas arrived at her home on Christmas Day, gunmen waiting on foot outside her house opened fire on her and her bodyguard, Maxime Seide. Montas had just entered her home and fell to the floor, but, as the front gate to the residence was shot, Seide found himself trapped on the street with the would-be assassins. He was shot and killed. Montas had previously noticed an upsurge in suspicious vehicles surveying Radio Haiti-Inter and had received warnings about a potential attack, though she had believed it would take place during Haiti's Carnival season, coming in two months.

Through his spokesman, Aristide denounced the attack, but in an interview referring to Montas's late husband on Radio Signal FM on December 26, Mario Andresol, the former head of Haiti's judiciary police, told listeners that, "Under the current government in Haiti, there will be no progress in the Dominique case"—this suggested that Dominique's murder was linked directly to Aristide and lambasted Minister Jocelerme Privert for corruption when he was head of Haiti's tax office.

WE CLIMBED THROUGH the mountains slowly, three Haitian journalists and I, as the sun was beginning to climb and spill its honeyed light down on the mountains steeping up to the Plateau Central. The others were heading to Hinche to conduct a training seminar for local reporters there, but I would only be accompanying them halfway. After about two hours of bumpy driving, we arrived at Cange, the squatter settlement at which the American doctor Paul Farmer had founded the Clinique Bon Saveur with a local priest, Father Fritz Lafontant, in 1983, while still a student at Harvard Medical School. The clinic had grown over the years to be the signal project of the Partners in Health (*Zanmi Lasante* in Kreyol) organization Farmer had formed in 1987 with another Harvard Medical School graduate, Jim Yong Kim. Even more so than the clinics they had opened up in southern Mexico, the slums of Lima or programs initiated in the prisons of Russia, it was this impressive creation that gave a glimpse of what public-health administration for the world's poor could be given dedication and a great deal of money. Farmer and I had been corresponding via email for the better part of a year, and I had been very impressed by his single-minded devotion to Haiti's poor. I knew something of his background, that he had gown up on Florida's Gulf Coast, with an eccentric father who, at various points, housed the family in a converted bus and a barely-seaworthy boat, and that he had won a scholarship to Duke University for his undergraduate studies. Something of it spoke to my own experience, growing up in a working-class family in southeastern Pennsylvania, and I was interested on a more personal level to see what fires drove him, and if they were the same ones the drove me, so far away from the environment in which he had been raised.

As the months had passed and the Aristide government had revealed itself to be more and more murderous and corrupt and less and less concerned with the well-being of the very people Farmer sought to help, Farmer's continued, unyielding advocacy for Aristide had caused our messages to grow more strained. Farmer would eventually be the subject of a supinely fawning biography by the American journalist Tracey Kidder, who knew little of Haiti and understood nothing of the power struggles it had undergone since Aristide had returned to power; but I believed, with so few people of good conscience concerned with the plight of the Haitians, it was our responsibility to keep a dialogue open on any subject we could.

In his book *The Uses of Haiti*, written at the height of violence against Aristide's supporters during his exile in the mid-1990s, Farmer describes U.S. policies in El Salvador in the 1970s and 1980s and offers them up for comparison with those used in Haiti around the time of the 1991 coup. "The killing of peasants is of a piece with the larger-project of U.S.-backed juntas, the destruction of Salvadoran civil society," Farmer writes. "[They] permitted the destruction of the non-violent popular movement, the independent press, the labor and peasant movements and human rights organizations." The analysis—sharp as always from such a scholarly and precise thinker—I had found oddly never turned on its head by the book's author to examine the results of Aristide's second term in office, during which the same traits that Farmer bemoaned as being propagated in El Salvador twenty years earlier were being displayed by the Aristide government in Haiti, albeit on a smaller scale but with considerable enthusiasm nonetheless, and one only needed to visit the MPP, an hour up the road, to see them in effect.

Significantly, in his extensive writings on Haiti, Farmer also never even addressed the wholesale slaughter of its merchant class by Dessalines or the century of internecine feuding between independence and the U.S. occupation of the early twentieth century as having in any way further helped impoverish the country. For Farmer, and Aristide's other apologists, it was as if no Haitian history transpired between the departure of the French and the arrival of the Americans in 1915—strange for a man with such a deep experience of Haiti. It was as if then, as now, the Haitians were little more than pawns of the larger world powers, with no ability to analyze and no responsibility for the events that swirled around them. Once, when asked to address a group of intellectuals in the Haitian capital interested in his work, Farmer looked out onto the audience and declaimed *"Kote pep la?"* ("Where are the people?"). One of those in attendance, the eminent and very self-made Haitian sociologist Laennec Hurbon, questioned, "Would he go to Harvard and say 'Where are the people?' I guess he feels safe talking to us like that because we are Haitians." The stark flaw in Farmer's analysis of Haiti seemed to be very similar to that of his close friend Aristide in that he viewed people as either victims, to be helped and protected, or victimizers, to be denounced and, in Aristide's view, killed. When one extended the analysis to the level that Aristide took it—that he himself was, above all, the symbol for all the victimized downtrodden of Haiti and that any attack against him, even if it came from that same disenfranchised sector, represented an assault on all the suffering of Haiti—the leap to a pernicious megalomania was not far off. Of course Farmer had devoted his life to helping, not destroying, the poor of Haiti, but in their writings and public pronouncements I found this urge toward absolutes, with themselves as the great leaders, was something Aristide and Farmer pointedly shared.

I descended from the car and bid my fellow travelers goodbye. Stepping onto the road and up around the clinic's high walls, it was hard not to feel that this spot on the road to Hinche, which I had passed many times before, visually, at least, had a slightly paradisiacal air, surrounded by tropical ferns and trees. I inquired as to where Polo, as Farmer was referred to by the Haitians, was. A young Haitian boy led me down a tree-lined path to a simple, two-room building painted in the bright pastel colors of the Haitian peasant shacks that surrounded it. I knocked on the door and a groggy woman answered in her nightgown. It was Farmer's sister-in-law, the sister of his Haitian wife, Didi, with whom he had a small daughter. Farmer was already at work across the road at the clinic, she explained. I thanked her and said I would go look for him there.

I walked through the expansive grounds of the clinic for a bit, watching the dozens of people arriving from all across the region for treatment. The AIDS clinic at Cange regularly monitored 1,500 HIV patients, and, relying on an extensive network of private donors, Farmer and his group had managed to keep the cost of retroviral treatment down to $1,500 per person per year—an extraordinary accomplishment. The center's ambulatory clinic often saw over three hundred patients daily, its optical clinic over ninety.

As I wandered into the compound's cafeteria, with Haitian and Cuban doctors—part of a public health initiative Fidel Castro had helped spearhead in Haiti—sitting and eating around a common table, Farmer walked in.

"Michael? I'm Polo," he said, shaking my hand.

A tall, slim man with thinning brown hair and glasses perched on his nose, Farmer gave off a curious air in his demeanor as I watched him interact—something between a serious academic and a priest. Obviously highly intelligent and displaying a real bond with the Haitian peasants surrounding him at the clinic, he could not be described as witty, though, a trait that set him apart from the Haitians.

"We're going to make a pass through the children's sick ward," he said. "Why don't you come along?"

I followed him as we entered a large room, which sat somewhat torporously in the Plateau's heat. There were rows of silent toddlers lying on cots, remarkable and disturbing given the volume at which most Haitian life is conducted.

The room was filled with peasants and their afflicted children, and Farmer began attending to a sick, emaciated teenage boy, whose eyes were alive with terror.

"He's in respiratory distress," said Farmer to the other physicians following in his wake, prescribing oxygen and other medicines. The boy was in the throes of multi-drug-resistant tuberculosis.

"We need to keep him breathing."

It was intriguing to watch Farmer work. He didn't just issue orders, but rather instructed attendants and interns on exactly what malady was afflicting a particular patient, why he was suggesting a particular course of treatment, and what the likely outcome would be.

As I stepped out the sick ward's door a moment before Farmer, two old peasant men approached me.

"Doctor, he has a little problem," said one man, motioning to the other. They seemed crestfallen and confused when I explained that I was only a journalist.

As Farmer stepped out and began writing notes on a Panasonic laptop covered with stickers of the Powerpuff girls, an otherwise healthy-looking Haitian man in his 40s who was HIV positive approached him, and Farmer showed and explained the man's CD4 (cluster of differentiation) charts, which measure the number of T-Cells in a blood sample, offering him a crash course on the main way of gauging HIV progress.

Quickly, we ducked into Farmer's office where the walls were adorned with his Harvard diplomas (in addition to his medical degree, Farmer also held a PhD. in anthropology) and a large photo of Aristide smiling with a small child, before beginning a walk across the compound toward a meeting Farmer was chairing about AIDS prevention and awareness strategies. Leaving his office, Farmer showed me a new under-construction respiratory unit, complete with high-power fans to circulate the air better and ultraviolet lights that work to kill the organism that causes tuberculosis. The unit was going to be the first of its kind in Haiti, and was slated to contain ten rooms for the worst TB cases. Cange had already become a national referral center for treatment of the disease. Institutions in the region with which Farmer's hospital in Cange worked with would be sharing in $2 million of the $67 million award secured by Haiti's Minister of Health, Henri-Claude Voltaire, last May from the Global Fund to Fight AIDS, Tuberculosis and Malaria.

"His mother died of AIDS," Farmer said, putting his hand on the shoulder of a small shyly smiling boy named Charlemagne who had run up to greet him as we walked through the compound. "He had TB himself, but we think he'll be fine now."

Another child of ten or eleven ran up to Farmer and, laughing, pulled up his t-shirt to reveal a deep scar running the length of his abdomen. The child had undergone open-heart surgery at Cange, attended to by a team of American and Haitian physicians, after suffering rheumatic heart disease that damaged his heart valves. The operation saved his life.

"Everything's alright now," the boy said, beaming. "Thank God for Dr. Farmer."

We walked to Farmer's meeting, passing gentle peasant men all the way from Thomassin standing outside the hospital discussing the well-being of their loved ones under broad-brimmed peasant hats, one of which was decorated with a jaunty ribbon. Across one stretch of earth inside the hospital grounds, a soccer field spread out, and in contrast to the surrounding hills stripped bare due to clearcutting, Cange seemed to retain a decent amount of forest. I sat and watched as Farmer chaired a meeting between clinic staff, representatives from the Ministry of Health, UNICEF and the PNH about AIDS prevention and awareness strategies. The meeting took place in an empty classroom, with representatives sitting on wooden chairs and brainstorming, taking notes to form a plan of action for continuing to tackle all aspects of the spread of the disease, from women's rights to poverty. During the meeting, a stray dog would wander into the classroom from time to time and lay down and go to sleep. As we emerged, a beautiful teenage girl came up and kissed Farmer on the cheek. The girl, it turned out, was a teenage sex worker who had recently discovered that she is also HIV positive. She had been sexually abused by a policeman at a young age, and the staff at Cange was working diligently to save her from the ravages her sickness could bring. In celebration, she had decided to go to school, for the first time in her life.

"I know my letters," she says, opening her purse to reveal dog-eared copies of books on Kreyol grammar and Haitian history. "Even if I can't read yet."

Later that night, I sat with Farmer in his two-room house. Books lined the walls from floor to ceiling, as did family pictures from grateful patients. A portrait of Farmer's wedding to his wife held a particular place of pride, as did a picture of the doctor's brother, who was a professional wrestler, done up in full battle gear, on the wall. As we spoke, Farmer drank from a jar of *tafia*, while I drank the by-now ubiquitous Prestige.

"So how did you first end up here?" I asked him.

"I was working with immigrant Haitian farm workers in Florida and the Carolinas in 1981," Farmer said, as peasants trudged past the shack in the gathering dark. "I was very shocked that anyone would ever chose to work in such desperate conditions that looked little better than slavery, When I asked the people why, they asked me 'Have you ever been to Haiti?'"

As Farmer spoke, we were joined by a local man in his mid 30s, Ti Jean Gabriel, who worked in the clinic and, it soon became clear, was much of a mind with Farmer on Haitian political matters. Following a discussion of the hospital and the work being done there—ground we had covered often before in our correspondence—we moved to political matters and I asked Farmer whether or not, given the excesses and abuses that Aristide had personally over-seen so far in his second term, he did not have any second thoughts about his unwavering support for such a government.

"That's not the real story," Farmer said forcefully, and launched into a litany of noxious Haitian rulers who had long been supported by the United States, including Francois Duvalier, who had received some $49 million from Wash-ington in 1961 as a reliable bulwark against Communism in the Caribbean. "What about the dictatorships and military governments to which aid flowed unfettered?"

Of course, Farmer was right, but none of that addressed the fact that the Aristide government was killing and exiling political opponents, cynically exploiting poor youths in the urban slum for its armed gangs, eviscerating the judiciary and politicizing the police. Changing tack, I asked Farmer if, given that he articulated many of the same progressive goals as Aristide at the time, if the government of René Préval, which also worked diligently on rural issues such as land-reform and health care—all the while being thwarted by a recalci-trant parliament and Aristide's machinations from Tabarre—was not more wor-thy of his defense than the regime currently in power?

"Around here, people just viewed him as a place-holder," Farmer said con-temptuously.

At this point, Ti Jean, a man whose bearing evidenced a great dignity and who spoke with great vigor and passion, joined the conversation, and he and Farmer both pointed out that the electrical wires littering the ground outside on the main road were evidence of the Aristide government's commitment to the peo-ple, that they were trying to install electricity for the peasants, the destruction of whose homes to construct the Peligre dam never brought a single kilowatt. I asked, though, if it didn't make sense that Aristide, always living proof that crazy didn't mean stupid, had cannily cultivated Farmer's support, stringing electri-cal lines to the villages around Cange for the first time in a measure of his "ded-ication" to "the people" while villages up and down the road and elsewhere on the Plateau Central did without, bullied and threatened by the government's police and gang-affiliated supporters.

"Everything they're saying about Aristide is lies," said Gabriel, a response that I found it hard to refute given its premise that everything I had seen happen over the last two years had not, in fact, happened. "Look at me, I am not getting any money from Aristide and I still support him."

It was late and I was very tired, my Kreyol faltering badly under a long back-and-forth of this nature, as I pointed out specific instances of the Aristide gov-ernment's complicity in retarding the development of and victimizing Haiti's poor and was met with steadfast denials of what I had seen with my own eyes. I asked, though, when a government was confronted with health problems as severe as Haiti's, how could it be justified to spend the money it did have on luxury SUVs, a multimillion-dollar foreign presidential security force and paying street gangs; what did that say about its priorities and good intentions? Could that all be blamed on disinformation and subversion allegedly spread by Haiti's foreign adversaries?

"If the white man doesn't leave us alone, if the white man doesn't let Aristide do the work he needs to do, then we will need to have 1804 all over again; all the foreigners will have to leave the country," said Gabriel, with the air of someone who finally got what he had wanted to say out after all. "They should take their visas away. We will have to do exactly what Dessalines did with the French and remove them from the country once and for all."

"I think he's a very dignified man," said Farmer, gazing at Gabriel placidly—a touch paternally, I thought. "If anyone should be upset by this, it's me, and I'm not."

I found Gabriel one of the most troubling, vexing figures that I met during my entire time in Haiti. Troubling because, on one hand, he seemed to be an ideologue who would brook no argument that Aristide was somehow at least partially responsible for the sorry state Haiti was in, but on the other hand, he was a man of great resolve and pure intentions for his country, a man who had been born into poverty but was working hard and with real dedication to try and improve the life of his community and the lives of his neighbors, in far more a concrete way that any of the politicians in Port-au-Prince ever had. He reminded me markedly of a rural version of the SOPUDEP activists I had come to know in Port-au-Prince, and his continued loyalty seemed to me to be the full measure of Aristide's betrayal.

As for Farmer, I could not explain or credit his willful ignorance of the events that were transpiring around the country with regards to those that he had devoted his life to protecting and helping—that is, the poorest of the poor—and how their victimization en masse by a criminal government served only to exacerbate the problems of instability, poverty, incompetence and corruption that made his presence in Haiti so necessary in the first place. His insistence that his own slice of Haiti—where thousands had benefited from a state-of-the-art hospital run by advocates of the regime, where the Aristide government savvily brought in improvement projects to confirm the existing views of the doctor and his staff—represented the entire country, represented something I found smacking not a little of colonial arrogance, despite its progressive trappings.

Suddenly, the sound of wailing went up from out on the road. Farmer and I looked up from our conversation, startled.

"*Woi! Woi!*" went a woman's voice, followed by a cacophonous shouting. They were not cries of joy.

In rural Haiti, when a person dies, a family member often performs a *rele*, an anguished cry that allows their neighbors to know that there has been a death in the area.

"The only time I ever heard that was when they took Aristide out in 1991 and when they put him back in 1994," Farmer said. "We better investigate."

Getting up from his house, we walked back down the darkened path where we were met by Ti Jean Gabriel, who had bolted up at the first sound of trouble.

"Ti Jean, what's going on?" Farmer asked, clearly concerned.

"A fire, doc."

Three of us descended an embankment down to Route Nationale 3 and there we saw for ourselves.

The home of a squatter woman that had been built across the street from the entrance to the clinic was engulfed in flames. Trying to run back into the house to save her meager belongings, the woman was being restrained by her neighbors, and her cries had brought a small crowd of onlookers, curious to see what was the matter.

Farmer walked over to the woman where she sat weeping by the roadside.

"It will be alright. We will take care of you," he told her. The woman cried, inconsolable. Farmer stood in the road, watching as the orange flames consumed the home and cindery ash floated off, glowing, into the darkened night sky. The consuming violence of the burning reflected itself in his glasses.

"Tell her we will rebuild it," Farmer said, putting his hand on the shoulder of Ti Jean, who was walking over to comfort the women. "Everything will be okay."

DESPITE HIS BEING lauded in the American press for his work among Haiti's poor, Farmer's quasi-Lavalassian approach to no-dissent, zero-option politics was not the only way to go about serving Haiti's beleaguered masses in their fight against infectious diseases, and others, with less of a slavish adherence to Aristide and his regime, had already pointed out alternate paths by which one could commit good works in Haiti.

In a Port-au-Prince clinic on the Carrefour Road just across from the Grand Ravine slum, the Groupe Haitien d'Etude du Sarcome de Kaposi et des Infections Opportunistes (GHESKIO) had worked since 1982 with the primary goal of comprehending the epidemiology of the then-strange new virus—HIV—that was afflicting the country, and in fact was the first location to begin documenting AIDS cases in the developing world in 1983. Under the direction of the Haitian physician Dr. Jean W. Pape—a graduate of Cornell Medical College and recipient of France's Legion d'Honneur for his work—GHESKIO is the second-oldest institution in the world, after the United States Centers for Disease Control, working to stem the spread of HIV/AIDS. Working with support from Dr. Pape's alma mater, the Pan American and World Health Organizations, USAID, UNICEF and the various administrations in Haiti's Ministry of Health for the last twenty-five years, GHESKIO has tended to over 100,000 children in its pediatric rehydration unit since its inception and trained over fourteen thousand healthcare workers. Some 100,000 patients visit annually for HIV/AIDS and tuberculosis testing, and the organization also established a Center for Female Reproductive Health and a program to stem maternal-infant HIV transmission with anti-retroviral drugs. Throughout all of this work, Dr. Pape and the GHESKIO staff maintained a resolutely low personal profile; although they may not be as wedded to Aristide's faux-populist rhetoric and as willing to provide snappy quotes in his defense as Farmer, their contribution to Haitian society—serving the poor alone rather than serving them with one hand and defending their oppressors with the other—often with little fanfare, is no less real than the work that publicity-savvy institutes like Partners in Health have done.

Later, before he cut all contact between us as the result of my continued insistence that he confront the reality of what Aristide's government was doing to the country, Farmer wrote in an email to me that, "All of these lessons you see in these cases here are about inequalities of power, the vast and unfettered power of the rich world, and the sharply constrained power of the poor. Health care and education need to be considered basic rights, because without them, this work is doomed and so are hundreds of millions of lives."

Of course, who could argue with that? But who could also argue that the lives of the patients Farmer had saved were worth any less—or any more—than the lives of the brother of Maxon Moreau, killed by Aristide's gunmen in Cité Soleil, or the high-school students gunned down in Petit Goave, or the students at the École Normale savaged by the police and the chimere, or the three brothers sent to such a criminal death in Carrefour?

Very much like Aristide, Farmer's over-romanticization of the "loyal" poor meant the individuals of modest means who had become educated to the point where they could actually challenge his analysis of their plight, such as Chavannes Jean-Baptiste or the student leaders in the capital or the provinces, were utterly worthless traitors to the cause of lower-class solidarity he had built up in his mind. It was utterly intolerable to him that products of Haiti's peasant heartland such as Jean-Baptiste and Charles Suffrard would dare voice an opinion that challenged his own. The idea that somehow the poor, such as those who lived in Cité Soleil and Hinche, were somehow less worthy as human beings because they dared criticize his hero was a repugnant one to me and one that I could not help but voice my opposition to.

AS THE NEW YEAR BEGAN, Haitians were stunned as gas prices rose 90 percent after the government ended long-standing fuel subsidies, with prices soon averaging $2.224 per gallon. The government said the end in subsidies was due to Haiti's budget deficit, which had reached nearly $80 million, as well as increasing oil prices on the world market—partially caused by a strike aimed at toppling Venezuelan President Hugo Chavez from power that was strangling oil exports from Haiti's main supplier.

By ending its support for artificially low prices, the Aristide government was also responding to demands from the International Monetary Fund that subsidies be halted before the disbursement of $50 million of $500 million in aid withheld since the disputed May 2000 elections. To compound the crisis, the Haitian currency, the gourde, had begun a downward spiral over the previous fall and had soon lost over 50 percent of its value even as inflation had climbed 16 percent during the previous year. The gas crisis, which had also seen spiraling prices for diesel and kerosene, had affected all aspects of daily life in Haiti, with taxis and tap-taps forced to raise their prices on cash-strapped passengers to pay for fuel, and even the fancy French-style pastry shops in Petionville displaying empty shelves due to lack of refrigeration.

At the CATH hall off Rue des Miracles on January 5, where the grime and heat seemed worlds away from the air-conditioned confines of the National Palace, the leaders of the leftist Mouvement Syndical Haitien announced that they were calling a general strike for January 7, saying that "after so many terrible struggles to improve the living conditions of Haitian workers, we have arrived at a decisive crossroads and a choice must be made." Decrying what they characterized as "the impoverishment of the population," the union leaders said that the rise in fuel prices had been the last straw. They called for a "peaceful march" to be held on January 10 and ended the conference with the declaration, *"Lavalas wete men'w nan poch pep la! Nou bouke! Se twop ato!"*

"We are announcing a general strike to force the government to withdraw the price increases we have witnessed since January 1st," said union leader Denise Almeuse, reading a prepared statement.

"We are also asking for all taxis, general transport and private vehicles to stay at home tomorrow between six a.m. and six p.m.," said another union leader, Fleurant Ancelot.

As I walked down Avenue Jean Paul II toward the Champs de Mars on strike day, the streets were eerily deserted in a manner reminiscent of the way they were when I descended along the same route after the December 17 attack on the Palace. Unlike some of the calls for strikes made by members of Haiti's petit-bourgeois political class in previous months, this strike took hold among the poorest sectors of Haitian society, who felt the bite of the price increases the worst. As people in Haiti live on such a thin margin from economic disaster, it takes an extraordinary amount of courage and will for them to take the financial hit of taking a day off from scrambling for money, but, nevertheless, this day they seemed willing to do so. With virtually no cars on the road and all visible businesses closed, I walked unimpeded down to the Champs de Mars, where I came upon one man, glumly trying to sell fried chicken from a kiosk.

"I don't blame them," said the man said about the strikes as he looked out on a street with thin foot traffic. "Gas is too expensive; we can't continue like this."

Some strike supporters took a more aggressive approach; a government Service Plus bus attempting to ply Delmas was attacked with bottles and rocks, and cars were turned back after similar assaults on the Bicentenaire section of Boulevard Harry Truman near the U.S. Embassy.

Had I ventured farther downtown that day, down near where my friend Herby lived near the National Stadium, I would have stumbled across the last act in the short life of Eric Pierre. Pierre, a 27-year-old medical student from Jacmel, was shot and killed while leaving the State University's Faculté de Medicine downtown that morning, with witnesses saying the attackers fled the scene in a car with official TELECO plates and even providing license numbers, one of which turned out to be a car frequently used by René Civil. Pierre, an electrician whose father had died when he was a young boy, had worked hard to put himself through university and hoped to become a physician. On the inside of the textbook Pierre had been carrying at the time of his murder were written the words *"Justice, quand?"*

The same day in Carrefour, seventeen-year-old Johnny Peter Ancy Oleus was shot and killed as he ran to his family home, chased by armed men who were accompanying Madame Cadet, who was the wife of the police commissioner of Jacmel, and who had evidently taken exception to the fact that the Oleus family was depositing their garbage near the front door of a property she owned in the neighborhood. Arrested the same day, Cadet was released within twenty-four hours by State Prosecutor Josue-Pierre Louis, who demurred that he had a "hierarchy to respect" and that he was releasing Cadet on Justice Minister Calixte Delatour's orders. Justice, it seemed, still did not come at all in Aristide's Haiti.

AS DEMONSTRATORS ERECTED barricades made of burning tires in the Decahos section of Gonaives on January 8, CIMO clearing the street shot and killed 25-year-old Saurel Volny. Following the killing, Ephraim Aristide (no relation to the president), the spokesman for a group calling itself the Front Citoyen pour la Liberation d'Haiti, told Radio Metropole that, "We will not be deterred; we'll continue this movement until Aristide goes." The next day in the city, a pedestrian was shot and killed as riot police and Cannibal Army members set upon a group of antigovernment protestors. As Gonaives erupted to the north, at Maxime Seide's funeral at the Sacre Coeur Church in the capital, which had been the scene of so much tragic drama over the years, some mourners wore t-shirts reading "Adieu Big Max," which featured the strapping Seide's smiling face and muscular physique. Michele Montas wept as she comforted Seide's mother, and the deceased man's widow shrieked and collapsed on the floor. In the front row, silent and shunned, Yvon Neptune, Gérard Dubreuil and Jean-Nesley Lucien sat stone-faced as the ceremony passed before them.

At a reception for visiting South African Foreign Minister Nkosazana Dlamini-Zuma on January 9, Aristide again laid the blame for the unrest that had roiled the country on the freeze on foreign aid, stating, rather obviously, that "if aid to the country would be unblocked, every Haitian will benefit. . . .

The opposition has a responsibility to help unblock the country and unfreeze the money." The same day, the labor unions, emboldened by their success of January 7, announced that they were going to conduct a massive march on the National Palace from the Portail Leogane bus terminal, linking up with an opposition march beginning in Christ Roi.

"According to the constitution," Aristide said when asked about the potential for violence at Friday's marches, "everyone is allowed to demonstrate."

"We will march to show solidarity with the worker's of the entire country, and we will mobilize together," said Evans Paul, when I reached him on the phone.

AS IT TURNED OUT, the march that promised to give the unions a chance to flex their muscles on January 10 never transpired. From early on that morning, the Portail Leogane bus terminal where the unions were to begin was filled with chanting, aggressive chimere, many high on marijuana and crack and drunk on *tafia* from the night before, dancing drunken jigs with shadows only they could see. The opposition march was left to take up the slack, and so I watched as Himmler Rebu, his chest thrust arrogantly forward, led about two hundred people down from the KID offices on Bourdon, and as they passed without incident down Lalue, though Evans Paul himself was conspicuously absent. The marchers passed through Champs de Mars under heavy police protection, including the everpresent Hermione Leonard, who walked alongside the marchers in concert with machine-gun carrying, hulking CIMO. As the marchers turned toward the National Palace in front of the Rex Theater, a contingent of Aristide supporters swept out of nowhere to hang over the fences separating the park from the street, shouting insults and invective. The crowd, liberally dosed with a contingent of Rebu's ex-FADH buddies, was not intimidated, and kept marching right along, giving as good as they got. Several blocks later, a storm of bottles and rocks descended on the marchers, with many hurling them back at their attackers. Fistfights broke out and gunfire soon erupted— from where originally no one was sure. After Radio Magik Stereo FM reporter Rosny Mathieu fell, his head gashed open by a rock, police began firing in the air and along the ground and lobbing tear-gas canisters at both the demonstrators and the chimere. Aristide's helicopter, carrying extra CIMO to the National Palace, swept low over the city, frightening residents even more, and at one point I found myself pushed along the high lip of a ravine of sewage by a group of people trying to escape the fighting. As the situation degenerated into something of a police riot, hulking PNH officers grabbed the *rigwaz* out of the chimere's hands and beat them with them, sending the often frail teenagers from the slums running for cover. Demonstrators and chimere dragged the injured among their number into Haiti's General Hospital, the latter threatening staff with automatic weapons and demanding medical attention. Echoing gunfire spread panic throughout the facility, chaotic on the calmest of days. At least one patient died from heart failure due to the stress and the hospital's medical staff immediately went on strike, demanding that the government take measures to protect them and arrest those who threatened them.

Livid at being shown up by the police, René Civil went on the radio. "They attacked us, they injured many of us; the police, the government bears responsibility for this!" he fumed, though he soon calmed down and was brought back into the fold.

Addressing the year's opening session of Haiti's contested parliament a few days later, Senate President Fourel Celestin, momentarily sober, addressed the chamber and spoke of Haiti's "fragile democracy," pledging that "we will find a solution to this crisis," before going on to denounce "terrorist demonstration in Cap Haitien, Petiti Goave and other cities."

Aristide sat, as was his habit, impassive with his hands clasped and fingers meeting in a steeple at his lips throughout the address before telling lawmakers that he expected to resolve the two-year-old electoral impasse by holding new elections, and he asked members of Haiti's political opposition to take part.

"We intend to have new elections in the first half of 2003, and we ask the opposition to participate," Aristide said, addressing the opening session of Haiti's contested parliament.

In what he characterized as a concession to the opposition, Aristide again noted that seven senators elected in the disputed elections had resigned and that two-thirds of the Chamber of Deputies, the parliament's lower body, had agreed to have their terms reduced by two years.

On January 14, though, Haitian judicial authorities issued an arrest warrant for one of those opposition leaders, Himmler Rebu, charging that he had drawn a firearm and shot Lavalas partisan Celange Antoine during the melee that erupted at the January 10 march. Rebu, who had been surrounded by Haitian police and reporters—myself included—during the majority of the demonstration, denied the charges.

"The government is trying to neutralize me," he said. "I call on the opposition to react strongly to these maneuvers."

The day following the announcement of the indictment, men who said they represented groups of demobilized Haitian soldiers visited radio stations around the capital to read a statement in support of Rebu.

"We warn the Aristide government not to arrest Colonel Rebu, because he is a citizen and has the right to participate in the political process," the statement said in part.

It was eventually revealed that Celange Antoine, the Lavalas militant claiming that Rebu had shot him in the foot, had in fact never actually been shot, but had been treated for a foot injury at the General Hospital several days before the January 10 melee. Nevertheless, Rebu lowered his profile considerably in the coming months.

ON THE NIGHT of the announcement of the arrest warrant against Rebu, I was in a taxicab talking with the driver, cruising down Rue Capois and looking out the open window at the glow of kerosene lamps.

"Things are getting expensive, huh?" I asked.

"Oh man, you don't know how expensive!" he said laughing.

"Are you going to strike tomorrow?"

"I don't think so. We did it last week, you know, but I need money, for my wife and my kids."

"Were you going to march?"

"You know, I drove down there on Friday, just to see what was happening. The chimere were all there and they surrounded my car. They were carrying Aristide posters and yelling 'Give us your money! Give us your money!' I told them that I had none, that I was just a poor chauffeur, so they started banging on the hood of my car and threatening to smash the windows. I got out of there fast."

"Why do you think Aristide spends so much money on the chimere?"

"To scare us. It's the same reason he sends the chimere from Grand Ravine over to terrorize the people in Carrefour and Martissant, and kidnap those kids. He wants to terrify people so they don't strike. But we're beyond that now, and this behavior can't continue."

ON JANUARY 14, hundreds of students from the Faculté de Medicine blocked streets in the capital and marched to protest the killing of Eric Pierre. Aristide, for his part, seemed unmoved, and held a farcical, chaotic book-signing of his new book *Shalom*, at the National Library in Port-au-Prince on January 17. About a hundred chimere were brought in for the event, waving copies of the book that many of them couldn't read and shouting *"Aristide a vie!"* sending frightened scholars and schoolchildren scurrying around machine gun-toting CIMO and white Steele Foundation bodyguards to the relative tranquility of the street. Aristide, in a tan suit, seemed well pleased with the event, and smiled broadly as he signed books for the young men shouting his name.

A NEW ENTITY ON the Haitian political scene, albeit one with many familiar faces in it, the Group of 184 (*san katreven kat* to the Haitians) portrayed itself as a middle ground between Haiti's warring political parties, asking them to eschew violence and for Aristide to reform his government before Haiti's crisis grew even graver. But in fact, many of the groups linked with it (its name referred to the 184 organizations it claimed as members) were cut from much the same well-to-do cloth as the Initiative de la Societé Civile group had been two years earlier. The Initiative had never entirely gone away, though, and the European Commission of the European Union had contributed 773,000 Euros (around US $890,374) to the Initiative help finance a human rights and democracy project between December 2001 and December 2003.[9] Though much would be made of this by Aristide's supporters, it was hardly an extraordinary sum when one considers that the Aristide government spent about US $1,732,785 in declared expenses on lobbyists over roughly the same time period. The Initiative's member bodies included the Fondation Nouvelle Haiti, which counted among its leading lights the Haitian businessmen Andy Apaid and Charles Baker, and the money was directed to be disbursed to some fourteen other human rights and civic organizations in Haiti, including Suzy Castor's CRESFED (whose archives had been torched by the chimere on December 17 2001) and Jean-Claude Bajeux's Centre Oecumenique des Droits Humains. The cash flow seemed to infuse a new sense of purpose among the organizers, prompting them, for the first time, to reach out to peasant groups such as the MPP, and student and union groups, who had all born the brunt of the Aristide government's thuggery and incompetence but had as yet been ignored by Haiti's political class. This time, perhaps not surprisingly given the country's state, it worked. In addition to such expected elite private-sector organizations like the Association des Industries d'Haiti (ADIH) and the Association Nationale des Distributeurs de Produits Pétroliers (ANADIPP), the group also succeeded in recruiting into its ranks the powerful CATH union, the MPNKP and MPP peasant unions, the Fanm Yo La feminist organization and such intellectual luminaries as the director Raoul Peck (who had served as René Préval's Minister of Culture) and the sociologist Laennec Hurbon. The group also announced that they would be touring Haiti in the coming months with a Caravane de l'Espoir (Caravan of Hope) to forge "a new social contract" that would "get rid of historical hindrances that have kept the Haitian people from making its national unity, and thus, have impeded the development of our country."

When the Group of 184 held its first large-scale press event in a crowded conference room at the capital's Hotel El Rancho on January 20, I showed up curious to see what this make-up would look like in person. At a long conference table covered with microphones and tape recorders, sat, among others, Maurice Lafortune, the head of the Chamber of Commerce and Industry of Haiti (CCIH); Pierre Emile Rouzier representing the Centre pour la Libre Entreprise et la Démocratie (CLED), Societé Civile head Rosny Desroches; Frankel Jeanrisca of the MPNKP and Marie Denise Saint-Clair Almeus representing CATH. Also in attendance to lend their support, I saw Jean-Claude Bajeux, Hans Tippenhauer, who was an economic advisor at the consulting firm Groupe Croissance and scion of one of Haiti's most respected families, and the novelist Gary Victor, who said he was there to represent the cultural sector. Interestingly, the majority of the people seated behind the speakers' tables in support were black, representing the black middle class that Aristide had succeeded in alienating as much if not more than any other group in the country. The group began its conference by singing "La Dessalinienne," hands over their hearts, and then observed a moment of silence "for all those who have fallen in the struggle."

Then, with Desroches taking the lead in speaking, those seated at the table took turns lambasting what they charged was "this climate of insecurity, politicization of the police force, the creation of armed bands that attack the population when they try to exercise their legitimate rights," and called on Aristide to disarm the street gangs in the government's employ, renounce hate speech, respect press freedom, end impunity, stem corruption and, finally, to attend to the catastrophic economic condition of the country. The group then announced a "new social contract with citizens in all nine departments and warned that "the elements don't exist for a fair, transparent and legitimate election in the country."

"Faced with our country's catastrophic situation, our 184 organization, representing all sectors of Haitian society, call a general strike in all nine departments for Friday, January 24," said Rouzier, reading from a written statement, to shout of "*nou bouke*" from those assembled behind. Desroches was quick to point out, however, that though the opposition to Venezuela's leftist president Hugo Chavez was simultaneously launching a series of strikes aiming at driving him from power, the Group of 184 was not as of yet asking for Aristide's resignation, but rather demanding that he ameliorate the situation in Haiti before it got any further out of control.

Daniel Morel, along with Agence France-Presse's Thony Belizaire, the dean of the local press-corps photographers, showed up to snap a few quick pictures of those seated around the table.

"They can't do anything about Aristide yet," he said, looking down at me (Daniel stood well over six feet tall) and running a hand through his wooly gray beard. "Except make life difficult. But he's used to that."

AT THE JANUARY 21 funeral for Eric Pierre, several thousand mourners— including Evans Paul and former President Leslie Manigat—weeping, waving banners and calling for René Civil's arrest paid tribute to Pierre's wreath-draped coffin at the state university's medical faculty. Civil, speaking on Radio Kiskeya, again denied the charge that he was responsible for Pierre's death.

"These charges are baseless invention designed to destroy me," Civil said. "They are complete fabrications and I plan to contact my lawyer to defend myself."

Still, Pierre's funeral was interrupted several times by groups of students calling for Civil's arrest and several students carried signs referring to the crime.

"The license number of the criminal's car is 0254," read one sign.

"When will we have justice?" asked another.

It was not a good time to run afoul of the authorities. When Judge Marcel Jean, the investigating judge in charge of the Amiot Metayer case in Gonaives, attempted to board a plane to the United States on January 22, he discovered that his name was on a list of those banned from leaving the country by Interior Minister Jocelerme Privert. Jean's passport was seized, and he was denied the right to leave the country. Many viewed the move as an attempt to force Jean to "legalize" Metayer's jailbreak of August 2 the previous year. Eventually, Jean slipped out of the country and went into exile.

That same day, the three murdered Carrefour brothers were finally laid to rest. I watched from a packed congregation at the capital's Christ Roi church as Father Max Dominique thundered against the slaughterhouse the country had become.

"These beautiful children were alive! No to impunity! No to insecurity! We demand justice!" he said to the applause of the assembled crowd.

A young girl of about fifteen looked at me and sadly shook her head. The look on the faces of those around her, including a handsome, graying middle-aged man in a suit, was one of heartbreak.

With the three simple wooden coffins placed in hearses by maroon-robed altar boys, white-clad mourners collapsed, wailing with grief, into the cars' paths. The funeral had been delayed for several weeks when officials refused to grant the NCHR human rights group the authorization to have autopsies performed on the brothers.

"This was an execution," said NCHR's director, Pierre Esperance, as we surveyed the scene together. "We're demanding the arrest of the police who took part in this."

A clutch of young men had been watching the service from outside the church grounds, and I thought I recognized one or two of them from pro-government demonstrations around the town. I walked up to them, introduced myself, and asked them what they thought.

"This government is garbage, nothing but murderers and thieves," said one dreadlocked man, not bothering to uncross his arms as he surveyed the scene.

We walked along slowly as the hearses and the hundreds of mourners following them snaked through the capital, across the expanse of Champs de Mars and to the very gates of the National Palace.

"Murderer!" they shouted, loud enough that Aristide could hear them inside. "We're finished with you!"

Though a PNH report had characterized the killing as "a crime of passion," it had nevertheless acknowledged the likelihood of police involvement and recommended the arrest of two officers. The officers were not taken into custody, with local police claiming they had fled. The police chief of the Carrefour commissariat was reassigned. To date, no one has been tried for the crime.

ALL THROUGH JANUARY, in the depths of the night, we would hear the wild dogs barking, louder than ever before, fighting and wilding away in the cool dark and the lightless ravines outside our doors. Many said that they were living off bodies that the Lavalas gangs were dumping in the ravines, and that the increase in number and ferocity of the canines was a measure of how much new sustenance the regime, which many now thought was approaching its death throes, was providing them.

THE GROUP OF 184'S strike to protest what they said was Aristide's failure to rein in his gunmen, take measures to address the tanking economy and create a secure climate for elections, was, as might have been expected, mainly divided along class lines. Large businesses closed in Port-au-Prince and Cap Haitien, and traffic in the capital was noticeably light as some disgruntled taxi and tap-tap drivers stayed home, but the market women were out as usual along Avenue Jean Paul II, and the vendors still lined the Champs de Mars.

All in all, the government was nonplussed. When I called to get his reaction, Lavalas spokesman Jonas Petit said, "The strike is not made with the interest of the population in mind. The majority of the population in this country is suffering because of destabilization, and they don't have money to fly away on an airplane, or buy a house abroad." An odd comment, I thought, from someone representing a government whose officials regularly did just that.

In the midst of all this, a four-man congressional delegation from the United States arrived in Haiti, promoting the Haitian Economic Recovery Opportunity (HERO) act and schmoozing with Haiti's right-wing business leaders, though also meeting with Aristide. Republican Senator Mike DeWine of Ohio, Democratic Senators Richard Durbin of Illinois and Bill Nelson of Florida and Democratic Congressman Kendrick Meek of Florida strolled through the neat, quiet aisles of the Caribbean Apparel Manufacturing Plant in Port-au-Prince's industrial park with Ambassador Curran, touting that the time was right to bring more low-wage factory jobs to Haiti.

"We wanted to see first-hand the opportunity the bill my colleagues and I are presenting will provide for the American people and also the Haitian people," said DeWine as I watched him tour the plant. He didn't make a big deal of it at the time, but when the delegation had gone to visit a hospital in the Artibonite Valley earlier in the day, locals spying the fifteen-car convoy as it passed Archaie promptly cut down several trees and laid them across the road in order stop the group on its way back, whether to force them to listen to their litany of problems or to collect "tolls" wasn't clear. A call by the senators' advance security solved things, though, and soon CIMO arrived to clear the obstruction forthwith.

Asked about the suspension of aid later at the apparel plant, DeWine said that not providing direct aid to the Aristide government was a policy that would continue "as long as this political impasse exists in Haiti today."

As the delegation got back into their heavily-guarded motorcade, the last ribbons of daylight sinking in scarlet away into Port-au-Prince's bay, I spoke with an aged and frail night watchmen to one of the neighboring factories, watching the headlights of the SUV's spring to life as the politicians prepared to leave.

"We are suffering here and there is no one to help us," the man said. "This is a good job, but I work seven days a week and I can barely feed my family because gas is so expensive, rice is so expensive."

He folded his arms, turned up his transistor radio playing compas and watched the cars pull away.

ON JANUARY 28, two former Haitian army colonels, Carl Dorelien and Herbert Valmond, were flown back to Haiti on a U.S. government aircraft. The pair, convicted in absentia in 2000 for their alleged role in the 1994 Raboteau massacre, were then immediately transferred to the National Penitentiary. Having lived in Florida since the mid-1990s, Dorelien had bought one of two winning tickets in a 1997 Florida State lottery that netted him half of a $6.3 million jackpot.

The government said they would have the right to a new trial with no presumption of guilt stemming from their previous convictions, but—given the fate of government opponents like Prosper Avril, still rotting in jail without trial over a year after being imprisoned, and Rosemond Jean—few took that promise seriously.

I WAS TRYING to get to the Canadian ambassador's house; my rental car snaking through a *rara* group several hundred strong marching past the Oloffson, with trumpets, drums and flags all at work marching down toward Place Jeremie, sounding for all the world like a New Orleans marching band. As I drove beyond them I passed a little boy walking down Lalue, sucking on an orange peel for sustenance and wearing a t-shirt that read "Jesus Will Save Me." Passing the dead-end corner near the Place Saint Pierre in Petionville where the bourgeois kids would go to score their coke, I crossed the square heading toward the Ambassador's residence, where a soiree was going to be held in honor of a departing Canadian diplomatic delegation. Entering the elegant, modernist structure, I found Evans Paul, Jonas Petit, Leslie Voltaire, Lionel Delatour and Léopold Bérlanger all present, drinking champagne, eating finger sandwiches and eyeing one another warily. Despite the civil tone at the reception, the government and those opposed to it were still at one another's throats in the media, which made the whole scene somewhat surreal.

"Yes, they're all very civilized aren't they?" said one Haitian employee of the embassy to me, dripping contempt, as she observed the utterly insincere pleasantries the men engaged in.

NAWOON MARCELLUS, the Lavalas deputy from Grande Rivière du Nord and one of the most prominent members of Haiti's burgeoning Muslim community, had begun an ironic campaign against the country's Arab merchants, declaring that they were "foreigners" and that the Ministry of Interior should haul them in for questioning to make sure "their papers were is order," a call which

Prime Minister Neptune enthusiastically echoed. Most dismissed it as a transparent attempt to harass the "Syrians" (as the Arabs were referred to regardless of national lineage) for participating in the general strikes against the Aristide government. Speaking to Radio Metropole and asked about his thoughts on the possibility of elections, Micha Gaillard said, "In the days of Duvalier it was impossible to have a good election with the Tontons Macoutes; during the coup d'etat, it was impossible to have a good election with FRAPH and the attachés. Today it is impossible to have a good election and form an electoral council with the chimere—the Cannibal Army, Domi Nan Bwa—running the streets."

As the atmosphere in Port-au-Prince continued to disintegrate, with the value of the gourde continuing to tumble as the cost of living began to climb ever higher, I began spending more and more time at a beach house near Jacmel that I was co-renting with the French photographer. Attempting to cleanse myself of the mental images of strikes, angry faces and frightened children, I would wake early in the morning to swim in the Caribbean, splashing feet away from my door, and spend my days reading histories of Haiti in a hammock and writing at a sturdy wooden table on the porch. At night, often, I would drive into Jacmel town for dinner and conversation at the home of the erudite European diplomat and filmmaker, and then walk alone through the bustling, busy streets of the once-grand town. Driving back to the beach late at night, I would cruise down deserted roads ringed by banana trees silhouetted in the moon, with gatherings of country people every few miles standing crowded around the kerosene glow of *ti machann*s frying up bananas and pork. Occasionally, the lights of boats would glitter just offshore.

ON JANUARY 31 the U.S. government released a statement saying that Haiti—along with Guatemala and Myanmar—had taken insufficient actions to stem drug trafficking in the past year. It was the second time Haiti had been so designated in as many years, and the United States described the country as a "path of least resistance" for narcotraffickers due to weak democratic institutions, corrupt officials and a fledgling police force. Since Aristide's return in 1994, the volume of cocaine passing through Haiti had nearly tripled, from 5 percent of the annual total imported into the United States to almost 15 percent.

That same week, *Le Nouvelliste* ran a list of officials whose visas had been allegedly revoked by the United States for suspected involvement in drug trafficking. The list included Aristide's chimere liaison in the PNH Hermione Leonard, Leonard's husband Rudy Therassan (head of the PNH's Brigade d'Intervention Rapide unit), director of the Administration Penitentiaire Nationale Clifford Larose, Aristide's Security Chief Oriel Jean, director of the National Palace motor pool Anthony Nazaire and Nawoon Marcellus. One of the defining legacies of his administration, the cocaine trade had exploded in Haiti under Aristide, and its trail led directly to the National Palace.

Beginning in 2001 and continuing throughout the next two years, Oriel Jean had been accepting large amounts of money and cocaine from Columbian drug traffickers based in the cities of Medellin and Barranquilla in exchange for allowing cocaine shipments to move through Haiti; feeling comfortable to be brazen enough, said a senior U.S. official familiar with the workings of the drug trade in Haiti, to pick up cash and cocaine in official National Palace cars, helpfully supplied by Nazaire. Haitian bank records also show that at the same time, Jean was the recipient of hundreds of thousands of dollars in unexplained payments from the General Administration of the National Palace, whose budget was under the direct discretion of the office of the President of the Republic, that went far beyond his salary as security chief there, totaling over $756,333 between May and December of 2001 alone.[10]

At the same time, PNH director general Jean-Nesley Lucien and PNH anti-drug chief Evintz Brillant had entered into business with Carlos Ovalle, a Colombian drug trafficker known as "Papi," who had moved to Haiti in the early 1990s and was married to a Haitian citizen. The relationship had begun in earnest after Lucien and Brillant seized $450,000 of Ovalle's drug profits at Port-au-Prince's airport in the summer of 2002. After taking $150,000 for themselves, the two police commanders had returned $300,000 to the Colombian and agreed to facilitate further movements of drugs and profits through the airport. Lucien then began tipping off drug traffickers when DEA agents became aware of shipments and routes were compromised.

For many years Aristide himself had been a close friend of Beaudoin "Jacques" Ketant, a Haitian drug trafficker and business partner of Ovalle's who had fled arrest in the United States in 1996 disguised as a woman on a Port-au-Prince-bound flight. Ketant, whom DEA officials said had first gotten involved in the drug trade with former Port-au-Prince Police Chief Michel Francois in the early 1990s, was indicted by a South Florida federal grand jury in 1997 on drug charges. Since returning to Haiti, he had continued with his drug business, acting as the chief Haiti contact for the Medellin, Cali and Norte del Valle cocaine cartels and managing an expansive operation that smuggled drugs into the United States in the hulls of Haitian ships plying the Florida Keys and Miami River, along with suitcases on international flights and "mules" who would ingest condoms filled with the drug. In 2001, Ketant had thrown a lavish christening party for Aristide's daughter Christine, at which the entire top command of the PNH, a roomful of Lavalas officials and Aristide himself were present, and Aristide pronounced Ketant his child's godfather. By early 2002, Ketant had amassed a fortune worth more than $15 million, including a luxury mansion in Port-au-Prince, a fleet of cars, rare art and scores of bank accounts and front businesses. According to those familiar with the arrangement, the police responsible for protecting the movement of Ketant's cocaine in and out of Haiti during Aristide's second term of office were none other than Rudy Therassan and Hermione Leonard, two of Aristide's closest disciples in the PNH.

Rumors about Aristide's alleged involvement in the drug trade had swirled from sources of varying levels of credibility stretching back to his days as a priest at Saint Jean Bosco, with murmurs that Aristide's public works initiatives such as the Lafanmi Selavi orphanage were partially financed through drug profits that the maverick priest had procured in cooperation with the Colombian cartels and some of his militant supporters along the capital's docks. Haiti's south coast, from which Aristide hailed, had, by the time of his return to office in 2001, become Haiti's virtual Cocaine Alley, with speedboats and runner ships depositing near-nightly loads of cocaine delivered from Colombia's Caribbean coast, a mere 380 miles away. While it could be theoretically possible that the entire top command of the PNH and his chiefs of security were deeply and flagrantly involved in drug trafficking and Aristide did not know about it, given Aristide's history with Ketant and, especially, the top-down micromanaging style of how he oversaw the operation of the Haitian government, that hypothesis would seem unlikely in the extreme. Someone had thrown open the doors of Haiti's young police force to the drug trade, and, by this point, the police force that Haitians had hoped so deeply would replace the brutal and corrupt army had become little more than the biggest chimere gang in the country.

Nor was the seductive influence of cocaine money limited to the police. On January 23, the judge Pierre Josiard Agnant authorized the release of Jean Salim "Johnny" Batrony, a drug trafficker from Jacmel who for years had allegedly been paying protection money to Fourel Celestin, Haiti's Senate president, to recruit and buy off police to help with his drug pick-ups from Colombia near the southern town, while Celestin also took a share of the profits. When Batrony stopped paying Celestin in a fit of pique, affidavits filed in U.S. District Court in Florida would later allege, Celestin told the local police to pick Batrony up, which they did in 2002, finding 58 kilograms of cocaine in his possession in the process. Batrony was down but not yet out, though, and after his release in the early weeks of 2003, many would charge that he had paid Judge Agnant some $350,000 in exchange for his freedom, a charge the U.S. took seriously enough to revoke Agnant's travel visa. Haiti's Justice Ministry, ever mindful of the interests of elected officials of the ruling party, suspended Agnant, but, in a low point for Haitian jurisprudence, a general strike by the other justices in Haiti's court system obtained his reinstatement shortly thereafter.

Following the visa announcement, some of those mentioned, including Clifford Larose, held news conferences confirming the revocation of their visas but denying their involvement in the drug trade. Nawoon Marcellus charged that the revocation of his visa was based on religious rather than criminal grounds.

"This is religious persecution," Marcellus, the Muslim, said at a press conference, citing by name, rather jarringly for me, an article I had written where he was mentioned as an example of the growth of the faith in the country. "They took my visa not because I am a drug trafficker, but because I am a Muslim."

A PHOTO OF ARISTIDE that ran in *Le Nouvelliste* on February 5 under the headline *"Aristide rejette la responsibilite sur les Etats Unis d'Amerique"* had him looking excessively predatory, eyes narrowed to slits behind gold-framed glasses and an expensive suit.

"He looks like the devil, doesn't he?" said a Haitian friend of mine—a longtime Aristide supporter from Les Cayes who had moved to the capital a decade ago—when he saw the paper laying on my coffee table. The same week, the paper carried the story of Ronald Cadet, a university student involved in the protest movement who had been living in semi-hiding since November 2002, and who was shot and killed by unknown assailants in the capital at the beginning of the month—a crime that was never solved. Faring slightly better in terms of actually living through his encounter with government hit men, the Reverend Manes Blanc, the director of Radio Shekina in Saint Marc, was shot twice in the stomach on February 4 by assailants who shouted pro-Lavalas slogans as they fired on him. Blanc survived.

Aristide had taken exception to the charge that his country had become a haven for drug traffickers and charged that the recent suspension of U.S. travel visas was not based on any concrete evidence.

"Haiti is not guilty of these charges. We are a poor country and we feel victimized by these actions," Aristide told reporters after meeting David Lee, chief of the OAS special mission to Haiti. "The U.S. Coast Guard patrolling our waters sees boat people, but they never see boats transporting drugs."

WHEN I VISITED Cité Soleil in early February, the mood was much calmer than it had been in the fall. Virtually the entire neighborhood was under the control of three pro-Lavalas groups and the hostile gang leaders were either dead or had been driven into exile in La Saline or other neighborhoods. The gangs were being paid well by the government for the work they were doing, and when I went down to visit them, several soldiers in Boston and Soleil 19 proudly showed me IDs the government had given them for no-show jobs at CAMEP, as the state water company was known, and at APN, the capital's port. Some of them said that they would have been happy to put down their weapons and continue to work at these jobs, but Aristide's representatives had informed them that there were no real jobs to give them. So they returned to the slum and awaited their next marching orders.

The Cité Soleil boys and the other chimere were very much in evidence at the rally that Aristide held—rather pointedly—at the Parc Industriel to celebrate his second year in office on February 7. James and I arrived together, and, as we disgorged ourselves from a public taxi, noted So Anne Auguste arriving in an official car. I laughed that leading the chimere reaps much richer rewards than working for Reuters, at least in the short term.

Thousands of people had crowded into the industrial park, which housed the factories of some of Aristide's bitterest enemies. Strolling the perimeter of a building near where he was speaking, I could hear Aristide's distinctive sing-song voice amplified over speakers. He announced that he was increasing the minimum wage to 70 gourdes a day, which at Haiti's ever-declining exchange rate measured out at a little over $1.50. He was also, much to my surprise, announcing the formation of a new electoral council.

"The electoral council is formed, and I call on you to applaud everyone, every person, every institution, every political party who has taken part in this. We expect all parties will react positively," Aristide told the overflow crowd in the factory hall. Scowling CIMOs were patrolling the park's perimeter as he spoke, and the presidential helicopter swooped overhead. Later, heading home, I heard Aristide's statement confirmed by an official communiqué signed by Aristide and Yvon Neptune sent to local media outlets.

As Aristide spoke, I saw a clutch of thin, dignified Haitian women standing in simple, worn dresses, straining to hear every word. I went toward them to speak but, just as I reached them, a group of about half a dozen chimere, drunk on *tafia* and staggering, interrupted me and began shouting *"Ariside a vie."* The women who had been walking toward me to chat, looked frightened of the chimere and backed away into a corner. With the group of drunken teenagers braying at my heels, I walked away and began a joking conversation with a group of blue-outfitted schoolgirls who had the day off for the occasion, with them asking me, "What is your name, *blan*?" before collapsing into giggles. As I spoke, I felt a tug on my shoulder and, turning around, saw the group of women, about half a dozen in all, who had followed me once the chimere had gone in to listen to Aristide.

I turned to them and we spoke in a corner of the park as Aristide's voice floated, melodious, over the gathering. From one corner of the compound, we could hear a *rara* band playing.

"We've come to see what President Aristide can do about our situation, if he can help us," said Martine Jean, a market vendor from La Plaine. She said she was thirty-three but looked much older, and as she spoke she held a small Haitian flag. The other women also carried flags, and some, small pictures of Aristide. "My husband has died and I cannot afford to send my boy to school. Life here is very hard."

After hailing another cab home that day, I descended long before I had arrived at my house, just at the shell of Port-au-Prince's old cathedral, burned by Aristide's supporters after Roger Lafontant's failed 1991 coup attempts. I walked over toward the newer, massive cathedral that towered above the poor houses spreading over the hills on either side of it and saw supplicants in white hats and blue robes, clutching Bibles and purple prayer beads, praying in the hot sun beneath a life-sized statue of Jesus nailed to the cross, suffering, as Haiti suffered, praying for salvation.

"Jesus, help me!"

"Jesus, can you hear me?"

They cried.

As I watched them, a beautiful young girl in a white dress and with a bandanna wrapped around her head turned and looked at me, giving one of those penetrating stares Haitians sometimes give foreigners. The white of the eye, the dark retinas burning into you from the dark pallor of the skin.

"I can't get no money, I can't get no job," said Gabriel Jean, a young man dressed in a dark suit in the roiling sun and walking up the steep hill toward the cathedral with his young son. "I went to school in the Bahamas and learned English, but now you can't get nothing in Haiti. If we could just get some jobs, this would be a lovely country."

Of course, no electoral council had been formed. Aristide had simply lied, again, and hoped that the parties he was negotiating with to form the body would not call his bluff. Instead of nine names—including representation for religious, judicial, private sector, human rights and opposition groups—the council put forth listed only seven with a vow that the other two representatives—from the Democratic Convergence and another from an unaligned political opposition group—would be named shortly.

"This is a decree that does not respect the rule of law," said Micha Gaillard when I spoke with him that night. "This move will fail as acceptable conditions for elections do not exist and the political parties, the civil society and the churches will not participate in a masquerade."

The council members themselves backed him up.

"At our last meeting, the president advised us that he would create the electoral council," Maurice Lafortune told Radio Metropole. "But our position is still the same, until the government creates a climate of security for elections, we will tell our members not to participate."

Evidently piqued that the council members wouldn't play ball, when TNH ran footage of the rally at the Parc Industriel that same evening, the camera denounced "economic coup d'etats" while panning over the white and brown faces of the industrialists as they watched Aristide deliver his address from the steps of their factories.

Deliverance, it appeared, would not be arriving yet.

ON FEBRUARY 14, PNH Inspector General Harvel Jean-Baptiste announced that Evintz Brillant, the director of the police department's anti-drug-trafficking brigade, had been arrested along with five other policeman. Though specifically charged with having overseen the landing of a Colombian airplane laden with nearly 2,000 pounds of cocaine on the capital's crime-ridden Route Neuf by setting up roadblocks and providing armed security for the delivery on February 6, Brillant had long been under investigation by DEA agents from the United States. The plane, it turned out, was in the employ of none other than the drug lord Jacques Ketant.

In most countries, this alone would have been top-billed news, but on this particular day, in what many viewed as a not-coincidental development, Hector Ketant, Jacques Ketant's brother, was dragged off a busy Petionville street with his business partner, Herman Charles, by masked men wearing t-shirts and jackets bearing police Brigade d'Intervention Rapide (BRI) insignias—the unit under the command of Hermione Leonard's husband, Rudy Therassan. Taken to the home of a woman they knew in the nearby Peguyville district, the men were executed in a hail of automatic weapons fire in the back yard.

A critical battle between gangs inside of the police fighting for control of the narcotics trade was being waged under the cover of fighting drugs. The police were awash with rumors. The Colombian cartels and the Ketants were said to have first reached out to Therassan and his wife Hermione Leonard, asking her to ensure their plane's safe landing as they had done before, but Evintz Brillant agreed to do it for less money. Therassan and Leonard and the National Palace itself were said to have reacted in a fury at this breech of protocol, which is why Therassan was ordered to kill Ketant's brother. When police spokesman Jean-Dady Simeon left the country that same week, it was said he did so because two men in his personal security detail were involved in the landing of the fabled drug plane and he feared for his safety. Adding to the tumult, several CIMO had threatened to rebel when they thought they were being transferred to Pernal so they could be killed, and the ex-military blamed. Aristide had visited them at the police academy on Saturday, it was said, and given them money to calm their fears.

One day later, Harvel Jean-Baptiste, who appeared to be waging a lone, nearly suicidal war against the drug trafficking that had taken hold like a cancer at the heart of the PNH, arrested four police officers closely connected with Jean-Nesley Lucien under suspicion of involvement in the drug trade. A day later, an irate Lucien arrived at the Cafeteria police commissariat where the men were being held in downtown Port-au-Prince with a group of armed policeman and forced officers to release them. Lucien, who lived in Tabarre near his patron Aristide and was said to have spread money and largess around to the criminal OPs in the area, was not about to back down and had won this confrontation with Haiti's police inspector general. Several days later, the radio announced that the four freed policeman had left the country on a plane bound for the United States. As the police scandal broke, news reached the street that Ronald Camille, once one of the Lavalas party's most valued gunmen and chimere leaders, had died of AIDS in the Azil Francais Hospital. He had been in jail nearly a year.

LATE THAT NIGHT, on one of the infrequent occasions I had a rental car at my disposal, Herby and I drove out to Bizoton to see Ti Papi at his peristyle, where he was initiating several new members. Ti Papi was looking dapper in a shiny black tank-top, black jeans and a black cowboy hat, and stood in the lane with his brother as we parked next to a decrepit red schoolbus before the temple. As we descended, we heard the drums already violently throbbing from inside.

"You never come to see me anymore!" he said, embracing me. "Listen to that, that's a petro rhythm!"

I gave Ti Papi a bottle of rum we had brought and the three of us walked inside. He took his place in a high, straight-backed chair to watch the ceremony commence, and Herby and I sat across the floor from him. The coffee-colored half-Israeli man I had seen marry Erzulie Dantor and Erzulie Freda a year earlier was seated at the *houngan's* right. The drummers tonight included a strapping, serious older man and a slim younger one whose seeming frailty belied his power, for he had *"vodou* in his arm," as the saying goes, and the trio were practically lifting themselves of the ground as they beat out the hot, fast *petro* rhythms. A whip was strung across the *poto mitan*, and, after a time, the leader of the ceremony took it down and cracked it violently on the ground.

By this point, Ti Papi was up, the cowboy hat off. A large gold medallion on a gold chain dangled from his neck as he danced, moving his large frame with great grace, saluting the *ounsis* who had gathered, and spitting perfume and rhum at the *poto mitan*. Above him, in place of the Haitian flags that often hung from the roof, were white and yellow doilies. Among those now chanting and dancing were some very butch-looking women in crew-cuts and jeans, and a handsome young man with an 1980s fade haircut and a gold chain, wearing a t-shirt that read, "*A Dieu Widmaer*" and bore a photograph of a serious-looking, fallen young friend. "Justice," read the back.

The drumming continued, faster and faster, and "Justice" began to furiously snap the whip as the *ounsis* brought out a series of *vodou* flags. As the lights in the peristyle went out, the music intensified. I could make out the outline of Ti Papi, taking great gulps from a bottle of Barbancourt and now snapping the whip. Herby and I watched as the initiates were led out. They climbed aboard the schoolbus for the next location of their induction, the cemetery. While Ti Papi said he wished that we could come, this part of the ceremony was done in secret. With an opening peel of the bus's faded yellow lights, they were off, lumbering through the night and toward the grave.

ON THE NIGHT of February 14, a group of armed men showed up at the family home in Carrefour of Goudou Jean Numa, the Radio Metropole reporter who had asked Aristide that peeving question about Haiti's corruption at the September press conference. Told that Numa was not home, they left, but returned later to set a car in the driveway of the residence on fire and begin chanting pro-Aristide slogans. Numa went into hiding.

Metropole's staff held a meeting at the station on Delmas that night and agreed to cease broadcasting for a day on February 18 in protest; in a statement read on the air that day, they said, "Here at Radio Metropole, we have always avoided protesting publicly against this intimidation, threats and physical and verbal attacks leveled against the members of the newsroom. However, the attack against our colleague Goudou Jean Numa was too much. We are doing this because we want to send a message because of these threats we've been receiving. We can't continue to work under these conditions. We want to send a message to those trying to destroy press freedom in Haiti."

Eventually, Numa would flee to Montreal, where he began reporting for the French-language radio station CPAM 1610, and where threats against his life by Aristide supporters continued to be phoned in frequently.

Having dinner with the Rotchild Francois—Metropole's news director and one of the best journalists in the country—in Petionville one night just after Numa's flight, he mused bitterly on the rhetoric coming out from the National Palace.

"Ah, my friend," said Rotchild, a supremely competent and courageous black reporter who had first made his name covering the brutality of the military junta that ousted Aristide in the mid-1990s. "They call us Radio Convergence, Radio Opposition, Radio Communanté Internationale. We have come to expect it."

The fallout from the climate of fear that stalked the press was not over, however, and on February 22, almost three years after her husband was killed, Michele Montas announced that Radio Haiti-Inter was going off the air because of the unending campaign of violence against it.

"We shut down tomorrow because we have been the subjects of constant threats," Montas said, the indignation audible in her voice. " We have lost three lives—Jean Dominique, Jean-Claude Louissant and Maxime Seide—and we refuse to lose another one."

Driving through Port-au-Prince in a taxicab that day, the white-haired driver passed a line of lethal fallen electrical cables drooping into the Canapé Vert road.

"They don't even bother to fix those wires before they fall, it's like we're animals to them," he said, turning to me.

We listened to Michele Montas's address from Radio Haiti, speaking in a voice that at times seemed to threaten to break into a sob.

"Those politicians are just *vakabons* and cannibals," said the driver as I paid him a handful of gourdes and disembarked in Petionville, switching the radio to another station. "They eat people's lives."

AS FEBRUARY CONTINUED dejectedly on, a trio of women's rights organizations—Dwa Fanm, Enfofanm and Kay Fanm—issued a scathing press release detailing the circumstances of eighteen year-old Natacha Jean-Jacques, a girl imprisoned at fifteen after she fought back and stabbed one among a number of a gang of rapists that had invaded her house in Carrefour. Arrested by the PNH despite the protests of her family, who had witnessed the attack, she was taken to the juvenile prison at Fort National. There, again, she was raped, this time by a health-care practitioner, and as a result became pregnant, giving birth to the child with no medical care in her cell with only the assistance of other inmates. Her violator, and all those who could bear witness to the crime, were transferred to other facilities throughout the island, the report said. Though the organizations had secured the girl's release the previous week, they were making the letter public, they said, in order to obtain formal release papers so that she would not be rearrested and also so that her attackers would be held accountable for their crime.

RESPITE. PLEASURE. It was Saturday night and the streets of Jacmel were full with revelers for the city's early carnival celebrations. The Group of 184 had held a meeting to present their social contract to about two hundred curious locals the night before, but all of that seemed old news now. Etzer, Herby, and I had slept out at the Ti Mouillage beach the night before, awakening to weather that was misty and warm, eternal waves crashing on the shore and pulling away. A group of masked children had been walking up and down the beach, carrying an effigy of a dead body and chanting, "There is no *loup garou* who can talk to us the way we look today," referring to the werewolf creature of Haitian legend. As we had driven into town, bright sunlight shone down on the jauntily painted houses and the carnival bands marching through the narrow lanes. The back streets saw strange goings on. A man painted yellow and dressed only in a grass skirt ran passed our car as we parked. A group of youths, *"Anges de Jacmel,"* walked past us beating drums and dressed in white. Now, at the Ambiance Restaurant looking down over Avenue Barranquilla in town, beautiful mulatta girls were dancing on the porch to music pumping out from giant speakers set up across the road. Earlier, I had searched the steep up-and-down streets, twisting, full of people and cars, for the mulatto doctor, a Jacmel native, before finally finding him in the hotel he owned at the entrance to the city, sprawled out and exhausted on his bed in the air-conditioning after partying all day long. As I walked back to the Ambiance, a troubadour band was playing on the steps of the Hotel de la Place, trying to compete with the strains of dancehall pumping from the bandstand. Down Rue du Commerce, several thousand people were following a *rara* band as it extolled the nonsense lyrics, "We want water but don't even try to touch our pussy with the water!" Jacmel was wonderful when it was like this: alive, vibrant, mysterious and sexy. Now, down below, throngs of people were dancing to the song of the year, by a Port-au-Prince group calling itself Ti Kriz ("Crisis").

The song was called "*Kale dada w jan w vle*" meaning "move your ass however you want" or, roughly, "do your thing," and it began with the monotonous chant "*ede mwen kriye, ede mwen rele*" ("Help me cry out, help me sing") before taking off on a skittering, calypso-syncopated keyboard line and a *vodou* rhythm tapped out on what sounded like a cowbell. The song then went on to chant a litany of how expensive things had become for Haiti's poor—clairin, rice, gas, buses, cell phones, even the staple *mayi moulen* cornmeal—and mocked politicians driving around in their fancy cars as Haiti's people suffered. The song, in the reeling, dangerous, almost nihilistic energy evoked by the title's near anarchic refrain, encapsulated the anger being felt at the government among the country's youths, the students, the lower middle class. For their trouble the group, along with Boukman Eksperyans, would be banned from that year's Carnival procession in Port-au-Prince by the Aristide government. Beneath us on the street, a group of men, painted black with tar and stripped to the waist, marched down the street, followed by an eerie, silent procession on horseback of men in masks representing deceased French soldiers and planters, complete with splendid cut-away coats and period footwear. Then in front of me, a lithe girl in low-rise hip-hugger jeans and a Che Guevara t-shirt swung her hips against an imaginary partner, her eyed closed and lips open in ecstasy as the Ti Kriz song played yet again.

"*Spectatum veniunt, veniunt spectentur ut ipsae*" observed the mulatto doctor, now roused from his slumber and taking part in the revelry, quoting Ovid. They come to watch, and in fact to be watched.

As the sun began to set in the west of the Bay of Jacmel, the Foula band marched, followed by the Fashion Band. Radio Ginen was broadcasting directly from on top of a truck across the street near the intersection of Avenue Barranquilla and Rue Ambroise.

Bringing up the rear of the procession marched a parade of figures in oversized papier-maché masks bearing the likenesses of Aristide (bringing up the front and waving) and behind him revelers in masks of Dany Toussaint, Minster of Justice Calixte Delatour, and other politicians, all holding their fingers extended to their lips.

"That means don't say a fucking word," said Herby solemnly as we watched them pass.

AS HAITI ATTEMPTED to forget its troubles, California Representative Barbara Lee, the former chief of staff for Aristide lobbyist Ron Dellums, on March 5 held a briefing on Haiti for liberal-leaning congressional members at the Rayburn House Office Building in Washington, DC, at which Mildred Aristide was the honored guest. Among the "experts" in attendance were Dellums himself, Selena Mendy Singleton (who served as the vice-president of Aristide booster Randall Robinson's TransAfrica forum), and Paul Farmer. Later that day in Congress, Lee introduced the Haiti Aid in Transition Initiative, which called international financial institutions to release the $145 million in previously withheld aid directly to the Aristide government.

Perhaps Aristide could have put that money to good use filling the cells of his jails with more dissidents or employing more killers in the police. In early March, on a road between the airport and Cité Soleil, human rights workers found a series of bodies that had been dumped and burned, and two that were fresh, restrained by police handcuffs. All had been shot at the spot there the night before, and another body was dumped at the same site a day later. The identity of the men was never determined. Attending a March 9 meeting of a microcredit organization near the old Duvalier death prison Fort Diminache on the border between Cité Soleil and La Saline, the women's rights advocate Carline Simone and her husband Serge were beaten and threatened by police working with Cité Soleil PNH Commander Xavier Brixon in an apparent attempt to extort money from them. When the attempt failed, they were imprisoned for a week without charge before finally being released, bruised and humiliated. When representatives of the Group of 184 attempted to enter Les Cayes on March 15, they were met by a bottle-and rock-throwing mob led by the government's departmental delegate, Jacques Mathelier. At the end of March, a small group of MPP peasants traversing the road between Papay and Hinche were set upon by a group of chimere—this time backed by PNH units—who beat them with clubs and whips, while others fired in the air.

It was thus against this backdrop that, on March 19, a delegation of OAS and CARICOM representatives met with Aristide at the National Palace and presented him with an ultimatum—steps the delegation said were necessary to ensure public security and create a climate for new elections. After the upheaval and violence of the previous fall, Aristide was told this was perhaps his last chance to avoid complete diplomatic isolation. Among the demands were new leadership for the PNH chosen in consultation with the OAS, the arrest of Amiot Metayer, the disarming of the chimere and a full implementation within ten days of OAS Resolutions 806 and 822. Adding weight to the deadline, the delegation included among its number were OAS Assistant Secretary General Luigi Einaudi, former U.S. Assistant Secretary of State for Western Hemisphere Affairs Otto J. Reich and the chairman of CARICOM's Council for Foreign and Community Relations, Julian Hunte.

In a typically flowery speech welcoming the delegation, Aristide praised Resolution 822, saying, "The violence must stop. It affects all sides. The attacks on opposition sympathizers are unacceptable. The attacks on government officials, judges, police, local officials and Fanmi Lavalas members are equally unacceptable, even if less publicized outside Haiti."

Aristide then committed himself to arresting Amiot Metayer, saying: "we reestablished control of the town . . . now we must enforce the law, by bringing the escapees, including Monsieur Metayer, to justice. We will do this and we will do it without bloodshed."

"I pledge to work with you to facilitate full implementation of Resolution 822 by all of the responsible parties. And I pledge, as well, to the people of Haiti, that I will continue to do everything within my power to reach out to Opposition parties and civil society to achieve the reconciliation, security and democratic elections that all Haitians desperately need and have a right to expect."

Leaving Haiti, though, the delegation remained firm. At Port-au-Prince airport on March 20, Julian Hunte told reporters that "the Delegation's message has been clear: the government of Haiti must implement OAS Resolution 822 now."

THE ABILITY OF ANYONE to believe in the Aristide government's commitment to the rule of law crumbled when Judge Bernard Sainvil sent his 33-page indictment in the Jean Dominique case to State Prosecutor Josué Pierre-Louis on March 21. In it, Saint-Vil accused Philippe Markington, Dymsley Millien, Jeudi-Jean Daniel, Ralph Léger, Ralph Joseph and Freud Junior Demarat of having taken part in the killing of Jean Dominique. Dany Toussaint was not charged, nor was Harold Sévère, a former assistant mayor of Port-au-Prince and member of Aristide's personal cabinet who was thought by many to be the key link in the crime. Though Sévère's name had originally appeared on the indictment, it had been removed following a meeting between Saint-Vil and Minister of Justice Calixte Delatour where Delatour insisted, on Aristide's orders, that Sévère's name be removed.

"It was incredible," said Michele Montas after the indictment became public. "As if they were saying these six nobodies killed Jean just for the hell of it."

Popular disgust at the indictment was high enough that, visiting the Anti-Riot Unit of the PNH on March 28 in commemoration of the 16th anniversary of Haiti's 1987 constitution, Aristide felt compelled to comment on the indictment.

"We're happy to see a good step made with the indictment issued regarding the assassinations of Jean Dominique and Jean-Claude Louissaint. For some people it is a good step forward, for others, it is a weak indictment," Aristide said, then continuing to lie placidly and tauntingly to the crowd. "Even though I think it has some weaknesses, I believe now there are more possibilities to continue a good investigation. I seize the opportunity to encourage the victims' family members, like Mrs. Michele Montas, who are thinking of appealing. . . . It is your right to do so and there must be security for all the victims who continue to look for justice according to the law. Your suffering is my suffering and when there is justice, our suffering is less."

The trial of one of those victims looking for justice, the long-suffering cooperative activist Rosemond Jean, finally commenced on March 24. Following a fitful beginning, Jean was conditionally freed from the prison cell where he had languished for six months with an order to return to court on April 7.

JEAN-NESLY LUCIEN and Harvel Jean-Baptiste both resigned from their posts at the PNH on March 24, and two days later, Jean-Claude Jean-Baptiste was inaugurated as the new Director General of the police at a ceremony at PNH headquarters in Pacot in the capital, under the eyes of his predecessor Lucien, Yvon Neptune, Secretary of State for Public Security Gérard Dubreuil and Minister of Justice Calixte Delatour. Jean-Baptiste had previously served as southern regional police commander, but he had never managed to distance himself from the accusations that he had orchestrated the murder of preacher and Aristide rival Sylvio Claude in Les Cayes in 1991, when he was serving as the first Aristide government's delegate in the city. The appointment was the subject of great controversy among Haiti's local human rights organizations and the foreign diplomatic core. Baptiste did nothing to assuage people's fears when he promptly named former Port-au-Prince mayor Harold Sévère, the man widely believed to be the key link between the recently absolved intellectual authors of the Jean Dominique murder and the actual triggermen, to his personal cabinet. Harvel Jean-Baptiste, who had been active and vocal in attempting to reign in the body's obvious links to the drug trade, had effectively been demoted and would eventually leave Haiti for Brasil, replaced by former traffic police director Evans Pierre Sainturné in the post of Inspector General. Sainturné's notoriety had previously been confined to the threats he had made against the life of Claudy Gassant when Gassant was investigating the Dominique killing. Jean-Dady Simeon, who had been the public image of the PNH on nightly newscasts and on the radio for some years, was transferred to head the constabulary's public relations office. No reason was given for the transfer, but police watchers viewed it as a step down. Jean-Claude Jean-Baptiste's new chief of the judicial police, Jude Perrin, quickly became an enthusiastic partner in the cocaine being trafficked through Port-au-Prince's airport with airport security director Romaine Lestin. Though Aristide had promised on March 19 to consult with the OAS Special Mission before naming a new PNH Director General and had reiterated that pledge at another meeting with OAS representatives the day before Jean Baptiste's swearing in, the move in fact came as a total surprise to the OAS team on the ground. Perhaps as their way of inaugurating Jean-Baptiste's tenure, in Petit Goave on March 27, PNH officers shot 21-year-old Ginette Pierre and then backed over her with their police car, believing her to be the daughter of a local Convergence leader. Pierre died at the scene and no one was ever prosecuted for the crime.

SHORTLY BEFORE I left Haiti for an extended period in New York and then Guatemala, I sat at the capital's Hotel Kinam having breakfast with Patrick Moynihan and Garry Delice, the director and headmaster, respectively, of the Louverture-Cleary School, a charter school for poor Haitian children located in the Port-au-Prince suburb of Santo and funded by American donations.

"You know I've always stopped myself from talking about politics, but it's gotten so bad for my staff, my students and their families that I'm just at my wit's end," said Patrick as we looked out onto the Kinam's pool and its latticed balconies.

Moynihan was a particularly American sort of dreamer. He had left a high-paying job as a trader with the firm Louis Dreyfus in Chicago five years earlier to work full-time improving the school after what he called a "spiritual awakening." That morning he was dressed as usual, in casual shorts and a polo shirt, sandy blonde hair falling over a ruddy Irish face.

The Louverture-Cleary School was a meritocracy (a novel notion in Haiti) that selected the top students from the poorest neighborhoods around the capital, like Cité Soleil, and provided them with an American-level education and encouraged them to remain in Haiti after their studies instead of traveling abroad to find work as many of their countrymen have been forced to do. The students would often go on to administrative or office jobs with placement help from the school while pursuing higher education at one of the capital's universities. Catholic-affiliated though open to all, the school was free except for a nominal meal fee that was paid through a work-study program if the student's family could not afford it.

"How does someone in the States 'earn' a car and someone here 'earns' dying of tuberculosis on an island in the Caribbean at seven years old?" Moynihan had asked me at the school one day, as we watched the students enter their classrooms. Same-sex dormitories rose three stories amid royal palms, and a short distance away, near a cafeteria, two buildings under construction rose from the brown earth. Students and teachers took turns during the school day helping a Haitian ladder crew with the less dangerous parts of building new classrooms and dorms. Earlier, I had watched a Catholic Mass celebrated in a mixture of English and Kreyol, and listened to hymns sung to the accompaniment of a student playing the traditional *rada vodou* drum. The school library featured volumes in several languages (students were encouraged to become conversant in English, French and Spanish as well as Kreyol), and posters of American civil rights leader Martin Luther King, Jr. and a gallery of Haitian presidents. Moynihan's growing family—his wife, two boys and two girls—often lived with him in Haiti while he administered the school. Though a 1998 World Bank report had found that, despite the fact that 53 percent of Haiti's children aged six through twelve were enrolled in school, by the time they reached thirteen to eighteen that number dropped to only 14 percent, Moynihan refused to despair.

"Yeah, most of these kids come from fiscally disadvantaged backgrounds," he had told me during that earlier visit, as we spoke over the din of the students finishing their breakfast and then rushing past us off to class. "But my dream is to have an alumni meeting with ten doctors, three senators and a couple of lawyers—people who have benefited from the education they got here and stayed to do something for the county."

"We work to educate these children so they will get out and help the community," said Garry Delice, a serious and dedicated educator, as we sat at the Kinam that morning. "But when they see someone like René Civil or Paul Raymond, who speak in such an uneducated manner, and they have cars, they have security guards, why should they think they need to stay in school?"

Later, driving out to the school, we passed women walking down Nazon and Delmas to work, their clean shirts pressed, their hair done, their high-heels and black shoes polished. When we arrived at the school compound, Haitian and American flags were fluttering together inside the school's wall, and wind was blowing down the dusty lane.

I WOULD LEAVE HAITI early on a Sunday morning in March and land in Miami on my way back to New York. Checking into a chic hotel on Collins Avenue, I took a long shower, which felt like trying to wash off the last traces of Haiti's dust, grime and dread from my body. Before I left, I had spoken to the mulatto doctor, at his office downtown across the street from the General Hospital, and he seemed somewhat drunk and depressed.

"You know this country is completely fucked up?" he asked.

And I went downtown to see Herby. I felt like I was saying goodbye, but little did I know I would be back before either of us knew.

Herby and I sat on a low wall on the Champs de Mars. The sun was dipping slowly away from Port-au-Prince, and around us preparations were under way to build the stands where revelers would watch the floats pass by for that year's Carnival.

"You know," Herby said, as he gazed at the scene before us, the Carnival workers, the beggars and street children, the National Palace losing some of its harsh white edges in the soft light. "What's happening with Aristide now is like what happens with a beautiful woman. When you first meet her and fall in love with her, all you can see is how beautiful she is; you can't see anything at all wrong with her, although those things might be there. But, little by little over time, as your love calms down, you can see more and more things about her that you maybe don't like, things she does wrong, maybe even bad things.

"That is what the Haitian people are seeing with Aristide now."

CHAPTER NOTES

1. "Des journalistes fuient la terreur de <<l'armee cannibale>>," *Le Nouvelliste*, December 2, 2002.
2. National Endowment for Democracy. 2000 Annual Report.
3. Data Sheet USAID Mission: Haiti, Program Title: Democracy and Governance.
4. Data Sheet USAID Mission: Haiti, Program Title: Democracy and Governance.
5. United States Department of Justice, Foreign Agents Registration Act (FARA) filings for Kurzban, Kurzban, Weinger & Tetzeli, P.A., 2000–2002.
6. United States Department of Justice, Foreign Agents Registration Act (FARA) filings for Dellums, Brauer, Halterman & Associates, LLC, 2001–2002.

7. United States Department of Justice,.Foreign Agents Registration Act (FARA) filings for Ross-Robinson & Associates, 1997–2000.
8. "Capitalizing on a Politician's Clout," *The Los Angeles Times*, December 19, 2004.
9. EUROPA—EuropeAid—European Initiative for Democracy and Human Rights. European Commission. Targeted Projects Report.
10. Banque de la Republique d'Haiti (BRH) internal report, May 2005.

| | |

10
The People's Pencil Has No Eraser

AT A CEREMONY at the National Palace on April 7 to mark the 200th anniversary of Toussaint Louverture's death in a French prison, Aristide delivered a speech calling on France to pay back the sum Haiti was forced to pay the French government for recognition of its independence in the nineteenth century. The indemnity agreed to by Jean-Pierre Boyer in 1825 under threat of bombardment by a French fleet in Port-au-Prince harbor saw Haiti pay France 150 million francs, and it was not finally paid off until the government of Lysius Salomon in 1880. To mark Haiti's upcoming bicentennial of independence, Aristide demanded the reimbursement in the sum of US $21,685,135,571.48—the equivalent of the sum factoring in account inflation and interest, he said. Aristide's sentiments were echoed by Minster of Foreign Affairs Antonio Joseph's comments on pro-government Radio Solidarité several days later. Aristide, it soon became clear, would make the celebration of Haiti's bicentennial, slated to occur on January 1, 2004, the touchstone project for his upcoming year in office. Though French President Jacques Chirac would eventually form a commission headed by veteran leftist adventurer Regis Debray on Franco-Haitian relations to, among other charges, investigate Haiti's claim for restitution, those familiar with the body said it was more to sound out the dynamics forming in the intensifying political crisis on the ground in the country than to dole out money to as corrupt and lethal a government as Aristide now ran. Over the coming months, though, Aristide would continue to crank up the rhetorical machine while government publications such as *L'Union*, the TNH state television network and the Agence Haitienne de Presse did their best to create the illusion that a huge cash payout to Haiti from France was just around the corner. In the meantime, a mordant joke took hold in the streets of Port-au-Prince that posited a conversation between Aristide and Mario Dupuy inside the National Palace:

"Mr. President, France has agreed to pay Haiti the 21 million, all except for the 48 cents! Isn't that wonderful?"

"But not the 48 cents?" the joke had Aristide responding. "But what will be left for the people?"

In other moves, in an April 4 presidential decree, Aristide had stated that heretofore all *vodou* practitioners and organizations would be allowed to file requests for recognition with the Ministry of Culture and Religious Affairs, and that if *vodou* priests would take an oath before a presiding (Aristide-appointed) judge of an appropriate civil tribunal, the priests would have the power to officiate baptisms, marriages and funerals. As *vodou* was already a central aspect in the lives of Haitians without state sanction, many of the faith's practitioners saw it as little more than one more government attempt to put yet another facet of Haitian life under its control, with sociologist and *vodou* authority Laennec Hurbon later telling a seminar marking the 212th anniversary of the Bois Cayman ceremony that "Aristide is only taking this move in order to manipulate *vodou*." Simultaneously, Aristide was also attempting an end-run around the university students who so hated him by redoubling his efforts to create his own university system with money donated to Haiti and the Aristide Foundation for Democracy by Taiwan. The Université Populaire de Tabarre, being built on the grounds of a former slave plantation near Aristide's mansion in Tabarre, was set to include a medical school as well as other facilities, but a noted Haitian cartoonist who used the name "Titosh" more accurately summed up general opinion of what the university's focus would be with a drawing showing a quizzical student viewing a course list offering, among other courses, "Lavalassian corruption" and "How to deceive great hopes." In what would prove to be one of the low points in his political career, former U.S. President Bill Clinton visited Haiti on April 8 and met with Aristide at the National Palace before a throng of photographers and reporters, but did not venture to Cité Soleil or La Saline to speak with the chimere and see what his handiwork had wrought.

Though the former U.S. president was entering, many more were leaving, and at least six Haitians died and dozens went missing when the boat they were in, carrying over 150 migrants, capsized off the north coast of the Dominican Republic when it struck a reef on April 14. A Dominican fisherman, spotting survivors floundering in the water, ferried many to shore. Of the survivors of the voyage, ninety-one deemed hardiest were unceremoniously repatriated to Haiti through Dajabon on the next day.

TWO INCIDENTS OF MENACE against the press and human rights workers in Haiti garnered little notice outside the country, but were illustrative of the direction in which the country was heading.

A young man quickly dropped an envelope at the reception area of Radio Kiskeya on April 30 before charging out the door and down the winding turns of Rue Villemenay. Upon opening the package, it was discovered that it was a bile-filled letter directed to program director Lilianne Pierre-Paul, assailing French president Jacques Chirac, demanding reparations for Haiti's colonial debt and threatening French citizens living in Haiti should the demands not be met. Pierre-Paul was given four days to read the letter or she "will reap the consequences on May 6th." Along with the letter was a bullet from a 12-gauge shotgun, a "preview" of what was to come. The letter was signed by Domi Nan Bwa and Bale Wouze, as well as three other Lavalas OPs.

From late April until early May, the country was both riveted and revolted by the story of a ten-year- old girl from Carrefour known only as "Ketou," who had been raped by a sixteen-year-old neighbor and then discovered to be pregnant several months after the crime. When Ketou's family attempted to bring their complaint before the Justice of the Peace in Carrefour, they were stonewalled over the course of several weeks by apparent collaboration between the assistant prosecutor there and the assailant's lawyer. Pierre Esperance's National Coalition for Haitian Rights was one of the driving forces supporting the girl and her family.

The incident might have been assigned away to a grim collective memory were it not for the events of May 14. On that day, Director Rose-André Bony of Social Services telephoned NCHR asking to know the whereabouts of the girl and her family, as she had a package for them. As Ketou and her family were at NCHR's offices on Rue Rivière in the capital, it was suggested that Bony come there. Upon arriving, Bony brought no package but rather an order signed by State Prosecutor Josué Pierre-Louis to take the child into the custody of Social Services. The NCHR representatives present cited legal procedure, saying they would convey the information to the family's lawyer and then proceed to the State Prosecutor's office with their response. Bony then left, somewhat huffily.

About an hour after NCHR's 4 p.m. closing time, Bony returned, this time with Justice of the Peace Nerva Simon, who was armed, and a group of police. Bullying the *gardien* she found at the gate, Bony demanded to know the child's whereabouts. Failing to discern that, the invaders searched the office and grounds of the human rights organization, in clear violation of Haitian law. Many speculated that the incident was simply a ruse for the government to gain a clear layout of the NCHR offices in preparation for an upcoming attack on the organization.

ARISTIDE'S ENEMIES, both within Haiti and without, had not stopped their plotting. In the border town of Dajabon on May 6, Dominican soldiers arrested Guy Philippe, former Haitian schoolteacher and Ambassador to the Dominican Republic Paul Arcelin, and three other Haitian nationals, alleging that they were "being investigated because of allegations that they are trying to reach Haiti with the aim of conspiring," according to Dominican General Fernando Cruz. The next day, in the early morning hours of May 7, gunmen in Haiti attacked the Peligre hydroelectric dam, killing two guards, setting fire to the control tower and temporarily shutting down operations at the plant that had proven itself so useless at providing power to the impoverished residents of Haiti's Plateau Central that surrounded it. That same day, PNH officers in the capital raided the home of Judith Roy, head of the Regroupement Patriotique pour le Renouveau National (REPAREN) party and former candidate for the mayorship of Port-au-Prince. The police claimed to have found a weapons cache, as well as documents referring to plans to attack the National Palace and Aristide's residence in Tabarre, but Roy denied the charges, and insisted that her party was nonviolent.

Despite all these intrigues, on May 8, Philippe and his cohorts were released, with the Dominicans sending them on their way under a warning they were "under no pretext to conspire," something that was greeted with derisive laughter by those in Haiti. Calling into Radio Vision 2000, Philippe denied he had been plotting to overthrow the Aristide government, but interviewed by the Associated Press in Santo Domingo several days later, he said "I would support a coup; we have to get rid of this dictator."

THOUGH THE PELIGRE ATTACK and the presence of Philippe and his henchmen across the border in Santo Domingo provoked a great outcry from the Aristide government and charges of conspiracy from its supporters, cross-border incursions were in fact an old gambit in Haitian politics. Francois Duvalier had been so unsettled by the number of exiles in the Dominican Republic plotting against him that in 1963 he evicted all peasants living along a swath of land ranging anywhere from three to five miles to the border, burned all structures found therein and declared it a *cordon sanitaire* in which any unauthorized persons moving would be shot. This didn't stop a combination of Haitian exiles, former Dominican soldiers and peasants led by an exiled Haitian general named Leon Cantave, from crossing into Haitian territory near the northern city of Fort Liberté in August 1963, and taking over the small town of Derac before fleeing back across the border when Duvalier learned of their plans. Two more attempts, in August and September, also ended in failure, and the rebels lost fifteen men in their final assault in an ill-advised frontal attack on Ouanaminthe. Fred Baptiste, another rebel, launched sustained raids against Duvalier from the Dominican Republic over a two-year period in the 1960s, but was captured in battle and hauled off to die in the Duvalier death jail Fort Dimanche.

An odd postscript to the attack at Peligre took place in Gonaives. An American missionary, James Glenn White, was arrested by PNH personnel at the port on May 8 only blocks away from Amiot Metayer's seaside redoubt of Raboteau. White, a 47-year-old Indiana native who had previously been employed as a carpenter, ran the "Sharing the Vision" missionary group in Cap Haitien; he was arrested after picking up a refrigerator that contained an AR15 assault rifle, a .40 caliber pistol, gun powder and bullet-reloading machine and a camouflage shirt emblazoned with the words "God's Army." A South Florida man, Jeremy Benenati, stepped forward to claim that the weapons in fact belonged to him, and that, as he couldn't manage to sell them in the United States, he had sent them along to Haiti ahead of his planned trip to join White's missionary group. Benenati claimed he had sent his permits ahead with White, who was told to present them once the weapons arrived. When he attempted to do so, the men claimed, White was arrested. Secretary of State for Communications Mario Dupuy denied the claims and accused White of having been part of the group that assaulted the Peligre dam, and the missionary was transferred from Gonaives to the National Penitentiary in Port-au-Prince. Imprisoned for two months and charged with attempting to illegally import weapons into the country, White finally appeared before a judge in the capital in July. Despite pleading his innocence, White was immediately convicted of the charges against him by Judge Bernard Sainvil and ordered out of the country.

ADDING TO THE GLOOM, Father Antoine Adrien, a grand old man of the Haitian democratic movement and a former mentor of Aristide's, passed away on May 12 at the age of eighty. Aristide had wanted Adrien's funeral to be held at the National Palace, but the deceased priest's Holy Ghost brothers refused, and at the funeral, Father Max Dominique, who had spoken so passionately at the Mass for the three slain Carrefour brothers the previous January, denounced what he charged was the repressive system Aristide had put in place and likened the chimere to the attachés and Macoutes of yore, stressing that Adrien had struggled all his life to plant a democracy, not a dictatorship, in Haiti. Dominique also assailed what he charged was a government plan to change the constitution so that Aristide could run for a second consecutive term in office. Later that night, a mob of some two dozen young men arrived at the compound where Dominique was staying, demanding the priest be turned over to them and were dissuaded only after prolonged negotiations by Father William Smarth. The next morning, the walls of nearby buildings were revealed to be covered in pro-Aristide graffiti.

STATE PROSECUTOR LOUISELME JOSEPH, doing what his predecessor Justice Marcel Jean had refused to do, on May 14 "legalized" Amiot Metayer's escape from the Gonaives prison, saying that no complaints had been filed against Metayer in the Jubilé house-burning incident he had originally been jailed for, or in the murder of Luc Mesadieu's bodyguards during the December 17 chimere rampage. Joining Metayer at liberty would be Lavalas deputy Jocelyn Saint-Louis, who was released from prison where he had been held briefly for his murder of Saint Raphael Mayor Sernand Sévère in January 2002.

Speaking at Archaie on May 18 (Flag Day), Aristide told his audience at the bicentennial anniversary of the creation of the Haitian flag that, "Poverty and freedom are like milk and lemon. As a squash doesn't give calabashes, poverty doesn't give freedom. And people who like freedom don't like poverty."

Then, referring to Haiti's arrears to the IDB, he denounced "plots to make

Haiti move backwards is to make it so that the debt of money cannot be paid. The murder and sabotage in Peligre is to make it so the debt of money cannot be paid. . . . To make a blockade in order to make the people become angrier is to make it so the debt of money cannot be paid. . . ."

And on it went like that, for quite some time.

At Father Jean-Marie Vincent Park, so named in honor of the fallen Catholic priest and peasant activist, Secretary of State for Public Security Gérard Dubreuil led a "symbolic" burning on May 29 of 233 weapons the government said were seized. Coming only a few days after police had killed five people in the Fort Liberté section of Petit Goave, some observers said the ceremony was symbolic chiefly because the guns appeared to be in utter disrepair and in many instances, unusable. An OAS report dismissed the government weapons-burning ceremonies by noting that "many of the weapons were in inoperable condition, with either missing or broken parts. Others were old and rusted, and some had seizure tags dating back as far as 1998. Most of the weapons were not suitable for ballistic testing." The OAS also observed the dramatic discrepancy between the inventory of seventy-seven seized weapons provided by the Secretary of State for Public Security and a report by Haiti's Ministry of Foreign Affairs that said 2,551 firearms had been seized in July and August of 2002 alone.

Having devoted the last years of his life to struggling against the Aristide government, on May 31, René Théodore, the veteran of Haitian communism who had matured into one of its most able and competent politicians and who bravely marched in the Vertières demonstration in Cap Haitien the previous November, died in Jackson Memorial Hospital in Miami at the age of sixty-two, losing his last fight to the tyrant of lung cancer.

AT THE END OF MAY, an incident at the exclusive Union School, a preparatory institution favored by wealthy Haitians and resident Americans located in Juvenat off of the winding Canapé Vert Road, would prove to have fateful consequences. At an end of the year party, a nephew of Jacques Beaudoin Ketant—the drug lord and Aristide associate whose brother had been killed by police the previous February—had his amorous intentions rejected by one of the school's pretty female students. Humiliated, the nephew, along with one of Ketant's sons, sought out the true object of the girl's intentions, beat him and threw him into the trunk of a car. Attempting to drive away with the boy still in the trunk, the pair was stopped at the school's gate by a security guard, who forced them to free the boy. Upon hearing of the assault, the Union School's principal expelled the pair. At this point, a few days later, an enraged Ketant showed up with several thugs, threatening the principal and an American teacher who was on hand and who decided to photograph the scene as a precautionary measure. Ketant smashed the camera and stormed off, threatening to have the school burned to the ground and the staff killed. When word of the incident reached U.S. Ambassador Brian Dean Curran, he was reportedly livid, and dispatched U.S. Marines to protect the school. After having played a cat-and-mouse game for some time, Ketant had finally shown himself in spectacularly unwise fashion and he was now firmly in America's sights. Still under a 1997 indictment in Miami accusing him of moving 15 tons of cocaine into the United States through Haiti, Ketant had lost his PNH protection following his attempted double-cross with the fabled Colombian cocaine plane the previous winter, and now made an attractive, and accessible, target for those parties interested in scooping him up.

A MAY IMF announcement had stated that Haiti had vowed to cut spending and stabilize the fluctuating gourd, and, as such, if it fulfilled its obligations within twelve months, the body would free up between $100 million and $150 million in IMF funds for antipoverty and employment programs. Given the signs that were coming out of the National Palace and the PNH at this point, this move baffled many, and Aristide must have sensed a backlash coming. Bowing to domestic and international pressure, at least publicly, in the runup to the general assembly meeting of the OAS set for June 8 in Santiago, Chile, the National Palace made public a letter they said was authored by Jean-Claude Jean-Baptiste, in which he offered to resign as interim director on the PNH after two months on the job.

"It is the time for me to leave and serve the nation elsewhere," read the letter, dated June 3. It was announced that Jean-Baptiste would become the Secretary of State for Public Works.

On June 6, Jean-Robert Faveur, a highly respected PNH officer, was sworn in as the PNH's interim director general. Addressing the OAS General Assembly in Santiago on June 10, U.S. Secretary of State Colin Powell praised Faveur's appointment, calling him "eminently qualified professionally" and saying that the U.S. was "encouraged" by the move. Roger Noriega, the U.S. Permanent Representative to the body, also lauded the selection of Faveur but warned that "the new Director General of the Haitian National Police must be permitted the independence of action accorded to him under Haitian law (and) must be allowed to act professionally without political interference from Haitian governmental authorities."

Things got off to a rocky start, though, when, at a meeting with Aristide preceding his inauguration as chief, the Haitian president told Faveur that he was to consult with Secretary of State for Public Security Jean Gérard Dubreuil and Jean-Claude Jean-Baptiste himself before making any decision about the management of the force. Aristide also lectured Faveur that nominations and transfers of departmental directors and officer assignments in the capital would be decided solely by the president himself, personally. Later that day, with Jean-

Claude Jean-Baptiste still busy signing promotion and transfer letters in violation of the law, the letters, illegally promoting PNH officers through the ranks beyond their grades and without the standard matriculation and competency assessments, were presented to Faveur for his signature. Complaining to Dubreuil, Faveur was told, "It is the president's order. You can change the form but the end result should be the same."

Faveur was informed on June 9 that he would not be able to sign checks paid out by the PNH to officers, as he had been led to believe, as that would be done by PNH official Jean-Robert Estère and the government's central and general services administrative and logistics director Patrick Valcin, both close Aristide loyalists. Again complaining to Dubreuil, Faveur was again told "I have no choice because that was decided by the president." Faveur pointed out that the arrangement was a clear violation of Article 23.7 of the law on the creation of the PNH, which clearly stated that among the PNH Director General's duties: "He will supervise and control the functioning of all expenses or outflow of funds, and prepare together with the administrative direction the pilot study of the yearly budget." Faveur then cited the law to Jean-Claude Jean-Baptiste, still acting very much as interim director general, and was told to "forget about that law."

When Lavalas Deputy Levy Joseph ordered Faveur to hire eighteen chimere as police officers in the Plateau Central, though they had no police training, Faveur vented his frustrations at a meeting of the PNH's Conseil Superiur with Yvon Neptune present on June 9.

"There is a difference between reality and the law," Neptune told him curtly. "Democracy is a utopia. What we have here is an authoritarian democracy, like Cuba's."

When Faveur turned on the radio on June 17 to hear the news that, much to his surprise, drug lord Jacques Ketant had been arrested and turned over to the United States in an operation of which he had no prior knowledge, he was already debating his dramatic next move.

ONE OF THE REASONS Faveur didn't hear about Ketant's seizure until the rest of the country did might have had to do with the peculiar arrangements that had been made to achieve it. Realizing that, following the school assault, Ketant had something of an unattractive liability, and having never forgotten Ketant's attempts to circumvent him the previous winter, Aristide made a secret deal with the United States Drug Enforcement Agency to hand them Ketant and partially take the heat off himself—a move that one of Aristide's security personnel with intimate knowledge of the deal characterized as "totally self-serving but typical Aristide." Rudy Therassan, the commander of the Brigade de Recherche et d'Intervention (BRI) of the PNH and husband of Aristide's chief PNH chimere organizer Hermione Leonard, was sent to fetch Ketant, despite being widely rumored to have engineered the operation that killed Ketant's brother Hector and drug dealer Herman Charles the previous February. When Therrassan showed up at Ketant's mansion in Petionville and told him that he was going to be taken to meet with Aristide to iron out some of the problems that had arisen recently, Ketant, eager to get back on good terms with his friend and sometimes partner Aristide, acquiesced. However, instead of meeting Aristide, Ketant was taken to a U.S. helicopter waiting at the helipad at Aristide's Tabarre home, making a last mad dash on foot in an attempt to escape when he realized something was amiss. It was futile, though, and the drug kingpin was whisked away to Guantánamo Bay Naval Facility in Cuba and from there to a federal prison cell in Miami. If there was ever any doubt that there was no one Aristide would not sell out in the name of political expediency, his treatment of his daughter's godfather would long be remembered by Haitians, for Ketant, thug though he was, was still a Haitian, and Aristide's handing him over to the *blan* in such a manner, still an unutterable treachery.

THE MONTH CONTINUED tensely when, on June 13, Viola Robert, the mother of the three brothers murdered by police in Carrefour the previous December, fled the country along with eight members of her family after receiving constant death threats for advocating for justice on her own behalf. Around the same time, a feared former FADH commander from Hinche who had been known as "Commander Zed" during the Cédras years and had been a frequent visitor to Tabarre in recent years, was kidnapped off a street in Port-au-Prince while walking to his home near the airport. Thrown into a black 4x4 pickup, he struggled with his assailants, but was overpowered and taken to Titanyen, where he was killed. Proving that Guy Philippe and his men were not resting after their May reversal, on June 21 about two dozen armed men killed four Lavalas partisans and attacked the police station in Lascahobas along the Dominican border.

IN THE DEAD OF NIGHT on Sunday, June 22, Jean-Robert Faveur had his driver take him to the Dominican frontier, where he walked across the border into exile. He left behind him a resignation letter, dated the previous day and sent to various radio stations around the capital, and a stunned and indignant Lavalas government, who mistakenly thought they could bully the police chief into submission. Beside themselves with rage, Haiti's Minister of Foreign Affairs Antonio Joseph charged that "international sectors and even diplomats" had facilitated Faveur's departure in an effort to "destabilize" the Aristide government, and Justice Minister Calixte Delatour called for Faveur to be arrested for "abandoning his post."

It has been two weeks of moral and physical suffering and two weeks of resistance that I have spent at the head of the PNH. I do not want to stay one more day," Faveur's letter, addressed to Aristide, read. "Mr. President, if you paid attention to what I was saying, you probably noticed that I have been making sacrifices for a long time so that I could safeguard the values that are now missing in the country, such as honor, integrity, dignity and character. Today, I have chosen the road of exile instead of letting myself be corrupted and enslaved.

Mr. President, the situation is not good at all within the PNH, and poverty is killing the country. I had thought that with my presence at the head of the PNH you would see a beginning of the solution to the crisis, but, unfortunately, you do not care about that. Those people who are making money around you are afraid to tell you that things are bad out there. I am glad that I did not betray the confidence that the people, the policemen, the large majority, the international community and some of your partners placed in me.

I seize the occasion to tell the prime minister, the finance minister, the secretary of state for public security, parliament, the international community, national policemen and the Haitian people that the documents attached to this letter prove the bad faith of our leaders and the permanent danger that my family and I were facing. All that explained my silence. I am leaving now but I will always be willing to serve my country in an honest manner without having dangers above me because of my character and my way of doing things. I have saved my life, my trust and my dignity.

Faveur's resignation marked the end of the PNH as a viable law enforcement body as long as Aristide remained in power. Jocelyne Pierre, up until this time the head of Port-au-Prince's civil court, was installed without much ceremony as new head of PNH on June 28, the same day gunmen thought to be allied with the former military killed three men in a car outside of Lascahobas. Becoming the third person to hold the post in less than a month, Pierre was never anything more than a figurehead, and the running of the PNH continued to be directed by Aristide's emissaries Jean-Claude Jean-Baptiste and Gérard Dubreuil. From thenceforth, as long as Aristide remained in the presidency, he would do everything he could to make sure the PNH would never be more than an emasculated and servile private army loyal to preserving his grip on power and the privileges of his party clique, attempting to wed their own security as closely to his own as Francois and Jean-Claude Duvalier had done with their supporters decades earlier. Sadly for the many decent, honest officers in the PNH who had signed up wanting to help build a new country and had instead found themselves caught in the middle of a murderous and criminal vise, they would often be the ones to pay the heaviest price at the hands of the population's revulsion at Aristide and his excesses. For those loyal officers who had signed on to the new institution in good faith, the next several months provided some brutal tests, indeed.

WE WERE SITTING in a garden near Haiti's National Palace, with the setting sun spilling through lilacs hanging over a low wall. My companion was a mid-level eight-year veteran of the PNH assigned to the Delmas 33 police commissariat, and as we listened to roosters crowing nearby, he mused about the transformation he says the force has undergone since Aristide's reelection in November 2000.

"In 1995, we formed the PNH with such confidence, to serve the people and respect human rights," said the man, who had worked at the Delmas station for two years following assignments in Petionville and Gonaives. "But the morale of the institution has deteriorated terribly. All of the heads of commissariats in the metropolitan area come from the National Palace; they do not have experience in PNH. It's not just Delmas, but every police station in the metropolitan area: Martissant, Port-au-Prince, Petionville, Croix de Bouquets. They're promoting and accrediting attachés directly as police officers."

Attaché. The word had come into vogue after the fall of Duvalier, when the military and police began the process of recruiting and arming civilians to work alongside the regular security forces, "attaching" themselves to the police and the army, and the practice had returned with great gusto since Aristide assumed office in 2001. The chief of the Delmas 33 police station, a bald-headed, slit-eyed thug named Emmanuel Mompremier, was a former National Palace security officer with no police training who had been assigned to head the station by Aristide after his predecessor, the equally brutal Camille Marcellus, was transferred to head the PNH in the Artibonite Valley from a base in Gonaives. In constant contact with Fritz Joseph, the Aristide-appointed ex-FRAPH mayor of Cité Soleil and groups of hired killers both there and in the *bas Delmas* region where the precinct was located, Mompremier presided over some of the most savage excesses of the sputtering regime.

"The situation in the PNH is not normal," said my companion, a solidly built, serious man in his mid-30s who spoke in a hushed voice and seemed very concerned with who might overhear us. "The people hired as police have no experience in this type of work, but the National Palace insists that they be hired. They make us work with chimeres and attachés. . . . They work in the same zones as the police and use their guns. There are political arrests, personal vendetta arrests (but) we have groups of officers against what is happening here."

The abuses had been legion. In May, a suspected thief named Félix Pierre had been brought late at night to the home of a local administrative council member, Jean Hernceau Morency, who locked him in the council office, saying he would take him to the commissariat in the morning. After Morency left however, two attachés from the Delmas 33 station, Isaac "Jonas" Jean-Louis and another who went by the name Ivanov, broke into the office, and when Morency happened on the scene and demanded to know what was going on, the two men announced they would implement "zero tolerance" against Pierre and shot the suspected criminal dead in the street. In June, two young men, Junior Jean and Mankès Anelus, were arrested by Delmas 33 attachés and never seen again; and another young man, Gueno Duchene, was executed in the street by black-clad men who drove away from the scene in a police pickup. Valbrun Vignet, a mechanic who lived in the Petite Place Cazeau area, fell into a dispute with two neighbors who were friends of the attaché Isaac "Jonas" Jean-Louis, and on the night of June 18, Jean-Louis appeared at Vignet's house and raked the door and windows with gunfire, sending Vignet scrambling over a wall to escape. Silendieu Esperance, a local merchant in the Petit Place Cazeau, was constantly being shaken down by attachés affiliated with the station. The most notorious killer at the Delmas 33 was a man in his early 40s named René Jean-Anthony, who went by the name Grenn Sonnen ("Ringing Testicles"), a former member of the Duvalier-era counterinsurgency Leopards battalion (as was the former colonel Himmler Rebu) who had never even officially matriculated into the PNH, but became known for torturing prisoners and summary executions conducted along the Adoquin in Delmas and Route Batimat near Cité Soleil.

Over the course of the summer, the situation deteriorated to the point that the National Coalition for Haitian Rights released a damning report on the progovernment death squads operating throughout the country titled "The Return in Full-Force of the Attaché Phenomenon," which assailed the Aristide government's human rights records.

"It has become blatantly obvious," the report said, "That the arbitrary practices that were forcefully denounced during the coup d'état period are resurfacing. The traditional methods used to control are reemerging, modified—intensified and used increasingly by the same individuals that once criticized them. The attaché phenomenon has thus become part of the repressive system put in place by those in power. . . . Judicial recourse becomes a privilege for certain political or social sectors that possess the necessary means. . . . It is imperative that something be done before it is too late. If this attaché phenomenon is not curtailed, Haiti runs the risk of being transformed into a bandit state living on the fringe of the civilized world."

As the sun set on Port-au-Prince and the attaches began their work again, my policeman friend agreed.

"We need the police to recover their independence. We must work to serve the people, not the politicians. We need to help our country and our police force because without that, we will have no democracy," he said, he voice breaking with emotion. "Is it a crime to speak out against this?"

AT THE TIME HAITI'S people of good conscience were fighting courageously and at great personal risk to defend their fragile institutions, with very few exceptions, the Caribbean community failed Haiti as roundly as any of its other so-called friends. Caribbean leaders such as Jamaican Prime Minister P.J. Patterson, St. Lucian Prime Minister Kenny Anthony and Prime Minister Ralph Gonsalves of St. Vincent and the Grenadines continued to fête and praise Aristide at occasions such as CARICOM's 24th Regular Meeting, held in Montego Bay, Jamaica on July 3, never pressing him on the violence being meted out to the Haitian people by his government but rather presenting him with yet another "presidential" photo opportunity. Some in the Caribbean intelligentsia, such as the Jamaican journalist John Maxwell—a man who had last visited Haiti a decade earlier and had never had bothered to go speak with the slum-dwellers that Aristide had sent out to kill or the peasants he had victimized—wrote pompous tracts defending his government and attacking his detractors, sitting safe and well clear of any danger at his home in Kingston, absolving the president of any culpability for the spiraling cycle of violence that Haiti was heading into in the summer and fall of 2003. Arrogant, blinded by facile regional and racial solidarity and insistent on ignoring the effects that state-sponsored violence and ruinous governmental policies were having on the poorest Haitians, these naysayers stuck with Aristide, holding on to him even as the boot of his criminality strangled the lives of his own people. One day, perhaps, when they look in the mirror, their consciences will spur them to some sort of reckoning for the part they played in giving succor to the regime. But perhaps not.

GIVEN THE CHAOS swirling within the PNH, the National Palace was not spared its own drama. In late June, rumors began to swirl throughout the capital regarding a trip taken to Canada by Aristide's Palace Security Chief, Oriel Jean—who was as close to the president as any official and deeply involved in the drug trade. Jean had left Haiti for Canada with his family on June 25 and two days later Radio Metropole ran a report implying that Jean had fled into exile just as Jean-Robert Faveur had done a week earlier. Calling Radio Kiskeya from Canada later that same day, Jean denied that he was going into exile and said that he was simply seeking medical treatment for a knee ailment, while his family went to visit relatives in North America. In the midst of the interview with Jean, Kiskeya then broadcast comments from United States Ambassador Curran stating that the U.S. had forwarded a "file" they had on Jean to the Canadian government. On June 30, with Radio Vision 200 broadcasting an erroneous report of his arrest, Jean opted to return to Haiti, where he arrived the next day and headed directly for the National Palace. Despite the fact that the rumors of Jean's exile and arrest turned out to be untrue, the tittering about his legal status served as an illustration of just how close to Aristide the U.S. charges of drug trafficking and official corruption were getting to the public realm.

BRIAN DEAN CURRAN, nearing the end of his tenure as U.S. Ambassador to Haiti, addressed the Haitian-American Chamber of Commerce in Port-au-Prince on July 9. Speaking in meticulous French in deference to his surroundings, the Kreyol-fluent ambassador launched into a scathing denunciation of the corruption and impunity that he said had infected all levels of Haitian society, shocking many of those in attendance. Calling for the arrest of Amiot Metayer, new leadership in the PNH and a credible disarmament campaign, Curran said that Washington accepted that Aristide was Haiti's only legitimate president until 2006, and the outlined the "four crisis" he saw facing the country: political, economic, humanitarian and moral crisis.

"Allow me, once again, to be clear and coherent concerning the American policy in Haiti," Curran began. "The United States accepts President Aristide as the constitutional president for the duration of his mandate which will end in 2006. We estimate that the legislative and territorial elections of May 2000 were sullied with errors and that the Haitian government has the responsibility first to rectify them.

Of the political crisis, he said, "the fundamental aspects are known of all. Electoral fraud. Violation of the human rights. Intolerance. Impunity. The solution is also known to all: new elections. But how does one arrive there from here? In negotiations having taking place during 2002, the OAS traced a way there to the elections. Resolution 822."

Chiding Haiti's political class for assuming that the solution to country's political problems "would be internationally imposed on it," Curran nevertheless could not resist a departing slap at the IRI, that had functioned as trying to portray itself as a parallel negotiating force to the ambassador's authority with the Aristide-hostile members of Haiti's *classe politique*.

"There were many in Haiti who preferred not to listen to me, the representative of the President, but rather listened to their own friends in Washington, the sirens of the extremists or the revanchists on a side or those of the apologists of the other," Curran said, "[who] don't have governmental functions. This is why I call them the chimere of Washington. Throw a glance over the two last years and if you make an honest evaluation of it, I hope that when you want to understand the American policy, you will listen to my successor, a proven and tested diplomat, and not the chimere."

Moving on to the country's economic crisis, Curran said that, "The impunity of criminals is like a stone around the neck of the Haitian economy. Business and commerce need an independent and strong legal system and a police force which neither is politicized nor corrupt. When justice is to be sold, the rights of the individuals suffer from it. A free market economy depends on the rights of ownership and the execution of the contracts. . . . In the final analysis, it is Haiti which profits the most by the state's adherence to rights and reinforced legal institutions.

It was the final section of the speech, though, on what he termed the country's "moral crisis," that attracted the most attention. Looking down on Haiti's elite business leaders, Curran began familiarly enough, making his views on the Aristide government's governmental practices crystal clear.

"I do not understand what is meant by moral values when senators demand the arrest of an ex chief of Police force because he dared to criticize or *lancer des fleches*," Curran said, in a clear reference to Jean-Robert Faveur. "I do not understand what is meant by moral values when elected officials benefit from the sale of the basic conveniences to the Haitian people, to the detriment of the taxpayers. I do not understand what is meant by moral values when the poor are encouraged to invest in co-operative swindles and then lose all or almost all their money, whereas the corrupt swindlers escape from the difficulty with complicity from certain officials."

But, it became apparent, those assembled would not be spared.

"I do not understand what has happened to the moral values of a company when drug trafficking is tolerated, and I do not speak only about the public sector. This is a subject which affects all to us. Or at least, it would claim that it does. . . . The traffickers are well-known. . . . They are supplied in your stores, you sell houses to them or construct new ones for them, you take their deposits, you educate their children, you elect them to positions in the Chamber of Commerce. . . . This battle cannot be left with the government. Without the support of the community, we cannot gain. But we will persevere; we cannot accept the intolerable; we will not be complacent."

"I hope sincerely that this dark scenario can be avoided," concluded Curran, who would take up a diplomatic posting in Italy at the end of the month and be replaced as ambassador by career diplomat James B. Foley, who had previously served as Deputy Permanent Representative of the United States to the UN. "The people deserve better. . . . The international community cannot save the democracy in Haiti. The Haitians alone can save it."

ARISTIDE'S CONCEPT of Haitian democracy was demonstrated quite clearly when, on July 14, Brigade de Recherche et d'Intervention (BRI) officers again arrested opposition politician Judith Roy and three other connected with her REPAREN party and took them to the National Police Academy in Freres. In an echo of the days of Prosper Avril's reign, two groups of men, one in civilian clothes and one in police uniform, took turns beating the prisoners, using their fists, clubs and iron bars. Roy herself was stomped on when she collapsed on the floor. The treatment continued for four days, and when Roy was transferred to the notorious Delmas 33 police station, the beating intensified. Finally taken before a judge on July 18, despite the fact that Haitian law required a detained to appear before a judge and be apprised of the charges against them within forty-eight hours of arrest, the charges against Roy still remained murky. She was remanded to the Petionville jail. When human rights activists from NCHR finally gained access to Roy at the Fort National prison, where she had again been moved, on July 21, they found her bruised and battered and unable to move her left hand. Her three co-detainees, visited by activists where they were being held at the Delmas police station, were found injured and bloodied and said they had been denied medical care.

ANDRÉ "ANDY" APAID, JR., the head of the Alpha Industries assembly plant who was emerging as the most visible spokesman for the Group of 184, liked to tell a story of a Haitian general who, when he saw two black people talking together, let it pass, saw two mulattos talking together and let it pass, but when he saw a black and a mulatto talking together, the general ordered "execute them." Apaid, who veered toward the white side of a mulatto complexion, had been born in New York City, the son of the Haitian industrialist (and later fierce Aristide opponent) André Apaid, Sr., who had founded the Alpha Sewing factory in the 1970s. The younger Apaid had returned to Haiti at four months old, but grew up on both sides of the Straits of Florida, attending the University of Miami for two years before graduating from Hofstra University in New York. Holding dual U.S.-Haitian citizenship, Apaid was fond of quoting Martin Luther King, Jr. and Mahatma Gandhi when it came time to explain the philosophy behind the Group of 184. Fluent in English, French, Kreyol and Spanish, Apaid was no naive dreamer, though, but was rather a very media-savvy leader for the organization and a figure who Aristide, from those who knew him, was said to hold in absolute contempt, the epitome of the light-skinned oligarchy he had built his rhetorical flourishes on cutting down even as he made deals with them when it suited his ends. Throughout the spring and summer, the Group of 184 felt they had gained some moderate success in presenting their *contrat social* in nine cities around Haiti, and so, on July 12, they intended to bring it to the heart of what remained of Aristide's power base and hold a meeting in Cité Soleil. The group had been invited to hold a forum at the Centre Sainte Thérèse d'Avila in Soleil 4, which had been run for many years by the elderly Haitian priest Arthur Volel.

As word spread of the intended rally and local radio stations advertised its existence, the National Palace was not at all pleased with the prospect of the group expounding their vision for a new Haiti on what Aristide viewed as his home turf. Several days before the rally was scheduled to take place, Minster of the Interior Jocelerme Privert called the gang leader Labanye on his cell phone and told him that "no matter what," the meeting of the Group of 184 should not be allowed to take place. As discussions commenced between Labanye's Boston base, James's Soleil 19 base and City Soleil Mayor Fritz Joseph on how to best thwart the event, the day before the rally, July 11, Hermione Leonard arrived in Cité Soleil on what would prove to be her final high-profile mission for Aristide, distributing freshly-printed t-shirts bearing the president's likeness, spray paint canisters and posters of Aristide, along with a meager amount of money for distribution among the chimere. Andy Apaid had also previously reached out to the gang leaders in an effort to insure the rally's security, but to no avail.

About two hundred people had gathered at Pere Volel's center, among them several observers from the foreign diplomatic missions at Haiti, including Luis Moreno, the deputy chief of mission at the U.S. Embassy, and Stephan Gruenberg, his French counterpart. Group of 184 members like Apaid and Charles Baker arrived, and the meeting was about to commence when, from the alleys of Cité Soleil, the chimere began filtering out and ringing the structure. What happened next would go down as one of the more spectacular examples of Aristide's bad judgment. The general consensus among the international observers there was that, were the meeting to go forward, it would have been fairly uneventful. But Aristide, ever mindful of any encroachments toward his power base, had no intention of letting these interlopers and their foreign protectors off that easily. Soon, rocks and bottles were raining down upon the center and those in attendance as the chimere, several hundred strong and many adorned in their new Aristide t-shirts, chanted that they were going to "cut the throats" of those inside. As the windows of the vehicles parked inside the compound began to shatter, a debate went on inside as to how best to proceed. The mob seemed larger and angrier than previous groups, and, despite a few scuffles with the police, seemed reined in only by their own sense of what they could get away with, and so the decision was made to evacuate the meeting. Journalists who went to speak with the chimere were told they were going to be killed.

As PNH officers opened the doors of the center so vehicles could get out of the courtyard and begin to drive away, about fifty chimere pushed past the assembled CIMO and began pelting a bus designed to transport attendees—and diplomats and journalists' vehicles—with stones. As the vehicles sped away through back lanes, they were also stoned. An ambulance attempting to ferry away the injured was attacked and barely escaped. The armored car belonging to the U.S. Embassy, the last vehicle to leave Cité Soleil, was nearly completely destroyed as it was pelted with boulder-sized rocks. The final toll would be forty civilians, six journalists and five policeman injured. Later, the government paper, *L'Union*, would print a typical piece of transparent propaganda on the incident, having "Cité Soleil residents" stating that, "They [the Group of 184] are the ones who killed Dessalines. . . . If they touch a hair on Aristide's head, the country will become a burning inferno."

The country would become a burning inferno soon enough, though by his actions such as those exhibited in the Cité Soleil attack, it would be Aristide himself who supplied the matches.

"Had Aristide just let it pass, Andy Apaid would have just been this somewhat pathetic guy with a megaphone," an American diplomat who had been present later told me. "But he couldn't let it pass, and so it became something else altogether."

GROWING EVER MORE BLOATED on the millions that Aristide was funneling to his Miami law firm, Haiti's government council, Ira Kurzban, opined in a press release from Miami on July 14 that the international community "must denounce also those who provoke violence. . . . A knowing provocation to violence under the guise of free speech is not protected under any country's laws, including the United States, and no one should expect governmental authorities in Haiti to tolerate such actions."[1] In other words, to the university students in the capital, the schoolchildren in Petit Goave and the journalists in Gonaives, it was really their fault anyway, so they got what they deserved. Despite his elite pedigree, Andy Apaid more accurately summed up popular sentiment in Haiti a day later when he told Haitian journalists that, "Mr. Aristide is in rebellion against the country."

When a suspicious fire tore through two blocks of warehouses in the capital on July 17, incinerating the livelihoods of some one hundred merchants, Prime Minister Yvon Neptue, speaking to reporters, pointed to the Group of 184, saying, "Certain people are speaking words of death and disaster."

Death came readily enough in Aristide's Haiti, though, that one did not need to speak about it beforehand, and on July 20, Roland Francois, the chimere leader from La Saline who had battled with Franco Camille's gang for control of the slum for several years, was picked up by the PNH, taken to the police station at Delmas 33, and executed by PNH officer Jean-Marie Dominique on the orders of Interior Minister Privert. Aristide, it appeared, was beginning to cut his links from the long-serving gunmen who knew so many of his secrets. The next day, Francois's body, pocked-marked with bullet holes, appeared in the city morgue. When Francois was buried two weeks later, members of his Fon Touron gang and hundreds of mourners followed his casket from the Église Saint Joseph, shouting "Aristide, look at what you've done to us!"

Another of Aristide's former associates, Jacques Ketant, stewing in a Miami prison cell, was ordered held without bail on July 9, and formally charged with having helped Colombian drug cartels move 33 tons of cocaine through Haiti on its way to the United States The five-count indictment also mentioned alleged payments Ketant had made to former Port-au-Prince police chief Michel Francois and airport employees in New York, Miami and Port-au-Prince.

ANDY APAID was summoned before the Parquet du Tribunal Civil in the capital on July 24 to answer charges from government judges that some "Cité Soleil residents" had claimed Apaid was responsible for the deaths of four people during the chimere attack on the Group of 184 there two weeks earlier. Apaid appeared to deny the charges, his lawyers called the whole proceeding a "political montage" and a number of civic organizations such as Kay Famn, Famn Yo La and NCHR had spoken out against the process as being baseless and nakedly political.

While Aristide was busy harassing his civic opposition, his cross-border adversaries operating in the Plateau Central scored another blow when a delegation from the Ministry of Interior traveling back from the swearing-in of a new mayor in the border town of Belladere fell victim to a roadside ambush on July 25. Four were killed and one seriously wounded. Yvon Neptune opined that the killers were a "group of terrorists aimed at destroying the foundation of Haitian democracy" while Dany Fabien, chief of staff for Secretary of State for Public Security Gérard Dubreuil, announced that the killings had been carried out by "the armed wing of the opposition." Interior Minister Jocelerme Privert charged that Judith Roy's Force de Protection Citoyenne group was a front for the Guy Philippe rebel gang, which had been such a headache to Aristide over the previous several years. Around the same time, the peasants around Pernal in the Plateau Central began complaining to the Haitian media that, following the attacks blamed on Philippe's men, they were essentially locked into their villages, unable to move freely or till their fields, and that anyone suspected of not being a Lavalas partisan was being, at best, harassed and roughed up by the police and, at worst, disappeared or killed.

In a ray of light for the government, at a press conference at the National Palace on July 25, Inter-American Development Bank (IDB) President Enrique Iglesias announced that the body would renew its cooperation with Haiti, highlighted by four programs with an estimated value of US $146 million. Aristide said that he wanted to express the "gratitude" of the Haitian people for the move.

IN THE LAST WEEK OF JULY, as a 16-year-old girl was killed in a gun battle in La Saline, outgoing U.S. Ambassador Brian Dean Curran told reporters that there was evidence of the Aristide government's collusion in organizing the attack on the Group of 184 and U.S. diplomats during the aborted July 12 rally in Cité Soleil. That same week, speaking to Radio Kiskeya from his exile in Florida, Johnny Occilius, a former employee of Cité Soleil Mayor Fritz Joseph, said that he, Labanye and Kolobri had been given several thousand dollars by Joseph in order to break up the rally and that Aristide's security chief, Oriel Jean, had also acted as the go-between for the National Palace and the Cité Soleil gangs. Additionally, Occilius said he had been party to conversations where Aristide partisans discussed orders from the president to kill the two gang leaders as well as police chief Hermione Leonard. Perhaps most disturbingly, Occilius charged that the disappearance of the newborn baby of one Nanoune Myrthil from the General Hospital on February 29, 2000, had been arranged by So Anne Auguste, who killed the child and then observed its burial by the missing Lavalas OP leader and former Port-au-Prince Cemetery Director Felix Bien-Aimé for the purposes of *vodou* sorcery to empower her patron Aristide. The charge was an eerie echo of a rumor that had surrounded the departure of the Duvalier family in 1986, where Gonaives *houngan* Hérard Simon was said to have sacrificed two infant boys on the couple's bed in the National Palace to ensure that none of their successors ever slept soundly there again. Bien-Aimé eventually threatened to expose the crime when he fell out with his Lavalas patrons, and so was picked up by the PNH and was himself killed, Occilius said.

Adding to the rumors swirling around the PNH since Jean-Robert Faveur's departure, in August Jean-Dady Simeon, the once affable public face of the police department's brutality, evidently sensing which way the wind was blowing for him from his former bosses, announced via a phone call to Radio Caraibes that he had chosen exile in Canada over remaining in Haiti after he had been threatened by fellow police officers. Simeon had never seemed comfortable after his transfer to the less-visible role of public relations head in May where, some thought, he would be far easier to eliminate as his face wouldn't be appearing on television every day. One of his former colleagues, the police officer Jean Panel Charles from the Delmas 33 commissariat, told Radio Metropole News Director Rotchild Francois in an interview that same month that, "Policemen are not able to exercise their authority, because of the armed civilians who have full control in that police station. . . . These attachés are responsible for the bad acts. . . . They arrest people, steal people's money, steal vehicles, put people in secret cells and kill them later on. Those people are so powerful that the policemen are not able to do their job as policemen."

Every week seemed to bring a new, troubling revelation about the Aristide government from its former backers. On August 13, speaking on Radio Metropole from exile in France, Jean-Michard Mercier, the former deputy mayor of Port-au-Prince under René Préval, charged that at meetings with Aristide at Tabarre prior to the May 2000 elections, Lavalas officials had plotted on how to best rig the legislative vote so they could get a "totality" not a "majority" of the vote; he also charged that his fellow deputy mayor at the time, Harold Sévère, whose name Aristide had removed from the Jean Dominique case indictment months before, had been personally present in one of the getaway cars at the scene of Dominique's murder. Echoing statements from Johnny Occilius the previous month, Mercier also gave a strikingly similar account of the alleged murder of the newborn baby stolen from the General Hospital by So Anne Auguste in 2000 and the murder of Felix Bien-Aimé for his threat to reveal the killing.

Another significant defection from the regime was announced in late August when Hermione Leonard resigned from her position as Directeur Départemental de l'Ouest and was replaced by Rudy Berthomieux. Evidently, Leonard had fallen afoul of Aristide's enforcer-in-chief, Jean-Claude Jean-Baptiste, still very much running the PNH from behind the scenes. Leonard had reportedly told acquaintances that she had begun to fear for her life after Johnny Occilius's declaration the previous month, and she ceased to show up for work from August 12 onwards. Rumors in the PNH of an apparent failed kidnapping attempt against Aristide's two daughters Christine and Michaelle by PNH officers under Leonard's command—foiled by Aristide's private security forces as they traveled to Tabarre—further inflamed matters. A week later, Leonard would surface in the Dominican Republic, living in Santo Domingo's chic Arroyo Hondo quarter.

Before the month was out, Dumay Carrier, a security guard for the APROFISA health organization that had been the target of so much government-sponsored harassment two years earlier, was gunned down by two armed men at the organization's headquarters in the Carrefour Feuilles neighborhood, in full view of a line of children waiting to be seen at the pediatric clinic there.

In the Maribaroux free-trade zone, Aristide's pet project, the Dominican Grupo M company, opened its first factory, hiring three hundred workers to assemble Levi's Jeans. Workers were forbidden to unionize or discuss politics while in the free trade zone. In place of their former lives farming one of Haiti's most fertile regions, the workers toiled from 7 o'clock in the morning until 7 at night with a single 45-minute break to eat lunch and use the bathroom. For their labors they were paid 432 gourdes (around US $10) per week.

IF ARISTIDE WAS FAZED by the announcements of his fugitive former supporters, he didn't let on when, speaking in Leogane on August 23, he brazenly, almost threateningly, promised "security" for any candidates willing to campaign in new elections and said that "elections will not help us have food, a home to live in or to obtain justice, but are essential for strengthening democratic institutions so that later on we can have more food, more houses to live in, more justice and better health conditions everywhere in the country."

During the ceremony in Leogane, the town's main Catholic priest, Fritz Sauvagère, lashed out from the pulpit against Radio Vision 2000 correspondent Peterson Milord, who had reported on local complaints that Sauvagère was extorting huge fees for burials and other ceremonies from locals and misappropriating Church funds. Sauvagère's remarks were broadcast on TNH, as Aristide sat impassively watching, and resulted in Milord being physically expelled from the church.

"All of the problems this country has are due to the press," thundered Sauvagère.

Haiti's Episcopal Council, the Association Nationale des Médias Haïtiens (ANMH) and NCHR all denounced the move and Aristide's silence in the face of it.

In the north of Haiti that same day, a Tropical Airways plane en route from Cap Haitien to Port de Paix, the same route and company I had been so nervous about traveling on the year before, crashed, killing all nineteen passengers and two pilots.

Despite a dip in protests in the capital following the Cité Soleil attack, in Cap Haitien the situation remained tense. On August 30, police fired tear gas to break up a rally of thousands of Aristide opponents sponsored by Jean-Robert Lalanne's Front de l'Opposition dans le Nord (FRON) and Frandley Julien's Initiative Citoyenne, saying the event was illegal, and on September 14 a similar demonstration left fifteen injured when a group of chimeres led by Jocelerme Privert's second-in-command, Bel Angelot, and Lavalas deputy Nawoon Marcellus attacked an opposition march in the city as police idly stood by. In the capital, to coincide with the twelfth anniversary of the 1991 coup against Aristide at the end of September, a demonstration organized at Aristide's request by Ben Dupuy, the leader of an infinitesimal and politically insignificant political grouping called the Parti Populaire National (PPN), chanted slogans against Haiti's journalists and accused the country's reporters of being part of a "macoute-bourgeois" conspiracy for reporting critically on the Aristide government. Dupuy, a political opportunist long supported in his intrigues by his wealthy white American ex-wife and her dilettante son, had first gained note lambasting Jean Dominique on the Duvalierist radio program Eddy Publicité in November 1980—at the height of Duvalierist terror and threats against Dominique and the Radio Haiti-Inter staff—and had long been mocked in Haiti for fawning in whatever direction assured him money and status.

Later that month, the Aristide government showed his support for Sauvagère and Dupuy's declarations when, in simultaneous interviews with television and radio stations in Port-au-Prince on September 21, Minister of Justice Calixte Delatour, Secretary of State for Communication Mario Dupuy and Conseil National des Telecommunications (CONATEL) head Jean Harry Ceant all said that there would be a move to revive a presidential decree passed by Jean-Claude Duvalier on October 12, 1977, which stated, "broadcast information must be precise, objective and impartial, and must come from authorized sources which are to be mentioned when broadcasting. Those who are responsible for the broadcasts have to control the programs to ensure that the information—even when it is correct—cannot harm or alarm the population by its form, presentation or timing. The broadcast stations will provide a channel for the broadcasting of official programs, if so required by the public powers. . . ." It was a naked assault on articles 28-1, 28-2 and 245 of Haiti's constitution, which forbids censorship and protects free speech and journalistic practices.

THE MEANS BY WHICH to implement OAS Resolution 822 and still maintain his advantage in firepower over Guy Philippe's cross-border insurgents and the unarmed student and civil society protesters had proved a thorny one for Aristide. La Saline gang leader Roland Francois had been dispatched to popular outcry earlier in the summer, but there were still stones weighing around Aristide's neck, keeping him from making the minimal headway necessary to regain the diplomatic advantage and hopefully unlock the international aid he had been salivating at the prospect of since his reelection in 2000. To that end, in mid-September, a representative sent on behalf of Aristide's right-hand man Jean-Claude Jean-Baptiste arrived in Gonaives to confer with Cannibal Army leader Amiot Metayer and Metayer's deputy, Winter Etienne, saying he was bringing an offer of $200,000 to Metayer if he would return to prison, presumably face a sham trial and eventual acquittal. If not, the emissary hinted darkly, the government would have no choice but to use "forceful means" to achieve that end. Metayer—not surprisingly, given his previous double-cross by the regime—declined, and he sent the envoy back to the National Palace with the warning that he would tell all that he knew about the government should the authorities try to arrest him again.

The conversation was evidently not foremost in Metayer's mind as he spent the day of September 21 in Gonaives with Odonel Paul, another Gonaives-based political activist who had served in the Aristide's Interior Ministry under Henri-Claude Ménard during the Cherestal government and had since remained close to the president. Paul had his own political movement, called the Mouvement Démocratique pour la Libération Nationale (MODLIN), and unbeknownst to Metayer had been seen visiting Aristide's wing on the National Palace several days earlier, though Raboteau's poverty-stricken residents did notice Paul's sudden seeming affluence and dapper clothes. Returning at around 7:30 p.m. that night, Metayer changed clothes and headed back out with Paul into the Artibonite night.

When the next day dawned and Metayer had still failed to return home, the Cannibal Army, aware that it was not their leader's custom to spend nights away from the district, began to worry—fears that were confirmed when Metayer's badly mutilated body was found at Bas Gros Morne, south of Gonaives on the road to Saint Marc. Metayer had been shot several times, and his eyes and heart had been removed, apparently excised by a bladed instrument. His body bore the signs of terrible torture. He had been thirty-nine years old.

Disbelief and agony greeted the news of their chief's demise in the lanes of Raboteau as Metayer's body was brought back to Gonaives on September 23. Metayer's brother, Butteur, who had previously worked at the Gonaives port, was visiting members of the Metayer family in Florida when he got the news and immediately headed home to see what had happened. The emotion in the city itself turned to rage, though, when some of Metayer's followers, phoning the National Palace to report the crime and seek Aristide's help, found out by way of the talkative secretary who answered the phone that none other than Odonel Paul himself had been at the Palace that morning. Paul had arrived to meet with Oriel Jean around 10 a.m. and left with Jean-Claude Jean-Baptiste around 3 p.m. Paul's family has already fled their home in Saint Marc, but Paul himself was never seen again. Whether he was killed on Aristide's orders after accomplishing his mission or slipped into exile remains unclear.

The following day, as news of Aristide's treachery swept through Gonaives, thousands of people flooded out of the slums in protests led by Butteur Metayer and the now-resurfaced Jean Tatoune, screaming that "Aristide killed Cubain!" and chanting "Tell Bush Aristide is in deep shit!" Though Jocelerme Privert told reporters in the capital that the government would conduct "a swift and thorough" investigation into the crime, the mob ransacked Odonel Paul's house and burned his belongings in the street. Frightened by the mob's anger and size, panicky PNH officers opened fire at several points during the day, wounding five people.

If anyone doubted that things in the city had turned an important corner, speaking on Radio Caraibes on September 24, Cannibal Army member Jules Andre launched an implacable threat to Aristide.

"Metayer is dead because Aristide thinks that Metayer's execution would resolve one of the key points of OAS Resolution 822," Andre said on the phone from Gonaives, as residents began to flee the city, fearing the inevitable showdown between the gangs and Aristide's security forces that seemed sure to come. "Aristide killed Amiot Metayer so that he can hold elections. That is why we are standing against him, to say elections will not take place. We want Aristide to leave office. . . . Our blood was shed so that Aristide could return to the country. That is what we stand for today."

FOR THE NEXT WEEK, protests continued in the city, with the Raboteau and Jubilé districts becoming barricaded with walls of burning tires and cars and buses that were set aflame. On September 26, 21-year-old Joseph Elisé was killed by gunfire, while on September 29, the PNH brutally dispersed a new march in the paralyzed city with tear gas and automatic-weapons fire.[2]

In the capital, demonstrating how wretchedly wedded to Aristide's survival they had become, Paul Raymond and René Civil in interviews with local media attempted to blame Metayer's killing on everyone from former French Ambassador Yves Gaudeul to the anti-Aristide Monsignor of Jacmel Guy Poulard and Himmler Rebu. They also announced that a new pro-government mobilization "Operation Stranglehold and Shield,' would stop in their tracks all demonstrations aimed at toppling the Aristide government, and that no large-scale demonstrations, á la Gonaives, would be permitted to pass. Back in Gonaives itself, Camille Marcellus, the lethal former commander of the Delmas commissariat in the capital who had been transferred by Aristide to command the PNH in the Artibonite in the months before Metayer's murder, was put in charge of organizing the government's response to the unrest. In an indication of how they planned to handle it, he summoned to Gonaives from the capital René Jean-Anthony, the notorious Delmas 33 police station killer called Grenn Sonnen, to help him oversee what was to come.

WHAT WAS TO COME was, in all its particulars, an atrocious repeat of the 1994 massacre that took place in Raboteau at the hands of the Haitian military and FRAPH, except that this time it would be carried out by Aristide's government against the same people who had bled and suffered for him for so long while he was in exile. In an assault led by Camille Marcellus and the attaché René Jean-Anthony and utilizing both Haitian Coast Guard boats, Aristide's private helicopter and Unité de Securite du Palais Nationale personnel under Aristide's direct command, government forces stormed Raboteau and Jubilé in the early morning hours of October 2 in an attempt to capture or kill Butteur Metayer and Jean Tatoune. After killing three locals in the initial assault, the Aristide forces then killed eight more, their deaths recorded at the Hopital la Providence in Gonaives throughout the day. Michelet Lozier, a mother of five, was gunned down by Jean-Anthony himself as she ran for cover, and empty boats bobbed on the sea from fishermen who locals say had gone out to sea around the time of the assault and never returned.

Speaking with Haitian journalist Gotson Pierre by phone from Gonaives and taunting the government for their failure to find him, Butteur Metayer again blamed Odonel Paul and Gonaives Police Commissioner Harold Adéclat for direct involvement in his brother's death and challenged Aristide to send "USP, the USGPN, the SWAT, the CIMO, to see whether or not we are joking."[3]

"We feel sorry for them, if they think they can take us by force," Metayer said, and darkly hinted that the Front had a "Phase 2" plan, which they would execute when ready.

"They have their strategy," Metayer said. "We have ours."

As Gonaives burned and bled under the ministrations of Camille Marcellus and René Jean-Anthony, the police and attachés at their former place of employment at the Delmas 33 commissariat kept in practice by arresting and torturing Faculté des Sciences Humaines student Nesly Numa the same day.

AMIOT METAYER was buried on October 6 in a crypt in the street in front of his home in Raboteau where he had fought his political battles all his life. After a ceremony at the Mormon chapel in Gonaives, thousands of protestors lead by Butteur Metayer carried "Cubain's" coffin through the streets of Gonaives, chanting "*Aba Aristide!*" and winding their way through the streets of the slums. At one point, rumors swirled through the crowd that police were going to try and seize Metayer's casket, and demonstrators hurled stones at PNH, who reacted by firing into the air and dousing the crowd with tear gas.[4] As Metayer's coffin was lowered into its crypt and the grave filled in with fresh cement, beneath an impressive gold-plate bust of the gang leaders that his loyalists had constructed above the tomb, Metayer's mother collapsed onto the hard concrete on top of her son's grave in the middle of the street, wailing, "Thanks, Odonel, a beautiful gesture! You ripped my Cubain apart!"

An October 8 Amnesty International bulletin warned that in Haiti, "Killings, violent attacks and threats—committed by political partisans and armed, politically-motivated groups—are of growing concern, as are violations committed by security forces in responding to political violence. In addition, attacks on freedom of expression continue."[5] As if to underline the report, on October 9, CIMO in Gros-Morne, clearing barricades set up in sympathy with Gonaives protestors, fired at a crowd of demonstrators, killing an eleven-year-old boy. In an October 11 interview with Haitian radio, Winter Etienne announced that the Cannibal Army would heretofore be known as the Front de Résistance des Gonaives pour le Renversement de Jean Bertrand Aristide (Gonaives Resistance Front for the Departure of Jean-Bertrand Aristide) and that they would work exclusively to drive the Haitian president from power. Two days later, police violently dispersed yet another antigovernment demonstration in Gonaives and a new, chaotic protest in Saint Marc organized by the Rassemblement des Militants Conséquents de Saint Marc group.

Unrest was sweeping the country. An October 15 antigovernment demonstration in Petit Goave was tear-gassed and broken up by the police. On the 197th anniversary of the assassination of Jean-Jacques Dessalines on October 17, Aristide attended a Mass at the ruler's former seat of power, Marchand Dessalines, that was led by Father Léobert Dieudonne, and he smiled as Dieudonne launched a bile-filled attack on the independent media as being part of a destabilization campaign against the country. In a press release, NCHR noted that some thirty journalists had fled into exile since Aristide had returned to power in 2001, and said that:

> The independent press in Haiti is facing a situation of cyclic terror. Whenever a government does not feel secure or comfortable, the repercussions can be felt by the members of the fourth [4th] power, and one could hardly imagine the cynicism with which this happens. These days the independent press faces revolting practices worthy only of the most reactionary dictatorships in the history of Haiti—it even looks as if all these successive governments are competing in cynicism and cruelty, in order to try and claim eventually the prize for having delivered the final blow to the press.[6]

In the capital, Danielle Lustin, a university professor, feminist activist and expert in microfinancing who worked with the *ti machanns* to help them obtain loans for their businesses, was murdered on October 22 under mysterious circumstances. Following a Mass held in her memory at the Sacre-Coeur on October 29, some thirty women held a sit-in at the Ministry of Justice to demand an investigation into Lustin's killing and an end to impunity. As they did so, a group of chimere descended from a white pickup bearing "Officielle" license plates and pummeled them with rocks and bottles, crying "*Viv Aristide*" and threatening them in the most base, misogynistic terms. The protestors were forced to flee.

DESPITE ARISTIDE'S ATTEMPTS to break the will of the population there, the people of Raboteau would not be cowed. An October 26 gunfight that erupted between Front members and PNH forces in the vicinity of the Gonaives commissariat succeeded in wounding the hated PNH director for the Artibonite Camille Marcellus, but a fourteen-year-old girl coming out of church was also killed. Butteur Metayer and Winter Etienne announced that the movement would henceforth be known, more succinctly, as the Artibonite Resistance Front.

Aristide responded with blind fury following the shooting of Marcellus, and on October 27, again using a combination of boats, state vehicles, and his presidential helicopter, the police once more attacked the slum neighborhoods near Gonaives's port, partially burning Amiot Metayer's house and assaulting it with a bulldozer and raking his monument with gunfire. A seventeen-year-old local girl, Josline Michel, was killed when police fired into her home, and several others were wounded. Police and attachés burned a dozen homes, incinerated fisherman's boats and killed any livestock they found in residents' yards. Yet again deprived of their quarry when the uprising's leadership escaped their grasp, government forces returned the next day, where they burned more homes in Raboteau, including one belonging to Micheline Limay, who managed to save her two-year-old son Judson from the flames but watched in horror as her month old baby girl was consumed by the fire. A dozen other people were also said to have died.

In the midst of the assault, in an October 27 op-ed in the *Miami Herald* by the ubiquitous American congresswoman Barbara Lee and Representative. John Conyers (D-Michigan), co-chairs of the Congressional Black Caucus Haiti Task Force, lauded the Aristide regime, writing that, "The government has invited international observers and police contingents from neighboring countries to enhance electoral security and guarantee fairness"—something that must have come as news to the savaged residents of Raboteau.

THE FATE OF AMIOT METAYER made the Cité Soleil chimere take a long, hard look at the government they had been serving, and many of them were slowly deciding that they did not like what they saw. While the attachés and gang leaders affiliated with the Delmas 33 police station and receiving the favor of Fritz Joseph sported new clothes and cars, the Cité Soleil militants still wallowed in poverty, and now it seemed that Aristide wanted to eliminate them—thus expunging the evidence that could tie him conclusively to the campaign of murder and intimidation he had waged over the years, and expose his brutal, cynical exploitation of the legitimate hopes of Haiti's poor. Labanye, whose doubts about Aristide had been prominent for some time, was the first to reach out, meeting with Andy Apaid in late September—at least the second meeting between to two since July. Labanye provided a pair of long cassette interviews to Apaid, during which he detailed and outlined many of the crimes the Aristide government had committed that he had been party to, including murders and details of other criminal activity. It was a ballsy, daring move but, despite his brutality, Labanye had always, in addition to being an extremely dangerous individual, been a somewhat clever guy, and for his efforts Apaid helped him obtain travel visas for both Jamaica and the Dominican Republic. Around the same time, my friend James, desperately poor and barely able to leave Cité Soleil for fear of being recognized and killed, particularly as a result of his contact with foreign journalists, met at the U.S. Embassy with Vice Consul Matthew Miller and the embassy's human rights officer in the vain hope of securing a travel visa to the United States. Junior Millard, the young militant I had met with James years earlier, had been killed and left facedown in a trash-strewn lane in the district a short time earlier, and James was feeling particularly vulnerable. The embassy officials pumped him for information on violent acts such as the December 17 chimere rampage or the July 12 Cité Soleil attack he had been involved in, but in the end they offered him no real hope of passage out of Haiti. Though the Cité Soleil chimere had finally begun to realize their expendability to their surrogate father Aristide, for some it was already too late.

On October 31, Rodson Lemaire, the 23-year-old Labanye deputy who went by the nom de guerre Kolobri, was gunned down in Cité Soleil in a joint operation by Dread Wilmé and Police Superintendent Bernard Saint-Louis, acting under the orders of Fritz Joseph, enthusiastically implementing his boss Aristide's request.

So poor at the time of his death that his family and friends had to take up donations around the neighborhood to pay for his funeral, Kolobri was nonetheless looked upon as a protector by enough people that, on November 4, hundreds of residents of Cité Soleil's Boston district gathered, chanting "Down with Aristide" in his memory.

"We are demanding that Aristide step down, because he ordered Dread Wilmé and these bastard policemen to shoot at the people of Cité Soleil and the people of Boston," one demonstrator told Radio Vision 2000. "May Dread Wilmé fuck his mother because he is a thief!"

"When I say that members of the government assassinated Kolobri, this is not something I'm presuming; it's a fact," a livid Labanye told Radio Metropole the same day. "There were two pickup trucks full of policemen. . . . There were attachés with the policemen."

We don't know why they eliminated Kolobri after all he did for the government. That is the way the Lavalas government is. The Lavalas authorities want to trample on the people's blood in order to celebrate 2004. The way things are now, Aristide is willing even to give away his own children so that he may celebrate 2004.

Fritz Joseph said that we would not have a chance to see 2004, and now what he said has come true. . . . They gave him a car so that he would ensure that Kolobri and I do not live to see 2004. So Kolobri has gone now.

They gave orders for us to break up the gathering of the Group of 184, they got us to do all kinds of things. Now they want us to do even more, and we have refused to do so, so they want to eliminate us. . . . Aristide is not playing games. As you can see, he gave away Jacques Ketant, and he is going to give away some more men, because he must celebrate 2004 by all means.

Aristide had pushed the population very far with his late spate of killings, and the rhetoric of those opposed to his role within Haiti was getting more and more violent. On November 1, a group based in Carrefour and calling itself the Front des Jeunes pour Sauver Haiti (FROJESHA), had told Radio Signal FM that, in response to Operation Stranglehold and Shield announced by René Civil, that the organization would soon rise up in armed opposition against Aristide; they called on members of the former military to support them.

"We're telling Aristide that civil war has been declared," the group's spokesman, David Cocy, declared. "We call on all former servicemen, all former soldiers that if you have *galils*, keep your *galils*, if you have heavy weapons, start loading your cartridges so we can revolt against Aristide."

AMIDST THIS TABLEAUX of treachery and violence, the Group of 184 announced that, despite the failure of their attempt to meet in Cité Soleil the previous July, they would present their social contract to the capital's population at a November 14 rally on the Champs de Mars. The Group had written to both Aristide and the Fanmi Lavalas party as a whole, asking for a private meeting to discuss the contract at the beginning of the month, but they were rebuffed. As had happened in Cité Soleil, though, when the 184 attempted to gather on the Champs de Mars they were met by a howling, stone-and-bottle throwing mob of chimere, about half of whom were children, who backed them into a corner near Haiti's National Museum of Art as tear-gas canisters exploded and clouds of noxious fumes wafted through the crowd. Of two police teams at the scene, one in front of the American consulate down the street watched the attack take place and another group nearer the scene left from their vehicle and went into a private home as the rock-throwing started. The attack, while significant, was

not unexpected and did not have as great an effect as the events that had proceeded it. Driving to the march with Andy Apaid's nephew, David, and two
other cars full of people, Vice President of the Association des Industries
d'Haiti (ADIH) Charles Baker was stopped by PNH officers, who asked him
to step out of his car while they searched it. Baker, whose life had been threatened on many occasions since he began accompanying the Group of 184's
"Caravan of Hope" around Haiti almost a year earlier, was well known to frequently carry a firearm and had made it a point at the beginning of demonstrations to show his pistol to the police along with his permit. When police found
three handguns in the vehicles, two with valid permits and one registered to
Apparel and Garment Contractors, the police asked Baker and about three
dozen others in the convoy to come with them to the police station. The men
were taken to the commissariat at Pompiers, near the National Palace, where
they sat from 11 a.m. until 5 p.m. that evening. Asked what was going on, the
policeman on duty responded to Baker by telling him, "We can't let you go, we've
received orders." Finally, near midnight, a police officer with a 4-bar ranking
on the shoulder of his uniform told a subordinate with a 2-bar ranking to write
Baker and the others up for arrest, all with the same charge—"Possession of
illegal weapons and police paraphernalia." The subordinate refused and
walked out of the station, and which point the officer with 4 bars said, "Look,
if I don't do it, someone else is going to do it," and wrote up the same charge
for all twenty-five arrested although there were only three weapons seized.
The group was then formally arrested and paraded before TNH and Tele Timoun government cameras by Port-au-Prince Police Commissioner Ricardo Etienne. That night, after the faces of the arrested men were broadcast to the
nation, the sister-in-law of one of the detainees was murdered and several of
their homes were ransacked. Twenty-one of the twenty-five men arrested were
eventually released, but Baker and David Apaid were held and interrogated
about the activities of the Group of 184 along with two former members of
Haiti's military, men who had been demobilized since the 1980s. Baker and
Apaid were sent to the Titanic Bloc of the National Penitentiary where the most
hardened criminals in the country were held in squalid, life-threateningly
unsanitary conditions, and where they would remain for seventeen days. Police
made no arrests among those who attacked the rally.

LARGE BUSINESSES, banks, gas stations and other mid-sized enterprises
closed on November 17 to protest the November 14 attack and the detention of
Baker and Apaid, though *ti machanns* and street vendors operated as usual. The
same day, Pierre-Honald Bonnet, chief of the Bureau des Affaires Criminelles
(BAC) and assistant director of the judiciary police in the PNH, was shot to
death in his car near the international airport by unknown assailants in a killing
that bore all the trademarks of an Aristide-ordered hit. Speaking in Cap Haitien

to commemorate the bicentennial of the battle of Vertières, Aristide told the crowd, "You are a victim, I am a victim, we are eight million victims. Victims who refuse to walk on our knees, or with shame in our hands. . . . This plot, this embargo is genocidal. We need a more human and more fraternal world. Social scourges on the planet scale are in fresh outbreak. . . . Respect, Restitution and Reparation for a civilization of Peace!" Echoing Aristide's rhetoric without apparent irony in the midst of the political murders and arbitrary detentions, Aristide's campaign that France pay Haiti restitution for its colonial debt was continuing, with a jingle running on state radio saying, *"Lafrans kale m lajan m!* (France, give me my money!) $21,685,135,571.48!"

In another indication of how Haitian society was coalescing against governmental misrule, Haiti's leading intellectuals and creative artists announced on November 20 that they were forming a new collective, called the *"NON"* collective, to prevent the undermining of civil liberties and in reaction to the spiraling violence that had taken hold of the country. Théodore "Lolo" Beaubrun of Boukman Eksperyans, sociologist Laennec Hurbon and the painter Pascale Monnin were among the group's fifty members.

A student demonstration in Petit Goave November 21 to mark the first anniversary of the shooting of the high school students there by the PNH was attacked by the same force, this time under the command of Jean-Marie Dominique, the rumored executioner of La Saline gang leader Roland Francois the previous July. Hervé Saintilus, the president of the Fédération des Étudiants Universitaires d'Haïti, was arrested and several demonstrators wounded by gunfire. Launching his own salvo, the often-dissenting Lavalas Senator Prince Pierre Sonson announced his distance from the Aristide government by publishing a book titled *Haiti: L'Etat de choc (Haiti: State of Shock)* in which he outlined what he characterized as the president's drift toward dictatorship and corruption and what he claimed were his own efforts to have the Lavalas movement remain true to its original ideals.

In addition to the rumblings caused by Sonson's book, other cracks were beginning to appear in the façade of Lavalas party unity. Dany Toussaint, who had been engaged in a complicated give-and-take with Aristide ever since the murder of Jean Dominique, charged in a pair of interviews on Radio Vision 2000 and Radio Kiskeya that, while he remained a Lavalas party member, he was growing ever-more estranged from the party's leader.

"Beware (Aristide) for the road you are taking is not a good one," Toussaint said, denouncing "despotic-anarchic" polices and the attack on the November 14 rally. Aristide's policies, said Toussaint, were leading him to "death, jail or exile."

"Today's regime resembles more and more those that preceded it," he concluded.

Toussaint told me later that he and Aristide hand been in "a cold war" since the May 2000 elections, when Aristide had put word out among the young political militants in the slums who had supported Toussaint's 2000 senatorial campaign to no longer rally for the senator in public, and that, as the Cité Soleil chimere had also said, Aristide had long been threatened by Toussaint's popularity among the Lavalas base.

THE CAPITAL'S RESIDENTS awoke on November 25 to find the severed head of a young man at the corner of Avenue Christophe and Rue Magny in downtown Port-au-Prince, surrounded by leaflets threatening opposition figures and the independent press. Later the same day, ten protestors entered and occupied the OAS headquarters demanding the release of Charles Baker and David Apaid. In Cap Haitien, Jean-Robert Lalanne, the anti-Aristide activist and owner of Au Cap's Radio Maxima, was attacked and injured when unknown intruders scaled the wall of his home.

Sensing how tenuous his situation was becoming and mindful how his recent slaughtering of gang leaders had served to unsettle his base in the capital's most populous slum, on Wednesday, November 26, Aristide called the warring Cité Soleil gang leaders to a meeting at the National Palace. Among the attendees were Labanye from Boston, Dread Wilmé from Bwa Neuf and James's Soleil 19 faction. Aristide told the gang leaders that they were his children, his last line of resistance against a coup. He promised them increased cooperation and status with regards to the police and that in order to defend their rights from the Group of 184 that they had to band together and face the enemy as one. All were convinced except Labanye, who had decided that this self-declared father was a false prophet and that he would do political work for him no more. The same day, Radio Signal FM carried news that the U.S. Embassy had revoked the American visas granted to Calixte Délatour, Jocelerme Privert and PNH director Jocelyne Pierre.

Labanye's new patron, Andy Apaid, again appeared at the Palace of Justice in the capital on November 27 to answer government charges that he was responsible for the deaths of four people during the aborted July Group of 184 rally in Cité Soleil. The appearance had been delayed several days after Apaid had allegedly been informed of a plot by Aristide loyalists to assassinate him on the courthouse steps. This time, Apaid was not arrested, but the government prosecutors seemed arrogantly sure they would proceed with the case against him.

After seventeen days in jail, finally, on December 1, a haggard and bearded Charles Baker and David Apaid emerged from prison, freed by Judge Joassaint St. Clair, who dismissed the charges against them. The protestors vacated the OAS office in the capital they had been occupying.

SHORTLY AFTER CHARLES BAKER'S release from prison, I sat down to speak with him at the offices of the Fondation Nouvelle Haiti in Petionville, behind high walls and patrolled by several security guards. Baker, a silver-haired white man in his late 50s, was descended from a British family that had emigrated to Haiti at the beginning of the twentieth century, and was still visibly, electrically angry over his detention, his fury at Aristide and the international community palpable. As we sat across from one another at a modern wooden conference table, he was blunt, nearly rude, about his views. Greeting me by telling me he knew that the foreign press had been "bought and paid for" by Aristide because they did not take the Haitian elite's change of heart and "social contract" seriously, in many ways during our interview (though not in our conversations and the demonstrations afterwards), Baker seemed to typify the whining self-pity of Haiti's oligarchy at its worst.

"It's going to get violent, and that's what we've been trying to avoid for a year now, well, three years now. If that's what the international community wants for things to change, I guess it's going to have to go that way, but we have to be clear on the fact that it's going to be the international community's fault," Baker told me in fluent, American-accented English perfected by years of living in California. "Twenty thousand troops brought back Mr. Aristide. He was at that time the elected president of Haiti, so I had no problems with that, but at the same time, when you give a guy total power . . . they give him the monopoly on terror and violence. What's happening now is a result of what they did in 1994. And they have the gall to come back and tell us it's a Haitian problem? Bullshit, it's not a Haitian problem. It's an international problem. I hear the U.S. is fighting against terrorism? Here's one, come and pick him up. He is terrorizing people into following his Lavalas movement and they're not buying it, period."

I asked him if he though the Group of 184 represented something truly new in Haitian politics, despite charges that it was simply a creation of the bourgeois to defend their interests.

"The 184? Aristide put us together because of the way he is terrorizing the Haitian people. I think we did a great thing in 1804. Blacks, whites, mulattos got together and abolished slavery and got out from under French rule. And from that time on, there's been division. That's the only thing I can thank Aristide for, that he's brought back unity to this country."

I asked him what effect being held in the squalor of Haiti's prison system had on him and if he had no worries that the government might now try other, less gentle ways of silencing him.

"People tell me, 'You're courageous.' Bullshit, I'm not courageous, the damn person who lives in the shantytown is courageous, because they've got to go home and face Aristide's terrorists with weapons in their hands."

"My going to jail for my country is no problem; they can take me back tomorrow. I'll get out in 2006 when Aristide is done if he stays that long. I'd go back in a second if it meant something would change in this country, and I think something has changed in this country since my arrest. I think my arrest showed the elites of Haiti that they're vulnerable. But it also showed the people of Haiti that someone in the elite cared about what was happening."

THE UNIVERSITY STUDENTS, watching the bourgeois elements of the Group of 184 increasingly radicalized by the arrests of Baker and Apaid, felt that it was time to ratchet up their own pressure on the regime and planned December 5 for a massive march in the capital.

Early that morning students had begun to congregate in preparation for the event at the Faculté des Sciences Humaines (FASCH) and Institut National de Gestion et des Hautes Etudes Internationales (INAGHEI) faculties in downtown Port-au-Prince, when a crowd of several hundred chimere appeared, attacking the FASCH with rocks and bottles in an effort to keep students from leaving; their efforts succeeded in trapping them inside the facility. Aristide's chimere leader Annette "So Anne" Auguste was seen traveling through the area in a car and pausing to chat with chimere there, including a group from Bel Air led by a young gang leader, Yvon "Zap Zap" Antoine. PNH forces on hand under the command of Police Commissioner Ricardo Etienne did nothing to stop the assaults, and things had reached an impasse when Pierre Marie Paquiot, the rector whose attempted dismissal had inflamed the student's passions in the first place over a year before, arrived at the FASCH in an attempt to calm the scene after having received a personal assurance from Prime Minister Yvon Neptune that his safety would be guaranteed. Paquiot entered through the front door of the compound with the Haitian news photographer Daniel Morel. Moments after he did so, the chimere, having succeeded in breaking a hole in the back wall of the structure, rushed in, beating and attacking anyone they found and turning the compound in an instant into a stampede of bleeding, terrified, running students and journalists. At least six people were shot, a dozen more stabbed and beaten. Paquiot himself was seized by chimere and beaten on the legs and back with iron bars until he could no longer walk. The university's Vice-Rector Wilson Laleau was beaten on the head with iron bars, and Rodson Jocelyn, a photographer with the Haiti Press Network, was also attacked. Moments later chimere raided INAGHEI and beat and assaulted students they found there. At both locations, rooms were sacked, books and equipment destroyed and at least two cars were torched in images broadcast live to the nation on the privately-owned Tele-Haiti network.

Employees of the nearby Fondation Connaissance et Liberté (FOKAL)—run by Michèle Pierre-Louis, the former sister-in-law of the slain priest Jean Pierre-Louis,—and a pair of visiting French diplomats watched the violence from the organization's headquarters on Avenue Christophe and later released a scathing press release in which they recounted the scene:7

We saw groups of pro-governmental militia . . . regroup in front of our building, visibly preparing to attack the student demonstration scheduled for that day. We saw their arms displayed, ranging from firearms, wooden and iron sticks, rocks and other objects capable of hurting and killing. We saw their chiefs, men and women, also armed, equipped with walkie-talkies and cellular phones, organize and give orders to the commandos that were to attack the students. We saw the police, not neutral as has been reported, but acting as accomplices to the militia. On several occasions, during that day of horror and shame, the police opened the way for the chimere attack and also covered their backs. We saw children aged between twelve and fifteen, some in school uniforms, used by the Lavalas militia to throw rocks and attack the students with fire arms.

It was an attack of unprecedented viciousness on one of the few institutions that ever gave Haiti's poor majority any hope of educating and bettering themselves, and when Yvon Neptune arrived at the at Canapé Vert Hospital to pay a face-saving visit to some of the injured that night, he was slapped and spat upon by students who chanted "Down with the government!" Neptune fled with security guards, who held the students at bay by clubbing them with their rifle butts; several more were arrested by PNH under the command of Rudy Berthomieux, though no one had yet been arrested for the attack itself. Mario Dupuy, speaking on Radio Kiskeya, attacked the independent press for spreading "misinformation." Watching in disbelief, a top official at the U.S. Embassy told me the attack was "a savage, stupid thing to do." The rector Pierre Marie Paquiot would never fully regain the use of his legs, being forced to use a wheelchair and canes afterwards.

THE NATION WAS REELING in shock from the bloodthirstiness of the assault when a December 8 demonstration in Gonaives saw several thousand students and Gonaives Resistance Front members form a united front for the first time, marching together, denouncing the assault and calling for Aristide's resignation. The same day Yvon Neptune also announced the formation of a commission of inquiry into the events of December 5, but he chiefly used the occasion to lecture schools and universities that "only through respect" of the law could citizens be expected to enjoy their right to protest. On International Human Rights Day (December 10), Aristide told reporters that:

A university is a sacred place; students should never see people violate the place where they are nurturing their intelligence so that they can serve the country tomorrow. . . . Democracy requires that we use dialectical arms and not deadly arms. Confrontation is excluded; we are open to dialogue to tackle the problems related to the holding of elections. And then, progressively, we reach a democratic compromise and we organize elections together, with security for all, of course.

But the time for Aristide's homilies was rapidly drawing to a close.

FOR THOSE SEEKING a reason to flee the sinking ship of state, the university attacks provided one. On December 11, in an announcement that had been long in coming but sent shock waves through the Haitian political establishment and chills through the National Palace, Dany Toussaint, perhaps the only man inside Haiti that Aristide was genuinely afraid of, announced in an interview with Radio Kiskeya that he was quitting the Fanmi Lavalas party and was calling on Aristide to reign.

"We have realized that we are faced with the power of one man," said Toussaint:

We have moved back to a state of nature where men are wolves against men, where people are killing one another, where people are fighting one another. We think that the time has come to stop that. There are people in the country who can stop it and we shall stop it. This means that we shall take part in all mobilizations going on to stop that. I gave the government a chance. I told it to watch out and make sure the train is on the right track. But instead of putting the train on the right track, it has done what it did on December 5th. As from today, I do not want anybody to associate my name with Fanmi Lavalas.

In the coming weeks, Minister of Education Marie-Carmel Paul Austin, Minister of the Environment Webster Pierre, Minister of Tourism Martine Deverson, Secretary of State for Public Health Pierre-Emile Charles and Haiti's ambassador to the Dominican Republic Guy Alexandre all resigned from the Aristide government in protest of the attack on the university, along with Lavalas Senator Prince Pierre Sonson, who finally, publicly broke with the leader he had so often been at odds with. The fealty of Lilas Desquiron, Aristide's Minister of Culture and Communications, to the regime, never appeared to waver, though, and, at the height of the controversy, she charged that the media was waging a "disinformation" campaign about the government. In the midst of this growing storm, in a hotel in Santo Domingo, a curious guest appeared at a political symposium sponsored by the International Republican Institute and attended by several lower-level representatives from Haiti's opposition political groups. Paul Arcelin, the former Haitian ambassador to the Dominican Republic and confidant of Guy Philippe, was spotted by local journalists leaving the conference—an interesting development to say the least.

FOLLOWING HIS PUBLIC BREAK with Aristide, Dany Toussaint's first public appearance at an antigovernment demonstration on December 12 had an electric effect on the movement, as now the students felt that someone Aristide feared was on their side and, despite his checkered past, Toussaint had maintained a low enough public profile over the preceding two years to not be too damagingly tarred by the regime's most extreme excesses. The government was not letting its enemies coast to victory, though, and on December 14, a car in Cap Haitien carrying Prince Pierre Sonson, in town for a book-signing, was fired upon. Sonson escaped unharmed. The attack came only days after Lavalas Deputy Nawoon Marcellus charged on local radio that Sonson wanted to bring weapons to opposition elements in the city and threatened to "act" against Sonson if he came to Au Cap. A day later in the capital, as police tear-gassed and beat hundreds of university students to crush a demonstration, the Group of 184, now having banded together with various political actors after the December 5 university attacks and calling itself the Democratic Platform, held a press conference where it urged a continued campaign of civil disobedience against the Aristide government, including the nonpayment of taxes. On the night of December 16, chimere backed by PNH riddled the Cap Haitien offices of Radio Maxima and Radio Vision 2000 with gunfire, while Nawoon Marcellus again took to the airwaves to utter threats, charging in an interview with Radio Ginen that journalist Valery Numa and Marie Lucie Bonhomme of Radio Vision 2000 and Sony Bastien and Lilianne Pierre-Paul of Radio Kiskeya were members of the Group of 184 and called for the l'Association Nationale des Médias Haitiens (ANMH) to move against them. TNH and Radio Nationale and the media outlets of Aristide-loyalist Venel Remarais, Radio Solidarité and Agence Haitian de Presse (AHP) also began cranking up a vitriolic propaganda machine. AHP produced articles lauding the Bale Wouze street gang in Saint Marc and warning Aristide's foes that "the population is ready to use all means to defend itself"; they also ran a December 17 article detailing how opposition marchers had a plan that "envisions the assassination of some of its own supporters with the idea of then attributing the blame for the killings to individuals close to the government," which in Haiti's climate was not much less than issuing a direct invitation to and attempt to deflect blame from the murder of the protesters. Indeed, the tone and bile of government-aligned media began more and more to mirror the tone of news outlets such as Radio Mille Collines and the newspaper *Kangura* in Rwanda, which paved the way for the 1994 genocide there, and the Nazi publisher Julius Streicher's anti-Semitic weekly *Der Stürmer*, in its dehumanizing of Aristide's enemies in an effort to legitimize attacks on them.

AS AN ANTI-ARISTIDE rally of several hundred people took place in front of the Haitian Embassy in Paris on December 17 (the second anniversary of the mysterious attack on the National Palace and the chimere rampage afterward), on the ground in Port-au-Prince another large antigovernment demonstration was broken up at various points by chimere firing at the crowd, wounding several people and attacking and chasing correspondents for Radio Ibo, Radio Vision 2000 and Radio Métropole. Armed chimere hanging from TELECO trucks and a van plastered with images of Aristide roamed the streets as CIMO fired into the air to further intimidate the demonstrators. Three gas stations in the capital were set aflame. At one point, enraged demonstrators attacked a vehicle of the Lavalas mouthpiece Radio Solidarité station and beat the channel's correspondent Alexis Eddy Jackson. Marchers in Jacmel and Saint Marc were also attacked.

Following the disintegration of the December 17 protest, the singer Théodore "Lolo" Beaubrun from Boukman Eksperyans returned home at around 4 p.m. the next day only to be stopped by a neighbor who warned him, "Don't come, there are people here to kill you." Lolo and his wife, Mimerose, a talented singer with the band who was also the sister of the recently resigned Minister of Environment Webster Pierre, discovered from neighbors living near their home that the gang leader Dread Mackenzie, who lead a pro-Aristide chimere band in the Bel Air slum near the National Palace and who Lolo had known since he was a boy, had staked out the couple's house for some hours—sent, it was said, on the orders of Jean-Claude Jean-Baptiste and Aristide to kill the singer before being eventually driven off by Beaubrun's irate neighbors. But many seemed sure the killer would return, and as a precaution Beaubrun began sleeping at a different house around the capital every night.

"I can't go on the street anymore, because they know what I look like," the six-foot-plus, dreadlocked Beaubrun told me after the plot was discovered.

In familiar rhetoric, in a December 18 press conference with René Civil at his side, Paul Raymond of the TKL told downtown merchants that "the anger of the people" would force them to open their stores if they followed any calls for a general strike, and accused the independent press and NCHR by name of working to destabilize the government.

Two days later, in an eloquent and impassioned declaration broadcast on Radio Metropole urging people to come out for the march on the 22nd, Andy Apaid said:

> In the name of the group that I represent, I send a message to all Haitians and foreigners to understand our movement.
>
> Jean Bertrand Aristide is the only actor of the situation in Haiti and that is why we send a special message to him in the way to ask him to put his ears down and listen to the voice of the Haitian people who believed in him. You and the Haitian people have another chance to resolve Haiti's problems and we could have peace because what we have now is not peace. We need YOU to stop killing people, stop beating

up the academics, stop the violation of our constitutional rights, stop corrupting the police and let us peacefully demonstrate to say to you what we feel. Do not lead the country in a fratricidal war, don't overlook history, leave peacefully. We won't give up, you've already had many chances. Now it's too late, you have to go.

Haitians, all of us can peacefully say NO. At the same time, we can rebuild a new Haiti with social justice and prosperity. We can—peacefully—stop all the armed bandits who surround the government. We are able and we must liberate ourselves from the slavery of the fear and intimidation. We are able and we must resist and liberate ourselves peacefully from all of this criminal action. All of this will still be a dream if we are not able to force Aristide and his clique to give up. . . . We ask again all Haitians to overcome their fear and go into the streets on Monday 22 December to give an answer to the Lavalas regime and the Aristide clique. We need to feel we are going to be liberated. We have the conviction that the victory of the people is not so far and this victory will be complete because it is the first time all the social categories demand something with a single voice. In this fact, we will find a new social contract and we will have a new country. Monday 22 December at 10, a unified population will rendezvous to Place Canapé Vert to denounce the criminal activities of Aristide's militia to protest against the inauguration of a brutal and retrograde dictatorship in Haiti. We are waiting for every one, our country needs that.

Do not come for someone, for some institution; come for yourselves and for your children. At this time we are certain the population will give a clear message to Aristide and he will know he needs to resign. Long live to the Haitian nation, great, inseparable and fraternal. Important notice: We ask all private sectors to facilitate it so that all their employees can come to this historic day.

The response to Apaid's call went beyond the opposition's wildest hopes. Despite chimere burning tractor tires at the end of the street he lived on throughout the night and shooting into the air, when Apaid and other members of the Democratic Platform took to the streets that day, they were joined by an estimated twenty thousand Haitians. Opposition politicians such as Evans Paul and Micha Gaillard, students, bourgeois businesspeople, peasants arriving into the capital and others joined Apaid, Charles Baker, Prince Pierre Sonson and a horde of other noted Haitians in a huge demonstration that snaked for miles through the capital's hilly streets, their voices raised thunderously as they called on Aristide to resign. The demonstration was met with violence by chimere gangs at several locations though, and as it approached the Post Marchand intersection near the Champs de Mars, a group of young gunmen, some of whom appeared to be in their early teens, fired on marches from an SUV that quickly sped away, a boy of about twelve clinging to its rooftop. When PNH officers escorting the march returned fire, they killed a chimere from Bel Air nicknamed Doudou—a Haitian term of endearment meaning "sweetie" or "baby." The protest broke up in confusion and billowing clouds of tear gas.

The same day as tens of thousands took to the streets in Haiti to demand Aristide's ouster, the government's lawyer, Ira Kurzban, writing again in the *Miami Herald*, advised U.S. readers that, "The president will not resign and disappoint the Haitian people. The vast majority of Haitians voted for and continue to support him. Instead of waiting for his resignation, U.S.-based critics should visit Haiti now and see that democracy is flourishing."

The day after the demonstration, in a gesture of artistic solidarity, the country's most famous musicians put on a free concert at the *Faculté des sciences humaines*, which had been the scene of such violence on December 5. Boukman Eksperyans, along with Sweet Micky, the Haitian reggae singer Jah Nesta and scores of other musicians sang songs of protest while surrounded by an exhibition of photos chronicling the chimere attack on the institution. Lolo Beaubrun stressed to me that the groups had wanted to perform at the place where the violence had taken place because, "You don't only have to have a street demonstration, you can also have a cultural demonstration." Despite fears that the chimere would return, the day passed peacefully.

THE LINKING UP of the university students, the peasantry, Haiti's progressive intellectual sector and disaffected poor victimized by his government with the well-financed and organized Group of 184 produced against Aristide a coalition of disparate elements that he had never before faced in his time as president. Coupled with the street courage of the radical students, there was now the suave, English-speaking bourgeois opposition, as typified by Hans Tippenhauer, the Group Croissance economic advisor who had been part of the Group of 184 since the beginning and who I now sat chatting with on December 27 at the Montana Hotel as it buzzed with journalists. I had returned to Haiti after a several-month stint reporting from New York and Central America, and between us and the still-stunning view from the hotel's terrace and amidst its gurgling fountain, sailors from South Africa's *SAS Drakensberg*, moored visibly in the capital's bay in the horizon, splashed about in the hotel pool. Though the heads of state of the Dominican Republic, Jamaica and even Cuba announced they would not be attending Haiti's highly-politicized upcoming bicentennial festivities, Thabo Mbeki, South Africa's imperious president, who frequently had warm words to say about the dictator Robert Mugabe in the neighboring African nation of Zimbabwe, announced that, human rights abuses or not, he would be attending the ceremony in Port-au-Prince, and in advance of his arrival had dispensed 10 million South African rands to the Aristide government as "material support" for the festivities. Mbeki also brought in a massive security force represented chiefly by the Drakensberg but also consisting of South African special forces and riot police, who arrived in Haiti told that they were being brought to protect the South African leader but quickly realized that they were in fact there to prop up the dictatorial Aristide and ensure that his moment in the sun for Haiti's anniversary was not interrupted by the rage of the populace against him. It was all very foolish on Mbeki's part, and a display that would earn him eternal enmity from great swathes of Haitian society; but, given the president's conciliatory attitude toward Mugabe, busy killing black political opponents and destroying white farms in South Africa's next-door neighbor, it was hardly surprising. Meanwhile, as Mbeki lavished praise and money on Aristide, the U.S. Embassy in Port-au-Prince, under the helm of its Ambassador James Foley, was frantically trying to negotiate a middle ground between Aristide and the opposition elements before things got any worse and the violence spiraled any farther out of control.

"After December 5, we told the students 'Whatever you do, we are behind you,'" said Tippenhauer, a coffee-complected mulatto with African features who I had known for several years. Today, he was dressed in a blue baseball cap and white shirt and had the air of someone energized for his cause. "We went from being an opposition where we were trying to negotiate to an opposition where we said there was no negotiation with this regime. And there is no negotiation point anymore."

"They're like an assassination team without a gun," said an American friend of mine who had lived off-and-on in Haiti for many years and was friends with many of the members of the Group of 184. It was hard to argue with him. After the December 5 university attack, perhaps the defining moment in crystallizing opposition to the regime, the dissidents' leaders smelled blood, and they showed no signs of backing down, even at the cost of their own comfortable lives and livelihoods, until they brought the Aristide regime tumbling down as surely as the walls of Jericho had fallen to Joshua's trumpet.

WITH HAITI'S MUCH-ANTICIPATED and potentially explosive bicentennial drawing ever nearer, I drove up to interview Andy Apaid at him home in the capital. I found myself driving up to the end of a long, winding road in the Mont Joli section of the capital—not at all far from my own neighborhood of Pacot, a neighborhood within easy each of the poor quarters downtown and quite removed from the mountainside retreats where Haiti's wealthiest traditionally lived. As I was ushered into the ranch-style building, I noticed Haitian art on the walls, fine oak tables and leather couches; but in truth, the residence was little more ostentatious than the residence a successful physician in Miami would own and not at all representative of the palatial homes of the country's wealthiest, Aristide included. Apaid was dressed in light slacks and a light yellow shirt and we sat in a study where a bowl of Haitian *pistache* nuts had been put on the circular table between us.

"The real tragedy of Mr. Aristide is that never in our history will we again have a president who can call, as Mr. Aristide could in '94-'95, every head of state on a first name basis and talk about the help that Haiti needs," he commenced, by way of analyzing the pass the country had come to. "Instead of concentrating on opening and modernizing his country he was concentrating on what kind of a machine he needed to put together to ensure sixty years of some kind of empire.

"We think it's time the U.S. put its weight on Mr. Aristide and tells him that he should resign," Apaid continued, evidencing a certain charisma despite his soft voice and somewhat cherubic appearance. Drawing an analogy to protests that were also swelling against Venezuela's left-wing president Hugo Chavez, he went on to say, "Mr. Aristide is no Chavez, and Haiti is no Venezuela. If he gets the U.S. request to pack and leave he will do that. The U.S. is simply not determined enough to do that."

I asked him what influence the now nearly two-year-old student protest movement had had on the Group of 184.

"The number-one tool used by Mr. Aristide is fear," he began. "Number two is division. Number three is corruption. On the first, fear is everywhere; its an institution in Haiti and this government is extremely good at using disinformation to frighten people when you don't do what they ask. Whether it is threatening with the frequency allowance for television and radio, or with the tax and customs offices, it uses the state apparatus to frighten people that want to see social and political modernism in Haiti. So when the students began to resist and not to be afraid to take to the streets and to protests, particularly after Aristide tried to take over the university, the students' determination and courage provoked the government into showing its real face, and that's what it did on the 5th of December. And out of fear that the student and civil society movements would gather strength, it violently reacted against their movement and simply fueled it. The issue was autonomy of the university, but it fueled a broader protest about how things are run."

"This government put together an occult criminal machine and one of its most damaging practices is that it keeps people very needy and then it asks them to cross the line of corruption, to do bad things, and when they do cross that line then its entices them through intimidation to cross the line of criminality. The more likely you are to commit crimes, the more likely you are to get promotion and access. And if you decide to go back on it, there are zero tolerance death squads who execute you. What do you say to a Metayer? He did something bad on the 17th of December and we asked that he be brought to court. No one asked to have him killed. Since the government can't get him to be quiet because he received orders from the National Palace, they executed him."

More measured in his words than Charles Baker, Apaid said he sought to differentiate the movement he was leading in Port-au-Prince from some of the more radical, armed elements in the Artibonite.

"Every demonstration is breaking up fear in specific neighborhoods, going a little bit deeper, a little bit deeper. We are nonviolent, we are exposing our lives. But at the same time we cannot blame anyone for practicing self-defense. I believe we are doing a very good job at keeping this. Every violent aspect to what has happened has come from the faction of Lavalas. We're hoping to keep it like that."

I asked him what he thought of those who saw the 184 as little more than a front for Haiti's elite and that they were cynically using the popular protests against Aristide in an effort to reassert their historic privileges in Haiti, which, in truth, had never been under any real threat from Aristide's government beyond the rampant criminality of his regime which threatened all facets of Haitian life with potentially violent interruption, most of all among the poor.

"We make no apologies for whatever money we have," Apaid responded, his voice keeping its same even keel. "We work hard, we have 4,200 employees, we provide good, clean jobs, we respect the law, we pay double the minimum wage and we are very proud of our role. If through our writings, our actions, our dialogue, we project an image that is not that of the past, shouldn't they be happy?"

"I think our generation should take some risk to make this a more livable place, and the risk is to be taken here, nowhere else."

It was an impressive performance and one that reinforced my perception that, in truth, Apaid was neither the humble, Bible-quoting conciliator he liked to portray himself as in the foreign press nor the pure product of a rancid oligarchy that Aristide liked to portray. He was, rather, an extremely adept and wily politician willing to put his personal safety at great risk to lead a cause that he desperately believed in, that of ousting Aristide from power. Whatever else one could say about him, and however one could legitimately second-guess his motives, Apaid's courage, which would continue to see him marching on rallies that became more and more fraught with peril as the weeks wore on, was something beyond dispute, and a measure of his commitment to his goal, and a sure sign that something significant had changed among Haiti's bourgeoisie.

As we walked to my car, I asked Apaid how he was planning on marking the coming New Year.

"I am not in a party mood," was his response.

I HAD NEVER SEEN Haiti so awash in rumors, and I could see no end in sight to the bloodshed of what had at once promised, at Aristide's first election, to be a movement that would engage and lift up this poor, beautiful country I had come to love. Speaking with Michele Montas at the United Nations shortly before I returned, we both lamented all the opportunities that Aristide had squandered and wasted until she finally said, by way of bringing us back to reality, "1990 is dead and, unfortunately, so are the hopes of so many people." A few days before the New Year, driving through Port-au-Prince in the direction of the cathedral, golden, liquid early morning sunlight was dropping on the city. I passed through the Bel Air and saw that hagiographic murals of Aristide had been painted with the words, *"Restitisyon pou Ayiti,"* echoing a huge billborad of Aristide put up outside the airport and another one of Aristide and Toussiant Louverture put up at Canapé Vert that read, "Two men, one vision." I spoke to Port-au-Prince Bishop Pierre André Dumas inside of the pink and white cathedral, listening to hymns being sung nearby; it was a conversation during which he bemoaned the Aristide government's human rights abuses and the direction in which the county was heading. On the streets, people had taken to using animal metaphors to describe the ways in which Aristide would cling to power, with some describing him as having the head of a snake with a scorpion's tail— with his adversaries thinking they had the head only to get stung—and others describing him as a jellyfish, sucking in all the energy of his diverse opposition while all the time behind the scenes preparing and laying the groundwork at all levels (local, national, international) for a new presidential campaign in 2005. I watched about a hundred or so chimere under the direction of René Civil gather with pro-Aristide banners in Petionville, with government Service Plus buses ferrying more people in. On the Champs de Mars, as stands were being built for spectators in front on the National Palace, hundreds of chimere, some in near rags, were hanging out by the front gates, with truckloads more guzzling from bottles of *tafia* and smoking huge spliffs of marijuana, cruising around. The chimere had recently taken to calling themselves *rat pa kaka* or "Rat's don't shit," which was evidently meant to evoke their bravery.

I GOT A FIRSTHAND taste of how radically the dynamic had shifted in Haiti during my months away when on December 30, I arrived at the Place Canapé Vert and saw several hundred members of Democratic Platform-aligned groups waiting to meet a student demonstration that was said to be moving up the hill from the university. That morning, the body of Doudou, the chimere who had been killed at the December 22 rally, had been taken from the Saint Antoine Church in Saint Martin to the National Cemetery by a howling mob of thugs wearing newly government-printed "Justice for Doudou" t-shirts and yelling that he was killed by Andy Apaid's security forces. The chimere went as far as to open the coffin, several times, revealing the dead body within, and shaking it back and forth so hard that the corpse nearly fell out. But here in Canapé Vert, the Platform looked supremely confident, and when I spied Hans Tippenhauer, he said he was looking forward to the march.

"We're here today to say no to what's happening. Right now, this is our way to say we don't accept the dictatorship that's being put in place by those guys," he told me. The Group of 184, who were officially sponsoring the march, had applied to the police and been approved for the march route on December 26, but as a group of 184 activists who had been doing last-minute negotiations with the police attempted to cut through Saint Martin after Doudou's funeral, they found chimere with weapons in their hands prowling the lanes, essentially locking the district down.

But all those fears seemed to evaporate with a charge of adrenaline as we turned to see thousands of university students running up to Canapé Vert from downtown to join the march. A huge cheer erupted from the crowd at the sight of the students and soon the crowd joined lustily along with the students own chant of *grenn nan bouda,* which literally translated into "balls in your ass" but colloquially meant a boast of "We've got balls."

Even a group of chimere throwing stones from cement houses crawling up the hill along Canapé Vert couldn't dampen the crowds' enthusiasm, and soon we were snaking over the hills of Bourdon, leading to Avenue Pan-Americaine, people cheering, standing on roofs, drivers blowing horns in support. The marchers were a see-saw of every shade of the color scale, from white to coffee-and-cream to (mostly) black, and many of them waved small Haitian flags as they marched.

"*Fok Aristide ale!*" they chanted. "Aristide must go."

"We are manifesting today to say that the youth of this country are fed up. No to impunity, no to the way the state is being governed," said a young, frail eighteen-year-old boy as we walked up Avenue Pan-Americaine and began to slope down toward the Delmas Road. "If we die, fine, but Aristide is not continuing on in Haiti."

"He brings these white African soldiers here to violate Haitian territory; we are accepting nothing like this in our country," said another boy. "Things must change in Haiti. This is not a bourgeois struggle. Haiti is a black country and this is a black struggle."

By the time the crowd had reached the wide lanes that ran back to downtown Port-au-Prince from Delmas, people were running out of their houses to join the march, swelling its ranks as the Caribbean sun burned hot in the sky. Jarringly, armed police were jogging at the front of the march, their automatic weapons out, and, as I looked down from a hill on one group of protesters I estimated to be over ten thousand bottlenecked at an intersection and stretching back over many hills, I watched as they waved palm fronds, which undulated like waves on the sea. I was surprised to look up and find Radio Kiskeya director Marvel Dandin standing next to me, the broad smile on his face of a journalist who knows he has found a big story, who told me that Butteur Metayer had said that a statement broadcast on government radio that day, where he told his men to lay down their arms was a fake, and that he wanted the struggle to continue. Finally, as the protestors were permitted to continue, they chanted "*Woi! Woi! Woi!*" as they snaked over hills. Drenched in sweat, I filed a story that from Richard Morse's computer at the office of the Hotel Oloffson, as his band Ram practiced in a nearby outbuilding, singing "We want justice."

ON NEW YEAR'S EVE, Aristide held a question-and-answer session with the foreign press at the National Palace with his wife, Mildred Trouillot, and the American congresswoman Maxine Waters—who had arrived in Haiti on December 28 and was staying in style at the luxurious Hotel Montana—at his side. He again reiterated that he would not step down, and assured reporters that the majority of the Haitian people were behind him.

Callers to Marvel Dandin's afternoon show on Radio Kiskeya painted a different picture of things, though, as they denounced the president almost to a one.

"Raboteau and Gonaives stay strong!" declared one caller. "We are with you!"

CHAPTER NOTES

1. "Counsel for the Government of Haiti Condemns Both Those Who Commit and Those Who Provoke Violence," PRNewswire, July 14, 2003.
2. "Manifestations brutalement dispersées par la police aux Gonaives," *AlterPresse*, September 29, 2003.
3. "Interview avec Buter Métayer, frere cadet de Amiot Métayer et un des principaux dirigeants de « L'Armée Cannibale »," *AlterPresse*, October 2, 2003.
4. "Funérailles de Amiot Metayer emmaillées d'incidents," *AlterPresse*, October 6, 2003.
5. Haiti: Human rights abuses on the rise. Amnesty International press release, October 8, 2003.
6. The Enemies of Democracy are Taking Aim : Haitian Press Under Fire. NCHR Report, October 25, 2003.
7. Public Outcry from Firsthand Witnesses of Brutality Against the Students, press statement of the Fondation Connaissance et Liberté (FOKAL) Open Society Institute Haiti in regards to the aborted student demonstration of December 5, 2003.

11
The Last Testament

IT WAS JANUARY 1, the bicentennial that Aristide had so long been waiting for, and as the day unfurled itself, a blazing sun began to rise over the parched fields to the north of Port-au-Prince. Arriving at the National Palace, I found about ten thousand Aristide partisans, mostly young male chimere drawn from the slums, cramming into the space directly in front of the Palace's brittle white gates, evidently to create the image of maximum popular support for the various TV crews and lower-level dignitaries assembled. One supporter carried a home-made painting of Aristide shaking hands with Dessalines. The crowd was small enough, however, that we were able to circle around the Palace without any problem, and I finally ended up entering the back gate of the building, where I had passed through so many times for Aristide's press conferences. Passing through the security check, which included bomb-sniffing dogs, I noted dozens of machine-gun wielding CIMO and as many South African security personnel patrolling the Palace grounds. Circling around the back to the front of the Palace, visitors today were greeted by the sound of racine music pumping out of speaker stacks set up in front of the building, and a huge Haitian flag banner ringing its length. Dozens of gold-painted teenage dancers stood on the Palace lawn, their bodies glittering in the sun. Up on the dais, Aristide sat passively with his wife, South African President Thabo Mbeki sitting to one side of him, Yvon Neptune to the other. Prime Minister Perry Christie of the Bahamas and Paul Farmer were also on the stage, and dozens of journalists and even more security personnel had spread out at the bottom of the steps immediately in front of the building's entrance. As I arrived at the front of the steps, so did a heavily made-up Maxine Waters, exiting a limousine. When asked what she, the only member of the Congressional Black Caucus to attend the ceremony, thought of the appropriateness of such an event given the political and social upheaval and huge antigovernment demonstrations the country was in the midst of, Waters responded in vintage fashion.

"I think we have to be careful that we don't have people that are attempting to have a coup d'etat and dress it up under the name of demonstrations and rallies," Waters responded, her lips pulled back into a despotic sneer. "I support demonstrations in a democracy all over the world, but we must be careful that they are peaceful demonstrations and that there are not those inside those demonstrations who are attempting coup d'etats!"

An English-speaking Haitian in a sharp suit and sunglasses that I had never seen before began peppering Waters with softball questions, though he carried no recording equipment nor pen nor notepad.

"What I'm trying to understand is at the White House in the United States, there are certain limits to where people can come?" he said to her, smiling conspiratorially.

"In the United Sates, we have peaceful demonstrations but we have rules. And the rules are that most of the time, you must get a license, you must follow the route, you must not violate the barricades, you must go where it is indicated. In Washington, DC, you don't get too close to the White House. Protestors who violate the rules and overcome the barricades are putting themselves at risk."

Asked her thoughts on the government gangs that were terrorizing the country, Waters opined that, "I don't know that there are paramilitary forces in the country. I can remember the reigns of Duvalier when they really did but I don't know that that is true here. I do know that there is opposition, however I don't know that there is [sic] paramilitary operations."

Following Waters, several exotically-robed African potentates ascended the steps, and the troupe of gold-painted teenaged dancers began to take their positions on the lawn in front of us. However, before the ceremony could began, in a move that some would later say had been choreographed by the government itself, the Palace's front security gate, groaning under the weight of the chimere hanging on it, collapsed, young men storming across the Palace lawn, terrifying the teenage dancers standing there. CIMO and South African security forces quickly formed a protective ring that prevented a deeper incursion toward the platform where Aristide and Mbeki sat, but for many the scene served as a grim illustration of a leader about to be overwhelmed by forces, internal and external, and reaping a whirlwind that he had sown, chaos overwhelming any attempt to portray himself as a statesman.

"*Aristide wa!*" the young men shouted. "Aristide is the king!"

"Do you feel safe?" asked Richard Bauer, Mexico City correspondent for the Swiss daily *Neue Zürcher Zeitung*, as we watched the scene.

"Not particularly," I said, and then we both went back to taking notes.

With white doves flying through a blue sky over the Champs de Mars, the Palace band ran through a too-fast "La Dessalinienne," as if terribly nervous, and the Haitian flag was raised. The gold-painted boys began blowing on conch shells, echoing the method by which slaves summoned one another for rebellion, and other boys, painted red, drummed a martial beat. Young girls in purple and red dresses danced to the music playing over a loudspeaker as helicopters (more than Aristide's ubiquitous single one this time) swooped low over the Palace grounds.

Bahamian Prime Minister Perry Christie rose to give a tasteful brief address in which he noted that, "No other nation of color can claim two hundred years as a sovereign nation." Then Thabo Mbeki, looking like a lost fool in a room full of gangsters, stood up to make his remarks.

"Together with the leadership and people of Haiti, we are determined to work together to address the problems facing this inspirational home of African freedom and achieve stability and prosperity in this important site of African heroism and wherever Africans are to be found," Mbeki said, standing just feet away from a man who had by this point helped to crush the inspiration of a generation of Haitians. "We trust and are confident that in both the leadership and people of Haiti we will find equally determined partners, so that together we can here help to recreate a model country, informed by the wise words of the 1805 constitution of Haiti that we have 'an opportunity of breaking our fetters, and of constituting ourselves as a people, free, civilized and independent.'"

Following Mbeki, Aristide rose from his gold-leafed chair and walked toward the microphone.

"*Bon anneé, bon anneé, bon anneé, bon anneé, bon anneé*," he repeated five times, counting off on his fingers, once for each year of his mandate. "After 1804 was debt, after 2004 is honey. Lavalas honey to everyone without distinction. We are putting our heads together as all Haitians."

I decided that I would listen to the speech, and the one that Aristide was scheduled to deliver, improbably, in Gonaives later that day, on the radio, and, picking my way past the groaning injured who had been hurt by the gate collapse and who were now being serviced by a harried-looking South-African medical team, I decided to try and find a way to the march scheduled for that day. Wandering around the Champs de Mars, I found Lionel Delatour, the Centre pour la Libre Entreprise et la Démocratie vice-president, who had been in attendance at the National Palace earlier, in the lobby of the Hotel Plaza. He was trying to reach his wife on her cell phone. She was in the midst of what sounded like a huge demonstration in Nazon and he was trying join her and make sure that she was alright. He offered me a lift there in his SUV and soon we were snaking the back way into the jagged hills of the zone until we came within a few blocks of the Nazon road, where we had to stop because of a huge crush of marchers in front of us. The radio told us that students demonstrating in Jacmel had just run to the cemetery there and were ringing the bell inside, as is done when someone dies, to signify the death of the Aristide regime. Getting out and walking to the intersection, we saw a solid wall of protesters stretching over the hills all the way from the Delmas Road past where my eyes could see toward Avenue John Brown. CIMO had set up positions in the trucks at various points along the route, but for some reason it seemed to have stalled, and the crowd was growing impatient. At various points people were flying Haitian flags and palm fronds, and chants of "Freedom or death" and "Everyone's surprised!" went up from the crowd. *"Non a la dictature totalitaire"* read one sign.

"We are mobilizing for Aristide to leave," a student at the faculty of economic sciences, Bartholy Julien, told me as we stood on a hill watching the protestors. "We are commemorating the bicentennial of our independence, but we will not celebrate with Aristide because he has brought the country to a situation of misery, especially Gonaives, where he burns little babies, in the hospital, where his killers attack us. He respects no one."

As we stood in Nazon, we had no way of knowing that the Aristide government had taken advantage of the bicentennial chaos to stage a jailbreak at the National Penitentiary. Clifford Larose, the prison director who for three years had overseen arbitrary detentions and torture in one of the most inhumane prison systems in the world, presided over one final betrayal of his duties to the Haitian people. At the sound of the passing *Gwo Lobo rara* band marching down the Rue des Casernes, over one hundred prisoners escaped, some through doors that had been unlocked and others through a hole burrowed into a wall. Most prisoners had been housed in the Hall district of the penitentiary, thereby facilitating an easier escape, and guards had left keys to some cells housing those sympathetic to the government with some detainees who simply walked through the front gate, others over a back wall abutting the College Bird and the Presses Nationales. Among those who fled that day were several pro-Aristide gangs' leaders, as well as Dymsley Millien, Jeudi-Jean Daniel and Philippe Markington, three of the men charged in the Jean Dominique slaying. Winston Jean-Bart, better known as Tupac, the older brother of the Cité Soleil gang leader James Petit-Frere and a well-known gang leader in his own right, got his first taste of freedom in two years and promptly headed back to Cité Soleil.

Back in Nazon, however, though the protestors had received approval for their march from the police three days earlier, the CIMO present declared the march illegal and began firing tear gas at the crowd. Andy Apaid and Charles Baker, midway in the march behind where I was and choking on the fumes, sat down in the middle of the street, refusing to move. Getting out of Lionel Delatour's car once more to get a better look at the situation down the hill, I was almost immediately hit in the face by a noxious wave of tear gas. Simultaneously, a blast of gunfire exploded and hundreds of people began scattering in all directors. Running into a side street, with people all around falling over one another looking for somewhere to go, I took refuge in a *lakou* with a poor family, where a worried young girl was braiding her mother's hair, looking up to hear the sound of automatic weapons fire that grew ever more fierce as the minutes wore on. At one point, Lolo Beaubrun also found himself on the street alone and dove into a nearby building where he found himself hiding with Charles Baker and a clutch of other marchers, and where Baker told him, "You can go; I'll take care of everybody here." Several attempts to emerge from the house I was in were met by waves of running, frightened people and the crackle of automatic weapons fire before I got down the block. I eventually had to thread my way past a diabolically hot wall of burning tires blocking an intersection before hitching a ride with a passing Haitian motorist back to Pacot, where I was staying. The final firefight of the day, this one between government-affiliated gang members and armed antigovernment protestors, occurred at Post Marchand, where the chimere Doudou had been killed on December 22. The groups exchanged small-arms fire across the Lalue road for nearly an hour before finally dispersing.

As protestors and journalists were being chased from the streets of Port-au-Prince, Aristide was getting a similar reception in Gonaives. Landing in the city by helicopter late and without Thabo Mbeki, whose security personnel refused to let him accompany the Haitian president to the rebellious town, Aristide landed in Haiti's City of Independence to find the Place d'Independence itself had been walled off with metal containers, as has been the Raboteau and Jubilé slums to keep the anti-Aristide street gangs, who had all but threatened to kill Aristide should he venture to the city, at bay. Arriving under volleys of exploding gunfire and detonating hand grenades, as hostile gangs attempted to lay siege to the square where he was speaking, the chaos conspired with wafts of tear gas to cut the president's speech to a mere fifteen minutes.

"You are happy to welcome me, just like I am happy to be as one with you to welcome our guests," Aristide told the frightened officials present, with no apparent irony.

"Congratulations, compliments, all of you who made patriotic sacrifices to prepare the 200th anniversary of liberty here. . . . What should be done? Is it a coup d'etat? No. Is it elections? Yes!

"As we are talking here, I see a Lavalas crowd of people coming from the street down there to come up. And I am certain that if I didn't have to go back to Port-au-Prince tonight to continue the ceremony, I would spend the afternoon with you and there would be no more room to put people because all of Gonaives's children, all of Artibonite's children, who want peace, who want security, when they feel the wind of peace, the wind of security blowing, they come closer."

Come closer they did, and, as it had been while landing, Aristide's helicopter was fired upon when taking off from the city.

Nerves rattled that night, I thought of what a young high-school student I had spoken to that day had said to me, telling me he would be unmoved by any more of Aristide's speeches.

"Thank you, Mr. President," he had said as we listened to Aristide talking on the radio. "Those were very beautiful words. We don't need to hear from you again. Bye-bye."

A FEW DAYS AFTER the mayhem and tear gas of January 1, Thomas Dworzak, a German photographer for the Magnum agency, and I decided to drive north to pay the naysayers in Gonaives a visit. Listening to the melodies of the Portuguese group Madredeus filtering through our rented car, we set out on the dusty and sun-blasted road early in the morning driving through the Artibonite Valley. Near the town of L'Estere, the fields turned gloriously green for a moment. Arriving at Gonaives after several hours drive, we found police roadblocks set up entering and leaving the city, metal containers still walling off Raboteau, and smoldering tires in the streets. The city's police station seemed almost deserted and *"Viv Cubain"* graffiti was scrawled on the destroyed Fanmi Lavalas headquarters in town, which had been littered with broken glass and partially burnt. Arriving at the Family Hotel, a prisonlike structure that I usually stayed in with an oddly elaborate swimming pool facing the bald, bare mountains on the outskirts of Gonaives, my traveling companion Thomas remarked that it reminded him of the former Taliban leader Mullah Omar's house in Kandahar, Afghanistan, where he had been the previous year. We found that the Family's restaurant, one of the few places to eat in the city, had closed. Its owner, a former Macoute named Eddy, told us that he had barely been able to save a friend of his, a policeman who had been surrounded by Front members, the day before.

"The police are hiding behind the walls of the commissariat because if they're caught alone on the street they'll be shot," he said.

When I asked him about Aristide's visit a few days earlier, his reply was succinct.

"If he would have stayed for fifteen minutes more they would have killed him."

Later, as we had arranged, a polite young man showed up at the hotel, and before long we were driving through the narrow back streets of Gonaives into a slum neighborhood, dusk falling and a bright descending sun hitting our windshield.

"Attache yo la," said the young man, directing us to avoid this road or that, warning us where Aristide partisans still roamed. We received many hard stares from people looking at us and our car from the roadside. Finally we came to a stop beside a group of men leaning against a low wall.

A serious, dapper young man stepped forward.

"I am Arios Jean-Charles," he said. He was a thirty-year-old computer programmer and spokesman for the Front who acted as something of a liaison between the tough longshoreman who had made up the Cannibal Army and the students they had banded together with after Amiot Metayer's killing, he said. As we spoke, we moved off the street to a small, tumbledown house. Entering its sitting room, I was greeted by a reflective mirror of Elvis Presley and posters of famous football players such as Thierry Henry and David Beckham. The shades were drawn, the front door locked, and we sat, about a dozen of us, around a narrow table.

"We do not accept the attempt of Aristide to install a dictatorial system in this country," Jean-Charles began, speaking in crisp, lucid Kreyol. "Professors, students, workers, political activists, we are telling the international community, the international press, human rights organizations, and the rest that the dictator Aristide is attempting to use his criminal power to violate and to rob the Haitian people. We will not accept this."

When I asked about the reception Aristide had received on January 1, the room exploded into laughter.

"He was here for ten or fifteen minutes, but the population didn't want him here and he was panicking," said a strapping older man with baseball cap and a mustache. "Gonaives symbolizes the liberty of Haiti, a place where oppression should not be allowed to enter again, so when he wanted to come here we mobilized the entire population."

"It was an historic day, a monumental day," said Arios Jean-Charles. "You have Toussaint, Dessalines, Christophe, and they sacrificed their blood for Haitian independence. Today, Gonaives is the same symbol of revolution.

"Today we are mobilizing the entire population of Gonaives to get rid of Aristide, because he is a dictator. Today Gonaives is a dying, wounded city," he continued. "We have no roads, we have no electricity, we have no drinking water. Aristide symbolized our hope, and he violated that hope. What we have now in the National Palace is just a small, fascist group. We will never accept that again, and from now on Gonaives will symbolize solid resistance to this. Aristide will never come back to Gonaives."

The next day, driving back at dusk, just before we entered Port-au-Prince south of the beach hotels and near the Tintanyen dumping ground, we got a flat tire and paused to change it. Around the corner of scrub brush where the road curved came a dark red truck with police license plates. The driver slowed down to a stop, and out hopped none other than the owner of the bar in Gonaives who had described to me the events of the liberation of Amiot Metayer from prison there some two years before. A pistol stuck in his waistband, the man, who was also the son of the Lavalassian mayor of Gonaives, approached me with a smile on his face.

"Here I am again man," he said, slapping me on the shoulder. "Always there to save your ass."

While his wife and child sat in the car, the bar owner and I joked about Gonaives, but one thing to him was no laughing matter.

"They were on the radio saying that I was running the bulldozer when they were attacking Cubain's house after he died," he said, scowling against the setting sun. "That shit ain't true."

As he turned to leave, he called over his shoulder back to me.

"I'm goin' back man, back to cowboy town." And he pulled off, heading north, dust dancing a trail behind his pickup. As we drove into Port-au-Prince, the moon was rising high in the sky.

I WENT TO SEE JAMES, for one last time, in Cité Soleil late that night. During my absence from Haiti, he had acquired a curious set of foreign hangers-on, a pair of drug-addled European twenty-somethings, one of whom, a woman working with an NGO in Cité Soleil, had taken to negotiating exorbitant fees on behalf of the boys in order to take timorous *blan* journalists down to see real live "chimere." James's brother, Tupac, had been sprung from jail in the January 1 jailbreak and now was back in Soleil 19. Some tension had built up between the two siblings as Tupac tried to return to his former role as gang leader. Tupac had also begun composing brilliant, incisive political rap songs while in jail, which took Haiti's leaders, both Lavalas and otherwise, to task for the agony they had inflicted on the country, while James still remained more or less a firm believer in Aristide's cause, if disappointed in the man himself. The whole thing made me a little uncomfortable.

Driving down through Cité Soleil with one of James's new clique under a full moon, we passed the rocky plane next to the burned-out Boulos market that marked the road to Bois Neuf, the place where Labanye's mortal enemy, Dread Wilmé, resided. Off to one side of the road, a park was being built, one of Aristide's cosmetic pet projects. As we stopped on a back road in Soleil 19, we came upon a group of young gunmen sitting in a circle, holding 9 mms and M1s, listening to King Posse and Sweet Micky on a loud ghetto blaster and drinking Prestige. A tall, striking-looking young man wearing his hair in cornrows, a huge gold and diamond crucifix set off against his tropical purple shirt open to the waist, approached us.

"I'm Tupac, man," he said to me, embracing my hand in his and addressing me in English. At the mention of his name, the gunmen cheered. "Everyone is glad that I'm back, man; you're safe here now. These are my men, my students, my people."

A decision was made to retire to James's room, and so, escorted by a du-rag wearing soldier named Dallas and another named Bling-Bling, we found our way through the back alleys to James's abode. After a moment, James arrived, and we embraced with emotion and he let us into his room.

We sat on the floor of the tiny space, watching a compas band play the old *"cigarette mwen, aliment mwen"* chestnut on a small television, a Haitian flag resting on top of it and James's M1 resting in the corner. A biography of Che Guevara that had been given to James recently by an American filmmaker sat propped up in a place of pride, the famous photograph of Che's face gazing sternly into the distance, looking out at us. This night, James was wearing a Bob Marley t-shirt and a smaller cross on his chest than his brother. He laughed and joked and shared *cremas*—the traditional Haitian New Year's celebratory drink—with Tupac, but he seemed much sadder and more hopeless than he had been.

"My dream is to change the situation, make the revolution and to make this country in a different way, Michael," he told me. "I want to do the same thing that Che Guevara did for Cuba. But I am too small now to make that work, but I am trying. That is my dream.

"I'm not really happy with the situation now; I don't understand where the country is going. In this country I have seen too much killing. But I know if I haven't died yet, I have a chance, and I will try."

As he spoke, half a dozen women filtered through the door into his small room, one wearing a bright red t-shirt with the words "Boy Crazy" written on it in bright white letters. As they entered, Tupac examined his newest purchase since leaving jail: a beautiful hand-crafted .44 bought for around H$2,000. Everyone was treating the brothers with absolute deference that night, and all the gangsters in the neighborhood came to peer through the front door and see the two chefs holding court. After a time, Tupac left for another assignation in Labanye's Boston neighborhood with several of the women, rolling off in a pickup so overloaded with teenage gunmen that they nearly fell into the street, weapons and all, when it hung a sharp right turn. Cité Soleil Mayor Fritz Joseph and Delmas 33 police chief Emmanuel Mompremier were throwing a huge party for the chimere and allied attaches that night in Cité Soleil, with plenty of liquor, women and guns present, distributing bullets and ammunition and preparing for the work they had to do the next day. Some of the boys asked me if I wanted to come along, but, sensing the reception I would likely get from the Lavalas officials present should I venture into such an atmosphere, I begged off. James was also leaving, and as we left him off at the road to Bois Neuf, I hugged him again.

"Take care of yourself, man," he said.

"Take care of yourself, too," I said.

"I'll see you soon," I added, and I hoped that it would true.

THE DEMONSTRATION the next day—January 7—started in violence and went downhill from there. Arriving at the Place St. Pierre in Petionville, where the march was set to begin, I spied Charles Baker, who turned toward me, his blue and white-striped shirt covered in blood, after just having helped to safety a middle-aged black protestor whose nose had been split open by a rock hurled by a chimere at the Église Saint Pierre's gates.

"Fortunately, it's not my blood," he said to me as we listened to a group of about thirty chimere shout insults and brandish rocks and bottles. Somewhat stupidly, I asked Baker what the march would be calling for that day.

"We are asking Jean-Bertrand Aristide to resign as dictator of Haiti," he responded.

Earlier that day, one of Dread Wilmé's gunmen, descending from Wilmé's Isuzu trooper, was killed when the chimere fired on a group of PNH officers around Delmas 62. The officers returned fire, killing the man and wounding three others. Cars bearing no license plates and carrying men wearing masks fired at marchers along the Delmas Road as an evangelical preacher, his car stuck in the demonstration, was dragged from his vehicle by chimere and beaten in the face until his jaw broke. Maxime Desulmond, a well-known student leader from Jacmel who was marching just behind Lolo Beaubrun, was shot in the neck and killed.

As TELECO and EDH vehicles ferried chimere around the city, a suspected Aristide gunmen was beaten, stabbed and thrown into a well near Avenue John Brown. Later, conflicting stories would say that the young man was in fact an opposition loyalist set upon and attacked by chimere. Again at Post Marchand, the march's PNH escort was fired upon by chimere and National Palace security personnel dressed in civilian clothes and as CIMO and PNH forces returned fire until one policeman finally told the marchers "Look, they're shooting at us; we can't protect you anymore."

Venturing to Canapé Vert to find the students who were set to march through there, I instead found chimere armed with clubs, knives and guns hunting demonstrators, and was chased into the Radio Ibo building as journalists from Radio Signal FM ran into the nearby offices of NCHR for cover. Security guards for the United Nations Development Program were held up at gunpoint and their weapons stolen and the Royal Market Turgeau and Star Mart off Avenue Martin Luther King were both looted. Nearby neighborhoods were covered in graffiti reading *"Baz Bwakayman/Viv Aristide 5 an,"* a reference to a chimere group that had been chased out of Gonaives by the Front and then came to Port-au-Prince. When it was all over, two were dead and dozens injured. That night, Front members, perhaps taking their revenge for that day's violence in the capital, torched the Gonaives home of Alina Sixto, a Lavalas activist based in Stamford, Connecticut.

In response to the chaos, U.S. State Department Spokesman Richard Boucher said in a written statement on January 9:

"The United States condemns the actions of the Haitian government in response to the political demonstration that occurred January 7 in Port-au-Prince. Although it is clear some elements of the police worked diligently to protect the demonstrators, it is also clear that other police officers collaborated with heavily armed, hired gangs to attack the demonstrators. Throughout the day, these same government-sponsored gangs rampaged through the streets of the capital, stealing cars, attacking radio stations, vandalizing businesses and harassing people. A government that wishes to be considered democratic cannot continue to use street gangs as an instrument of terror and intimidation."

The body count continued to rise. Claude Bernard "Billy" Lauture, a Haitian engineer and businessman who had been consistently at the front of the marches calling for Aristide's resignation, was kidnapped outside of the Ecko Depot store he owned just off the airport road on January 6. After his family was contacted with a ransom demand of $100,000, Lauture's body, bearing the signs of savage torture and nine bullet wounds, was found at the morgue of the State University hospital four days later. In Cap Haitien, PNH Inspector General Edner Jeanty was killed on January 10, only three days after being named to the post of Directeur Départemental de la Police du Nord, responsible for commanding the PNH throughout the entire region. Jeanty, a former Unite de Securite de la Garde du Palais National d'Haiti (USGPNH) official, was found dead alone in his car, and the circumstances of his demise were never fully explained by the government.

BEGINNING WITH AN extraordinary Mass at the Cathedral Saint Pierre in Petionville, which saw Port-au-Prince Bishop Pierre André Dumas declaring, "God bless this demonstration!" and Andy Apaid weeping in prayer as young women handed out key chains of the Virgin Mary, the march on January 11 took off in a rolling advance down the steep Delmas Road, with participants waving palm fronds and chanting, "We're going to dress Aristide as a red devil and send him away!" Spying Lolo Beaubrun, I pulled him aside to ask him what he thought of the display.

"It's important that we continue to mobilize because we can no longer accept compromise and negotiation," he said, marching as his gray dreadlocks flew in the air. "This government has gone too far with their crimes and they have to go."

Picking up marchers along the way, the crowd swelled to an estimated size of around twenty thousand, the biggest total yet, before heading toward the Place Canapé Vert.

Hoping to be in a good position for their arrival, I hitched a ride in a taxi, and again went to wait for the march at Place Canapé Vert, standing next to an outdoor bar with about half a dozen other clients lounging in chairs and sipping a Coke as *Bon* cart ice cream vendors nervously hugged the sidewalks, ringing on their bells trying to attract customers. As we sat watching and listening for signs of the march, a white Toyota pickup without license plates pulled away from the Canapé Vert police station on the other side of the plaza, followed a few minutes later by a Nissan pickup, also without plates, with chimere hanging off it flashing the "5 Years" sign with five outstretched fingers. Several minutes later, another pickup, this one with tinted windows and no plates, began slowly circling the plaza, and the men who had been chatting at the open-air bar began scattering wildly, running to-and-fro to get out of sight, as the barman pulled down his screen and hid inside.

Despite these tactics, and thanks in no small part to local radio, which broadcast such announcements as the one run on Radio Metropole stating that a pickup with hooded men in it was headed toward the Place from Avenue John Brown, and requesting police to help, the march came off largely without violence, aside from some sporadic clashes toward the end, and many marchers shouted encouragement to the police for protecting the demonstrators.

With large antigovernment demonstrations also reported in Petit Goave, Marigot and Miragoane that day (the latter marred by the killing of one pro-government activist and government partisans responding by setting fire to several homes rumored to be affiliated with opposition figures there), that night state televisions TNH broadcast a program called "Les Grands Débats," which featured archive footage of crowds from old Aristide speeches during the 1990 campaign interspersed with recent addresses to create the illusion that president still summoned similarly huge, enthusiastic support. The difference in footage, fashion, attire and at times even location was obvious to anyone watching. Following a fifteen minute propaganda montage extolling Aristide's virtues and accomplishments and attacking the opposition and civil society, the station played over and over the gruesome footage of the man beaten, stabbed and thrown into the deep gully during the January 7 demonstration as well as footage of bullet-riddled body of policeman Edner Jeanty shot in Cap Haitien. Tiring of the broadcast, I stepped out into the night from the house I was staying at in the Croix Desprez district, walking past *"Viv Jean Claude/Chef PNH"* graffiti as I did so. Walking through the bidonville up the hill from where I was staying to buy a soda from a kerosene-lit boutique, I heard the word *"blan,"* pronounced in wonder instead of anger, issue from a tiny voice. Turning around, I saw a little girl, ribbons in her hair and a new white dress, running toward me, her mother at her side, smiling. She ran into my arms and I lifted her up into the star-streaked night sky, both of us laughing as for a moment all of Haiti's demons receded away.

BEFORE HE DEPARTED for a conference he was scheduled to attend in Mexico, Aristide called the press to the capital's airport on January 12 for a strange address that he wanted to give. Driving to the airport, there were no supporters—paid or otherwise—lining the route, a new thing, and no ministers were gathered to bid the president farewell, as was customary. In the newly redone departure lounge, an assortment of domestic and foreign journalists waited, observing much furious discussion among the president's underlings of where the Haitian flag should be hung behind the podium, until Aristide himself arrived with now inevitable entourage of his wife, Yvon Neptune and several hulking Steele Foundation security guards.

Launching into a rambling speech about Claire Heureuse, the wife of Jean-Jacques Dessalines, Aristide said that, "When there are victims, I suffer, my heart bleeds. When there are condolences we all feel hit because we are children of the same family. . . . May the light of peace shine everywhere in the country with the wisdom of Claire Heureuse so that when I come back we may continue to intensify this peace that is essential for our land."

The gathered reporters sat transfixed, not by the president's words so much as by a large black moth floating above Aristide's head and then plastering itself on the wall behind him as he spoke—a chilling omen if there ever was one in vodou-superstitious Haiti.

As a farewell gift to the president, Dany Toussaint took to the airwaves later that day to say that he had obtained a list (though he declined to say from whom) of people to be murdered by the Aristide government, which included himself, Andy Apaid, Evans Paul, Nawoon Marcellus, the gang leader Labanye and my friend James, among others. Asked about his sudden reappearance after two weeks of silence, Toussaint responded that, "Sometimes I am visible, sometimes I am invisible."

"I'm here to give support to the students," he continued. "I have a surprise and President Aristide is going to have a surprise when he comes back from Mexico. He says he will go in peace. Yes, no problem, he will go in peace."

OVER THE NIGHT of January 13, in a move that Lavalas OP leader Roger "Béry" Binry would later say was planned in concert with Agathe Delone, a member of Aristide's private cabinet, and Jean-Claude Jean-Baptiste, Fritz Innocent, a member of the Unité de Sécurité du Président de la République, led a group of armed men to the site of the city's radio transmitters in Boutilliers, in the hills above Port-au-Prince. Tying up the guard there, they smashed transmitters and broke antennas serving Radio Galaxie, Radio Kiskeya, Radio Melodie, Radio Magik-Stereo, Radio Plus and Radio Signal FM, which all went off the air. Radio and Television Timoun, owned by the Aristide Foundation for Democracy, were also interrupted, but the silencing of the latter two was apparently an accident, as nothing differentiated their antennas from those of the private stations. A rumor also spread that, at the same meeting where it had been decided to knock down the transmitters, a plot had been hatched to kill four of the country's most well-known journalists, including Lilianne Pierre-Paul of Radio Kiskeya and Rotchild Francois, news director of Radio Metropole.

As Haiti's radio stations went silent, its parliament did as well, with the body rendered powerless on January 13 as the terms of most of the legislators elected in the disputed May 2000 elections expired. In the twenty-seven-seat Senate, the terms of four senators expired in addition to the eight who had previously resigned, leaving only fifteen sitting members of the body, and the terms of all eighty-three members of the Chambers of Deputies expired. From thenceforth, Aristide would rule by decree. As the legislature closed its doors, Dany Toussaint, speaking to a Haitian radio station in Miami, again reiterated that, "President Aristide had three options: prison, exile or death. Today, there remain only two available to him, namely prison or death. . . . The demonstrators of the opposition are determined to pass in front of the National Palace and I sincerely doubt that they would pass by there without invading the building."

On January 16, hundreds of highly radicalized university students nearly succeeded in doing just that, as they carried the coffin bearing the body of the murdered student leader Maxime Desulmond to the National Palace after a funeral service at the Sacré-Cœur Church. As they crossed Champs de Mars and approached the palace, CIMO fired in the air and lobbed tear-gas canisters at the protestors while chimere cruising through the square shot at the marchers. Students torched cars and threw rocks at the gunmen, before driving the coffin to a university building and finally releasing the body to Desulmond's family.

A MARCH ON JANUARY 18, which saw demonstrators carrying signs declaring that *"La Pres Endependan Ak Pep La Se Marasa"* ("The independent press and the people are one") ended when marchers were fired upon by gunmen shooting from the TNH building on Delmas. A planned protest from the State University's medical faculty on January 28 was broken up by police firing tear gas and stone-throwing chimeres, but not before students had burned a coffin in front of the American Embassy with the words "Lavalas" written on it. One student was struck by a tear-gas canister that lodged in his chest, and was taken to the Canapé Vert hospital, where he later died when it exploded. The hospital filled with students and the dead man's family, and some protestors set up flaming barricades in the streets outside. As darkness fell, police stormed the hospital, chasing students, staff, and visiting journalists inside from the parking lot or out into the night, opening fire on the crowd within the hospital grounds and killing at least two. In Cap Haitien three days later, police and chimere led by Nawoon Marcellus attacked and dispersed a large antigovernment march in that city.

Under the pressure, Aristide's mask of preternatural calm—maintained, many said, by a steady diet of pharmaceutical drugs—was showing signs of beginning to crack. When Radio Vision 2000 journalist Alex Régis asked the Haitian president his reaction on February 4 to the demonstrations taking place across the country demanding he resign, Aristide responded by saying that Régis was likely a paid member of the opposition and a liar to boot. Aristide's attitude with the Haitian press stood in marked contrast with his response to CNN's Anderson Cooper, who asked him the same question and was met with a measured and courteous response, another example of Aristide wearing one face abroad and another one at home. In response to Aristide's attack on one of their members, which in Haiti's charged political climate was little more than a signal that the reporter was now fair game to be targeted for a violent attack, the Association Nationale des Médias Haitiens declared that they would suspend any coverage of National Palace events until Aristide apologized.

THE HAMMER FINALLY FELL on the government in Gonaives on February 5. As hundreds of gunmen loyal to Butteur Metayer and Jean Tatoune flooded out of Raboteau and Jubilé and laid siege to the Gonaives police commissariat, they burned the Lavalas mayor's residence and succeeded for the first time in driving all of the PNH forces from the city in brutal fighting that left seven dead and over twenty injured. Some of the Front gunmen were swathed in the camouflage outfits associated with the disbanded FADH, while others wore Caribbean hip-hop apparel, shorts and American sports jerseys. One of the rebels, Wilfort Ferdinand—a diminutive, jherri-curled man whose slight stature gave him the nickname "Ti Will"—had in fact been in charge of the arms depot of the Gonaives commissariat, and he distributed the weapons to Front members once the police had fled. After freeing prisoners from the commissariat's jail, the rebels sacked and burned, eventually completely leveling, the police station that had become such a nexus for terror and fear throughout the region for so long. Going on national radio, Front spokesman Winter Etienne declared Gonaives a "liberated city" and promised that more cities would soon follow the town's example and rise up against Aristide.

Two days later, on February 7, over one hundred PNH and CIMO tried to retake Gonaives from the Front and its allies. Allowed to enter deep into the city, crawling alongside the cars that they were using as shields, they were then set upon and caught in a murderous barrage of gunfire coming from gang members hiding behind barricades, in narrow alleys and in doorways. Attempting to fight back, government forces ventured several bold incursions toward the city center, but were beaten back each time, with the Front now having in their possession prime weaponry such as brand new M16s looted from the Gonaives police station. When two policeman fired at Wilfort Ferdinand, he fell and rolled in a debris-strewn ditch, feigning death. When the policeman walked past the "corpse," Ferdinand leapt up and let loose with a shower of bullets from his M16, killing both men instantly and cementing his reputation as the fiercest fighter in a fierce group of men. The police, finally forced to retreat, left at least nine dead comrades in their wake, which crowds set upon, mutilating the bodies with knives and rocks and dragging through the streets, images that were broadcast throughout Haiti and the world. If there was ever any doubt that this uprising against Aristide was different than all of those that had come before it, or that the Gonaives gangs that Aristide had for so long propped up were now going for a solution of either death or victory against his rule, those scenes put an end to any speculation. There were now only two possible outcomes to the rebellion: the complete destruction of Gonaives, or Aristide's removal from power.

The same day in Saint Marc, just south of Gonaives, the anti-Aristide group Rassemblement des militants conséquents de Saint-Marc (Ramicos), based in the neighborhood of La Scierie, took advantage of the chaos to the north to use the weapons at their disposal—mostly light sidearms and pistols—to overrun the Saint Marc police station, where they freed all the prisoners before setting the structure on fire. Ironically, Ramicos had originally come into being partially through the patronage of Lavalas Senator Medard Joseph, but had gradually grown into something of a underdeveloped opposition force to Bale Wouze, the fierce pro-Lavalas OP in the town headed by Lavalas Deputy Amanus Mayette, whose term of office had expired in January. As police fled, hundreds of people began looting Saint Marc's port. Word filtered down from the Artibonite and around that populations had also attacked and sacked the police stations in the towns of Anse Rouge, Ennery, Gros Morne, Petite Rivière de l'Artibonite, L'Estere and Trou du Nord. Unrest then began spreading through the north of the country when, in the early morning hours of February 8, arsonists burned down the two-story building in Cap Haitien that housed the studios for Radio Vision 2000 in the city. Succeeding where they had failed in Gonaives, government forces managed to retake much of Saint Marc on February 9, with a noticeable exception being the Ramicos stronghold of La Scierie and the town's port, where looting continued unabated. As night began to fall, Yvon Neptune landed in Saint Marc in Aristide's helicopter and toured the gutted police station. Afterwards, Neptune paused to tell reporters that the violence "was connected to a coup attempt" and that "the national police force alone cannot reestablish order," an apparent reference to the legions of armed Bale Wouze members that were patrolling the town with M14s and glocks. Throughout that night and into the next day, reporters saw streams of frightened refugees flowing south out of Saint Marc, clearly terrified at reprisal killings that had already taken place and worried that worse was yet to come.

REACTING TO SUCH roiling violence, the U.S. Embassy authorized the departure of family members and nonemergency employees on February 10, the same day Haiti's Secretary of State for Communications Mario Dupuy said that local and foreign correspondents working in Haiti were "attachés of the terrorists" in Gonaives, and said that all the city's problems came from the false and deceptive reports being brought back from there. A demonstration of high-school students that day in Jacmel was attacked by chimere, and beginning that evening, chimere bands set up flaming barricades outside of Cap Haitien as the city descended into a state of blackout with no fuel arriving, north-south traffic in the country being effectively cut off following the fall of Gonaives to rebel forces. Drunk and high at their roadblocks, the chimere attacked approaching vehicles with rocks and prevented deliveries from the UN World Food Program from being distributed from the city. The next day, White House Press Secretary Scott McClellan said in a press briefing that the Bush government was "extremely concerned about the wave of violence spreading through Haiti and we certainly deeply regret the loss of life. We call on the government to respect the rights, especially human rights of the citizens and residents of Haiti."

TO THE NORTH of the capital, in Saint Marc, a terrible day of killing had arrived. As Bale Wouze members under the command of Lavalas Deputy Amanus Mayette, members of the PNH and armed men from the Unite de Securite de la Garde du Palais National d'Haiti—sent under Aristide's express order to Saint Marc—attempted to take the Ramicos stronghold of La Scierie on the morning of February 11, gunfire erupted throughout the town. Though Ramicos attempted to build a roadblock barring entrance to the neighborhood, the reinforced government partisans quickly overran it. As Ramicos members attempted to flee over the Morne Calvaire that rose imposingly behind the city, a foreign news photographer watched as government forces, with the aid of a helicopter Aristide had sent from the National Palace, chased them down, shooting several in the back, including Ramicos members Leroy Joseph and Francky Narcisse. Entering La Scierie, they set the Ramicos headquarters, located in a building housing several other businesses, ablaze.

That same morning in Saint Marc, Leroy Joseph, a twenty-three-year-old Ramicos member who had recently returned his .22 revolver to the organization because its presence in the house troubled the mother of his small child, went out to fetch something from his mother's house. Shortly after he left their home, his common-law wife, inside the house they shared with their baby and several other children, heard gunfire coming from the street, followed by shouts of "Come out!" that sounded to be just outside her door. As she shouted that it was only herself and the children who were home, Bale Wouze members broke down the door and stormed in. Amanus Mayette, wearing gray pants, sandals and a red *cagoule* (mask) entered the house and, pulling off his *cagoule*, asked the woman if she recognized him. Terrified, she said no. He then held a gun to her head in front of her children and said that he was going to kill her. Two other men, Ronald Dauphin (better known in Saint Marc as "Black Ronald") and a feared Bale Wouze member who went by the name Somoza were also present, both masked, though she recognized their voices. Black Ronald put a gun under her heart and told her that he was going to kill her, but one of the others argued for mercy. Demanding to know where Joseph was, they punched and slapped her. As they did so, they saw Joseph returning from his mother's house and ran out, seizing him. They bound the woman's wrists behind her back and made her lie on the ground with the children, and they watched as the three men pistols-whipped Joseph and administered slashing blows to his back with a machete. Dragging him to the already-smoldering Ramicos headquarters, Somoza then administered a coup de grace by decapitating him with a machete.

Elsewhere in the town, Amazile Jean-Baptise, after going out early in the day to attempt to sell goods at Saint Marc's market, finally made her way back to her small, tumbledown house through the chaos of the city streets. There she found her son, Kenol St. Gilles, a twenty-three-year old carpenter who was not a member of Ramicos, groaning with a bullet in each thigh. Taking him to the nearby home of Pastor Naulet Dameus, whose wife was a nurse, she sat outside with him on the porch as the pastor ran to get material to dress the wounds. Upon returning, having seen the condition of the city, the pastor ordered everyone inside. However, seven armed men, including three Jean-Baptiste thought might be police, had seen them and demanded they open the door. The men entered the house and ordered everyone down on the floor. Kenol St. Gilles, still in agony from his wounds, was half hidden behind a bed in the next room. The men searched the house and found him, dragging him out as he protested that he was only a carpenter, but the men said no, he had shot at them. Amazile Jean-Baptiste then watched as they dragged her son away. Terrified, she ran after the men, hiding on the way, and watched as her son was dragged to a cement depot that Bale Wouze had set ablaze, shot and thrown—injured but still alive—into the fire there.

Fritzner Moise, a twenty-four-year-old with no political affiliation, was forced at gunpoint to leave his seventeen-year-old wife and work for Bale Wouze that day, pulling down Ramicos barricades and carrying dead bodies. He was also forced to carry bags of cement the group had looted to reinforce the police commissariat. As he did so, the town seemed one great charnel house of flames and the dying. An estimated thirty homes were burned that day.

Though the spasm of murder—which, given the presence of National Palace security forces was certainly carried out with Aristide's knowledge and forethought—was most intense on the 11th, it would continue on in fits and starts for two weeks. A man named Yveto Morancy was killed by Bale Wouze's Somoza on February 13, and a list of men—Ramicos second-in-command Nixon Francois, Gaston St. Fleur, Laurestre Guillaume, Guernal Joseph, over twenty in all—would be seized by Bale Wouze and the government forces over the coming days, never to be seen again. Bodies littered the city's Autorité Portuaire Nationale parking lot, and the scrub-covered mountains surrounding it, where witnesses such as Radio Kiskeya correspondent Jean Max Blanc told of dogs feasting on corpses bloated by the sun.

What happened in Saint Marc that February was not unique—over the preceding three years there had been hundreds of killings of Aristide opponents by armed factions around the country—but it was the most extreme example of the logical outcome of Aristide's fomenting of armed pressure groups, outside the law and outside any real fear of retribution—as his bulwark against that threats that he was convinced he faced in his dual quests for control of the Haitian political machine and personal wealth. It was indeed in that blind quest that those he had claimed to represent—people like Leroy Joseph, Kenol St. Gilles and Amazile Jean-Baptiste—were forced to endure imaginable agony so that one man—with the aid of a small cadre of killers for hire, corrupt officials and cynical, avaricious foreign advocates—could attempt to build his own personal empire on the ruins of what was once a country.

WITH WORD OF THE MASSACRE still filtering out of Saint Marc as a delegation from the Plateforme des Organisations Haïtiennes des Droits Humains (POHDH) and the National Coalition for Haitian Rights (NCHR) visited the town that afternoon, after meeting with his Canadian counterpart, Bill Graham, on February 13, Colin Powell told reporters in Washington that "We will accept no outcome that in any way illegally removes the elected president of Haiti," adding "What we need from Aristide now is action, and not only words and expressions of support. . . . There is no plan, and we [have] discussed no plan here, for military or other kinds of intervention." The same day, the New York-based organization Human Rights Watch issued a press release calling on Aristide to "ensure that the country's security forces respect international human rights standards on the use of lethal force."

AS THE FRONT celebrated its victory over the police in Gonaives on February 14, Haitian radio listeners were stunned to hear the identities of the newest additions to the rebellion against the government. That day, a Radio Signal FM reporter told listeners that none other than former Cap Haitien police chief Guy Philippe, architect of so many attempts to topple Aristide in the past, and former FRAPH leader Louis Jodel Chamblain, who had also been living in exile in the Dominican Republic, had arrived in Gonaives "with two trucks full of weapons and men." The pair told reporters that they had arrived in the country to help the Gonaives rebels, and that they intended to seize Saint Marc before heading on to Port-au-Prince. Two of Aristide's most implacable foes were now back on Haitian soil, and they showed every indication of being willing to fight with the Gonaives rebels right up until the bitter end.

"Guy Philippe," said a Haitian ex-military man who was intimately involved in the restructuring of the police force after Aristide's return in 1994. "Well, Aristide always had a problem with these guys who studied in Ecuador; he targeted the professional aspect of the police force. But I can't put my hand in the fire for Guy Philippe. He had a very violent personality; he believed in extra judicial executions against criminals. Besides that aspect, he and the other 'Ecuadorians' were the best investigative policeman we had, but, and you wouldn't think it to look at him, Philippe was very aggressive, a crazy motherfucker."

Louis Jodel Chamblain, who had hated Aristide ever since a pro-Aristide mob had killed his pregnant wife in 1990, would later tell reporter Pastor Vasquez from the Dominican newspaper *Hoy* that he, Philippe, former Croix-des-Bouquets Police Chief Gilbert Dragon, and two other former soldiers had crossed the border into Haiti at the town of Elias Pina, unarmed, dressed in civilian clothes and mingling with the Haitians there for the town's busy market. Chamblain said the group then made its way through the mountains to a base of sympathizers in the Haitian town of Pernal, where they picked up another fifty men, and moved north, to the outskirts of Cap Haitien, where they arrived on February 7. Deciding they didn't have the strength to attack the Cap, the group instead entered Saint-Michel de la Atalaye, whose population had already ousted its Lavalas mayor and driven off the police, on February 8. Chamblain said that he and his men were virtually broke when they began the rebellion, but that a rich citizen at Saint-Michel gave them 10,000 gourdes to buy food and supplies for their troops. Taking the hamlets of Pilvorot, Cerca-la-Source, Limbé and Lacour-du-Nord, after rendezvousing with the Front in Gonaives, Chamblain set off with a contingent of men for Hinche, leaving the majority at Saint-Michel. Rejecting any suggestions that the group had gotten help from anyone on the Dominican side of the border, Chamblain told Vasquez that the first he even told his Dominican wife of his plans was when he called her after the border crossing to tell her, "I'm fighting in Haiti."

Dominican Armed Forces Secretary General José Miguel Soto Jimenez would later tell reporters that the Dominican government had informed Aristide of rebels groups training inside of Haiti some eight months earlier—a fact that the Haitian government was careful to obscure in the coming days.

For the moment, at least rhetorically, the men with guns in Haiti's north were on their own, with Andy Apaid telling Radio Metropole that while he supported the calls of "the people of the North" for Aristide's resignation, Chamblain represented "a vision of the past." A vision of Haiti's future was played out the same day at the FOKAL organization in Port-au-Prince, which was stormed by police officers, led by the dreaded Jackson "Gwo Jack" Bernard, who pointed their weapons at a board meeting of the foundation's directors and threatened to open fire unless those assembled explained the purpose of the event. Police took down the names of all those in attendance, and the incident prompted twenty-four organizations, including NCHR, TÉt Kole, Fanm Yo La and POHDH, to issue a press release two days later declaring that, "In 2004, 200 years of independence, we cannot accept that the reign of terror settles again. It is high time that the Haitian populations enjoy all finally their rights."

As the violence intensified, eight PNH officers were among ten Haitians rescued from their 15-foot sailboat by fishermen off the coast of the parish of Portland in Jamaica. The officers surrendered their firearms to Jamaican authorities and told a Jamaican constable that "We don't want to die just because we are policemen."

SPEAKING TO A RADIO INTERVIEWER in the United States on February 16, a mere four days after the Saint Marc massacre, Maxine Waters asserted that, "These so-called peaceful marches are not peaceful; they are creating the violence and Aristide is being blamed. . . . [Aristide] cannot just allow these things and opposition to take over these towns. . . . He will have to do something." Two days later in a February 18 press release, Waters, whose trips to Haiti consisted of staying at the capital's luxurious Hotel Montana and being feted by the Aristide government, opined about what an authority she was on the Haitian situation; she obsessed at length about the supposed violence being committed by the protestors calling for Aristide's removal and her fixating, consuming hatred of Andy Apaid, accusing the demonstrators of causing "tumult and havoc" and being responsible for all the violence.

"The so-called opposition is supported by many of the same people who were content with the brutal dictators of Haiti's past," Waters wrote of the students and slum dwellers and peasants who trudged for miles or rode in the back of tap-taps from humble homes without electricity and running water to march against a man they viewed as a tyrant. She then went on to denounce the rebellion in Gonaives, never mentioning that it had begun because of Aristide's betrayal of a group he himself had armed.

It was unfortunate that Waters was not on hand to witness the chaotic, surreal scene that played itself out in Hinche that day, when, around noon, a convoy of rebels led by Louis Jodel Chamblain arrived in jeeps and pickup trucks, carrying mostly pump-actions shotguns and some more sophisticated weaponry they had looted from police stations around the country. With Chamblain leading the attack on the town's police station, the rebels, which also included a well-known former FADH sergeant from the region named Joseph Jean-Baptiste, killed the town's police chief Maxime Jonas and another officer when the two attempted to fight back, as well as a prisoner who was caught in the crossfire. As the rest of the police fled, the rebels freed all the prisoners from the town's jail before setting it on fire. Before entering Hinche, the rebels had also burned down police stations in Maissade and Pandiassou, and the police forces in Thomonde. Belladere and Savannette had fled, leaving the town of Mirebalais, midway between Hinche and the capital, alone as the only staffed police garrison in the Plateau Central, mostly defended by chimere dressed in police uniforms. In Hinche, as they previously had been on their route, almost unbelievably for a man who had been one of the public faces of the FRAPH death squads, Chamblain and his men were cheered by the local population, with people running out of their homes and chanting, "Thank God for Gonaives" and "Mothers, keep your babies safe! Aristide has not left yet!"—a measure of just how desperately those in Haiti's countryside wanted to be liberated from Aristide's rule.

When the rebels arrived at a meeting MPP leader Chavannes Jean-Baptiste had organized outside of town, though, many attendees fled in fear. Chavannes met with rebel commander Joseph Jean-Baptiste (no relation) but declined to come out in public support of the rebels, insisting that the MPP was nonviolent.

"We know the strength of MPP in this region; we took the police barracks in Hinche, and we have come to see how we can collaborate," the rebel Jean-Baptiste told him. "We want to have a demonstration of support immediately and we want you to immediately name people to run the public administration."

"Collaboration isn't possible," Chavannes responded. "You lead an armed group; MPP is an organization struggling against Aristide but struggling peacefully. Just before you took over the police barracks, some members of MPP were there negotiating for security for a march we have organized for the February 17. But these events which have occurred require us to cancel this march to avoid the appearance that this is a show of support for the former military. "

The meeting ended cordially, but with no resolution to the rebel's request. Rebels returned again the next day, and Chavannes again told them the MPP would not march under pressure. On the 20, the MPP finally held their march, for which the rebels gave them their requested wide berth, and some ten thousand people showed up.

"We cannot make an alliance with this group just because we are both against Aristide," Chavannes said in a press release several days later. "An alliance requires more than that. . . . We don't know what plan the Front has. We have problems with the origin of all the sectors which form the Front. We see former military who tortured MPP militants during the coup d'etat, FRAPH which caused all the militants of MPP to go into hiding, the Cannibal Army mistreats and kills Aristide supporters. . . . [But] Aristide is a criminal, an assassin, a thief, a liar, a traitor, a gang leader, a dictator. There is no hope with him. All sectors of national life are finished with him. No compromise with him is possible. Democracy is not possible with Aristide. It is over. We must remove him from power. The presence of the Front cannot make us accept anything with Aristide. Aristide must leave. That is the principal objective of the Haitian people at this time. We must cut out this cancer."

Speaking to reporters at the National Palace that night after Hinche had fallen, Aristide told them that February 16, "Blood has flowed in Hinche. . . . A group of terrorists are breaking democratic order."

FOLLOWING THE KILLING of two Dominican soldiers and the theft of their weapons near Dajabon over the weekend, possibly by rebels, the Dominican Republic sealed its border with Haiti on February 17. The same day, in a tape recording broadcast over several stations around the country, Père Joachim Samedi, a Catholic priest and former Curé of the parish of Saint-Hélène in Jérémie in the Grande Anse region, said that Aristide was "insane, sick, like a trapped animal" and said that Lavalas Senator Louis Gérald Gilles had confided to him that Aristide wanted to "physically eliminate" René Préval, Bishop of Jacmel (and fierce Aristide critic) Guy Poulard, Radio Kiskeya director Lilianne Pierre-Paul and Radio Cariabes journalist Euvrard Saint Armand. Speaking to

Radio France-Inter, French Foreign Minister Dominique de Villepin seemed to pledge increased international involvement in the crisis, saying that, "We have the means—and many friendly countries are mobilized and ready to act. We have to find a way to do this in liaison with the different Haitian parties." Speaking in the capital on February 19 at the funeral for some of the officers killed in Gonaives, Aristide said, "I'm ready to give my life if that's what it takes to defend my country." The same day, the U.S. State Department urged all U.S. citizens to leave Haiti. In Gonaives itself, the Artibonite Resistance Front and the ex-military and police officers who had crossed the Dominican border announced they were forming a unified military alliance under the overall command of Guy Philippe.

FLYING BACK INTO Port-au-Prince on an American Airlines flight from Miami on February 20 after a brief trip to the States, my traveling companions included a four-man U.S. Embassy security team carrying four large bags labeled "Department of Defense." Halfway through the flight, the captain came on and announced, "I just spoke with our security personnel on the ground in Port-au-Prince and they assure us that all is secure." One's interpretation of security could vary however, as, exiting the airport upon landing, just outside of the arrival gate, a group of about a dozen chimere in Aristide t-shirts, drinking beer and guzzling Courvosier cognac out of the bottle, sat on two cars, listening to blaring rap music and moving M16s in full public display between the two vehicles. Stuck at the airport for an hour when my ride failed to materialize, I was nevertheless in better shape than my colleagues attempting to cover a student march in Canapé Vert, which was broken up by gun- and machete-wielding chimere and which injured over twenty people, including Mexican journalists attacked by chimere and chased into the stalls at the outdoor market there. As the demonstration dispersed, U.S., French, OAS and CARICOM diplomats held meetings with government and opposition representatives, and U.S. Ambassador James Foley told Aristide in a meeting that he needed to accept a proposal whereby he would install a new prime minister and cabinet—that it was the only way to save his presidency. The next day, perhaps sensing that he was rapidly running out of straws to clutch at, Aristide accepted the CARICOM plan, which called on him to name a government heavily populated by opposition figures, disarm the chimere, and for the rebels to lay down their arms. Aristide announced his decision with his wife Mildred and Maxine Waters at his side at a news conference at the National Palace. During the morning and afternoon, as various diplomats met with Haiti's opposition to try and get them to also accept the plan, Ambassador Foley put what one observer of the talks called "tremendous pressure" on the Democratic Platform to concede to the plan, but to no avail, leading one U.S. Embassy official to comment later that "maybe the opposition knew a lit bit more about the rebel's military plans than they were letting on." The Americans even added a guarantee clause for the opposition that if Aristide didn't follow through with his commitments that he must resign; but it was still not enough, and the Democratic Platform asked to be given until the end of business on Monday, two days later, to announce their decision. Given little choice, Foley and the other diplomats accepted.

At a press conference announcing the status of the talks at the Hotel Montana, Roger Noriega, then serving as the Bush administration's top envoy for the Western Hemisphere, OAS Haiti chief David Lee, Ambassador Foley and Bahamian Foreign Minister Fred Mitchell all looked grim, but tried to put the best face possible on the situation.

"The meetings began this morning with President Aristide. There was a frank exchange of views," Mitchell said to the assembled press corps. "The president agreed to proceed on the basis of the plan. . . . [The opposition] has agreed to get back to us by the close of business on Monday. Once again, I would characterize the discussions with the opposition as being very frank and, I think, useful."

Meanwhile, as armed Lavalas gunmen manned roadblocks and patrolled Cap Haitien that same day, shooting into the Hotel Roi Christophe where foreign journalists were ensconced, Elie Sam Pierre, director of Au Cap's Radio Hispaniola as well as Radio Metropole's correspondent in the city, was shot in the neck by Aristide partisans who recognized him as he was driving through the city with one of his young sons.

AGAIN LED BY Louis Jodel Chamblain, Haiti's rebel forces entered Cap Haitien in a convoy of vehicles shortly before midday on Sunday, February 22. Exchanging fire with chimere throughout Au Cap's narrow, historic lanes, the insurgents quickly overran their defenses.

"There are no police defending Au Cap, only chimere," said a caller from the city to Radio Vision 2000.

The rebels seized the police station and looted and torched the building that housed Radio Africa FM, owned by the feared former Lavalas Deputy Nawoon Marcellus. Marcellus himself, swept up in the panic spreading through the Aristide partisans in the city, hijacked a plane at gunpoint from Cap Haitien's small airport and flew back to Port-au-Prince, leaving the structure to be burned by the town's new masters. Looting broke out at the Cap's food warehouses.

"We are not terrorists," Chamblain told reporters as he paraded through the town amidst the surreal scene of its residents cheering his arrival.

As the rebels consolidated their grip on the city, the wires carried the unlikely picture of Louis Jodel Chamblain helping to load the gravely wounded journalist Elie Sam Pierre on a humanitarian-aid helicopter to airlift him to Port-au-Prince.

The same day, as exhausted OAS and CARICOM negotiators left the country without an agreement, rebels also attacked the police post in Terre Rouge between Mirebelais and the capital. Residents of the capital's northern Cazeau and Bon Repos neighborhoods reported that weapons were being distributed to chimere from the police stations there throughout the evening.

This time around, I would be working with a gifted photographer from Trinidad, Alex Smailes, and, with the help of some generous Haitian-American friends, we secured an excellent base from which to work, with high-speed Internet and a reliable generator in the mountain suburb of Thomassin, off the Kenscoff Road above the capital. Driving down to the Champs de Mars to observe the beginning of the city's Carnival celebrations that night, we found the square nearly empty this year, with CIMO clutching their weapons and standing on trucks, as clutches of Aristide's drunken male supporters danced as the Brothers Posse sang a song with the refrain *"W pa resiste chime yo"* ("You can't resist the chimere"). The National Palace was lit up in the red-and-blue colors of the Haitian flag, and off the park someone had scrawled graffiti that read *"Aristide 50 An Prizon."*

WITH RUMORS ALREADY SWIRLING that rebels had infiltrated the city and were preparing to attack, and with increasingly intimidating barricades being manned by armed and often drunken Aristide partisans at the Croix de Bouquets and Bon Repos northern approaches to the city, on Monday the Democratic Platform called a press conference at the Villa Creole hotel in Petionville where they announced their rejection of the CARICOM plan, despite a last-minute phone call from U.S. Secretary of State Colin Powell pressuring the group to accept it.

With Andy Apaid, Paul Denis and Micha Gaillard looking on, Evans Paul—who had assumed an increasingly visible role as the Platform's spokesman as he felt his revenge on his old nemesis Aristide approaching—told dozens of reporters that, while the Platform remained a "nonviolent, democratic, pacifist" movement, "we can accept no solution where Jean-Bertrand Aristide continues in power."

"Aristide created this violence and now the violence is coming back to him," Paul said. "With what happened in Cap Haitien yesterday and what could happen in Port-au-Prince today or tomorrow, the international community has to understand that Haiti has arrived at a difficult crossroads and that Aristide must go."

Noting that Aristide had already agreed to and broken OAS Resolutions 806 and 822, Paul Denis said that Aristide had a "deficit of credibility" and called for new directors of all police divisions and state industries, as well as a new interim prime minister to take the reins after being appointed by a "council of eminent persons."

As thirty-two more Haitian refugees arrived in Jamaica by boat, that night the capital's dread deepened when a fourteen year-old girl was killed and twenty-one people injured when an explosion tore through a crowd of Carnival revelers in front of the Rex Theater on the Champs de Mars. Conflicting reports blamed the explosion on, alternately, a grenade, a homemade bomb and a faulty electrical transformer.

With Au Cap now in rebel hands and the CARICOM plan to ensure that he continued in office rejected out of hand by the opposition, a mood of panic began to set over the Palace. Aristide, writing to Jamaican Prime Minister P.J. Patterson, requested the latter's assistance in procuring from the sympathetic government of South Africa more weaponry with which he could defend his faltering regime, now facing a rebel movement equipped with the high-powered arms seized from the slew of police stations they had overrun. The *Jamaican Observer* newspaper later reported that Patterson, sympathetic to Aristide's request, wrote to South African President Thabo Mbeki the same day, and, when Mbeki responded in the affirmative, immediately sent a faxed letter back to Aristide saying the shipment would arrive within days.[1]

ON TUESDAY, FEBRUARY 24, as fifty U.S. Marines landed to help secure the U.S. Embassy, setting up sandbagged machine-gun nests on its roof and around its perimeter, and as groups of armed Aristide partisans continued to man roadblocks around the capital's northern approaches, the Democratic Platform called another press conference.

"One man cannot hold a nation hostage," said Andy Apaid, as he sat with the other members of the group. "He must resign."

"We feel trapped," Apaid added, "between two groups: an armed movement coming from the North and an armed movement coming from the terrorizing and criminal government in the National Palace."

Despite the Platform's claims to nonviolence, it soon became clear that they weren't above using the rebel advance as leverage for achieving their ultimate goal of forcing Aristide from power.

"The first element in any negotiation is Mr. Aristide's leaving power," Hans Tippenhauer said in his remarks. "Everywhere these so-called rebels go, the population receives them as liberators. The voice of the Haitian people is clear: they want Mr. Aristide to leave."

As news filtered down from the northern city of Port-de-Paix that rebels had sacked and burned the police station there and seized the municipality, Alex and I toured the capital's perilous streets. Passing the Behrman Motors building, partially burned down but not completely destroyed by arsonists, we made our way to the Sant Alfabetizasyon Organizasyon Wayom Bondye Etabli Soulate (God's Kingdom Literacy Organization), a government literacy center in a rundown neighborhood near Haiti's Parliament.

"The opposition doesn't want Haiti to go forward, but Aristide realizes that people are suffering," said Murat Rosier, a dreadlocked man smoking a large ganja spliff, who we found sitting outside the deserted building and who said he acted as a literacy councilor.

With the road in front of the Faculté des Sciences Humaines building of the State University blocked by the hulks of burned-out cars, Alex and I got out and walked into the facility, where we found a clutch of students immersed in a reading of, appropriately, Machiavelli's treatise on political methodology, *The Prince*. The students echoed the opposition's call for Aristide to step down, saying they would not let up on their drive to oust him, though they distanced themselves from the rebels' violent methods.

"In our society now we have no rights, no right to expression of criticism [against Aristide]," said one young boy, a social sciences student. "We will continue with our movement against Aristide even though we have no guns; we have nothing but our peaceful voice."

Driving in front of the National Palace, we found Albert Mangones's iconic *"Le Marron Inconnu"* statue desecrated with graffiti reading *"Viv eleksyon,"* and at the Palace's rear gate, we found chimere lounging with assault rifles and beer bottles. On a side street, a few hundred people noisily demonstrated their support for Aristide, with one woman who said she represented a group called Radical Women in Action screaming that, "We chose Aristide for five years! We will defend him to the death!" On the capital's courthouse nearby, the graffiti read, "Aristide: Cut off the heads and burn down the houses of the bourgeoisie," an echo of Dessalines's cry against the French some two hundred years earlier.

Attempting to disingenuously portray himself as the voice of reason in the crisis, Aristide told reporters at the Palace, referring to Chamblain, Philippe and company, that, "They are back with the same methods. They prefer to use weapons to kill the dream of democracy, killing the people who vote."

Also speaking that day, Yvon Neptune had another message for radio listeners in the country, saying in reference to the chimere gangs roaming the capital that, "The population has the right to defend themselves. We call on the population who want peace to mobilize to end this spiraling violence."

As Alex and I passed *"Aristide Mikrob Social"* graffiti in Canapé Vert on our way home to our mountain retreat that night, we paused near the Petionville police station to watch as black-suited government riot police stole tap-taps and quarry trucks, forcing their drivers and passengers out facedown in the street at gunpoint and then used the vehicles to barricade the commissariat against any possible attack. Fortunately, our battered pickup was spared.

THE NEXT DAY, descending past the Thomassin police station, we saw new *"Viv lame Aba Aristide"* ("Long live the army/Down with Aristide") graffiti scrawled along the Kenscoff Road. We found barricades manned by young men in long dreadlocks and Rasta tams along Nazon and the Delmas Road and a row of burned-out market stands around Delmas 33.

"It's a terrible situation, there is too much misery and danger in the country," a middle-aged man in ragged clothing said to me as he nervously eyed the barricades with other people waiting in line for petrol.

Up and down Delmas, truckloads full of armed chimere, brandishing shotguns, pistols and automatic rifles, cruised unhindered. The PNH were nowhere in evidence. As we traveled further toward the port, the road was nearly empty save for gangs of armed Aristide partisans guarding blockades made of flaming tires, hulks of burned-out cars and overturned market stands, many barricades constructed under the ubiquitous billboards of Aristide. We found similar roadblocks were also in evidence throughout the Croix de Bouquets and Tabarre neighborhoods.

"Aristide will stay for five years! We are mobilizing now for him and the rebels will never come to Port-au-Prince!" said a young man, his head swathed in a red bandanna as he manned a roadblock at the end of Delmas and waved to a truckload of shotgun-toting, pro-government militants speeding by in the back of a pickup.

"Aristide or death!" the others chanted. *"Rat pa ka ka!"*

The U.S. Embassy and consulate had closed, and groups of men near the parliament were reported to be throwing stones at passing cars in an attempt to block traffic.

Not that far away from Haiti's travails, as he was sentenced to twenty-seven years in prison and leveled with $30 million in fines and forfeitures by U.S. District Judge Federico A. Moreno in Miami, drug trafficker and former Aristide confidant Beaudoin "Jacques" Ketant lashed out in a memorable tirade against his former friend in the courtroom.

Calling Aristide "a drug lord" who "controlled the drug trade in Haiti," the 42-year-old Ketant said that, "It's a one-man show, your honor. You either pay him or you die. He turned the country into a narco-country [and] he betrayed me just like Judas betrayed Jesus."

When Judge Moreno explained to Ketant that that had no bearing on why he was before him, and that Aristide himself had not yet been charged with anything, Ketant had his response prepared.

"Not yet, your honor. You will be seeing him pretty soon," Ketant retorted, before being led away to his cell.

As Alex and I returned home that night, the police manning the roadblock at the Thomassin commissariat shone torches in our eyes, the flames illuminating the guns that surrounded us.

WE AWOKE ON FEBRUARY 26 to a chilly morning in Thomassin and the echo of a report of automatic weapons fire from the valley below. We had decided to drive to Saint Marc that day, to examine the government's last line of defense against the rebels who now controlled half the country. As we drove down through Petionville, there seemed to be many more people on the streets and riding tap-taps and camionettes than there had been the day before. Slinking through menacing but unmanned barricades made of downed trees and remnants of burned-out cars on the road through Canapé Vert, we picked up Herby and the mulatto doctor downtown before continuing, our pickup truck now full for the day. Roadblocks of tires and cement blocks ringed the roads out by the airport and Tabarre, and the situation seemed very tense along the stretch between Tabarre and Croix des Missions, with only one person, an old man, smiling at us as we passed by. Cabaret was busy, crowded with tap-taps and market women bringing baskets of plantain, and beyond the small town we passed a seaside vodou temple with dozens of flags fluttering about it in the breeze.

The news for Aristide this morning was not good. In Washington and Ottawa, the respective governments there began for the first time to seem to suggest that the Haitian president should consider resigning, a shift that did not go unnoticed among the civil opposition in the capital and the rebels in the north.

"Whether or not he is able to effectively continue as president is something he will have to examine carefully in the interests of the Haitian people," U.S. Secretary of State Colin Powell told reporters in Washington, and he again reiterated that U.S. troops would take part in a peacekeeping force only to enforce any political settlement reached before their deployment. Canadian Foreign Minister Bill Graham told journalists there that, "Clearly Mr. Aristide has to accept that the conditions in his country are deteriorating. He also has to examine all the possible [options] for the well being of his people." Despite Jamaican Foreign Minister Keith D. Knight's plea to the UN Security Council in New York that, "The member-states of the CARICOM community seek the direct and immediate intervention of the United Nations within the context of the U.N. charter," the council declined to rescue the Haitian leader, instead only adopting a draft resolution that said the body would consider a peacekeeping force after the president and his opponents hammered out some sort of agreement. Up until this point, the UN didn't even have a senior diplomat in Haiti. On the ground in Port-au-Prince, American Airlines announced it was suspending flights between Haiti and the United States due to fears for the security of its staff; and in Petit Goave, the Domi nan Bwa chimere OP sacked Radio Echo 2000, the station where the murdered journalist Brignol Lindor had worked.

As we entered Saint Marc that day, we were confronted by the face of what Aristide and his loyalists referred to as "the population," or, rather, the element of it he was counting on to defend his government. Outside of the small police commissariat that marks the entrance to the city at Portail Montrouil, military-fatigued members of Bale Wouze were lounging, holding M14s, shotguns and automatic pistols. Glaring at passersby from behind mirrored sunglasses, they were stopping and searching cars at will, shouting orders at terrified civilians and communicating loud and clear that, for the moment at least, Saint Marc remained in government hands. I asked Alex to slow down. I wanted to talk to these men. Parking about 100 meters from the police station, I got out of the car while Alex, Herby and the mulatto doctor remained inside. The armed men at the police station glared at me hostilely.

I introduced myself to one man who stood fingering an assault rifle, his head wrapped in a black du-rag. He gave his name as No Limit and said that he was from the USGPNH, the Unite de Securite de la Garde du Palais National d'Haiti, Aristide's personal security force at the Palace. Motioning to a clutch of like-camouflaged, armed men near our parked car, he identified them as Bale Wouze.

"Terrorists came into the town and attacked the people here with their weapons. They wanted to intimidate people here. We came back to town and chased them away," he said, never for a moment slackening his grip on his weapon. "Every day there's a rumor that they'll come back, they'll return to the city, they'll take it hostage. If you see that we look kind of fierce (*nou kanpe yon ti jan rong*), it's because of them. We're not here to intimidate the press. We're making a stand here to intimidate the terrorists, those who want to intimidate the people."

As he spoke, I turned to see Herby being dragged into the street by a shouting, camouflaged Bale Wouze member with a 9 millimeter pistol stuck in his belt, frisking him and forcing him to begin to strip. I ran back, tape recorder in one hand, Palace-issued press ID in the other hand, telling him to stop, that Herby was with us and we had a right to be there.

"Put that fucking thing away," he yelled, pointing his gun at his tape recorder and then at my head. "Put it away now!"

I shoved it in my pocket. He turned back to Herby.

"Why the fuck are you with these white men?" He glared at myself, Alex and the mulatto doctor. I turned to look back at No Limit, who had been surveying the scene. I turned my palms up as if to say, "Help us," and, finally, he came striding over.

"They can proceed," he said to the other man.

After the less-than-warm welcome, we proceeded to the hospital, where the mulatto doctor thought he might know some of the physicians working. However, the green-and-white facility was almost deserted, ghostly and eerie, with only one nurse and an attendant present, stitching the wound of a tiny street boy who had been beaten by his playmates. They told us that Bale Wouze had been there, looking for the injured, and frightened people from coming back. Driving to the northern edge of the town, several large metal containers had been thrown across the road, augmented with the jacknifed chassis of a large tap-tap. Dozens of cars and buses had queued up, attempting to negotiate passage, and people were crawling on their hands and knees through a small space between the two. Two men, sweating in their dark suits, were attempting to find a way to attend a funeral in Gonaives.

As we entered La Scierie, pink stucco and plain wooden houses sat empty, scorched black from the fire, their windows shattered and doors broken down. Frightened residents asked us not to speak with them when I tried to talk to them, and a young man on a motorcycle sat at the end of one block, picking his teeth and watching us. At the African Snack Bar, a mural of a spliff-smoking Rasta in red, gold and green colors had been decorated with "*Aba Aristide*" graffiti, and the lanes were littered with the remnants of burned cars and tires. At Saint Marc's main police station, which had been partially burned by antigovernment forces after they occupied the city, a PNH officer, who gave his name as Lestor Octaves and sat swathed in black pants and t-shirt and holding an automatic rifle and surrounded by scowling, armed Bale Wouze members, said that the links between the police and the paramilitary forces were a good thing.

"We have an armed bandit group operating from Gonaives; it's an illegal force," Octaves said, as a shotgun-toting Bale Wouze member nodded in agreement. "If they attack us here today or tomorrow, we will have more people to meet them. We must protect the security of the populace."

As Octaves spoke, another Bale Wouze gunmen, apparently staggeringly drunk, dropped his M14 from his shoulder and it bounced several times on the ground, miraculously not going off. He picked it up, smiling stupidly.

We drove on to the cool confines of Saint Marc's impressive gray and white Catholic church and a slim, serious man of about thirty came to the room where we were sitting. He introduced himself as Father Arnal Metayer, vicar of the Catholic parish of Saint Marc.

"The tension began on February 7, after the people sacked the commissariat," he said, sitting in a straight-back chair, his hands folded across his lap, his voice barely above a whisper. "They assaulted the commissariat and the police were forced to leave. Following that, on February 11, Wednesday, the government sent other police to retake control of the city and when the police came, they committed many acts of brutality. They assaulted the headquarters of Ramicos and a lot of them died."

I asked him why the city seemed nearly deserted.

"Many people, after they witnessed those events, where they went into the Ramicos headquarters, many young people fled. Those that ran, they followed them; they killed them and the next day, they set fire to a lot of buildings, to people's houses. Since then people have been really frightened and they have left the city to protect themselves. They've gone into hiding."

Coming back to an earlier aside the mulatto doctor had made about our incident at the roadblock, the priest explained the collusion underway between regular and irregular government forces:

"Since February 11, the police have been working with Bale Wouze. People are afraid. They have been many disappearances. Two people died in the Paultre house. There were more than ten killed on the mountain there, where the police chased them and killed them. Since the police came here, the city of Saint Marc has been a dead city. These people don't make arrests; they kill.

"There has been terrible suffering in this town, many people have fled and are afraid to return. The Bale Wouze burned people to death in their houses. Those people slept in their houses and they died there as well."

We then sat in silence, briefly, as a washerwoman banged pots around in the church's kitchen nearby, and a boy's voice called from outside. We shook hands, and then went back to our truck.

As we drove slowly along, a man slept in the ruins of the burned-out pharmacy Clinique D'Esculape, and we spied a little girl hiding behind a gate nearby who overcame her shyness and walked into the road, smiling and giving a quick wave to some visitors.

"This is terrible," muttered the mulatto doctor, looking out at the girl. "These children shouldn't have seen what happened here."

The day after our visit, 21-year-old Ketia Paul, mother of a one-month-old baby, went along with another woman to the burned-out commissariat where we had spoken to police. They had gone to plead for the release of a friend held there. Arriving early in the morning, they found Ronald "Black Ronald" Dauphin and several men they didn't recognize inside the building, wearing the gray uniforms associated with CIMO and helmets. Dauphin asked the girl if she would sleep with him in order save her friend's life, and, when she laughed nervously, he punched her in the mouth, breaking off one her teeth. Then Dauphin and the men dragged Paul and her friend to two rooms in the back of the commissariat where they took turns gang-raping them over the course of the next seven hours. Eventually, the women were freed, but Paul's breast milk dried up after the rape. No one, its seems—none of the PNH or USPGNH officers present, and certainly none of the Bale Wouze members—had ever lifted a finger to help her.

BY FRIDAY, the capital was in a state of near-collapse, with looting breaking out at the port and automatic weapons fire echoing on the Rue de Cesars and near the Promobank on Lalue. Petionville was nearly completely deserted. Banks, schools and businesses around the city were all shuttered tight. Chimere, including many teenagers, had taken over the police station at Gressier, robbing motorists, assaulting people and extorting "tolls" for passage, while others, also armed, rode around Champs de Mars with Aristide posters taped to their windshields. That morning, several dead bodies had appeared around the capital, their hands bound, dead from execution-style bullet wounds to the head. That night, a wounded chimere had been brought into the Canapé Vert hospital where the doctor was forced to operate at gunpoint, and still could not save the young man. The front of Radio Vision 2000 was raked by gunfire as word reached the capital that the rebels had finally succeeding in taking Mirebalais, only thirty-five miles to the northeast and their last major obstacle on the drive toward Port-au-Prince. Rumors, unusually detailed rumors, had it that Aristide was planning his own *semaine sanglante*, and that large-scale, lethal attacks on the mulatto business class and his political enemies were only hours away.

That morning, an editorial in the *Miami Herald* had called for Aristide to step down, writing that, "Listening to no one but paid sycophants, Mr. Aristide has been left to rule by decree, with street toughs acting as political enforcers. It's too bad that none of the president's advisors told him that his own credentials as a democrat would expire with the death of democracy."[2] An editorial a day earlier in the *South Florida Sun Sentinel* had sent a similar message, writing that, "The rejection of a diplomatic compromise by Haitian opposition leaders leaves the international community with no choice but to intervene and it leaves President Jean-Bertrand Aristide with no alternative but to resign."[3]

"I've seen nine bodies over the last few days," said a man playing cards in Nazon, where Alex, the French photographer and I, driving around trying to get the pulse of the city, had stopped to chat for a while. That morning, Alex and I had waited in a queue of cars thirty deep to try and get gas for our pickup off the Canapé Vert road. We finally ended up filling the tank of our vehicle for over US$50. As word came over the radio that the population of Cayes Jacmel had set the police station there aflame, we decided that, with the afternoon dragging on, we better head back up the hill to relative safety soon. The French photographer had to get a change of clothes and photo equipment from her home in Pacot (she had been sleeping in a spare bed at the Hotel Montana and did not like venturing the return home at night), and we ended up spending about another thirty minutes at her apartment.

We were extremely nervous about deciding which route to take back to the Montana. The Avenue Pan-Americaine was the most direct route, but there had been reports of shooting there all morning. The Canapé Vert road would get us into Petionville quicker, but it abutted the police station there—always a sketchy place in the best of times—and the warren of poor homes that had served as a hideout for the chimere in recent weeks. Earlier in the day, a reporter from the *New York Daily News* had been car-jacked in front of the General Hospital, and that afternoon a carload of Canadian journalists were robbed and threatened at gunpoint by a group of some thirty chimere at Croix des Bouquets.

Finally, after some discussion, we decided to chance driving past the Canapé Vert police station as the road was quicker back and the route up Pan-Americaine had grown rather monotonous. It was late afternoon, around five o'clock, and we figured that, as long as the sun was still up, passing through the chimere nest that the neighborhood had become would be alright.

Approaching the Place Publique, we saw a tap-tap ahead of us make a sharp left down a side street, and, before we know what was happening, we heard the distinctive click-click of a cocking shotgun. Alex brought the car to a screeching halt as a group of descending men, their hands on their pistols, moved out from behind a barricade toward the car. One man, jittery and glassy-eyed, held a shotgun level with my head.

"We are just trying to pass," I said to them in Kreyol.

"Get out, we're going to search the car," said their apparent leader, a young man with a purple felt beret and mirrored sunglasses.

"We're not getting out of this car," I said under my breath to Alex and the French photographer, and explained to the man in sunglasses that I had been issued an ID by the National Palace to work as a journalist in Haiti, pulling it out of my wallet to show them. The man seemed unimpressed.

"Get out of the car. We need to search it. We are here to protect the police station."

The man with the shotgun kept staring at us, his finger on the trigger, poised to shoot.

"Listen, I am a journalist, these two men are journalists, we have a long time in the country and we are just trying to get home," the French photographer piped up from the back seat.

Letting the French photographer, with her long experience in the country, continue on chatting with the leader, we finally succeeded in being able to pull away from the roadblock, slinking down toward Avenue Pan-Americaine, feeling lucky not to have lost our vehicle, not to mention other, far more important possessions.

"A cup of coffee and a baguette would be good right about now," Alex said as we sped up the hill.

WITH THE STREETS of Port-au-Prince in chaos and increasingly dangerous, by Saturday the U.S. Embassy had split into two camps. Ambassador Foley and several senior staff were sequestered at the ambassador's residence in the hills above Port-au-Prince, while Deputy Chief of Mission Luis Moreno, several other staff members and a contingent of U.S. Marines held down the fort at the embassy building on Avenue Bincentenaire, which roadblocks and tit-for-tat killings had transformed into a dangerous no-man's land. Moreno, who had previously served as the military affairs officer at the U.S. Embassy for a period after Aristide's return in 1994, had left Haiti to work as the director of Narcotics Affairs Section of Plan Colombia from a base in Bogota, returning to Haiti in August 2001. Though he had initially been skeptical after his return to Haiti that Aristide, someone he said always conducted himself with "great dignity and graciousness" in their dealings, had gone as bad as his colleagues at the embassy said he had, Moreno, who many whispered was a possible station chief for the Central Intelligence Agency in the Caribbean, concluded fairly soon after his return that, "Aristide wasn't ruling a country, he was running a crime syndicate."

Despite a huge pro-government demonstration that swept through the capital's streets from Bel Air that afternoon, Aristide, feeling the net closing in on him, was growing frantic. Although later charges would be leveled that the U.S. State Department had blocked a new detachment of Aristide's Steele Foundation security personnel from arriving in the country, the State Department had in fact approved the request (made a week before), but Steele had never sent them.

"I think the American contractors saw the writing on the wall," said a Western diplomat in Port-au-Prince.

Fearful of the "apocalyptic" orders Aristide had given to the chimere in the event of a rebel attack on the city, U.S. Embassy officials had contacted Guy Philippe on the latter's cell phone in the field on Friday night and successfully argued for him to delay his planned assault on the Haitian capital for forty-eight hours, in order to give negotiations with Aristide more time. Philippe's thirty-sixth birthday was Sunday, and he had frequently said that he wanted to be in the capital to celebrate it.

As Saturday drew into evening, Aristide, who always had a shrewd instinct for assessing political realities despite his rhetoric, sent an emissary to the U.S. ambassador's residence, stating that he and his wife were looking, under the most secretive circumstances, to leave the country (Aristide had already sent his two young daughters to the United States some days before). No doubt realizing that he was faced with all but certain death should Philippe and Chamblain's men ever find him, and perhaps looking on his departure as no more than a tactical retreat, Aristide greeted his envoy when the latter returned to Tabarre with the message that, yes, the U.S. would help the Aristides leave the country. A series of telephone conversations (at least four) between Aristide and U.S. Ambassador Foley discussing the details of the departure began, which lasted until close to midnight when a final call came that an agreement had been reached and Aristide was ready to leave. As the fax machine in the ambassador's residence wasn't functioning, Aristide faxed his resignation letter to the U.S. Embassy building in downtown Port-au-Prince, where it was received by Luis Moreno around 2:15 a.m. Sunday. The letter, written in Kreyol and bearing Aristide's signature, read as follows:

7 February 2001,
I took an oath to respect and have the constitution respected.
Tonight, 28 February 2004, I am still determined
To respect and have the constitution respected.
The constitution guarantees life and peace.
The constitution can't be drowned in the blood of the Haitian people.
It's for that, tonight I am resigning in order to avoid a bloodbath.
I accept to leave, and hope there will be life, not death.

Life for everyone.
Death for no one.
In respect for the constitution,
And in the face of respecting the constitution,
Haiti will have life and peace.
Thank you,
Jean-Bertrand Aristide.

With the letter in hand, and a U.S. military transport plane speeding to take Aristide into exile, Moreno took off the from the embassy downtown to Tabarre. Wearing no bullet-proof vest and carrying no sidearm, Moreno and a convoy of four cars, including six security personnel, made their way through what he later described as "a very intimidating atmosphere. There were abandoned barricades everywhere and quite a few dead bodies in the streets."

Arriving at Tabarre, the gates of Aristide's mansion were opened for the convoy by one of Aristide's Steele Foundation security detail, and the U.S. officials found themselves facing around twenty Steele security personnel armed with MP5 submachine guns and around three dozen Haitian CIMO and SWAT personnel. The embassy envoys were heavily outgunned.

As they entered, Aristide stood in the doorway of his residence dressed in a suit with a set of bags and his wife, Mildred, at his side. He was speaking to a tall, light-skinned Haitian man wearing a bullet-proof vest and holding a radio. That man was Aristide's personal security director, Frantz Gabriel.

Descending from his car, Moreno approached Aristide.

"You know why I'm here, Mr. President," Moreno said, addressing Aristide in Spanish.

"Yes, I know," Aristide replied.

"I need the original copy of that letter."

"Yes, I know," Aristide said. "I will give it to you when we reach the airport. *Mi palabra es mi palabra.*"

The convoy entered the airport through a side gate and drove to the tarmac, waiting for the plan to land. At this point, the U.S. personnel on the ground didn't even know where the plane with Aristide was going, only that the U.S. government was attempting to find a place that would take him.

As Aristide waited to board the plane, he placed a phone call to some of his security staff—who would later confirm the call to me—including the pilot of the helicopter that had ferried him around the country over the last three years, and, in a calm, clear voice, told them he was leaving and wished them well. He also called Yvon Neptune. As he did so, Luis Moreno, growing restless at still not having the original copy of Aristide's resignation letter in his possession even as the plane was scheduled to land at any moment, got out of the vehicle he was traveling in and walked up to Aristide's SUV, rapping lightly on the tinted back-seat windows. The window rolled down automatically and Aristide peered out at Moreno.

"I need that letter, Mr. President."

Aristide shrugged and turned to his wife, Mildred, and nodded. Opening her purse, Madame Aristide removed the original copy of Aristide's resignation letter from it. Moreno handed it to a Kreyol-speaking U.S. Embassy employee who confirmed that it was the same as the one that had been faxed to the embassy hours before. Standing there with Aristide as the first glow of dawn began to streak across the sky, Moreno—a voluble Colombian-American from Brooklyn—attempted to break the uncomfortable silence as he stood outside of Aristide's vehicle by noting to the president that, as military liaison officer at the U.S. Embassy in 1994, he had been responsible for organizing airport security for Aristide's triumphant return to Haiti in October of that year. He said that he found it both ironic and saddening, that he was seeing the Haitian president off from the country under these circumstance. Aristide looked at him and shrugged his shoulders, resigned.

"Sometimes life is like that," Aristide replied in English.

Aristide's backers abroad had sought to defend him, and to abet further murder of his fellow Haitians, one last time, but their help had come too late. That very morning, a South African Boeing 707 had arrived in Norman Manley Airport in Kingston, Jamaica to refuel, bound for Haiti with a cargo of some 150 R1 assault rifles, five thousand rounds of ammunition, smoke grenades and bullet-proof vests. In responding to Jamaican Prime Minister P.J. Patterson's request and running to the defense of the Aristide regime, South African President Thabo Mbeki had circumvented the usually weeks-long approval process of his own country's National Conventional Arms Control Committee (NCACC) to approve and set in motion the arms distribution in a matter of days. The plane eventually returned to South Africa with its cargo intact.4

Aristide boarded the aircraft that would take him into exile with his wife, Frantz Gabriel and several Steele Foundation employees, including Mark Moore, a former Marine who had been on Aristide's security detail for some time. Around 6:15 a.m., the plane took off roaring over Cité Soleil before it veered left, heading over the Caribbean and, eventually, Africa.

THE CALL CAME just as dawn was creeping up over the chilly hills of Thomassin. My cell phone buzzed just a few minutes after seven. When I answered, the line went dead, but the caller-ID said that it was the German photographer Thomas Dworzak, who had traveled with me to Gonaives and wisely sequestered himself at the Hotel Plaza just off the Champs de Mars downtown. Instinctively, at this hour on a Sunday, I knew what it meant: Aristide was gone. Almost simultaneously as the thought crossed my mind, a tremendous crackle of gunfire went off down the road. Time to move.

I grabbed Alex out of a sound sleep and we jumped in the truck and started careening at breakneck speed down toward the capital. The Thomassin police station appeared completely deserted, its doors hanging wide open. All along the side of the road, crowds of people, mostly poor mountain peasants, had gathered. Some looked angry and defiant. Others were celebrating and drinking. One big, burly man with a thick mustache and a baseball cap on leapt in the air as we passed, laughed and held up three fingers in mocking reference to the Aristide partisans "five years!" chant. From the valleys on either side of the Kenscoff Road, volleys of gunfire erupted all the way down to Petionville.

Speeding down toward Petionville with Alex at the wheel, we decided to make a quick swing past the Hotel Montana to see if any other journalists had heard anything. We arrived to an army of cars honking their horns and backing to and fro in the Montana's long driveway and parking lot. Hopping out, I saw first the French photographer, a Comme il Faut Haitian cigarette in one hand and a portable radio pressed up to her ear in the other. When she saw me she gave me a quick, wry smile, and then a hug. Behind her was Gerry Hadden, the National Public Radio reporter who had traveled with me to Gonaives two years before. We embraced. Scott Wilson, a reporter from the *Washington Post*, came charging out of the lobby. At some point I leapt into a car, I forget whose, and a caravan of journalists headed down to the prime minister's office where Yvon Neptune and Haiti's soon-to-be new president, Supreme Court Justice Boniface Alexandre, were announced to be giving a press conference momentarily.

We arrived at the prime minister's office to find a crowd of angry onlookers gathered outside the front gate and the grounds ringed by American special forces personnel, U.S. Marines and CIMO. Entering the ground floor of the building, dozens of reporters were herded into a conference room where, on one side of a long, finely-polished wooden table, Neptune and Alexandre sat, as U.S. Ambassador Foley stood behind them.

"Today is an extremely difficult day for us," Neptune began, speaking in Kreyol, without notes. "Today President Jean-Bertrand accepted again to make a huge sacrifice on behalf of the Haitian people."

After reading a copy of Aristide's resignation letter and announcing that Alexandre would be sworn in as Haiti's new president "as the constitution demands," Neptune then continued:

"Today we are encourage the entire Haitian population, every political sector, every socio-economic category, for their lives, we are asking for their understanding to follow the example of President Jean-Bertrand Aristide so Haiti can continue to live and so peace can exist in the country of Haiti. We do not need looting; we need understanding and peace."

Neptune said he would continue in his office and contribute in any way he could until the appointment of an interim prime minister.

"Dear fellow citizens," Alexandre, a big man with a high, nasal voice began, speaking in French. "Our society is in a crisis, of justice, of economy, but today I exhort you to scrupulously respect the right to live of all citizens. I exhort you to keep your calm. I ask you, the Haitian people, to help me build a new Haiti."

As the floor was opened to questions, Neptune began addressing the foreign press corps in English.

"Indeed it is a very dangerous moment for Haiti and the Haitian people," he said, taking the press assembled before him in with a withering gaze. "President Aristide wanted it otherwise, but unfortunately it didn't happen that way.

"But despite all the problems that may be looming on the horizon, we are confident that the people of Haiti will understand the sacrifices made by President Aristide, and will understand and share the words of President Aristide."

"I know it is a difficult moment," Neptune continued, his voice catching with emotion. "I know it is an unexpected moment; I know it is not what the vast majority of the people of Haiti would have wished to have happened, but I'm sure that what President Aristide would want is for all of us to understand this grave situation and do whatever we can do.

"President Aristide and myself, we have always asked for those who hold illegal weapons to hand them to the police," Neptune said with no apparent irony. "Guns, especially when they are implicated in political activities, are a dangerous instrument."

As Foley then tried to usher the men out of the room (and Alexandre to his swearing-in as Haiti's new president), he was surrounded by journalists, asking about the manner of Aristide's departure and Haiti's future.

"The important changes that are ushered in now by the resignation of President Aristide open the possibility for a new and more hopeful chapter in the history of Haiti," Foley said, announcing that a tripartite commission would be formed by one member each from the Lavalas government, the Democratic Platform and the international community, a commission that would then be responsible for selecting a seven-member "council of eminent persons" that would choose a new prime minister. Foley announced the imminent arrival of a multinational military peacekeeping force, including forces of the United States, called on Guy Philippe and his men to disarm, and appealed to "the poor majority of Haitians" that "there is hope finally for a better tomorrow."

"President Aristide made a decision, for the good of Haiti and I think he spoke eloquently about his reasons in his letter of resignation," the ambassador then concluded. "As I understand, President Aristide was particularly concerned about where the country was heading, towards further and further violence. He indicated that by his resignation, by this personal sacrifice, he could help begin to heal the country, he could encourage people rapidly to stop the violence and he felt that this was his responsibility. Haiti is going to change."

And with that, they were gone, followed by a small army of American and Haitian security personnel.

Downtown, however, all hell was breaking loose, with chimere shooting at anything that moved, and journalists trapped in the Hotel Plaza. An abandoned vehicle marked "Presse" sat with its doors open in front of the National Palace and throughout Bel Air and along Grand Rue, Aristide loyalists were burning down gas stations and looting banks.

"No, don't come down, man," said one photographer I spoke to who said that a pair of journalists who had ventured out to the Champs de Mars had run back inside after being shot at.

Within hours, small groups of armed men claiming to be fighters of Guy Philippe's rebels appeared in Port-au-Prince. On the road outside of the Hotel El Rancho, where Aristide's political opposition was scheduled to give a news conference, armed men descended from cars with Front Liberation d'Haiti insignias taped to their windshields.

"We are with Guy Philippe's team, and we are here to make sure that everything can function normally," said a strapping, mustachioed man who gave his name as Faustin Radeux, marching through the intersection clutching an Uzi submachine gun with a clutch of like-armed individuals. Small groups of residents clapped in their wake.

"We've freed the people," the armed men cheered.

One Haitian assistant to foreign news crews in Haiti, a brawny tattooed former U.S. Marine who had fled the United States to avoid a conviction for dealing in controlled substances, promptly told his charges, "Look, I'm sorry, but I've got to go change into my uniform and join them." Minutes later, he reappeared in combat fatigues, clutching an Uzi and giving interviews to, among others, CNN, in English. He had been a rebel sleeper in the capital all along. Crowds of rebels were also milling about in front of the Petionville police station along with curious onlookers, where many people on the streets were cheering, and car horns sounding.

Arriving at the garish, neo-modern Hotel El Rancho, we saw Andy Apaid, Victor Benoit and Evans Paul emerging from a conference room near the hotel's casino.

"You did it!" the French photographer exclaimed as Paul arrived and stopped to say hello to us.

"Yes, we did it, but it wasn't easy," he said, smiling his thin smile.

But it was really Andy Apaid's moment, and, using his media savvy and eloquence for all it was worth, with Paul and Benoit on either side of him, he spoke to journalists by the El Rancho's pool, as gunfire echoed in the distance:

> We want to remember all those who spilled their blood, all those who risked their lives or who gave their lives for this nonviolent, peaceful movement and for some of the areas where some of our brothers and

sisters expressed themselves in different ways but lost their lives, on both sides.

We take a commitment in front of the international community that us, political parties, civil society members, private sector, citizens, peasants, union members, we all take the commitment to never, never again return to a dictatorship in Haiti."

[We will] take the necessary steps to have a society that orients itself to a democracy for the well-being of the eight million Haitians and of their children to come. We are determined to contribute our part in a way that will show that we can and we will build a new Haiti. Thank you to the international community for its support, and thank you to the international press for allowing the world to see what our fight was about. And we will do everything for those who have guns to deposit their guns and those who are in despair today, to find hope so we can build a new Haiti of which we will all be proud.

OR SO ONE would have hoped. As March 1 dawned, we saw hundreds of people gathered in front of the Petionville police station singing "Bon anneé!" People were returning looted items to the station, and hundreds of men were waiting hoping to sign up for what they hoped would be the reconstituted army. Camouflaged rebels were already rolling through the streets with rifles at the ready. In front of the National Palace downtown, where U.S. Marines had parked their Humvees on the Palace lawn, we saw tens of thousands of Haitians flooding the Champs de Mars, waving Haitian flags and hoisting camouflaged rebels onto their shoulders. One man carried a dead rat that he said represented the departed president. Guy Philippe was there in front of the Palace, in a green shirt, smiling with his men.

"When Aristide was here, we couldn't come here!" sang one group of students.

Later, at the Hotel El Rancho, the press descended when Philippe, now clad in military fatigues, said he was going to make an important announcement. Arriving at the hotel, I found Louis Jodel Chamblain lunching on *poisson gros sel* in the El Rancho's restaurant as waitstaff and others came up to shake his hand and pat him on the back. A guy in a PNH hat stood talking to Syrian-looking mulatto carrying a Galil, and various groups of rebels posed with their weapons and bottles of Barbancourt rum.

Paul Arcelin, Philippe's political advisor and a former Haitian ambassador to the Dominican Republic stood, attired in military fatigues, barely able to control his rage at the press corps assembled. Arcelin, who had been among those arrested and then released for allegedly plotting a coup against Aristide from across the border the previous May, saved special venom for the Americans.

"You don't see the anarchy in this county? All what Aristide has left in this country?" Arcelin shouted at me when I tried to interview him. "Thanks to those who occupied our country some years ago, when Aristide asked them to come in our country to put him back in power? That is the crime they have done to this country, by putting in this crazy guy who has made this country a narco-state! We are going to put order in this country!"

As the press waited for the promised press conference, amid reports that the bodies of Aristide loyalists were being found in the suburb of Carrefour, hands bound, shot in the head execution-style, Philippe all of a sudden rapidly swept up the El Rancho's stairs, heading for the building's foyer and waiting cars parked outside.

"He has to leave urgently," said Arcelin, as Aristide partisans were reportedly rioting throughout the city. "There is disorder throughout the city, and he has to put this disorder down."

Despite swirling conspiracy theories that were developing among his apologists abroad that Aristide's departure had been arranged by the U.S. Embassy and that the Americans had provided support of one kind or another to Philippe and his men, American officials on the ground in Port-au-Prince, whose chief desire had been to keep an emasculated Aristide on as President of Haiti until the 2006 elections, reacted to the appearance of the rebels with disgust and alarm.

"They're a bunch of drug traffickers," a senior embassy official told me one day shortly after Aristide had fled as we sat lunching in Petionville, guarded by U.S. Marine personnel. "Guy Philippe's record as a drug trafficker, especially in Cap Haitien, speaks for itself. He really wants to be president and we can't let that happen."

Halfway around the world, Aristide arrived at around one in the morning on March 1 in Bangui, the bullet-riddled and war-wracked capital of the Central African Republic (CAR). Speaking to state-run radio in the country, Aristide said that, "In overthrowing me, they cut down the tree of peace, but it will grow again, because the roots are well-planted." His arrival had been negotiated by the United States and France with the help of the West African nation of Gabon. The CAR was at the time led by a military dictator, Francois Bozize, who had taken power in a March 2002 coup. Speaking to CNN and the Associated Press after arriving, Aristide said he had been "forced to leave" by "white American, white military" personnel who threatened to "start shooting" if he didn't go. In addition to claiming that he had been kidnapped, Aristide had Ira Kurzban issue a press release saying that he had been denied access to a telephone, despite the fact that Aristide had chatted with a host of supporters and media after his arrival. The whole theater prompted CAR government spokesman Parfait M'Bay to memorably tell Agence France Presse that "He's already started to embarrass us. He's scarcely been here 24 hours, and he's causing problems for Central African diplomacy."

In the days following his flight, the reaction of Aristide's supporters in the United States, with the former president's connivance, was also predictable. Maxine Waters went on the radio the day after Aristide left with TransAfrica's

Randall Robinson—the latter never mentioning how handsomely his family had profited from its relationship with Aristide—claiming that Aristide had been kidnapped and said he had called them to inform them of his plight early on Monday morning. Speaking to the overly-credulous host Amy Goodman on Pacifica Radio in the United States, which had served as a longtime source for uncritical pro-Aristide public relations ploys, Waters claimed she had been called by Mildred Aristide around 6 a.m. that morning and told that "the coup d'etat has been completed." Talking with Aristide himself and then Mildred again, Waters said that she had been told that Luis Moreno and U.S. soldiers arrived at Tabarre and Moreno had told Aristide that "Guy Philippe and the Marines" would come to Port-au-Prince, Aristide would be killed, and that many Haitians would also die. Waters also claimed that Aristide's "brother" had been kidnapped, an apparent reference to Mildred Aristide's brother, who was with them, as Aristide didn't have a male sibling, and went on to fulminate against "this bourgeoisie mulatto class of people who own everything, who want to take control of government so they can be control of the next election."

"He did not resign; he was kidnapped," Robinson added solemnly.

It was a pathetic performance, but a fitting coda for those who had consumed their last vestiges of credibility by their continued fawning over a criminal and outlaw regime. In Kingston, Jamaican Prime Minister P.J. Patterson, whose attempt to help South Africa arm Aristide had come too late, released a statement on March 1 saying that:

"President Aristide has submitted his resignation as the President of Haiti and has left the country for an undisclosed destination. We are bound to question whether his resignation was truly voluntary, as it comes after the capture of sections of Haiti by armed insurgents and the failure of the international community to provide the requisite support, despite the appeals of CARICOM. The removal of President Aristide in these circumstances sets a dangerous precedent for democratically-elected governments anywhere and everywhere, as it promotes the removal of duly-elected persons from office by the power of rebel forces. CARICOM has no desire to abandon the people of Haiti and would wish to see the quick restoration of peace and stability in that country, and the earliest return to constitutional democracy." But abandon them they would.

That night, driving back to our base in Thomassin on the Kenscoff Road, Alex and I were greeted by a burning car that had been pushed in the middle of the narrow road, flames roaring up and licking the low-hanging branches of trees.

THE NEXT DAY, life appeared to be returning to the capital. Our drive down Kenscoff Road saw smiling people walking the mountain roads again, and a ladder crew working on a building with their pails. We again passed the Petionville police station where, unknown to us at the time, Dany Toussaint was celebrating by having Franco Camille summarily released from custody. The man viewed by many as one of the key links between the murder of Jean Dominique and the Aristide government walked out of jail a free man. Outside of the jail, a doctor, who said his father was in prison for thirty-three months on Fort Dimanche under Jean-Claude Duvalier, regarded the scene and said he had hope for the future.

"Everyone has his own skills," he said. "Everyone can bring his own particles of sand to help build the wall."

With U.S. military personnel in combat fatigues still patrolling the grounds of the National Palace, Guy Philippe had to be satisfied with taking over the old FADH headquarters, which now housed the Musée de l'Indépendance and sat across the Champs de Mars from the Palace. As Philippe waved to thousands of former soldiers and supporters from the balcony, his men looted the museum's priceless collection of art, burning paintings by André Eugène and Edouard Duval Carrié among others, and at one point, in an eerie scene, throwing out and tearing to pieces a child-sized coffin. One supporter who attempted to scale a wall to get to Philippe was shot and killed by a rebel soldier. Afterwards, a throng of rebels charged up the hill to the prime minister's office, declaring that they were going to arrest Yvon Neptune, only to be met by U.S. Marines and CIMO guarding the building and turned back. The move to seize Neptune infuriated the U.S. Embassy, with one embassy official telling me that, "It was a very brave thing Neptune did. He stood up to the plate and was a patriot and probably saved thousands of lives and now these guys want to put him in jail."

Following their failure to get their hands on the prime minister, the rebels and former soldiers then held a huge rally at Petionville's Place Boyer square, where Philippe, the mask of media-savvy calm he had worn so well during the rebellion falling to reveal the dangerous, angry man beneath, called out to his armed supporters:

"People of Cité Soleil and La Saline, we haven't forgotten you! We can't let the chimere do whatever they want! Despite the oligarchy's attempts to hold us back, we will go in and crush the chimere!"

Speaking at a press conference earlier in the day, when asked if he would disarm as the Americans had requested, Philippe was unequivocal in his response, his voice bristling with emotion:

"I'm not taking any pressure from anyone. The only pressure I'll take is from the Haitian people. If they want to kill me, I'm here they can come and kill me. But I'm here to defend my people and I will defend them, whatever it takes, whatever it costs. I'm ready to die for my country. I will fight until death for my country and my people and we're ready to die."

CHAPTER NOTES

1. "Jamaica Returns Arms to South Africa," *Jamaica Observer*, March 5, 2004.
2. "President Aristide should step down," *The Miami Herald*, February 27, 2004.
3. "U.S. Has No Other Choice," *The South Florida Sun-Sentinel*, February 26, 2004.
4. "Jamaica Returns Arms to South Africa," *Jamaica Observer*, March 5, 2004.

|||

Paths Away

GUY PHILIPPE'S GRAND PLANS to seize power in Port-au-Prince, however, soon ran into the formidable obstacle of the U.S. Embassy, which, with U.S. and French forces deploying on Haitian soil throughout the day of March 3, called Philippe in and read him the riot act, telling him he absolutely could not stay in the capital and continue parading around with his armed band of merry men.

That afternoon, Alex and I drove up a long, heavily-forested road in an obscure corner of Petionville where we arrived at the Hotel Ibo Lele, where Philippe was ensconced with dozens of other rebels. Arriving at the hotel, we found insurgents in military fatigues lounging around the hotel's entrance with their weapons. As we walked through the brown-paneled hallway, old photos of famous personalities who had visited the hotel in the 1950s decorated the walls. From a higher vantage point than the Hotel Montana, the hotel still had similarly sweeping views of the city, bay, and denuded mountains to the north. A mural depicted a Haitian peasant woman walking in front of narrow houses built before lush, fecund hills. Earlier in the day, we had seen a dejected group of rebels driving away from the parking lot, with one telling me, "The Americans don't want us, so we're going back to Gonaives."

At the Ibo Lele, Philippe appeared in military fatigues with Gilbert Dragon at his side, and sat at a table before a forest of microphones. Philippe, a slight man in a small brown chair, seemed to be in a calmer frame of mind than the previous day, and laughed and looked amused as reporters vied to put their tape recorders before him.

"As President Aristide was the principal problem for democracy and for the people, and the principal problem that kept the people from moving forward," he began, speaking in Kreyol. "And now that foreign soldiers are protecting the Haitian people, and are giving us a guarantee of security, we will lay down our arms. There will no longer be patrols in the streets. This is a decision made for the benefit of the Haitian people."

Philippe then said he would depart for Cap Haiten the next day. He took no questions. He would later announce the formation of his political party, the

Front de Reconstruction Nationale, and its intention to field candidates in Haiti's next general election, scheduled for November 2005. Philippe's comrade-in-arms, Louis Jodel Chamblain, turned himself over to the Haitian police and was eventually tried and acquitted (along with Jackson Joanis) for the Antoine Izmery killing in a one-day proceeding as farcical as the one that had convicted him nearly a decade earlier.

Despite Philippe's tactical bow to the U.S. Embassy, revenge was not long in coming to the former officials and partisans of Aristide's regime. In the capital, Aristide's residence at Tabarre and the homes of Yvon Neptune and Fanmi Lavalas spokesman Jonas Petit were sacked by angry mobs. Petit himself and former government official Lovinsky Pierre-Antoine were ferried to the United States on a special plane chartered by the U.S. government, while in Saint Marc, the city's population took its vengeance on Bale Wouze, chopping the killer known as Somoza into pieces and carrying him around town and torching the group's headquarters. Bale Wouze's leader, the former Lavalas deputy Amanus Mayette and the killer Ronald "Black Ronald" Dauphin fled to Port-au-Prince where they were arrested by the PNH and thrown in jail. Minister of Finance Gustave Faubert, Minister of Public Health Henri-Claude Voltaire and Aristide's Palace security chief Oriel Jean all entered the Dominican Embassy in Port-au-Prince for protection, and from there were ferried to Santo Domingo by helicopter. The Democratic Platform announced a huge rally to be held on the Champs de Mars on March 7 to celebrate Aristide's departure and called on "every sector of society" to participate.

For the second time in little over a decade, Aristide was gone, and U.S., French, Argentine and Chilean troops continued to land. The interim force was put under the command of Brigadier General Ronald Coleman, a soft-spoken 55-year-old African-American Philadelphia native, who told me after his arrival:

"I've been to a lot of different countries in my time, but this is the one that hurts the most. Seeing the condition of Haiti has hurt me more than anything ever has. Especially being a black person. But the best thing I've seen here is the Haitian people. I've not seen one person slumped over. The thing that hurts me the most is to see how poor everyone is, but the thing that impresses me the most is the resolve and the resilience and the pride in the Haitian people. You'll never take their pride away."

One morning several days after Aristide had left, as we sat on my couch in Pacot after a day spent shopping for a mosquito net downtown, my friend Herby spoke of the great weight that rested on his shoulders.

"I have to be everything, man. I have to be *grenn nan bouda*, I have to be *rat pa ka ka*, I have to be Aristide, I have to be Dany Toussaint, I have to be Lavalas, I have to be Group of 184. All of this in my little head.

"When people ask me what group I belong to, I tell them I belong to the group that wants to leave Haiti, because I don't believe in Aristide and I don't believe in the opposition because they don't know what they're looking for, if they knew, they would find a way for Haiti."

Then, Herby pulled out a Bible that I had often seem him with. It had been given to him by an American soldier when U.S. Forces had landed to return Aristide in 1994.

"Frank Atwood, U.S. Army, 28 Nov 94, 3:31 AM," the inscription read.

"After almost ten motherfucking years, they came back," Herby said, before returning the Bible securely in his backpack.

"WE NEED TO GET his money so he cannot continue to act from abroad," said the sociologist Laennec Hurbon, as we sat in his backyard in the Belville suburb of the capital. Hurbon, the author of such treatises as *Les Mysteres du Vaudou* and a professor at the Centre National de la Reserche Scientifique in Paris, was one of the leading lights of the intellectual movement against Aristide and now was still worried about Aristide's ability to influence events on the ground in Haiti.

"Most of his victims were black, most of his victims were poor and yet the newspapers in the United States continued to insist he was popular. This I don't understand. Those gangs would rob market women. These people were more victimized than the middle class and the elite. Aristide finally represented the exclusion of the masses from political life which was the exact opposite of what he was supposed to realize.

"I think if it would have continued, he was planning on doing exactly Pol Pot did to Phnom Penh, to destroy all the commerce, all the business, all the middle class and all the political parties. This kind of behavior was the real signature of the regime. The true face of the Aristide regime was the destruction and disorder we saw in this city."

Hurbon was an intelligent man, as well-versed and comfortable among Haiti's peasant traditions as he was in the rarefied airs of European academia and his words proved to be apt.

When March 7—the day of the planned celebratory demonstration—arrived, the outpouring was truly astonishing. Larger crowds than I had ever seen in Haiti, even at the height of the opposition protest movement, were streaming down to the Champs de Mars along Lalue and the Delmas Road. *"Aristide prizon, chimere lekol"* the crowds chanted, while others carried blue and red signs (the colors of the Haitian flag) reading *"Jugez Mario Dupuy," "Jugez Yvon Neptune," "Jugez Jocelerme Privert,"* and so on.

As the Danish filmmaker Asger Leth and I arrived at the intersection of Lalue and Nazon, we found it guarded by French paratroopers, in camouflage with French tricolour patches on their arms, operating machine guns off their APCs. I saw Pierre Esperance, the director of NCHR, standing talking on his cell phone as he watched the marchers and a vendor was threading his way through the crowd, calling out *"dlo, dlo, dlo"* as he tried to sell little plastic baggies full of water.

"The power of the chimere is finished and they won't return," said a man in a striped shirt and jeans, clapping his hands together as he looked at the troops.

"They need to begin disarming the chimere now: this is their most important mission," said another man, pressing a radio to his ear.

The mood of the crowd seemed upbeat and joyous rather than angry and a cheer went up when word filtered around that marchers had succeeded finally in burning a huge Aristide billboard that had loomed over the Canapé Vert road for some months. Passing over to the Delmas Road, I spied Hans Tippenhauer with a throng of thousands of marchers and I remarked that the mood seemed quite positive given the violence that had proceeded it.

"Maybe it's because there's much more freedom, people are really happy," he said. "If we march successfully and there is no violence at all, it will be a new beginning in Haiti."

Walking across the Champs de Mars under the blazing sun later, I saw clutches of several hundred people standing before the National Palace, waiting for the march to arrive. I saw the French photographer and Gerry Hadden again.

"These are some of the people who were throwing bottles at us and they are looking very stern," she said, perusing the unsmiling crowd.

I started to speak to a young man, thin, intense and articulate, who said his name was David Oxygen, from the Young Revolutionaries of Haiti and he read to me from a paper he had composed in Spanish about what had transpired a week earlier.

"Aristide was the legitimate president of the Haitian people," it read in part. "This was a coup on the part of the United States. In the poor neighborhoods, we will be with Aristide until death. Long live democracy in small countries, long live the Haitian constitution, long live peace in Haiti and long live Aristide, the second black Toussaint Loverture!"

As the celebratory crowd kept coming, filling the Champs de Mars and getting bigger and bigger, the PNH also began arriving in larger numbers, smiling, holding their weapons, some in the crowd even running up and embracing them as if they were finally allowed to do their job. An old mulatto women held up a picture of the Virgin Mary as music emanated from her car, while two other mulatto men stood in t-shirts bearing the image of the slain businessman Billy Lauture. A small boy in a Brazilian football jersey carried a sign that said *"Jugez Aristide"* while a black couple, a man and woman, lay asleep together in one another's arms in the shade of a tree just at the edge of the tumult.

"I think it's important to demonstrate today because Jean Dominique fell struggling for us," said a middle-aged black man in a Dominique t-shirt and Haitian flag head scarf who said he was from Cité Soleil. "To everyone who suffered crimes under the government, Jean Dominique and all the other people, we march for justice. We think Aristide should be returned to Haiti to be judged."

But Aristide had not yet run out of cards to play. As the popular DJ Fan Fan was manning a Carnival float that was gradually snaking toward the Champs de Mars, where people stood blasting compas and reggae from car radios, groups of chimere who had previously sequestered themselves inside the Rex Movie Theater across the park and in other buildings leading up to the Bel-Air slum opened fire on the crowd. U.S. Marines and Haitian police responded with withering blasts of their own, but the gunmen had already managed to kill two people on the plaza. Michael Laughlin, a photographer for the *South Florida Sun Sentinel*, was shot in the shoulder and neck by gunmen standing on top of a building across the street Rue Lamarre. After Laughlin was helped into a nearby home by several Haitian bystanders and the photographer Daniel Morel, a reporter with the Spanish television network Antennae 3, Ricardo Ortega, stepped out into the back courtyard of the house, where he was fatally shot by a gunman firing down from one of the neighboring buildings. Later rumors that Ortega was shot by U.S. Marines were dismissed as groundless to those who witnessed the killing and it seems likely that he was killed by a gunman from the same chimere gang that had attacked Laughlin. Ortega became the first foreign journalist to be killed in Haiti since Dominican cameraman Carlos Grullon was murdered during the Ruelle Vaillant election-day massacre in November 1987.

THE SPECIAL COUNCIL set up to oversee the country's transitional government eventually selected Gerard Latortue, a rotund and jovial former World Bank official living in Boca Raton, Florida, to serve as Haiti's interim prime minister under Boniface Alexandre. At an official March 14 welcoming ceremony for the multinational military force, set to cede control to United Nations troops three months later, Latortue said that Aristide's had been a "a democratically elected government that didn't know how to govern according to the rules of democracy. The government I am leading will do its utmost to plant the seeds of democracy."

Latortue almost immediately became embroiled in a diplomatic flap with CARICOM when, in addition to refusing to recognize his government, P.J. Patterson offered Aristide and his wife temporary exile in Kingston, which the deposed president gratefully accepted, arriving back in the Caribbean on March 15 and staying until he left for permanent exile in South Africa at the end of May. Furious, Latortue recalled Haiti's ambassador to Jamaica and began a spat with CARICOM—many of whose leaders had done so much to shelter and protect Aristide over the years—which continues to this day.

Emboldened by Aristide's proximity and fortified by regular phone calls from the former president, the chimere gangs of Bel Air launched a chaotic protest march to mark Haiti's Flag Day on May 18, swooping down toward the National Palace before being tear-gassed by CIMO. Watching the demonstration from in front of the Eglise Notre Dame du Perpetuel Secours in Bel Air, I saw convoys of U.S. Marines rolling through the hilly streets as heavily-armed CIMO set up cordons to the south of the neighborhood and residents watched from their doorways.

"This is an illegal demonstration. . . . Return to your homes immediately," said an announcement broadcast over loudspeakers to the crowd.

At one point, the Radio Metropole van was surrounded by an angry group of young men that rocked it back and forth and pounded on it with their fists, and, as I accepted a ride from Radio Kiskeya's Marvel Dandin down to the Champs de Mars, the crowd charged down the hill, only to be teargassed. A jittery CIMO pointed his weapon at us as he saw our car approach, only to lower it when he saw we were journalists. One civilian was killed in the melee, though the circumstances of his death have never been made clear.

WITHIN A FEW MONTHS of his departure, many of Aristide's top officials found themselves in prison cells. In Haiti itself, Yvon Neptune, former Minister of Interior Jocelerme Privert, chimere leader Annette "So Anne" Auguste and Bale Wouze's leader Amanus Mayette all found themselves in Haitian prisons after Aristide's departure, awaiting trial for crimes that occurred during his tenure in office. Jocelyn Saint-Louis, the Lavalas deputy who had murdered the mayor of Saint Raphael, was himself gunned down in mysterious circumstances in the Haitian capital in July 2004. Dread Mackenzie, the Bel Air gang leader who was sent to stake out Lolo Beaubrun's house and kill him, was killed by rival gang members in December 2004. Dymsley Millien and Jeudi-Jean Daniel, who had been charged in connection with the Jean Dominique murder and escaped in the January 1 prison break, were recaptured in August 2004. Another indicted conspirator, Philippe Markington, remains at large.

Further afield, Oriel Jean, Aristide's former Palace security chief would be arrested attempting to enter Canada on a flight from the Dominican Republic and deported to the United States; Jean-Nesly Lucien, former director of the PNH, would be arrested at his home in Miami, and Fourel Celestin, after running away on foot from PNH and DEA agents who raided his Port-au-Prince home, turned himself over to the American Embassy. All three were arraigned in Miami on drug-trafficking charges, where they awaited trial along with Aristide's former anti-drug czar Evintz Brillant and former Brigade d'Intervention Rapide unit head Rudy Therassan. Jean-Nesly Lucien would eventually plead guilty in April 2005 to money laundering, with prosecutors agreeing to recommend a reduction in his possible twenty-year sentence in exchange for cooperating with a joint DEA, FBI and IRS investigation into drug smuggling and corruption by Aristide's government. Oriel Jean, who had received hundreds of millions of dollars in unexplained payments from Aristide's National Palace during his tenure as head of security there, pleaded guilty to a similar charge in exchange for cooperating, and Rudy Therassan would plead guilty to conspiring to import cocaine to the United States and money laundering, agreeing to work with investigators in exchange for a shortening of his ten-year sentence. One wonders if they have had the chance to meet with Jacques Ketant yet. Hermione Leonard, Therassan's wife who had served as director of the PNH in the West Department and liaison between Aristide and the street gangs he employed, was arrested in the Dominican Republic in June 2004. René Civil and Paul Raymond, along with Haiti's former prison director, Clifford Larose, were all arrested in the Dominican Republic at the outset of 2005, but freed before they could be deported back to Haiti under circumstances the Dominican judicial system never satisfactorily explained. Another of the regime's most lethal figures, Jean-Claude Jean-Baptiste, a man responsible for some of the most sickening excesses of Aristide's last days, has disappeared and is rumored to be in Venezuela. Gérard Pierre-Charles, the intellectual luminary of the OPL who had helped Aristide found the original Lavalas party in 1995, died in October 2004 of heart failure in Cuba, where he had been flown to be treated for a lung infection. He was sixty-eight. Butteur Metayer, whose rage against Aristide for the murder of his brother had helped spark the rebellion that eventually toppled him, was felled by his legendary fondness for rum and died of kidney failure in Gonaives in June 2005.

Former Lavalas Senate President Yvon Feuillé, former Senator Gerard Gilles and former Chamber of Deputies president Rudy Herivaux were all arrested and later released after an explosion of violence by Aristide partisans commenced at the end of September 2004, to coincide with the anniversary of the 1991 coup. The movement, which saw chimere gangs killing civilians, decapitating policemen and torching swaths of the capital, became known as "Operation Baghdad," claiming nearly seven hundred lives, and a prominent Lavalas leader from the capital's Martissant slum, Wench Luc, would later go on Radio Kiskeya to denounce what he charged was Aristide's financial and moral support of the rebellion from South Africa, echoing a charge made by the Latortue government shortly after the violence began.

Adding to the litany of charges laid at the former regime's feet, in a taped statement broadcast on Radio Vision 2000, Labanye charged that former Port-au-Prince Assistant Mayor Harold Sévère, Annette Auguste and the Camille brothers had been the ones responsible for formulating and carrying out the Jean Dominique murder on Aristide's orders, employing the services of Guy "Ti Ponyet" Benson, a downtown gang leader who was also later murdered, to silence his knowledge of the crime.

It was during this period of unrest, while I was working in Brasil, that tragic news reached me about James Petit-Frere and his brother Tupac. The brothers, along with Dread Wilmé, Labanye and other gang leaders in Cité Soleil, had attempted to make peace with the international forces in the country and turned in some seventy weapons, announcing their desire to reintegrate into society as "good citizens," but they realized they had made many enemies over the years, and went into exile shortly after Aristide's departure, Tupac in the Dominican Republic and James in Belize. The two brothers quickly burned through the money that had been given to them by a European diplomat in Haiti sympathetic to their plight and then found themselves back in Cité Soleil, James lured back by Aristide's promise that a new rebellion was brewing but almost defenseless without their old authority and forced to strike a strategic alliance with Dread Wilmé, now Aristide's top enforcer in the district.

As the brothers marched past the Boston section of Cité Soleil, on their way to take part in a massive pro-Aristide demonstration, they were fired upon by Labanye's gang, now protected from arrest due to his friendship with Andy Apaid, and a contingent of Haitian police. Tupac, the warm, witty, elegant young man who wanted nothing more than to tell the story of the struggles of the slum in his rap songs, was hit and bled to death on its streets. He had been free only nine months. James, seeking to avenge his brother, was wounded badly in the stomach and taken to the hospital, where he was dragged out of bed by a group of CIMO and disappeared. Frantically trying to track down his whereabouts, I found out finally that he had survived, injured but alive, at the Port-au-Prince police commissariat, and succeeded in getting a Haitian doctor I was friends with in to tend to his wounds. He remained in jail without charge until February 19, 2005, when he, along with some 350 other inmates, broke out of Port-au-Prince's National Penitentiary. Having failed to track him down during subsequent visits to Haiti, and hearing conflicted stories, some of which recounted his execution by police, of his fate after escape, I am left with my prayers. If he is still in this world, I hope he remains safe and that some day I will be able to help find a new life for him, his girlfriend and his two children. If he has departed from this mortal realm, I hope he has found the peace that so eluded him in life. Despite all he did that could be considered violent or wrong, I considered him my friend, and I will miss him.

Labanye himself, who had ruled for so long as the most powerful boss in Cité Soleil, was betrayed by two of his deputies who had been paid off by Dread Wilmé and was shot down on the last day of March 2005. Wilmé's men then dragged Labanye's body through the streets, crushed its head with stones and placed a dead dog on it before dismembering him and, in a moment of doubtlessly drug-fueled fury, feasting on the remains, so near where Dessalines had met a similar fate at the hands of his foes so many years before. Labanye was a brutal man who had caused much misery for many people, yet the image of his broken corpse lying in the lanes of Cité Soleil that I later saw in photos could not help but make me wince. Dread Wilmé met his own end on July 6 2005, when some three hundred UN troops stormed Cité Soleil looking for him and engaged in a three-hour gunbattle with his men, which finally ended his life in a shower of bullets. The mercurial ex-FADH sergeant Ravix Rémissainthe, one of the rebel leaders during the rebellion against Aristide and the alleged mastermind behind the massacre of a Lavalas official's family in June 2000, eventually became a bitter critic of the Latortue government and squared off in several firefights with PNH and UN forces before being cornered and killed near the airport in April 2005. The notorious Delmas 33 attaché René Jean-Anthony, better known as Grenn Sonnen, branched out in entrepreneurial banditry and murder after his patron Aristide's flight and was killed by the PNH the same month only blocks away from the commissariat where he had tormented so many people.

ARISTIDE, THOUGH, despite his flight, had no intention of going quietly. Having saved his own skin and having left his supporters in the slums to their fates for the second time, Aristide began a slick public relations campaign from South Africa, spearheaded by his Miami attorney Ira Kurzban and the Kurzban-directed Bureau des Avocats Internationaux lawyers group headed by the attorney Brian Concannon, which transformed into something calling itself The Institute for Justice in Democracy and Haiti. The organization continues the BAI's human-rights-as-political-lobbying tradition, denouncing the interim government and agitating for Aristide's return to Haiti, and has been responsible for several bogus "human rights" reports, all led or authored by attorneys who continue to be employed by or are sympathetic to Aristide. The most notorious example, a report released under the auspices of the University of Miami (home of Aristide's former advisor Irwin Stotzky) and headed up by Philadelphia lawyer Thomas Griffin, cannily omitted to mention the fact that the only other attorney listed in the report's voluminous pages was a longtime BAI employee. The report was so scurrilous, in fact, and so obviously designed for an audience abroad rather than to reflect realities on the ground, that the head of the Comité des Avocats pour le Respect des Libertés Individuelles (CARLI) in Haiti, Renan Hédouville, referred to extensively in its findings, felt the need to take to Radio Metropole, denying the accuracy of the conclusions attributed—erroneously he said—to CARLI and saying that the report did "not reflect Haiti's reality at all."

And the struggle against misinformation continues. In a typically pompous and deliberately evasive March 2005 essay on Haiti in which he extensively quoted his disciple Paul Farmer, the American academic Noam Chomsky laid most of Haiti's problems on the "establishment press," which must have played well from Chomsky's well-paid and sheltered academic life at the Massachusetts Institute of Technology, where he served as a professor, but had little impact on the lives of the terrorized and oppressed people I met in Haiti's slums and its countryside. Characteristically of Aristide's apologists and of his own intellectually dishonest, sweeping critiques of history elsewhere in the Americas, in his essay Chomsky turns the clock back to Aristide's first election in 1990 to repeat the well-documented antipathy of the first Bush administration and the Haitian elite to Aristide's election, and then even further back to the U.S. occupation at the beginning of the twentieth century in an attempt to lay bare the "true story" of what had happened in Haiti. No attempt is made to address the terrible cost Aristide's second term in office had exacted on Haiti's poorest to provide men like Chomsky with a platform for their facile defenses of his reign, and, like many defenders of dictatorship, Chomsky abstracts its human cost in a flurry of numbers, quotes and adages. The dead peasants aren't really dead; they are marionettes to be manipulated for political purposes. Chomsky and those like him continue to write about Aristide as if none of the dead of Haiti had ever flooded a room with laughter, ever felt their faces go flush with anger under the Caribbean sun, ever held anyone's hand.

SO MANY DEATHS, so many wasted lives and dashed dreams. How does one go on? How do the Haitians, in their warmth and bravery and tears and infinite capacity to love among all this destruction continue on? Seldom has a leader betrayed the legitimate hopes of so many so thoroughly. In all of its essentials—the killing of civilians, restriction of personal and professional liberty, the subjugation of all state institutions to the whim of an executive branch that disregarded even the most cursory adherence to such fundamental principals as human rights and due process—the Aristide government deserved to be overthrown as much as any in Haitian history. He took a generation of desperately poor slum children whose heads were filled with idealistic notions about changing their country, put weapons in their hands and turned them into killers. But the way in which Aristide's departure was achieved, his flight into exile in the middle of the night, the continuation of armed groups such as the former rebels and the chimere to operate in Haiti afterwards, the massive and well-financed propaganda campaign that began as soon as he arrived in South Africa, and the weakness and inability of the Haitian judicial system to deal with the high-profile cases concerning members of his regime—the Haitians have as of yet been deprived of having justice for the terrible crimes Aristide submitted them to.

"We can't have reconciliation in Haiti without justice," Pierre Esperance told me shortly after Aristide's fall. "This is the big error we made after the coup d'etat in 1991. The human rights organizations and the civil society didn't do enough to help those victims under the military dictatorship to find justice, that is why we had the same situation under Aristide's government. Now it is time to help the Aristide government's victims to find justice."

Who will help them? After they achieved their goal of ousting Aristide, Haiti's elite businesspeople—the Apaids, the Bakers and the rest—returned to their factories, and, despite all their lofty talk of a new "social contract" with their fellow

Haitians, they showed no intention of ever addressing in any meaningful way the brutal deprivation that afflicted the majority of their countrymen and gave rise to Aristide in the first place. Having piggybacked on the popular outrage against Aristide to successfully drive him from the National Palace, the Haitian bourgeois apparently felt they had no more responsibility at all to their country, and the dialogue between the social classes they had spoken so eloquently of during the 2003/2004 protests remained but a vain hope for those really looking for a reconciliation within Haitian society. A short-sighted and self-interested reaction to a momentary victory, the indifference of Haiti's ruling class to the poverty— to the economic violence, really—that grinds down the majority of their countrymen, will surely give rise to another Aristide, or worse, if they continue to ignore it. They will likely then be caught directly in the sights of the oncoming steamroller as surely as Aristide and his cronies were, and all their pleas for understanding will likely fall on deaf ears. Without a more responsible civic spirit, Haiti's elite is doomed to be revisited by Duvaliers and Aristides time and again, and only a massive outlay of capital—political, financial and moral—to break the cycles of poverty and exclusion in Haiti will save them from that fate. Their hour is growing late, and they must act before it is all but extinguished.

Haiti's hope remains that perhaps it will yet produce a leader who is cognizant, even if only for self-interest, of two salient facts: that power and progress are only as sure as the strength of the institutions on which they rest, and that Haiti must find a way to address its peasant majority and shift the balance of power away from Port-au-Prince, teeming as it is with would-be politicians and armies of desperately poor young men easily exploited by the country's political actors. Haiti must devolve her power from the imperial presidency, which Aristide raised to such a garish level during his time in office, and address substantially the demands that its peasant groups have been making for decades, for substantial government and international involvement in finding a way to make agricultural cultivation sustainable on the land again, lest the tradition of migration to the urban centers of the country, where no jobs await the populace no matter how much they may hope, continue.

Haiti has been failed on many levels, and, much like Haiti's elite, the country's friends abroad must realize the dangers of their apathy and inaction or be ready to face a similar scenario as that which played itself out in the months leading up to Aristide's resignation in the future. In September 2004, Tropical Storm Jeanne devastated Haiti and the Artibonite Valley and Gonaives in particular, killing some three thousand people and leaving some 200,000 homeless. CARICOM, which had strenuously protested Aristide's fall in the months since February, didn't lift a finger to help their Caribbean brethren and offered no assistance—financial, technical or moral—to help the Haitians in the face of such a tragedy, but rather continued to debate whether or not to recognize the Latortue government. Such inaction is inexcusable.

Further afield, Haiti's more significant partners have also failed to have their actions match their words. The International Republican Institute attempted to set itself up, first in Port-au-Prince and then with its cross-border conferences in the Dominican Republic, as a parallel diplomatic force on par with the U.S. ambassador in Port-au-Prince, a breach of protocol and an undermining of the U.S. envoy's power in negotiating with the Haitian opposition that helped to further polarize the political situation there. The international left failed Haiti, as the greatest trick Aristide ever played was convincing progressives that he was one of them, even as he implemented a neoliberal economic program designed to benefit only him, his family and his party cadre, attacked unions with armed government partisans, drove peasants off their land and tried to kill their representatives. The failure of his supports abroad to see him for what he was, a refusal that indeed persists to this day, is something that must be confronted by anyone who truly wishes to see Aristide's legacy for what it is.

Of the $1.08 billion pledged to Haiti by international donors at a July 2004 conference in Washington, DC, by March 2005 only $220 million—less than a fifth of the total—had been disbursed. The United Nations peacekeeping force, led by a contingent of troops from Brasil, took over from the U.S.-lead multinational force in June 2004 and took until early 2005 to come up to full troop strength of eight thousand. The understaffed command was thus woefully ill-equipped to deal with the Aristide-inspired insurrection or the natural calamities that befell Haiti the fall of 2004. Bands of armed men from Haiti's former military calling for the reinstatement of the army continued to maintain bases throughout the country into 2005 and fought several fatal skirmishes with the UN forces before being dislodged. Haiti will take a commitment of time, money and manpower that the international community must be willing to make if they do not wish to be called yet again to help put out a house on fire. Haiti is populated by some of the most resourceful, hard-working and decent people in the world, despite the face the political culture presents to the casual observer, but they cannot change the country on their own.

There is an ache within me for Haiti that will be with me for as long as I live. Really, it's a great love. There is a part of me that will, wherever I am in the world, be looking for signs of the *lwa's* presence, reflections of the women walking down with their produce in the early morning stillness to market and the peasants slowly riding their donkeys into the vastness of the mountains. And there will be a piece of me left there, eternally running from the bullets in Petit Goave, eternally walking with James and his friends in all their youth through the solarizing brightness of Cité Soleil, and eternally walking through the night with a girl at my side toward the thunder of distant music. And Haiti will hang, like a tear, like a rough-hued diamond on the ocean, and its mountaintop fastness, quiet valleys and exhaust-choked city lanes will say, "This is where we were."

IT WAS ON A LONELY, collapsing stretch of road between Hinche and Maissade in the Plateau Central, several months after Aristide had resigned. The sun shone high in the sky, but the spring rains had unleashed torrents across the island and the road now disappeared under alternately swift-moving and placidly-still brown water. Tremendous potholes had rutted the wheels of our truck immobile in the mud and further passage seemed unlikely. As we stood beside our car pondering what to do, two men came walking by, leading a bull by a rope tied around its neck. They regarded us curiously as they approached but, discovering that we spoke Kreyol, stopped to chat about the things that had come to pass in their country.

"Look at the roads, and you can understand our situation," said one of the men, in his late twenties, as he gave the bull a playful pat and looked down at the mud surrounding his plastic sandals. "We have no roads, its very difficult economically. We lack about everything, just name it. "

We asked them how the security situation was for them since the end of February.

"We used to have some bandits around here, but now not so much," said the other man, clad in a blue guayrabara shirt and tan slacks but, like his friend, wearing cheap plastic sandals. "But here, to tell you the truth, we are mostly suffering from being cut off from the rest of the country."

"So what do you see in the future?" I asked them.

"We are democrats," said the first man. "But we aren't belonging to any party. Whatever government was there, they always forgot about us, especially here. We are forgotten, whatever government was in charge. So, we'll take what's coming up and we'll judge ourselves. We'll take what's coming up and if it's good for us, it's good. We will have to see for ourselves."

Bibliography

Abbott, Elizabeth. *Haiti: The Duvaliers and Their Legacy*. New York: McGraw Hill, 1988.

Alexis, Jacques Stephen. *General Sun, My Brother*. Charlottesville: University Press of Virginia, 1999.

Aristide, Jean-Bertrand. *Tout Homme Est Un Homme*. Paris: Editions du Seuil, 1992.

Avril, Gage. *A Day for the Hunter, A Day for the Prey: Popular Music and Power in Haiti*. Chicago: University of Chicago Press, 1997.

Avril, Prosper. *Le Livre Noir d l'Insecurite*. Port-au-Prince: Imprimerie Le Natal, 2001.

Bazin, Henri. *Le Secteur Prive Haitien a l'oree du Troisieme Millenaire*. Port-au-Prince: Imprimeur II, 1999.

Blancpain, Francois. *Louis Borno: President d'Haiti*. Port-au-Prince: Editions Regain, 1993.

Castor, Suzy. *L'Occupation Americaine D'Haiti*. Port-au-Prince: Imprimerie Henri Deschamps, 1988.

Cuello, Jose Israel. *Contraction de Mano de Obra Haitiana Destinada a la Industria Azucarera Dominicana 1952-1982*. Santo Domingo: Biblioteco Taller, 1997.

Diedrich, Bernard and Burt, Al. *Papa Doc: Haiti and Its Dictator*. New Jersery: Waterfront Press, 1991.

Deren, Maya. *The Divine Horsemen: The Living Gods of Haiti*. New York: McPherson and Company, 1953.

Farmer, Paul. *The Uses of Haiti*. Maine: Common Courage Press, 1994.

Farmer, Paul. *Infections and Inequalities: The Modern Plagues*. Berkeley: University of California Press, 1999.

Franco Pichardo, Franklin. *Sobre Racismo y Antihaitianismo (y Otros Ensayos)*. Santo Domingo: Impresora Vidal, 1997.

Gaillard, Roger. *Hinche Mise En Croix*. Port-au-Prince: Imprimerie Le Natal, 1982.

Gaillard, Roger. *La Guerilla de Batraville*. Port-au-Prince: Imprimerie Le Natal, 1983.

Heinl, Robert Debs and Heinl, Nancy Gordon. *Written in Blood: The Story of the Haitian People, 1492–1995*. Maryland: University Press of America, 1996.

Hurbon, Laennec. *Voodoo: Search for the Spirit*. Harry N. Abrams Inc, 1994.

James, C. L. R. *The Black Jacobins*. New York: Vintage, 1989.

Laferriere, Dany. *Dining With the Dictator*. Toronto: Coach House Press, 1994.

Loederer, Richard A. *Voodoo Fire In Haiti*. New York: The Literary Guild, 1935.

Metraux, Alfred. *Voodoo in Haiti*. New York: Schocken Books, 1972.

Roumain, Jacques. *Masters of the Dew*. Oxford: Heinemann, 1978.

Seabrook, William. *The Magic Island*. New York: Paragon House, 1929.

Thoby-Marclin, Philippe and Marcelin, Pierre. *The Beast of the Haitian Hills*. New York: Rinehart & Company, 1946.

Thomson. Ian. *Bonjour Blanc: A Journey Through Haiti*. 2nd edition. London: Vintage, 2004.

Wilentz, Amy. *The Rainy Season*. New York: Simon & Schuster, 1989.

Haiti: Jamais, Jamais Plus! Port-au-Prince: Atelier de Droits Humains du CRESFED, 2000.

Mouvman Peyizan Papaye (MPP) Bilan 25 an 1973-1998. Port-au-Prince: Imprimeur II, 1998.

Ochan Pou Jean-Marie Vincent. Port-au-Prince: Imprimerie Le Natal, 1995.

Index

MICHAEL DEIBERT first visited Haiti in 1997 and served as the Reuters correspondent in Port-au-Prince from 2001 until 2003. His writing on Latin America and the Caribbean has appeared in *Newsday,* the *Miami Herald, The Village Voice, The Economist Intelligence Unit, Salon,* and *The Guardian,* among other publications.

RAOUL PECK was minister of culture during the Préval presidency in Haiti (1996–1997). Celebrated as one of the world's great contemporary filmmakers, his films include *Lumumba* and *Sometimes in April* (HBO), among many others. He is also the recipient of the Human Rights Watch 2001 Irene Diamond Lifetime Achievement Award.